DATE DUE

MAY 0 8 2002			
NO 1. 03			

Legends and Lore of the American Indians

Legends and Lore
of the
AMERICAN
INDIANS

Edited by Terri Hardin

BARNES
&NOBLE
BOOKS
NEW YORK

1993 Barnes & Noble Books

Book design by Charles Ziga, Ziga Design

ISBN 1-56619-039-8

Printed and bound in the United States of America

M 9 8 7 6 5 4 3 2 1

CONTENTS

PART II · TALES FROM THE CENTRAL & GREAT LAKES REGION

Part III · Tales from the Southwest Region

PART IV · TALES FROM COASTAL CALIFORNIA & THE NORTHWEST REGION

LIST OF TRIBAL NATIONS AND THEIR REGIONS

North & Pacific Northwest

CANADA & ALASKA
Aleut
Athabascan
Bear Lake
Beaver
Bella Coola
Chigmiut
Chuga
Cree
Haida
Han
Hare
Ingalik
Inuit
Kaska
Kawkiutl
Koyukon
Kutchin
Malemiut
Nootka
Salish
Sekani
Slave
Tagish
Tanana
Tlingit
ALSO ESKIMO

IDAHO
Bannock (Shoshone)
Coeur d'Alene
Flathead
Kootenai
Nez Perce
Paiute
Palouse
Shoshone
Skitswish
Spokan

MICHIGAN
Menominee
Chippewa
Ojibwa
Ottawa

MINNESOTA
Chippewa
Dakota
Sac and Fox
Sioux (Lower, Upper, Shakopee, Satee)
Wahpeton

OREGON
Cayuse
Clatsop
Coos
Des Chutes
John Day
Kalapoola
Klamath
Modoc
Paiute
Shosoni
Siletz
Siuslaw
Tenino
Tilkuni
Umatilla
Umpqua
Walla Walla
Wasco

WASHINGTON
Chehalis
Chinook
Clallam
Colville
Hoh
Kalispel
Klickitat
Lummi
Makah
Methow
Nespelim
Nez Perce
Nisqually
Nooksak
Okinagan
Palouse
Puyallup
Quileute
Quinault
Sanpoil
Senijextee
Skagit
Skitswish
Skokomish
Spokan
Squaxon
Stillaguamish
Suquamish
Wasco
Wenatchee
Yakima

WISCONSIN
Mahican
Menominee
Munsee
Ojibwa
Oneida
Potawatomi
Sac and Fox
Winnebago

Northeast

CONNECTICUT
Mashantucket Pequot
Mohegan (Mahican?)
Paugusset
Pequot
Schaghticoke

DELAWARE
Maliseet
Nanticoke
Nipmuck
Passamaquoddy
Wampanoag

MAINE
Abnaki
Passamaquoddy
Algonkian
Penobscot

MASSACHUSETTS
Massachusetts
Wampanoag
Pequot

NEW HAMPSHIRE
Pennacook

NEW JERSEY
Delaware

NEW YORK
Adirondaks
Akwesasne
Algonkian
Cayuga
Hanhasset
Iroquois
Iroquois Confederacy (Six Nations)
Manhatten
Mohawk

Mohican
Montauk
Oneida
Onondaga
Seneca
Shinnecock
Tuscarora
Wappinger

PENNSYLVANIA
Erie
Munsee
Delaware
Susquehanna

RHODE ISLAND
Narragansett

VERMONT
Mohawk
Iroquois

Midwest

ILLINOIS
Cahokia
Illinois
Kaskaskia
Kickappoo
Poeria
Shawnee

INDIANA
Miami
Wea
Yuchi

MISSOURI
Shawnee

OHIO
Erie
Shawnee
Wyandot

South

ARKANSAS
Caddo
Quapaw
Nachitoches

FLORIDA
Apalachee
Calusa
Miccosukee
Pensacola
Seminole
Takesta
Timucha

GEORGIA
Chatot
Cherokee
Creek
Okmulgee
Quale
Yamasee

LOUISIANA
Caddo
Chitmacha
Coushatta
Houma
Nachitoches
Natchez
Tunica-Biloxi
Washa

MARYLAND
Nanticoke

MISSISSIPPI
Biloxi
Catawba
Cherokee
Chickasaw
Choctaw
Pascagoula
Yazoo

NORTH CAROLINA
Catawba
Cheraw
Cherokee
Chowanoc
Hatteras
Pamlico
Saponi
Sugeree
Tuscarora
Woccon

SOUTH CAROLINA
Catawba
Coosa
Creek
PeeDee
Santee

TENNESSEE
Cherokee
Chickasaw
Chickmunga
Yuchi

TEXAS
Alabama-Coushatta
Apache (Lipan)
Atakapa
Comanche
Isleta
Karan
Kawa
Kickapoo
Kiowa

Mescalero
Tonkawa
Wichita
Ysleta del Sur Pueblo

VIRGINIA
Chickahominy
Chowanoc
Manahoac
Mattaponi
Monacan
Pamunkey
Powhatan
Tuscarora
Tutelo

WEST VIRGINIA
Manahoac
Tutleo

Southwest

ARIZONA
Ak-Chin
Apache (Mohave-, Yavapai-)
Chemehuevi
Chiricahua
Cocopah
Havasupai
Hohokam
Hopi
Hualapai
Kaibab-Paiute
Maricopa
Mohave
Navajo
Paiute (Kaibab-)
Papago
Pima
Quechan
Tonto
Walapai
Yaqui

Yavapai
Yuma
Zuñi

COLORADO
Arapaho
Cheyenne
Jicarilla Apache
Ute

NEW MEXICO
Acoma
Apache (Chiricahua-, Jicarilla,
  Mescalero)
Conchiti
Keresan
Manso
Mogollon
Piro
Pueblo (numerous)
Tesuque
Tewa
Tiwa Tano
Zuñi

UTAH
Bear River
Goshute
Navajo
Pahvant
Shoshone
Ute

Plains

IOWA
Iowa
Mesquakie
Omaha
Sac and Fox
Winnebago
Yangton Sioux

KANSAS
Iowa
Kansa
Kaw
Kickapoo
Kiowa
Osage
Oto
Wichita

NEBRASKA
Arapaho
Omaha
Oto
Pawnee
Sioux
Winnebago

NORTH DAKOTA
Arikara
Chippewa
Hankpapa
Hidatsa
Mandan
Sioux (Yankton)

OKLAHOMA
Apache
Arapaho
Caddo
Cherokee
Cheyenne
Chicaksaw
Choctaw
Commanche
Creek
Delaware
Iowa
Kiowa
Kiowa-Apache
Miami
Modoc
Osage
Ottawa

Pawnee
Peoria
Ponca
Potawatomi
Quapaw
Sac and Fox
Seminole
Seneca-Cayuga
Shawnee
Sioux (Kaw, Oto, Missouri)
Susquehanna
Tonkawa
Wichita
Wyandot
Yuchi

SOUTH DAKOTA
Miniconjou
Ponca
Sioux (Dakota, Oglala)

WYOMING
Arapaho
Cheyenne
Crow
Gros Ventre
Lakota
Shoshone

West

CALIFORNIA
Achomawi
Atseguwi
Cabazon (Mission)
Cahto
Cahuilla (Mission)
Chemeheuvi
Chumash (Mission)
Coast Miwok
Cumash

Diegueño (Mission)
Esselen
Hoopa
Ipai
Karok
Kumeyaay Nation
Luiseno (Mission)
Maidu
Mojave
Mono
Morongo (Mission)
Ohlone (Mission)
Paiute
Pomo
Serrano
Shasta
Shoshone
Tache Yokuts
Talawa
Tipai
Tolowa
Tygh
Wailaki
Wappo
Wintun
Wiyot
Yahi
Yokuts
Yuki
Yurok

NEVADA
Gosute
Paiute (Shoshone, Moapa)
Panaca
Shoshone (Paiute)
Washo
Winnemucca

Pacific
Hawaiians

INTRODUCTION

Native American folklore began to be preserved as a part of our national heritage at the end of the nineteenth century. It was at that time that interest in and concern for the Indian tribes was revived, and attempts were made to preserve the native peoples and their legends, history, and customs. This book brings together an extraordinary collection of Native American legends and lore drawn from the wealth of material collected by these nineteenth-century scholars and storytellers.

Legend is the accumulation of experience, thus there is no rule that says legends must begin or end in a certain time and place. While some of the legends in this collection are ancient, others concern horses and rifles—which are only about a century old. Native American legends and lore have continued to develop during our own century.

Much Native American belief revolved around the creation of the world and humanity, and the hunting and gathering of food. Although not all tribes cultivated crops, for those who did, clement weather was essential for survival. The gods of sky, sun, and rain were importuned with song, ritual, and greatest of all, the sacred tobacco. Legends grew up around the cultivated plants, and ceremonies were established to aid and celebrate maize, beans, and other valuable crops. Plants were also grown for medicinal purposes, and these bore their own legends.

Animals were not only a source of food, but of clothing, utensils, and lodge coverings. Deer, rabbits, and bears were important to the tribes of the northwest, and the buffalo was essential to the tribes of the plains and prairies. To the peoples of the west and Pacific northwest, the coyote was an integral part of their lore; and the beaver was important to all the north, since its pelt was the basis of barter with European traders. Since most of the animals were vital to survival, myths that described the tribes' relationship with them flourished. Many legends concern animals as sentient beings with whom it was necessary to establish rapport. Animals had knowledge of their own, which they would share with chosen humans. Through fasting or by other means, a human might have a vision of his or her animal "protector." This protector would become the person's spiritual guide, a link between nature and being.

For the purposes of this book, the United States is divided—perhaps arbitrarily—into four separate sections: the Northeastern and Southeastern Regions, the Central and Great Lakes Region, the Southwest Region, and coastal California and the Northwest Regions. Tribal lore and legend is organized within the geographic area where a particular tribe lived at the turn of the century. The apportioning here of certain tribes to distinct regions of the United States can only be an approximation, since most tribes migrated over a large area, and territory seized in war could be dominated without being inhabited. Each section presents its own regional folklore under the headings of creation and nature myths, gods and goddesses, core beliefs, tribal history and customs, and tribal legends. The specific tribal reference (or a more general designation, such as "various" to represent a type of legend shared among many tribes) occurs at the beginning of each legend or sub-legend. A list of tribes is also offered for each region.

The careful reader will note an occasional variable spelling or reference; this is indicative of the wide range of source material used and is not intended to compromise the material, but rather to enhance it by offering all the variables of storytelling, oral legend, and transliteration.

C. M. Skinner wrote in his *Myths and Legends of Our Own Land* that the Native American "is a great story-teller. Every tribe has its traditions, and the elderly men and women like to recount them, for they always find listeners." In *Legends and Lore of the American Indian,* a bountiful crop of Native American folklore and stories has been made available for generations to come.

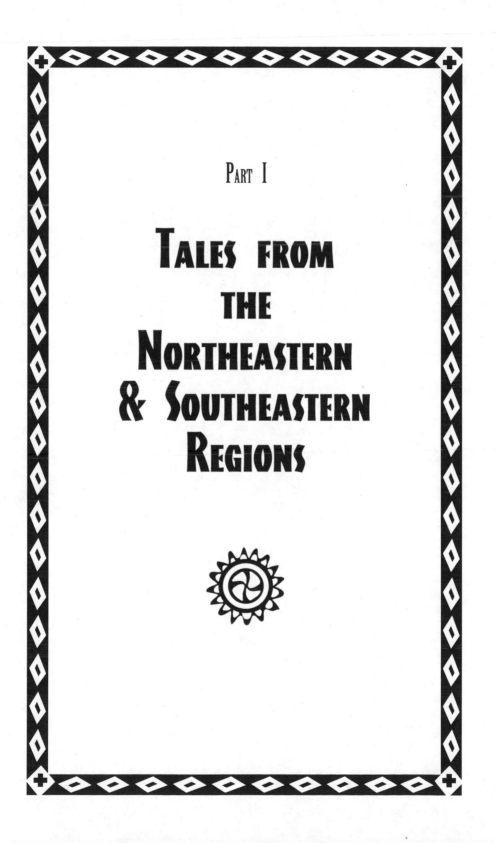

Part I

Tales from the Northeastern & Southeastern Regions

CHAPTER 1

CREATION AND NATURE MYTHS

THE MUSKHOGEAN CREATION-STORY
(Muskhogean)

The Muskhogean Indians believe that in the beginning the primeval waste of waters alone was visible. Over the dreary expanse two pigeons or doves flew hither and thither, and in course of time observed a single blade of grass spring above the surface. The solid earth followed gradually, and the terrestrial sphere took its present shape. A great hill, Nunne Chaha, rose in the midst, and in the center of this was the house of the deity *Esaugetuh Emissee,* the "Master of Breath." He took the clay which surrounded his abode, and from it molded the first men, and as the waters still covered the earth he was compelled to build a great wall upon which to dry the folk he had made. Gradually the soft mud became transformed into bone and flesh, and Esaugetuh was successful in directing the waters into their proper channels, reserving the dry land for the men he had created.

This myth closely resembles the story in the Book of Genesis. The pigeons appear analogous to the brooding creative Spirit, and the manufacture of the men out of mud is also striking. So far is the resemblance carried that we are almost forced to conclude that this is one of the instances in which Gospel conceptions have been engrafted on a native legend.

CREATION-MYTH
(Algonquin)

In many other Indian mythologies we find the wind brooding over the primeval ocean in the form of a bird. In some creation-myths amphibious animals dive into the waters and bring up sufficient mud with them to form a beginning of the new earth. In a number of these tales no actual act of creation is recorded, but a reconstruction of matter only. The Algonquins relate that their great god Michabo, when hunting one day with wolves for dogs, was surprised to see the animals enter a great lake and disappear. He followed them into the waters with the object of rescuing them, but as he did so the lake suddenly overflowed and submerged the entire earth. Michabo despatched a raven with directions to find a piece of earth which might serve as a nucleus for a new world, but the bird returned from its quest unsuccessful. Then the god sent an otter on a like errand, but it too failed to bring back the needful terrestrial germ. At last a muskrat was sent on the same mission, and it returned with sufficient earth to enable Michabo to recreate the solid land. The trees had become denuded of their branches, so the god discharged arrows at them, which provided them with new boughs. After this Michabo married the muskrat, and from their union sprang the human race.

THE FOUR BROTHERS
(Algonquin)

The Indians tell that, in a time so long ago no one can tell when, four brothers were born on this earth.

The first was Menabozho, who is the friend of all the human race. The second was Chibiabos, who cares for the dead and lives in the Country of Souls. The third was Wabose. He ran far away to the north and was changed into a rabbit, but is still very powerful. The fourth was Chokanipok, the Man of Flint.

Menabozho did not love his fourth brother, the stone man, and had many battles with him. These battles were long and terrible. Traces of them can be found to this day. Chokanipok's body was as large as a mountain. In one of these battles Menabozho's arrows tore off many pieces of flesh from him. These changed into flint stones when they touched the earth, and men made fire by striking two of them together.

At last Menabozho conquered, for he had more love for man in his heart than had his brother, and the great firestone giant fell, and his pieces are scattered everywhere.

This gave Menabozho courage, and he traveled all over the earth teaching men how to use stone and bone. He taught them how to make stone axes. He showed them how to make snares and traps so as to catch fishes and birds. He taught the women how to weave mats and beautiful baskets.

While he traveled he saw the huge creatures whose bones are now dug up from far under the ground. Menabozho slew these animals himself and hid them away. He opened the pathway for the rivers between the hills and mountains. He made the earth ready for the Indian.

Menabozho placed four spirits at the four sides of the heavens. The spirit which he put in the north sends snow and ice so that the Indian may hunt during the cold moons. The spirit in the south sends the warm wind and gives the red man corn, melons, and tobacco. The spirit that stands in the west sends the rain, and the spirit in the east gives light to the earth.

Some Indian legends say that Menabozho now lives on an ice mountain in the great sea. If he, by any chance, were driven from his home all things would burn if he should touch his feet to the ground to spring into the air. The end would come, for the sun could never shine again without Menabozho to guide it from the east to the west.

Chapter 2

Gods and Goddesses

The Battle of the Twin-Gods
(Iroquois)

Two brothers, *Ioskeha* and *Tawiscara,* or the White One and the Dark One, were twins, whose grandmother was the moon. When they grew up they quarrelled violently with one another, and finally came to blows. Ioskeha took as his weapon the horns of a stag, while Tawiscara seized a wild rose to defend himself. The latter proved but a puny weapon, and, sorely wounded, Tawiscara turned to fly. The drops of blood which fell from him became flint stones. Ioskeha later built for himself a lodge in the far east, and became the father of mankind and principal deity of the Iroquois, slaying the monsters which infested the earth, stocking the woods with game, teaching the Indians how to grow crops and make fires, and instructing them in many of the other arts of life. This myth appears to have been accepted later by the Mohawks and Tuscaroras.

Esaugetuh Emissee
(Creek)

The great life-giving god of the Creeks and other Muskhogeans was *Esaugetuh Emissee,* whose name signifies, "Master of Breath." The sound of the name represents the emission of breath from the mouth. He was the god of wind, and, like many another divinity in American mythology, his rule over that element was allied with his power over the breath of life—one of the forms of wind or air. Savage man regards the wind as the great source of breath and life. Indeed, in many tongues the words "wind," "soul," and "breath" have a common origin. We find a like conception in the Aztec wind-god Tezcatlipoca, who was looked upon as the primary source of existence.

MENABOZHO
(Chippewa)

Menabozho, the great land manitou, did not like the water manitous or spirits. One day he saw the chief of the water manitous asleep on a rock, and he shot and killed him with a magic arrow; then the little water manitous called the big rivers to help them and chased Menabozho up a high hill.

The water reached halfway up the hill; the water manitous called all the little rivers then to help them. The water chased Menabozho to the top of the high hill. He climbed up a tall pine tree, but the water came up to his chin; it could not go over his head, for there is not water enough in the whole world to drown the great Menabozho.

He waited a long time while he stood on the top of the pine tree. The rivers would not go back, and he could not see any land.

A loon flew over his head and then dived into the great water. Menabozho said: "Brother Loon, come to me. I must make land for us to stand on. Will you dive down and bring me a little sand?"

The loon put down his head and went through the deep water, but it was too deep even for the great loon-bird. He came up again, but he had left his breath in the deep water. Menabozho caught him as he floated by the pine tree, but he found no sand in his bill nor on his feet.

An otter put his head out of the water close by Menabozho.

"Brother Otter, dive down and bring me up a few grains of sand. We must have land to put our feet upon."

The otter knew he must do as Menabozho told him, so he put his head down into the deep water. He came up, but he had no life any more, and Menabozho could not find any sand in his paws.

A muskrat came swimming by just then. "Brother Muskrat, you are very brave. Will you dive down to the sand under this deep water and bring me a few grains? I must make land for my brothers," said Menabozho.

The muskrat was brave, for he dived down, but he came up just like the otter. He had no more life, but he had a little sand in one front paw.

Menabozho held the sand in his own hand and dried it in the sunshine. He blew it with his breath far out on the water, and it made a little island. Menabozho called the sand back to him. He dried it in his hand again and then blew it to its place on the deep water. He did this for two days, and the island grew larger every time it was sent back. Menabozho left the tree and walked on the land.

He called to his brothers, who are the trees, animals, and everything on the land, to come and live on this land. The water had to go back to its place.

MICHABO
(Algonquin)

The Great Hare is the principal deity of the Algonquins. In the accounts of the older travelers we find him described as the ruler of the winds, the inventor of picture-writing, and even the creator and preserver of the world. Taking a grain of sand from the bed of the ocean, he made from it an island which he launched in the primeval waters. This island speedily grew to a great size; indeed, so extensive did it become that a young wolf which managed to find a footing on it and attempted to cross it died of old age before he completed his journey. A great "medicine" society, called Meda, was supposed to have been founded by Michabo. Many were his inventions. Observing the spider spread its web, he devised the art of knitting nets to catch fish. He furnished the hunter with many signs and charms for use in the chase. In the autumn, ere he takes his winter sleep, he fills his great pipe and smokes, and the smoke which arises is seen in the clouds which fill the air with the haze of the Indian summer.

Some uncertainty prevailed among the various Algonquian tribes as to where Michabo resided, some of them believing that he dwelt on an island in Lake Superior, others on an iceberg in the Arctic Ocean, and still others in the firmament, but the prevalent idea seems to have been that his home was in the east, where the sun rises on the shores of the great river Ocean that surrounds the dry land.

That a being possessing such qualities should be conceived of as taking the name and form of a timid animal like the hare is indeed curious, and there is little doubt that the original root from which the name Michabo has been formed does not signify "hare." In fact, the root *wab,* which is the initial syllable of the Algonquian word for "hare," means also "white," and from it are derived the words for "east," "dawn," "light," and "day." Their names proceeding from the same root, the idea of the hare and the dawn became confused, and the more tangible object became the symbol of the god. Michabo was therefore the spirit of light, and, as the dawn, the bringer of winds. As lord of light he is also wielder of the lightning. He is in constant strife, nevertheless, with his father the West Wind, and in this combat we can see the diurnal struggle between east and west, light and darkness, common to so many mythologies.

Modern Indian tales concerning Michabo make him a mere tricksy spirit, a malicious buffoon. It is in the tales of the old travelers and missionaries that we find him in his true colors as a great culture-hero, Lord of the Day and bringer of light and civilization.

THE ADVENTURES OF GLOOSKAP
(Various)

THE STORY OF GLOOSKAP
(Penobscot)

Glooskap gave names to everything. He made men and gave them life, and made the winds to make the waters move. The Turtle was his uncle; the Mink, *Uk-see-meezel,* his adopted son; and *Moninkwessos,* the Woodchuck, his grandmother. The Beaver built a great dam, and Glooskap turned it away and killed the Beaver. At Moose-tchick he killed a moose; the bones may be seen at Bar Harbor turned to stone. He threw the entrails of the Moose across the bay to his dogs, and they, too, may be seen there to this day; and there, too, in the rock are the prints of his bow and arrow.

OF GLOOSKAP'S BIRTH AND OF HIS BROTHER MALSUMSIS, THE WOLF
(Wabanaki)

Now the great lord Glooskap, who was worshiped in after-days by all the *Wabanaki,* or children of light, was a twin with a brother. As he was good, this brother, whose name was *Malsumsis,* or Wolf the younger, was bad. Before they were born, the babes consulted to consider how they had best enter the world. And Glooskap said, "I will be born as others are." But the evil Malsumsis thought himself too great to be brought forth in such a manner, and declared that he would burst through his mother's side. And as they planned it so it came to pass. Glooskap as first came quietly to light, while Malsumsis kept his word, killing his mother.

The two grew up together, and one day the younger, who knew that both had charmed lives, asked the elder what would kill him. Now each had his own secret as to this, and Glooskap, remembering how wantonly Malsumsis had slain their mother, thought it would be misplaced confidence to trust his life to one so fond of death, while it might prove to be well to know the bane of the other. So they agreed to exchange secrets, and Glooskap, to test his brother, told him that the only way in which he himself could be slain was by the stroke of an owl's feather, though this was not true. And Malsumsis said, "I can only die by a blow from a fern-root."

It came to pass in after-days that *Kwah-beet-a-sis,* the son of the Great Beaver, or, as others say, Miko the Squirrel, or else the evil which was in himself, tempted Malsumsis to kill Glooskap; for in those days all men were wicked. So taking his bow he shot *Ko-ko-khas* the Owl, and with one of his feathers he struck Glooskap while sleeping. Then he awoke in anger, yet craftily said that it was not by an owl's feather, but by a blow from a pine-root, that his life would end.

Then the false man led his brother another day far into the forest to hunt, and, while he again slept, smote him on the head with a pine-root. But Glooskap arose unharmed, drove Malsumsis away into the woods, sat down by the brook-side, and thinking over all that had happened, said, "Nothing but a flowering rush can kill me." But the Beaver, who was hidden among the reeds, heard this, and hastening to Malsumsis told him the secret of his brother's life. For this Malsumsis promised to bestow on Beaver whatever he should ask; but when the latter wished for wings like a pigeon, the warrior laughed, and scornfully said, "Get thee hence; thou with a tail like a file, what need hast thou of wings?"

Then the Beaver was angry, and went forth to the camp of Glooskap, to whom he told what he had done. Therefore Glooskap arose in sorrow and in anger, took a fern-root, sought Malsumsis in the deep, dark forest, and smote him so that he fell down dead. And Glooskap sang a song over him and lamented.

Preparing for the Great Battle
(Passamaquoddy)

G looskap is living far away; no one knows where. Some say he sailed away in his stone canoe beyond the sea, to the east, but he will return in it one day; others, that he went to the west. One story tells that while he was alive those who went to him and found him could have their wishes given to them. But there is a story that if one travels long, and is not afraid, he may still find the great sagamore. He lives in a very great, a very long wigwam always making arrows. One side of the lodge is full of arrows now. When it is all quite full, he will come forth and make war. He never allows any one to enter the wigwam while he is making these arrows.

He will make war on all, kill all; there will be no more world,—world all gone. Dunno how quick,—mebbe long time; all be dead then, mebbe,—guess it will be long time.

Some say world all burn up some day, water all boil all fire; some good ones be taken up in good heavens.

How Glooskap Caught the Summer
(Algonquin)

A very beautiful myth tells how Glooskap captured the Summer. The form in which it is preserved is a kind of poetry possessing something in the nature of meter, which until a few generations ago was recited by many Algonquian firesides. A long time ago Glooskap wandered very far north to the Ice-country, and, feeling tired and cold, sought shelter at a wigwam where dwelt a great giant—the giant Winter. Winter received the god hospitably, filled a pipe of tobacco for him, and entertained him with charming stories of the old time as he smoked. All the time Winter was casting his spell over Glooskap, for as he talked drowsily and monotonously he gave forth a freezing atmosphere, so that Glooskap first dozed and then fell into a deep sleep—the heavy slumber of the winter season. For six whole months he slept; then the spell of the frost arose from his brain and he awoke. He took his way homeward and southward, and the farther south he fared the warmer it felt, and the flowers began to spring up around his steps.

At length he came to a vast, trackless forest, where, under primeval trees, many little people were dancing. The queen of these folk was Summer, a most exquisitely beautiful, if very tiny, creature. Glooskap caught the queen up in his great hand, and, cutting a long lasso from the hide of a moose, secured it around her tiny frame. Then he ran away, letting the cord trail loosely behind him.

The tiny people, who were the Elves of Light, came clamoring shrilly after him, pulling frantically at the lasso. But as Glooskap ran the cord ran out, and pull as they might they were left far behind.

Northward he journeyed once more, and came to the wigwam of Winter. The giant again received him hospitably, and began to tell the old stories whose vague charm had exercised such a fascination upon the god. But Glooskap in his turn began to speak. Summer was lying in his bosom, and her strength and heat sent forth such powerful magic that at length Winter began to show signs of distress. The sweat poured profusely down his face, and gradually he commenced to melt, as did his dwelling. Then slowly nature awoke, the song of birds was heard, first faintly, then more clearly and joyously. The thin green shoots of the young grass appeared, and the dead leaves of last autumn were carried down to the river by the melting snow. Lastly the fairies came out, and Glooskap, leaving Summer with them, once more bent his steps southward.

This is obviously a nature-myth conceived by a people dwelling in a climate where the rigors of winter gave way for a more or less brief space only to the blandishments of summer. To them winter was a giant, and summer an elf of pigmy proportions. The stories told during the winter season are eloquent of the life led by people dwelling in a sub-arctic climate, where the traditional tale, the father of epic poetry, whiles away the long dark hours, while the winter tempest roars furiously without and the heaped-up snow renders the daily occupation of the hunter impossible.

THE MOOSE OF MOUNT KINEO
(Passamaquoddy)

G looskap, god of the Passamaquoddies, gave names to things, created men, filled them with life, and moved their wonder with storms. He lived on the rocky height of Blomidon, at the entrance to Minas Basin, Nova Scotia, and the agates to be found along its foot are jewels that he made for his grandmother's necklace, when he restored her youth. He threw up a ridge between Fort Cumberland and Parrsboro, Nova Scotia, that he might cross, dry shod, the lake made by the beavers when they dammed the strait at Blomidon, but he afterward killed the beavers, and breaking down their dam he let the lake flow into the sea, and went southward on a hunting tour. At Mount Desert he killed a moose, whose bones he flung to the ground at Bar Harbor, where they are still to be seen, turned to stone, while across the bay he threw the entrails, and they, too, are visible as rocks, dented with his arrow-points. Mount Kineo was anciently a cow moose of colossal size that he slew and turned into a height of land, and the Indians trace the outline of the creature in the uplift to this day. Little Kineo was a calf moose that he slew at the same time, and Kettle Mountain is his camp-caldron that he flung to the ground in the ardor of the chase.

Of Glooskap and the Sinful Serpent
(Passamaquoddy)

O f old time it befell that Glooskap had an enemy, an evil man, a sinful beast, a great sorcerer. And this man, after trying many things, made himself a great serpent, hoping so to slay the Master.

Of old time Glooskap met a boy whose name was 'Nmmokswess, the Sable. And the boy had a flute: whoever played on it could entice unto him all the animals. And once, when the Master was afar, the boy broke the flute, and in his great sorrow he would not return home, but wandered away into the wilderness. Now Glooskap knew in his heart that the flute was broken: he who is a magician knows at once of a great evil. And coming home, he asked of the grandmother where the boy was, and she could only weep. Then the Master said, "Though I roam forever, yet will I find the boy." So he went forth, and he tracked him in the snow for three days; and on the third night he heard some one singing in a hollow; and it was a magic song, that which the m'téoulin sings when he is in dire need and death is near. And making a circle around about the place, Glooskap looked down and saw a wigwam, and heard the voice more distinctly as he drew nearer; and it was the voice of the boy, and he was singing a song against all of the snake kind. And he was wandering about the wigwam, seeking a straight stick.

Then Glooskap understood all the thing, and how the boy had been enticed into the wilderness by the evil arts of At-o-sis, the Snake, and that the Great Serpent was in the wigwam, and had sent him out to seek a straight stick. Then Glooskap, singing again softly, bade him get a very crooked one, and told what more to do. So the boy got an exceedingly crooked one; and when he entered, the Snake, seeing it, said, "Why hast thou got such a bad stick?" And the boy, answering, said, "Truly, it is very crooked, but that which is crookedest may be made straightest, and I know a charm whereby this can be done; for I will but heat this stick in the fire, and then I will make it quite straight, as you shall see." Now At-o-sis was very anxious to behold this wonderful thing, and he looked closely; but the boy, as soon as the end of the stick was red-hot, thrust it into his eyes and blinded him, and ran forth. Yet the Snake followed him; but when he was without the wigwam he met the Master, who slew him out of hand.

Of old times. This is an end of the story.

Glooskap's Battle Against the Giant Sorcerors
(Penobscot)

T his is a story of Glooskap. There was a father who had three sons and a daughter: they were m'téoulin, or mighty magicians; they were giants; they ate men, women, and children; they did everything that was wicked and horrible; and the world grew tired of them and of all their abominations. Yet when this family was young, Glooskap had been their friend; he had made the father his adopted father, the brothers his brothers, the sister his sister. Yet as they grew older, and he began to hear on every side of their wickedness, he said: "I will go among them and find if this be true. And if it be so, they shall die. I will not spare one of those who oppress and devour men, I do not care who he may be."

This family was at *Samgadihawk,* or Saco, on the sandy field which is in the Intervale or the summer bed of the Saco River, in the *El-now-e-bit,* the White Mountains, between Geh-sit-wah-zuch and K'tchee penahbesk, and near *Oonahgemessuk weegeet,* the Home of the Water Fairies.

Now the old man, the father of the evil magicians and his adopted father, had only one eye, and was half gray. And Glooskap made himself like him—there was not between them the difference of a hair; and having this form, he entered the wigwam and sat down by the old man. And the brothers, who killed everybody, not sparing one living soul, hearing a talking, looked in slyly, and seeing the newcomer, so like their father that they knew not which was which, said, "This is a great magician. But he shall be tried ere he goes, and that bitterly."

Then the sister took the tail of a whale, and cooked it for the stranger to eat. But as it lay before him, on the platter and on his knees, the elder brother entered, and saying rudely, "This is too good for a beggar like you," took it away to his own wigwam. Then Glooskap spoke: "That which was given to me was mine; therefore I take it again." And sitting still he simply *wished* for it, and it came flying into the platter where it was before. So he ate it.

Then the brothers said, "Indeed, he is a great magician. But he shall be tried ere he goes, and that bitterly."

When he had eaten, they brought in a mighty bone, the jaw of a whale, and the eldest brother, with great ado, and using both his arms and all his strength, bent it a little. Then he handed it to Glooskap, who with his thumb and fingers snapped it like a pipe-stem. And the brothers said again, "Truly, this is a great magician. But he shall for all that be tried ere he goes, and that bitterly."

Then they brought a great pipe full of the strongest tobacco; no man not a magician could have smoked it. And it was passed round: every one smoked; the brothers blew the smoke through their nostrils. But Glooskap filled it full, and, lighting it, burnt all the tobacco to ashes at one pull, and blew all the smoke through his nostrils at one puff. Then the brothers said again in anger, "This is indeed a great magician. Yet he shall be tried again ere he goes, and that bitterly." But they never said it again.

And they still tried to smoke with him, and the wigwam was closed; they hoped to smother him in smoke, but he sat and puffed away as if he had been on a mountain-top, till they could bear it no longer. And one said, "This is idle; let us go and play at ball." The place where they were to play was on the sandy plain of *Samgadihawk,* or Saco, on the bend of the river. And the game begun; but Glooskap found that the ball with which they played was a hideous skull; it was alive and snapped at his heels, and had he been as other men and it had bitten him, it would have taken his foot off. Then Glooskap laughed, and said, "So this is the game you play. Good, but let us all play with our own balls." So he stepped up to a tree on the edge of the river-bed and broke off the end of a bough, and it turned into a skull ten times more terrible than the other. And the magicians ran before it as it chased them as a lynx chases rabbits; they were entirely beaten. Then Glooskap stamped on the sand, and the waters rose and came rushing fearfully from the mountains adown the river-bed; the whole land rang with their roar. Now Glooskap sang a magic song, which changes all beings, and the three brothers and their father became the *chinahmess,* a fish which is as long and large as a man, and they went headlong down on the flood, to the deep sea, to dwell there forever. And the magicians had on, each of them, a wampum collar; wherefore the chinahmess has beneath its head, as one may say, round its neck, the wampum collar, as may be seen to this day. And they were mighty m'téoulin in their time; but they were tried before they went, and that bitterly.

How Glooskap Bound Wuchowsen
(Passamaquoddy)

The Indians believe in a great bird called by them *Wochowsen* or *Wuchowsen,* meaning Wind-Blow or the Wind-Blower, who lives far to the North, and sits upon a great rock at the end of the sky. And it is because whenever he moves his wings the wind blows they of old times called him that.

When Glooskap was among men he often went out in his canoe with bow and arrows to kill sea-fowl. At one time it was every day very windy; it grew worse; at last it blew a tempest, and he could not go out at all. Then he said, "Wuchowsen, the Great Bird, has done this!"

He went to find him; it was long ere he reached his abode. He found sitting on a high rock a large white Bird.

"Grandfather," said Glooskap, "you take no compassion on your *Koosesek,* your grandchildren. You have caused this wind and storm; it is too much. Be easier with your wings!"

The Giant Bird replied, "I have been here since ancient times; in the earliest days, ere aught else spoke, I first moved my wings; mine was the first voice,—and I will ever move my wings as I will."

Then Glooskap rose in his might; he rose to the clouds; he took the Great Bird-giant Wuchowsen as though he were a duck, and tied both his wings, and threw him down into a chasm between deep rocks, and left him lying there.

The Indians could now go out in their canoes all day long, for there was a dead calm for many weeks and months. And with that all the waters became stagnant. They were so thick that Glooskap could not paddle his canoe. Then he thought of the Great Bird, and went to see him.

As he had left him he found him, for Wuchowsen is immortal. So, raising him, he put him on his rock again, and untied one of his wings. Since then the winds have never been so terrible as in the old time.

GLOOSKAP'S PUNISHMENT
(Passamaquoddy)

You know *At-o-sis,* the Snake? Well, the worst of all is Rattlesnake. Long time ago the Rattlesnakes were saucy Indians. They were very saucy. They had too much face. They could not be put down by much, and they got up for very little.

When the great Flood was coming Glooskap told them about it. They said they did not care. He told them the water would come over their heads. They said that would be very wet. He told them to be good and quiet, and pray. Then those Indians hurrahed. He said, "A great Flood is coming." Then they gave three cheers for the great Flood. He said, "The Flood will come and drown you all." Then these Indians hurrahed again, and got their rattles, made of turtle-shells, in the old fashion, fastened together, filled with pebbles, and rattled them and had a grand dance. Afterwards, when the white men brought cows and oxen into the country, they made rattles of horns.

Yes, they had a great dance. The rain began to fall, but they danced. The thunder roared, and they shook their rattles and yelled at it. Then Glooskap was angry. He did not drown them in the Flood, however, but he changed them into rattlesnakes. Nowadays, when they see a man coming, they lift up their heads and move them about. That's the way snakes dance. And they shake the rattles in their tails just as Indians shake their rattles when they dance. How do you like such music?

GLOOSKAP AND THE BABY
(Algonquin)

Glooskap, having conquered the *Kewawkqu',* a race of giants and magicians, and the *Medecolin,* who were cunning sorcerers, and *Pamola,* a wicked spirit of the night, besides hosts of fiends, goblins, cannibals, and witches, felt himself great indeed, and boasted to a certain woman that there was nothing left for him to subdue.

But the woman laughed and said: "Are you quite sure, Master? There is still one who remains unconquered, and nothing can overcome him."

In some surprise Glooskap inquired the name of this mighty individual.

"He is called Wasis," replied the woman; "but I strongly advise you to have no dealings with him."

Wasis was only the baby, who sat on the floor sucking a piece of maple-sugar and crooning a little song to himself. Now Glooskap had never married and was quite ignorant of how children are managed, but with perfect confidence he smiled to the baby and asked it to come to him. The baby smiled back to him, but never moved, whereupon Glooskap imitated the beautiful song of a certain bird. Wasis, however, paid no heed to him, but went on sucking his maple-sugar. Glooskap, unaccustomed to such treatment, lashed himself into a furious rage, and in terrible and threatening accents ordered Wasis to come crawling to him at once. But Wasis burst into direful howling, which quite drowned the god's thunderous accents, and for all the threatenings of the deity he would not budge. Glooskap, now thoroughly aroused, brought all his magical resources to his aid. He recited the most terrible spells, the most dreadful incantations. He sang the songs which raise the dead, and which sent the devil scurrying to the nethermost depths of the pit. But Wasis evidently seemed to think this was all some sort of a game, for he merely smiled wearily and looked a trifle bored. At last Glooskap in despair rushed from the hut, while Wasis, sitting on the floor, cried, *"Goo, goo,"* and crowed triumphantly. And to this day the Indians say that when a baby cries *"Goo"* he remembers the time when he conquered the mighty Glooskap.

GLOOSKAP'S DEPARTURE FROM THE WORLD
(Micmac)

N ow Glooskap had freed the world from all the mighty monsters of an early time: the giants wandered no longer in the wilderness; the cullo terrified man no more, as it spread its wings like the cloud between him and the sun; the dreadful Chenoo of the North devoured him not; no evil beasts, devils, and serpents were to be found near his home. And the Master had, moreover, taught men the arts which made them happier; but they were not grateful to him, and though they worshiped him they were not the less wicked.

Now when the ways of men and beasts waxed evil they greatly vexed Glooskap, and at length he could no longer endure them, and he made a rich feast by the shore of the great Lake Minas. All the beasts came to it, and when the feast was over he got into a great canoe, and the beasts looked after him till they saw him no more. And after they ceased to see him, they still heard his voice as he sang; but the sounds grew fainter and fainter in the distance, and at last they wholly died away; and then deep silence fell on them all, and a great marvel came to pass, and the beasts, who had till now spoken but one language, were no longer able to understand each other, and they fled away, each his own way, and never again have they met together in council. Until the day when Glooskap shall return to restore the Golden Age, and make men and animals dwell once more together in amity and peace, all Nature mourns. And tradition says that on his departure from Acadia the Great Snowy Owl retired to the deep forests, to return no more until he could come to welcome Glooskap; and in those sylvan depths the owls even yet repeat to the night *Koo-koo-skoos!* which is to say in the Indian tongue, "Oh, I am sorry! Oh, I am sorry!" And the Loons, who had been the huntsmen of Glooskap, go restlessly up and down through the world, seeking vainly for their master, whom they cannot find, and wailing sadly because they find him not.

But ere the Master went away from life, or ceased to wander in the ways of men, he bade it be made known by the Loons, his faithful messengers, that before his departure years would pass, and that whoever would seek him might have one wish granted, whatever that wish might be. Now, though the journey was long and the trials were terrible which those must endure who would find Glooskap, there were still many men who adventured them.

Now ye shall hear who some of these were and what happened to them.

When all men had heard that Glooskap would grant a wish to any one who would come to him, three Indians resolved to try this thing; and one was a Maliseet from St. John, and the other two were Penobscots from Old Town. And the path was long and the way was hard, and they suffered much, and they were seven years on it ere they came to him. But while they were yet three months' journey from his dwelling, they heard the barking of his dogs, and as they drew nearer, day by day, it was louder. And so, after great trials, they found the lord of men and beasts, and he made them welcome and entertained them.

But, ere they went, he asked them what they wanted. And the eldest, who was an honest, simple man, and of but little account among his people, because he was a bad hunter, asked that he might excel in the killing and catching of game. Then the Master gave him a flute, or the magic pipe, which pleases every ear, and has the power of persuading every animal to follow him who plays it. And he thanked the lord, and left.

Now the second Indian, being asked what he would have, replied, The love of many women. And when Glooskap asked how many, he said, "I care not how many, so that there are but enough of them, and more than enough." At hearing this the Master seemed displeased, but, smiling anon, he gave him a bag which was tightly tied, and told him not to open it until he had reached his home. So he thanked the lord, and left.

Now the third Indian was a gay and handsome but foolish young fellow, whose whole heart was set on making people laugh, and on winning a welcome at every merry-making. And he, being asked what he would have or what he chiefly wanted, said that it would please him most to be able to make a certain quaint and marvelous sound or noise, which was frequent in those primitive times among all the Wabanaki, and which it is said may even yet be heard in a few sequestered wigwams far in the wilderness, away from men; there being still here and there a deep magician, or man of mystery, who knows the art of producing it. And the property of this wondrous sound is such that they who hear it must needs burst into a laugh; whence it is the cause that the men of these our modern times are so sorrowful, since that sound is no more heard in the land. And to him Glooskap was also affable, sending Marten into the woods to seek a certain mystical and magic root, which when eaten would make the miracle the young man sought. But he warned him not to touch the root ere he got to his home, or it would be the worse for him. And so he kindly thanked the lord, and left.

It had taken seven years to come, but seven days were all that was required to tread the path returning to their home, that is, for him who got there. Only one of all the three beheld his lodge again. This was the hunter, who, with his pipe in his pocket, and not a care in his heart, trudged through the woods, satisfied that so long as he should live, there would always be venison in the larder.

But he who loved women, and had never won even a wife, was filled with anxious wishfulness. And he had not gone very far into the woods before he opened the bag. And there flew out by hundreds, like white doves, swarming all about him, beautiful girls, with black burning eyes and flowing hair. And wild with passion the winsome witches threw their arms about him, and kissed him as he responded to their embraces; but they came ever more and more, wilder and more passionate. And he bade them give way, but they would not, and he sought to escape, but he could not; and so panting, crying for breath, smothered, he perished. And those who came that way found him dead, but what became of the girls no man knows.

Now the third went merrily onward alone, when all at once it flashed upon his mind that Glooskap had given him a present, and without the least heed to the injunction that he was to wait till he had reached his home drew out the root and ate it; and scarce had he done this ere he realized that he possessed the power of uttering the weird and mystic sound to absolute perfection. And as it rang over many a hill and dale, and woke the echoes of the distant hills, until it was answered by the solemn owl, he felt that it was indeed wonderful. So he walked on gayly, trumpeting as he went, over hill and vale, happy as a bird.

But by and by he began to weary of himself. Seeing a deer he drew an arrow and stealing silently to the game was just about to shoot, when despite himself the wild, unearthly sound broke forth like a demon's warble. The deer bounded away, and the young man cursed! And when he reached Old Town, half dead with hunger, he was worth little to make laughter, though the honest Indians at first did not fail to do so, and thereby somewhat cheered his heart. But as the days went on they wearied of him, and, life becoming a burden, he went into the woods and slew himself. And the evil spirit of the night-air, even Bumole, or Pamola, from whom came the gift, swooped down from the clouds and bore him away to 'Lahmkekqu', the dwelling place of darkness, and he was no more heard of among men.

OF OTHER MEN WHO WENT TO GLOOSKAP FOR GIFTS
(Micmac)

Of the old times: this is a story of Glooskap. Now there went forth many men unto Glooskap, hearing that they could win the desires of their hearts; and all got what they asked for, in any case; but as for having what they wanted, that depended on the wisdom with which they wished or acted.

The good Glooskap liked it not that when he had told any one evenly and plainly what to do, that man should then act otherwise, or double with him. And it came to pass that a certain fool, of the kind who can do nothing unless it be in his own way, made a long journey to the Master. And his trials were indeed many. For he came to an exceeding high mountain in a dark and lonely land, where he heard no sound. And the ascent thereof was like a smooth pole, and the descent on the other side far worse, for it hung over the bottom. Yet it was worse beyond, for there the road lay between the heads of two huge serpents, almost touching each other, who darted their terrible tongues at those who went between. And yet again the path passed under the Wall of Death. Now this wall hung like an awful cloud over a plain, rising and falling at times, yet no man knew when. And when it fell it struck the ground, and that so as to crush all that was beneath it.

But the young man escaped all these trials, and came to the island of the Great Master. And when he had dwelt there a certain time, and was asked what he would have, he replied, "If my lord will, let him give me a medicine which will cure all disease." More than this he asked not. So the Master gave him a certain small package, and said, "Herein is that which thou seekest; but I charge thee that thou lettest not thine eyes behold it until thou shalt reach thy home." So he thanked the Master, and left.

But he was not far away ere he desired to open the package and test the medicine, and, yet more, the truth of the Master. And he said to himself, "Truly, if this be but a deceit it was shrewdly devised to bid me not open it till I returned. For he knew well that once so far I would make no second journey to him. Tush! if the medicine avail aught it cannot change in aught." So he opened it, when that which was therein fell to the ground, and spread itself like water everywhere, and then dried away like a mist. And when he returned and told his tale, men mocked him.

Then again there were three brothers, who, having adventured, made known their wishes. Now the first was very tall, far above all his fellows, and vain of his comeliness. For he was of those who put bark or fur into their moccasins, that they may be looked up to by the little folk and be loved by the squaws; and his hair was plastered to stand up on high, and on the summit of it was a very long turkey-tail feather. And this man asked to become taller than any Indian in all the land.

And the second wished that he might ever remain where he was to behold the land and the beauty of it, and to do naught else.

And the third wished to live to an exceeding old age, and ever to be in good health.

Now the three, when they came to the island, had found there three wigwams, and in two of these were dwellers, not spoken of in other traditions. In one lived *Cool-puj-ot,* a very strange man. For he has no bones, and cannot move himself, but every spring and autumn he is "rolled over with handspikes" by the order of Glooskap, and this is what his name means in the Micmac tongue. And in the autumn he is turned towards the west, but in the spring towards the east, and this is a figure of speech denoting the revolving seasons of the year. With his breath he can sweep down whole armies, and with his looks alone he can work great wonders, and all this means the weather—frost, snow, ice, and sunshine.

And in the other wigwam dwelt *Cuhkw,* which means Earthquake. And this mighty man can pass along under the ground, and make all things shake and tremble by his power.

Now when Glooskap had heard what these visitors wished for, he called Earthquake, and bid him take them all three and put them with their feet in the ground. And he did so, when they at once became three trees: as one tradition declares, pines; and another, cedars.

So that he that would be tall became exceeding tall, for his head rose above the forest; and even the turkey-feather at the top thereof is not forgotten, since to this day it is seen waving in the wind. And he who will listen in a pine-wood may hear the tree murmuring all day long in the Indian tongue of the olden time,—

"Ee nil Etuchi nek m'kilaskitopp
Ee nil Etuche wiski nek n'kil ooskedjin."

Oh, I am such a great man!

Oh, I am such a great Indian!

And the second, who would remain in the land, remains there; for while his roots are in the ground he cannot depart from it.

And the third, who would live long in health, unless men have cut him down, is standing as of yore.

OF GLOOSKAP AND THE THREE OTHER SEEKERS
(Micmac)

Of old time. Now when it was noised abroad that whoever besought Glooskap could obtain the desire of his heart, there were three men who said among themselves, "Let us seek the Master." So they left their home in the early spring when the bluebird first sang, and walked till the fall frosts, and then into winter, and ever on till the next midsummer. And having come to a small path in a great forest, they followed it, till they came out by a very beautiful river; so fair a sight they had never seen, and so went onward till it grew to be a great lake. And so they kept to the path which, when untrodden, was marked by blazed trees, the bark having been removed, in Indian fashion, on the side of the trunk which is *opposite* the place where the wigwam or village lies towards which it turns. So the mark can be seen as the traveler goes towards the goal, but not while leaving it.

Then after a time they came to a long point of land running out into the lake, and, having ascended a high hill, they saw in the distance a smoke, which guided them to a large, well-built wigwam. And, entering, they found seated on the right side a handsome, healthy man of middle age, and by the other a woman so decrepit that she seemed to be a hundred years old. Opposite the door, and on the left side, was a mat, which seemed to show that a third person had there a seat.

And the man made them welcome, and spoke as if he were *weleda'asit kesegvou*— well pleased to see them—but did not ask them whence they came or whither they were going, as is wont among Indians when strangers come to their homes or are met in travel. Erelong they heard the sound of a paddle, and then the noise of a canoe being drawn ashore. And there came in a youth of fine form and features and well clad, bearing weapons as if from hunting who addressed the old woman as *Kejoo,* or mother, and told her that he had brought game. And with sore ado—for she was feeble—the old dame tottered out and brought in four beavers; but she was so much troubled to cut them up that the elder, saying to the younger man *Uoh-keen!,* "My brother," bade him do the work. And they supped on beaver.

So they remained for a week, resting themselves, for they were sadly worn with their wearisome journey, and also utterly ragged. And then a wondrous thing came to pass, which first taught them that they were in an enchanted land. For one morning the elder man bade the younger wash their mother's face. And as he did this all her wrinkles vanished, and she became young and very beautiful; in all their lives the travelers had never seen so lovely a woman. Her hair, which had been white and scanty, now hung to her feet, dark and glossy as a blackbird's breast.

Then, having been clad in fine array, she showed a tall, lithe, and graceful form at its best.

And the travelers said to themselves, "Truly this man is a great magician!" They all walked forth to see the place. Never was sunshine so pleasantly tempered by a soft breeze; for all in that land was fair, and it grew fairer day by day to all who dwelt there. Tall trees with rich foliage and fragrant flowers, but without lower limbs or underbrush, grew as in a grove, wide as a forest, yet so far apart that the eye could pierce the distance in every direction.

Now when they felt for the first time that they were in a new life and a magic land, he that was host asked them whence they came and what they sought. So they said that they sought Glooskap. And the host replied, "Lo, I am he!" And they were awed by his presence, for a great glory and majesty now sat upon him. As the woman had changed, so had he, for all in that place was wonderful.

Then the first, telling what he wanted, said, "I am a wicked man, and I have a bad temper. I am prone to wrath and reviling, yet I would fain be pious, meek, and holy."

And the next said, "I am very poor, and my life is hard. I toil, but can barely make my living. I would fain be rich."

Now the third replied, "I am of low estate, being despised and hated by all my people, and I wish to be loved and respected." And to all these the Master made answer, "So shall it be!"

And taking his medicine-bag he gave unto each a small box, and bade them keep it closed until they should be once more at home. And on returning to the wigwam he also gave to each of them new garments; in all their lives they had never seen or heard of such rich apparel or such ornaments as they now had. Then when it was time to depart, as they knew not the way to their home, he arose and went with them. Now they had been more than a year in coming. But he, having put on his belt, went forth, and they followed, till in the forenoon he led them to the top of a high mountain, from which in the distance they beheld yet another, the blue outline of which could just be seen above the horizon. And having been told that their way was unto it, they thought it would be a week's journey to reach it. But they went on, and in the middle of the afternoon of the same day they were there, on the summit of the second mountain. And looking from this afar, all was familiar to them—hill and river, and wood and lakes—all was in their memory. "And there," said the Master, pointing unto it,—"there is your own village!" So he left them alone, and they went on their way, and before the sun had set were safe at home.

Yet when they came no one knew them, because of the great change in their appearance and their fine attire, the like of which had never been seen by man in those days. But having made themselves known to their friends, all that were there of old and young gathered together to gaze upon and hear what they had to say. And they were amazed.

Then each of them, having opened his box, found therein an unguent, rich and fragrant, and with this they rubbed their bodies completely. And they were ever after so fragrant from the divine anointing that all sought to be near them. Happy were they who could but sniff at the blessed smell which came from them.

Now he who had been despised for his deformity and weakness and meanness became beautiful and strong and stately as a pine-tree. There was no man in all the land so graceful or of such good behavior.

And he who had desired abundance had it, in all fullness, his wish. For the moose and caribou came to him in the forest, the fish leaped into his nets, all men gave unto him, and he gave unto all freely, to the end.

And he that had been wicked and of evil mind, hasty and cruel, became meek and patient, good and gentle, and he made others like himself. And he had his reward, for there was a blessing upon him as upon all those who had wished wisely even unto the end of their days.

Chapter 3

Core Beliefs

The Cherokee River Cult
(Cherokee)

From the beginning of knowledge, Fire and Water, twin deities of the primitive pantheon, have occupied the fullest measure of man's religious thought, holding easy precedence over all other divinities. Others were gods of occasion, but these twain were the gods of very existence, and in a hundred varied and varying forms, whether as beneficent helpers in the cheering blaze and the soft-falling rain, or as terrible scourges in the consuming conflagration or the sweeping torrent, they were recognized always as embodiments of power, masters and conservators of life itself. If they differed in degree of honor, the first place must be given to water, without which life was impossible. In every cosmogony the world itself is born from the water, and the symbolic rite of purification by ablution was so much a part of the ancient systems that even the great teacher of Galilee declares that except a man be born of water he cannot enter the kingdom.

As the reverence for fire found its highest and most beautiful expression in sun worship, so the veneration for water developed into a cult of streams and springs. From the east to the extremest west, primitive man bowed low to the god of the river and the fountain, and a newer religion consecrated the rite that it could not destroy. The sacred river of the Hindu, the holy wells of Ireland, have their counterpart in the springs of the Arapaho and the Navajo, with their sacrificial scarfs and pottery fastened upon the overhanging branches or deposited upon the sandy bank.

In Cherokee ritual, the river is the Long Man, a giant with his head in the foothills of the mountains and his foot far down in the lowland, pressing always, resistless and without stop, to a certain goal, and speaking ever in murmurs which only the priest may interpret. In the words of the sacred formulas, he holds all things in his hands and bears down all before him. His aid is invoked with prayer and fasting on every important occasion of life, from the very birth of the infant, in health and sickness, in war and love, in hunting and fishing, to ward off evil spells and to win success in friendly rivalries. Purification in the running stream is a part of every tribal function, for which reason the town-house, in the old days, was always erected close to the river bank.

We shall speak here of ceremonial rites in connection with the running stream, saying nothing of the use of water in the sweat-bath or in ordinary medico-religious practice, beyond noting the fact that in certain cases the water used by the doctor must be dipped out from a waterfall. Two distinct formulistic terms are used for the rite, one of which signifies "plunging into the water," the other "dipping up the water," nearly corresponding to our own "immersion" and "sprinkling" in baptism. Whenever possible, the priest selects a bend in the river where he can face toward the east and look upstream while performing the ceremony, which usually takes place at sunrise, both priest and petitioner being still fasting.

When the newborn child is four days old, the mother brings it to the priest, who carries it in his arms to the river, and there, standing close to the water's edge and facing the rising sun, bends seven times toward the water, as though to plunge the child into it. He is careful, however, not to let the infant's body touch the cold water, as the sudden shock might be too much for it, but holds his breath the while he mentally recites a prayer for the health, long life, and future prosperity of the child. The prayer finished, he hands the infant back to the mother, who then lightly rubs its face and breast with water dipped up from the stream. If for any reason the ceremony cannot be performed on the fourth day, it is postponed to the seventh, four and seven being the sacred numbers of the Cherokee.

At regular intervals, usually at each recurring new moon, it is customary among the more religiously disposed of the old conservatives, for the whole family to go down together at daybreak, and fasting, to the river and stand with bare feet just touching the water, while the priest, or, if properly instructed, the father of the household, stands behind them and recites a prayer for each in turn, after which they plunge in and bathe their whole bodies in the river. One of my interpreters, whose father was an acknowledged medicine-man, told me, with shivering recollection, how, as a child, he had been compelled to endure this ordeal every month, even in the depth of winter, when it was sometimes necessary to break a hole in the ice for the purpose. Following is a literal translation of one of the regular ritual prayers used on this occasion:—

"Listen! O, now you have drawn near to hearken, O Long Man at rest. O helper of men, you let nothing slip from your grasp. You never let the soul slip from your grasp. Come now and take a firmer grasp. I originated near the cataract, and from there I stretch out my hand toward this place. Now I have bathed in your body. Let the white foam cling to my head as I go about, and let the white staff be in my hand. Let the health-giving *âya* await me along the road. Now my soul stands erect in the seventh heaven. *Yû!*"

The declaration that the suppliant himself originated "near the cataract" is intended to emphasize his claims upon the assistance of the Long Man, who is held to speak to the initiated in the murmurs of the stream and the roar of the waterfall. The idea intended to be conveyed by the latter part of the prayer is that the petitioner, having bathed in the stream, comes out with the white foam still clinging to his head, and taking in his hand the "white staff"—symbolic of old age and a long life—begins his journey to the seventh upper world, the final abode of the immortals. At first his progress is slow and halting, but strengthened by the health-giving *âya* (ambrosia) set out for him at intervals along the road, he is enabled at last to reach the goal, where his soul thereafter stands erect.

It is well-nigh impossible to render into English all the subtle meaning of the Cherokee formulistic original. Thus the verb translated here, *stands erect,* implies that the subject is now at last standing erect, after having for a long time staggered or crept along, like a sick man or an infant. Philologists acquainted with Indian languages will appreciate this difficulty. Moreover, many of the formulistic expressions occur only in the sacred rituals and are unintelligible to the laity. In the color symbolism of the tribe, *white* is emblematic of peace and happiness; *red,* of power and success; *blue,* of trouble and defeat; and *black,* of death.

When a member of a family dies, it is believed that the spirit is loath to leave the scenes of life and go alone upon the long journey to the Darkening Land in the west. It therefore hovers about for a time, seeking to draw to it the souls of those it has most loved on earth, that it may have company in the spirit land. Thus it is that the friends of the lost one pine and are sorrowful and refuse to eat, because the shadow-soul is pulling at their heartstrings, and unless the aid of the priest is invoked their strength will steadily diminish, their souls will be drawn from them, and they too will die. To break the hold of the spirit and to wash away the memory of the bereavement, so that they may have quick recovery, is one of the greatest functions of the medicine-man.

Following is one of the prayers used for this purpose, the address being to the Ancient White (the Fire), the Long Man (the River), and *Gĕ′hyăgúga* (the Sun):—

THIS IS TO TAKE BEREAVED ONES TO WATER.

Sgĕ! O Ancient White, where you have let the soul slip from your grasp, it has dwindled away. Now his health has been restored and he shall live to be old. *Kû!*

Sgĕ! O Long Man, now you had let the soul slip from your grasp and it had dwindled away. Now his health has been restored and he shall live to be old.

In the first upper world, O Gĕ′hyăgúga, you have the tables. The white food shall be set out upon them. It shall be reached over and pushed away (*i.e.,* the client shall eat of the "white" or health-giving food, reaching across the tables in his eagerness, and pushing the food away from him when satisfied). His health has been restored and he shall live to be old.

In the second upper world, O Gĕ′hyăgúga, you have the tables. The white food shall be set out upon them. It shall be reached over and pushed away. His health has been restored and he shall live to be old.

In the third upper world, O Gĕ′hyăgúga, you have the tables. The white food shall be set out upon them. It shall be reached over and pushed away. His health has been restored and he shall live to be old.

In the fourth upper world, O Gĕ'hyăgúga, you have the tables. The white food shall be set out upon them. It shall be reached over and pushed away. His health has been restored and he shall live to be old.

In the fifth upper world, O Gĕ'hyăgúga, you have the tables. The white food shall be set out upon them. It shall be reached over and pushed away. His health has been restored and he shall live to be old.

In the sixth upper world, O Gĕ'hyăgúga, you have the tables. The white food shall be set out upon them. It shall be reached over and pushed away. His health has been restored and he shall live to be old.

In the seventh upper world, O Gĕ'hyăgúga, you have the tables. The white food has been set out upon them. It has been reached over. It has been pushed away. His health has been restored and he shall live to be old. *Yû!*

The first paragraph, addressed to the Fire, the "Ancient White," is recited by the priest inside the house of his clients, while standing in front of the fire and looking down into it, with his back turned to the members of the family, who stand in line with their backs turned toward him and their eyes looking out the door. He has with him an assistant, who, at the conclusion of the final paragraph, ejaculates *Kû!* when the members of the family start in procession to go down to the water, followed by the doctor and the attendant.

On arriving at the stream, the persons for whose benefit the ceremony is intended stand in line side by side close to the water's edge, with their eyes intently fixed upon the stream, while the priest stands behind them with his hands outstretched and his eyes looking straight forward. He then recites the prayer to the "Long Man," the River, followed by the seven paragraphs addressed to Gĕ'hyăgúga, the Sun, represented as the owner of tables spread with "white," or peace-bringing food, which the client eats and is restored to health. During this part of the ceremony the attendant is closely watching the appearance of the water in front of the clients for the distance of a "hand-length" (*awâ'hilû,* a formulistic term, not always to be taken literally) from the shore. Should a stick, fish, or other object come within this limit during the recitation of the prayer, it is a sign that the death in the family was due to witchcraft. By certain signs in connection with the appearance of the object, the priest is enabled to guess the whereabouts, or even the name, of the secret enemy, who must then be proceeded against in another ceremony to neutralize any further evil conjurations. On the other hand, should the water appear clear, the death was due to ordinary circumstances, and no further ceremony is necessary.

As the priest mentions each in turn of the seven upper worlds,—each of which is figuratively said to be a "hand-length" above the last,—he raises his hands gradually higher, until, at the concluding paragraph, they are stretched high above his head. At the final *Yû!* his clients bend down with one accord, and, dipping up the water in their hands, lave their heads and breasts, or else, wading out into the stream, plunge their bodies completely under seven times.

Each "upper world" or heaven symbolizes a definite period, usually one year or one month, according to the nature of the formula. In ceremonies for obtaining long life, the period is commonly one year. Should the omens in the water be propitious up to the mention of the third, fourth, or fifth upper world, the client will live three, four, or five years longer. If all goes well until he is raised up to the seventh or highest heaven, he may expect at least a seven years' lease of life, for beyond this limit the mental vision of the seer is unable to pierce the future. If, on the contrary, an unfavorable omen is perceived in the water during the recital, for instance, of the paragraph which raises the client to the fifth upper world, the priest knows that some great danger, possibly death itself, threatens the man in five months or five years to come. This necessitates the immediate performance of another ceremony, accompanied by fasting and going to water, to turn aside the impending peril. The final result is generally successful, as the priest seldom ceases from his labors until the omens are propitious. Should it still be otherwise, after all his effort, he informs his client, who is often so completely under the force of the delusion that he not infrequently loses all courage, believing himself doomed by an inexorable fate, broods, sickens, and actually dies, thus fulfilling the prediction.

Chief among the sacred paraphernalia of the priests and conjurers are the beads used in connection with certain water ceremonies, more especially those for counteracting the evil spells of a secret enemy, or for compassing the death of a rival. The beads formerly used were the small glossy seeds of the Viper's Bugloss, superseded now by the ordinary beads of glass or porcelain. They are called by the formulistic name of *sû'nikta,* the regular term being *adéla.* They are of different symbolic colors, and are kept carefully wrapped in buckskin—or in cloth, in these degenerate days of calico—until needed in the ceremony, when they are uncovered and laid upon a whole buckskin spread out upon the ground, or, more often now, upon a piece of new cloth furnished by the client, and which is afterward claimed by the priest as the fee for his services.

There are many formulas for conjuring with the beads, and differences also in the details of the ceremony, but the general practice is the same in nearly all cases. Let us suppose that it is performed for the benefit of a man who believes himself to be withering away under a secret spell, or who desires the death of a hated rival.

Priest and client go down together at early daybreak to the river, and take up their position at the point where they can look up-stream while facing the rising sun. The client then wades out to where, in ceremonial language, the water is a "hand-length" in depth and stands silently with his eyes fixed upon the water and his back to the shaman upon the bank, while the latter unfolds upon the sand a white and black cloth, and lays upon the first the red beads—typical of success and his client—and upon the other the black beads, emblematic of death and the intended victim.

The priest now takes a red bead, representing his client, between the thumb and index finger of his right hand, and a black bead, representing the victim, in a like manner, in his left hand. Standing a few feet behind his client he turns toward the east, fixes his eyes upon the bead in his right hand, and addresses it as the *Sû'nikta*

Gǐgagéǐ, the Red Bead, invoking blessings upon his client and clothing him with the red garments of success. The formula is repeated in a low chant or intonation, the voice rising at intervals, after the manner of a revival speaker. Then, turning to the black bead in his left hand, he addresses it in a similar manner, calling down withering curses upon the head of the victim. Finally looking up, he addresses the stream, under the name of *Yû'ñwǐ Gûnahíta,* the "Long Man," imploring it to protect his client and raise him to the seventh heaven, where he shall be secure from all his enemies. The other, then stooping down, dips up water in his hand seven times and pours it over his head, rubbing it upon his shoulders and breast at the same time. In some cases he dips completely under seven times, being stripped, of course, even when the water is of almost icy coldness. The priest, then stooping down, makes a hole in the ground with his finger, drops into it the fatal black bead, and buries it out of sight with a stamp of his foot. This ends the ceremony.

While addressing the beads the priest attentively observes them as they are held between the thumb and finger of his outstretched hands. In a short time they begin to move, slowly and but a short distance at first, then faster and farther, sometimes coming down as far as the first joint of the finger or even below, with an irregular serpentine motion from side to side, returning in the same manner. Should the red bead be more lively in its movements and come down lower on the finger than the black bead, he confidently predicts for the client the speedy accomplishment of his desire. On the other hand, should the black bead surpass the red in activity, the spells of the shaman employed by the intended victim are too strong, and the whole ceremony must be gone over again with an additional and larger quantity of cloth. This must be kept up until the movements of the red bead give token of success, or until it shows by its sluggish motions or its failure to move down along the finger that the opposing shaman cannot be overcome. In the latter case the discouraged plotter gives up all hope, considering himself as cursed by every imprecation which he has unsuccessfully invoked upon his enemy, goes home and—theoretically— lies down and dies. As a matter of fact, however, the priest is always ready with other formulas by means of which he can ward off such fatal results, in consideration of a sufficient quantity of cloth.

Should the first trial prove unsuccessful, the priest and his client fast until just before sunset. They then eat and remain awake until midnight, when the ceremony is repeated, and if still unsuccessful it may be repeated four times before daybreak, both men remaining awake and fasting throughout the night. If still unsuccessful, they continue to fast all day until just before sundown. Then they eat and again remain awake until midnight, when the previous night's program is repeated. As the enemy and his shaman are supposed to be industriously working counter- charms all the while, it now becomes a trial of endurance between the two parties, each being obliged to subsist upon one meal per day and abstain entirely from sleep until the result has been decided one way or the other. Failure to endure this severe strain, even so much as closing the eyes in sleep for a few moments, or partaking of the least nourishment excepting just before sunset, neutralizes all the previous work and places the unfortunate offender at the mercy of his more watch- ful enemy. If the priest be still unsuccessful on the fourth day, he acknowledges himself defeated and gives up the contest. Should his spells prove the stronger, his victim will die within seven days, or, as the Cherokees say, seven nights. These "seven nights," however, are interpreted figuratively, to mean *seven years,* a rendering which often serves to relieve the conjurer from a very embarrassing position.

With regard to the oracle of the ceremony, the beads do move; but the explanation is simple, although the Indians account for it by saying that the beads become alive by the recitation of the sacred formula. The priest is laboring under strong though suppressed emotion. He stands with his hands stretched out in a constrained position, every muscle tense, his breast heaving and his voice trembling from the effort, and the natural result is that, before he is done praying, his fingers begin to twitch involuntarily and thus cause the beads to move. As before stated, their motion is irregular, but the peculiar delicacy of touch acquired by long practice probably imparts more directness to their movements than would at first seem possible.

We give one of the formulas used in connection with the beads when performing the purification rite for a family preparatory to eating the new corn. It will be noted that the form of the prayer is assertive rather than petitional. In this case, as always in connection with the Green Corn Dance, the principal bead is white, symbolic of health, happiness, and gentle peace; instead of red, significant of triumph over another. The ceremony is performed for each member of the family in turn, and should the movements of the beads foreshadow sickness to any one of them, the priest at once takes the necessary steps to avert the misfortune.

THIS IS FOR USING THE BEADS.

Sgĕ! O now you have drawn near to listen, O Long Man, in repose. You fail not in anything. My paths lead down to the edge of your body. The white cloth has come and is resting upon the white seats. The white beads are resting upon it (the cloth). The soul restored has now ascended to the first upper world.

In the second upper world, where the white seats have been let down, the white cloth has come and rested upon them. The white beads are resting upon it. The soul restored has now ascended to the second upper world.

In the third upper world, where the white seats have been let down, the white cloth has come and rested upon them. The white beads are resting upon it. The soul restored has now ascended to the third upper world.

In the fourth upper world, where the white seats have been let down, the white cloth has come and rested upon them. The white beads are resting upon it. The soul restored has now ascended to the fourth upper world.

In the fifth upper world, where the white seats have been let down, the white cloth has come and rested upon them. The white beads are resting upon it. The soul restored has now ascended to the fifth upper world.

In the sixth upper world, where the white seats have been let down, the white cloth has come and rested upon them. The white beads are resting upon it. The soul restored has now ascended to the sixth upper world.

In the seventh upper world, where the white seats have been let down, the white cloth has come and rested upon them. The white beads are resting upon it. He is called *thus* (*iyústĭ*, mentioning name). His soul, made pleasing, has now been examined. His soul has now gone to the seventh upper world and appeared there in full view. He shall recover by degrees. *Yû!*

The next formula, used also in connection with the beads, is rather peculiar, and is intended to ward off the evil presaged by dreams of sudden death, as by falling from a cliff, drowning in the river, or any similar accident. Such dreams are regarded as the result of the hostile conjurations of some secret enemy, and it is believed that the calamity shadowed forth will actually befall unless the proper ceremony is performed to avert it. The client is specially mentioned by name and clan, and the prediction is read from the appearance of the water and the movements of the beads.

THIS IS WHEN THEY HAVE BAD DREAMS.

Sgĕ! His clan is *this* (insert name). He is called *thus* (*iyústĭ*—name). Evil things were being allotted for him. Where is the assigner of evil located?

Sgĕ! Oh, now you have drawn near to listen, O Brown Beaver. Evil was being allotted for him, but now it has been taken away. The body is called *thus.* The evil has been taken away. Where people are many, there you have gone and allotted that evil shall remain. He is called *thus.* His soul is now released. His soul has now been lifted up. His soul has become renewed. His soul has now been lifted up.

Sgĕ! His clan is *this.* He is called *thus.* Evil things were being allotted for him. Where is the assigner of evil located?

Sgĕ! O White Beaver, reposing up the stream, quickly you have arisen. Evil things were being allotted for him, but now it has been taken away. The evil allotted has now been turned aside. It has been scattered about where people are many. It shall utterly disappear. His soul has now been renewed. His pleasure-filled soul has now been lifted up. In the seventh upper world his soul has now arisen to its full height. *Yû!*

The priest stands upon the bank, while the client, stripped of all clothing excepting his shirt, wades out into the shallow water. Before beginning the prayer, the priest inquires of his client to what place he wishes to send the evil foreshadowed in the prophetic dream, for it is held that such dreams must be fulfilled, and that all that the priest can do is to divert their accomplishment from the intended victim. The client names some distant settlement as the place where he wishes the blow to fall, and the priest at once summons the Beaver to bear the "evil thing" (*tsâstâ*) to that place and leave it there, "where people are many." As every Cherokee settlement is situated upon a stream, and the "evil thing," when exorcised, is thrown into the water, it is quite natural that the Beaver should be chosen to assist in the matter. Should the priest find himself unable to send the calamity so far, the client names some nearer settlement, and a second attempt is made, and so on until a resting place is found for the tsâstâ, even though it be necessary to send it to another clan or family within the settlement of the client himself. These successive trials are made by working the beads, using one color for the client and the other for the vicarious victim, as already described. After each recitation the client stoops and laves his face in the water. When the beads show that the evil is finally banished, he wades far out into the stream and plunges under seven times. At the seventh plunge, while still under water, he tears the shirt from his body and lets it float down the stream, carrying with it all the evil of the dream, to go where the Beaver wills.

THE UNDER LAND
(Chatot)

W hen the Chatas looked into the still depths of Bayou Lacombe, Louisiana, they said that the reflection of the sky was the empyrean of the Under Land, whither all good souls were sure to go after death. Their chief, Opaleeta, having fallen into this bayou, was so long beneath the water that he was dead when his fellows found him, but by working over him for hours, and through resort to prayers and incantations of medicine men, his life returned and he stood on his feet once more. Then he grieved that his friends had brought him back, for he had been at the gates of the Under Land, where the air is blithe and balmy, and so nourishing that people live on it; where it is never winter; where the sun shines brightly, but never withers and parches; and where stars dance to the swing of the breezes. There no white man comes to rob the Indian and teach him to do wrong. Gorgeous birds fly through changing skies that borrow the tints of flowers, the fields are spangled with blossoms of red and blue and gold that load each wind with perfume, the grass is as fine as the hair of deer, and the streams are thick with honey.

At sunset those who loved each other in life are gathered to their lodges, and raise songs of joy and thankfulness. Their voices are soft and musical, their faces are young again and beam with smiles, and there is no death. It was only the chiefs who heard his story, for, had all the tribe known it, many who were old and ill and weary would have gone to the bayou, and leaped in, to find that restful, happy Under Land. Those who had gone before they sometimes tried to see, when the lake was still and dappled with pictures of sunset clouds, but the dead never came back—they kept away from the margin of the water—lest they should be called again to a life of toil and sorrow. And Opaleeta lived for many years and ruled his tribe with wisdom, yet he shared in few of the merrymakings of his people, and when, at last, his lodge was ready in the Under Land, he gave up his life without a sigh.

ONONDAGA WITCHCRAFT
(Onondaga)

A t Onondaga there are persons who pretend to identify and distinguish ailments of which witchcraft is the cause; to determine who is the witch implicated, and even, when consulted in time, to effect a cure. In the absence of a better word these may, for the sake of convenience, be called witch-doctors. Once when a young girl died a witch-doctor advised the mother to search carefully near the house, and, if she found any scraps of cloth, to keep them and watch for a woman wearing a dress which matched the pieces. Should such a woman be discovered, she would, without doubt, be the person who had bewitched the child. Soon after a piece of cloth was found which corresponded with a dress worn by a Seneca woman living among the Onondagas, who, though protesting her innocence, is still regarded with distrust by the mother and friends of the dead girl.

As to the cure of persons bewitched, there are several courses adopted by these witch-doctors or conjurors. A general belief seems to be that the victim is killed by the presence of a foreign substance which has, so to speak, been shot or otherwise introduced into the body, in some mysterious way. One man spoke of actually putting the object into a gun (presumably a magic gun of some sort, and noiseless) and shooting it into the person whom it was intended to kill. Accounts differ on this point, but the cure is usually wrought by removing the fatal missile or charm. This is done by deceiving the spectators through the employment of trickery. At times the afflicted part is bandaged, especially if it be one of the limbs, when on the following day, upon the removal of the cloths by the witch-doctor, "a few gray and black hairs," "a bit of shawl fringe," or a "small coal of wood neatly sharpened at both ends," any or all of these, or similar objects, are found to have been drawn out by the bandages.

Another method, which partakes more of the nature of a surgical operation, is the following: A woman who was suffering severe pain in her side called in the old man already referred to, and asked his advice. He examined her side, and, having ascertained the woman was a victim of witchcraft, told her that he could cure her, but the operation being an exceedingly difficult one, he would have to bring a stronger man to assist him, and a pint of whiskey must be provided for their use to keep up their strength. An incision was made at the point where the pain was most intense, and the large end of a horn applied to it. Then through a hole in the smaller end of the horn the men sucked violently for a long time, drawing much blood and perspiring profusely with fatigue, relieving one another from time to time, and occasionally taking a drink of whiskey. Finally, a stony object of a whitish color, and soon after a small bunch of yarn, were sucked through. The doctor carried these away with him, and the woman recovered. The old man was probably cunning enough to foresee the beneficial effect of this barbaric cupping process, while it is quite possible that the imagination may have contributed to produce a favorable result.

The power of bewitching appears to belong only to those who are witches by profession—to those who have gone through the initiation or preparation necessary in order to become a witch. Some say that the candidate must promise to sacrifice, as the price of his tuition, a member of his own family, as a sister, brother, or cousin, before he may become master of the art.

As soon as the power of witchcraft is obtained, the individual seems to be able, by mere volition, to injure his victim; nor do charms and spells appear, in most cases, necessary. If a dispute occurs, in which a witch threatens or curses his antagonist, he has only to be in earnest in what he says to cause the malediction to take effect. If the person bewitched is able to anticipate the evil, or can discover the guilty one, he may make an appeal, through a third person, to have the malediction revoked. An instance of this kind occurred under my own observation as recently as last August. A woman, whose child had unwittingly offended the wife of a neighbor (a reputed witch), was caused much anxiety by the fear that, in retaliation, some member of her family might be bewitched. In order to prevent this she sent a friend to tell the witch that she was mistaken in accusing the child, and to ask her not to think harshly of any of the family. The witch, being notified in this way that he is discovered, is presumably forced to discontinue his evil practices, for fear of exposure and punishment. If, however, the cause of the trouble is not suspected, or is discovered too late, the victim is doomed, unless a cure can be effected by ordinary remedies, which is usually impossible.

Charms do not seem to be in common use, though the St. Regis Indians are said to make a small wooden peg, which they drive into the ground, or into a log or tree. The victim lives as long as the peg lasts, but wastes away gradually as it decays, and dies when it has rotted completely. Tobacco sometimes is burned in a fire, the witch meanwhile addressing it in a low tone, and exhorting it to efficacy. This seems to possess something of the character of a spell. It is equally possible that this may be some form of sacrificial offering.

Witches are supposed to meet at night in the woods and bushes, taking temporarily the form of dogs or other animals to better conceal themselves. For this reason the howling of dogs at night and lights moving in the woods are looked upon with suspicion and dread.

The enumeration of the above facts suffices to prove that a strong belief in witches exists at the present time.

In addition to witches, these Indians believe that there exists a race of supernatural evil beings or demons, whom they call *Hat-do'-ĭ, Hon-do'-ĭ* in the plural.

These Hon-do'-ĭ afflict human beings with illness and other misfortunes, but, notwithstanding their hostility to mankind, they can be propitiated and persuaded not only to withdraw the evil they themselves have caused, but also to grant aid and protection against the witches, to whom they appear to be antagonistic. They are said to inhabit a cave, which opens at the stone quarries on the north edge of the reservation, and extends through a narrow cleft in the rock to a similar cavern near Jamesville, NY.

In this cave, according to the Indian belief, are stone images supposed to represent the Hon-do'-ĭ, and the whole inner atmosphere of the place is charged with a malign influence. An old man and some boys visited the cave one Sunday afternoon. They remained there several hours; so long, in fact, that when at last they emerged their candles were nearly consumed. One of the boys for days afterward was annoyed by a swollen face, the swelling being so great that his eyes were almost closed. This was ascribed to the resentment of the devils. But these evil beings, if flattered and humored, become less troublesome, and will even withdraw for a time the evil or sickness they have caused. Dances in their honor ("devildances") and offerings of tobacco and food are the usual means adopted to pacify them. The dancers, masked and attired in the most uncouth and tattered garments, imitate by weird groanings, grunting, and eccentric movements the actions of the demons. Their masks are of several kinds, principally of wood, but some of husk, buffalo-skin, muslin, and occasionally the coarse papier maché masks of the toy-shops. The wooden masks are the most interesting, often artistic, and very hideous, and are held in the highest esteem, some of them having been in use for from twenty to one hundred years. The older ones are by far the more characteristic, but there are comparatively few of them now in existence. The eyes are usually made of discs of tin or brass set into the wood, while the expression of the mouth is occasionally heightened by the addition of hog's teeth or chips of bone or shell. A wig of horse-tail, a strip of buffalo-robe, or a braid of corn-husks is sometimes fastened to the mask when in use, and helps to disguise the wearer as well as to make the general effect more frightful. The rest of the costume consists of old, torn clothes, corn-husks, old buffalo-robes, and even at times articles of female attire. Baskets, pans, bundles of cloth, or other bulky objects are stuffed under the garments, with cords tied around the body above and below them, so as to produce the appearance of humps or deformities. In fact, any device is used which contributes to make the disguise unsightly. Heavy moccasins, made of old boot-legs, are generally worn in winter. A rattle, *Us-ta-wä^{n}s'-ha,* made of the shell of a snapping-turtle, with the head, neck, and entire skin except the legs and tail, is carried by some of the dancers. Others carry clubs or rough staffs, four or five feet long, and from an inch and a half to two inches in diameter. A few carry both staffs and rattles, or substitute for the club a wooden pestle, such as is used in grinding corn. Formerly the pestles figured more commonly than at present.

Chapter 4

Tribal History and Tribal Customs

The Celestial Bear
(Algonquin)

T he two stellar groups which seem to have played decidedly the most conspic uous part in Algonquin legends are the Pleiades and the Great Bear. Turning our attention to the latter group, we can easily imagine the astonishment of the early missionaries when they pointed out its stars to the Algonquins, and received the reply, "But they are our Bear Stars too."

The minds of these worthy men were already impressed by the discovery in other parts of America of native traditions of a deluge, a passage through divided water, and a hero miraculously born, as well as a ritual, including baptism, confession, communion, and the use of the cross as a sacred symbol. Doubtless, therefore, they regarded the identity of the Algonquin Bear and their own as only another proof that an apostle had at some time visited this continent. While that explanation is not tenable today, the interesting question remains as to what this identity does mean.

The answer is best found by an examination of the traditions associated with this stellar group. Its stars seem to have been called the Bear over nearly the whole of our continent when the first Europeans, of whom we have knowledge, arrived. They were known as far north as Point Barrow, as far east as Nova Scotia, as far west as the Pacific Coast, and as far south as the Pueblos.

Some tribes within these boundaries, however, seem to have called the group by other names. When we seek legends connected with the Bear, we find that in spite

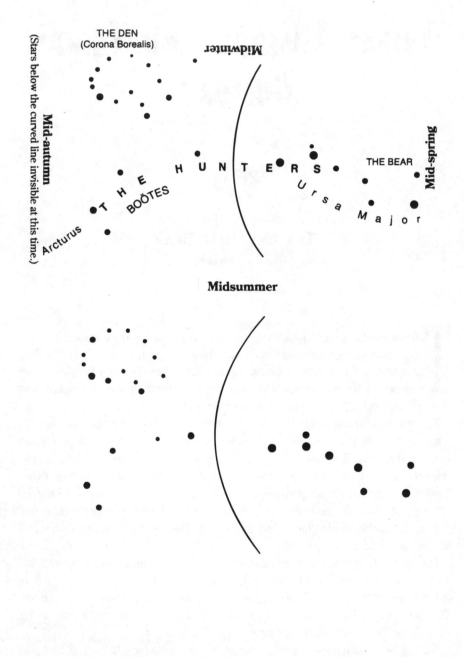

THE DEN
(Corona Borealis)

Midwinter

Mid-autumn
(Stars below the curved line invisible at this time.)

THE BEAR

Mid-spring

THE HUNTERS

BOÖTES

Arcturus

Ursa Major

Midsummer

of the widespread knowledge of the name there is by no means a wealth of material.

The best known legend is that common to the tribes of the Algonquin and Iroquois families. It has been related to me many times, in what is perhaps its most complete and extensive form, by the Micmacs of Nova Scotia, as we sat beside the camp-fire in the glorious summer evenings of that land, and they pointed out overhead the stars of which they spoke. Let us preface the legend with the following table:—

DRAMATIS PERSONÆ

ENGLISH	MICMAC	SPECIES	STARS
The Bear,	Mooin,	Ursus Americanus,	α, β, γ, δ, Ursae Majoris.
The Hunters,	Ntóoksooinook,		
The Robin,	Quipchowwéch,	Merula migratorius,	ε Ursae Majoris.
The Chickadee,	Chŭgegéss,	Parus atricapillus,	ζ Ursae Majoris.
The Moose Bird,	Mikchăgŏgwéch,	Perisoreus Canadensis,	η Ursae Majoris.
The Pigeon,	Pŭlés,	Ectopistes migratorius,	γ Boötis.
The Blue Jay,	Wŏlŏwéch,	Cyanurus cristatus,	ε Boötis
The Owl,	Kookoogwéss,	Strix cinerea,	Arcturus.
The Saw-whet,	Kŏpkéch,	Nyctale Acadica,	η Boötis.
The Pot,	Wo,		Alcor.
The Den,	Mskegwŏm,		μ, δ, Boötis.
			α, β, γ, δ, ε, ζ, θ, κ, λ, ρ, Coronæ Borealis.

Comparing the above list with the accompanying chart, we observe that the Bear is represented by the four stars in the bowl of what we call the Dipper. Behind are seven hunters who are pursuing her. Close beside the second hunter is a little star. It is the pot which he is carrying, so that, when the bear is killed, he may cook the meat therein. Just above these hunters a group of smaller stars form a pocket-like figure—the den whence the bear has issued.

Late in spring, the bear waking from her long winter sleep, leaves her rocky hillside den and descends to the ground in search of food. Instantly the sharp-eyed chickadee perceives her, and, being too small to undertake the pursuit alone, calls the other hunters to his aid. Together the seven start after the bear, the chickadee with his pot being placed between two of the larger birds so that he may not lose his way. All the hunters are hungry for meat after the short rations of winter and so they pursue eagerly, but throughout the summer the bear flees across the northern horizon and the pursuit continues. In the autumn, one by one, the hunters in the rear begin to lose their trail. First of all the two owls, heavier and clumsier of wing than the other birds, disappear from the chase. But you must not laugh when you hear how Kŏpkéch, the smaller owl, failed to secure a share of the bear meat, and you must not imitate his rasping cry, for if you disregard either warning, be sure that wherever you are, as soon as you are asleep he will descend from the sky with a birch bark torch and set fire to whatever clothing covers you. Next the blue jay and the pigeon also lose the trail and drop out of the chase. This leaves only the robin, the chickadee, and the moose bird, but they continue the pursuit, and at last, about mid-autumn, they overtake their prey.

Brought to bay, the bear rears up on her hind feet and prepares to defend herself, but the robin pierces her with an arrow and she falls over upon her back. The robin being himself very thin at this season is intensely eager to eat some of the bear's fat as soon as possible. In his haste he leaps upon his victim, and becomes covered with blood. Flying to a maple-tree near at hand in the land of the sky, he tries to shake off this blood. He succeeds in getting all off save a spot upon his breast. "That spot," says the garrulous chickadee, "you will carry as long as your name is robin."

But the blood which he does shake off spatters far and wide over the forests of earth below, and hence we see each autumn the blood-red tints on the foliage; it is reddest on the maples, because trees on earth follow the appearance of the trees in the sky, and the sky maple received most of the blood. The sky is just the same as the earth, only up above, and older.

Some time after these things happened to the robin, the chickadee arrived on the scene. These two birds cut up the bear, built a fire, and placed some of the meat over it to cook. Just as they were about to begin to eat, the moose bird put in his appearance.

He had almost lost the trail, but when he regained it he had not hurried, because he knew that it would take his companions some time to cook the meat after the bear was slain, and he did not mind missing that part of the affair so long as he arrived in time for a full share of the food. Indeed, he was so impressed with the advantages of this policy, that ever since then he has ceased to hunt for himself, preferring to follow after hunters and share their spoils. And so, whenever a bear or a moose or other animal is killed today in the woods of *Megumaage,* Micmac Land, you will see him appear to demand his share. That is why the other birds named him *Mikchagogwech,* He-who-comes-in-at-the-last-moment, and the Micmacs say there are some men who ought to be called that too.

However that may be, the robin and chickadee, being generous, willingly shared their food with the moose bird. Before they ate, the robin and moose bird danced around the fire, while the chickadee stirred the pot. Such was the custom in the good old times, when Micmacs were brothers all to all and felt it a duty to share their food together, and to thank each other and the Universal Spirit for their present happiness.

But this does not end the story of the bear, though one might think so. Through the winter her skeleton lies upon its back in the sky, but her life-spirit has entered another bear who also lies upon her back in the den, invisible, and sleeping the winter sleep. When the spring comes around again, this bear will again issue forth from the den to be again pursued by the hunters, to be again slain, but again to send to the den her life-spirit, to issue forth yet again, when the sun once more awakens the sleeping earth.

TALE OF THE PLEIADES
(Onondaga)

The Huron-Iroquois seem to have taken little note of the stars, though the sun and moon had a prominent place in their mythology and customs. The north star could not well escape their attention, and they called it the star which always stands still. The Great Bear was not entirely overlooked, but the Pleiades formed their favorite constellation.

Indeed, the Indians along the Atlantic coast displayed much the same judgment. They called the Great Bear by its familiar name, and they had another for the belt of Orion. Some called the Pleiades the Seven Stars, and others the Brooding Hen, or literally, "They sit apart from others," or are grouped together. The women there are the most experienced star-gazers; there is scarcely one of them but can name all the stars; their rising and setting; the position of the Arctos, that is the wagon, is as well known to them as to us, and they name them by other names.

Among the Onondagas a single star is *O-chis-tan-oo-kwa,* adding *i-nune* in the plural, "Spotting the sky." It is of the Pleiades, or *Oot-kwa-tah,* "There they dwell in peace."

A long time ago a party of Indians went through the woods toward a good hunting-ground, which they had long known. They traveled several days through a very wild country, going on leisurely and camping by the way. At last they reached *Kan-ya-ti-yo,* "the beautiful lake," where the gray rocks were crowned with great forest trees. Fish swarmed in the waters, and at every jutting point the deer came down from the hills around to bathe or drink of the lake. On the hills and in the valleys were huge beech and chestnut trees, where squirrels chattered, and bears came to take their morning and evening meals.

The chief of the band was *Hah-yah-no,* "Tracks in the water," and he halted his party on the lake shore that he might return thanks to the Great Spirit for their safe arrival at this good hunting-ground. "Here will we build our lodges for the winter, and may the Great Spirit, who has prospered us on our way, send us plenty of game, and health and peace." The Indian is always thankful.

The pleasant autumn days passed on. The lodges had been built, and hunting had prospered, when the children took a fancy to dance for their own amusement. They were getting lonesome, having little to do, and so they met daily in a quiet spot by the lake to have what they called their jolly dance. They had done this a long time, when one day a very old man came to them. They had seen no one like him before. He was dressed in white feathers, and his white hair shone like silver. If his appearance was strange, his words were unpleasant as well. He told them they must stop their dancing, or evil would happen to them. Little did the children heed, for they were intent on their sport, and again and again the old man appeared, repeating his warning.

The mere dances did not afford all the enjoyment the children wished, and a little boy, who liked a good dinner, suggested a feast the next time they met. The food must come from their parents, and all these were asked when they returned home. "You will waste and spoil good victuals," said one. "You can eat at home as you should," said another, and so they got nothing at all. Sorry as they were for this, they met and danced as before. A little to eat after each dance would have made them happy indeed. Empty stomachs cause no joy.

One day, as they danced, they found themselves rising little by little into the air, their heads being light through hunger. How this happened they did not know, but one said, "Do not look back, for something strange is taking place." A woman, too, saw them rise, and called them back, but with no effect, for they still rose slowly above the earth. She ran to the camp, and all rushed out with food of every kind, but the children would not return, though their parents called piteously after them. But one would even look back, and he became a falling star. The others reached the sky, and are now what we call the Pleiades, and the Onondagas *Oot-kwa-tah*. Every falling or shooting star recalls the story, but the seven stars shine on continuously, a pretty band of dancing children.

TALE OF THE NORTHERN LIGHTS
(Wabanaki)

O ld Chief *M'Sartto* (Morning Star) had an only son, so different from the other boys of the tribe as to be worry to old chief. He would not stay and play with the others, but would take his bow and arrows, and leave home for days at a time, always going towards the north. When he came home they would say, "Where you been—what you see?" but he say nothing. At last old chief say his wife, "The boy must be watched. I will follow him." So next time M'Sartto kept in his path and travel for long time. Suddenly his eyes closed an' he could not hear; he had a curious feeling, then *know* nothing. By'm-by his eyes open in a queer light country, no sun, no moon, no stars, but country all lighted by this peculiar light. He saw many beings, but all different from his people. They gather 'round and try to talk, but he not understand their language. M'Sartto did not know where to go nor what to do. He well treated by this strange tribe; he watched their games and was 'tracted to wonderful game of ball he never saw before; it seemed to turn the light to many colors, and the players all had lights on their heads, and all wore very curious kind belts, called *Menquan,* or Rainbow belts. In few days an old man came and speak to M'Sartto in his own language, and ask him if he knew where he was. Old chief say "No." Then old man say, "You are in the country of *Wa-ba-ban* (northern lights). I came here many years ago. I was the only one here from the 'lower country,' as we call it; but now there is a boy comes to visit us every few days." Then M'Sartto ask how old man got there—what way he come. Old man say, "I follow path called Spirits' Path, *Ket-à-gus-wowt* (Milky-Way)." "This must be same path I come," said old chief. "Did you have queer feeling as if you lost all knowledge when you traveled?" "Yes," say old man, "I could not see nor hear." Then say M'Sartto, "We did come by same path. Can you tell me how I can get home again?" "Yes, the chief of Wa-ba-ban will send you home safe." "Well, can you tell me where

I can see my boy?—the boy that comes here to visit you is mine." Then old man tell M'Sartto, "You will see him playing ball if you watch." Chief M'Sartto very glad to hear this, and when man went 'round to wigwams telling all to go have game ball, M'Sartto go too. When game began he saw many beautiful colors in the playground. Old man ask him, "Do you see your boy there?" Old chief said he did: "The one with the brightest light on his head is my son." Then they went to Chief of Northern Lights, and the old man said, "The chief of the Lower Country wants to go home, and also wants his boy." So Chief of Northern Lights calls his people together to bid goodbye to M'Sartto and his son, then ordered two *K'che Sipps* (great birds) to carry them home. When they were traveling the Milky-Way he felt the same strange way he did when going, and when he came to his senses he found himself near home. His wife very glad he come, for when boy told her his father was safe she pay no notice, as she afraid M'Sartto was lost.

ORIGIN OF THUNDER
(Passamaquoddy)

Of old times. Once an Indian went forth to hunt. And he departed from the east branch of the Penobscot, and came to the head of another branch that leads into the east branch, and this he followed even to the foot of Mount Katahdin. And there he hunted many a day alone, and met none, till one morning in midwinter he found the track of snow-shoes. So he returned to his camp; but the next day he met with it again in a far-distant place. And thus it was that, wherever he went, this track came to him every day. Then noting this, as a sign to be observed, he followed it, and it went up the mountain, *Katahdin,* which, being interpreted, means "the great mountain," until at last it was lost in a hard snow-shoe road made by many travelers. And since it was hard and even, he took off his *agahmook,* or snow-shoes, and went ever on and up with the road; and it was a strange path and strange was its ending, for it stopped just before a high ledge, like an immense wall, on a platform at its foot. And there were many signs there, as of many people, yet he saw no one. And as he stayed it seemed to grow stranger and stranger. At last he heard a sound as of footsteps coming, yet within the wall, when lo! a girl stepped directly out of the precipice upon the platform. But though she was beautiful beyond belief, he was afraid. And to his every thought she answered in words, and that so sweetly and kindly and cleverly that he was soon without fear, though he saw that she had powerful *m'téoulin,* or great magic power. And they being soon pleased one with the other, and wanting each other, she bade him accompany her, and that by walking directly through the rock. "Have no fear," said she, "but advance boldly!" So he obeyed, and lo! the rock was as the air, and it gave way as he went on. And ever as they went the maiden talked to him, answering his thoughts, so that he spoke not aloud.

And anon they came to a great cavern far within, and there was an old man seated by a fire, and the old man welcomed him. And he was very kindly treated by the strange pair all day: in all his life he had never been so happy. Now as the night

❖ 43 ❖

drew near, the old man said to his daughter, "Can you hear aught of your brothers?" Then she went out to the terrace, and, returning, said, "No." Then anon he asked her again, and she, going and returning as before, replied, "Now I hear them coming." Then they listened, when lo! there came, as at the door without, a crash of thunder with a flash of lightning, and out of the light stepped two young men of great beauty, but like giants, stupendous and of awful mien. And, like their father, their eyebrows were of stone, while their cheeks were as rocks.

And the hunter was told by their sister that when they went forth, which was every few days, their father said to them, "Sons, arise! it is time now for you to go forth over the world and save our friends. Go not too near the trees, but if you see aught that is harmful to those whom we love, strike, and spare not!" Then when they went forth they flew on high, among the clouds: and thus it is that the Thunder and Lightning, whose home is in the mighty Katahdin, are made. And when the thunder strikes, the brothers are shooting at the enemies of their friends.

Now when the day was done the hunter returned to his home, and when there, found he had been gone seven years.

ORIGIN OF CORN
(Various)

A mong the Iroquois they, with the pumpkin, are known as Our Life, or Our Supporters, collectively, and the Seneca word for this is *De-o-há-ko*. The Onondagas call them *Tune-hā-kwe* (Those we live on), and they are the special gift of Hawenneyu, having a proper place in their thanksgiving feasts. Corn was originally of easy culture, abundant yield, and rich in oil. The envious Evil Spirit cast a blight upon it, and the yield became small and poor. This may be a reminiscence of the time when the Iroquois lived farther west and south. In another story, the Great Spirit gives corn to the Mohawks, squashes to the Onondagas, and beans to the Senecas, thus dividing the three among the three Elder Brothers. The others have less important gifts. In a story of Hiawatha, none of the three are mentioned in this way, but the Senecas are commended for their skill in raising corn and beans. Their crops of these were large indeed.

As has been said, corn was raised on a large hill, on which beans and squashes, or pumpkins, were planted later. The bean clung closely to the corn, while the pumpkin vine rambled over the field. On this fact is founded the Onondaga story and in this the three do not appear as sisters; indeed, one is a young man, while no relationship appears between the other two. The foliage and flowers represent their dresses, and habits of life are simply brought out.

A fine young man lived on a small hill, and being there alone he wished to marry. He had flowing robes, and wore long and nodding plumes, so that he was very beautiful to behold. Every morning and evening he came out of his quiet house, and three times he sang, *"Che hen, Che hen. Sone ke kwah no wah ho ten ah you ke neah.* Say it, Say it. Some one I will marry;" and he thought he cared not at all who it might be. For a long time he kept this up, every morning and night, and still he was a lonesome young man.

At last a tall young woman came, with long hair neatly braided behind, as is the Indian style. Her beads shone like drops of dew, and her flowing green mantle was adorned with large golden bells. The young man ceased to sing, and she said, "I am the one for whom you have been looking so long, and I am come to marry you." But he looked at her and said, "No! you are not the one. You wander so much from home, and run over the ground so fast, that I cannot keep by your side. I cannot have you." So the pumpkin maiden went away, and the young man was still alone, but kept on singing morning and night, hoping his bride would come.

One day there appeared a slender young woman, of graceful form and fair of face. Her beautiful mantle was spotted here and there with lovely clusters of flowers, and groups of bangles hung upon it. She heard the song and drew near the singer. Then she said she could love dearly one so manly, and would marry him if he would love her in turn. The song ceased; he looked at her and was pleased, and said she was just the one he wished, and for whom he had waited so long. They met with a loving embrace, and ever since the slender bean twines closely around the corn, he supporting her and she cherishing him. Perhaps it might be added that they are not divided in death, for beans make a part of Indian corn bread.

Another Indian corn story is as follows. The great magician called *Masswaweinini,* or the Living Statue, remained on the Manitoulin Islands after his friends had left. While hunting one day, he came suddenly to a wide prairie, across which he proceeded. There he met a small man, wearing a red feather on his head, and they smoked together. A wrestling match followed, with doubtful fortunes, but at last the small man was thrown. As directed, the victor cried out, "I have thrown you; *wa ge me na;"* and his opponent at once disappeared. In his place there lay on the ground a crooked ear of *mondamin,* or Indian corn, with a red hairy tassel at the top. A voice was heard, directing him to strip the body and throw the fragments all around. The spine, which gave these parts support, was also to be broken up and scattered near the edge of the wood. In one moon he was to return. This he did, and found the plain filled with growing corn. From the broken cob grew luxuriant pumpkin vines. At the end of summer he was on the wrestling ground again where the corn was in full ear and the pumpkins of great size. Of these he gathered a good store, and the voice was heard again: "Masswaweinini, you have conquered me, and thus saved your own life. Victory has crowned your efforts, and now my body shall forever nourish the human race." Thus came the gift of corn and pumpkins, and the gift of wampum followed closely, brought about by the good fairies of that enchanted land.

An old Odjibwa custom was to have the wife, some dark night, divest herself of clothing, and drag her principal garment around the cornfield. This was a safeguard against pests, and insured an abundant crop. If a young woman found a red ear in husking, this was typical of a brave lover, and a fit present for some young warrior. If it was crooked and tapered to a point, it was the symbol of an old man thievishly entering the field. Every one laughed and shouted *"Wa ge min!"*

THE FALSE FACES
(Onondaga)

After the making of the world and its people by Rawen Niyoh, he left it for a time, but when he returned he was one day walking through an open place, following the sun, overlooking his own work, and examining the ground where the people were going to live, when his eye caught a strange, long-haired figure coming in the opposite direction. The face of this figure was red and twisted, the mouth being pulled up at the left corner.

Rawen Niyoh said to him, "Where did you come from?" to which the False Face replied, "I am the real owner of this world—I was here before you."

Rawen Niyoh said, "I think *I* am the owner of this place, because I made it."

"That may be quite true," the False Face assented, "but I have been here a long time, and I have a good claim to it, and I am stronger than you are."

"Show me how you can prove this," demanded Rawen Niyoh.

The False Face suggested that they should retire to a valley not far from two high mountains. The False Face ordered one of the mountains to come nearer, and it moved close to them. Rawen Niyoh was very much surprised at the result, upon which he ordered the other mountain to approach, which it did—the two remaining so nearly together that Rawen and the False Face had barely room to get out.

Each was satisfied with this exhibition of power on the part of the other, and Rawen Niyoh said, "I think it would not be well for you to be seen here by the people who are coming to this place, because you are so ugly, for everybody would follow you to look at you."

Ah k'on wa-rah (the False Face) agreed to this on condition that he should be allowed to claim the new people as his grandchildren and they were to call him Grandfather. "I will help all I can," said he, "to drive away sickness from among the new people, and I am able to protect them from storms by causing the winds to go up high into the sky."

Rawen Niyoh replied, "I am sure you have much power to help the people, and you must keep this power as long as they live. We will make a bargain. They shall be your grandchildren, and you their Grandfather. They must observe a dance— the False Face Dance—at the Longhouse, forever. Now we make this bargain, which shall last as long as you, and I, and the people, and the world shall last."

Ah k'on wa-rah replied, "It is well, and I want you to know that I am going to get much help in my good work among the people, from my brother who is black, and who will be with me, as well as from my cousin who always goes with us. He is half black and half red."

Rawen Niyoh and Ah k'on wa-rah then separated, the former saying, "I am going towards the setting sun," and the Red False Face saying, "I go where the sun rises."

It will be seen from this story that even Rawen Niyoh is not supreme. His power is equalled by that of Ah k'on-wa-rah, and both are able to transport themselves to any part of the world at pleasure.

The fact that there are only three False Faces—one red, one black, and one half-and-half is suggestive of connection with the sun-myth.

It is to be observed, also, that although nothing is here mentioned respecting the power of the False Faces to exert evil influences on mankind, it is to be understood, according to the general belief, that they have this power, and exercise it, too.

OTHER VERSIONS

For a long time many hundreds of years ago, there was no being of any kind on this island (continent?) but one False Face.

One day the Creator appeared on the scene and told the False Face that some other beings were soon going to come into the world and it would be necessary for him to keep out of the way. The False Face objected very much to this suggestion, declaring that he had been in possession for such a long time that he didn't think it was fair to remove him for the convenience of newcomers, and he succeeded so well in convincing himself of his rights that he at last refused flatly to be displaced.

After a good deal of argument on both sides, the Creator told him it was no use to talk any more about the removal—He had decided that the False Face should go, and go he must. The Creator then told him that a hard and fast line must be drawn between their two territories. The Creator insisted on his right to mark the boundary without any interference on the part of the False Face, indeed he ordered him to turn himself away while the marking out was going on, so that he might know nothing of it until it was settled.

The False Face, with very bad grace, complied by looking in the opposite direction, but he was too much interested to remain in this position, and continued to give sly glances sidewise for the purpose of finding out how the line was being drawn. Becoming bolder after a little he turned right about to see the work, when the Creator catching him in the act, struck him such a blow on the cheek as to knock his mouth out of shape, and so it has remained until this day!

Another way of it is that the first being, who was not a man although he looked like one, had a face red on one side and black on the other.

One day he had a talk with Rawen Niyoh, who told him that very soon real people would inhabit the earth, and there would not be any use for beings like him, although he was the only one of his kind. He objected very seriously to make way for men and women, but when he saw there was no way out of the difficulty he requested that he might be allowed to live away by himself, promising that he would allow the coming race to make masks imitating his face, the effect of which would be to charm away disease and witchcraft.

He exists, but even the Creator knows nothing regarding his origin; and where he lives there is no human being.

Among the old Ojibwas it was the custom to paint one side of the face black and the other red when asking the manitous for anything very desirable.

THANKSGIVING DANCE
(Delaware)

Traditions of the Delaware people as far back as the memories of their tribe are that they always had a Thanksgiving Dance. That many, many generations ago they came from a far-off country in the northwest; came across a land of ice and snow, until they reached the Great Fish River, or Mississippi River, where they found many people living in that valley who fiercely opposed their progress, but, after a long war, they completely overcame these people, and proceeded on their journey until they finally settled in that country watered by the Susquehanna and the Delaware Rivers, their territory extending from the mountains to the tide water. Here all the Algonquin Tribes lived near them, and they became powerful and rich, so much so that they forgot to give thanks to the Great Spirit.

About that time there was a great famine or drought. Following this great earthquakes came, rivers went dry, streams and springs started up in places where water had scarcely been seen before. Mountains came and disappeared and great fear prevailed among the people.

About this time there came to the head chief, or sachem, of the Delawares a little boy, who told the chief that his people had treated him very badly; that they would make him do more work than he was able to do and would give him but little to eat; that he had felt very badly about the way he was treated, but had put up with it. Finally, one day his people told him to go out and gather some wild sweet potatoes, which were considered a great delicacy. He went, and, to show that he was industrious, and thinking to get a little praise, or if not that, at least, to escape blame by bringing home a bountiful supply, he worked hard and got all he could carry.

He reached home as early as possible, and his people put the potatoes on to cook in a large kettle at noon. They cooked them until the evening star went down, but before this time they made the little boy go to bed without any supper. After he had been in bed some time they began to eat the potatoes and other food. They called the boy, and he answered, and jumped quickly from the bed, thinking he was invited to take part in the feast. He was only abused, however, called a glutton and told to go away. So, heart-broken and in despair, he left the house and wandered aimlessly until he was utterly exhausted. He then went to sleep. Before this he was moaning to himself over his unfortunate lot. He cried out to the Great Spirit to give him relief. He began his supplication with *O-oo* and heard twelve voices with the same sound.

When he went to sleep there came to him a man with his face painted red, and as he emerged from the darkness only half of his face showed. This man talked to him and told of the great things there were in the world beyond; that his people were wicked, not only his own family but all his tribe; that they had forgotten the Great Spirit, which was the reason why the earthquakes and other trouble had been visited upon them, and that more would follow, if they did not repent. The boy asked why he heard twelve voices answer his prayer, and the spirit to whom he was talking replied that he would have to pass through twelve worlds or spheres before he could get to the home of the Great Spirit; that in each sphere there was a Manitou ruling, and that no prayer could reach the Great Spirit that did not come through the twelve spheres; that his cry had reached the first, who transmitted it to the second, and he in turn to the third, and so on until the twelfth delivered it to the Great Spirit himself.

He was told to go to the head chief or sachem and tell him that the people should return thanks each autumn to the Great Spirit, and when the people all met he should say that the Great Spirit sent him to talk to them; that he was a medicine man, made so this night; that he had received the gift of the Great Medicine from the Great Spirit himself. He was to tell the people they should never be discouraged when trials and tribulations came to them, for it was under those circumstances, and when in that condition, that the Great Spirit took compassion upon mortals, and made them superior and possessed of great influence over their fellow men; that none of the tribe had gone through as great trials as he had.

The chief or sachem called the people together, and renewed the Thanksgiving Dance of the Delawares. The little boy told what he had seen. He told them that they were to prepare a long, large house, and inside this house were to be twelve posts, each with a face carved on it, half the face to be painted red and the other half black. There should also be a center post with four faces carved on it. These posts were to represent the twelve Manitous who guarded the twelve spheres through which the people should pass to reach the Happy Hunting Ground. The center post represented the Great Spirit, who saw and knew all things.

Every year after that they were to return thanks to the Great Spirit in the time of the autumn full moon, when nature had painted the forest in brilliant hues and the harvest was over. The dance was to last twelve days, which was the time it would take the twelve Manitous to convey their thanks and prayers to the Great Spirit.

All the people are to enter at the east and retire the same way. When they come in they are to pass to the right of the fire and each clan takes its place, sitting on the ground (skins or robes are thrown down for them to sit on) next to the wall.

The Turtle clan on the south, the Turkey on the west, and the Wolf on the north, and, in no case, shall any one pass between the center post and the east door, but must go around the center post to go to the north side of the dance house. The medicine man shall lead the dance. A tortoise shell, dried and polished, and containing several pebbles, is to be placed in the southeast corner, near the door, in front of the first person, known as the orator. If he has anything to say, he will take the shell and rattle it, and an answer shall come from the south of the dance house from the singers who hit on a dry deer hide. Then the parties who had the tortoise shell shall make a talk to the people, and thank the Great Spirit for their blessings, and then proceed to dance, going to the right and around the fire, followed by all who wished to dance, and, finally, coming to the center post, stop there. All the people shall shake hands with him, and return to their seats. Then the shell should be passed to the next person, who shall either pass it on or rattle it, as he chooses. They shall have a doorkeeper and a leader, and twelve oshkosh to sweep the ground with turkey wings, make fires, and serve as messengers. The ashes should always be taken out of the west door. In front of the east door, outside, should be a high pole, on which venison should hang. The oshkosh shall distribute food among the people. The officers and oshkosh are to be paid in wampum for their services. In no case shall they allow a dog to enter the dance house, and no one should laugh inside or in any way be rude. The orators repeat the traditions, but each party is allowed to speak and tell his dream or give advice. Every one has a guardian spirit. Sometimes representations of it come in the form of some bird, animal, or anything; at times we see it in dreams, and at other times by impression; and it tells us what to do or what will happen, etc. The guardian spirit is sent from the Great Spirit. It is the inward voice.

The last thing, when the dance is over, all the people are to go out and stand in a line east and west, with their faces south, and bow down and thank the Great Spirit, and then go home.

Some of the Delaware Indians still keep up this dance, but the dance house is not so large as it used to be, and the attendance now is not more than one hundred. Any Indian of any tribe can participate in the dance.

At the dance all who take part repeat what the leader says, both the song and the exhortation. The leader often repeats the story of the little boy, comparing the tribe's trials to that of the little boy who had met with disappointments, but telling that after a while the Great Spirit sent him gifts, by which he was enabled to overcome these disappointments, or be strong enough to bear them.

Sometimes in their dreams or visions they see men, sometimes birds or animals, and in telling of them they do not say they had a dream, but say: "There came to me this," etc.

These dreams and impressions are sometimes used as illustrations by the orator before repeating the orations that have been handed down from memory. There are quite a number of these orations. On the following pages are some expressed as nearly as can well be translated.

The historical or opening oration gives one a fair idea of what their faith is. Each night the orations are different, and each night several dances take place; and preceding the dance will be an oration of instructions, an oration of thanks, an oration of praise and encouragement, or an address in which the speaker gives his impressions, and speaks generally for the good of the assembly.

Before the dance closes each night hominy is passed around, and all partake of it and say: "For this we are thankful."

Fire is made with the use of fire sticks by friction, which they call pure fire. Smoking is permissible in the dance house, but the smoker must use the fire that is burning in the center, and made by the oshkosh, which is called pure fire. No matches are allowed to be used.

When the Manitou appeared to the little boy his face was painted red, but as he emerged from utter darkness only one-half of his face showed, and he was singing—

"These Delawares are my own people, and here is where I bring them in their days of tribulation that they make supplications to my Maker, the Creator."

ORIGIN OF THE MEDICINE PLANT
(Various)

HOW THE INDIANS CAME TO KNOW MEDICINE PLANTS
(Tuscarora)

M any winters ago a poor, sickly old man came to an Indian village. In front of each
wigwam was placed a skin on a pole to show what totem belonged to the family.
Over some wigwams hung a beaver skin; that was the totem or sign of the tribe of
Beaver Indians. Over other wigwams hung deerskins; that was the totem of the
Deer tribe.

The old man stopped at each wigwam and asked for food and a place to sleep
during that night. He looked so sick that the families who had the Wolf, the Turtle,
and the Heron totems all refused him a chance to enter their wigwams.

He went the whole length of the village, and at last he saw a wigwam with a
bearskin hanging over it. A kind old squaw came out of this wigwam and brought
food to him, and spread out skins for his bed. The old man felt very sick. He told
her what plants to gather in the woods to make him well.

The squaw gathered these plants and did as he told her with them; the sores on
his feet were healed and he was better very soon. She promised not to forget the
secret of the healing plants.

In a few days he was taken with a fever; again he told the old squaw what plants
and leaves to go out and gather for him. She did so, and it was not long before he
was well. She promised again not to forget what she had learned.

Many times he fell sick; each time it was with a new sickness. Each time he told
the squaw what to find that would heal him. The squaw learned more than all her
nation knew of medicine.

One morning the old man told her that he had come to her village just to teach
the people the secrets which she now knew. No one had welcomed him but the
Bear band.

The old man said: "I am going away from this people now. I came to do them
good. No one but you would show kindness to the stranger. When you see the sun
again, you will find a young hemlock tree growing by the door of your wigwam. It
will grow taller than any tree that you or your tribe have seen.

"This will show that the Bear tribe is the greatest. All the tribes shall come to the
Bear tribe for help in sickness. You will show them the plants, roots, and leaves that
can heal their sick people."

When the old man was done talking he went out of sight. No one has ever seen
him since that morning. The Bears have become strong, and their warriors are
very brave. Their medicine men can do more than the medicine men of other
tribes.

A Medicine Legend
(Seneca)

A similar legend is told by the Senecas to account for the origin of their "medi-cine." Nearly two hundred years ago—in the savage estimation this is a very great period of time—an Indian went into the woods on a hunting expedition. One night while asleep in his solitary camp he was awakened by a great noise of singing and drum-beating, such as is heard at festivals. Starting up, he made his way to the place whence the sounds came, and although he could not see any one there he observed a heap of corn and a large squash vine with three squashes on it, and three ears of corn which lay apart from the rest. Feeling very uneasy, he once more pursued his hunting operations, and when night came again laid himself down to rest. But his sleep was destined to be broken yet a second time, and awaking he perceived a man bending over him, who said in menacing tones:

"Beware: what you saw was sacred. You deserve to die."

A rustling among the branches denoted the presence of a number of people, who, after some hesitation, gathered round the hunter, and informed him that they would pardon his curiosity and would tell him their secret. "The great medicine for wounds," said the man who had first awakened him, "is squash and corn. Come with me and I will teach you how to make and apply it."

With these words he led the hunter to the spot at which he had surprised the medicine-making operations on the previous night, where he beheld a great fire and a strange-looking laurel-bush, which seemed as if made of iron. Chanting a weird song, the people circled slowly round the bush to the accompaniment of a rattling of gourd-shells. On the hunter's asking them to explain this procedure, one of them heated a stick and thrust it right through his cheek. He immediately applied some of the medicine to the wound, so that it healed instantly. Having thus demonstrated the power of the drug, they sang a tune which they called the medi-cine-song, which their pupil learnt by heart.

The hunter then turned to depart, and all at once he saw that the beings who surrounded him were not human, as he had thought, but animals—foxes, bears, and beavers—who fled as he looked at them. Surprised and even terrified at the turn matters had taken, he made his way homeward with all speed, conning over the prescription which the strange beings had given him the while. They had told him to take one stalk of corn, to dry the cob and pound it very fine, then to take one squash, cut it up and pound it, and to mix the whole with water from a running stream, near its source. This prescription he used with very great success among his people, and it proved the origin of the great medicine of the Senecas. Once a year at the season when the deer changes his coat they prepare it as the forest folk did, singing the weird song and dancing round it to the rhythmic accompaniment of the gourd-shell rattles, while they burn tobacco to the gods.

The Good Hunter
(Iroquois)

In ancient times a war broke out between two tribes. On the one side the forces were jointly led by a great warrior and a noted hunter. The latter had killed much game for the skins, the remains being left for beasts and birds of prey. The battle was going against his side, and he saw that to save his own life he must quit the field. As he turned, the body of a great tree lay across his path. He came up to it, when a heavy blow felled him. On recovering he found, strangely enough, that he could as easily pass through as over the obstruction. Reaching home, his friends would not talk with him; indeed they seemed quite unaware of his presence. It now occurred to him that he, too, had been killed, and was present in spirit only, human eyes not seeing him. He returned to the place of conflict, and there, sure enough, lay his mortal part quite dead, and its scalp gone. A pigeon-hawk, flying by, recognized the disembodied hunter, and gratefully offered to restore his scalp; so, stretching away in its flight to the retiring victors, he plucked it from the bloody pole. The other birds had, meantime, prepared a medicine which soon united the scalp to the head, when bears and wolves gathered around and joined in the dance. The hunter got well and lived many years, his experience strengthening their religious faith, and teaching them how to use the remedies so strangely acquired, which, to this day, are among the most efficacious known to the Indians.

In another version the good hunter appears as before, as one noted for kindness and generosity to all, even beasts and birds. Though a hunter, he was considered the protector of these. On one occasion he went out with a war party. The battle was furious, and in the most desperate struggle he was struck down, scalped, and left for dead.

A fox came along when the conflict was over, and recognized this friend of bird and beast lying lifeless on the field. Shocked by the sight, he raised the death lament, and called all the beasts together. Their cries were heard in the forest; they came by hundreds to the spot and tried to revive their friend. Vain were all their efforts, and he remained lifeless. As they sat down on their haunches to hold a council, they raised their heads, and a dolorous cry rent the air. Then the bear was called to speak, as being the nearest relative and best friend of man. He appealed to each and all for any medicine they had, but though each had his own, none did any good. Again they lifted up their heads and howled a mournful requiem, long continued, and with many varying notes.

This sad lament, wild as the Highland coronach, brought the oriole to the spot. He was told of their sad plight, and in turn went and called a council of the birds. There was a flapping of wings everywhere, and all came, from the eagle to the wren, in response to the call. With beak and with claw they made every effort, but nothing came of it. The hunter was dead, stubbornly dead, and his scalp was gone. The eagle's head had become white in his long and wise life, and from his lofty eyrie he had looked down, and knew every force of nature and all the events of life.

This white-headed sage said that the dead would not revive unless the scalp was restored.

First of all the fox went to seek it. He visited every hen-roost and every bird's-nest, but no scalp did he find. The pigeon-hawk took up the search, but soon returned. She flew so swiftly that no one expected her to see much, for birds have characters as well as men. The white heron flew more slowly, and said he would do better, but he came to a field of luscious wild beans, which tempted him to stop. He fed and slept, and fed again, while the council waited his return in vain. At last the crow took the mission. The warrior who had the scalp knew of the council, but feared nothing when he saw the crow flying near. He was accustomed to that. She saw the scalp stretched to dry in the smoke above his cabin, and after a time carried it off. Great was the rejoicing when she came back successful. At once they put the scalp on the dead man's head, but so dry and warped had it become that it would not fit.

Here was a new trouble. The animals did their best, but could not moisten it, having no patent lubricator. Then the great eagle said that on the high rocks, where he lived, the mountain dew had collected on his back, and perhaps this might serve. He plucked one of his long feathers, dipped it in this dew, and applied it to the scalp. It was at once effectual, and the scalp became moist again. The animals brought other things for the cure. The scalp was placed on the head, to which it closely adhered, and then the hunter revived and recovered his strength. They gave him the compound which had restored him, as the gift of the Great Spirit, and then there was a pattering of feet and a rustle of wings as the council dispersed. The medicine was always cherished.

It was used in this way: a wooden goblet is taken to a running stream, and filled by dipping down the stream. When brought back to the house it is placed near the fire, with some tobacco. Then there are prayers while the tobacco is gradually thrown on the fire. The smoke is grateful to the Great Spirit, and with this American incense their prayers arise. The medicine-man then places a piece of skin near the cup, and on this the medicine is laid. He takes up a little of the pulverized compound with a wooden spoon, such as was recently used, and dusts it on the water in three spots *₊* in the form of a triangle. This is closely watched. If it spreads over the water and whirls about on the surface, the sick person will recover. If it sinks at once, where it was placed, the sick will die, and nothing can be done. In the one case the medicine is given, in the other all the water is thrown away.

This is not the only medicine. One day a hunter heard the sweetest music in the woods, but the most thorough search did not reveal its source. Charmed by the sound, he went again and again, but with no better success. Not a note was heard. At last the Great Spirit came to him in a dream, and told him what to do. He was to purify himself before he sought it, and this he at once did. The forest path was taken, the ravishing strain fell upon his ear, and he listened attentively till he could sing every note himself. Then he drew nearer. A tall, green plant stood before him, with long and tapering leaves. This he cut down, but it was immediately healed, and became as before. He did this repeatedly, with the same results, and then knew it as medicine especially good for wounds. Rejoicing in his great discovery, he took part of the plant home, where it was dried and pulverized. Then he touched it to a bad wound which a man had received, and it was healed at once. In this way did the Great Spirit bestow this great medicine upon men, and very grateful were they.

This medicine is used very differently, and the following describes the feast to which it belongs. Once in six months there is a great feast at the hunting season, and these come in the spring and in the fall. On the night of the feast, as soon as it is dark, all concerned assemble in one room. Lights are extinguished, and even the coals are carefully covered. The medicine is placed near these, and tobacco is laid beside it. Then all begin to sing, proclaiming that the crows are coming to the feast, and the other birds and beasts whose brains form part of the first great medicine, the one which originated when they revived the good hunter. At the end of the song their calls are imitated. Thrice during the night prayers are offered, and during these tobacco is thrown on the smothered embers. In these it is asked that all may be protected from harm, and that this medicine may heal injuries of every kind. To preserve due solemnity and prevent interruption the doors are locked when the ceremonies begin. None are allowed to enter or go out, and none to fall asleep. Anything like this would spoil the medicine.

The actual feast begins just before daybreak. The past observances being here described as in the present, the master of ceremonies first takes a deer's head and bites it, imitating the call of a crow. He then passes it to another, who bites it in turn, and imitates some other beast or bird. Thus it goes around. When it begins to be light the master of ceremonies takes a duck's bill and dips it full of the medicine. Some of this he gives to each one present, who puts it into a piece of skin, wrapping it in several covers. This is kept for the next feast, six months later. The panther's skin was preferred for the first cover, when it could be had.

Those who take active part in this feast are all medicine-men, but chiefs may be present, and those who at any time have been cured by the medicine. While these things are going on within the house, the young people are having a merry time outside, and the remnants of the feast are given to them when those inside are done. When this medicine is used the tune heard at its discovery is sung, both at the feast and at its administration. The ceremonies are thought to make it effective. Each medicine-man has a large quantity, which he keeps in a bag. To this he sometimes adds pulverized corn roots or squash vines, if he fears its exhaustion, and when it is given several assemble and sing. Both kinds were deemed especially useful in healing wounds received in war. These were the great medicines; there were others less important.

The origin of the Seneca medicine has some resemblance to this: A hunter is awakened by singing and the sound of a drum. He followed the sound and came to a place apparently inhabited. There a hill of corn had three ears, and a squash vine bore three squashes. The next night he heard the sound again, and a man threatened his life for looking on forbidden things. Others gathered around and said he should not die, but they would impart to him their secret medicine. This was contained in the squashes and corn.

He was led to a spot where many were dancing around a fire. They heated an iron and thrust it through his cheek, and then at once healed it. They burned his leg, and did the same, but all the time they sang the medicine song, which he also learned. As he turned homeward he found that these were not men, as he had supposed, but a great gathering of birds and beasts. It seems in this a variant of the good hunter story.

He had been shown how to prepare the medicine. He was to take one stalk of corn and dry the cob and pound it very fine, and to take one squash, cut it up and pound that, and they then showed him how much for a dose. He was to take water from a running spring, and always from up the stream, never down.

Of course the giving of it varies little. The people sing over its preparation every time the deer changes his coat, and when it is administered to a patient they sing the medicine song, while they rattle a gourd-shell as accompaniment, and burn tobacco.

In another story, an old man applied for hospitality at several lodges in turn, and was repulsed. He found shelter at last, and was kindly treated. Being sick, he desired his hostess to go for certain herbs, which she prepared as he told her, and he was soon cured. Then he had a fever, and other herbs were brought for his cure. One after another he had all the ailments known to the red man, and recourse to every healing herb. When the cure of all diseases had been taught he went away, and was seen no more, leaving a blessing behind.

THE WAMPUM STRING
(Seneca)

A pretty little legend concerning the origin of wampum is that told by the Senecas at night around the fire when the pipe is passed and smoke is made to the earth and sky. So the legend runs: Many, many moons ago, when our old men were but whispers in the woods and their fathers and mothers played the game of sticks at the lake side and the fish swam to meet the spear, a great trouble came upon the Senecas. From the north came a warlike tribe, the O-jeb-wa, and fell upon the villages and killed young warriors and took away the most beautiful maidens. Many war parties followed brave chiefs to find and rescue the maidens, but alas! they, too, were swept away. The head chief, the wise Da-ga-now-e-da, called a council, and taking his stand before his old men and warriors, spoke long and earnestly of the ruin wrought by the fierce O-jeb-wa and the futility of giving battle to so strong a people. Thus he recommended: "Send my son, the eloquent and brave Ha-o-a-tha, southward to the tribes friendly to us and lay before them this vital matter, and that by union we may be able to break the power of these fierce northern warriors and peace will ensue to our people." The old men smoked in silence until a venerable chief arose and in a wise speech gave his approval to the words of his chief. Murmurs of satisfaction came from all quarters and the council adjourned. In the gray of the dawning young Ha-o-a-tha stepped into his light canoe and turning his face toward the south, departed upon his journey. When the noon day sun beat upon him he turned the bow of his canoe to the margin of the stream and, as the light craft shelved the beach, he stepped ashore, and, after a frugal meal, sat long and silently, thinking over his mission, and, fully realizing the great importance of presenting the case in the most appealing form, rehearsed in his mind what words and arguments he should use. His thoughts flowed slowly, but at last he felt satisfied and stepping aboard his canoe he shot out into the stream. As the current caught and carried him along he sought to again grasp the ideas that had so recently presented themselves. Alas! they were gone, and try as he would they returned not. Again he turned to the shore and as the canoe grated the pebbles he plunged his paddle into the sandy beach and brought it dripping across the boat. Bowing his head in his hands he was again lost in meditation. Slowly the ideas came, but would not remain. Sadly he turned his head and his gaze fixed upon the blade of the paddle, on which were some small shells glittering in the sunlight. Picking up a small white shell he idly turned it in his palm; a small hole through its center attracted his gaze, and fingering the fringe of his girdle, he slowly strung the shell upon the thong. As a flash came an inspiration. A thought was represented by the small white shell. Another black shell was drawn into place beside the former one. At last his speech was a fixture in his mind, and as he ran the shells through his fingers his thoughts ran in unison. Gaily he left the shore, and ere night-fall was among the sought for allies of his father's tribe. The council met, and never before had the chiefs listened to such eloquence. The day was won. Home departing, young Ha-o-a-tha carried the assurance of assistance to his people, and soon runners arrived from the on-coming allies, who recited the wonderful and eloquent appeal of the young chief. To his father he confided his secret and thus was adopted the conveyance of messages and thought by means of pierced shells or wampum.

NATURAL BRIDGE
(Mohegan)

Though several natural bridges are known in this country, there is but one that is famous the world over, and that is the one which spans Clear Creek, Virginia— the remnant of a cave-roof—all the rest of the cavern having collapsed. It is two hundred and fifteen feet above the water, and is a solid mass of rock forty feet thick, one hundred feet wide, and ninety feet in span. Thomas Jefferson owned it; George Washington scaled its side and carved his name on the rock a foot higher than any one else. Here, too, came the youth who wanted to cut his name above Washington's, and who found, to his horror, when half-way up, that he must keep on, for he had left no resting-places for his feet at safe and reachable distances— who, therefore, climbed on and on, cutting handhold and foothold in the limestone —until he reached the top, in a fainting state, his knife-blade worn to a stump. Here, too, in another tunnel of the cavern, flows Lost River, that all must return to, at some time, if they drink of it. Here, beneath the arch, is the dark stain, so like a flying eagle that the French officer who saw it during the Revolution augured from it a success for the united arms of the nations that used the eagle as their symbol.

The Mohegans knew this wonder of natural masonry, for to this point they were pursued by a hostile tribe, and on reaching the gulf found themselves on the edge of a precipice that was too steep at that point to descend. Behind them was the foe; before them, the chasm. At the suggestion of one of their medicine-men they joined in a prayer to the Great Spirit for deliverance, and when again they looked about them, there stood the bridge. Their women were hurried over; then, like so many Horatii, they formed across this dizzy highway and gave battle. Encouraged by the knowledge that they had a safe retreat in case of being overmastered, they fought with such heart that the enemy was defeated, and the grateful Mohegans named the place the Bridge of God.

OLD INDIAN FACE
(Tahawi)

On Lower Ausable Pond is a large, ruddy rock showing a huge profile, with another, resembling a pappoose, below it. When the Tahawi ruled this region their sachem lived here at "the Dark Cup," as they called this lake, a man renowned for virtue and remarkable, in his age, for gentleness. When his children had died and his manly grandson, who was the old man's hope, had followed them to the land of the cloud mountains, Adota's heart withered within him, and standing beneath this rock, he addressed his people, recounting what he had done for them, how he had swept their enemies from the Lakes of the Clustered Stars (the Lower Saranac) and Silver Sky (Upper Saranac) to the Lake of Wandah, gaining a land where they might hunt and fish in peace. The little one, the Star, had been ravished away to crown the brow of the thunder god, who, even now, was advancing across the peaks, bending the woods and lighting the valleys with his jagged torches.

Life was nothing to him longer; he resigned it. As he spoke these words he fell back, and the breath passed out of him. Then came the thunder god, and with an appalling burst of fire sent the people cowering. The roar that followed seemed to shake the earth, but the medicine-man of the tribe stood still, listening to the speech of the god in the clouds. "Tribe of the Tahawi," he translated, "Adota treads the star-path to the happy hunting-grounds, and the sun is shining on his heart. He will never walk among you again, but the god loves both him and you, and he will set his face on the mountains. Look!" And, raising their eyes, they beheld the likeness of Adota and of his beloved child, the Star, graven by lightning-stroke on the cliff. There they buried the body of Adota and held their solemn festivals until the white men drove them out of the country.

BALANCED ROCK
(Atotarhos)

Balanced Rock, or Rolling Rock, near Pittsfield, Massachusetts, is a mass of limestone that was deposited where it stands by the great continental glacier during the ice age, and it weighs four hundred and eighty tons (estimated) in spite of its centuries of weathering. Here one of the Atotarhos, kings of the Six Nations, had his camp. He was a fierce man, who ate and drank from bowls made of the skulls of enemies, and who, when he received messages and petitions, wreathed himself from head to foot with poison snakes. The son of this ferocious being inherited none of his war-like tendencies; indeed, the lad was almost feminine in appearance, and on succeeding to power he applied himself to the cultivation of peaceful arts. Later historians have uttered a suspicion that he was a natural son of Count Frontenac, but that does not suit with this legend.

The young Atotarho stood near Balanced Rock watching a number of big boys play duff. In this game one stone is placed upon another and the players, standing as far from it as they fancy they can throw, attempt to knock it out of place with other stones. The silence of Atotarho and his slender, girlish look called forth rude remarks from the boys, who did not know him, and who dared him to test his skill. The young chief came forward, and as he did so the jeers and laughter changed to cries of astonishment and fear, for at each step he grew in size until he towered above them, a giant. Then they knew him, and fell down in dread, but he took no revenge. Catching up great boulders he tossed them around as easily as if they had been beechnuts, and at last, lifting the balanced rock, he placed it lightly where it stands to-day, gave them a caution against ill manners and hasty judgments, and resumed his slender form. For many years after, the old men of the tribe repeated this story and its lesson from the top of Atotarho's duff.

Chapter 5

Tribal Legends

The Origin of the Thunder-Bird
(Onondaga)

A story of the old times. Two men desired to find the origin of thunder. They set out and traveled north, and came to high mountains. These mountains drew back and forth, and then closed together very quickly. One of the men said to the other, "I will leap through the cleft when it opens, and if I am caught you can follow and try to find the origin of thunder." The first one passed through the cleft before it closed, and the second one was caught. The one that went through saw, in a large plain below, a group of wigwams, and a number of Indians playing ball. After a little while these players said to each other, "It is time to go." They went to their wigwams and put on wings, and took their bows and arrows and flew away over the mountains to the south. The old men said to the Indian, "What do you want? Who are you?" He told his mission, and they deliberated what to do. Finally they took him and put him in a mortar and pounded him up so that all his bones were broken. Then they took him out and gave him wings and a bow and arrows, and sent him away. They told him he must not go near the trees, for if he did he would go so fast that he could not stop, but would get caught in the crotch of a tree.

He could not get to his home because the bird Wochowsen blew so hard that he could make no progress against it. As the Thunder-Bird is an Indian, the lightning from him never strikes one of his kind.

This is the same bird one of whose wings Glooskap once cut when it had used too much force. There was for a long time, the story goes, no moving air, so that the sea became full of slime, and all the fish died. But Glooskap is said to have repaired the wing of Wochowsen, so that we now have wind alternating with calm.

O-KWEN-CHA
(Onondaga)

There was once, a long time ago, a little boy named *O-kwen-cha,* or Red Paint, who lived with his old grandmother in an old *ka-no-sah hon-we,* or wigwam, which had no windows, and but one doorway. The door was made out of the skins of wild animals, such as deer, bears, wolves, and foxes. The old skin door was so old that nearly all the fur had disappeared, and the smoke-stack was so large that a little way off the old wigwam seemed to have no roof. This smoke-stack was its window and chimney. But the old *ka-no-sah hon-we* had a roof of bark, covered with moss. The bark was so old that a young maple was growing on the roof, and the moss so thick that the bark could not be seen from the outside. The inside of the old wigwam had no floor, and the fireplace was in the center, on the bare ground. On one side of its walls were hung dried venison and bears' meat. On another were war-clubs, bows and arrows, feather heads, and buckskin leggings, moccasins, and buckskin coats. These had not been used for many moons. There was also a *ga-na-cho-we,* or Indian drum, and many other things used in hunting, dancing, and war were hung on these old bark walls.

O-kwen-cha's grandmother did all the work, brought all the wood, and killed the game. Many a time she returned with a deer or a bear on her back, and sometimes brought a string of fish, so that they always had plenty to eat. O-kwen-cha's grand-mother went away every day, but one thing she always told him when about to leave, he must not touch the Indian drum that hung upon the wall.

O-kwen-cha, or Red Paint, was a very small boy, about knee-high, and his clothes were made out of the skins of different wild animals. The coat which he wore was a fox-skin, and his leggings the skin of a white weasel. His belt was a rattlesnake's skin, and his feather head-dress was made of the feathers of a partridge. In his belt were stuck a war-club, a stone tomahawk, and a bone scalping-knife. On his back hung his arrow-pouch, full of arrows, which his uncles had made for him many moons ago. His bow was made from the rib of a *Ka-ya-kwa-ha,* or Mammoth Bear. All his face was painted with streaks of red, that could not be washed off. This was why he was called O-kwen-cha, or Red Paint.

So you can imagine how O-kwen-cha looked, with his wild Indian dress. He was never allowed to go out of this *ka-no-sah hon-we,* or wigwam, so he amused himself, day by day, shooting at the flies and fleas, and sometimes at his grandmother's old moccasins.

In this wigwam were four beds that no one had slept in for many moons. O-kwen-cha had his mind full of these things, and sometimes would sit and think what the beds were for, and why he was so often told not to touch the Indian drum, and why he was not allowed to go hunting with his grandmother, and be out of doors. While in these deep thoughts he would get up and give a little war-whoop, and then say to himself that he was a young man, and as good a runner as any warrior; that he could hunt, as he had killed many flies and bugs. This made him bold, and sometimes he would say, "I could kill a bear like this." Then he would take an arrow from his pouch and shoot at the dry bear's meat on the wall. Then he would pull the arrow out of the meat, and look at the point for fresh blood.

One day, getting tired with his games, he thought he would amuse himself with something new. Thinking what it should be, he set his mind on the *ga-na-cho-we,* or Indian drum. So he got upon the bed, and reached the drum. As soon as he got down he said to himself, "This is the way I think my uncles used to do." Then he began to drum and to chant his war-song, *"Ha-wa-sa-say! Ha-wa-sa-say!"* etc. Then came his uncles from under the four beds, dancing the war-dance. When O-kwen-cha's uncles danced, the dancing was heard throughout the world. His grand-mother was at the end of the world when he danced with his uncles, and she heard the beating of the drum and the dancing, as plainly as if she had been in her own wigwam. So she ran home at once, and whenever O-kwen-cha's grandmother ran, her steps were heard throughout the world. So the world and its people and the bad men with magic powers heard the beating of the *ga-na-cho-we,* or Indian drum, and the dancing, and the running of the old woman. Then the people of the world said, *"He, Ha!"* (*i.e.,* Ho, ho!) "So *Cho-noo-kwa-a-nah* (*i.e.,* Uncombed Coarse Hair) is in trouble again. We will soon know which of the men with magic powers will try to take her life, or her children's life, if she has any more left."

While he was beating his drum, O-kwen-cha heard his grandmother running for her wigwam. He got right down and put the drum in its place; but he was real sorry to do this, for he had lost the fun he had had with his uncles. When the drum was hung up they were no more to be seen. He looked under the four beds whence he saw his uncles come, but they were not to be found there. So he went back and put more wood on the fire, listening for his grandmother's footsteps. At last she came, with the sweat on her face, and all out of breath. "Oh, my grandchild," she said, "what have you been doing? Oh, you have caused my death! You have killed me! What have you been doing?"

O-kwen-cha replied, "Oh, nothing; only I have been making your old moccasins dance. Oh, it was real fun to see your moccasins dance!" But Cho-noo-kwa-a-nah, his grandmother, said, "But whose foot-tracks are these on the dust?" "Oh, those are your moccasin tracks," he said; "just see what I can do." So he went to a corner and got his grandmother's old moccasins, putting them in a row, and then taking his bow and arrows. He then began to beat on the string of his bow, and sung his war-song, "Ha-wa-sa-say! Ha-wa-sa-say!" and the old moccasins danced till the wig-wam was full of dust. "Oh!" said his grandmother, "O-kwen-cha is quite a witch!"

She went off the next day, and he had the dance of his uncles again. Again the world heard the drum and dancing, and the running of Cho-noo-kwa-a-nah. When his grandmother came he repeated the moccasin dance. On the third day he made his uncles dance again, and the world heard the drum and dancing, and the run-ning of Uncombed Coarse Hair.

This time Coarse Hair had not been very far, so she caught O-kwen-cha with his Indian drum still in his hands when she came into the wigwam. She had hardly said a word when a very tall man appeared. He was so tall that he could not walk into the wigwam where Red Paint and his grandmother lived, but when he came in he had to crawl on his hands and knees, and he stooped down while he talked. This was what he said: "Three days from today you are to appear at my place, and be ready for a grand wrestling match. We are to bet for our heads. If I throw you three times I will cut your head off; and if you throw me three times you may cut my head off, and save your life." This tall man's name was *Sus-ten-ha-nah,* or "He Large Stone," for he lived on a very large, flat stone. He lived on human flesh, and never was beat in wrestling. He cut off the heads of all whom he threw, and ate their flesh.

As soon as Sus-ten-ha-nah left Coarse Hair's house she made ready for her journey to the large, flat stone. It was three days' journey to this. As she left her wigwam she said to O-kwen-cha, "You must stay here and not go out of doors, for you have plenty to eat and plenty of wood. Only hope that I may throw and kill Sus-ten-ha-nah when we wrestle." So she went away, feeling very sorry, for she knew that her days had now come to an end.

She journeyed a day. In the evening she made a fire, ate her dried bear's meat, and stayed over night. In the morning she ate again, and took her journey. About noon, on the third day, Coarse Hair reached the place where Sus-ten-ha-nah lived. He was anxious for her coming, for he was now very hungry. He had eaten up all that came in his way, all that lived near and far, and all the game he could find. He was a great eater. He would eat a whole bear or deer at a single meal, and now he had eaten nothing for a long time.

Coarse Hair got up on the flat stone. Hardly had she done this when He Large Stone seized her by the neck, and was going to throw her on the stone. Just then he heard some one calling to him, "Here, here! that is not the way to wrestle! Here, here! give me the chance, grandmother!" Sus-ten-ha-nah stopped to see where the voice came from, and said, "Ho, ho! plenty of game today!" He was looking afar off, when the hallooing was repeated, "I say, grandmother, give me the chance!" Coarse Hair was also looking around to see whence the voice came, when O-kwen-cha appeared, coming through the stone, and saying, "Give me the chance! give me the chance to wrestle!"

Red Paint, small as he was, was now very powerful in magic. "Ho, ho!" said He Large Stone, "so you want to wrestle with me, do you? What do you amount to?" said he, at the same time catching Red Paint by the legs. He tore his body in two pieces, and threw them aside. Then he went at Coarse Hair again, but up came O-kwen-cha once more, crying, "Give me the chance, grandmother!" So she let him try again.

He threw He Large Stone three times, and then Sus-ten-ha-nah said, "Now you can cut off my head." So he knelt down to give O-kwen-cha a chance to cut his head off. As soon as this was done the head flew high up in the air, and Red Paint and his grandmother wondered when it went up so high. The body remained kneeling. While they looked the head came down again, and stuck to the body. Then O-kwen-cha took his bone scalping-knife and cut off the head again. Then the head flew up again, for three times. The third time, when the head flew up, O-kwen-cha said to his grandmother, "Let us draw the body to one side;" and they laid it on the flat stone. When the head came down it struck on the stone, and that flew into a thousand pieces, which were scattered all over the world. That is why we have stones lying about everywhere. The head also broke into a thousand pieces, which flew all over the earth, and the brains became snails, and that is why they are found everywhere (*Ge-sen-weh*, brains, is the Onondaga name for snails also.) Thus O-kwen-cha killed Sus-ten-ha-nah.

His grandmother said, "Now we have killed our enemy we will go home." Red Paint replied, "No! we have lived below long enough. Now I have to go after my uncles." Then he told her to go home alone. When she had gone, he went to work and gathered all the bones that lay there, of those whom Sus-ten-ha-nah had killed, and put them all together in a row—all that he could find. Then he went to a big hickory tree which stood there, and called out, "*Euch! Euch!*" or "Take care! take care! This tree will fall over you; you had better get out of the way." He pushed hard on the tree and the big tree fell, and the bones came to life, and all began to run away. Some had short backs, and some short legs, and some had big heads on little bodies, or little heads on big bodies; while some had the heads of bears, and others of deer or wolves, for the right bones had not always come together.

When Red Paint saw how oddly they looked he made them exchange heads and bodies, and all other parts that did not match; so that the men looked like men, and the bears and deer as bears and deer should. Then the people wanted Red Paint to stay with them, and be their chief; but he said, "No. Go back to your own homes and your own people, your fathers and your mothers." He found one of his uncles in the crowd, and told him to go home to his grandmother. "Tell her," said he, "I am going to find my other three uncles." Then all the people went to their homes, and Red Paint made his journey again.

When the evening came he built a little fire, and lay down for the night. On the third day of his journey he heard an Indian drum somewhere, he could not tell where. In the evening he built a fire again, and heard the drum all the time. Then he went to sleep, but when he woke again he found himself a great way from his fire, and dancing. He was going towards the drum. He said, "He, he! the old fellow is quite a witch!" When he journeyed in the morning he went towards the drum again, and heard it all the day, but did not see it. He stopped again and made a fire.

The same thing happened again, and he found himself dancing in the morning. The sound grew louder, and the third day he came to an opening, where there was a great crowd. A big man was beating the drum very hard, as he sat by a kettle of boiling soup. The people were dancing around, very hungry, and waiting for him to give them some soup. Every little while he grabbed one of them and ate him, while Red Paint stood a little way off to see what he was doing.

Then Red Paint took his war-club and ran at the man, whose name was *Kah-nah-chu-wah-ne,* or "He Big Kettle." When he ran at him he hit him on the forehead with his club, but he seemed not to notice it at all. He hit him again, and the third time Kah-nah-chu-wah-ne looked up, and scratched his forehead, saying, "It seems to me the mosquitoes bite." Red Paint called out, "They do bite, and I will show you some more of that." He Big Kettle tried to catch him, but Red Paint got hold of him, and they began fighting. In the midst of this O-kwen-cha took his bone scalping-knife again and cut off his head, throwing it into the big kettle of soup. The people were very glad when they saw this, and wanted Red Paint to be their chief, but he said he could not, for he had something else to do. Then they wanted something to eat, but he said, "If you eat the soup in the kettle you will all die." So he sent them away to their own homes, their fathers and mothers, their wives and their children.

After the people had gone away, he broke in pieces the big kettle and the big drum. Also he made a big fire, and when he had cut Kah-nah-chu-wah-ne's body in pieces he threw it in the fire. When everything was destroyed, he gathered all the bones and placed them in a row on the ground, near a big pine tree. He gathered all he could find, and arranged them as well as he could, by their appearance. Then he pushed hard against the tree, and called out, *"Euch! Euch!* Look out! look out! this tree is going to fall on you!" Then the bones came to life and ran out of the way. But some had long arms and some short; the heads had sometimes got on the wrong bodies, and he had to exchange different parts, until all appeared as men, deer, and bears should. He found one of his uncles there and said, "You must go home to my grandmother, and tell her I am going to find my other two uncles." So he sent them all to their homes, and went on alone, going west all the time.

When he had traveled three days he heard the barking of a dog, as though it were a great way off. He went in that direction all day, without seeming to come near him. He built a fire and camped that night, but when he had traveled all the next day he had not seen the dog. On the third day he met a tall man, whose flesh was eaten on the legs from his feet to his thighs. When O-kwen-cha first saw the man he stopped and looked, and he was a great way off. Then he saw the dog running after the man and biting great pieces of flesh from his legs. The man cried out as if in great pain, every time the dog bit him.

Then Red Paint said, "I wish my dogs were here to fight this dog." So he whistled for his dogs to come. His dogs were *Ok-wa-e,* or Bear, and *Ku-hah-sen-tea-tah,* or Lion. These were his dogs, as he called them. He set them on the big dog which bit the man. Lion and Bear pitched on the dog, killed him, and tore him in pieces. Then Red Paint said to his dogs, "Go back to your places till I call you again."

He then put spittle on the tall man's legs, and the flesh healed up, until all was right again. Then he saw that he had found his third uncle. He told him to go back to his grandmother, for there would be no dangers on the way. All dangers were now over. He said, too, "I am going to find my other uncle. Tell my grandmother I will soon be back."

Red Paint then went on. He had journeyed three days when he came to a settlement, and went at once to find one of the people who was very poor. On one side of the reservation he found a little boy at play, and made friends with him. They became great friends in a little while, and the little boy asked him to go to his home and stay with him. He lived with him quite a time, and they often went out hunting with their bows and arrows. The little boy had a small bow, but O-kwen-cha's was of the rib of the Mammoth Bear. He was a good hunter and killed much game.

At last these boys became such good hunters that they came back with partridges or wild turkeys almost every day. Sometimes they had a deer or bigger game. The little boy's mother liked Red Paint very much, because he was such a good hunter, and would have been very sorry to part with him if he had wished to go home.

One day the little boy, Red Paint's friend, said to him that there was to be a great feast at the long house (council-house) that night. There would be dancing and many things to amuse the people. There would be big kettles of soup for the feast, and they would make wampum, too. O-kwen-cha said, "How is this, that the people are going to make wampum?" His friend answered, "They are going to hang up a human being's skin on a long pole. This skin the people have had for a great many moons back. When they want to make wampum they take the soup and pour it in the mouth of the skin, and as it passes through it turns into wampum and falls down."

Now this skin was the very one that O-kwen-cha was after.

He asked his little friend to go with him that night when they held their grand feast, and he replied, "I'll ask my mother and see what she says about it." But his mother said, "No; you two had better stay at home. The people will run around so that I am afraid they will run over you." But on the night when the dance was to be, O-kwen-cha had already made up his mind what to do.

Quite late in the evening, when the whole nation was gathered at the long house, he went over, and there he saw a great crowd of people. Then he said, "I wish *Tah-hun-tike-skwa,* the bat, would come here. Then I wish that *Che-ten-ha,* the mouse, would be here. And I wish that *Tah-hoon-to-whe,* the night-hawk, would be here, too." So these little creatures came, and he told them what to do. He said to Tah-hun-tike-skwa, the bat, "You may amuse the people in the long house by flying around, so that they will chase you." He told Che-ten-ha, the mouse, to climb up on the pole and gnaw off the cords which held up his uncle's skin. He told Tah-hoon-to-whe, the night-hawk, to fly to and fro between him and the mouse, to tell him how the mouse got along.

So the bat went into the council-house, and the people had great sport running around and trying to catch him. After a while Tah-hoon-to-whe came to O-kwen-cha, and said, "The cords are almost broken now." The night-hawk also went into the long house, and told the bat that the work was about done. Then the night-hawk and bat flew off and left the people, who were almost out of breath. The sweat poured from their brows, so lively a time had they had in chasing the bat. When they had cooled off, a leading man made a speech about the ceremony now to take place, but while he was speaking, O-kwen-cha went and took the skin of his uncle away. When he did this he stopped and thought, "I wish all the people would go to sleep in the long house."

He went back to the council-house and found them all asleep. Then he said, "I'll pay you for taking my uncle's skin." So he went in and cut off the leading man's head, taking it with him, and hiding his uncle's skin. He had gone but a little way when the people woke up again, and found the principal chief's head had been cut off and carried away. When they went to find the skin, that was gone too. Then there was a big stir, and some said they knew Red Paint was on the reservation and had done this, for they had seen him on one side of the village with the little boy. Then there was a greater stir, and some cried, "Where is he? Look for him! Search for him! Kill him!" Then Red Paint pretended to be looking too, and hallooed from where he was in the dark, but a little way off, "Here he is! here he is!" Then they began to chase him. He ran ahead of the rest, calling on them to follow. "There he is!" said he, "there he is over yonder!" But he carried the chief's head all the time, while pretending to be one of them. They ran a long way off, and some got out of breath and went back, giving up the chase.

Then O-kwen-cha went back to the council-house too, reaching it about day-break. "There," said he, "I have killed the man who stole the skin! I have killed the man who cut off our chief's head!" So they thought it was Red Paint's head, and when he threw it into the crowd they kicked it around, having a game of football with it. While they did this he slipped off, and got his uncle's skin from the place where he had left it. When he had run very far off some one noticed the head, and said, "Why, this is our chief's head, and not O-kwen-cha's!" When they lifted it, so it was. Then they said, "Red Paint has cheated us again!" There was another great stir, and they shouted, "Chase him! Kill him!" They threatened to catch him and take his skin off, too. But Red Paint was very far off by this time, and when they chased him it was too late.

When he was going towards home by himself, he found it very lonesome. "Why should I not have company?" he said to himself, "while I have my uncle with me?" Then he began to breathe in the mouth of the skin, and the last of his four uncles came to life again. So they journeyed homeward together, having a pleasant time.

When he got to his grandmother's, she had fastened the old door very tight, so that no one could come in. He rapped at the door and begged and begged her to open it. He said, "Grandmother, I have got back now, with my fourth uncle;" but all the answer was a cry out of the old *ka-no-sah hon-we*. They begged and begged again, for a very long time, but all the answer they got was the cry of his old grandmother. At last they broke the door in.

When they got inside the wigwam, Red Paint found his grandmother had become a very old woman, and was bending over a little fire trying to warm herself. The dust and ashes lay on her back about an inch thick. She always cried now when any one rapped at the door, because, after Red Paint was gone, the rabbits would come and rap at the door. Sometimes the squirrels would come, and would say, "Grand-mother, I have got back." This they did to fool her, making her think it was Red Paint. When she opened the door, away would run a rabbit or a squirrel. This made her cry when any one came and rapped, for she said, "It is only a rabbit, a squirrel, or a coon. You are fooling me;" for she was a very old woman.

When he saw her so old, Red Paint said, "I will make a young woman out of my grandmother yet." Then he took a little stick and stuck it in the back of her head under the loose skin, and twisted it until all the wrinkles were straightened out, and her face became smooth again. His grandmother looked up, and there was not a wrinkle on her face, and she seemed a handsome young woman. Then she turned around and saw Red Paint standing there. She knew him at once, and this made her so glad that she felt young again all over.

O-kwen-cha said, "Now we will fix up the old house." He went around and looked at it, and said, "I want it such a size," and at once there was a nice new house, where the old *ka-no-sah hon-we* had been. Just then the other three uncles came along. They had been hunting on the way, and had not traveled fast, but they brought plenty of bear's meat, which they had dried on the hunting grounds. So O-kwen-cha restored his family, and they are all living happily.

TALES OF PASSACONAWAY
(Various)

PASSACONAWAY'S RIDE TO HEAVEN
(Pennacook)

The personality of Passaconaway, the powerful chief and prophet, is involved in doubt, but there can be no misprision of his wisdom. By some historians he has been made one with St. Aspenquid, the earliest of native missionaries among the Indians, who, after his conversion by French Jesuits, traveled from Maine to the Pacific, preaching to sixty-six tribes, healing the sick and working miracles, returning to die at the age of ninety-four. He was buried on the top of Agamenticus, Maine, where his manes were pacified with offerings of three thousand slain animals, and where his tombstone stood for a century after, bearing the legend, "Present, useful; absent, wanted; living, desired; dying, lamented."

By others Passaconaway is regarded as a different person. The Child of the Bear —to English his name—was the chief of the Merrimacs and a convert of the apostle Eliot. Natives and colonists alike admired him for his eloquence, his bravery, and his virtue. Before his conversion he was a reputed wizard who sought by magic arts to repel the invasion of his woods and mountains by the white men, invoking the spirits of nature against them from the topmost peak of the Agiochooks, and his native followers declared that in pursuance of this intent he made water burn, rocks move, trees dance, and transformed himself into a mass of flame.

Such was his power over the forces of the earth that he could burn a tree in winter and from its ashes bring green leaves; he made dead wood blossom and a farmer's flail to bud, while a snake's skin he could cause to run. At the age of one hundred and twenty he retired from his tribe and lived in a lonely wigwam among the Pennacooks. One winter night the howling of wolves was heard, and a pack came dashing through the village harnessed by threes to a sledge of hickory saplings that bore a tall throne spread with furs. The wolves paused at Passaconaway's door. The old chief came forth, climbed upon the sledge, and was borne away with a triumphal apostrophe that sounded above the yelping and snarling of his train. Across Winnepesaukee's frozen surface they sped like the wind, and the belated hunter shrank aside as he saw the giant towering against the northern lights and heard his death-song echo from the cliffs. Through pathless woods, across ravines, the wolves sped on, with never slackened speed, into the mazes of the Agiochooks to that highest peak we now call Washington. Up its steep wilderness of snow the ride went furiously; the summit was neared, the sledge burst into flame, still there was no pause; the height was gained, the wolves went howling into darkness, but the car, wrapped in sheaves of fire, shot like a meteor toward the sky and was lost amid the stars of the winter night. So passed the Indian king to heaven.

THE LOSS OF WEETAMOO
(Pennacook)

Winnepurkit, sagamore of the coast settlements between Nahant and Cape Ann, had married Weetamoo, daughter of Passaconaway, king of the Pennacooks, and had taken her to his home. Their honeymoon was happy, but old ties are strong, and after a little time the bride felt a longing to see her people again. When she made known this wish the husband not only consented to her visit, but gave her a guard of his most trusty hunters who saw her safe in her father's lodge (near the site of Concord, NH), and returned directly. Presently came a messenger from Passaconaway, informing his son-in-law that Weetamoo had finished her visit and wished again to be with her husband, to whom he looked for an escort to guide her through the wilderness. Winnepurkit felt that his dignity as a chief was slighted by this last request, and he replied that as he had supplied her with a guard for the outward journey it was her father's place to send her back, "for it stood not with Winnepurkit's reputation either to make himself or his men so servile as to fetch her again."

Passaconaway returned a sharp answer that irritated Winnepurkit still more, and he was told by the young sagamore that he might send his daughter or keep her, for she would never be sent for. In this unhappy strife for precedent, which has been repeated on later occasions by princes and society persons, the young wife seemed to be fated as an unwilling sacrifice; but summoning spirit to leave her father's wigwam she launched a canoe on the Merrimack, hoping to make her way along that watery highway to her husband's domain. It was winter, and the stream was full of floating ice; at the best of times it was not easy to keep a frail vessel of bark in the current away from the rapids, and a wandering hunter reported that a canoe had come down the river guided by a woman, that it had swung against the Amoskeag rocks, where Manchester stands now, and a few moments later was in a quieter reach of water, broken and empty. No more was seen of Weetamoo.

HIAWATHA
(Iroquois)

Many, many moons ago three Indians sat on the bank of the great river with many islands. These three Indians had come on a long trail from their country, and it was a new trail, for they had made it themselves. Nobody had been on it before they cut their way through the thick forest.

The fathers of these Indians had been told of this river in the north which was filled with islands. The three Indians had said to their fathers that they would seek it; now they sat on a little hill, and it was before them.

The night sun had changed into a shape like a canoe three times since they had started on the long trail. Their moccasins were torn, and their feet were very tired; but the river was very beautiful, and it made their eyes glad to see it.

While the three Indians sat watching the river, they saw a white canoe coming straight toward the little hill where they sat. It seemed to come from the place of the setting sun.

The three Indians saw a white-haired chief alone in the canoe, and he had no paddle. The canoe came very fast, but it needed no help. The white-haired chief told the canoe to stop by the little hill on the shore where sat the three Indians; it came there and stopped.

The three Indians knew by the strange canoe that the Great Spirit had sent him, and they were afraid.

The white-haired chief said: "I am Hiawatha. I will help you and your people. Tell me what your nation can do. Tell me of your hunting."

The three arose and told Hiawatha of their nation. They had thought their people very strong; now they seemed like wild rabbits for weakness. They told him of their hunting, but they were not proud, for Hiawatha was wiser than any chief, and he knew what was in their hearts.

Hiawatha said: "Go back to your people. I shall come, and you will see me when you have made my lodge ready. I knew you were coming, for I saw you in the dark forests. I saw you on the great rocks in the forests. Go back and tell your people I am coming. Tell them to make a wigwam for Hiawatha."

The three Indians could not talk to each other. Their hearts were full. They found the trail they had made and followed it back to their own land; there they told their chiefs of the wise one in the white canoe. The chiefs made ready for his coming.

"He will come in a white stone canoe," said the chiefs.

The wigwam was built by a lake, and it was made of the finest skins of the deer. It was a white wigwam, with the door left open. No one watched to see who should shut the door.

One morning the door was shut, and a strange white canoe was in the water. The people came out of their lodges, and soon the doorway of skins in the white wigwam was opened. Hiawatha had come to the Onondaga nation. His wigwam was on the shore of Tiota or Cross Lake, in the land of the Onondagas.

Heyanwatha means the Wise Man. Hiawatha the people call him now. He taught the Onondagas many things, for he had lived with the Great Spirit. He was sent to help the Indian tribes.

Hiawatha taught the people how to plant corn and beans. They learned much about planting, and they learned how to store food for winter time.

While he was with the Onondagas the runners brought word that a great band of warriors was coming to fight them. The young braves put on their war paint.

"Call a great council of all the tribes," said the wise Hiawatha. "Let them meet on the hill by the lake." It was Onondaga Lake.

Swift runners carried word to four tribes. Their chiefs and great braves met on the hill by the lake, and their wives waited with them. All the people waited for three days, but Hiawatha did not come to the council. The chiefs sent men to Hiawatha on the morning of the fourth day to ask why he made them wait.

Hiawatha answered: "The Holder of the Heavens has shown me that if I go to this council great sorrow will come to me. I was sent to teach you peace. I shall show you how to make war. I will come."

Then Hiawatha stepped into his white stone canoe, and it went to the place of the great council, where the chiefs waited.

All the great chiefs and the people shouted when Hiawatha came. He stood still in the council circle. His daughter stood beside him, but no one had seen her before. When her father looked at her she went to her place among the women.

The first day of the council the chiefs told their plans, and Hiawatha listened. The second day he arose in the council, and the people listened. Hiawatha said wise words. All the chiefs remembered the words of Hiawatha. He made this speech:

"My brothers: You are from many tribes. You have come here for one cause. It is to live in safety. We must join ourselves together. The tribes that are on the warpath are strong. Not one tribe here is equal to that great people. Make yourselves a band of brothers. Then you will be stronger than they.

"The Mohawks that sit in council by that great tree shall be the first nation. They are the warlike people.

"The Oneidas who sit by the great stone that cannot be moved shall be the second nation. They are a wise people.

"The Onondagas that live at the foot of the great hills shall be the third nation. They are great in speech making.

"The Senecas who live in the forest, and whose trails are found all over the land, shall be the fourth nation, for they have much wisdom in hunting.

"The Cayugas live in the open country. Their wigwams are the finest, and their beans and corn grow like the grass on the plains. Their name is known for great wisdom; they shall be the fifth nation."

Hiawatha sat down in the council, and the third day the chiefs talked with one another; then they all said: "We will do this thing. We will be one nation. We will be called the Five Nations."

The council was ended. Hiawatha went to his canoe and called softly to his daughter.

As she left the women a great cloud came in the sky. It was a thunder-bird. The great cloud took the daughter of Hiawatha, and she was gone.

The white stone canoe came to the landing place. There was music in the air like the wind blowing through the pine trees. All the sky was filled with the sweet music.

The people mourned for Hiawatha, for he was gone. His wigwam by the lake Tiota was empty, and he was never seen again.

The Five Nations say that he went to the Islands of the Happy Ones. Owayneo, the Great Spirit, called him. His daughter had gone before him.

The Five Nations were strong. They were a wise people. Many moons after the white men came the Tuscaroras sat with them around the council-fire. Then they were known as the Six Nations. The white people have often called them the Mingos.

TALES OF MASTER LOX OR LEUX
(Various)

How Master Lox Froze to Death
(Passamaquoddy)

O f old times it came to pass that Master Lox, the Wolverine, or Indian Devil, he who was slain many times and as often rose from the dead, found himself deeply down in luck; for he was crossing a wide and dismal heath in winter-time, being but poorly provided in any way for travel. The wind blew like knives; the snow fell; sleet, frost, hail, and rain seemed to come all together in bad company, and still Lox was not happy, although he had no blanket or fur coat beyond his own. Yet this evil-minded jolly companion with every vice had one virtue, and that was that of all the beasts of the forest or devils in P'lamkik' he was the hardest hearted, toughest, and most unconquerable, being ever the first to fight and the last to give in, which even then he did not, never having done it and never intending to; whence it happened that he was greatly admired and made much of by all the blackguardly beasts of the backwoods,—wherein they differed but little from many among men.

Now as of all rowdies and rascals the wolves are the worst, we may well believe that it was with great joy Lox heard, as the darkness was coming on, a long, sad howl, far away, betokening the coming of a pack of these pleasant people; to which he raised his own voice in the wolf tongue,—for he was learned in many languages, —and soon was surrounded by some fifteen or sixteen lupine land-loafers, who danced, rolling over, barking and biting one another, all for very joy at meeting with him. And the elder, he who was captain, or the sogmo, said, "Peradventure thou wilt encamp with us this night, for it is ill for a gentleman to be alone, where he might encounter vulgar fellows." And Lox thanked him as if he were doing him a favor, and accepted the best of their dried meat, and took the highest place by their fire, and smoked the chief's choicest tomawe out of his best pipe, and all that with such vast condescension that the wolves grinned with delight.

And when they laid them down to sleep he that was the eldest, or the sogmo, bade the younger cover their guest Lox over very carefully. Now the tail of the wolf has broad-spreading, shaggy hair, and Lox, being sleepy, really thought it was a fur blanket that they spread, and though the night was cold enough to crack the rocks he threw the covering off; twice he did this, and the chief who looked after him, with all the rest, admired him greatly because he cared so little for the cold or for their care.

And having eaten after they arose, when in the morning they would wend away, the Wolf Chief said unto Lox, "Uncle, thou hast yet three days' hard travel before thee in a land where there is neither home, house, nor hearth, and it will be ill camping without a fire. Now I have a most approved and excellent charm, or spell, by which I can give thee three fires, but no more; yet will they suffice, one for each night, until thou gettest to thy journey's end. And this is the manner thereof: that thou shalt take unto thee dry wood, even such as men commonly burn, and thou shalt put them together, even as boys build little wigwams for sport, and then thou shalt jump over it. And truly, uncle, this is an approved and excellent charm of ripe antiquity, kept as a solemn secret among the wolves, and thou art the first not of our holy nation to whom it hath been given." So they parted.

Now Lox trudged on, and as he went westwards kept thinking of this great secret of the pious and peculiar people, and wondering if it were even as the Wolf said, or only a deceit; for however kindly he was treated by people, he always suspected that they mocked him to scorn, or were preparing to do so; for as he ever did this thing himself to every condition of mankind or beasts, he constantly awaited to have it done to him. And being curious withal, and anxious to see some new thing, he had not walked half an hour ere he said, "Tush! let me try it. Yea, and I will!" So building up the sticks, he jumped over them, and at once they caught fire and blazed up, and it came to pass even as the Wolf had prophesied.

Now having solaced himself by the heat, Lox went on. And anon it grew cold again, and he began to think how pleasant it was to be warm; and being, like most evil people, wanting in a corner of wisdom, he at once put the sticks together again and jumped over them, and as before there rose a blaze, and he was happy. And this was the second fire, and he had still three cold nights before him before he could reach his home.

And yet this Wolverine, who was so wise in all wickedness and witty in evil-doing, had not walked into the afternoon before he began to think of the third fire. "Truly," he said to himself, "who knows but the weather may take a turn to a thaw, and give us a warm night? Hum! ha! methinks by the look of the clouds the wind will soon be southwesterly. Have I not heard my grandmother say that such a color, even the red, meant something?—I forget what, but it might be a warm change. Luck be on me, I will risk the odds." And, saying this, he set up the sticks again; and this was the last fire, though it was not even the first night.

And when he came after dark to the first camping place it grew cold in earnest. Howbeit Lox, thinking that what was good for once must be good forever, made him his little pile of sticks and jumped over them. It was of no avail. Finally, when he had jumped twenty or thirty times more, there arose a little smoke, and, having his heart cheered by this, he kept on jumping. Now it is said that there can be no smoke without fire, but this time it went not beyond smoke. Then Lox jumped again, and this time the Indian Devil came up within him, and he swore by it that he would jump till it blazed or burst. So he kept on, and yet there came no comfort, not even a spark; and being at last aweary he fell down in a swoon, and so froze to death. And so the Devil was dead, and that was the last of him for that turn; but he got over it, for he has been seen many a time since.

How Master Lox Played a Trick on Mrs. Bear
(Micmac)

D on't live with mean people if you can help it. They will turn your greatest sorrow to their own account if they can. Bad habit gets to be devilish second nature. One dead herring is not much, but one by one you may make such a heap of them as to stink out a whole village.

As it happened to old Mrs. Bear, who was easy as regarded people, and thought well of everybody, and trusted all. So she took in for a house-mate another old woman. Their wigwam was all by itself, and the next neighbor was so far off that he was not their neighbor at all, but that of some other folks.

One night the old women made up a fire, and lay down and went to sleep Indian-fashion,—*witkusoodijik,*—heads and points, so that both could lie with their back to the fire.

Now while they were sound asleep, Lox, the Wolverine, or Indian Devil, came prowling round. Some people say it was Hespuns, the Raccoon; and it is a fact that Master Coon can play a very close game of deviltry on his own account. However, this time it must have been Lox, as you can see by the tracks.

While they were both sound asleep Lox looked in. He found the old women asleep, heads and points, and at once saw his way to a neat little bit of mischief. So, going into the woods, he cut a fine long sapling-pole of *ow-bo-goos,* and poked one end of it into the fire till it was a burning coal. Then he touched the soles of Mrs. Bear; and she, waking, cried out to the other, "Take care! you are burning me!" which the other denied like a thunder-clap.

Then Master Lox carefully applied the end of the hot pole to the feet of the other woman. First she dreamed that she was walking on hot sand and roasting rocks in summer-time, and then that the Mohawks were cooking her at the death-fire; and then she woke up, and, seeing where she was, began to blame Mrs. Bear for it all, just as if she were a Mohawk.

Ah, yes. Well, Master Lox, seeing them fighting in a great rage, burst out laughing, so that he actually burst himself, and fell down dead with delight. It was a regular side-splitter.

In the morning, when the women came out, there lay a dead devil at the door. He must indeed have looked like a Raccoon this time; but whatever he was, they took him, skinned him, and dressed him for breakfast. Then the kettle was hung and the water boiled, and they popped him in. But as soon as it began to scald he began to come to life. In a minute he was all together again, alive and well, and with one good leap went clear of the kettle. Rushing out of the lodge, he grabbed his skin, which hung on a bush outside, put it on, and in ten seconds was safe in the greenwood. He just saved himself with a whole skin.

Now Master Lox had precious little time, you will say, to do any more mischief between his coming to life and running away; yet, short as the allowance was, he made a great deal of it. For even while jumping out his wits for wickedness came to him, and he just kicked the edge of the pot, so that it spilled all the scalding hot water into the fire, and threw up the ashes with a great splutter. They flew into the eyes of Dame Bear and blinded her.

Now this was hard on the old lady. She could not go out hunting, or set traps, or fish any more; and her partner, being mean, kept all the nice morsels for herself. Mrs. Bear only got the leanest and poorest of the meat, though there was plenty of the best. Mrs. Bear might have fared better if she had used her eyes earlier.

One day, when she was sitting alone in the wigwam, Mrs. Bear began to remember all she had ever heard about eyes, and it came into her head that sometimes they were closed up in such a way that clever folk could cut them open again. So she got her knife and sharpened it, and, carefully cutting a little, saw the light of day. Then she was glad indeed, and with a little more cutting found that she could see as well as ever. And as good luck does not come single, the very first thing she beheld was an abundance of beautiful fat venison, fish, and maple-sugar hung up overhead.

Dame Bear said nothing about her having recovered her eyesight. She watched all the cooking going on, and saw the daintiest dinner, which all went into one platter, and a very poor lot of bones and scraps placed in another. Then, when she was called to eat, she simply said to the other woman, who kept the best, "Well, you have done well for yourself!"

The other saw that Mrs. Bear had recovered her sight. She was frightened, for Dame Bear was by far the better man of the two. So she cried out, "Bless me! what a mistake I've made! Why, I gave you the wrong dish. You know, my dear sister, that I always give you the best because you are blind."

After this Mrs. Bear kept her eyes open on people in two ways.

BLACK CAT AND THE SABLE
(Passamaquoddy)

Cooloo, the great bird that overspreads all with his wings, was a chief. His wife was named Pookjinsquess. The Sable and the Black Cat went in a stone canoe to a place where they make maple sugar. In this journey they were lost, and separated from each other. Sable in his wanderings came to a peculiarly shaped wigwam. He went in and found within a large Snake. The Snake said he was glad the Sable had come, as he was very hungry. The Snake told him to go into the woods and get a straight stick, so that when he pierced him he would not tear open his entrails. Sable then went out and sang in a loud voice a song which he hoped his brother the Black Cat would hear and come to his aid. The Black Cat heard him and came to him. Then the Sable told the Black Cat the trouble he was in, and how the Snake was going to kill him. The Black Cat told Sable not to be afraid, but that he would kill the big Snake. He told him that he would lie down behind the trunk of a hemlock tree which had fallen, and that Sable should search out a stick that was very crooked, obeying the commands of the big Snake. When he had found a stick, he should carry it to the Snake, who would complain that the stick was not straight enough. The Black Cat instructed Sable to reply that he would straighten it in the fire, holding it there until the steam came out of the end. While the Snake was watching the process of straightening the stick and the exit of the steam, Black Cat told Sable that he should strike the Snake over the head. The Sable sought out the most crooked stick he could find, and then returned to the wigwam where the Snake was. The Snake said the stick was too crooked. The Sable replied, "I can straighten it," and held it in the fire. When it was hot he struck the Snake on the head and blinded him. The Snake then followed the Sable, and, as he passed over the hemlock trunk, Black Cat killed him, and they cut him in small fragments. Black Cat and Sable called all the animals and birds to the feast; the caribous, wild horses, and swift animals and birds were first to arrive at the feast. The Turtle was the last, and got only the blood. Then the Black Cat and Sable returned home to Cooloo, whose wife was Pookjinsquess. She thought she would like to have for her husband Black Cat if she could get rid of Cooloo. But Black Cat offended Pookjinsquess and made her angry. To make way with him she invited him to go with her for gulls' eggs. She took him across the water in a canoe to an island which was very distant. There they filled baskets with eggs and started home in the canoe. A large, very beautiful bird flew over them. They both shot their arrows at it. The bird fell, and Black Cat jumped into the water to get what they had shot. When he got to where the bird fell he could not find it. Pookjinsquess went off, singing as she went and left Black Cat on the island.

In another version of this story Pookjinsquess leaves Black Cat on the island, and paddles away, singing songs. In this story, Black Cat was carried off from the island by the Fox, who swam out to get him.

Black Cat called to the gulls to defile Pookjinsquess with their dung. They flew over her, and as she looked up they covered her face with bird-lime. They then burst out in a laugh, which they still have, when they saw how changed her face was.

Black Cat wandered about the island, until at last he found a wigwam of the grandfather, the "Morning Star," who told him he was on a very dangerous island. He told him it was the habit of the Great Beaver to destroy every one who came to the island.

He told the Black Cat to climb a tree, and when he needed help to call out for him. Night coming on, water began to rise about the base of the tree, and the Giant Beaver came and began to gnaw at its base. The friendly ants tried to keep the tree upright, but the water continued to rise and the Beaver kept on gnawing. Then the Black Cat in his sore dilemma called out, "Grandpa, come!" The grandfather responded, "I am coming; wait till I get my moccasins." The water rose higher. Again Black Cat called out, "Come, grandpa, come!" "I am coming," his grandfather said; "wait till I get my cap." Again Black Cat called, "Hurry, grandpa!" "Wait until I get my pipe," said the grandparent. But the waters had reached him. The tree swayed to and fro. "Come, grandpa, come!" said Black Cat for the last time. Then he said, "I am coming; wait till I open my door;" and then he opened the door of his wigwam and the Morning Star came forth, the water began to recede, and the Beaver swam away. Then Black Cat's grandfather told him to come down, and he would send him over the water to the other shore on the back of the Wewillemuck. Black Cat thought that Wewillemuck was too small to carry him over, but his grandfather told him to seat himself between his horns, and when he wished Wewillemuck to go faster he should tap him on the horns. The grandfather then gave his grandson a small bow and arrows, and put him on the snail's back between his horns.

As they were crossing the channel, Wewillemuck said to the Black Cat, "When we get near shore tell me." But Black Cat gave Wewillemuck a sharp rap on the horns, and the snail jumped forward and went so far that both went a far distance inland. Wewillemuck said, "Why did you not tell me we were near the land? Now I cannot get back to the water again." But Black Cat took his small bow and arrows, and with them carried Wewillemuck back to the water. So pleased was he that he said, "Scrape from my horns some fine dust, and, whatever you wish, put this powder upon it and it is yours." So Black Cat scraped off some powder from the horns of Wewillemuck.

The Raven was told to build a wigwam for Cooloo, who was chief. *Pogump* (Black Cat) went to see the chief, and killed him with the powder. Black Cat went to see Pookjinsquess; he scattered a ring of powder around her wigwam, and then set it on fire. It blazed up and ignited the wigwam, burning up the old woman Pookjinsquess, whose ashes, blown about by the winds, made the mosquitoes.

RABBIT STORY
(Omaha)

T he Rabbit and the Grizzly Bear had been friends for some time. One day the Rabbit said to the Grizzly Bear, "Come and visit me. I dwell in a very large brier patch." Then he departed home. On his arrival he went out and gathered a quantity of young canes, which he hung up. Meanwhile the Grizzly Bear had reached the abode of the Rabbit, and was seeking the large brier patch; but the Rabbit really dwelt in a very small patch. When the Rabbit perceived that the Grizzly Bear was near, he began to make a pattering sound with his feet. This scared the Grizzly Bear, who retreated to a distance and then stopped and stood listening. As soon as the Rabbit noticed this he cried out, "Halloo! my friend, was it you whom I treated in that manner? Come and take a seat." So the Grizzly Bear complied with the Rabbit's request. The Rabbit gave the young canes to his guest, who soon swallowed them all, while the Rabbit himself ate but one, that is, the Rabbit minced now and then at one piece of cane while the Grizzly Bear swallowed all the others. "This is what I have always fancied," said the Grizzly Bear, as he was about to depart. Said he to the Rabbit, "Come and visit me. I dwell in a large bent tree." After his departure, the Rabbit started on his journey to the home of the Grizzly Bear. He spent some time in seeking the large bent tree, but all in vain, for the Grizzly Bear was then in a hollow tree, where he was growling. The Rabbit heard the growls and fled in terror, going some distance before he sat down. Then said the Grizzly Bear, "Halloo! my friend, was that you whom I treated in that manner? Come hither and sit down." So the Rabbit obeyed him. "You are now my guest," said the Grizzly Bear, "but there is nothing here for you to eat." So the Grizzly Bear went in search of food. He went to gather young canes. As he went along he was eating the small black insects which stay in decayed logs. These are called "Bessie bugs" by the white people, and *A-ki-di-sīp'-si-wé-di* by the Biloxi, from the noise (*"Sp! sp!"*) which they make when they are disturbed. After a long absence he returned to his lodge with a few young canes, which he threw down before the Rabbit. Then he walked in a circle around the Rabbit. In a little while the Grizzly Bear said "Oh!" and turned back toward the Rabbit, before whom he vomited up the black insects which he had devoured. "Swallow these," said he to the Rabbit. "I have never eaten such food," replied his guest. This offended the Grizzly Bear, who said, "When you entertained me, I ate all the food which you gave me, as I liked it very well; but now when I give you food, why do you treat me thus? Before the sun sets, I will kill you and lay down your body." As he spoke thus the Rabbit's heart was beating rapidly from terror, for the Grizzly Bear stood at the entrance of the hollow tree in order to prevent the Rabbit's escape. But the Rabbit, who was very active, managed to dodge, and thus he got out of the hollow tree. He ran at once to the brier patch and took his seat, being very angry with the Grizzly Bear. Then he shouted to the Grizzly Bear, "When they are hunting for you, I will go towards your place of concealment." For that reason it has come to pass ever since that day that, when dogs are hunting a rabbit, they find a grizzly bear, which is shot by the hunter.

THE TERRAPIN AND THE TURKEY
(Choctaw)

The Choctaws called all fables *shukha anump* (hog talk) as a mark of derision and contempt. Some of their fables, handed down by tradition through unknown generations, were similar in the morals taught by those of the famous Aesop. One of these shukha anumpas was that of the turkey and the terrapin. A haughty turkey gobbler, with long flowing beard and glossy feathers, meeting a terrapin one bright and beautiful spring morning, thus accosted him with an expression of great contempt: "What are you good for?" To which the terrapin humbly replied "many things." "Name one," continued the turkey. "I can beat you running," said the terrapin. "What nonsense! I thought you were a fool, now I know it," continued the turkey.

"I repeat it, I can beat you running, distance half a mile," continued the terrapin. "To prove you are a fool in believing such an absurdity, I'll run the race with you," responded the turkey with marked disgust. The day was appointed, the distance marked off, and the agreements entered into, one of which was, the terrapin was to run with a white feather in his mouth by which the turkey might be able to distinguish him from other terrapins; another was, the turkey was to give the terrapin the advantage of one hundred yards in the start. In the intervening time of the race, the wily terrapin secured the assistance of another terrapin to help him. Therefore, he secretly placed his assistant, with the white insignia also in his mouth, at the terminus to which the race was to be run. Early on the morning of the day agreed upon, the competitors were at their posts—the contemptuous turkey at the goal, and the dispassionate terrapin a hundred yards on the line. The turkey was to give the signal for starting by a loud gobble. The signal was given, and the race was opened. The turkey soon came up with the terrapin, who had gotten but a few feet from his goal, and shouted derisively as he passed by "What a fool!"

To which the terrapin ejaculated—"Not as big as you imagine." The confident turkey ran on about half way, and then stopped and turned off a little distance to secure his breakfast, but kept an eye on the track that the terrapin might not pass unobserved. After feeding about some time and not seeing anything of the terrapin, he began to fear he had passed him unobserved; therefore, he started again at full speed; and not overtaking the terrapin as he expected, he redoubled his exertions and reached the goal breathless, but to find the terrapin with the white feather in his mouth (his supposed opponent) already there. Moral.—The scornful are often outwitted by those upon whom they look with contempt.

Little Men Stories
(Various)

The Little Men
(Mohegan)

It is still a matter of discussion just how much credence can be placed in our Indian traditions. That is, credence in their soundness and verity in attempting to deal with affairs that have transpired in the past. In some cases their assertions are verifiable, while in others they manifestly lack accuracy, to no greater an extent, however, than those of other peoples. Believing, then, that the traditions of the Mohegans were not entirely fictionary, I decided to gather such as treated upon the existence of a race of "little people" about whom we had often heard the older and wiser folk speak. They had mentioned that these "little men" originally occupied the region bordering the Thames River where the Mohegans now dwell. In fact the oldest legends said that when the Pequots emigrated from the upper Hudson River country and worked their way down the Connecticut to the Sound, this race of pygmies was about extinct. Little was seen of them by the Indians and less was known, until after the disruption of a fractious band under Uncas, prior to 1630, which thenceforth became known as Mohegans. Uncas, with his cohort of renegades, proceeded up the Thames, or Pequot River as it was in early times, and there established himself and followers permanently. These are the tribal accounts. It seems then that before long the newcomers, the Mohegans, discovered that another people, a smaller and lighter people were the rightful tenants of their adopted home. And from this period, date the first memoirs relating to the mysterious originals. Owing to their diminutive size they received the name of *"muhkeahweesug"* from the Indians. Those of them that were seen must have been the last survivors, for they soon died out leaving nothing but weird reminders in the shape of a few relics and memories among the Mohegans. Constantly, however, tangible evidences of their existence have been disclosed. There are the copper kettles unearthed by old *"Wegun,"* the Good, while plowing near home, and the groups of dwarfed human bones occasionally revealed by some washout or excavation, and the old rock, now destroyed by omnipresent road-makers, that bore inscriptions claimed by the Indians to have been carved not by themselves, but by some "other people." The evidence of the kettles, though, is disputed by some claiming that they belonged to Mohegans who obtained them in the early days by barter with the whites. If the uninvestigated testimony of many significant mounds in the region were accepted, it would be an easy matter to give credence to the traditions, and believe with the Mohegans, that the east central part of Connecticut has seen within the last three hundred years, the passing away of a race that may have been somewhat akin to the Mound-builders.

One Mohegan's tale about them is as follows: The little men were here then. They used to tell about them; my grandmother and the rest. It was long before my time, but my grandmother knew of them from her grandmother. Folks saw more things in the woods then, than they do nowadays. Well it's different. Anyhow, *"nonnuh"* my grandmother's grandmother, saw the "little men" when she was a child. She was coming down the Yantic river in a canoe with her father and mother. There they were, the *"muhkeahweesug,"* the "little men," running on the shore. A pine woods came down to the water there and she could see them through the trees. But her mother told "nonnuh;" "Don't look at those "little men." They will point their fingers at you, then you cannot see them." So she turned her head away. There were not many of them.

And the "little men" would come to your house, so they used to say, asking for something to eat. You must always give them what they wanted, for if you didn't they would point at you, then, while you couldn't see them, they would take what they wanted. That is what the old people told the children about the "little men."

They told their children about those things. Then, once, an Indian and his wife lived here. They were Mohegan. They saw a "little man" too. It was in this way. One wild, stormy night, a rap on the door. The wind blew very hard when the squaw opened it. Someone was standing outside. But she didn't know who it was. When she found out what he wanted, she told her husband that he wanted her to go and take care of a sick woman, a long way off. She then told her husband that she was going, and that she would be back before long. So she packed up a few things, and out through the storm the person led her. This small person was a "little man," but she thought it was a boy. They went on and on through the storm. It was a bad night, even the squaw didn't know where she was being taken. But at last she saw a light before them, and soon there was a house. The "little man" said nothing but led her in, and showed her a "little woman" lying ill on a bed of skins. This "little man" and "woman" were *"muhkeahweesug;"* and the squaw then saw that they were. But she took good care of the "little woman." For a long time she stayed with them, not saying much but doing very well. By and by the "little woman" got better, and pretty soon she was well. After this the squaw was ready to go, for she had been away from home long enough. So they gave her presents, and she packed her bundle. Then the "little man" wound a piece of skin over her eyes so that the squaw couldn't see, and led her back to her husband's wigwam. You see, the "little people" treated her well. But when the squaw got to her house and took the skin from her eyes, she couldn't see where the "little man" had gone. He was gone. This squaw and her husband wanted to find the "little man" but they couldn't. So they gave it up. The "little people" died out. I guess these were the last. They lived way back in the woods. They kept away from the Indians. All this happened a long time ago, before the white people came down here. My grandmother told it to me.

The Little People of the Senecas
(Iroquois)

Two Indians from the Seneca Reservation went hunting; they went on a long trail, but at last found a place where the deer come to eat the salt that is in the sand; it is called a "salt lick." The Indians waited in the trees until many deer came; they shot at the deer, which fell like wild ducks when the rice is ripe.

The Indians had to throw away much meat in order to save the skins for leather. There was more meat than the wolves could eat, but the hunters shot many deer every day, until no more came.

The hunters went on carrying great rolls of deerskin, which were very heavy. They were hungry, but found nothing but acorns to eat. They became very weak and said: "Our wigwams will see us no more. We shall starve, and the deerskins will never be used."

They sat by a great rock. One of the hunters hit the rock with a stick, and a little man appeared.

The little one said: "You are starving because you killed and did not eat. You fed the wolves; now the wolves will feed on you. We have driven the deer to another forest, where they may live and be found by other hunters. You were selfish. You wanted all the deerskins in the forest. You were not wise."

"What shall we do to get food?" said the hunters.

"You may have meat if you will give up all the deerskins. My people have said it," said the little one.

"We must have the skins, and we must have food. Ask your chief to let us have the skins for our wigwams. We will be wise when we see the deer again at the salt licks," said the older hunter.

"I will go to my chief. Hit on this rock again when you want me," said the little one.

The Indians rapped on the rock again when the sun was setting. The little one came and led the way to a great cave filled with food and furs. They ate and slept. At midnight they were awakened by many of the little people, who said that the hunters might take their packs of skins and all the food they wished from the cave if they would never again shoot the deer to feed the wolves. The hunters promised and soon were in a strange, sound sleep. When they awoke they were near their homes.

THE DEMON OF CONSUMPTION
(Cherokee)

In the olden days, before the white man's foot had ever crossed the Blue Ridge, there resided in a cave in the Tusquittee Mountain, in what is now Clay County, NC, a demon with an iron finger, who had the power to assume the exact form and image of any one whom he chose to represent. His food was human lungs and livers, which he procured by his power of personating any absent member of a family and the aid of his iron finger. His method was to watch till some one of a family would be absent for an hour or so without notice. The demon would then enter the house in the form of the absent one, select his victim, begin fondling his head, run his soft fingers through his hair until the unsuspecting victim would go to sleep. Then with his iron finger would he pierce the victim's side and take his liver and lungs, but without pain. The wound would immediately heal, leaving no outward mark.

The one thus robbed would, on awaking, go about his usual occupation, entirely unconscious of the injury at the time, but would gradually pine away and die.

The monster, of course, did most of his mischief in the immediate neighborhood of his home. So terrible became his depredations that the beautiful valley of the Tusquittee was almost depopulated, and the whole tribe of the Cherokees became aroused, and determined at all hazards to destroy their dreadful enemy. After a long search, they at length found him in his cave; but no one would venture in to lay hands on him, for fear of the iron finger. He laughed at all their devices to allure him from his cave. They then undertook to destroy him by shooting him with arrows. This only the further provoked his mirth. The more they shot at him the louder he laughed, and the more he taunted them. As the arrows would pierce him, he would draw them out of his body and toss them back at the men who shot them, his wounds healing the instant the arrows were withdrawn. Thus the fight went on for a long time, the Indians shooting the arrows and the demon throwing them back. What was war with them was sport to him. But when the Indians were nearly exhausted and almost ready to give up the struggle, a little bird sang out to them, "Shoot him on his iron finger." At once they began to aim at that. The demon's mirthfulness left him. He raged and fumed, and tried every device to avoid the arrows aimed at his finger, but in vain. In a short time an arrow struck the iron finger and the monster fell and expired. Since that day the little bird, the wren, is sacred to the Cherokees, and on no account will they harm it.

For a long time the wasting sickness was stayed; but at length some of the demon's descendants learned the art and occasionally secured a victim, but none of them ever attained either the power or malignity of the demon of the iron finger.

Snake Lovers
(Various)

Lover of At-o-sis
(Passamaquoddy)

Far away, very far in the north, there dwelt by the border of a great lake a man and his wife. They had no children, and the woman was very beautiful and passionate.

The lake was frozen over during the greater part of the year. One day when the woman cut away the ice, she saw in the water a bright pair of large eyes looking steadily at her. They charmed her so that she could not move. Then she distinguished a handsome face; it was that of a fine slender young man. He came out of the water. His eyes seemed brighter and more fascinating than ever; he glittered from head to foot; on his breast was a large shining silvery plate.

The woman learned that this was *At-o-sis,* the Serpent, but she returned his embraces and held conversation with him, and was so charmed with her lover that she not only met him more than once every day, but even went forth to see him in the night.

Her husband, noticing these frequent absences, asked her why she went forth so frequently. She replied, "To get the fresh air."

The weather grew warmer; the ice left the lake; grass and leaves were growing. Then the woman waited till her husband slept, and stole out from the man whom she kissed no more, to the lover whom she fondled and kissed more than ever.

At last the husband's suspicions being fairly aroused, he resolved to watch her. To do this he said that he would be absent for three days. But he returned at the end of the first day, and found that she was absent. As she came in he observed something like silvery scales on the logs. He asked what they were. She replied, "Brooches."

He was still dissatisfied, and said that he would be gone for one day. He went to the top of a hill not far distant, whence he watched her. She went to the shore, and sat there. By and by there rose up out of the lake, at a distance, what seemed to be a brightly shining piece of ice. It came to the strand and rose from the water. It was a very tall and very handsome man, dressed in silver. His wife clasped the bright stranger in her arms, kissing him again and again.

The husband was awed by this strange event. He went home, and tried to persuade his wife to leave the place and to return to her people. This she refused to do. He departed; he left her forever. But her father and mother came to find her. They found her there; they dwelt with her. Every day she brought to them furs and meat. They asked her whence she got them. "I have another husband," she replied; "one who suits me. The one I had was bad, and did not use me well. This one brings all the animals to me." Then she sent them away with many presents, telling them not to return until the ice had formed; that was in the autumn.

When they returned she had become white. She was with young, and soon gave birth to her offspring. It consisted of many serpents. The parents went home. As they departed she said to them, "When you come again you may see me, but you will not know me."

Years after some hunters, roaming that way, remembered the tale, and looked for the wigwam. It was there, but no one was in it. But all the woods about the place were full of great black snakes, which would rise up like a human being and look one in the face, then glide away without doing any harm.

THE SERPENT AND THE THUNDERERS
(Oneida)

A long time ago, in an Indian settlement, were two wigwams, not far apart, and in these lived two squaws who were very good friends. They had two children of about the same age, who played together, and when they had little bows and arrows they shot together. As they grew bigger they wanted stronger bows and arrows, and their uncles made some for them. They used these every day, and became skillful in killing birds and small game, and then asked for some still stronger, that they might kill larger animals. They were now young men and good hunters. One of them, being handsome and kind, was very much liked by the women, and some of the maidens would have married him, but he refused all offers. At last his friend talked with him, and told him he had better marry, or something might happen for which he would be sorry. This troubled him, and he said he would soon choose a wife, but first they would have a long hunt together.

They got ready for this, telling their mothers they were going away on a great hunt, far from their village, and might be gone many days. So their mothers took some corn and roasted it, and then pounded this into meal in their wooden mortars. This was light, and would keep a long time. The young men filled their sacks, took their bows, and went to their hunting-ground. They walked all day, and camped in the woods. They walked all the next day, and camped on the hunting-ground, where they soon built a wigwam.

After this they hunted every day, and one was lucky and brought home a great deal of game, but the one whom the young squaws liked came home without any and said very little. This happened for several days, and the one who had been so happy and such a favorite seemed sorry all the time. Every morning they went off to hunt in opposite directions, and one day his friend thought he would follow him and see what he did. They went out as before, and after he had walked a little way the lucky hunter turned back into the other's path. He soon saw him running very fast through the woods, and hurried after him, calling to him to stop; but he did not. They ran till they came to a lake, and the first one plunged into the water and swam across, while his friend went around the shore. The swimmer got there first, paying no attention to his loud calls. They ran on to a second smaller lake, where they did the same, but this time the one on shore got ahead. The sorry young man then turned back, and his friend ran past both lakes, and hid in the bushes when the other came ashore. As the swimmer entered the woods the other jumped out and caught him, asking him what was the matter and why he acted so strangely.

At first the young man could say nothing and seemed to know nothing, but soon came to his senses. He told his friend that he was going to be married, and must leave him all alone, for he could not go back to his home. If he wished to see him at any time, he might come to the lake, bringing fresh Indian tobacco and clean clay pipes. These things he must lay on bark just from the tree, and then say to the lake, "I want to see my friend."

So he went off another way, and married the big serpent in the lake. When he had gone his friend went back to the wigwam, and he, too, was now very sorry, and did not wish to hunt. He built a fire and sat down alone.

It was very still for a long time, and then he heard some one coming. When he turned around a young man stood in the doorway dressed in white and with white feathers on his head. The visitor said, "You seem to be in trouble, but for all that you are the only one that can help us. My chief has sent me to invite you to our council." Then he gave him wampum, to show that he brought a true message. The hunter said, "Where is the council?" The young man in white answered, "Why, you came right by our wigwam in the woods, though you did not see it. Follow me, and you will find it quite near." So he went with him, not very far, till he saw smoke rising from the ground, and then a wigwam. Going in he saw eight chiefs sitting quietly on the ground. All had white feathers on their heads, but the principal chief had larger feathers than the rest. They gave him a place, and the hunter sat down and smoked with them. When the pipe came round to the principal chief, he rose and spoke to the young man.

"You have come to help us, and we have waited for you a long time." The young man said, "How can I help you?" The chief answered, "Your friend has married the big serpent in the lake whom we must kill. He has told you how to call him when you want to see him, and we will furnish the tobacco and pipes." The chiefs then gave him clean pipes and fresh tobacco, and the hunter took these and went to the lake. The principal chief said also, "When your friend comes you must ask to see his wife. She will want to know if the sky is clear. When she comes you must take them a little way from the lake and talk to them there. The chiefs will come in the form of a cloud,—on the lake, not in the sky."

So he took the fresh tobacco, the clean bark, and pipes, and laid them by the shore. Then he stood by the water and called loudly for his friend, saying he was going away, and wished to see him once more. Soon there was a ripple out on the lake, and the water began to boil, his friend coming out of it. He had a spot on his forehead, and looked like a serpent and yet like a man. His friend talked with him, asking what he should say to his mother when he got home. Then he asked to see his wife, that he might tell his mother what she was like. The serpent man said that she might not wish to come, but he would try. So he went to the shore and lay down, placing his lips to the water and beginning to drink. Then the hunter saw him going down through the water, not swimming like a man, but moving like a snake. Soon the water boiled again, and he came back, saying that his wife would come; but she did not. Then he looked around to see if the sky was clear, and went to the shore once more, drinking again and going down in the water like a snake.

Now a greater sight was seen. The lake boiled again, not in one spot, but all over, and great waves rolled up on the shore, as though there had been a strong wind, but there was none. The waves grew larger, and then the serpent man's wife came out of the water. She was very beautiful and shone like silver, but the silver seemed like scales. She had long hair falling all around her, as though it had been gold and silver glittering in the sun. Her husband came with her through the waves and up on the shore, and all three sat down on a log and talked together.

The hunter remembered the chief's words, and at last saw something like a cloud a great way off, moving upon the water, and not through the sky. Then he asked them to go into the woods, where the sun was not so hot, and there talk with him. When they did this he said he must step aside, and then he ran away, as the chiefs had told him. As he ran, a great cloud came at once over everything, and terrible thunder and lightning followed where they had sat, with rain everywhere.

At last all was quiet again, and the hunter went back to the lake, where a big and a little serpent lay dead upon the ground. They were the serpent woman and his friend. The eight chiefs were there, too, and had a great dance, rejoicing over their dead enemy. When this was over they cut up both serpents, making eight equal bundles of them. Each chief put one on his back, and then they were ready to go. All thanked the young man for what he had done, and told him he should always be lucky, saying, "Ask us for what you want at any time, and you shall have it." Then they went off through the woods in Indian file, and as he looked they seemed to step higher and higher, until they went up to the sky. Then there was a great thunder-storm, for the chiefs were the Thunderers.

The hunter went back to his wigwam, but it was quiet and lonesome, and he was sad; so he took down part of his meat, carrying it a half day's journey into the woods, where he hung it up on the trees. Then he returned for more, doing the same with the rest until he got home, where he told the story to the mother of his friend. She was very sorry for the death of the son whom she had loved but adopted him in his place, and so the young man had two mothers.

CHAHNAMEED'S WIFE
(Pequot-Mohegan)

Long ago there lived a man upon an island some distance from the mainland. His name was *Chahnameed,* the great eater, the glutton. On the island he had a house, and in a cove near by he kept two canoes. One day, as he stood on the beach looking toward the mainland, he saw something moving, but he could not make out what it was. He looked for some time, and then saw that it was a beautiful young girl walking along the beach. He said to himself: "She is looking for shells to put on her dress;" for her garment was of buckskin covered with colored beads, shells, and fringe. She was very beautiful, and Chahnameed thought so. So he put his hands about his mouth, and called to her. When she looked up, he called to her, and asked her to come over and live with him. The girl hesitated, but Chahnameed urged her, and at last she consented. Then he got into one of the canoes, and paddled to the mainland. When he got there, the girl said: "I will come back, but first I must go and get my mortar and pestle." So she went away to her village, and Chahnameed waited for her. When she came back, she had a mortar, a pestle, and some eggs. Then he took her in the canoe, and paddled to the island, and after that they lived together for a long time.

Now Chahnameed was accustomed to stay away from home for long periods, during which his wife did not know what he did, or where he went. She did not like this, but said nothing to him about it. After a while, however, she made up her mind that she would leave him, for she did not like to be left alone so long. Quietly she set about making some dolls. She made a great many, decorating them with paint and shells, but one doll was made larger than the rest. These she put away, so that her husband should not find them. Waiting until he had departed as usual one day, she took her mortar and pestle and some eggs down to the canoe. This canoe Chahnameed had left at home. Then she went back to the house, and got the dolls, which she put against the walls in different places, all facing the center. The large one she put in the bed, and covered it up with robes. Before she left, she put a little dried dung about each doll, and then crawled into the bed, and voided her excrement where the large doll lay. She then left her handiwork, went down to the canoe, and paddled away towards the mainland. In the canoe were the mortar, pestle, and eggs.

By and by Chahnameed came home. When he got to the house he looked for his wife, but did not find her. Then he went in and looked around. He saw the dolls, and went over towards one. Immediately the one against the wall behind him began to scream. When he turned around to look at it, the first one began to scream. Every time he turned to look at one doll, the one that was behind him would begin to scream. He did not know what they were. Soon he saw that something was in the bed, and, taking a big stick, he went over to it. He struck the large doll that was under the robes, thinking that it might be his wife. The large doll then screamed louder than the others. He pulled down the robes, and saw that it was only a doll. Then he threw down his stick, and ran down to his canoe. He knew that his wife had departed, for he saw that the mortar and pestle were gone.

When he got to the shore, he put his hands to his eyes, and looked for a long time toward the mainland. Soon he saw her paddling very hard for the land. He leaped into his canoe, and went after her. He soon began to gain, and before long he was almost up to her, and would have caught her, had she not suddenly crept to the stern of her canoe, and, lifting up the mortar, thrown it out into the water. Immediately the water where the mortar fell became mortars. When Chahnameed got there, he could go no farther. But he jumped out of his canoe and dragged it over the mortars, then pushed it into the water and jumped into it again. He paddled very hard to catch her up. His wife paddled very hard, too. But again he began to gain, and soon almost caught her. As before, however, she crept back to the stern, and raising the pestle, threw it over. Where it fell, the water became pestles. Then she paddled on again, very hard. Chahnameed could not pass these pestles either, so he jumped out and dragged the canoe over them; then jumped in and paddled as hard as he could to catch up. Again he began to gain, and almost caught her. But his wife crept to the stern of her canoe, and threw out all the eggs. Where the eggs fell, the water turned to eggs. Chahnameed could not get through these either. So he jumped out and dragged the canoe over them as before. This time he had to work very hard to get through the eggs, but at last succeeded. He paddled harder than ever, and soon began to catch up again. Now he would have caught her, for she had nothing more to throw out. But she stopped paddling, and stood up. Quickly she raised her hand to her head, and from the top pulled out a long hair. Then she drew it through her fingers, and immediately it became stiff like a spear. Chahnameed thought he was going to catch her now; he did not see what she was doing. When he got quite near, she balanced the hair-spear in her hand, and hurled it at him. She threw it straight; it hit him in the forehead, and he fell out of the canoe, and sank. He was dead. This all happened a very long time ago, back in the beginning of the world. The woman went back to her people. She was a Mohegan.

A Witch-Story
(Abenaki)

An old "witch" was dead, and his people buried him in a tree, up among the branches, in a grove that they used for a burial-place. Some time after this, in the winter, an Indian and his wife came along, looking for a good place to spend the night. They saw the grove, went in, and built their cooking fire. When their supper was over, the woman, looking up, saw long dark things hanging among the tree branches. "What are they?" she asked. "They are only the dead of long ago," said her husband, "I want to sleep." "I don't like it at all. I think we had better sit up all night," replied his wife. The man would not listen to her, but went to sleep. Soon the fire went out, and then she began to hear a gnawing sound, like an animal with a bone. She sat still, very much scared, all night long. About dawn she could stand it no longer, and reaching out, tried to wake her husband, but could not. She thought him sound asleep. The gnawing had stopped. When daylight came she went to her husband and found him dead, with his left side gnawed away, and his heart gone. She turned and ran. At last she came to a lodge where there were some people. Here she told her story, but they would not believe it, thinking that she had killed the man herself. They went with her to the place, however. There they found the man, with his heart gone, lying under the burial tree, with the dead "witch" right overhead. They took the body down and unwrapped it. The mouth and face were covered with fresh blood.

THE TERRIBLE SKELETON
(Onondaga)

In old times the Onondagas lived on a much larger reservation than now, a great land, but they made hunting parties to the North Woods. A party went off in which were an old man, his daughter and her husband, and their little boy. They went one day and camped, and another day and camped, and then separated. The old man, his daughter, and her husband turned one way, but the little boy accidentally went the other way with his uncle. The three kept on, and late in the day found an empty cabin in a clearing. There was an Indian bedstead on each side within, and as no one seemed to live there they resolved to stay for the night. They gathered plenty of fuel, stripping long pieces from the shag-bark hickory built a fine fire, spread their deerskins on the bedsteads, and they went to sleep; the old man on one side, and the man and his wife on the other. When the fire became low, and it grew dark in the cabin, the young people were awakened by a sound like a dog gnawing a bone. They stirred about, and the noise ceased, but was followed by something like rattling bones overhead. They got up and put on more fuel, and were going back to bed when they saw something like water flowing from the other couch. It was blood, and the old man was dead. His clothes were torn open, and his ribs broken and gnawed. They covered him up and lay down again. The same thing happened the second time, and this time they saw it was a terrible skeleton, feeding on the dead man. They were frightened, and in whispers devised a plan of escape. They made a greater fire, and the wife said, "Husband, I must go to the spring and get some water; I am so thirsty." So she quietly went out, but when she had got a little way she ran with all her might towards her own country.

When her husband thought she had a good start, he made a very big fire, to last a great while, and then he said, "What has become of my wife? I am afraid she is drowned in the spring. I must go and see." So he went out, and when he had got some way he ran with all his might, too, and when he overtook his wife he caught her by the arm, and they both ran on together. By and by the fire went down, and the skeleton came again, and when he found they were gone he started in chase. Soon they heard him howling terribly behind them, and they ran faster.

It happened that night that the Onondagas were holding a feast, and it now drew near morning. The man and woman heard the drum sounding afar off, *tum-tum, tum-tum,* and they ran harder, and shouted, but the skeleton did the same. Then they heard the drum again, *tum-tum, tum-tum,* and it was nearer, and they shouted again. Their friends heard the distress-hallo, and came to their rescue with all their arms. The skeleton fled. The fugitives fell down fainting, and did not regain their senses for four hours; then they told their story.

A council was held, and the warriors started for the dreadful spot. They found the hut, and a few traces of the old man. In the loft were some scattered articles, and a bark coffin in which was the skeleton of a man, who had been left unburied by his friends. They determined to destroy everything, and fuel was gathered on all sides and fire applied. Then the warriors stood with raised tomahawks and bended bows to destroy the terrible skeleton if he burst forth upon them. The fire grew hot, the cabin fell in, and out of the flames rushed a fox, with red and fiery eyes, which burst through the ranks and disappeared in the forest. The dreadful skeleton was never heard of more.

But what had the little boy to do with all this?

Oh, that is to show how well it was he went the other way.

THE PARTRIDGE WITCH
(Passamaquoddy)

Two brothers, having hunted at the head of the Penobscot until their snow-shoes and moccasins gave out, looked at each other ruefully and cried, "Would that there was a woman to help us!" The younger brother went to the lodge that evening earlier than the elder, in order to prepare the supper, and great was his surprise on entering the wigwam to find the floor swept, a fire built, a pot boiling, and their clothing mended. Returning to the wood he watched the place from a covert until he saw a graceful girl enter the lodge and take up the tasks of housekeeping.

When he entered she was confused, but he treated her with respect, and allowed her to have her own way so far as possible, so that they became warm friends, sporting together like children when the work of the day was over. But one evening she said, "Your brother is coming. I fear him. Farewell." And she slipped into the wood. When the young man told his elder brother what had happened there—the elder having been detained for a few days in the pursuit of a deer—he declared that he would wish the woman to come back, and presently, without any summons, she returned, bringing a toboggan-load of garments and arms. The luck of the hunters improved, and they remained happily together until spring, when it was time to return with their furs.

They set off down the Penobscot in their canoe and rowed merrily along, but as they neared the home village the girl became uneasy, and presently "threw out her soul"—became clairvoyant—and said, "Let me land here. I find that your father would not like me, so do not speak to him about me." But the elder brother told of her when they reached home, whereon the father exclaimed, "I had feared this. That woman is a sister of the goblins. She wishes to destroy men."

At this the elder brother was afraid, lest she should cast a spell on him, and rowing up the river for a distance he came upon her as she was bathing and shot at her. The arrow seemed to strike, for there was a flutter of feathers and the woman flew away as a partridge. But the younger did not forget the good she had done and sought her in the wood, where for many days they played together as of old. "I do not blame your father: it is an affair of old, this hate he bears me," she said. "He will choose a wife for you soon, but do not marry her, else all will come to an end for you." The man could not wed the witch, and he might not disobey his father, in spite of this adjuration; so when the old man said to him, "I have a wife for you, my son," he answered, "It is well."

They brought the bride to the village, and for four days the wedding-dance was held, with a feast that lasted four days more. Then said the young man, "Now comes the end," and lying down on a bear-skin he sighed a few times and his spirit ascended to the Ghosts' road—the Milky Way. The father shook his head, for he knew that this was the witch's work, and, liking the place no longer, he went away and the tribe was scattered.

THE STORY OF TIJAIHA, THE SORCERER
(Huron)

When the French came the missionaries tried to prevail on the Indians to receive their religion. They asked the Indians if they knew anything about God. The Indians replied that they did; that three or four times a year they had meetings, at which the women and children were present, and then the chiefs told them what to do and warned them against evil practices. The missionaries said that this was good, but that there was a better way, which they ought to know. They ought to become Christians. But the Indians said, "We have many friends among the creatures about us. Some of us have snake friends, some eagles, some bears, and the like. How can we desert our friends?" The priests replied, "There is only one God." "No," said the Indians, "there are two gods, one for the Indians and the other for the whites." The discussion lasted three days. Finally, the priests said it was true,— there were two Gods, Jesus and the Holy Ghost. One of these might be the same as the Indian God. The Indians could follow all his commands which were good, and also obey the commands of Jesus. But they would have to give up their allies among the brutes.

Some of the Hurons became Christians, but others refused to accept the new religion. Among these was a noted warrior, a young man, named Tijaiha. On one occasion he left the town with his family to hunt on the Huron River. One day, coming to a deep pool near the river, he beheld a violent commotion in the water, which was evidently made by a living creature. Of what nature it might be he did not know, though he believed it to be a great serpent, and to be possessed, like many of the wild creatures, of supernatural powers. Thereupon, after the fashion of the Indians, he fasted for ten days, eating occasionally only a few morsels to preserve life; and he prayed to the creature that some of its power might be bestowed on him. At the end of the tenth day a voice from the disturbed pool demanded what he wanted. He replied that he wanted to have such power given to him that he could vanquish and destroy all his enemies. She (the creature) replied that this power should be conferred upon him if he would grant her what she desired. He asked what this was, and was told that she would require one of his children. If he would grant this demand, he might come at night and learn from her the secret which would give him the power he sought for. He objected to this sacrifice, but offered, in place of the child, to give an old woman, his wife's mother. The creature accepted the substitute, and the bargain was concluded.

That night Tijaiha returned to the pool, and learned what he had to do. He was to prepare a cedar arrow, with which he must shoot the creature when she should appear, at his call, above the water. From the wound he could then draw a small quantity of blood, the possession of which would render him invincible, and enable him to destroy his enemies. But as this blood was a deadly poison, and even its effluvia might be mortal, he must prepare an antidote from the juice of a plant which she named. On the following day he procured the plant, and his wife—who knew nothing of the fatal price he was to pay—assisted him in making the infusion. He also made a cedar arrow, and, with bow in hand, repaired to the pool.

At his call the water began to rise, boiling fearfully. As it rose, an animal came forth. It proved to be a large bird, a "diver," and the warrior said, "This is not the one," and let it go. The water boiled and rose higher, and a porcupine came out. "Neither is this the one," said the warrior, and withdrew his arrow from his bow. Then the water rose in fury to the level of the bank, and the head of a huge horned serpent, with distended jaws and flaming eyes, rose and glared at Tijaiha. "This is the one," he said, and shot the creature in the neck. The blood gushed forth, and he caught, in a vessel which he held ready, about half a pint. Then he ran toward his lodge, but before he reached it he had become nearly blind and all but helpless. His wife put the kettle to his lips. He drank the antidote, and presently vomited the black poison, and regained his strength. In the morning he called to his wife's mother, but she was dead. She had perished without a touch from a human hand. In this manner he became possessed of a talisman which, as he believed, would give him a charmed life, and secure him the victory over his enemies.

But in some way it became known that he had been the cause of the mother's death. This crime excited the indignation of his people, and he dared not go back to them. He took refuge with the Iroquois, and became a noted war-chief among them. After some time he resolved, in an evil hour, to lead an attack against his own people. He set forth at the head of a strong party of warriors, and arrived at the Wyandot settlement, near the present town of Sandwich. It was the season of corn-planting, and two of Tijaiha's aunts had come out on that day to plant their fields. They were women of high rank in the tribe, and Tijaiha knew that their death would arouse the whole tribe. He ordered his followers to kill them. This they did, and then retreated into the forest to the northward, carefully covering their tracks, to escape pursuit. Their leader's expectation was that the Huron warriors would go off in another direction in search of their enemies, thus leaving their defenceless town at his mercy.

When the Hurons found the bodies they were greatly excited. They searched for ten days without discovering any trace of the murderers. Their chief then consulted a noted soothsayer, who promised that on the following day he would tell him all. During the night the soothsayer made his incantations, and in the morning informed the Hurons that the deed had been done by a party of Iroquois, under the lead of Tijaiha. The enemy, he said, was lurking in the woods, and he could guide them to the spot; but they must wait ten days before starting. The Hurons waited impatiently until the ten days had expired, and then placed the old soothsayer on horseback, and followed him. He led them through the forest directly to the encampment of their enemies. On seeing them they waited till evening, and then through the night, till daybreak. Then, according to their custom, they shouted to their sleeping foes, and rushed upon them. They killed every man in the camp; but on examining carefully the bodies, they were annoyed to find that Tijaiha was not among them.

Being hungry, they seated themselves to eat, and the chief, feeling thirsty, told his son to take his kettle and bring him some water. "Where shall I find water here?" asked the boy. "These men must have had water," replied his father. "Look for the path they have made to it." The lad looked, and found the path, and, following it, came to a deep spring or pool under a tree. As he was stooping down to it a man rose partly out of the pool, and bade the youth take him prisoner. The affrighted boy ran to the camp and told what he had seen. All shouted "Tijaiha," and rushed to the pool, where they dragged him forth by the hair. He stood defiant and sneering, while they attempted to kill him. Their blows seemed powerless to injure him. He caught the tomahawks which were aimed at him, and hurled them back. At length a warrior, exclaiming, "I will finish him," plunged a knife into his breast and tore out his heart. Thrown on the ground, it bounded like a living thing, till the warrior split it open with his knife. Thus ended Tijaiha's evil career. His contract with the serpent had only led him to crime and death.

DANCES OF OLD AGE
(Various)

THE MAGIC OF THE WEEWILLMEKQ'
(Passamaquoddy)

Of old times. There lived in a village many Indians. Among them was a handsome young man, very brave, a great hunter. And there was a beautiful girl. What was her name? Mahli-hahn-sqwess, or Kaliwahdazi,—I don't remember which. But she was proud and high-tempered, and, what was worse, a great witch, but nobody knew it. She wanted the young man to marry her, but he was very busy getting ready for the fall and winter hunt, and had no time to attend to such a thing; and told her so very plainly.

Yes, he must have been very plain with her, for she was very angry, and said to him, "You may go; but you will never return as you went." She meant that he would be ill or changed. He gave no heed to her words; he did not care for her nor fear her. But far away in the woods, far in the north, in midwinter, he went raging mad. The witch had struck him, when far away, with her magic.

He had with him an elder brother, a great brave, a very fierce man. He, not being able to do aught else, did the most desperate thing a Wabanaki Indian can do. He went down to the river, and sang the song which calls the *Weewillmekq'*.

> *"We que moh wee will l'mick,*
> *We que moh m'cha micso,*

Som'awo wee will l'mick!
Cardup ke su m'so wo Sawo!"

I call on the Wee-will-l'mick!
I call on the Terrible One!
On the One with the Horns!
I dare him to appear!

It came to him in all its terrors. Its eyes were like fire; its horns rose. It asked him what he wanted. He said that he wished his brother to be in his right mind again.

"I will give you what you want," said the Weewillmekq', "if you are not afraid."

"I am not afraid of anything," said the Indian.

"Not of me?"

"Not of you nor of *Mitche-hant,* the devil himself."

"If you dare take me by my horns and scrape somewhat from one of them with your knife," said the monster, "you may have your wish."

Now this Indian was indeed as savage and brave as the devil; and he had need to be so to do this, for the Weewillmekq' looked his very worst. But the man drew his knife and scraped from the horn till he was told that he had enough.

"Go to your camp," said the Worm. "Put half the scrapings into a cup of water. Make your brother drink it."

"And the other half?" asked the Indian.

"Give it to the girl who made all this trouble. She needs medicine, too."

He returned to camp, and gave the drink to his brother, who recovered. When the hunt was at an end they went home.

They arrived at night. There was an immense lodge in the town, and a dance was going on. The younger brother had prepared a cool drink,—sweet with maple-sugar, fragrant with herbs,—and in it was the powder of the horn of the Weewillmekq'. The witch, warm and very thirsty from dancing, came to the door. He offered her the cup. Without heeding who gave it, she drank it dry, and, turning to her partner, went on in the dance.

And then a strange thing happened. For at every turn of the dance she grew a year older. She began as a young girl; when at the end of the room she was fifty years of age; and when she got back to the door whence she started she fell dead on the floor, at the feet of him who gave her the drink, a little wrinkled, wizened-up old squaw of a hundred years.

This is the story of the Dance of Old Age. But you may call it *Sektegah,* the Dance of Death, if you like it better.

ANOTHER VERSION OF THE DANCE OF OLD AGE
(Passamaquoddy)

It was in the autumn, the time when Indians go up the rivers to their hunting-grounds, that two young men left home. They ascended the stream; they came to a branch, where they parted: one going alone, another with his married brother. This latter, with the brother, had left in the village a female friend, a witch, who had forbidden him to go hunting, but he had not obeyed her.

And she had cause to keep him at home, for, when he was afar in the woods, and alone, he met one day with a very beautiful girl, who fascinated him, and gave herself to him. And when he said that he did not know how to conceal her from his friends she told him that she was a fairy, and could make herself as small as a newly born squirrel, and that all he need do was to wrap her up in a handkerchief and carry her in his pocket. When alone, he could take her out, enjoy her company, and then reduce and fold her up and put her away again.

He did so, but from that hour, while he carried the fairy near his heart, he began to be wicked and strange. This was not caused by her, but by the girl at home. He was entirely changed; he grew devilish; he refused to eat, and never spoke. His sister-in-law began to fear him. When she offered him food he cried out, "Unless I can devour one of your children I will have nothing!"

When his brother returned and heard all this, he, too, offered him meat, but met with a refusal and the reply, "Give me one of your little children." To which he answered, "The child is so small that it will not satisfy you. Let me go and get a larger one." Then he ran to the village and informed his friends of what had come over the brother. And as they knew that he was about to become a *kewahqu'* (*chenoo*) they resolved to kill him.

But there was a young man there, a friend of the sufferer, who said that he could save him. So all who were assembled bade him try.

And when night came he went apart, and began to sing his *m'téoulin,* or magic song. When it ended there was a loud sound as of some heavy body falling and striking the earth, which fairly shook. The next morning he called all his friends and the married brother, and showed them a human corpse. "Now leave me," he said. "Go to my friend and tell him that I have food for him." The Indians did so, and in horror left the two cannibals to devour their disgusting meal. When the insane youth was satisfied, his friend asked, "Have you had enough?" He replied that he had. Then the magician said, "You are bewitched by the girl who forbade you to go hunting; she knew you would find a maid better than she is. Now come with me."

They went to a small lake; they sat down by its side; the sorcerer began his magic song. And as he sang the waters opened; from the disturbed waves rose a huge *Weewillmekq',* a creature like an alligator, with horns. And, as the terrible being came ashore, the magician said, "Go and scrape somewhat from his horn and bring it here!" The young man had become fearless; he went and did as he was bid: he scraped the horn, and brought the scraping.

"Now, my friend," said the magician, "let us try this on a tree." There was a large green beech growing by them. It was simply touched with the fragment from the horn when another color spread all over the bark as rapidly as the eye could follow it: in an instant it was dead, and in a few minutes more it fell to the ground, utterly rotten, as if it were a century old.

"Now," said the sorcerer, "we will experiment with this on the witch who wishes to destroy you." So as it was night they went to the village. A dance was being held, and the beautiful tall witch having paused to rest, the two men approached her. The young man placed his hand on her head; he held in it a scraping of the horn of the weewillmekq'. As he did so she grew older in an instant,—she became very old; a pale color rippled all over her; she fell, looking a hundred years, dead on the floor, shriveled, dried, and dropped to powder.

"She will not trouble you any more," said the sorcerer. "Her dance is over."

LOVERS
(Various)

THE GIRL WHO MARRIED MOUNT KATAHDIN
(Penobscot)

O f the old time. There was once an Indian girl gathering blueberries on Mount Katahdin. And, being lonely, she said, "I would that I had a husband!" And seeing the great mountain in all its glory rising on high, with the red sunlight on the top, she added, "I wish Katahdin were a man, and would marry me!"

All this she was heard to say ere she went onward and up the mountain, but for three years she was never seen again. Then she reappeared, bearing a babe, a beautiful child, but his little eyebrows were of stone. For the Spirit of the Mountain had taken her to himself; and when she greatly desired to return to her own people, he told her to go in peace, but forbade her to tell any man who had married her.

Now the boy had strange gifts, and the wise men said that he was born to become a mighty magician. For when he did but point his finger at a moose, or anything which ran, it would drop dead; and when in a canoe, if he pointed at the flocks of wild ducks or swans, then the water was at once covered with the floating game, and they gathered them in as they listed, and through that boy his mother and every one had food and to spare.

Now this was the truth, and it was a great wonder, that Katahdin had wedded this girl, thinking with himself and his wife to bring up a child who should build up his nation, and make of the Wabanaki a mighty race. And he said, "Declare unto these people that they are not to inquire of thee who is the father of thy child; truly they will all know it by seeing him, for they shall not grieve thee with impertinence." Now the woman had made it known that she would not be questioned, and she gave them all what they needed; yet, for all this, they could not refrain nor restrain themselves from talking to her on what they well knew she would fain be silent. And one day when they had angered her, she thought, "Truly Katahdin was right; these people are in nowise worthy of my son, neither shall he serve them; he shall not lead them to victory; they are not of those who make a great nation." And being still further teased and tormented, she spake and said, "Ye fools, who by your own folly will kill yourselves; ye mud-wasps, who sting the fingers which would pick ye out of the water, why will ye ever trouble me to tell you what you well know? Can you not see who was the father of my boy? Behold his eyebrows; do ye not know

Katahdin by them? But it shall be to your exceeding great sorrow that ever ye inquired. From this day ye may feed yourselves and find your own venison, for this child shall do so no more for you."

And she arose and went her way into the woods and up the mountain, and was seen on earth no more. And since that day the Indians, who should have been great, have become a little people. Truly it would have been wise and well for those of early times if they could have held their tongues.

THE INVISIBLE ONE
(Micmac)

There was once a large Indian village situated on the border of a lake,—*Names-keek' oodun Kuspemku*. At the end of the place was a lodge, in which dwelt a being who was always invisible. He had a sister who attended to his wants, and it was known that any girl who could see him might marry him. Therefore there were indeed few who did not make the trial, but it was long ere one succeeded.

And it passed in this wise. Towards evening, when the Invisible One was supposed to be returning home, his sister would walk with any girls who came down to the shore of the lake. She indeed could see her brother, since to her he was always visible, and beholding him she would say to her companions, "Do you see my brother?" And then they would mostly answer, "Yes," though some said, "Nay,"— *alt telovejich, aa alttelooejik*. And then the sister would say, *"Cogoowa' wiskobook-sich?"* "Of what is his shoulder-strap made?" But as some tell the tale, she would inquire other things, such as, "What is his moose-runner's haul?" or, "With what does he draw his sled?" And they would reply, "A strip of rawhide," or "A green withe," or something of the kind. And then she, knowing they had not told the truth, would reply quietly, "Very well, let us return to the wigwam!"

And when they entered the place she would bid them not to take a certain seat, for it was his. And after they had helped to cook the supper they would wait with great curiosity to see him eat. Truly he gave proof that he was a real person, for as he took off his moccasins they became visible, and his sister hung them up; but beyond this they beheld nothing not even when they remained all night, as many did.

There dwelt in the village an old man, a widower, with three daughters. The youngest of these was very small, weak, and often ill, which did not prevent her sisters, especially the eldest, treating her with great cruelty. The second daughter was kinder, and sometimes took the part of the poor abused little girl, but the other would burn her hands and face with hot coals; yes, her whole body was scarred with the marks made by torture, so that people called her *Oochigeaskw* (the rough-faced girl). And when her father, coming home, asked what it meant that the child was so disfigured, her sister would promptly say that it was the fault of the girl herself, for that, having been forbidden to go near the fire, she had disobeyed and fallen in.

Now it came to pass that it entered the heads of the two elder sisters of this poor girl that they would go and try their fortune at seeing the Invisible One. So they clad themselves in their finest and strove to look their fairest; and finding his sister at home went with her to take the wonted walk down to the water. Then when He came, being asked if they saw him, they said, "Certainly," and also replied to the question of the shoulder-strap or sled cord, "A piece of rawhide." In saying which, they lied, like the rest, for they had seen nothing, and got nothing for their pains.

When their father returned home the next evening he brought with him many of the pretty little shells from which *weiopeskool,* or wampum, was made, and they were soon engaged *napawejik* (in stringing them).

That day poor little *Oochigeaskw',* the burnt-faced girl, who had always run barefoot, got a pair of her father's old moccasins, and put them into water that they might become flexible to wear. And begging her sisters for a few wampum shells, the eldest did but call her "a lying little pest," but the other gave her a few. And having no clothes beyond a few paltry rags, the poor creature went forth and got herself from the woods a few sheets of birch bark, of which she made a dress, putting some figures on the bark. And this dress she shaped like those worn of old. So she made a petticoat and a loose gown, a cap, leggins, and handkerchief, and, having put on her father's great old moccasins,—which came nearly up to her knees,—she went forth to try her luck. For even this little thing would see the Invisible One in the great wigwam at the end of the village.

Truly her luck had a most inauspicious beginning, for there was one long storm of ridicule and hisses, yells and hoots, from her own door to that which she went to seek. Her sisters tried to shame her, and bade her stay at home, but she would not obey; and all the idlers, seeing this strange little creature in her odd array, cried, "Shame!" But she went on, for she was greatly resolved; it may be that some spirit had inspired her.

Now this poor small wretch in her mad attire, with her hair singed off and her little face as full of burns and scars as there are holes in a sieve, was, for all this, most kindly received by the sister of the Invisible One; for this noble girl knew more than the mere outside of things as the world knows them. And as the brown of the evening sky became black, she took her down to the lake. And erelong the girls knew that He had come. Then the sister said, "Do you see him?" And the other replied with awe, "Truly I do,—and He is wonderful." "And what is his sled-string?" "It is," she replied, "the Rainbow." And great fear was on her. "But, my sister," said the other, "what is his bow-string?" "His bow-string is *Ketaksoowowcht*" (the Spirits' Road, the Milky Way).

"Thou hast seen him," said the sister. And, taking the girl home, she bathed her, and as she washed all the scars disappeared from face and body. Her hair grew again; it was very long, and like a blackbird's wing. Her eyes were like stars. In all the world was no such beauty. Then from her treasures she gave her a wedding garment, and adorned her. Under the comb, as she combed her, her hair grew. It was a great marvel to behold.

Then, having done this, she bade her take the *wife's seat* in the wigwam,—that by which her brother sat, the seat next the door. And when He entered, terrible and beautiful, he smiled and said, *"Wajoolkoos!"* "So we are found out!" *"Alajulaa."* "Yes," was her reply. So she became his wife.

Love and Treason
(Nantucket)

The tribes that inhabited Nantucket and Martha's Vineyard before the whites settled the country were constantly at war, and the people of the western island once resolved to surprise those of Nantucket and slay as many as possible before they could arm or organize for battle. The attack was to be made before daybreak, at an hour when their intended victims would be asleep in their wigwams, but on rowing softly to the hostile shore, while the stars were still lingering in the west, the warriors were surprised at finding the enemy alert and waiting their arrival with bows and spears in hand. To proceed would have been suicidal, and they returned to their villages, puzzled and disheartened. Not for some years did they learn how the camp had been apprised, but at the end of that time, the two tribes being at peace, one of their young men married a girl of Nantucket, with whom he had long been in love, and confessed that on the night preceding the attack he had stolen to the beach, crossed to Nantucket on a neck of sand that then joined the islands, and was uncovered only at low tide, sought his mistress, warned her of the attack, that she, at least, might not be killed; then, at a mad run, with waves of the rising tide lapping his feet, he returned to his people, who had not missed him. He set off with a grave and innocent face in the morning, and was as much surprised as any one when he found the enemy in arms.

An Event in Indian Park
(Saranac)

It was during the years when the Saranacs were divided that Howling Wind, one of the young men of Indian Carry, saw and fell in love with a girl of the family on Tupper Lake. He quickly found a way to tell his liking, and the couple met often in the woods and on the shore. He made bold to row her around the quieter bays, and one moonlight evening he took her to Devil's Rock, or Devil's Pulpit, where he told her the story of the place. This was to the effect that the fiend had paddled, on timbers, by means of his tail, to that rock, and had assembled fish and game about him in large numbers by telling them that he was going to preach to them, instead of which moral procedure he pounced upon and ate all that were within his grasp.

As so often happened in Indian history, the return of these lovers was seen by a disappointed rival, who had hurried back to camp and secured the aid of half a dozen men to arrest the favored one as soon as he should land. The capture was made after a struggle, and Howling Wind was dragged to the chief's tent for sentence. That sentence was death, and with a refinement of cruelty that was rare even among the Indians, the girl was ordered to execute it. She begged and wept to no avail. An axe was put into her hands, and she was ordered to despatch the prisoner. She took the weapon; her face grew stern and the tears dried on her cheeks; her lover, bound to a tree, gazed at her in amazement; his rival watched, almost in glee. Slowly the girl crossed the open space to her lover. She raised the tomahawk and at a blow severed the thongs that held him, then, like a flash, she leaped upon his rival, who had sprung forward to interfere, and clove his skull with a single stroke. The lovers fled as only those can fly who run for life. Happily for them, they met a party from the Carry coming to rescue Howling Wind from the danger to which his courtship had exposed him, and it was even said that this party entered the village and by presenting knives and arrows at the breast of the chief obtained his now superfluous consent to the union of the fugitives. The pair reached the Carry in safety and lived a long and happy life together.

SAFE HARBOR
(Pequot)

H ither came a band of Delawares with Pequot captives, among them a young chief to whom had been offered not only life but leadership if he would renounce his tribe, receive the mark of the turtle on his breast, and become a Delaware. On his refusal, he was bound to a tree, and was about to undergo the torture, when a girl among the listeners sprang to his side. She, too, was a Pequot, but the turtle totem was on her bosom, and when she begged his life, because they had been betrothed, the captors paused to talk of it. She had chosen well the time to interfere, for a band of Hurons was approaching, and even as the talk went on their yell was heard in the wood. Instant measures for defence were taken, and in the fight that followed both chief and maiden were forgotten; but though she cut the cords that bound him, they were separated in the confusion, he disappearing, she falling captive to the Hurons, who, sated with blood, retired from the field. In the fantastic disguise of a wizard the young Pequot entered their camp soon after, and on being asked to try his enchantments for the cure of a young woman, he entered her tent, showing no surprise at finding her to be the maiden of his choice, who was suffering from nothing worse than nerves, due to the excitement of the battle. Left alone with his patient, he disclosed his identity, and planned a way of escape that proved effective on that very night, for, though pursued by the angry Hurons, the couple reached "safe harbor," thence making a way to their own country in the east, where they were married.

THE HEALING WATERS
(Iroquois)

T he Iroquois have a touching story of how a brave of their race once saved his wife and his people from extinction.

It was winter, the snow lay thickly on the ground, and there was sorrow in the encampment, for with the cold weather a dreadful plague had visited the people. There was not one but had lost some relative, and in some cases whole families had been swept away. Among those who had been most sorely bereaved was Nekumonta, a handsome young brave, whose parents, brothers, sisters, and children had died one by one before his eyes, the while he was powerless to help them. And now his wife, the beautiful Shanewis, was weak and ill. The dreaded disease had laid its awful finger on her brow, and she knew that she must shortly bid her husband farewell and take her departure for the place of the dead. Already she saw her dead friends beckoning to her and inviting her to join them, but it grieved her terribly to think that she must leave her young husband in sorrow and loneliness. His despair was piteous to behold when she broke the sad news to him, but after the first outburst of grief he bore up bravely, and determined to fight the plague with all his strength.

"I must find the healing herbs which the Great Manitou has planted," said he. "Wherever they may be, I must find them."

So he made his wife comfortable on her couch, covering her with warm furs, and then, embracing her gently, he set out on his difficult mission.

All day he sought eagerly in the forest for the healing herbs, but everywhere the snow lay deep, and not so much as a blade of grass was visible. When night came he crept along the frozen ground, thinking that his sense of smell might aid him in his search. Thus for three days and nights he wandered through the forest, over hills and across rivers, in a vain attempt to discover the means of curing the malady of Shanewis.

When he met a little scurrying rabbit in the path he cried eagerly: "Tell me, where shall I find the herbs which Manitou has planted?"

But the rabbit hurried away without reply, for he knew that the herbs had not yet risen above the ground, and he was very sorry for the brave.

Nekumonta came by and by to the den of a big bear, and of this animal also he asked the same question. But the bear could give him no reply, and he was obliged to resume his weary journey. He consulted all the beasts of the forest in turn, but from none could he get any help. How could they tell him, indeed, that his search was hopeless?

On the third night he was very weak and ill, for he had tasted no food since he had first set out, and he was numbed with cold and despair. He stumbled over a withered branch hidden under the snow, and so tired was he that he lay where he fell, and immediately went to sleep. All the birds and the beasts, all the multitude of creatures that inhabit the forest, came to watch over his slumbers. They remembered his kindness to them in former days, how he had never slain an animal unless he really needed it for food or clothing, how he had loved and protected the trees and the flowers. Their hearts were touched by his courageous fight for Shanewis, and they pitied his misfortunes. All that they could do to aid him they did. They cried to the Great Manitou to save his wife from the plague which held her, and the Great Spirit heard the manifold whispering and responded to their prayers.

While Nekumonta lay asleep there came to him the messenger of Manitou, and he dreamed. In his dream he saw his beautiful Shanewis, pale and thin, but as lovely as ever, and as he looked she smiled at him, and sang a strange, sweet song, like the murmuring of a distant waterfall. Then the scene changed, and it really was a waterfall he heard. In musical language it called him by name, saying: "Seek us, O Nekumonta, and when you find us Shanewis shall live. We are the Healing Waters of the Great Manitou."

Nekumonta awoke with the words of the song still ringing in his ears. Starting to his feet, he looked in every direction; but there was no water to be seen, though the murmuring sound of a waterfall was distinctly audible. He fancied he could even distinguish words in it.

"Release us!" it seemed to say. "Set us free, and Shanewis shall be saved!"

Nekumonta searched in vain for the waters. Then it suddenly occurred to him that they must be underground, directly under his feet. Seizing branches, stones, flints, he dug feverishly into the earth. So arduous was the task that before it was finished he was completely exhausted. But at last the hidden spring was disclosed, and the waters were rippling merrily down the vale, carrying life and happiness wherever they went. The young man bathed his aching limbs in the healing stream, and in a moment he was well and strong.

Raising his hands, he gave thanks to Manitou. With eager fingers he made a jar of clay, and baked it in the fire, so that he might carry life to Shanewis. As he pursued his way homeward with his treasure his despair was changed to rejoicing and he sped like the wind.

When he reached his village his companions ran to greet him. Their faces were sad and hopeless, for the plague still raged. However, Nekumonta directed them to the Healing Waters and inspired them with new hope. Shanewis he found on the verge of the Shadow-land, and scarcely able to murmur a farewell to her husband. But Nekumonta did not listen to her broken adieux. He forced some of the Healing Water between her parched lips, and bathed her hands and her brow till she fell into a gentle slumber. When she awoke the fever had left her, she was serene and smiling, and Nekumonta's heart was filled with a great happiness.

The tribe was for ever rid of the dreaded plague, and the people gave to Nekumonta the title of "Chief of the Healing Waters," so that all might know that it was he who had brought them the gift of Manitou.

THE PEACE QUEEN
(Oneida)

A brave of the Oneida tribe of the Iroquois hunted in the forest. The red buck flashed past him, but not swifter than his arrow, for as the deer leaped he loosed his shaft and it pierced the dappled hide.

The young man strode toward the carcass, knife in hand, but as he seized the horns the branches parted, and the angry face of an Onondaga warrior lowered between them.

"Leave the buck, Oneida," he commanded fiercely. "It is the spoil of my bow. I wounded the beast ere you saw it."

The Oneida laughed. "My brother may have shot at the buck," he said, "but what avails that if he did not slay it?"

"The carcass is mine by right of forest law," cried the other in a rage. "Will you quit it or will you fight?"

The Oneida drew himself up and regarded the Onondaga scornfully.

"As my brother pleases," he replied. Next moment the two were locked in a life-and-death struggle.

Tall was the Onondaga and strong as a great tree of the forest. The Oneida, lithe as a panther, fought with all the courage of youth. To and fro they swayed, till their breathing came thick and fast and the falling sweat blinded their eyes. At length they could struggle no longer, and by a mutual impulse they sprang apart.

"Ho! Onondaga," cried the younger man, "what profits it thus to strive for a buck? Is there no meat in the lodges of your people that they must fight for it like the mountain lion?"

"Peace, young man!" retorted the grave Onondaga. "I had not fought for the buck had not your evil tongue roused me. But I am older than you, and, I trust, wiser. Let us seek the lodge of the Peace Queen hard by, and she will award the buck to him who has the best right to it."

"It is well," said the Oneida, and side by side they sought the lodge of the Peace Queen.

Now the Five Nations in their wisdom had set apart a Seneca maiden dwelling alone in the forest as arbiter of quarrels between braves. This maiden the men of all tribes regarded as sacred and as apart from other women. Like the ancient Vestals, she could not become the bride of any man.

As the Peace Queen heard the wrathful clamour of the braves outside her lodge she stepped forth, little pleased that they should thus profane the vicinity of her dwelling.

"Peace!" she cried. "If you have a grievance enter and state it. It is not fitting that braves should quarrel where the Peace Queen dwells."

At her words the men stood abashed. They entered the lodge and told the story of their meeting and the circumstances of their quarrel.

When they had finished the Peace Queen smiled scornfully. "So two such braves as you can quarrel about a buck?" she said. "Go, Onondaga, as the elder, and take one half of the spoil, and bear it back to your wife and children."

But the Onondaga stood his ground.

"O Queen," he said, "my wife is in the Land of Spirits, snatched from me by the Plague Demon. But my lodge does not lack food. I would wive again, and thine eyes have looked into my heart as the sun pierces the darkness of the forest. Will you come to my lodge and cook my venison?"

But the Peace Queen shook her head.

"You know that the Five Nations have placed Genetaska apart to be Peace Queen," she replied firmly, "and that her vows may not be broken. Go in peace."

The Onondaga was silent.

Then spoke the Oneida. "O Peace Queen," he said, gazing steadfastly at Genetaska, whose eyes dropped before his glance, "I know that you are set apart by the Five Nations. But it is in my mind to ask you to go with me to my lodge, for I love you. What says Genetaska?"

The Peace Queen blushed and answered: "To you also I say, go in peace," but her voice was a whisper which ended in a stifled sob.

The two warriors departed, good friends now that they possessed a common sorrow. But the Peace Maiden had for ever lost her peace. For she could not forget the young Oneida brave, so tall, so strong, and so gentle.

Summer darkened into autumn, and autumn whitened into winter. Warriors innumerable came to the Peace Lodge for the settlement of disputes. Outwardly Genetaska was calm and untroubled, but though she gave solace to others her own breast could find none.

One day she sat by the lodge fire, which had burned down to a heap of cinders. She was thinking, dreaming of the young Oneida. Her thoughts went out to him as birds fly southward to seek the sun. Suddenly a crackling of twigs under a firm step roused her from her reverie. Quickly she glanced upward. Before her stood the youth of her dreams, pale and worn.

"Peace Queen," he said sadly, "you have brought darkness to the soul of the Oneida. No longer may he follow the hunt. The deer may sport in quiet for him. No longer may he bend the bow or throw the tomahawk in contest, or listen to the tale during the long nights round the camp-fire. You have his heart in your keeping. Say, will you not give him yours?"

Softly the Peace Queen murmured: "I will."

Hand in hand like two joyous children they sought his canoe, which bore them swiftly westward. No longer was Genetaska Peace Queen, for her vows were broken by the power of love.

The two were happy. But not so the men of the Five Nations. They were wroth because the Peace Queen had broken her vows, and knew how foolish they had been to trust to the word of a young and beautiful woman. So with one voice they abolished the office of Peace Queen, and war and tumult returned once more to their own.

ARROW AND LENAWEE
(Saranac)

B rightest flower that grows beside the brooks is the scarlet blossom of the Indian plume: the blood of Lenawee. Hundreds of years ago she lived happily among her brother and sister Saranacs beside Stony Creek, the Stream of the Snake, and was soon to marry the comely youth who, for the speed of his foot, was called the Arrow. But one summer the Quick Death came on the people, and as the viewless devil stalked through the village young and old fell before him. The Arrow was the first to die. In vain the Prophet smoked the Great Calumet: its smoke ascending took no shape that he could read. In vain was the white dog killed to take aloft the people's sins. But at last the Great Spirit himself came down to the mountain called the Storm Darer, splendid in lightning, awful in his thunder voice and robe of cloud. "My wrath is against you for your sins," he cried, "and naught but human blood will appease it."

In the morning the Prophet told his message, and all sat silent for a time. Then Lenawee entered the circle. "Lenawee is a blighted flower," she sobbed. "Let her blood flow for her people." And catching a knife from the Prophet's belt, she ran with it to the stream on which she and the Arrow had so often floated in their canoe. In another moment her blood had bedewed the earth. "Lay me with the Arrow," she murmured, and, smiling in their sad faces, breathed her last. The demon of the quick death shrank from the spot, and the Great Spirit smiled once more on the tribe that could produce such heroism. Lenawee's body was placed beside her lover's, and next morning, where her blood had spilt, the ground was pure, and on it grew in slender spires a new flower,—the Indian plume: the transformed blood of sacrifice. The people loved that flower in all years after. They decked their hair and dresses with it and made a feast in its honor. When parents taught their children the beauty of unselfishness they used as its emblem a stalk of Indian plume.

BIRD'S DEATH
(Saranac)

B ack from his war against the Tahawi comes the Sun, chief of the Lower Saranacs, —back to the Lake of the Clustered Stars, afterward called, by dullards, Tupper's Lake. Tall and invincible he comes among his people, boasting of his victories, Indian fashion, and stirring the scalps that hang at his breast. "The Eagle screams," he cries. "He greets the chief, the Blazing Sun. Wayotah has made the Tahawi tremble. They fly from him. Hooh, hooh! He is the chief." Standing apart with wistful glance stands *Oseetah,* the Bird. She loves the strong young chief, but she knows that another has his promise, and she dares not hope; yet the chief loves her, and when the feasting is over he follows her footprints to the shore, where he sees her canoe turning the point of an island. He silently pursues and comes upon her as she sits waving and moaning. He tries to embrace her, but she draws apart. He asks her to sing to him; she bids him begone.

He takes a more imperious tone and orders her to listen to her chief. She moves away. He darts toward her. Turning on him a face of sorrow, she runs to the edge of a steep rock and waves him back. He hastens after. Then she springs and disappears in the deep water. The Sun plunges after her and swims with mad strength here and there. He calls. There is no answer. Slowly he returns to the village and tells the people what has happened. The Bird's parents are stricken and the Sun moans in his sleep. At noon a hunter comes in with strange tidings: flowers are growing on the water! The people go to their canoes and row to the Island of Elms. There, in a cove, the still water is enamelled with flowers, some as white as snow, filling the air with perfume, others strong and yellow, like the lake at sunset.

"Explain to us," they cry, turning to the old Medicine of his tribe, "for this was not so yesterday." "It is our daughter," he answered. "These flowers are the form she takes. The white is her purity, the yellow her love. You shall see that her heart will close when the sun sets, and will reopen at his coming." And the young chief went apart and bowed his head.

The Envy of Manitou
(Delaware)

B ehind the mountains that gloom about the romantic village of Mauch Chunk, PA, was once a lake of clear, bright water, its winding loops and bays extending back for several miles. On one of its prettiest bits of shore stood a village of the Leni Lenape, and largest of its wigwams, most richly pictured without, most luxurious in its couching of furs within, was that of the young chief, Onoko. This Indian was a man of great size, strength, and daring. Single-handed he had slain the bear on *Mauch Chunk* (Bear Mountain), and it was no wonder that Wenonah, the fairest of her tribe, was flattered when he sued for her hand, and promptly consented to be his wife. It was Onoko's fortune in war, the chase, and love that roused the envy of Mitche Manitou.

One day, as the couple were floating in their shallop of bark on the calm lake, idly enjoying the sunshine and saying pretty things to each other, the Manitou arose among the mountains. Terrible was his aspect, for the scowl of hatred was on his face, thunder crashed about his head, and fire snapped from his eyes. Covering his right hand with his invincible magic mitten, he dealt a blow on the hills that made the earth shake, and rived them to a depth of a thousand feet. Through the chasm thus created the lake poured a foaming deluge, and borne with it was the canoe of Onoko and Wenonah. One glance at the wrathful face in the clouds above them and they knew that escape was hopeless, so, clasping each other in a close embrace, they were whirled away to death. Manitou strode away moodily among the hills, and ever since that time the Lehigh has rolled through the chasm that he made. The memory of Onoko is preserved in the name of a glen and cascade a short distance above Mauch Chunk.

It is not well to be too happy in this world. It rouses the envy of the gods.

Star-Crossed Lovers
(Cherokee)

A century ago this rough eminence, a dozen miles from Chattanooga, TN, was an abiding place of Cherokee Indians, among whom was Arinook, their medicine-man, and his daughter. The girl was pure and fair, and when a white hunter saw her one day at the door of her father's wigwam he was so struck with her charm of person and her engaging manner that he resolved not to return to his people until he had won her for his wife. She had many lovers, though she favored none of them, and while the Cherokees were at first loath to admit a stranger to their homes they forgot their jealousy when they found that this one excelled as a hunter and fisherman, that he could throw the knife and tomahawk better than themselves, and that he was apt in their work and their sports.

They even submitted to the inevitable with half a grace when they found that the stranger and the girl of whom they were so fond were in love. With an obduracy that seems to be characteristic of fathers, the medicine-man refused his consent to the union, and the hearts of the twain were heavy. Though the white man pleaded with her to desert her tribe, she refused to do so, on the score of duty to her father, and the couple forlornly roamed about the hill, watching the sunset from its top and passing the bright summer evenings alone, sitting hand in hand, loving, sorrowing, and speaking not. In one of their long rambles they found themselves beside the Tennessee River at a point where the current swirls among rocks and sucks down things that float, discharging them at the surface in still water, down the stream. Here for a time they stood, when the girl, with a gush of tears, began to sing—it was her death-song. The white man grasped her hand and joined his voice to hers. Then they took a last embrace and flung themselves into the water, still hand in hand.

When the river is low you may sometimes hear their death-song sounding there. The manitous of the river and the wood were offended with the medicine-man because of his stubbornness and cruelty, although he suffered greatly because of the death his daughter died, and he the cause of it. For now strange Indians appeared among the Cherokees and drove the deer and bear away. Tall, strong, and large were these intruders, and they hung about the village by day and night— never speaking, yet casting a fear about them, for they would throw great rocks farther than a warrior could shoot an arrow with the wind behind him; they had horns springing from their heads; their eyes were the eyes of wild-cats, and shone in the dark; they growled like animals, shaking the earth when they did so, and breathing flame; they were at the bedside, at the council-fire, at the banquet, seeming only to wait for a show of enmity to annihilate the tribe.

At length the people could endure their company no longer, and taking down their lodges they left Wallen's Ridge and wandered far away until they came to a valley where no foot had left its impress, and there they besought the Great Spirit to forgive the wrong their medicine-man had done, and to free them from the terrible spirits that had been living among them. The prayer was granted, and the lodges stood for many years in a safe and happy valley.

OCKLAWAHA AND WINONAH
(Ocala)

In the long ages ago there dwelt in the region of Silver Springs, two neighboring tribes of the Vitachuco Indians, the Ocalas and the Kanapahas. In the dense and fertile forests near the springs lay the village of the Ocalas, while not far distant on the winding, dazzling river, dwelt the tribe of Kanapaha. But though dwelling so close together there was war and hatred between these tribes. Indeed one may well wonder at the ferocity of these noble Indians, for noblest of all the Floridian Indians were they, and it is not to be wondered that none but the noblest should dwell in a region so beautiful as Silver Springs. Onto its waters one soft, salubrious evening in May came Ocklawaha, son of Oluskee, chief of the Kanapahas. Ocklawaha, the greatest pride of the old chief's heart, skilled in every pursuit of the warrior and having already tasted of Cassine, the black drink, was indeed worthy of the devotion of his tribe. Tall and powerful was he, with skin of an olive hue and hair as black as the raven's wing.

In the depths of his dark eyes lay a slumbering gleam of ferocity, which needed only to be aroused, and the firm lines of his mouth showed a character, strong and unrelenting.

Braided into his trussed up hair was the scarlet feather of the flamingo which proclaimed his rank, while the only clothing which he wore was a loin cloth of well tanned deer skin and moccasins of the same. Suspended over his breast were small sticks of engraved gold and silver and at his side hung a quiver of arrows. This day, on which he, intent upon his fishing, had drifted, unknown, into the region of his enemies, it seemed that all nature had united in making one perfect day.

The sun, sinking to rest behind the whispering pines, cast a golden glow o'er the world. The pebbles at the bottom of the spring took the rainbow colors of the sky above, and the huge, overhanging trees pictured a forest below. So pellucid were the waters that Ocklawaha, in his canoe, seemed suspended in midair. The whip-poor-wills darted here and there in the twilight, swooping down o'er the spring to dip their wings in the water, and the heron overhead flew wearily home to his nest. Here, in this romantic setting, Ocklawaha first saw the daughter of Suwannee, chief of the Ocalas. Standing at the edge of the dusky forest with the last rays of the sun throwing a golden halo about her, she seemed to him the creature of another world. Her features were of the most delicate molding and her soft, black hair hung in freedom, reaching almost to her knees. She was clothed in a skirt and cloak woven of Spanish moss which was so delicate in texture as to resemble silk. This cloak was drawn around the upper part of her small, lithe body and fastened over one shoulder with a golden clasp. Her neck and arms were bare except for the necklaces and bracelets of most exquisite pearls which encircled them, and her tiny feet were encased in deer skin moccasins. Her large dark eyes gazed straight into those of Ocklawaha and he, with dripping oar half raised, gazed back with a new and tender light in his eyes.

"*Hitanachi* (beautiful)," he murmured, "who art thou?"

"Winonah," she answered, in a low, sweet voice. And the nodding pines whispered softly "Winonah, Winonah."

"Goodbye," said she and again the whispering pines echoed, "goodbye."

"Goodbye, Winonah," he answered softly, and springing into his canoe, he paddled away into the evening, and the eyes of the little Indian maiden followed him till he disappeared in the gathering darkness.

But this was not goodbye, for Ocklawaha, drawn by that overwhelming power, love, paddled secretly every evening to the spot of their first meeting, and there always found Winonah, gazing with wistful eyes from beneath the towering oak.

Fiercely did he struggle to overcome that power, but alas, he himself was overthrown, and one evening, just as the shades of night were falling, Ocklawaha, casting discretion to the winds, crushed Winonah in his mighty arms and whispered, fiercely:

"Winonah, my little one, I love thee! Dost thou love me?"

And Winonah, yielding with a happy sigh, to his embrace, nodded and softly murmured, "Un-cah."

Then the moon came out and the two lovers, bathed in its silvery beams, vowed to the Great Spirit, to be forever true to one another. Then every night, before the rising of the moon, Ocklawaha and Winonah met in the dark shadows, beneath the sheltering oak. Wildly happy were they, in their lovers' oblivion, until there came a fatal day. This night, Ocklawaha waited long and patiently for Winonah. After many weary hours had passed, Winonah, slipping noiselessly through the forest shadows, cast herself into her lover's arms.

Then she, whispering, told him that they were being secretly watched by Hiatiqui, the medicine man.

An important man was Hiatiqui in the village of the Ocalas. He cured the sick and healed the wounded with his herbs, and was the leader in all religious ceremonies. He might easily be distinguished by his grave and solemn countenance and dignified step, as he strolled about the village, singing to himself, songs or hymns in a low sweet voice. But keen were his eyes as the eyes of *Ya-chi-la-ne,* the eagle, and his heart was cunning and cruel as the heart of *Chitta,* the snake.

Swiftly Winonah related her discovery to Ocklawaha, and he, taking her in his arms, soothed her and subdued her fears.

Then they planned to escape on the following night to the peace town of the Chattahoochees. This night had been set apart by the warriors for the ceremony of moon worship, and at the signal from Ocklawaha, Winonah was to slip away from the worshippers and meet him beneath their trysting oak.

He was now loath to leave her, but as it was very late he held her close for a moment, then sprang into his canoe and disappeared into the darkness. Winonah slipped back into the village and spent a long and sleepless night, praying to the Great Spirit to watch over them and deliver them from danger. The following night found a strange scene within the palisade of the village. In the center of the enclosure a short distance from the dwelling of the chief, the warriors squatted in a circle upon the ground. By the dim light of the rising moon their faces, bedaubed with war paint, appeared fierce and grotesque in strange contrast to the soft, gentle faces of the women, in the background. When the moon appeared above the tree tops, Hiatiqui rose and standing in the center of the group with his face towards the sacred orb, began an utterance of the most hideous noises, which echoed and re-echoed throughout the silent forest. Then he acted as a mad man for fully the space of a half hour, while the remainder of the men looked on with stolid expressionless faces and the women thrilled with pride and reverence at the religion of their men. Winonah, alone, was inattentive.

Suddenly, at the signal of Suwannee, the warriors sprang from the ground and danced around in a circle, uttering the noises of various animals. Amidst the din there came from away in the forests the cry of *Huppe,* the great owl, and Winonah slipped silently from the group of onlookers, unseen by any eyes except those of the watchful Hiatiqui. A few moments later there came a louder hoot, and Hiatiqui abruptly paused in his demonstrations and listened. Loud murmurs of dissent rose from the warriors and Suwannee, voicing their resentment, spoke to Hiatiqui:

"Hast my brother mistaken the hoot of Huppe for the war cry of the enemy?" he asked gravely.

"Nay, not mistaken," answered the priest, "Unless Ocklawaha, son of Oluskee, has taken to himself the form of the great owl."

"Why dost my brother speak thus?" questioned the chief.

"Why dost Winonah absent herself from our sacred ceremony at the cry of Huppe?" returned Hiatiqui.

"Winonah!" called Suwannee, turning towards the group of wondering women. "Winonah, come, my little one."

But no answer came to him, for Winonah had gone.

Then there arose from the warriors a terrible cry of revenge. Meanwhile Winonah sped with fast beating heart towards her lover. Trembling violently, she flung herself into his arms, but when he would have fondled her, she drew away and taking his hand, pressed him to hasten. Thus they set forth upon their journey. Swiftly and silently they slipped through the woods and had begun to breathe with ease, when suddenly, there broke from the surrounding forests a blood-curdling yell which seemed to check the very life blood of the lovers' hearts. Indeed for a moment, they seemed frozen to the spot, but Ocklawaha, the first to recover, seized Winonah's hand more firmly and darted into the bushes. Then began the most thrilling chase that the old pines of this region had ever looked upon. The faithful moon, ever a friend of lovers, slid behind a cloud and darkness prevailed over the forest. On and on fled Ocklawaha and Winonah, slipping backwards and forwards, always eluding the grasp of their blood thirsty pursuers, who in terrifying yells gave vent to their anger. Finally the yells subsided and all grew still. The lovers crept towards the water, where lay Ocklawaha's canoe, to carry them into safety. They reached the high cliff which overlooks the springs and stood there to seek out the canoe in the darkness. At this moment the terrifying yell of triumph that arose on all sides made known to them their discovery. Ocklawaha, knowing there to be now no escape from those merciless and unrelenting pursuers, turned and gazed into the soft, fearless eyes of Winonah.

Then the moon, to witness the scene, slid from beneath the cloud, and shed her silvery light about the lovers. Their figures stood out against the landscape, one a tall powerful Indian youth, the other a small, graceful Indian maiden. Heedless of the oncoming savages with lifted tom-a-hawks, they gazed long and tenderly into each other's eyes, then Ocklawaha, seizing the frail form of Winonah in his arms, leaped into the spring and the limpid waters closed o'er them.

A deep silence reigned o'er the forest; the moon shone on, outwardly undisturbed; from the oak came the call of *Huppe,* the great owl; from the air came the cry of *Nutcha,* the hawk; and through the woods, whistled *Hulalah,* the wind. Alone on the bank, face towards the glowing moon and arms uplifted, stood Suwannee, chief of the Ocalas, praying the great Spirit to receive in his realm of the beautiful the soul of the lost Winonah, the little Indian maiden.

CREATING THE "NEW WORLD"
(Various)

THE SPRINGS OF BLOOD AND WATER
(Unidentified)

A great drought had fallen on Long Island, and the red men prayed for water. It is true that they could get it at Lake Ronkonkoma, but some of them were many miles from there, and, beside, they feared the spirits at that place: the girl who plied its waters in a phosphor-shining birch, seeking her recreant lover; and the powerful guardians that the Great Spirit had put in charge to keep the fish from being caught, for these fish were the souls of men, awaiting deliverance into another form. The people gathered about their villages in bands and besought the Great Spirit to give them drink. His voice was heard at last, bidding their chief to shoot an arrow into the air and to watch where it fell, for there would water gush out. The chief obeyed the deity, and as the arrow touched the earth a spring of sweet water spouted into the air. Running forward with glad cries the red men drank eagerly of the liquor, laved their faces in it, and were made strong again; and in memory of that event they called the place the Hill of God, or Manitou Hill, and Manet or Manetta Hill it is to this day. Hereabouts the Indians settled and lived in peace, thriving under the smile of their deity, making wampum for the inland tribes and waxing rich with gains from it. They made the canal from bay to sea at Canoe Place, that they might reach open water without dragging their boats across the sand-bars, and in other ways they proved themselves ingenious and strong.

When the English landed on the island they saw that the Indians were not a people to be trifled with, and in order to properly impress them with their superiority, they told them that John Bull desired a treaty with them. The officers got them to sit in line in front of a cannon, the nature of which instrument was unknown to them, and during the talk the gun was fired, mowing down so many of the red people that the survivors took to flight, leaving the English masters at the north shore, for this heartless and needless massacre took place at Whale's Neck. So angry was the Great Spirit at this act of cruelty and treachery that he caused blood to ooze from the soil, as he had made water leap for his thirsting children, and never again would grass grow on the spot where the murder had been done.

THE WHITE DEER OF ONOTA
(Onota)

B eside quiet Onota, in the Berkshire Hills, dwelt a band of Indians, and while they lived here a white deer often came to drink. So rare was the appearance of an animal like this that its visits were held as good omens, and no hunter of the tribe ever tried to slay it. A prophet of the race had said, "So long as the white doe drinks at Onota, famine shall not blight the Indian's harvest, nor pestilence come nigh his lodge, nor foeman lay waste his country." And this prophecy held true. That summer when the deer came with a fawn as white and graceful as herself, it was a year of great abundance. On the outbreak of the French and Indian War a young officer named Montalbert was despatched to the Berkshire country to persuade the Housatonic Indians to declare hostility to the English, and it was as a guest in the village of Onota that he heard of the white deer. Sundry adventurers had made valuable friendships by returning to the French capital with riches and curiosities from the New World. Even Indians had been abducted as gifts for royalty, and this young ambassador resolved that when he returned to his own country the skin of the white deer should be one of the trophies that would win him a smile from Louis.

He offered a price for it—a price that would have bought all their possessions and miles of the country roundabout, but their deer was sacred, and their refusal to sacrifice it was couched in such indignant terms that he wisely said no more about it in the general hearing. There was in the village a drunken fellow, named Wondo, who had come to that pass when he would almost have sold his soul for liquor, and him the officer led away and plied with rum until he promised to bring the white doe to him. The pretty beast was so familiar with men that she suffered Wondo to catch her and lead her to Montalbert. Making sure that none was near, the officer plunged his sword into her side and the innocent creature fell. The snowy skin, now splashed with red, was quickly stripped off, concealed among the effects in Montalbert's outfit, and he set out for Canada; but he had not been many days on his road before Wondo, in an access of misery and repentance, confessed to his share of the crime that had been done and was slain on the moment.

With the death of the deer came an end to good fortune. Wars, blights, emigration followed, and in a few years not a wigwam was left standing beside Onota.

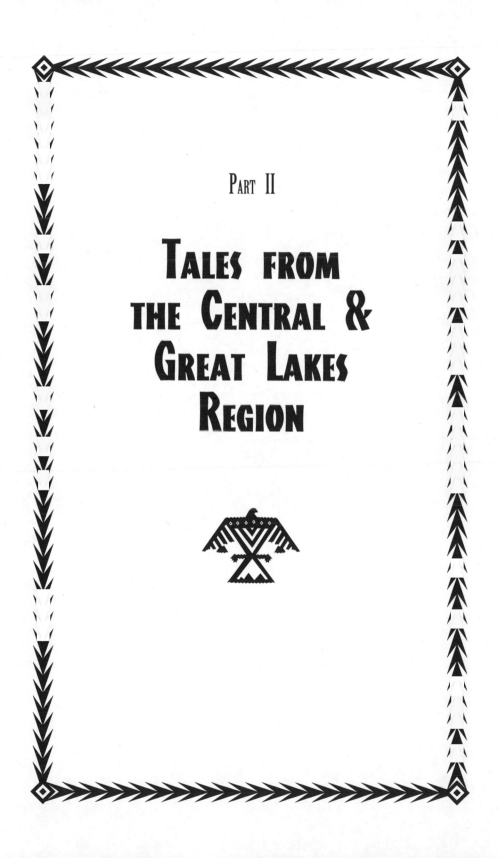

Part II

Tales from the Central & Great Lakes Region

CHAPTER 6

CREATION AND NATURE MYTHS

THE BLACKFOOT GENESIS
(Blackfoot)

All animals of the Plains at one time heard and knew him, and all birds of the air heard and knew him. All things that he had made understood him, when he spoke to them,—the birds, the animals, and the people.

Old Man was traveling about, south of here, making the people. He came from the south, traveling north, making animals and birds as he passed along. He made the mountains, prairies, timber, and brush first. So he went along, traveling northward, making things as he went, putting rivers here and there, and falls on them, putting red paint here and there in the ground,—fixing up the world as we see it today. He made the Milk River (the Teton) and crossed it, and, being tired, went up on a little hill and lay down to rest. As he lay on his back, stretched out on the ground, with arms extended, he marked himself out with stones,—the shape of his body, head, legs, arms, and everything. There you can see those rocks today. After he had rested, he went on northward, and stumbled over a knoll and fell down on his knees. Then he said, "You are a bad thing to be stumbling against;" so he raised up two large buttes there, and named them the Knees, and they are called so to this day. He went on further north, and with some of the rocks he carried with him he built the Sweet Grass Hills.

Old Man covered the plains with grass for the animals to feed on. He marked off a piece of ground, and in it he made to grow all kinds of roots and berries,—camas, wild carrots, wild turnips, sweet-root, bitter-root, sarvis berries, bull berries, cherries, plums, and rosebuds. He put trees in the ground. He put all kinds of animals on the ground. When he made the bighorn with its big head and horns, he made it out on the prairie. It did not seem to travel easily on the prairie; it was awkward and could not go fast. So he took it by one of its horns, and led it up into the mountains, and turned it loose; and it skipped about among the rocks, and went up fearful places with ease. So he said, "This is the place that suits you; this is what you are fitted for, the rocks and the mountains." While he was in the mountains, he made the antelope out of dirt, and turned it loose, to see how it would go. It ran so fast that it fell over some rocks and hurt itself. He saw that this would not do, and took the antelope down on the prairie, and turned it loose; and it ran away fast and gracefully, and he said, "This is what you are suited to."

One day Old Man determined that he would make a woman and a child; so he formed them both—the woman and the child, her son—of clay. After he had moulded the clay in human shape, he said to the clay, "You must be people," and then he covered it up and left it, and went away. The next morning he went to the place and took the covering off, and saw that the clay shapes had changed a little. The second morning there was still more change, and the third still more. The fourth morning he went to the place, took the covering off, looked at the images, and told them to rise and walk; and they did so. They walked down to the river with their Maker, and then he told them that his name was *Na'pi,* Old Man.

As they were standing by the river, the woman said to him, "How is it? will we always live, will there be no end to it?" He said: "I have never thought of that. We will have to decide it. I will take this buffalo chip and throw it in the river. If it floats, when people die, in four days they will become alive again; they will die for only four days. But if it sinks, there will be an end to them." He threw the chip into the river, and it floated. The woman turned and picked up a stone, and said: "No, I will throw this stone in the river; if it floats we will always live, if it sinks people must die, that they may always be sorry for each other." The woman threw the stone into the water, and it sank. "There," said Old Man, "you have chosen. There will be an end to them."

It was not many nights after, that the woman's child died, and she cried a great deal for it. She said to Old Man: "Let us change this. The law that you first made, let that be a law." He said: "Not so. What is made law must be law. We will undo nothing that we have done. The child is dead, but it cannot be changed. People will have to die."

That is how we came to be people. It is he who made us.

The first people were poor and naked, and did not know how to get a living. Old Man showed them the roots and berries, and told them that they could eat them; that in a certain month of the year they could peel the bark off some trees and eat it, that it was good. He told the people that the animals should be their food, and gave them to the people, saying, "These are your herds." He said: "All these little animals that live in the ground—rats, squirrels, skunks, beavers—are good to eat. You need not fear to eat of their flesh." He made all the birds that fly, and told the people that there was no harm in their flesh, that it could be eaten. The first people that he created he used to take about through the timber and swamps and over the prairies, and show them the different plants. Of a certain plant he would say, "The root of this plant, if gathered in a certain month of the year, is good for a certain sickness." So they learned the power of all herbs.

In those days there were buffalo. Now the people had no arms, but those black animals with long beards were armed; and once, as the people were moving about, the buffalo saw them, and ran after them, and hooked them, and killed and ate them. One day, as the Maker of the people was traveling over the country, he saw some of his children, that he had made, lying dead, torn to pieces and partly eaten by the buffalo. When he saw this he was very sad. He said: "This will not do. I will change this. The people shall eat the buffalo."

He went to some of the people who were left, and said to them, "How is it that you people do nothing to these animals that are killing you?" The people said: "What can we do? We have no way to kill these animals, while they are armed and can kill us." Then said the Maker: "That is not hard. I will make you a weapon that will kill these animals." So he went out, and cut some sarvis berry shoots, and brought them in, and peeled the bark off them. He took a larger piece of wood, and flattened it, and tied a string to it, and made a bow. Now, as he was the master of all birds and could do with them as he wished, he went out and caught one, and took feathers from its wing, and split them, and tied them to the shaft of wood. He tied four feathers along the shaft, and tried the arrow at a mark, and found that it did not fly well. He took these feathers off, and put on three; and when he tried it again, he found that it was good. He went out and began to break sharp pieces off the stones. He tried them, and found that the black flint stones made the best arrow points, and some white flints. Then he taught the people how to use these things.

Then he said: "The next time you go out, take these things with you, and use them as I tell you, and do not run from these animals. When they run at you, as soon as they get pretty close, shoot the arrows at them, as I have taught you; and you will see that they will run from you or will run in a circle around you."

Now, as people became plenty, one day three men went out on to the plain to see the buffalo, but they had no arms. They saw the animals, but when the buffalo saw the men, they ran after them and killed two of them, but one got away. One day after this, the people went on a little hill to look about, and the buffalo saw them, and said, "Saiyah, there is some more of our food," and they rushed on them. This time the people did not run. They began to shoot at the buffalo with the bows and arrows Na'pi had given them, and the buffalo began to fall; but in the fight a person was killed.

At this time these people had flint knives given them, and they cut up the bodies of the dead buffalo. It is not healthful to eat the meat raw, so Old Man gathered soft dry rotten driftwood and made punk of it, and then got a piece of hard wood, and drilled a hole in it with an arrow point, and gave them a pointed piece of hard wood, and taught them how to make a fire with fire sticks, and to cook the flesh of these animals and eat it.

They got a kind of stone that was in the land, and then took another harder stone and worked one upon the other, and hollowed out the softer one, and made a kettle of it. This was the fashion of their dishes.

Also Old Man said to the people: "Now, if you are overcome, you may go and sleep, and get power. Something will come to you in your dream, that will help you. Whatever these animals tell you to do, you must obey them, as they appear to you in your sleep. Be guided by them. If anybody wants help, if you are alone and traveling, and cry aloud for help, your prayer will be answered. It may be by the eagles, perhaps by the buffalo, or by the bears. Whatever animal answers your prayer, you must listen to him."

That was how the first people got through the world, by the power of their dreams.

After this, Old Man kept on, traveling north. Many of the animals that he had made followed him as he went. The animals understood him when he spoke to them, and he used them as his servants. When he got to the north point of the Porcupine Mountains, there he made some more mud images of people, and blew breath upon them, and they became people. He made men and women. They asked him, "What are we to eat?" He made many images of clay, in the form of buffalo. Then he blew breath on these, and they stood up; and when he made signs to them, they started to run. Then he said to the people, "Those are your food." They said to him, "Well, now, we have those animals; how are we to kill them?" "I will show you," he said. He took them to the cliff, and made them build rock piles; and he made the people hide behind these piles of rock, and said, "When I lead the buffalo this way, as I bring them opposite to you, rise up."

After he had told them how to act, he started on toward a herd of buffalo. He began to call them, and the buffalo started to run toward him, and they followed him until they were inside the lines. Then he dropped back; and as the people rose up, the buffalo ran in a straight line and jumped over the cliff. He told the people to go and take the flesh of those animals. They tried to tear the limbs apart, but they could not. They tried to bite pieces out, and could not. So Old Man went to the edge of the cliff, and broke some pieces of stone with sharp edges, and told them to cut the flesh with these. When they had taken the skins from these animals, they set up some poles and put the hides on them, and so made a shelter to sleep under. There were some of these buffalo that went over the cliff that were not dead. Their legs were broken, but they were still alive. The people cut strips of green hide, and tied stones in the middle, and made large mauls, and broke in the skulls of the buffalo, and killed them.

After he had taught those people these things, he started off again, traveling north, until he came to where Bow and Elbow rivers meet. There he made some more people, and taught them the same things. From here he again went on northward. When he had come nearly to the Red Deer's River, he reached the hill where the Old Man sleeps. There he lay down and rested himself. The form of his body is to be seen there yet.

When he awoke from his sleep, he traveled further northward and came to a fine high hill. He climbed to the top of it, and there sat down to rest. He looked over the country below him, and it pleased him. Before him the hill was steep, and he said to himself, "Well, this is a fine place for sliding; I will have some fun," and he began to slide down the hill. The marks where he slid down are to be seen yet, and the place is known to all people as the "Old Man's Sliding Ground."

This is as far as the Blackfeet followed Old Man. The Crees know what he did further north.

In later times once, Na'pi said, "Here I will mark you off a piece of ground," and he did so. Then he said: "There is your land, and it is full of all kinds of animals, and many things grow in this land. Let no other people come into it. This is for you five tribes (Blackfeet, Bloods, Piegans, Gros Ventres, Sarcees). When people come to cross the line, take your bows and arrows, your lances and your battle axes, and give them battle and keep them out. If they gain a footing, trouble will come to you."

Our forefathers gave battle to all people who came to cross these lines, and kept them out. Of late years we have let our friends, the white people, come in, and you know the result. We, his children, have failed to obey his laws.

CREATION
(Pawnee)

Tiráwa is the creator. He made the mountains, the prairies, and the rivers.

The men of the present era were not the original inhabitants of the earth. They were preceded by another race—people of great size and strength. These were so swift of foot, and so powerful, that they could easily run down and kill the buffalo. A great bull was readily carried into camp on the back by these giants, and when a calf or a yearling was killed, the man thrust its head under his belt and carried it dangling against his leg, as the men of today carry a rabbit. Often when these people overtook a buffalo, they would strike it with their hands, or kick it with the foot, to knock it down, and today, the Arikaras say, you can see the marks of these blows—the prints of the hands and the feet—on the flesh of the buffalo beneath the skin, where these people kicked and scratched the animals.

The race of giants had no respect for the Ruler. On the contrary, they derided and insulted him in every way possible. When the sun rose, or when it thundered and rained, they would defy him. They had great confidence in their own powers, and believed that they were able to cope with the Creator. As they increased in numbers they grew more defiant, and at length became so bad that Tiráwa determined to destroy them. This he attempted to do at first by shooting the lightning at them; but the bolts glanced aside from their bodies without injuring them. When he found that they could not be killed by that means, he sent a great rain, which destroyed them by drowning. This was a deluge, which submerged the high hills and the mountains, and the tradition of the Arikaras is the same. This does not agree with the story from the Pawnees. They say that the ground became water-soaked and soft, and that these large and heavy people sank into it and were engulfed in the mire. The great fossil bones of mastodons, elephants, and *Brontotheridae* are said by the Pawnees to be the bones of these giants; and that such remains are often found sticking out of cut banks, or in deep cañons, buried under many feet of earth, is deemed conclusive evidence that the giants did sink into the soft earth and so perish.

After the giant race had passed away, Tiráwa created a new people, a man and a woman, who were like those now on the earth. These people were at first poor, naked, and were without any knowledge of how they should live; but after a time the Creator gave them the corn, the buffalo, and the wild roots and fruits of the prairie for food, bows and arrows to kill their game, and fire-sticks to furnish a means of cooking it. Where they originated the Ruler provided for them these various things, such as trees bearing fruits, and things that grow in the ground, artichokes, wild turnips, and other roots. In the rivers he put fish, and on the land game. All these things, everything good to eat found on the plains or in the timber, was given to them by Tiráwa.

All these gifts were presented to the Pawnees in the country in which they were originally created, and which, as clearly appears from the statements of the oldest men, was far to the southwest. It was in this original country that the Pawnees received their sacred bundles. When they were given them the people knew nothing of iron, but used flint knives and arrow-heads. The bundles are said to have been handed down from the Father, though in certain cases special stories are told of how particular bundles came to be received.

A more detailed account of the creation and the doings of the original people is given by the Arikaras, but it is not in all respects like that told by the Pawnees, for these two tribes separated long ago. This story, which is generally known in the Arikara tribe, has come from various sources. Two Crows,—the Chief Priest and the fountain of sacred learning for the tribe,—*Pahukatawá,* Fighting Bear, and others have given portions of this history.

In the beginning *Atíuch* (= Pawnee *Atíus*) created the earth and a people of stone. These people were so strong that they had no need of the Creator, and would not obey him. They even defied him; so he determined to put an end to them. He therefore caused a great rain, which fell continuously for many days, until the land was all covered with water, and the trees were dead and the tops of the hills were submerged. Many of these people being big and heavy, and so able to move only slowly, could not reach the tops of the hills, to which all tried to escape for safety, and even those who did so were drowned by the rising waters, which at last covered the whole land. Everything on the earth was dead. [Today in the washed clay bluffs of the bad lands, the horizontal lines of stratification are shown as marking the level of the waters at various times during this flood, and the hard sandstone pinnacles which cap the bluffs, and which sometimes present a rude semblance of the human form, are pointed out as the remains of these giants.]

Now when everything was dead, there was left a mosquito flying about over the water and a little duck swimming on it. These two met, and the duck said to the mosquito, "How is it that you are here?" The mosquito said: "I can live on this foam; how is it with you?" The duck answered: "When I am hungry I can dive down and eat the green weed that grows under the water." Then said the mosquito: "I am tired of this foam. If you will take me with you to taste of the things of the earth, I shall know that you are true." So the duck took the mosquito under his wing, where he would keep dry, and dived down with him to the bottom of the water, and as soon as they touched the ground all the water disappeared. There was now nothing living on the earth.

Then Atíuch determined that he would again make men, and he did so. But again he made them too nearly like himself. They were too powerful, and he was afraid of them, and again destroyed them all.

Then he made one man like the men of today. When this man had been created he said to himself: "How is it now? There is still something that does not quite please me." Then Atíuch made a woman, and set her by the man, and the man said: "You knew why I was not pleased. You knew what I wanted. Now I can walk the earth in gladness." Atíuch seems to have made men and the animals up above in the sky where he lives, and when he was satisfied with what he had made, he resolved to place them upon the earth. So he called the lightning to put them on the earth, and the lightning caused a cloud to come, and the cloud received what Atíuch had made. But the lightning, acting as he always does, set them down on the earth with a crash, and as the ground was still wet with the water that had covered it, they all sank into the soft earth. This made the lightning feel very badly and he cried, and to this day whenever he strikes the earth he cries. That is what we hear when it thunders.

Now all living things were under the ground in confusion and asking one another what each was; but one day, as the mole was digging around, he broke a hole through, so that the light streamed in, and he drew back frightened. He has never had any eyes since; the light put them out. The mole did not want to come out, but all the others came out on to the earth through the hole the mole had made.

[In some versions this is understood to have taken place in the country now occupied by the Rees, but older men say it happened "in the far south country, by the big water."]

After they had come out from the ground, the people looked about to see where they should go. They had nothing. They did not know what to do, nor how to support themselves. They began to travel, moving very slowly; but after their third day's camp, a boy, who had been left behind asleep at the first camp that they had made, overtook the company, carrying in his arms a large bundle. The people asked him what this was. He replied that when he woke up and found the people gone, he cried to Father for help, and Father gave him this bundle, which had taught him to find the way to his people. Then the people were glad, and said that now they would find the way, and they went on.

After they had gone a long way, they came to a deep ravine with high steep banks, and they could not cross it. There they had to stop. All came to this place, but they could not get over it. They asked the boy what they should do, and he opened the bundle, and out of it came a bird with a sharp bill,—the most sacred of all birds, the bone striker. Wherever this bird strikes its bill it makes a hole. This bird flew over the ravine and began to strike the bank with his bill, and flew against the bank again and again, and at last the dirt fell down and filled up the ravine, and made a road for the people to pass across. A part of them passed over, but before all had done so the road closed up, and the ravine became as it had been at first. Those who were behind perished. They were changed into badgers, snakes, and animals living in the ground. They went on farther, and at length came to a thick wood, so thick that they could not pass through it. Here they had to stop, for they did not know how they could pass through this timber. Again they asked the boy what should be done, and he opened the bundle, and an owl came out from it, and went into the wood and made a path through it. A number of the people got through the wood, but some old women and poor children were lagging behind, and the road closed up and caught them, and these were changed to bears, wild-cats, elks, and so on.

[Another version says that a mole came out of the bundle and tunneled a passage beneath the forest, and when this passage closed up those who were caught in it changed into moles, muskrats, beavers, and other animals that live under ground.]

The people went on farther, and came to a big river which poured down and stopped them, and they waited on the bank. When they went to the bundle, a big hawk came out of it. This bird flew across the river and caused the water to stop flowing. They started across the dry river bed, and when part had gone across and were on this side, and some old women and poor children were still in the stream bed, the water began to flow again and drowned them. These people were turned into fishes, and this is why fishes are related to men. [The order in which these obstacles to their progress were encountered differs in different versions of the story.]

They went on until they came to some high hills called the Blue Mountains, and from these mountains they saw a beautiful country that they thought would be good to live in; but when they consulted the boy who carried the bundle he said: "No, we shall see life and live in it." So they went on.

Soon after this some people began to gamble, and one party won everything that the others had, and at last they began to quarrel and then to fight, and the people separated and went different ways, and the animals, which had all this time been with them, got frightened and ran away. But some of the people still remained, and they asked the boy what they should do, and he went to the bundle and took from it a pipe, and when he held up the pipe the fighting ceased. With the pipe was a stone arrow-head, and the boy told them they must make others like this, for from now on they would have to fight; but before this there had been no war. In the bundle also they found an ear of corn. The boy said: "We are to live by this. This is our Mother." The corn taught them how to make bows and arrows.

Now the people no longer spoke one language, and the eight tribes who had run away no longer understood each other and lived together, but wandered about, and the Mother (*Atiná* = Pawnee *Atíra*) no longer remained with them, but left them alone. The ninth or remaining band—which included the Rees, Mandans, and Pawnees—now left the Blue Mountains and traveled on until they reached a great river, and then they knew what the boy meant by saying "We shall see life and live in it." Life meant the Missouri River, and they said: "This is the place where our Mother means us to live." The first night they stayed by the river, but they went off in the morning and left behind them two dogs asleep. One was black, the other white; one was male, the other female. At the third camp they said: "This is a good place; we will live here." They asked the boy what they should do, and he told them that they should separate into three bands; that he would divide the corn among them, and they could plant it. He broke off the nub and gave it to the Mandans, the big end and gave it to the Pawnees, and the middle of the ear he gave to the Rees.

To this day the Mandans have the shortest corn, the Rees next in size, and the Pawnees the best and largest. He also took from the bundle beans, which he divided among the people, and the sack of a buffalo's heart full of tobacco. Here by the river they first planted and ate, and were well off, while the eight bands that had run away were dying of hunger. When they got here they had no fire. They knew nothing of it. They tried to get it from the sun, and sent the swallow to bring it. He flew toward the sun, but could not get the fire, and came back, saying that the sun had burned him. This is why the swallow's back is black today. The crow was sent. He used to be white, but the sun burned him too. Another kind of bird was sent, and he got the fire.

After this they traveled again, and as they traveled they were followed by two great fires that came up on the hills behind them and shut them in, so that they did not know how to escape. The bundle told them to go to a cedar-tree on a precipice, and that if they held fast to this they would not be hurt by these two great bad things. They did so and escaped, but all cedars have been crooked ever since. These two great fires were the two dogs that had been left behind at their first camp. These dogs then came to them and said: "Our hearts are not all bad. We have bitten you because you left us without waking us up, but now we have had our revenge and we want to live with you." But sickness and death have followed the people ever since they first left these dogs behind.

The dogs were taken back into the company and grew old. The female dog grew old and poor, and died first, and was thrown into the river, and after that the male dog died; but before he died they said to him: "Now you are going to die and be with your wife." "Yes," he replied. "But you will not hate us. From this time you will eat us, and so you will think well of us. And from the female dog's skin has come the squash, and you will like this, and on this account, also, you will not hate us." So ever since that day dogs have been raised as friends, and afterwards eaten for revenge, because of their treachery.

After this, they looked out on the prairie and saw some great black animals having horns, and they looked as though they were going to attack them. The people dug a hole, and got in and covered it over, and when the buffalo rushed on them they were safe, though their dwelling trembled and the people thought the roof would fall in. Finally some one looked out and saw the buffalo standing around. They did not look very fierce, so forty men, women, and children ventured out; but the buffalo attacked them, tore off their arms and ate them, and tore off their hair. Ever since that time there has been a lock of Rees's hair in the buffalo's mouth, hanging down from his chin. One handsome young woman was carried off by the buffalo. They held a council to know what they should do with her. She said she could not travel, and they did not wish to kill her. They did not wish to let her go either. But one night when she was sleeping in the midst of the band, a young bull came to her and pulled her sleeve, and told her to follow him, that he would show her the way back to her people. He did so, and his parting words to her were: "Tell your people that we do not like the bows and arrows that they make, and so we have attacked you."

The young woman was gladly received. They asked the boy with the bundle what should be done with the buffalo. He answered: "The buffalo are to be our food. They ate us first, so now we will always follow them for food. We must make arrows like the one Tinawá gave us with the pipe, and fight the buffalo with them." After making many arrows of the flint they use for striking fires, they all came out of the hole in the earth and lived by planting and hunting.

The Rees have always kept near the Missouri River, and have lived by planting. The bundle reputed to have been given to the boy in the beginning is now in the house of Two Crows. It is still powerful. It contains the ear of corn which was first given to the Rees. When a great young man dies—a chief's son—and the people mourn, the relations are asked to the Rees medicine lodge, and the ear of corn is taken from the bundle and put for a short time in a bucket of water and then replaced in the bundle. As many as drink of that water are cured of sad hearts, and never mourn their friends again.

THE STORY OF THE EARTH
(Cheyenne)

The earth rests on a large beam or post. Far in the north there is a beaver, as white as snow, who is a great father of all mankind. Some day he will gnaw through the support at the bottom; we shall be helpless, and the earth will fall. This will happen when he becomes angry. The post is already partly eaten through. For this reason one band of Cheyennes never eat beaver, or even touch the skin. If they do touch it, they become sick.

STORY OF THE FIRST MAN AND WOMAN
(Chippewa)

The Great Manitou had his home in the Land of Peace. Before he became a man and his face was cut in the stone, he was a great bird and his nest was in the pipestone rocks.

He fed on the wild buffaloes that lived on the prairies. He could carry two buffaloes in his claws; he always ate them near his nest; this is why the rocks are red.

The tracks of the manitou bird can be seen near the Land of Peace. The Indians know where to find these tracks and will show them to the white man.

The Great Serpent is older than mankind. He was alive before the first man was made. He found the nest of the manitou bird; there was one egg in the nest. The manitou heard the egg move. He was miles away, but he flew with a great rock in his claws and killed the serpent. The rock broke open the egg, and out of it came a grown man, but the rock lay upon his feet and he could not walk. He had to stand in one place, for the manitou bird would not set him free until he knew many things.

The man learned how to hunt the buffalo, for he could see many miles. He learned how to tan and use the buffalo skin; he learned the language of birds; they would come when he would call their names; he learned how to make and use the bow and arrow.

The manitou bird covered the man with a great buffalo skin, but his head was not covered, for he had much black hair. The first man was slow to learn and he stood many moons in his place in the pipestone rocks; nothing came to hurt him.

When he had learned much, he woke one morning and found a woman standing beside him. The manitou bird pulled away the stone from the feet of the man. He shook his wings and the man and woman ran to the prairie.

These two were the first of all people. They were Indians. All mankind know they were the first to live on the earth.

DEATH

(Cheyenne)

When first created, the people gathered to see if they were to live or to die. If a stone floated in water, they were to live; if it sank, they were to die; but to a buffalo chip opposite conditions were attached. The stone was thrown in. For a moment it remained at the surface, and all the people rejoiced, thinking to live forever; then it sank. So the chip was thrown in, and for a moment it sank out of sight, and again they rejoiced; but then it rose and drifted away. The short time that the stone floated and the chip sank represents the shortness of man's life before lasting death.

CHAPTER 7

GODS AND GODDESSES

SUN AND MOON
(Cheyenne)

The Sun and the Moon disputed as to their superiority. The Sun said that he was bright and light; that he ruled the day, and that no being was superior to him. The Moon in answer said to the Sun that he ruled the night, and was without a superior; that he looked after all things on earth, and that he kept all men and animals from danger. The Sun said: "It is I who light up all the world. If I should rest from my work, everything would be darkened; mankind could not do without me." Then the Moon replied: "I am great and powerful. I can take charge of both night and day, and guide all things in the world. It does not trouble me if you rest." Thus the Sun and the Moon spoke to each other; but both were great rulers. The day on which they disputed became almost as long as two days, so much did they say to each other. At the end the Moon said that there were a great many wonderful and powerful beings on his side. He meant the stars in the sky.

ATÍUS TIRÁWA
(Pawnee)

Atíus Tiráwa was the great god of the Pawnees. He also was a creative deity, and ordered the courses of the sun, moon, and stars. As known today he is regarded as omnipotent and intangible; but how far this conception of him has been colored by missionary influence it would be difficult to say. We find, however, in other Indian mythologies which we know have not been sophisticated by Christian belief many references to deities who possess such attributes, and there is no reason why we should infer that Atíus Tiráwa is any other than a purely aboriginal conception.

THE ADVENTURES OF ICTINIKE
(Various)

ICTINIKE AND THE RABBIT
(Iowa)

M any tales are told by the Iowa Indians regarding *Ictinike,* the son of the sun-god, who had offended his father, and was consequently expelled from the celestial regions. He possesses a very bad reputation among the Indians for deceit and trickery. They say that he taught them all the evil things they know, and they seem to regard him as a Father of Lies. The Omahas state that he gave them their war-customs, and for one reason or another they appear to look upon him as a species of war-god. A series of myths recount his adventures with several inhabitants of the wild. The first of these is as follows.

One day Ictinike encountered the Rabbit, and hailed him in a friendly manner, calling him "grandchild," and requesting him to do him a service. The Rabbit expressed his willingness to assist the god to the best of his ability, and inquired what he wished him to do.

"Oh, grandchild," said the crafty one, pointing upward to where a bird circled in the blue vault above them, "take your bow and arrow and bring down yonder bird."

The Rabbit fitted an arrow to his bow, and the shaft transfixed the bird, which fell like a stone and lodged in the branches of a great tree.

"Now, grandchild," said Ictinike, "go into the tree and fetch me the game."

This, however, the Rabbit at first refused to do, but at length he took off his clothes and climbed into the tree, where he stuck fast among the tortuous branches.

Ictinike, seeing that he could not make his way down, donned the unfortunate Rabbit's garments, and, highly amused at the animal's predicament, betook himself to the nearest village. There he encountered a chief who had two beautiful daughters, the elder of whom he married. The younger daughter, regarding this as an affront to her personal attractions, wandered off into the forest in a fit of the sulks. As she paced angrily up and down she heard some one calling to her from above, and, looking upward, she beheld the unfortunate Rabbit, whose fur was adhering to the natural gum which exuded from the bark of the tree. The girl cut down the tree and lit a fire near it, which melted the gum and freed the Rabbit. The Rabbit and the chief's daughter compared notes, and discovered that the being who had tricked the one and affronted the other was the same. Together they proceeded to the chief's lodge, where the girl was laughed at because of the strange companion she had brought back with her. Suddenly an eagle appeared in the air above them. Ictinike shot at and missed it, but the Rabbit loosed an arrow with great force and brought it to earth. Each morning a feather of the bird became another eagle, and each morning Ictinike shot at and missed this newly created bird, which the Rabbit invariably succeeded in killing. This went on until Ictinike had quite worn out the

Rabbit's clothing and was wearing a very old piece of tent skin; but the Rabbit returned to him the garments he had been forced to don when Ictinike had stolen his. Then the Rabbit commanded the Indians to beat the drums, and each time they were beaten Ictinike jumped so high that every bone in his body was shaken. At length, after a more than usually loud series of beats, he leapt to such a height that when he came down it was found that the fall had broken his neck. The Rabbit was avenged.

ICTINIKE AND THE BUZZARD
(Iowa)

One day Ictinike, footsore and weary, encountered a buzzard, which he asked to oblige him by carrying him on its back part of the way. The crafty bird immediately consented, and, seating Ictinike between its wings, flew off with him.

They had not gone far when they passed above a hollow tree, and Ictinike began to shift uneasily in his seat as he observed the buzzard hovering over it. He requested the bird to fly onward, but for answer it cast him headlong into the tree-trunk, where he found himself a prisoner. For a long time he lay there in want and wretchedness, until at last a large hunting-party struck camp at the spot. Ictinike chanced to be wearing some racoon skins, and he thrust the tails of these through the cracks in the tree. Three women who were standing near imagined that a number of racoons had become imprisoned in the hollow trunk, and they made a large hole in it for the purpose of capturing them. Ictinike at once emerged, whereupon the women fled. Ictinike lay on the ground pretending to be dead, and as he was covered with the racoon-skins the birds of prey, the eagle, the rook, and the magpie, came to devour him. While they pecked at him the buzzard made his appearance for the purpose of joining in the feast, but Ictinike, rising quickly, tore the feathers from its scalp. That is why the buzzard has no feathers on its head.

ICTINIKE AND THE CREATORS
(Iowa)

In course of time Ictinike married and dwelt in a lodge of his own. One day he intimated to his wife that it was his intention to visit her grandfather the Beaver. On arriving at the Beaver's lodge he found that his grandfather-in-law and his family had been without food for a long time, and were slowly dying of starvation. Ashamed at having no food to place before their guest, one of the young beavers offered himself up to provide a meal for Ictinike, and was duly cooked and served to the visitor. Before Ictinike partook of the dish, however, he was earnestly requested by the Beaver not to break any of the bones of his son, but unwittingly he split one of the toe-bones. Having finished his repast, he lay down to rest, and the Beaver gathered the bones and put them in a skin. This he plunged into the river that flowed beside his lodge, and in a moment the young beaver emerged from the water alive.

"How do you feel, my son?" asked the Beaver.

"Alas! father," replied the young beaver, "one of my toes is broken."

From that time every beaver has had one toe—that next to the little one—which looks as if it had been split by biting.

Ictinike shortly after took his leave of the Beavers, and pretended to forget his tobacco-pouch, which he left behind. The Beaver told one of his young ones to run after him with the pouch, but, being aware of Ictinike's treacherous character, he advised his offspring to throw it to the god when at some distance away. The young beaver accordingly took the pouch and hurried after Ictinike, and, obeying his father's instruction, was about to throw it to him from a considerable distance when Ictinike called to him: "Come closer, come closer."

The young beaver obeyed, and as Ictinike took the pouch from him he said: "Tell your father that he must visit me."

When the young beaver arrived home he acquainted his father with what had passed, and the Beaver showed signs of great annoyance.

"I knew he would say that," he growled, "and that is why I did not want you to go near him."

But the Beaver could not refuse the invitation, and in due course returned the visit. Ictinike, wishing to pay him a compliment, was about to kill one of his own children wherewith to regale the Beaver, and was slapping it to make it cry in order that he might work himself into a passion sufficiently murderous to enable him to take its life, when the Beaver spoke to him sharply and told him that such a sacrifice was unnecessary. Going down to the stream hard by, the Beaver found a young beaver by the water, which was brought up to the lodge, killed and cooked, and duly eaten.

On another occasion Ictinike announced to his wife his intention of calling upon her grandfather the Muskrat. At the Muskrat's lodge he met with the same tale of starvation as at the home of the Beaver, but the Muskrat told his wife to fetch some water, put it in the kettle, and hang the kettle over the fire. When the water was boiling the Muskrat upset the kettle, which was found to be full of wild rice, upon which Ictinike feasted. As before, he left his tobacco-pouch with his host, and the Muskrat sent one of his children after him with the article. An invitation for the Muskrat to visit him resulted, and the call was duly paid. Ictinike, wishing to display his magical powers, requested his wife to hang a kettle of water over the fire, but, to his chagrin, when the water was boiled and the kettle upset instead of wild rice only water poured out. Thereupon the Muskrat had the kettle refilled, and produced an abundance of rice, much to Ictinike's annoyance.

Ictinike then called upon his wife's grandfather the Kingfisher, who, to provide him with food, dived into the river and brought up fish. Ictinike extended a similar invitation to him, and the visit was duly paid. Desiring to be even with his late host, the god dived into the river in search of fish. He soon found himself in difficulties, however, and if it had not been for the Kingfisher he would most assuredly have been drowned.

Lastly, Ictinike went to visit his wife's grandfather the Flying Squirrel. The Squirrel climbed to the top of his lodge and brought down a quantity of excellent black walnuts, which Ictinike ate. When he departed from the Squirrel's house he purposely left one of his gloves, which a small squirrel brought after him, and he sent an invitation by this messenger for the Squirrel to visit him in turn. Wishing to show his cleverness, Ictinike scrambled to the top of his lodge, but instead of finding any black walnuts there he fell and severely injured himself. Thus his presumption was punished for the fourth time.

The four beings alluded to in this story as the Beaver, Muskrat, Kingfisher, and Flying Squirrel are four of the creative gods of the Sioux, whom Ictinike evidently could not equal so far as reproductive magic was concerned.

Nā′nībōjū′

(Mississaga)

Nā′nībōjū′ was walking along a sandy shore, and after a while he became hungry. It was in the fall of the year. He saw something moving towards him. It was a bear. He pulled up a sapling, and, hiding himself, got ready to club the bear with it. When the latter came near enough he killed it with one blow. He then built a fire, singed the bear's hair, and roasted the carcass. When it was sufficiently roasted, he cut the meat up into small pieces with the intention of eating it leisurely. Before he began to eat he was annoyed by the squeaking of a tree, to put a stop to which he climbed the tree, and, while endeavoring to separate a split crotch, his hand was caught in it. While he was trying to get his hand out, a pack of wolves ran down to the shore and came towards him. Nā′nībōjū′ kept working hard, trying to release his hand. Meanwhile the wolves began to eat his meal, paying no attention to him, although he shouted in order to scare them away. When the wolves had eaten up all the meat, he got his hand out of the crotch of the tree and came down. He found nothing left to eat, except the brain in the skull, which, however, he could not get out. So he said: "I will change myself into a little snake, and enter the skull to eat the brain." He did so, but when he got through eating he could not get out of the skull. So Nā′nībōjū′ went along the shore without seeing, and at last fell into the lake. He swam under the water, and when he came up to the surface he heard voices saying: "There is a bear swimming, let us kill him!" There was a chase on the lake. When the parties came up they struck the bear on the head, splitting it open, whereupon Nā′nībōjū′ jumped out and got to the dry land. He continued his walk along the shore. The lake was calm, and the water began to freeze. Nā′nībōjū′ walked on the newly-formed ice, and liked the sound the ice made. He saw a "fisher" coming towards him. The fisher made up his mind to make fun of Nā′nībōjū′. Running to the shore, he peeled some basswood bark, and with it tied two stones, attaching them to his hind legs, so that every time he leaped, the stones, falling upon the ice, made a sort of musical sound. He then ran towards Nā′nībōjū′, who said: "Kwē! What are you doing with the basswood on your legs?" "Nothing," said the fisher; "it being a fine day I thought I would attach the stones to my legs." The fisher passed Nā′nībōjū′, making music with the noise of the stones falling upon the newly-formed ice. Nā′nībōjū′ listened to the ice-music for some time, until the fisher got out of sight on the lake. He then went ashore, peeled basswood bark, tied two stones with it, and, making two holes through the lower part of his body, put the bark through and tied it. As he walked along, the stones made a loud noise on the ice, which at first pleased him. But in course of time the stones made very little music on the ice, which caused him to look back. He saw that the stones were far behind, and that he was dragging a part of his entrails upon the ice. He cut this part off, and threw it on an elmtree, saying: "That will be called by my nephews [that is, the Indians] in the future *pemâtig* (a species of climbing vine). They will use it when they have nothing else for food."

This is one of the most interesting episodes of the Nā'nĭbōjū' cycle of myth-stories.

LAKE SUPERIOR WATER GODS
(Chippewa)

There were many water gods about Lake Superior to whom the Indians paid homage, casting implements, ornaments, and tobacco into the water whenever they passed a spot where one of these manitous sat enthroned. At Thunder Cape, on the north shore, lies Manibozho, and in the pillared recess of La Chapelle, among the Pictured Rocks, dwelt powerful rulers of the storm to whose mercy the red men commended themselves with quaint rites whenever they were to set forth on a voyage over the great unsalted sea. At Le Grand Portal were hidden a horde of mischievous imps, among whose pranks was the repetition of every word spoken by the traveler as he rested on his oars beneath this mighty arch. The Chippewas worked the copper mines at Keweenaw Point before the white race had learned of a Western land, but they did so timidly, for they believed that a demon would visit with injury or death the rash mortal who should presume to pillage his treasure, unless he had first bestowed gifts upon him. Even then they went ashore with fear, lighted fires around a surface of native copper, hacked off a few pounds of the softened metal, and ran to their canoes without looking behind them.

There was another bad manitou at the mouth of Superior Bay, where conflicting currents make a pother of waters. This spirit sat on the bottom of the lake, gazing upward, and if any boatman ventured to cross his domain without dropping a pipe or beads or hatchet into it, woe betide him, for his boat would be caught in a current and smashed against a rocky shore. Perhaps the most vexatious god was he who ruled the Floating Islands. These islands were beautiful with trees and flowers, metal shone and crystals sparkled on their ledges, sweet fruits grew in plenty, and song-birds flitted over them. In wonder and delight the hunter would speed toward them in his canoe, but as he neared their turfy banks the jealous manitou, who kept these fairy lands for his own pleasure, would throw down a fog and shut them out of sight. Never could the hunter set foot on them, no matter how long he kept up his search.

Stories of Menabozho

(Various)

Hiawatha or Menabozho

(Chippewa)

The story of Hiawatha—known about the lakes as Menabozho and in the East as Glooskap—is the most widely disseminated of the Indian legends. He came to earth on a Messianic mission, teaching justice, fortitude, and forbearance to the red men, showing them how to improve their handicraft, ridding the woods and hills of monsters, and finally going up to heaven amid cries of wonder from those on whose behalf he had worked and counseled. He was brought up as a child among them, took to wife the Dakota girl, *Minnehaha* ("Laughing Water"), hunted, fought, and lived as a warrior; yet, when need came, he could change his form to any shape of bird, fish, or plant that he wished. He spoke to friends in the voice of a woman and to enemies in tones like thunder. A giant in form, few dared to resist him in battle, yet he suffered the common pains and adversities of his kind, and while fishing in one of the great lakes in his white stone canoe, that moved whither he willed it, he and his boat were swallowed by the king of fishes. He killed the creature by beating at its heart with a stone club, and when the gulls had preyed on its flesh, as it lay floating on the surface, until he could see daylight, he clambered through the opening they had made and returned to his lodge.

Believing that his father had killed his mother, he fought against him for several days, driving him to the edge of the world before peace was made between them. The evil Pearl Feather had slain one of his relatives, and to avenge that crime Hiawatha pressed through a guard of fire-breathing serpents which surrounded that fell personage, shot them with arrows as they struck at him, and having thus reached the lodge of his enemy he engaged him in combat. All day long they battled to no purpose, but toward evening a woodpecker flew overhead and cried, "Your enemy has but one vulnerable point. Shoot at his scalp-lock." Hiawatha did so and his foe fell dead. Anointing his finger with the blood of his foe, he touched the bird, and the red mark is found on the head of every woodpecker to this day. A duck having led him a long chase when he was trying to capture it for food, he angrily kicked it, thus flattening its back, bowing its legs, despoiling it of half of its tail-feathers, and that is why, to this day, ducks are awkward.

In return for its service in leading him to where the prince of serpents lived, he invested the kingfisher with a medal and rumpled the feathers of its head in putting it on; hence all kingfishers have rumpled knots and white spots on their breasts. After slaying the prince of serpents he traveled all over America, doing good work, and on reaching Onondaga he organized a friendly league of thirteen tribes that endured for many years. This closed his mission. As he stood in the assemblage of chiefs a white bird, appearing at an immense height, descended like a meteor, struck Hiawatha's daughter with such force as to drive her remains into the earth and shattered itself against the ground. Its silvery feathers were scattered, and these were preserved by the beholders as ornaments for their hair—so the custom of wearing feather head-dresses endures to our time. Though filled with consternation, Hiawatha recognized the summons. He addressed his companions in tones of such sweetness and terms of such eloquence as had never been heard before, urging them to live uprightly and to enforce good laws, and—unhappy circumstance!—promising to come back when the time was ripe. The expectancy of his return has led to ghost-dances and similar demonstrations of enmity against the whites. When he had ended he entered his stone canoe and began to rise in air to strains of melting music. Higher and higher he arose, the white vessel shining in the sunlight, until he disappeared in the spaces of the sky.

Incidents of the Hiawatha legend are not all placed, but he is thought to have been born near the great lakes, perhaps at Mackinack. Some legends, indeed, credit him with making his home at Mackinack, and from that point, as a center, making a new earth around him. The fight with his father began on the upper Mississippi, and the boulders found along its banks were their missiles. The south shore of Lake Superior was the scene of his conflict with the serpents. He hunted the great beaver around Lake Superior and brought down his dam at the Sault Sainte Marie. A depression in a rock on the southern edge of Michipicotea Bay is where he alighted after a jump across the lake. In a larger depression, near Thunder Bay, he sat when smoking his last pipe. The big rocks on the east side of Grand Traverse Bay, near Antrim City, MI, are the bones of a stone monster that he slew.

So trifling an incident as the kicking of the duck has been localized at Lake Itasca. [It is worth passing mention that this name, which sounds as if it were of Indian origin, is held by some to be composed of the last syllables of *veritas* and the first letters of *caput,* these words—signifying "the true head"—being applied by early explorers as showing that they were confident of having found the actual source of the Mississippi.] Minnehaha lived near the fall in Minneapolis that bears her name. The final apotheosis took place on the shores of Lake Onondaga, NY, though Hiawatha lies buried under a mountain, three miles long, on the east side of Thunder Bay, Lake Superior, which, from the water, resembles a man lying on his back. The red man makes oblation, as he rows past, by dropping a pinch of tobacco into the water. Some say that Hiawatha now lives at the top of the earth, amid the ice, and directs the sun. He has to live in a cold country because, if he were to return, he would set the earth on fire with his footsteps.

MENABOZHO CAUGHT
(Chippewa)

Menabozho killed a large moose when hunting. He put the meat in boxes made of birch bark and hid the boxes by a sweet-water tree, which the white men call a maple tree.

There was much moose meat, and it would last many weeks. There was much moose fat, so Menabozho made more birch-bark boxes and hid the fat in them near an oak tree. He hung the mooseskin in the branches of the tree.

Menabozho sat on the ground and ate much moose meat; while he was eating he heard a noise over his head and saw that two trees were pulling each other. A tall tree had fallen into the top of a small tree, and it was caught. The wind tried to pull the tall tree away, but the little tree held it tight, and the branches made a noise like something alive. Menabozho did not like to hear such a loud noise when he was eating.

He climbed into the little tree and tried to pull the tall tree away. His arm was caught between the two trees, and he was like a bear in a trap. The two trees pinched Menabozho's arm very hard.

While he was in the trap trying to get loose, a wolf came along under the trees; she had two young wolves with her.

"Look out!" said Menabozho; "don't go near that sweet-water tree. There is nothing for you in these woods."

The old mother wolf knew Menabozho and his tricks. She found the birch-bark boxes and called to her little ones.

"Come down and eat, Brother Menabozho," said the old wolf. She knew she was safe, for the trees held him close.

The wolf and her young ones played with the empty boxes when the meat was gone; they broke them all, then ran toward the oak tree.

"Don't go there; the tree may fall on you!" said Menabozho.

"Come, children," said the wolf, "use your noses and you will find more food."

They found the moose fat in the other boxes. Wolves can eat all the time. These wolves ate up the sweet moose fat, and Menabozho fought with the trees to get out of the trap they made for him. He tried to pull up the tree he was in by the roots, but he could not do it with one hand.

When the wolves were done eating, a great wind came and blew the trees apart. Menabozho came down the tree very fast, but the wolf and her young ones were very strong from their good dinner. They ran away where no one could find them.

Menabozho liked to play tricks on everything. He did not like it when they played tricks on him, and now he had no meat nor fat. There was only the moose head left.

He put his head into the moose head to eat the meat. He could not get out, and there he was caught again in a trap, and this time he could not see, but he could use his arms and feet.

"I don't care," said Menabozho. "It is a good trick. I will get away."

He ran against a tree. Menabozho put his arm around the tree and said: "What is your name, Brother Tree?"

"My name is White Oak," was the answer.

"White Oak does not grow near water; I must go further," said Menabozho.

Soon his moose head struck another tree. "O my brother, what is your name?" asked Menabozho.

"My name is Basswood," said the tree.

"Basswood grows near water," said Menabozho.

He ran along a little further and fell over the bank into a river, and he swam with the strong current down the stream. He knew there were many Indians in a tipi village near that river, and they would help him.

Menabozho kept the moose head out of the water and made a great noise. He heard the Indian boys whoop and knew they had seen him. The hunters got their canoes and came out to him with their tomahawks, for they thought it was a moose and they would get much fat meat.

The Indians broke the moose head with their tomahawks and found Menabozho. He was always good to the Indians, and many times he helped them in their hunting.

"It is a good trick," they all said; then Menabozho laughed, and they were glad to see him.

The chief made a great feast in his tipi. Menabozho told many stories, but he did not tell how the wolves, the trees, and the moose head all played tricks on him.

Menabozho Swallowed By a Large Fish
(Chippewa)

One day Menabozho went fishing with hook and line in Gitchee Gumee, the Big Sea Water. A large fish came along and swallowed the hook and line, swallowed Menabozho and his canoe, swallowed everything, just like a big sea cave.

When Menabozho woke out of his sleep he saw a squirrel sitting on the canoe beside him. The fish had swallowed him, too.

Menabozho said: "Brother Squirrel, where are we?"

The squirrel answered: "Menabozho, we are in a great fish."

Menabozho found his bow and arrows in the canoe and shot an arrow upward. It killed the great fish. The body of the fish began to rise to the top of the water. Menabozho prayed to the Great Manitou that the wind might blow from the south. The Great Spirit heard his prayer and sent the south wind. It blew the great fish to the north shore of Gitchee Gumee, where Nokomis lived.

The great fish floated on the water like a little sunfish; when it touched the shore the birds fed on its flesh, and Menabozho came out and went to his grandmother, Nokomis.

After their greeting was over Menabozho went back and found the birds still feeding on the fish.

"Go away, my little brothers," he said.

Each bird took a piece of the fish and flew away, and Menabozho then cut up the great creature and made much fish oil; he had a great plan in his mind and was glad to have this oil.

A wicked manitou lived on an island in Gitchee Gumee. This island had miles of blackest pitch on all of its shores; not even a water manitou could swim through this pitch. Menabozho carried the fish oil over and poured it on the pitch; wherever the oil touched the pitch it was never sticky again.

Menabozho found the wigwam of the wicked manitou. All day long he shot arrows at this wigwam. The manitou came out and laughed at him.

A woodpecker called out, "Hit him in the back, Menabozho!"

The manitou just then turned to run, and Menabozho hit him and he fell. The woodpecker flew down by Menabozho. His white feathers were stained by the pitch, but Menabozho painted his head with war paint. He is one of Menabozho's brothers.

CHAPTER 8

CORE BELIEFS AND RELIGION

FEASTS
(Chippewa)

A fter the spring trade was over, the traders would start with their furs and
peltries for their homes. The old Chippewa men would take a frolic (at this
time their young men never drank). When this was ended, the next thing to
be done was to bury their dead (such as had died during the year). This is a
great *medicine feast*. The relations of those who have died, give all the goods they
have purchased, as presents to their friends—thereby reducing themselves to poverty, to show the Great Spirit that they are humble, so that he will take pity on
them. They would next open the cashes, and take out corn and other provisions,
which had been put up in the fall,—and then commence repairing their lodges. As
soon as this is accomplished, they repair the fences around their fields, and clean
them off, ready for planting corn. This work is done by the women. The men,
during this time, are feasting on dried venison, bear's meat, wild fowl, and corn,
prepared in different ways; and recounting to each other what took place during the
winter.

The women plant the corn, and as soon as they get done, the men make a feast,
and dance the *crane* dance, in which the women join them, dressed in their best,
and decorated with feathers. At this feast the young braves select the young woman
they wish to have for a wife. He then informs his mother, who calls on the mother
of the girl, when the arrangement is made, and the time appointed for him to come.
He goes to the lodge when all are asleep (or pretend to be), lights his matches,
which have been provided for the purpose, and soon finds where his intended
sleeps. He then awakens her, and holds the light to his face that she may know him
—after which he places the light close to her. If she blows it out, the ceremony is

ended, and he appears in the lodge next morning, as one of the family. If she does not blow out the light, but leaves it to burn out, he retires from the lodge. The next day he places himself in full view of it, and plays his flute. The young women go out, one by one, to see who he is playing for. The tune changes, to let them know that he is not playing for them. When his intended makes her appearance at the door, he continues his *courting* tune, until she returns to the lodge. He then gives over playing, and makes another trial at night, which generally turns out favorable. During the first year they ascertain whether they can agree with each other, and can be happy—if not, they part, and each looks out again. No indiscretion can banish a woman from her parental lodge—no difference how many children she may bring home, she is always welcome—the kettle is over the fire to feed them.

The crane dance often lasts two or three days. When this is over, they feast again, and have their *national* dance. The large square in the village is swept and prepared for the purpose. The chiefs and old warriors take seats on mats which have been spread at the upper end of the square—the drummers and singers come next, and the braves and women form the sides, leaving a large space in the middle. The drums beat, and the singers commence. A warrior enters the square, keeping time with the music. He shows the manner he started on a war party—how he approached the enemy—he strikes, and describes the way he killed him. All join in applause. He then leaves the square, and another enters and takes his place. Such of the young men as have not been out in war parties, and killed an enemy, stand back ashamed—not being able to enter the square.

What pleasure it is to an old warrior, to see his son come forward and relate his exploits—it makes him feel young, and induces him to enter the square, and "fight his battles o'er again."

This national dance makes the warriors.

When the national dance is over—the corn-fields hoed, and every weed dug up, and our corn about knee-high, all the young men would start in a direction towards sun-down, to hunt deer and buffalo—being prepared, also, to kill Sioux, if any are found on their hunting grounds—a part of the old men and women to the lead mines to make lead—and the remainder of our people start to fish, and get mat stuff. Every one leaves the village, and remains about forty days. They then return: the hunting party bringing in dried buffalo and deer meat, and sometimes *Sioux scalps,* when they are found trespassing on our hunting grounds. At other times they are met by a party of Sioux too strong for them, and are driven in. If the Sioux have killed the Sacs last, they expect to be retaliated upon, and will fly before them, and vice versa. Each party knows that the other has a right to retaliate, which induces those who have killed last, to give way before their enemy—as neither wish to strike, except to avenge the death of their relatives. All the wars are predicated by the relatives of those killed; or by aggressions upon their hunting grounds.

The party from the lead mines bring lead, and the others dried fish, and mats for their winter lodges. Presents are now made by each party; the first, giving to the others dried buffalo and deer, and they, in exchange, presenting them with lead, dried fish and mats. This is a happy season of the year—having plenty of provisions, such as beans, squashes, and other produce, with our dried meat and fish, we continue to make feasts and visit each other, until our corn is ripe. Some lodge in the village makes a feast daily, to the Great Spirit. Every one makes his feast as he thinks best, to please the Great Spirit, who has the care of all beings created. Others believe in two Spirits; one good and one bad, and make feasts for the Bad Spirit, *to keep him quiet!* If they can make peace with him, the Good Spirit will not hurt them.

When the corn is getting ripe, the young people watch with anxiety for the signal to pull roasting ears—as none dare touch them until the proper time. When the corn is fit to use, another great ceremony takes place, with feasting, and returning thanks to the Great Spirit for giving them corn.

They next have their great ball play—from three to five hundred on a side, play this game. They play for horses, guns, blankets, or any other kind of property they have. The successful party take the stakes, and all retire to their lodges in peace and friendship.

They next commence horse-racing, and continue their sport and feasting, until the corn is all secured. They then prepare to leave their village for their hunting grounds. The traders arrive, and give them credit for such articles as the Chippe-was want to clothe their families, and enable them to hunt. They first, however, hold a council with the traders, to ascertain the price for their skins, and what they will charge for goods. They inform the traders where they intend hunting—and tell them where to build their houses. At this place, the Indians deposit part of their corn, and leave their old people. The traders have always been kind to them, and relieved them when in want. The traders were always much respected—and never since they have been a nation, has one of them been killed by any of the nation.

They disperse, in small parties, to make their hunt, and as soon as it is over, they return to their traders' establishment, with their skins, and remain feasting, playing cards and other pastimes, until near the close of the winter. The young men then start on the beaver hunt; others to hunt raccoons and muskrats—and the remain-der of the people go to the sugar camps to make sugar. All leave their encampment, and appoint a place to meet on the Mississippi, so that they may return to their village together, in the spring. They always spent their time pleasantly at the sugar camp. It being the season for wild fowl, they lived well, and always had plenty, when the hunters came in, that the Chippewas might make a feast for them. After this is over, the Indians return to their village, accompanied, sometimes, by their traders. In this way, the year rolled round happily. But these are times that were!

THE SACRED BUNDLE
(Pawnee)

In the lodge or house of every Pawnee of influence, hanging on the west side, and so opposite the door, is the sacred bundle neatly wrapped in buckskin, and black with smoke and age. What these bundles contain we do not know. Sometimes, from the ends, protrude bits of scalps, and the tips of pipe stems and slender sticks, but the whole contents of the bundle are known only to the priests and to its owner—

perhaps, not always even to him. The sacred bundles are kept on the west side of the lodge, because, being thus furthest from the door, fewer people will pass by them than if they were hung in any other part of the lodge. Various superstitions attach to these bundles. In the lodges where certain of them are kept it is forbidden to put a knife in the fire; in others, a knife may not be thrown; in others, it is not permitted to enter the lodge with the face painted; or again, a man cannot go in if he has feathers tied in his head.

On certain sacred occasions the bundles are opened, and their contents form part of the ceremonial of worship.

No one knows whence the bundles came. Many of them are very old; too old even to have a history. Their origin is lost in the haze of the long ago. The sacred bundles were given long ago. No one knows when they came.

All the sacred bundles are from the far off country in the southwest, from which the Pawnees came long ago. They were handed down to the people before they started on their journey. Then they had never seen anything like iron, but they had discovered how to make the flint knives and arrow points. There was nothing that came to through the whites. It all came through the power of Ti-ra′-wa. Through his power they were taught how to make bows and stone knives and arrow heads.

It was through the Ruler of the universe that the sacred bundles were given to them. They look to them, because, through them and the buffalo and the corn, they worship Ti-ra′-wa. They all, even the chiefs, respect the sacred bundles. When a man goes on the warpath, and has led many scouts and brought the scalps, he has done it through the sacred bundles. There were many different ceremonies that they used to go through. The high priest performs these ceremonies.

The high priestship was founded in this way: The black eagle spoke to a person, and said to him, "I am one of those nearest to Ti-ra′-wa, and you must look to me to be helped; to the birds and the animals—look to me, the black eagle, to the white-headed eagle, to the otter and the buffalo."

The black eagle sent the buzzard as a messenger to this person, and he gave him the corn. The secrets of the high priestship and the other secrets were handed down at the same time. The buzzard, because he is bald, stands for the old men who have little hair. The white-headed eagle also represents the old men, those whose hair is white. These are the messengers through whom Ti-ra′-wa sends his words to the people. The Wichitas also had these secrets, and so have the Rees.

FASTING
(Sac and Fox)

In olden times the Indians knew that there was God. When a man's children were old enough to learn, they were taught to mind. They were made to fast one, two, three, four, or sometimes ten days. They were told that God would take pity upon them and would make something great stand up before them and talk to them plainly. It will be the sun or moon, or stars of night, or any sort of animal. They are told that if they can remember the wonderful thing they saw at fasting-time, when in danger during war, if they say "God had pity upon me once, and I will depend on it, they will be helped. In the case of a boy, the father will teach him to be brave and tough, to face his enemies in war;" to die on the battle-field and not in his tribe; to fight his enemies, and not fight in the tribe, or over women. The Indians teach their children everything (except reading, writing, etc.), just like white people. They teach them to be good and polite to everybody, to respect everybody, to be smart and active. In olden times they taught the boys to be brave, for then the Indians used to kill one another. He who killed the most men in battle would be ruler over his people, next to the chief. The Indians say that when God made the people he made also the chief to rule them. Today, when they have a quarrel with a chief who isn't a real chief, they will tell him he is no real chief, but only acting one.

About girls. They let them fast to have good luck in helping their people out of danger in time of war, etc., to aid them when they give birth to children, and to help out other women who have a hard time. Here is the true story of a woman who helped her people out of danger:—

The Sac and Fox Indians of Iowa were bad. One or two Indians would go to a tribe and kill somebody or steal horses and then return home. Once two men went to the Kickapoo village and made fun of a blind boy. They made believe he was running them, and that they were afraid of him and his bow and arrow. He would aim at them and they would run away, saying he was very brave. They bothered him a long time, and when they got tired they killed him. They told the blind boy's father that his son was killed, that he was pretty brave, and ran them a good while until he got killed. The father commenced to fast all winter, and he felt very bad, crying every time he fasted. He stuffed a pipe full of tobacco and took it to four or five villages of other tribes. They smoked the pipe, which meant that they were willing to help the old man. He appointed a time two or three years off. These Indians mixed with the Sacs and Foxes, so that they were thought to be Sacs and Foxes of the Mississippi. They were called *Ma-squ-hee* in Indian. Their language was different from that of the Sacs, but they had married among them, so they called them Sacs and Foxes. There was a big war, four or five tribes together against two, but the smaller side began to lose. Their enemies made up their minds to kill every one of them. So they kept it up day and night. Some of the women and children starved to death. Soon there was only a small tribe left. They were pursued a long way and surrounded by their enemies, who watched them all night so that they could not get away. So they whispered to one another, and passed the pipe round, and told of their dreams and the wonderful things they had seen when fasting and the dangers they had escaped. The pipe kept passing round until at last one woman and one man got up and said that they would try to get the people out of their great danger. The woman said, "Find me an ear of corn," and they found her one. She took it in her arms and treated it as if it were a baby. She sang for it, just as if it were her own baby, and tried to put it to sleep. In so doing she put all the people around them to sleep. At the same time the man was acting his part (as an elk), and made it foggy so nobody could see far. Then they took each other's hand (so as not to get lost), and the woman led all her people that were left out of danger. They traveled all night, having jumped over their sleeping enemies, one after another. It was so dark that nothing could be seen, but their enemies remained sound asleep, and they managed to escape. Soon they came across a village and were afraid, but it turned out to be the village of the Iowas. When they told them their story, the Iowas were very sorry for them and angry besides. The Iowas welcomed them and told them not to be afraid, as they would fight for them. But their enemies never followed them up. So the Sacs and Foxes were saved. They have increased a great deal since that time. Doubtless on that terrible night some of them may have strayed away and got lost. This they never knew for certain. There have been some Indians heard of in the far west who talked the Sac language. The oldest men used to tell us to remember that their only friends were the Iowas. So, as long as they live, the Indians must be good to them; even if it is only an Iowa dog and wants anything they must feed it. While their enemies were after them the Sacs and Foxes had a very hard time of it day and night. Many of the women and children starved to death. Often the babies would drop from their backs at night. They were so hungry that, whenever there was time they would eat roots (and even dirt), bark, herbs, anything they thought was fit for food.

PAWNEE CEREMONIES
(Pawnee)

The Ski-di, one of the four bands composing the Pawnee tribe of Indians as it is known today, trace their origin and organization to the stars, and most of their ceremonies are connected with this definite belief. As a result, the rites are necessarily limited in their scope, and this limitation has left an impress upon the people who not only took part in the ceremonies, but relied upon them for personal and tribal welfare. The fact that for numberless generations the thought and attention of the entire community have been directed toward a special aspect of nature, the firmament with its stars, clouds, and winds, renders the Ski-di an unusually interesting field for the comparison of the lore of the people with the lore of the priests.

While the data at present in hand are insufficient for a final comparison of these lores, yet the material already secured, a part of which is here presented, clearly points to their interacting influence, and may be of interest to students of folk-lore.

The dual forces, male and female, had, according to the Ski-di rituals, their places in the heavens. The west was female, the east was male. The source of all life, the power which permeated all forms, dwelt in the zenith, in "the silence of the blue sky, above and beyond all clouds." This central power, whose abode was where the east and west conjoined, could not be seen or heard or felt by man, and yet it was to this power that man must address his wants. Ti-ra-wa was the name of this power in common use by the people and in the public ceremonies. The old and venerable men, the leaders in the sacred rites, called this power *"A-ti-us Ti-ra kit-ta-ko"* (A-ti-us, "father;" Ti-ra, a part of Ti-ra-wa, "the highest power;" ki-ta, "above;" ko, a part of ti-ko, "sitting;" "Father Ti-ra-wa sitting above"). This name must be uttered in the lowest of tones or in a whisper. The priest explained: "That the mysterious being who instructed our fathers said, that this is the name by which men must think of the highest power, and when one takes his child aside, and teaches it quietly, then, too, he must think of this power as Ti-ra-wa father sitting above."

Ti-ra-wa approached man through the lesser or under powers which were called *"Ti-ra-wa-wa-ri-ki-u-ra-wi'-hi-ri"* (*Ti-ra-wa,* "power;" *wa-ri-ki,* "standing;" *u-ra,* a part of hu-ra-ru, "earth, ground;" *wi'-hi-ri,* "touching.") The word implies that these powers are standing below or under the highest power, which sits above, and are able to move and to touch, to come in contact with the earth, here spoken of by the term which signifies its life-giving power. The term in common use for the dwelling-place of all the powers above, the highest as well as the under powers, was *Ti-ra-wa-hut.*

Many of the under powers, those which can come near to man and be seen, heard, or felt by him, were believed to dwell in particular stars. Several of these stars had their shrines in certain villages, and had also bestowed the sacred objects kept within the shrines, authorized the ceremonies connected with them, and inaugurated a priesthood.

It is a current belief among the people, and, as they say, "it often happens that when a person goes out on the hills at night to fast and to pray to the powers above, he will, as he is praying, become conscious that a particular star is looking at him. Then he will have a vision from that star, and the star will have control of his life." Sometimes the effect of a star was disastrous. For instance: "A lad was made crazy by a star. His friends sent for a doctor, and when he came, he waited for the star to rise which had caused the trouble. As soon as it was discerned above the horizon, the doctor took the lad out under the open sky, painted his body black with white spots, wrapped a fawn skin, which had still the spots upon it, about the boy, and then painted a star on his forehead. As long as the painted star remained on his forehead, the youth was sane, but when it wore off, he became crazy again."

A certain star in the west, which cannot now be designated, was believed to be the abode of the potential female element. The ceremonies of the shrine of this star led in the series of yearly ceremonies which culminated with the rites belonging to the red morning star. "There are two morning stars, brothers; the elder is red, and it is he to whom the human sacrifice is made; the younger is white, he is kind, and does not share in these rites." Some of the rituals speak of the red morning star as "a man, who stands facing the west. His body is red, and the right side of his face, that is, the side toward the north, is painted black, the left side, toward the south, is painted red. The downy, 'breathing' (as it is called) feather is tinged with red, and tied to his hair over the coronal suture. He wears his robe in the sacred manner, with hair outside. His arms are crossed over his breast, his hands closed, and grasped in the right hand is a club."

The people say that "once when a man was with a war party, he lay on the top of a mountain. (The place is sometimes designated as one of the Wichita mountains.) He heard a voice telling him not to go away, for he was at the place where the stars passed. The stars are people. As he lay there, he saw them file by, all going from the east to the west. At the last came a great warrior, painted red, carrying a club in his folded arms, and having on his head a downy feather, painted red. This was the red morning star."

This morning star is called *Ho-pi-ri-ku-tzu*. The word is made from *ho-pi-rit,* "star;" *ko-ri-tu,* "fire;" and *ku-tzu,* "large, great, mighty." The name signifies "the mighty star of fire."

The person to be sacrificed to the morning star was considered as having no future, as no longer belonging to the living. From the time of dedication to the star until the actual sacrifice of the life took place, the victim belonged to the star-god, was kept in seclusion, and not permitted to be touched by the people.

This fact was known even to the children, who, when they wished to ostracize a playmate, would cry *"Pi-ra ho-pi-ri-ku-tzu!"* ("child set apart to the morning star").

There is a story told of the use of a like term which turned the tide of war:—

In a time of scarcity of game, the Ski-di secured an abundance by means of a ceremony connected with the shrine of the star in the west. This aroused the ire of one of the other bands of the Pawnee, and a plan was made to kill the priest who had so much power, so that the Ski-di should not fare any better than the rest of the tribe. This plan was carried out, and the Ski-di was aroused to war upon the band which had killed the priest. In the fight a Ski-di warrior pointed to the leader of the offending band, and shouted the words that dedicated him to the morning star. Instantly the man ceased fighting, and pleaded for his life; he begged that he might be killed at once, but no one would listen. Then he appealed to his own party, but they fled from him in fear, leaving the field to the Ski-di, in seeking to escape from the man thus dedicated to sacrifice, for he no longer belonged to the living.

The rituals state that the first human beings were borne to the earth from the star of the west by the wind.

The people say, "When a child is born during the night, the relatives take notice of the stars. If the wind does not blow, and the next day is clear, then the parents are assured that the child will probably live without sickness or trouble."

The ancient instructor of the priests said, "The wind, *hu-tu-ru,* would divide, and there would be places where the different winds would dwell." This statement does not refer to the four winds which guard the paths at the four quarters down which the lesser powers descend to man.

There are seven winds, each of which has its name and peculiar function:—

The east wind, *hu-tu-ru-ha-wit* (*hu-tu-ru,* "wind;" *ha-wit,* the sacred name for east, the meaning lost). This is the wind which comes with the dawn; it brings life to the body, but it does not bring help to the spirit.

The west wind, *hu-tu-ru-wa-rux-ti* (*hu-tu-ru,* "wind;" *wa-rux-ti,* "mysterious, wonderful!"). This wind comes from the mysterious being to whom Ti-ra-wa gave power to put life into all things, to have direct communication with man, and to direct his life. In the west are the powers which bring rain to cool and vivify the earth, in the west we hear the thunders sound; there dwell the powers which carry out the commands of Ti-ra-wa. Because of this, we call the wind sent from this power, *hu-tu-ru-wa-rux-ti.*

North wind, *hu-tu-ru-ru-chow-wi-ri-ki* (*hu-tu-ru,* "wind;" *ru-chow-wi,* "placed permanently;" *ri-ki,* "standing"). From the character of the name of this wind it would seem to be connected with the north star, *ho-pi-ri-ka-ra-wi'-wa-ri,* "the star that does not move." This star is one of the lesser powers, and was made a chief. Ti-ra-wa told this chief that he was always to stand there, where he was placed, and to watch the earth. This Le-cha-ru, chief, must not move, for if he should do so, all the other stars, as they pass over the heavens, would become confused, and know not which way to go.

The wind of the spirits, *Hu-tu-ri'-kot-tsa-ru* (*hu-tu,* a part of hu-tu-ru, "wind;" *ri-kot-tsa-ru,* "a shadowy image of a person, a ghost"). This wind takes the spirits of the dead from the north, from some star in the north to which the dead immediately pass from the earth, and blows or drives the ghosts along the way, to the star at the southern end of the path. The Milky Way is called *ru-ha-ru'-tu-ru-hut* (*ru-ha,* "bright, light;" *ru,* first syllable of ru-hut, "a long stretch;" *tu-ru,* a part of hu-tu-ru, "wind," hut, the last syllable of ru-hut, "a long stretch," as across the heavens). The Milky Way is the path taken by the spirits as they pass along, driven by the wind which starts at the north, to the star in the south, at the end of the way. This star is named *ho-pi-ri-ka'-hu-ri-ri-wi-si-su* (*ho-pi-ri,* a modification of ho-pi-rit, "star;" *ka-ru,* a part of ka-ru-ra, "the earth, as the dwelling-place of man;" *ri-ri-wi-si-su,* "midway from east to west"). The word tells that the star is the dwelling-place of those who once lived on the earth, and that its length is east and west, it being narrow in width, north and south. As most people linger in their death through sickness, so the path they tread is the long path we see across the sky, while the short path (the short fork of the Milky Way) is the path made by those whose life is cut short by sudden death, as in battle.

South wind, *Ra-ri-tu-ru.* This wind comes from the star in the south where the spirits of the dead dwell. It is connected with the Milky Way and with the wind that drives the spirits of the dead to the south star. This wind accumulates at the south, and their ancestors were told (so the priest said) that some day this wind will rise up in the south, and make its way back to the north, doing much damage as it goes. When this shall come to pass, the people must remember that this wind has come from the place where the dead dwell, and as they see it coming, they must show it respect and offer it tobacco.

In the old days the Pawnee did not know cyclones; but when they came to know them, they called them *Ra-ri-tu-ru.* They remembered what we had been told of the return of the south wind from the star of the dead, and we offered tobacco. The Pawnee always do this, and it is wonderful to see how the cloud will rise and go off in another direction, and the people escape all harm. The modern name for the south wind is where the sun goes.

Hu-tu-ru-ka'-wa-ha-ru is the wind that sends the game. This wind comes from one of two stars that are close together, and are back of the north star, nearer to the horizon toward the east. The name *Ka'-wa-ha-ru* occurs in the rituals, and seems to be a personification of the attribute of willingness to give.

Among the people when a man is about to shoot at game, he will call upon *ka'-wa-ha-ru* to give the game to him, to make his shot successful. A woman will call upon this power to help her husband when he is hunting. A little boy, when he is learning to use the bow and arrow, calls upon ka'-wa-ha-ru to give him good fortune. When a person is successful in any matter, secures that which he desires, particularly when hunting, he says by way of thanks, *"Hu-tu-ru-ka'-wa-ha-ru-u-ti-*

kis!" *U-ti-kis* is that which assists in time of need. A man sometimes uses this term toward his son, as implying one upon whose assistance the father can depend.

Hu-tu-ru-hi'-hus-su is the wind that drives. This wind comes from the other of the two stars that are back of the north star (*hu-tu-ru,* "wind;" *hi'-kus-su,* "the sudden expelling of breath"). This wind is associated with the wind which sends the game, *hu-tu-ru-ka'-wa-ha-ru,* it drives the animals toward the camp, so that the people can secure the game given them by *ka'-wa-ha-ru.* When the people have secured the game, that has been thus driven toward their camp, they give thanks to this wind by saying: *"Na-wa-i-ri Ti-wa-chi-riks hu-tu-ru-hi'-kus-su!"* (*Na-wa-i-ri,* "we give thanks;" *ti-wa-chi-riks,* "uncle;" *hu-tu-ru-hi'-kus-su,* "wind that drives").

The constellation Corona borealis is said to be a council of chiefs, and the star in the center of the circle, the servant cooking over the fire, preparing the feast.

Ursa Major represents four men carrying a sick or dead man, and Ursa Minor, four persons carrying a sick baby. In reference to these groups of stars: "The people took their way of living from the stars, so they must carry their sick or their dead as shown, the mourners following."

Various animals are seen in the skies. The rabbit is a group east of the lower end of the Milky Way; a bird's foot is discerned on the path itself. To the south and near the galaxy is a cluster called the bear. In the south toward the east is a bright star; this is the head of the serpent; many little stars are to be seen on its body, which lies close to the horizon. Farther north, in the east are three deer, one following the other. The bow is to be seen among the stars, but "it is difficult to locate."

The notion that rewards and punishments are meted out to men at their death, the good being transported to the stars, and the bad, as in one instance, turned to stone, are importations from the white race. Many of these ideas have been spread by means of the ghost dance, and already the fancy of the folk has crystallized about these new ideas; but these modern bits are easily distinguished from the lore that has its roots in the native mind.

Chapter 9

Tribal Origins

The Origin of the Crane Tribe
(Chippewa)

The Great Spirit sent two cranes from the world above the sky. They came through an opening between the clouds and tried to find a place upon the earth. The Great Spirit told them when they were suited with some spot to fold their wings closely to their sides and wait; a change would come over them.

The pair of cranes flew down to the earth and began to search for a home. They went to the prairies and tasted the buffalo meat. It was good, but there were many days when no buffalo was in sight. They feared that the food would not last, and the two cranes flew to a great forest.

In the forest they tasted of the flesh of the elk, the deer, and many other animals. It was good meat, but it was hard work to hunt, and many days there were neither elk nor deer in sight.

Then the two cranes flew to the Great Lakes. They tasted of many kinds of fish. They came to the rapids in the outlet of the lake white men call Lake Superior. Many fish were in this outlet; every day the fish seemed more plentiful than the day before.

"We will find food here forever. We will make our home here," said the two cranes.

They flew away from fishing in the waters. The two cranes stood on a little hill near the rapids and folded their wings closely to their sides. The Great Spirit saw their faith, and they were changed into a man and a woman. Among the Ojibways there is a tribe called the Cranes, who believe they are the children of these two cranes sent by the Great Spirit to the earth.

ORIGIN OF THE SIOUX
(Sioux)

The Mandan tribes of the Sioux suppose that their nation lived in a subterranean village near a vast lake. Hard by the roots of a great grape-vine penetrated from the earth above, and, clambering up these, several of them got a sight of the upper world, which they found to be rich and well stocked with both animal and vegetable food. Those of them who had seen the new-found world above returned to their home bringing such glowing accounts of its wealth and pleasantness that the others resolved to forsake their dreary underground dwelling for the delights of the sunny sphere above. The entire population set out, and started to climb up the roots of the vine, but no more than half the tribe had ascended when the plant broke owing to the weight of a corpulent woman. The Mandans imagine that after death they will return to the underground world in which they originally dwelt, the worthy reaching the village by way of the lake, the bad having to abandon the passage by reason of the weight of their sins.

The Minnetarees believed that their original ancestor emerged from the waters of a lake bearing in his hand an ear of corn, and the Mandans possessed a myth very similar to that of the Muskhogees concerning their origin.

CHAPTER 10

TRIBAL HISTORY AND TRIBAL CUSTOMS

HOW LIGHT, FIRE, AND WATER ORIGINATED
(Chippewa)

L ong time ago the only place where light could be seen was in the tipi of one old chief.

This chief had light, fire, and water. All the other Indians in the whole world suffered from cold and darkness and had no water.

All the Indians came to this old chief's tipi and begged for a little light. He would not give them any. The Indians went away and told the wild animals, and asked their help.

The animals and the Indians held a great dance around the old chief's tipi. They chanted songs and all begged for light. Each one sang his own song.

One young fox kept singing, *"Khaih! Khaih!"* which means "light." He believed it would bring light, and the men and the animals were helped, he was so strong. Their voices made a great noise.

At last a faint color was seen in the east. The old chief came out and drove the little light away.

Then the young fox called, *"Khaih! Khaih!"* louder than before. The men and the animals began again. They called and called for the light to come.

At last a little color was seen in the east again. The old chief had not slept. He was tired and he said: "You may have all the light you want."

Now the light comes every morning. Some of the animals still call for it to come before it is day.

A young caribou said that he would get the fire from the old chief's tipi. The

Indians tied a great dry branch to his big antlers. The young caribou put his head into the fire tipi and tried to reach the coals, but he could not do it. The wise chief drove him away.

But when the old chief was driving back the young caribou, a muskrat crept into the tipi. He reached the precious coals of fire and caught one in his mouth. He ran back into the woods with it. Before he could reach his own burrow he had to drop the burning coal. It fell on the dry leaves and set the woods on fire. You can see now where the muskrat burned himself.

All the world had fire now, and there has always been enough since the muskrat dropped the first coal.

The fire melted the ice in the rivers and lakes. The light showed every one where to find water.

The old chief has never been seen since that time.

THE PLEIADES
(Various)

VERSION I
(Cheyenne)

A chief had a fine-looking daughter, who had a great many admirers. At night she was visited by a young man, but did not know who he was. She worried about this, and determined to discover him. She put red paint near her bed. At night he crawled on her bed, wearing a white robe. She put her hand into the paint and then on his back. The next day she told her father to call all the young men to a dance in front of his tent. They all came, and the whole village turned out to see them. She watched all that came, looking for the mark she had made. As she turned, she saw one of her father's dogs, with the mark on his back. This disheartened her, so that she went straight into her tent. This broke up the dance. The next day she went into the woods near the camp, with the dog on a string, and hit him. He finally broke loose. She was very unhappy. Several months later she bore seven pups. She told her mother to kill them, but her mother was kind toward them, and made a little shelter for them. They began to grow, and at night the old dog sometimes came to them. After a time, the woman began to take interest in them, and sometimes played with them. When they were big enough to run, the old dog came and took them away. When the woman went to see them in the morning, they were gone. She saw the large dog's tracks, and several little ones, and followed them a distance. She was sad, and cried. She came back to her mother, and said: "Mother, make me seven pairs of moccasins. I am going to follow the little ones, searching for them." Her mother made seven pairs of moccasins, and she started out, tracking them all the way. Finally, in the distance, she saw a tent. The youngest one came to her, and said: "Mother, father wants you to go back. We are going home; you cannot come." She said: "No. Wherever you go, I go." She took the little one, and carried him to the tent. She entered, and saw a young man, who, however, took no notice of her. He gave her a little meat and drink, which did not grow less however much she ate. She tied the little pup to her belt with a string. Next morning, she was left alone, and the tent was gone. She followed and again came to them. Four times this happened in the same way; but the fourth time the tracks stopped. She looked up, and there she saw seven pups (*Manootóxtcioo*); they were stars (the Pleiades).

Version II
(Cheyenne)

S even men were on the warpath. As they went along, they found a young woman who lived alone, in a solitary tent. These seven men were brothers. They remained with her and called her sister. They hunted and killed much game. The girl made seven buffalo robes for her seven brothers. She embroidered them all with porcupine quills; and she embroidered moccasins also. She worked very much for her brothers, and they were very kind to her and loved her very much. Six of the brothers used to go out hunting, and the youngest, who was only a boy, always stayed with his sister. When his brothers returned with game, he always ran to meet them and welcome them. Once the brothers went hunting again. The boy was outside, a little way from the tent where his sister was. He had a bow and arrows, and was hunting birds. He aimed at a red-bird, and shot it through the breast. The bird flew away, carrying with it his arrow. The boy ran after, to get both the bird and his arrow. Thus he pursued, always thinking he was going to catch the bird, until he had gone far from the tent. Then a powerful buffalo came to the tent and took the girl to be his wife, and made her go along with him, for she was afraid of his power. He took her westward, where there were many buffalo. The brothers returned, bringing game, but they did not see the boy coming to meet them. So they knew at once that something had happened. At the same time the boy came back, and told his brothers what had happened: how he had run after a red-bird which he had shot, and which flew away with his best arrow. The brothers looked all about the tent until they found their sister's tracks, and saw that she had been taken away when she was alone. So they went in the direction in which she had gone. The boy shot off one of his arrows toward the west. When they got to where it fell, there was a large village. The boy went to it, and found an old woman living in a tent by herself. He asked her if she had heard any news. She told him that she had heard that a powerful buffalo had passed that day, taking a fine girl with him to the westward. The boy returned to his brothers and told them what the old woman had said to him. Thus they passed through four villages, always learning the same, until they found where their sister was. They saw a large tipi, in which she was with the powerful buffalo; but all about the tent were buffalo. They stopped and considered what it was best to do. The boy was powerful too. He turned himself into a ground-rat, and dug a hole to where the tent stood. In a short time he dug to where his sister sat alone and sad. Then the boy received her in his hole and took her back to his brothers, who kissed her. Then they returned. As soon as they arrived at their home, they made an iron fence or wall. This enclosure surrounded them fourfold. Then the boy shot an arrow far up toward the sky, and there stood an iron tree in the middle of the enclosure. The sister climbed up first, and then, one after another, all the brothers. Then the whole herd of buffalo came, and surrounded the iron fence, intending to get back the powerful buffalo's wife. They tried to batter down the fence, but they broke their horns. At last they succeeded in breaking it down. Then the great bull tried to overthrow the tree. But now the boy at last succeeded in killing him. These seven men then were raised to the sky, and are said to be a group of seven stars (the Pleiades).

STAR NAMED BEAVER
(Cheyenne)

Among the people who lived generations ago there was a young man as handsome as might be. Almost all the girls and young women liked him very much, and always talked of him. Once, as night came on, there came a very beautiful girl. She had come from the sky, and was a bright star in the west. But the young man did not know this; and at night they both ran off together. He told his family that he was married, and they were glad to hear this. But she was a star just come from the sky to be a woman. So they married. Then the girl took him far off, and she told him that she was a bright western star. They both went to the sky, and the man also became a star. His name had been Beaver, and so a star in the western sky is still called Beaver.

ANIMAL TRAITS
(Various)

WHY BEARS HAVE NO TAILS
(Cheyenne)

Some hunters found some young bears. They amused themselves with them, and cut their ears and tails. Then one of the cubs sang that his father and mother were away, while he was maltreated, and that they might know it. As soon as he sang, the old bears heard his voice. The mother stood up, and tried her might on a large tree, and broke it in two. The father said to himself: "I am great and powerful. Who has come to take away my child?" And he rolled a huge stone, and broke it in two. At once they both ran to their hole. This hole is called the Bears' Lodge, and is in Yellowstone Park. The bears arrived here, and saved their young. But ever since, bears are tailless.

HOW PEOPLE WERE ABLE TO EAT BUFFALO
(Cheyenne)

The buffalo formerly ate men. The magpie and the hawk were on the side of the people, for neither ate the other. These two flew away from a council that was being held between the animals and men, and brought it about that there was to be a race, the winners to eat the losers. The course was a long one, around a mountain. The swiftest of all the buffalo was a cow called *Neika^n sa^nniia^nme-yox sts* (swifthead). She thought that she would win, and consented to race. On the other hand, the people were afraid, on account of the long distance. They were trying to get medicine to prevent them from becoming tired or winded. All the birds and animals painted for the race, and since that time they are colored. Even the water turtle put red paint around his eyes. The magpie painted himself white on head, shoulders, and tail. At last all were ready and stood in a row. Then they ran, all making some noise, in place of singing, to help them. All the small birds, the turtles, rabbits, coyotes, wolves, flies, ants, insects, and snakes were soon left behind. When they approached the mountain the buffalo-cow was ahead; then came the magpie, then the hawk, then the people; the rest were strung out. So thickly did the dust rise that nothing could be seen. All around the mountain the cow led, but the two birds knew that they could win, and merely kept up with her until they got near the starting-place, and then both went by her and won the race for man. When they arrived, they saw animals and birds all over the course, running themselves to death, and the ground and rocks turned red from the blood of these. Then the buffalo told their young to hide, as the people were going to hunt them, and told them to take some dried human flesh with them, for the last time. They did this, and stuck the meat in front of their chest, under the throat. Therefore the people do not eat that part, saying that it is human flesh. From the day of the race men began to hunt. But as hawks, magpies, nighthawks, crows, and buzzards were on their side in the race, they do not eat them, but use their feathers for ornament.

Another version says that when the coyote, who was on the side of the buffalo, came in, the magpie, who beat even the hawk, said to him: "We will not eat you, but we will use your skin."

WHY THE WOLVERINE BECAME A THIEF
(Athabascan)

A man went out hunting with a wolverine. They were out three nights, and during the third night the wolverine rose and threw the man's shoes into the fire. In the morning the wolverine deserted the man, leaving him unable to travel. The wolverine then went out with another man, and served him in the same treacherous manner. He went hunting with a third man, and during the first and second nights he was very careful to provide for the man's wants. The third evening they took off their shoes and hung them before the fire, as is the custom of the country. The man soon rose and put on his shoes and again laid down. Later the wolverine got up, and, seeing a pair of shoes, thought they belonged to the man, and threw them into the fire. The next morning, as they rose, the wolverine said, "Where are your shoes?" "On my feet," replied the man. "I have lost mine," said the wolverine; "lend me yours, and I will go and get a pair for you." But the man refused. Just as he was leaving the camp the wolverine put his forefoot in the fire and burned it. "I will never hunt for myself again, but will always live by robbing the caches of the people." And that is why the wolverine is such a thief.

ORIGIN OF THE PINE
(Athabascan)

There were a number of Indians in a camp who went away one by one and were lost. At last only one remained, and he also decided to leave the camp. He soon encountered a wolverine, which said, "I know who you are; you will have to go before me." As they went along they came out upon the river at a point where the bank was very steep. The wolverine said, "You must slide down." So the Indian slid down the bank, and the wolverine ran around through a ravine. When the man reached the bottom, he caused his nose to bleed, and put some of the blood on a spear, and then laid down and feigned death. When the wolverine reached the spot where the man lay, he took him up and carried him to his camp across the river. After placing him in the middle of the camp he began to sharpen his knife. The man soon opened his eyes and looked for a stick; when he found a stick he sprang up and killed all the wolverines except one young one which ran up a tree. The man blew his nose and threw the phlegm at the tree, and it was transformed into a pine. The wolverine then said, "That will do for your arrows; now you must leave me alone."

ORIGIN OF CORN
(Various)

GIFT OF THE BUFFALO
(Osage)

The Hanga clan regulates corn-planting. Corn is a mother, and the buffalo is a grandfather, and in the Osage tale corn was the gift of four buffalo bulls. In the harvest, one of the keepers of the sacred tents selects a number of perfect red ears, and lays them by for the spring planting. In the spring a Hanga crier is sent through the village announcing the planting time, and carrying the sacred corn. This has been shelled, and two or three grains are given to each household to be mixed with the ordinary seed. Then all may plant, but some of the people never eat red corn. It is prepared for food much as in the East.

It is said that the people came from the lower world and took different roads, having many adventures. Four buffalo bulls came near. The first one rolled, and, as he arose an ear of red corn and a red pumpkin fell from his left hind leg. A young man was told to pick them up, and his elder brother said, "These will be good for the children to eat. Their limbs will stretch and increase in strength." The second bull rolled, and as he came to his feet an ear of spotted corn and a spotted pumpkin dropped from his left hind leg. These were approved. From the third bull came dark corn and a dark pumpkin, and from the fourth these were white.

The Giver of Corn
(Chippewa)

A Manitou lived alone in the land. Wunaumon was his name. He was brave. All the animals feared him. He was a great hunter and the son of Menabozho.

Wunaumon walked all the day through a great woods. When he came out of the woods he saw a great prairie; it was wide, like a lake of land. Wunaumon saw trees on the further side of the prairie.

"I will see what is in that forest," he said. His steps were long, and he was soon almost across the prairie.

Wunaumon stopped like a deer that is startled. He was not afraid, but he saw a strange sight. A stranger came out of the forest across the prairie. He came to meet Wunaumon.

"Where are you going?" said the stranger. Then he lifted a pipe of peace, and Wunaumon took it. They were friends now.

The stranger was short. He had a red feather in his scalp lock. His coat was stiff and shiny. He did not wear deerskin. They sat down on the prairie. They smoked the pipe of peace.

"I am very strong," said Wunaumon. "How strong are you?"

"I am strong as a man," said the stranger.

"My name is Wunaumon; what is yours?"

"We will wrestle. If you throw me, I will tell you my name. You will win much from me if I fall. Let us try our strength."

Wunaumon stood up on the prairie. He was very tall and strong.

"Come, Red Feather," he said.

"That is not my name," the stranger answered. "If I fall, you shall know my name. You shall have a great gift. You must conquer me. The gift is for all your people."

It was morning when the two began to wrestle. They were both very strong. One could not make the other fall. They had no more breath. They stopped and began again. They did this many times. It was a great battle.

The sun began to go down. Wunaumon thought that the sun was ashamed to see his weakness. Wunaumon put his feet very hard on the ground. He grew very fierce. His arms were strong like the legs of a bear. There was a great noise. "Red Feather, I have made you fall," said he; "what is your name?"

"My name is Mondahmin. My body is my gift to you. Cover me with the fine dust where we have wrestled. Come to this place often. You will see me again. I will bring gifts out of this prairie to your people."

Wunaumon covered Mondahmin. He went into the forest and waited one moon. He came back to the place of wrestling. Two green feathers were waving in the air above the little hill he had made. A voice like singing came out of the green plumes.

"This is the corn, the gift of Mondahmin. Watch this plant and take the seeds to the tribe that lives nearest you. Tell them to make a feast to Mondahmin in the Moon of Fruits."

Wunaumon took the corn in the month of fruits. He told the tribe to keep the feast. The gift of Mondahmin was good. It saved the people from hunger.

THE MARRIAGE
(Pottawottomi)

The old chiefs tell the young men, and all who will listen, that two great spirits rule the world. One is very good, but the other does only wicked things. The Good Spirit made the world and filled it full of men and women. The wicked spirit would not let one person thank the Good Spirit for his gifts to them.

All tribes had much food, for there were many deer, elk, and buffalo, and the rivers were full of fish. Water, light, and fire were given to every one; but not one gave thanks for these things. They forgot the Good Spirit and the bad spirit was glad. He showed them how to fight and to make war.

The Good Spirit did not like to have men forget him. He lifted up the whole world and dropped it into a great lake. All the people were drowned excepting one young chief who had kindness in his heart. He gave thanks for his life, and a sister was given to him, for the wigwams were empty and he was alone. He called his sister White Earth.

The young chief dreamed that five strangers came to see his sister. The Good Spirit whispered to his heart that she must not see nor speak to one of them until the fifth one came to her wigwam. If she did not say anything nor see them, they would give her greater gifts than she could ask. She must not be afraid if they fell down with no more life in them when she did not answer. But all the world would be happy if she smiled and welcomed the fifth stranger.

They came the next day. The first one was tall and wore a green blanket. White Earth did not look nor answer him when he spoke.

The stranger stood very still, and then his blanket changed into leaves, and *Usama* the tobacco plant fell down to the ground.

The next visitor was very short and round. He could not walk fast. The girl did not say one word when he asked her to look at him. She did not see him, but her brother was watching, and he laughed when *Wapako* the pumpkin rolled over and down the hill. The girl was very wise and knew how to keep silent.

Eshkossim the melon and *Kokees* the bean came together and called to White Earth the maiden to welcome them. She did not answer, and they fell down the same as the two who had come before them.

Soon she heard a strong voice calling to her the fifth time. The girl untied the strings that fastened her door, and looking up she saw a very tall chief with feathers in his scalp lock. She loved his voice, for it was like the wind in the pine trees. She said: "You are welcome, Dahmin. I will take you to my brother. He will call you Mondahmin."

The brother gave his sister White Earth to Mondahmin, for the Good Spirit had sent him to her.

After the wedding feast a great wind came, and then much rain. In a few days the ground was covered with the green leaves of growing plants. *Usama* the tobacco had come with all of his tribe to give gifts to the great chief Mondahmin the corn plant. *Wapako* the pumpkin, *Eshkossim* the melon, and *Kokees* the bean, all brought many gifts to Mondahmin and his wife. They promised to bring the same gifts each year as long as the rains should come and the sun give his light and make them warm.

Mondahmin and his wife gave thanks to the Good Spirit. They taught their children these things. The Indians call Mondahmin their grandfather, and they do all the things he told them. The Indians do not forget to give thanks for the corn, bean, pumpkin, and melon.

THE BULL DANCE AND SONG
(Blackfoot)

The people had built a great pis'kun, very high and strong, so that no buffalo could escape; but somehow the buffalo would not jump over the cliff. When driven toward it, they would run nearly to the edge, and then, swerving to the right or left, they would go down the sloping hills and cross the valley in safety. So the people were hungry, and began to starve.

One morning, early, a young woman went to get water, and she saw a herd of buffalo feeding on the prairie, right on the edge of the cliff above the pis'kun. "Oh!" she cried out, "if you will only jump off into the pis'kun, I will marry one of you." This she said for fun, not meaning it, and great was her wonder when she saw the buffalo come jumping, tumbling, falling over the cliff.

Now the young woman was scared, for a big bull with one bound cleared the pis'kun walls and came toward her. "Come," he said, taking hold of her arm. "No, no!" she replied pulling back. "But you said if the buffalo would jump over, you would marry one; see, the pis'kun is filled." And without more talk he led her up over the bluff, and out onto the prairie.

When the people had finished killing the buffalo and cutting up the meat, they missed this young woman, and her relations were very sad, because they could not find her. Then her father took his bow and quiver, and said, "I will go and find her." And he went up over the bluff and out on the prairie.

After he had traveled some distance he came to a wallow, and a little way off saw a herd of buffalo. While sitting by the wallow—for he was tired—and thinking what he should do, a magpie came and lit near him. "Ha! *Ma-me-at'-si-kim-i,*" he said, "you are a beautiful bird; help me. Look everywhere as you travel about, and if you see my daughter, tell her, 'Your father waits by the wallow.'" The magpie flew over by the herd of buffalo, and seeing the young woman, he lit on the ground near her, and commenced picking around, turning his head this way and that way, and, when close to her, he said, "Your father waits by the wallow." "Sh-h-h! sh-h-h!" replied the girl, in a whisper, looking around scared, for her bull husband was sleeping near by. "Don't speak so loud. Go back and tell him to wait."

"Your daughter is over there with the buffalo. She says 'wait!'" said the magpie, when he had flown back to the man.

By and by the bull awoke, and said to his wife, "Go and get me some water." Then the woman was glad, and taking a horn from his head she went to the wallow. "Oh, why did you come?" she said to her father. "You will surely be killed."

"I came to take my daughter home; come, let us hurry."

"No, no!" she replied; "not now. They would chase us and kill us. Wait till he sleeps again, and I will try to get away," and, filling the horn with water, she went back.

The bull drank a swallow of the water. "Ha!" said he, "a person is close by here."

"No one," replied the woman; but her heart rose up.

The bull drank a little more, and then he stood up and bellowed, *"Bu-u-u! m-m-ah-oo!"* Oh, fearful sound! Up rose the bulls, raised their short tails and shook them, tossed their great heads, and bellowed back. Then they pawed the dirt, rushed about here and there, and coming to the wallow, found that poor man. There they trampled him with their great hoofs, hooked him and trampled him again, and soon not even a small piece of his body could be seen.

Then his daughter cried, *"Oh! ah! Ni'-nah-ah! Oh! ah! Ni'-nah-ah!"* (My father! My father!) "Ah!" said her bull husband, "you mourn for your father. You see now how it is with us. We have seen our mothers, fathers, many of our relations, hurled over the rocky walls, and killed for food by your people. But I will pity you. I will give you one chance. If you can bring your father to life, you and he can go back to your people."

Then the woman said to the magpie: "Pity me. Help me now; go and seek in the trampled mud; try and find a little piece of my father's body, and bring it to me."

The magpie flew to the place. He looked in every hole, and tore up the mud with his sharp nose. At last he found something white; he picked the mud from around it, and then pulling hard, he brought out a joint of the backbone, and flew with it back to the woman.

She placed it on the ground, covered it with her robe, and then sang. Removing the robe, there lay her father's body as if just dead. Once more she covered it with the robe and sang, and when she took away the robe, he was breathing, and then he stood up. The buffalo were surprised; the magpie was glad, and flew round and round, making a great noise.

"We have seen strange things this day," said her bull husband. "He whom we trampled to death, even into small pieces, is alive again. The people's medicine is very strong. Now, before you go, we will teach you our dance and our song. You must not forget them." When the dance was over, the bull said: "Go now to your home, and do not forget what you have seen. Teach it to the people. The medicine shall be a bull's head and a robe. All the persons who are to be 'Bulls' shall wear them when they dance."

Great was the joy of the people, when the man returned with his daughter. He called a council of the chiefs, and told them all that had happened. Then the chiefs chose certain young men, and this man taught them the dance and song of the bulls, and told them what the medicine should be. This was the beginning of the *I-kun-uh'-kah-tsi.*

MORE BANDS AND DANCES
(Blackfoot)

For a long time the buffalo had not been seen. The pis'kun was useless, and the hunters could find no food for the people. Then a man who had two wives, a daughter, and two sons, said: "I shall not stop here to die. Tomorrow we will move toward the mountains, where we shall perhaps find deer and elk, sheep and antelope, or, if not, at least we shall find plenty of beaver and birds. Thus we shall survive."

When morning came, they packed the travois, lashed them on the dogs, and then moved out. It was yet winter, and they traveled slowly. They were weak, and could go but a little way in a day. The fourth night came, and they sat in their lodge, very tired and hungry. No one spoke, for those who are hungry do not care for words. Suddenly the dogs began to bark, and soon, pushing aside the door-curtain, a young man entered.

"O'kyi!" said the old man, and he motioned the stranger to a sitting-place.

They looked at this person with surprise and fear, for there was a black wind which had melted the snow, and covered the prairie with water, yet this person's leggings and moccasins were dry. They sat in silence a long time.

Then said he: "Why is this? Why do you not give me some food?"

"Ah!" replied the old man, "you behold those who are truly poor. We have no food. For many days the buffalo did not come in sight, and we shot deer and other animals which people eat, and when all these had been killed, we began to starve. Then said I, 'We will not stay here to starve to death'; and we started for the mountains. This is the fourth night of our travels."

"Ah!" said the young man. "Then your travels are ended. Close by here, we are camped by our pis'kun. Many buffalo have been run in, and our parfleches are filled with dried meat. Wait; I will go and bring you some."

As soon as he went out, they began to talk about this strange person. They were very much afraid of him, and did not know what to do. The children began to cry, and the women were trying to quiet them, when the young man returned, bringing some meat and three pis-tsi-ko'-an.

"Kyi!" said he. "Tomorrow move over to our lodges. Do not be afraid. No matter what strange things you see, do not fear. All will be your friends. Now, one thing I caution you about. In this be careful. If you should find an arrow lying about, in the pis'kun, or outside, no matter where, do not touch it; neither you, nor your wives nor children." Having said this, he went out.

Then the old man took his pipe and smoked and prayed, saying: "Hear now, Sun! Listen, Above People. Listen, Under Water People. Now you have taken pity. Now you have given us food. We are going to those strange ones, who walk through water with dry moccasins. Protect us among those to-be-feared people. Let us survive. Man, woman, child, give us long life; give us long life!"

Once more the smell of roasting meat. The children played. They talked and laughed who had so long been silent. They ate plenty and lay down and slept.

Early in the morning, as soon as the sun rose, they took down their lodge, packed up, and started for the strange camp. They found it was a wonderful place. There by the pis'kun, and far up and down the valley were the lodges of meat-eaters. They could not see them all, but close by they saw the lodges of the Bear band, the Fox band, and the Badger band. The father of the young man who had given them meat was chief of the Wolf band, and by that band they pitched their lodge. Ah! That was a happy place. Food there was plenty. All day people shouted out for feasts, and everywhere was heard the sound of drums and song and dancing.

The new-comers went to the pis'kun for meat, and one of the children found an arrow lying on the ground. It was a beautiful arrow, the stone point long and sharp, the shaft round and straight. All around the people were busy; no one was looking. The boy picked up the arrow and hid it under his robe. Then there was a fearful noise. All the animals howled and growled, and ran toward him. But the chief Wolf said: "Hold! We will let him go this time; for he is young yet, and not of good sense." So they let him go.

When night came, some one shouted out for a feast, saying: *"Wo'-ka-hit! Wo'-ka-hit! Mah-kwe'-i-ke-tum-ok-ah-wah-hit. Ke-tŭk'-ka-pŭk'-si-pim."* ("Listen! Listen! Wolf, you are to feast. Enter with your friend.") "We are asked," said the chief Wolf to his new friend, and together they went to the lodge.

Within, the fire burned brightly, and many men were already there, the old and wise of the Raven band. Hanging behind the seats were the writings of many deeds. Food was placed before them,—pemmican of berries and dried back fat; and when they had eaten, a pipe was lighted. Then spoke the Raven chief: "Now, Wolf, I am going to give our new friend a present. What say you?"

"It is as you say," replied the Wolf. "Our new friend will be glad."

Then the Raven chief took from the long parfleche sack a slender stick, beautifully dressed with many colored feathers; and on the end of it was fastened the skin of a raven, head, wings, feet, and all. "We," he said, "are the *Mas-to-pah'-ta-kiks* (Raven carriers, or those who bear the Raven). Of all the above animals, of all the flyers, where is one so smart? None. The Raven's eyes are sharp. His wings are strong. He is a great hunter and never hungry. Far, far off on the prairie he sees his food, and deep hidden in the pines it does not escape his eye. Now the song and the dance."

When he had finished singing and dancing, he gave the stick to the man, and said: "Take it with you, and when you have returned to your people, you shall say: Now there are already the Bulls, and he who is the Raven chief says: 'There shall be more, there shall be the I-kun-uh'-kah-tsi, so that the people may survive, and of them shall be the Raven carriers.' You will call a council of the chiefs and wise old men, and they will choose the persons. Teach them the song and the dance, and give them the medicine. It shall be theirs forever."

Soon they heard another person shouting for a feast, and, going, they entered the lodge of the Sin'-o-pah chief. Here, too, were the old men assembled. After they had eaten of that set before them, the chief said: "Those among whom you are newly arrived are generous. They do not look at their possessions, but give to the stranger and pity the poor. The Kit-fox is a little animal, but what one is smarter? None. His hair is like the dead prairie grass. His eyes are sharp, his feet noiseless, his brain cunning. His ears receive the far-off sound. Here is our medicine, take it." And he gave the stick. It was long, crooked at one end, wound with fur, and tied here and there to it were eagle feathers. At the end was a fox's skin. Again the chief said: "Hear our song. Do not forget it; and the dance, too, you must remember. When you get home, teach them to the people."

Again they heard the feast shout, and he who called was the Bear chief. Now when they had smoked, the chief said: "What say you, friend Wolf? Shall we give our new friend something?"

"As you say," replied the Wolf. "It is yours to give."

Then said the Bear: "There are many animals, and some of them are powerful. But the Bear is the strongest and bravest of all. He fears nothing, and is always ready to fight." Then he put on a necklace of bear claws, a belt of bear fur, and around his head a band of the fur; and sang and danced. When he had finished, he gave them to the man, saying: "Teach the people our song and dance, and give them this medicine. It is powerful."

It was now very late. The Seven Persons had arrived at midnight, yet again they heard the feast shout from the far end of camp. In this lodge the men were painted with streaks of red and their hair was all brushed to one side. After the feast the chief said: "We are different from all the others here. We are called the *Mŭt'-siks*. We are death. We know not fear. Even if our enemies are in number like the grass, we do not turn away, but fight and conquer. Bows are good weapons. Spears are better, but our weapon is the knife." Then the chief sang and danced, and afterwards he gave the Wolf's friend the medicine. It was a long knife, and many scalps were tied on the handle. "This," he said, "is for the I-kun-uh'-kah-tsi."

Once more they were called to a feast and entered the Badger chief's lodge. He taught the man the Badger song and dance and gave him the medicine. It was a large rattle, ornamented with beaver claws and bright feathers. They smoked two pipes in the Badger's lodge, and then went home and slept.

Early next day, the man and his family took down their lodge, and prepared to move camp. Many women came and made them presents of dried meat, pemmican, and berries. They were given so much they could not take it all with them. It was many days before they joined the main camp, for the people, too, had moved to the south after buffalo. As soon as the lodge was pitched, the man called all the chiefs to come and feast, and he told them all he had seen, and showed them the medicines. The chiefs chose certain young men for the different bands, and this man taught them the songs and dances, and gave each band their medicine.

THE FOX BAND AND DANCE
(Cheyenne)

A man had once gone out on the warpath. Finally he started home. But a blizzard came, he lost his way, and nearly perished. At last he was met by some one and taken into a tent. This was full of a large company, all of them dressed up, while their dancing apparel hung on every tent-pole. It was the fox company. They commenced to teach the man their dance. They showed him how to paint, and what to wear, and the songs to be sung. They had four young girls with them in their company. On the fourth morning, when he had learned all, the storm was over, and it had grown warm. The dance broke up, and some one was sent to guide him home. As the company scattered, he saw they were wolves and coyotes. A wolf guided the man, and he returned in safety. Then he instituted the fox-company, whose dance has continued to the present day.

LEGEND OF RED COULEE
(Blackfoot)

There lies in a "coulee" near the Marias River, on the road that leads from Macleod to Benton, a large "medicine stone," venerated by the Indians belonging to the Blackfoot Confederacy. The "coulee" is named by the Indians the "Red Coulee." When the Blackfeet came from the north, the Snake Indians, who at that time inhabited the country, told the Blackfeet that there was a large medicine stone on the top of a hill, close to a ravine.

Several years after they were told this, a Blackfoot chief with fifty men went southward on the war-path. They all went to this stone, and the chief, being skeptical about the mysterious powers possessed by it, laughed at his men for exhibiting such childishness as to believe in it. In derision he hurled the stone down the mountainside into the ravine, and then departed. They engaged in a battle with some Indians in the South, and all of them were killed, only one man returning to tell the fate of his comrades.

Ever since that time the Indians have called the place the "Red Coulee," and as they travel to and fro, they never forget to go there and present their offerings, to insure safety in battle and protection by the way.

LEGEND OF RED STONE
(Blackfoot)

On the river flat at the mouth of one of the ravines at Lethbridge, and not many yards distant from the coal mine, lies a stone, which oftentimes been painted, and surrounded by numerous Indian trinkets, which had been offered to it by the Indians. The Blood Indians call it *"Mikiotouqse;"* that is the Red Stone. Tradition states that a long time ago, a young man lay down beside this stone, and fell asleep, and as he lay there he dreamed that the stone spoke to him, and said, "Am I the Red Stone?" And the young man said, "Yes, you are the Red Stone." When he awoke, he felt that this must be a mysterious stone, that could thus converse with him, and he made offerings to it. Until the present day these offerings are made, the Indians believing that by giving to it reverence they will be blessed in all things that concern them in this life.

LEGEND OF SHEEP CREEK
(Blackfoot)

N apioa, which means "The Old Man," who is the Secondary Creator of the Blackfeet, was traveling one day with the Kit-fox, near Sheep Creek, which is located about twenty-five miles south of Calgary, in the Provisional District of Alberta. As they traveled together they saw a large rock, and Napioa felt constrained to make an offering of his robe to it. He presented the robe and, with the Kit-fox as his companion, departed. He had not proceeded far upon the way, when, perceiving that it was going to rain, he told his companion to return, and ask the rock to give him back his robe, as he was afraid of being drenched with the rain. The rock refused to give the robe to the Kit-fox, and then Napioa, becoming angry, said, "That old rock has been there for a long time and never had a robe. It has always been poor. I will go back myself and take away my robe."

He returned and took the robe by force, and then the rock became very angry, and followed them, determined to punish them. Napioa fled southward toward High River, and the Kit-fox, anxious for his own safety, hid in a hole in the ground. Napioa saw an old buffalo bull, and he called to him for help; but when the buffalo came to his rescue, the rock ran over him and crushed him to death. Then two bears came to help Napioa, and they too were killed by the rock. Two small birds, with very large strong bills, came to help him, and they attacked the rock, breaking off pieces from it, as they suddenly pounced upon it, and then flew upward. In a short time they killed the rock, and Napioa was saved. The Indians then named the stream "Oqkotokseetuqta, the Rock Creek, or Stony Creek," but it is called by the white people at the present day, "Sheep Creek."

LEGEND OF TONGUE CREEK
(Blackfoot)

T ongue Creek is situated between Sheep Creek and High River, about nine miles south of Sheep Creek. In the distant past Napioa was traveling in the vicinity of Tongue Creek, when he espied a band of elk sporting themselves on its banks. They came to a place where the bank was steep, and they all leaped down, seeking a sandy resting-place in the bed of the stream. Napioa reached the creek, and, lighting a piece of wood, he threw the firebrand over the bank. The elk heard him, and asked him what he wanted. "Oh," said he, "I was laughing when you spoke to me, and I could not answer; but that is a very nice spot down there, and I want to go down, for there is abundance of beautiful clean sand." When the elk saw the fire-brand they became frightened, and, rushing headlong over each other, broke their necks. A single young elk escaped, but Napioa said, "Never mind, there are many more elk in the country; that one can go." Napioa pitched his lodge, and erected a pole with a flag upon it. He skinned the elk, filled his lodge with the meat, and made preparations to camp there and have a feast. While thus engaged, a coyote entered his lodge and asked him for something to eat, but he would not give any. He noticed that the coyote had on a necklace of shells, and said he, "If you will give me that necklace, I will give you something to eat." The coyote replied, "I cannot do that, for this is my medicine (amulet) and it is very strong." Napioa then said, "Well, I will run a race with you, and if you beat me I will give you some of the meat." But the coyote refused, and as he did so he held up a bandaged foot, and said, "I cannot run for I am lame!" and the two went off together, the coyote protesting that he had a sore foot, and could not run. He managed to get Napioa a long distance from the lodge, and then quickly unloosing the bandage from his foot, he ran back to the lodge. Napioa followed, a long distance behind, shouting, "Save me some of the meat!" When the coyote reached the lodge, he called aloud for his fellow coyotes, who speedily came and devoured all the meat. Napioa had placed the tongues upon the top of the pole, but a mouse ran up the pole and ate them all. When Napioa found that the meat was all gone he said, "Then I will have the tongues, for the coyote could not get them." But as he took down the remaining portions, he threw them away, saying, "They are not good!" The Indians call this creek *"Matsinawustam,* The Tongue Flag," but the white people call it "Tongue Creek."

DEVIL'S LAKE
(Sac and Fox)

M any of the noble rivers and secluded lakes of Wisconsin were held in esteem or fear by the northern tribes, and it was the now-forgotten events and superstitions connected with them, not less than the frontier tendency for strong names, that gave a lurid and diabolical nomenclature to parts of this region. Devils, witches, magicians, and manitous were perpetuated, and Indians whose prowess was thought to be supernatural left dim records of themselves here and there—as near the dells of the Wisconsin, where a chasm fifty feet wide is shown as the ravine leaped by chief Black Hawk when flying from the whites. Devil's Lake was the home of a manitou who does not seem to have been a particularly evil genius, though he had unusual power. The lake fills what is locally regarded as the crater of an extinct volcano, and the coldness and purity kept by the water, in spite of its lacking visible inlets or outlets, was one cause for thinking it uncanny.

This manitou piled the heavy blocks of Devil's Door-Way and set up Black Monument and the Pedestaled Boulder as thrones where he might sit and view the landscape by day—for the Indians appreciated the beautiful in nature and supposed their gods did, too—while at night he could watch the dance of the frost spirits, the aurora borealis. Cleft Rock was sundered by one of his darts aimed at an offending Indian, who owed his life to the manitou's bad aim. The Sacrifice Stone is shown where, at another time, a girl was immolated to appease his anger. Cleopatra's Needle, as it is now called, is the body of an ancient chief, who was turned into stone as a punishment for prying into the mysteries of the lake, a stone on East Mountain being the remains of a squaw who had similarly offended. On the St. Croix the Devil's Chair is pointed out where he sat in state. He had his play spells, too, as you may guess when you see his toboggan slide in Weber Cañon, UT, while Cinnabar Mountain, in the Yellowstone country, he scorched red as he coasted down.

The hunter wandering through this Wisconsin wilderness paused when he came within sight of the lake, for all game within its precincts was in the manitou's protection; not a fish might be taken, and not even a drop of water could be dipped to cool the lips of the traveler. So strong was this fear of giving offense to the manitou that Indians who were dying of wounds or illness, and were longing for a swallow of water, would refuse to profane the lake by touching their lips to it.

Vision of Rescue
(Sauk)

Surmounting Red Banks, twelve miles north of Green Bay, WI, on the eastern shore, and one hundred feet above the water, stands an earthwork that the first settlers found there when they went into that country. It was built by the Sauks and Outagamies, a family that ruled the land for many years, rousing the jealousy of neighboring tribes by their wealth and power. The time came, as it did in the concerns of nearly every band of Indians, when war was declared against this family, and the enemy came upon them in the darkness, their canoes patroling the shore while the main body formed a line about the fort. So silently was this done that but one person discovered it—a squaw, who cried, "We are all dead!"

There was nothing to see or hear, and she was rated for alarming the camp with foolish dreams; but dawn revealed the beleaguering line, and at the lifting of the sun a battle began that lasted for days, those within the earthworks sometimes fighting while ankle-deep in the blood of their fellows. The greatest lack of the besieged was that of water, and they let down earthen jars to the lake to get it, but the cords were cut ere they could be drawn up—the enemy shouting, derisively, "Come down and drink!" Several times they tried to do so, but were beaten back at every sally, and it seemed at last as if extermination was to be their fate.

When matters were at their darkest one of the young men who had been fasting for ten days—the Indian custom when divine direction was sought—addressed his companions to this effect: "Last night there stood by me the form of a young man, clothed in white, who said, 'I was once alive, but I died, and now I live forever. Trust me and I will deliver you. Be fearless. At midnight I will cast a sleep on your enemies. Go forth boldly and you shall escape.'" The condition was too desperate to question any means of freedom, and that night all but a handful of disbelievers left the fort, while the enemy was in a slumber of exhaustion, and got away in safety. When the besiegers, in the morning, found that the fort had been almost deserted, they fell on the few that remained to repent their folly, and put them to the knife and axe, for their fury was excessive at the failure of the siege.

THE SNAKES AND PIEGANS
(Blackfoot)

In those days there was a Piegan chief named Owl Bear. He was a great chief, very brave and generous. One night he had a dream: he saw many dead bodies of the enemy lying about, scalped, and he knew that he must go to war. So he called out for a feast, and after the people had eaten, he said:—

"I had a strong dream last night. I went to war against the Snakes, and killed many of their warriors. So the signs are good, and I feel that I must go. Let us have a big party now, and I will be the leader. We will start tomorrow night."

Then he told two old men to go out in the camp and shout the news, so that all might know. A big party was made up. Two hundred men, they say, went with this chief to war. The first night they traveled only a little way, for they were not used to walking, and soon got tired.

In the morning the chief got up early and went and made a sacrifice, and when he came back to the others, some said, "Come now, tell us your dream of this night."

"I dreamed good," said Owl Bear. "I had a good dream. We will have good luck."

But many others said they had bad dreams. They saw blood running from their bodies.

Night came, and the party started on, traveling south, and keeping near the foot-hills; and when daylight came, they stopped in thick pine woods and built war lodges. They put up poles as for a lodge, and covered them very thick with pine boughs, so they could build fires and cook, and no one would see the light and smoke; and they all ate some of the food they carried, and then went to sleep.

Again the chief had a good dream, but the others all had bad dreams, and some talked about turning back; but Owl Bear laughed at them, and when night came, all started on. So they traveled for some nights, and all kept dreaming bad except the chief. He always had good dreams. One day after a sleep, a person again asked Owl Bear if he dreamed good. "Yes," he replied. "I have again dreamed of good luck."

"We still dream bad," the person said, "and now some of us are going to turn back. We will go no further, for bad luck is surely ahead." "Go back! go back!" said Owl Bear. "I think you are cowards; I want no cowards with me." They did not speak again. Many of them turned around, and started north, toward home.

Two more days' travel. Owl Bear and his warriors went on, and then another party turned back, for they still had bad dreams. All the men now left with him were his relations. All the others had turned back.

They traveled on, and traveled on, always having bad dreams, until they came close to the Elk River. Then the oldest relation said, "Come, my chief, let us all turn back. We still have bad dreams. We cannot have good luck."

"No," replied Owl Bear, "I will not turn back."

Then they were going to seize him and tie his hands, for they had talked of this before. They thought to tie him and make him go back with them. Then the chief got very angry. He put an arrow on his bow, and said: "Do not touch me. You are my relations; but if any of you try to tie me, I will kill you. Now I am ashamed. My relations are cowards and will turn back. I have told you I have always dreamed good, and that we would have good luck. Now I don't care; I am covered with shame. I am going now to the Snake camp and will give them my body. I am ashamed. Go! go! and when you get home put on women's dresses. You are no longer men."

They said no more. They turned back homeward, and the chief was all alone. His heart was very sad as he traveled on, and he was much ashamed, for his relations had left him.

Night was coming on. The sun had set and rain was beginning to fall. Owl Bear looked around for some place where he could sleep dry. Close by he saw a hole in the rocks. He got down on his hands and knees and crept in. Here it was very dark. He could see nothing, so he crept very slowly, feeling as he went. All at once his hand touched something strange. He felt of it. It was a person's foot, and there was a moccasin on it. He stopped, and sat still. Then he felt a little further. Yes, it was a person's leg. He could feel the cowskin legging. Now he did not know what to do. He thought perhaps it was a dead person; and again, he thought it might be one of his relations, who had become ashamed and turned back after him.

Pretty soon he put his hand on the leg again and felt along up. He touched the person's belly. It was warm. He felt of the breast, and could feel it rise and fall as the breath came and went; and the heart was beating fast. Still the person did not move. Maybe he was afraid. Perhaps he thought that was a ghost feeling of him.

Owl Bear now knew this person was not dead. He thought he would try if he could learn who the man was, for he was not afraid. His heart was sad. His people and his relations had left him, and he had made up his mind to give his body to the Snakes. So he began and felt all over the man,—of his face, hair, robe, leggings, belt, weapons; and by and by he stopped feeling of him. He could not tell whether it was one of his people or not.

Pretty soon the strange person sat up and felt all over Owl Bear; and when he had finished, he took the Piegan's hand and opened it and held it up, waving it from side to side, saying by signs, "Who are you?"

Owl Bear put his closed hand against the person's cheek and rubbed it; he said in signs, "Piegan!" and then he asked the person who he was. A finger was placed against his breast and moved across it zigzag. It was the sign for "Snake."

"Hai yah!" thought Owl Bear, "a Snake, my enemy." For a long time he sat still, thinking. By and by he drew his knife from his belt and placed it in the Snake's hand, and signed, "Kill me!" He waited. He thought soon his heart would be cut. He wanted to die. Why live? His people had left him.

Then the Snake took Owl Bear's hand and put a knife in it and motioned that Owl Bear should cut his heart, but the Piegan would not do it. He lay down, and the Snake lay down beside him. Maybe they slept. Likely not.

So the night went and morning came. It was light, and they crawled out of the cave, and talked a long time together by signs. Owl Bear told the Snake where he had come from, how his party had dreamed bad and left him, and that he was going alone to give his body to the Snakes.

Then the Snake said: "I was going to war, too. I was going against the Piegans. Now I am done. Are you a chief?"

"I am the head chief," replied Owl Bear. "I lead. All the others follow."

"I am the same as you," said the Snake. "I am the chief. I like you. You are brave. You gave me your knife to kill you with. How is your heart? Shall the Snakes and the Piegans make peace?"

"Your words are good," replied Owl Bear. "I am glad."

"How many nights will it take you to go home and come back here with your people?" asked the Snake.

Owl Bear thought and counted. "In twenty-five nights," he replied, "the Piegans will camp down by that creek."

"My trail," said the Snake, "goes across the mountains. I will try to be here in twenty-five nights, but I will camp with my people just behind that first mountain. When you get here with the Piegans, come with one of your wives and stay all night with me. In the morning the Snakes will move and put up their lodges beside the Piegans."

"As you say," replied the chief, "so it shall be done." Then they built a fire and cooked some meat and ate together.

"I am ashamed to go home," said Owl Bear. "I have taken no horses, no scalps. Let me cut off your side locks?"

"Take them," said the Snake.

Owl Bear cut off the chief's braids close to his head, and then the Snake cut off the Piegan's braids. Then they exchanged clothes and weapons and started out, the Piegan north, the Snake south.

"Owl Bear has come! Owl Bear has come!" the people were shouting.

The warriors rushed to his lodge. *Whish!* how quickly it was filled! Hundreds stood outside, waiting to hear the news.

For a long time the chief did not speak. He was still angry with his people. An old man was talking, telling the news of the camp. Owl Bear did not look at him. He ate some food and rested. Many were in the lodge who had started to war with him. They were now ashamed. They did not speak, either, but kept looking at the fire. After a long time the chief said: "I traveled on alone. I met a Snake. I took his scalp and clothes, and his weapons. See, here is his scalp!" And he held up the two braids of hair.

No one spoke, but the chief saw them nudge each other and smile a little; and soon they went out and said to one another: "What a lie! That is not an enemy's scalp; there is no flesh on it. He has robbed some dead person."

Some one told the chief what they said, but he only laughed and replied:—

"I do not care. They were too much afraid even to go on and rob a dead person. They should wear women's dresses."

Near sunset, Owl Bear called for a horse, and rode all through camp so every one could hear, shouting out: "Listen! listen! Tomorrow we move camp. We travel south. The Piegans and Snakes are going to make peace. If any one refuses to go, I will kill him. All must go."

Then an old medicine man came up to him and said: "*Kyi,* Owl Bear! listen to me. Why talk like this? You know we are not afraid of the Snakes. Have we not fought them and driven them out of this country? Do you think we are afraid to go and meet them? No. We will go and make peace with them as you say, and if they want to fight, we will fight. Now you are angry with those who started to war with you. Don't be angry. Dreams belong to the Sun. He gave them to us, so that we can see ahead and know what will happen. The Piegans are not cowards. Their dreams told them to turn back. So do not be angry with them any more."

"There is truth in what you say, old man," replied Owl Bear; "I will take your words."

In those days the Piegans were a great tribe. When they traveled, if you were with the head ones, you could not see the last ones, they were so far back. They had more horses than they could count, so they used fresh horses every day and traveled very fast. On the twenty-fourth day they reached the place where Owl Bear had told the Snake they would camp, and put up their lodges along the creek. Soon some young men came in, and said they had seen some fresh horse trails up toward the mountain.

"It must be the Snakes," said the chief; "they have already arrived, although there is yet one night." So he called one of his wives, and getting on their horses they set out to find the Snake camp. They took the trail up over the mountain, and soon came in sight of the lodges. It was a big camp. Every open place in the valley was covered with lodges, and the hills were dotted with horses; for the Snakes had a great many more horses than the Piegans.

Some of the Snakes saw the Piegans coming, and they ran to the chief, saying: "Two strangers are in sight, coming this way. What shall be done?"

"Do not harm them," replied the chief. "They are friends of mine. I have been expecting them." Then the Snakes wondered, for the chief had told them nothing about his war trip.

Now when Owl Bear had come to the camp, he asked in signs for the chief's lodge, and they pointed him to one in the middle. It was small and old. The Piegan got off his horse, and the Snake chief came out and hugged him and kissed him, and said: "I am glad you have come today to my lodge. So are my people. You are tired. Enter my lodge and we will eat." So they went inside and many of the Snakes came in, and they had a great feast.

Then the Snake chief told his people how he had met the Piegan, and how brave he was, and that now they were going to make a great peace; and he sent some men to tell the people, so that they would be ready to move camp in the morning.

Evening came. Everywhere people were shouting out for feasts, and the chief took Owl Bear to them. It was very late when they returned. Then the Snake had one of his wives make a bed at the back of the lodge; and when it was ready he said: "Now, my friend, there is your bed. This is now your lodge; also the woman who made the bed, she is now your wife; also everything in this lodge is yours. The parfleches, saddles, food, robes, bowls, everything is yours. I give them to you because you are my friend and a brave man."

"You give me too much," replied Owl Bear. "I am ashamed, but I take your words. I have nothing with me but one wife. She is yours."

Next morning camp was broken early. The horses were driven in, and the Snake chief gave Owl Bear his whole band,—two hundred head, all large, powerful horses.

All were now ready, and the chiefs started ahead. Close behind them were all the warriors, hundreds and hundreds, and last came the women and children, and the young men driving the loose horses. As they came in sight of the Piegan camp, all the warriors started out to meet them, dressed in their war costumes and singing the great war song. There was no wind, and the sound came across the valley and up the hill like the noise of thunder. Then the Snakes began to sing, and thus the two parties advanced. At last they met. The Piegans turned and rode beside them, and so they came to the camp. Then they got off their horses and kissed each other. Every Piegan asked a Snake into his lodge to eat and rest, and the Snake women put up their lodges beside the Piegan lodges. So the great peace was made.

In Owl Bear's lodge there was a great feast, and when they had finished he said to his people: "Here is the man whose scalp I took. Did I say I killed him? No. I gave him my knife and told him to kill me. He would not do it; and he gave me his knife, but I would not kill him. So we talked together what we should do, and now we have made peace. And now (turning to the Snake) this is your lodge, also all the things in it. My horses, too, I give you. All are yours."

So it was. The Piegan took the Snake's wife, lodge, and horses, and the Snake took the Piegan's, and they camped side by side. All the people camped together, and feasted each other and made presents. So the peace was made.

For many days they camped side by side. The young men kept hunting, and the women were always busy drying meat and tanning robes and cowskins. Buffalo were always close, and after a while the people had all the meat and robes they could carry. Then, one day, the Snake chief said to Owl Bear: "Now, my friend, we have camped a long time together, and I am glad we have made peace. We have dug a hole in the ground, and in it we have put our anger and covered it up, so there is no more war between us. And now I think it time to go. Tomorrow morning the Snakes break camp and go back south."

"Your words are good," replied Owl Bear. "I too am glad we have made this peace. You say you must go south, and I feel lonesome. I would like you to go with us so we could camp together a long time, but as you say, so it shall be done. Tomorrow you will start south. I too shall break camp, for I would be lonesome here without you; and the Piegans will start in the home direction."

The lodges were being taken down and packed. The men sat about the fireplaces, taking a last smoke together. They were now great friends. Many Snakes had married Piegan women, and many Piegans had married Snake women. At last all was ready. The great chiefs mounted their horses and started out, and soon both parties were strung out on the trail.

Some young men, however, stayed behind to gamble a while. It was yet early in the morning, and by riding fast it would not take them long to catch up with their camps. All day they kept playing; and sometimes the Piegans would win, and sometimes the Snakes.

It was now almost sunset. "Let us have one horse race," they said, "and we will stop." Each side had a good horse, and they ran their best; but they came in so close together it could not be told who won. The Snakes claimed that their horse won, and the Piegans would not allow it. So they got angry and began to quarrel, and pretty soon they began to fight and to shoot at each other, and some were killed.

Since that time the Snakes and Piegans have never been at peace.

Chapter 11

Tribal Legends

Story of the Twins
(Sac and Fox)

Once upon a time a man and his wife lived all alone in a little shanty. The man used to go hunting at daylight. He told his wife once that a man would come who would do everything and say everything to make her look at him, but she must not listen to him, else it would not be good for her. "All right," said she, "I will not." One day the man came, and said everything to her, but she did not notice him, and he went off. He kept coming for three days, and the fourth time he came she looked at him as he was going out of the shanty. He had two faces, and turned back into the shanty, saying, "I thought you wouldn't be very hard." Taking out his bow and arrow, he shot at her until she was dead. He then cut her open and there were little twins in her. Thinking it was about time for her husband to return, he then went away. When the husband returned he found his wife dead, but the little twins were still alive, so he took care of them. They were boys. He kept them for a few days, and, thinking that the smaller one was not going to live, he threw it away under a big log. The days went by, and this little boy grew fast; the years went by and he was big enough to take care of the house, while the man went hunting. One day he heard somebody singing. The voice came nearer and nearer, and it said, "Lonlay's got father and he eats meat; but I eat only wild beans because I've got grandmother." The boy that was singing was his brother who had been thrown away. The rat had carried him into its hole, and the old rat had raised him. He was singing for his brother. After the father had gone hunting he used to come and play with his brother, and they would muss the house all up. When he thought it was time for their father to return he would go back to his rat grandmother's to sleep. When the father came home he would see everything scattered all about the house.

He said, "My son, it looks as if you had been playing with somebody, the way the house looks." The boy said nothing, and the father went away the third time. When he came back in the evening, he said, "Have you been playing with somebody? You'll set the house on fire, my son." Said the boy, "Yes, father. A little boy always comes right after you go off. He is always singing, and says, 'Lonlay's got a father, and he always eats meat, but I've got a grandmother, so I eat wild beans.' " Said the father, "Oh, my son, that's your brother. The next time he comes, seize his scalp lock, wind it round your hand, and holloa for me. I will come and cut it off, so that he won't go away again, and you will have company." So, the next morning, he made ready, sharpened his butcher knife, went off a little distance, and hid himself. The boy came, but wouldn't go inside the shanty. He had some idea that the father was near. His brother said, "Come in, come in." But he said, "No, I am afraid." Said the other, "Why, my father went long ago." At last he came in, and after they had begun playing his brother seized the plait of hair and wrapped it around his hand, and called for his father. The father came and cut the plait off. The little boy tried to get away, but the man talked with him, and told him he was the father of both of them. He told them the whole story of the killing of their mother. He told him he must stay with his brother, because their father had to go off hunting most of the time. When the boys grew to be of a pretty good size, their father said to them, "You must never go to that big bank, because nobody ever goes there." But as soon as their father had gone off hunting one of the boys, the smaller, said, "Let's go." Said the other, "Where?" The younger said, "You know; where that big bank is." Said his brother, "Oh, no." Said other, "Why?" "Because our father told us not to," said the older. "Well, give me my hair-plait, and I'll go home," said the other. "Well, let's go then," said the older one. So they went, and when they got there they found nothing but snakes. "Oh, what nice things!" they said, and took a lot of them home. Some they cut up and cooked for their father. Others they hung up about the shanty (the rattlesnakes inside), some on the door, etc. When their father came in through the door he was frightened, and when he sat down the snakes touched him on his head and back, so that he was almost scared to death. He ran out of the house. "Oh, my sons," he said, "you naughty boys, you just take them back where they belong." They did this. When their father went out hunting next morning, he told them not to go to a certain other place. "All right," they said, "we won't." But after he had gone, the younger one said, "Let's go." Said the other, "Where?" Said the younger, "Where our father said; you know he told us to go there." Said the other, "Oh, no, he told us not to go there." Said the younger, "Well, give me my scalp-lock; I'll go home, if you don't want to go." Said the other, "All right, I'll go with you." So they went to the place, a big high rock. "Well, grandmother," said the boys to the biggest rock there was there, "we have come after you. Come with us. We will 'pack' you on our backs. There is to be a great council, and every one must be there." "I will 'pack' you, grandmother," said the younger. "Very well, my grand-son," said the old rock. So he got it upon his back and carried it home. When he got home he couldn't get it off his back. And when their father came home in the evening, he found that one of the boys had a big rock on his back. "Why, my sons," said he, "what are you doing with your grandmother here? Take her back where she belongs." So they took her back where they got her, and the rock came off of itself. Next day when their father went off hunting as usual, he told them not to go to a certain place, where there was a white bull that no one could ever kill. "All right," they said. But as soon as he had gone, the younger son said, "Well, let's go now." Said the other, "Oh, no. Our father told us not to go." Said the younger, "Well, if you don't want to go, just give me my lock, and I'll go home to my grandmother." Said the other, "Well, all right; I'll go with you." So they went to the place. They never were without their bows and arrows, and when the white bull came after them, they just stood there, and kept shooting at him till they killed him. They skinned him and took the hide home. Then they stuffed it and set it before the door, where it looked very lifelike. When their father came home in the evening, and saw the wonderful thing standing before the door, he just ran for his life. But the boys called after him, telling him that the bull was dead. When he came back, he said, "Oh, my boys, how did you kill him? Didn't I tell you not to go there?" Said they, "We thought what a kind-looking creature he was, when you said nobody could kill him." Next morning when he went out hunting, he told them not to go to another certain place. But just as soon as he was off they went to the place and found three angels which they brought home. When their father came home in the evening and saw them, he scolded his sons, and told them to take the angels back where they belonged. This they did. By this time the father had got to be rather afraid of his sons, and thought he would run away from them. So next morning he got ready and went off. But the boys knew all the time what he was doing. He traveled all day until dark, when he thought he would lie down to sleep. So he tied his gun to a tree and lay down by a log and fell asleep. Next morning the boys woke him up, and said, "Why, father, what are you trying to do? Why didn't you lie in bed right and sleep better?" When he got up and looked around, he found himself sleeping right in the shanty by the fire-log, with his gun tied to the post inside the shanty. He tried three times in vain to get away. The fourth time he started off, he never slept any, but traveled day and night, and so got away. These boys were "regular devils," but they killed all the "devils" around them.

LITTLE HAIRY MAN
(Athabascan)

The Loucheux Indians once cached a quantity of meat, which the Polar Bear (So') discovered and began to eat. The people were unable to kill the animal themselves, so they called upon the Little Hairy Man. The bear came to rob the cache (tsi) at night, and the Little Man concealed himself in a tree to await the coming of the thief. The people were to give the Little Man a big knife if he killed the bear; he took this knife with him into the tree, and when the bear appeared he jumped down upon and easily killed it, thus gaining possession of the knife. The Little Man left the place, and continued his wanderings as usual. As he went along, he came upon two brothers who were separated from the rest of the tribe, so he asked them what they were doing. They replied that they were just traveling about, and in turn they asked the Little Man what he was doing. "I am wandering about also; let us journey together." The Little Man called one of his companions "Breaking Mountain" and the other "Breaking Sticks." They asked him what his name was, and he replied that he had no name, but that anything that they asked of him would be granted. They decided to call him Little Hairy Man. As they went along together, they came upon two deserted houses, which they occupied for a time. Little Man and Breaking Mountain went off to hunt and cut wood, while Breaking Sticks stayed at home to attend to the cooking. When the hunters returned they found no dinner cooked, but Breaking Sticks was lying in his blanket groaning. The following day Little Man and Breaking Sticks went out, leaving Breaking Mountain to take care of the camp, but as he repeated his brother's experience Little Man said, "You two go and cut wood and I will stay at home and get the dinner." As soon as they were gone a strange pigmy entered the house and said, "What are you doing here? Who gave you permission to stop here?" The stranger tried to whip Little Hairy Man, but the latter was too quick for him, snatched the whip away and drove the fellow out and into a hole under the other house. When the two brothers returned a dinner was awaiting them, and the Little Man said, "So that is what troubled you two. The pigmy gave you a whipping." "You must have caught it yourself today," they replied. "No, I whipped him and chased him into his burrow under the other building." After they had dined they went to examine the retreat of the mysterious stranger. By means of a strong cord and an old kettle, Breaking Mountain was lowered into the hole. He came back saying that he had seen a door at the bottom of the pit. Breaking Sticks next went down and reported the finding of the corpse of the pigmy. Little Hairy Man then went down, taking his big knife with him. He knocked on the door which he found and a voice answered, "Come in!" On entering he was met by a two-headed individual, who asked, "Are you the person who killed my son?" "Yes," replied the Little Hairy Man. At this the monster rushed upon him, and tried to kill him. Little Man succeeded in cutting off both the heads with his big knife. He then noticed another door to the apartment, on which he knocked, and received the invitation to enter as before. This time he was met by a creature with three heads, who asked the same question, and upon receiving an affirmative reply tried to kill him. Little Man overcame his opponent and chopped off his three heads. To this apartment there was a door, at which he knocked and entered to find a four-headed being, whom he killed after a severe struggle. Before him stood yet another door, through which he passed to find three pretty women. He was much pleased with the appearance of the prettiest one, who gave him a ring. He took them to the entrance, and sent them up one by one in the kettle. When it came the turn of the Little Man to be hauled out, Breaking Sticks, who thought Little Man would want all the women for his own wives, said, "Let us cut the line." "No," said Breaking Mountain, "he helps us very much, and does things which we cannot do." But before he had finished speaking his brother had cut the line, allowing the kettle to fall with the Little Hairy Man to the bottom of the shaft. A small dog that had belonged to the pigmy came and licked the wounds of Little Man, brought him bread, and finally showed him the way to escape. Little Man found that the brothers and the women whom he had rescued were gone, so he took his big knife and set off after them. As he was passing through some thick woods, he heard the sounds of a struggle, and soon came upon the dead body of a moose, *tĭng-ĭk,* over which a woodpecker, a wasp, and a little wood-worm were fighting. Little Man wished to settle their differences for them, so he divided the carcass, giving the meat to the wasp, the fat to the woodpecker, and the bones to the wood-worm. Then he started off, but the woodpecker flew after him, and called him back. They all thanked him, and told him if he ever got in trouble he might turn into a woodpecker, a wasp, or a little worm. He thanked them and went on his way. Little Man came to a big lake; to avoid the long journey around, he wished himself a woodpecker, and in that form flew out over the lake. When he was half way across he became very tired, and, seeing a stick of driftwood, wished to be a worm. He crawled into the stick, where he remained until he felt it strike against the shore. Then he came out and found a large quantity of fresh chips around him. He soon caught sight of a small house and wished to be transformed into a wasp. In this guise he entered the house and found the brothers and the three women inside. The girl whom he had chosen was cooking food. Little Man went back into the forest and resumed his natural shape, then he returned with his big knife to the house. He asked the girl what she was doing, and she said she was cooking. "May I help you?" "Yes," said she, after consulting her master. Little Hairy Man helped her place the food, and he arranged it in six portions. "Why do you set six places?" said she; "the cooks do not eat with their masters." But he replied, "We will eat with them this once to talk about old times." Her master said, "Very well." When they sat down to eat, he placed the ring she had given him beside the plate of his sweetheart, who recognized it at once, and turned pale as she concealed it. Breaking Mountain began to tell the story of their desertion of Little Man, and said he was sorry, because Little Man was so useful. Breaking Sticks laughed and said, "Well, I laughed when I heard the kettle rattling down, and the Little Man squealing." At this the Little Man jumped up and killed them all. Little Man left the house and went on his way again.

He found a small house in the forest, and on entering discovered a pretty woman in it. He asked her to marry him, but she said that she was married and her husband was away. She was afraid of her husband, and dared not run away with Little Man. He said, "I will kill him," but she declared that no one could do that. When the husband returned she asked him how any one could kill him, and he answered: "First, there is a mountain-lion; if you kill it, a bear will come from the carcass, then a wolf will come from the bear, a wolverine from the wolf, a rabbit from the wolverine, a partridge from the rabbit, an egg from the partridge: only by striking me on the forehead with that egg can you kill me." The next day, when the man was away, the woman told Little Hairy Man how he could kill her husband. He killed the mountain-lion and all the other animals, and obtained the egg, which he took to the woman. When her husband came home she wanted to hunt lice in his head; while his head was in her lap she struck him with the egg and killed him. She and Little Hairy Man were married and lived [happily] together.

THE BEAR MAIDEN
(Ojibwa)

There was an old man and woman who had three daughters, two older ones, and a younger one who was a little bear. The father and mother got very old and could not work any longer, so the two older daughters started away to find work in order to support themselves. They did not want their little sister to go with them, so they left her at home.

After a time they looked around, and saw the little Bear running to overtake them. They took her back home, and tied her to the door-posts of the wigwam, and again started away to find work; and again they heard something behind them, and saw the little Bear running toward them with the posts on her back. The sisters untied her from them and tied her to a large pine-tree. Then they continued on their journey. They heard a noise behind them once more, and turned around to find their younger sister, the little Bear, running to them with the pine-tree on her back. They did not want her to go with them, so they untied her from the pine-tree and fastened her to a huge rock, and continued on in search of work.

Soon they came to a wide river which they could not get across. As they sat there on the shore wondering how they could cross the river, they heard a noise coming toward them. They looked up and saw their younger sister running to them with the huge rock on her back. They untied the rock, threw it into the middle of the river, laid a pine-tree on it, and walked across. This time the little Bear went with them.

After a short journey they came to a wigwam where an old woman lived with her two daughters. This old woman asked them where they were going. They told her that their parents were old, and that they were seeking work in order to support themselves. She invited them in, gave them all supper, and after supper the two older sisters and the two daughters of the old woman went to sleep in the same bed.

The old woman and the little Bear sat up, and the little Bear told many stories to the old woman. At last they both appeared to fall asleep. The little Bear pinched the old woman, and finding her asleep went to the bed and changed the places of the four sleeping girls. She put the daughters of the old woman on the outside and her own sisters in the middle. Then she lay down as though asleep. After a short time the old woman awoke and pinched the little Bear to see whether she slept. She sharpened her knife and went to the bed and cut off the heads of the two girls at the outer edges of the bed. The old woman lay down and soon was sleeping. The little Bear awoke her sisters, and they all three crept away.

In the morning when the old woman got up and found that she had killed her two daughters, she was very angry. She jumped up into the sky, and tore down the sun and hid it in her wigwam, so that the little Bear and her sisters would get lost in the dark. They passed on and on, and at last met a man carrying a light. He said he was searching for the sun. They passed on, and soon came to a large village where all of the men were going around with lights. Their chief was sick because the sun had vanished.

He asked the little Bear whether she could bring back the sun. She said: "Yes, give me two handsful of maple-sugar and your oldest son." With the maple-sugar she went to the wigwam of the old woman, and, climbing up to the top, threw the sugar into a kettle of wild rice which the old woman was cooking. When the old woman tasted the rice she found it too sweet, so she went away to get some water to put in the kettle, and the little Bear jumped down, ran into the wigwam, grabbed up the hidden sun, and threw it into the sky. When the little Bear returned to the village, she gave the oldest son of the chief to her oldest sister for a husband.

The old woman was angry, very angry, to find that the sun was again up in the sky, so she jumped up and tore down the moon. The good old chief again became sick because the nights were all dark. He asked the little Bear whether she could bring back the moon. She said: "Yes, if you give me two handsful of salt and your next oldest son." She took the salt, climbed on top of the wigwam of the old woman, and threw it into her boiling kettle. Again the old woman had to go away for water. The little Bear then ran into the wigwam, and, catching up the moon, tossed it into the sky. The little Bear returned to the village and gave the chief's second son to her other sister.

Again the old chief got sick, and he asked the little Bear whether she could get him his lost horse which was all covered with bells. She answered: "Yes, give me two handsful of maple-sugar and your youngest son." The little Bear went to the old woman's wigwam, and, doing as she had done before, she made the old woman go away for water. She then slipped into the wigwam and began taking the bells from the horse which was there. She led the horse outside, but she had neglected to take off one bell. The old woman heard the bell, and ran and caught the little Bear. She put the bells all back onto the horse, and put the little Bear into a bag and tied the bag to a limb of a tree. When this was done she went far away to get a large club with which to break the little Bear's neck.

While she was gone the little Bear bit a hole in the bag and got down. This time she took all of the bells from the horse, and then she caught all of the dogs and pet animals of the old woman, and put them and her dishes into the bag, and tied it to the limb. Pretty soon the old woman returned with her large club, and she began to beat the bag furiously. The little Bear could see from her hiding-place, and could hear the animals and hear the dishes breaking as the old woman struck the bag.

When the little Bear took the horse to the chief, he gave her his youngest son. They lived close to the other two brothers and sisters. The little Bear's husband would not sleep with her, so she became very angry, and told him to throw her into the fire. Her sisters heard the noise, and came in to see what the matter was. The young man told them what their sister had ordered him to do. When they went away he turned toward the fire, and a beautiful, very beautiful maiden sprang out from the flames. Then this beautiful maiden would not sleep with her husband.

GUARDIAN OF THE COPPER MINE
(Slave)

Many years ago, a woman of the Yellow (or Red) Knife tribe got separated from her people and was left at the edge of the woods, from which the open lands stretch away to the north. She was found by a party of Inuits, who took her with them to the salt sea on the other side of the open country. Having reached the sea, they took her across it in a boat made of skins, to a country still farther away.

She was in that country for several winters, but became very tired of it, and longed to see her own people once more. One day in spring she was sitting on the shore looking south across the water and crying for her people. A friendly wolf came towards her, wagging its tail. "My poor woman," said the wolf, "why do you cry?" At the same time he licked the tears from her cheeks. She told him she wished to cross the sea, so that she might try to walk to her own tribe. "I can help you to do that," said the wolf. "But," the woman answered, "you have no boat." "Never mind, follow me," was the reply. She followed him along the shore for some distance, and then he commenced to wade out into the water. He knew the shallow places for crossing the sea. The woman found the water not too deep. In some parts it was not much above her ankles. She got safely to the south side, and the wolf returned by the way they had come. She then started to walk over the open country. After traveling thus all alone for two moons she came to a river and sat down upon its bank. Among the stones at her feet she saw some pieces of red metal. She selected a thin one and made it into a bracelet, which she polished till it looked very beautiful, and then put it upon her arm. She then continued her journey toward the south. For several days after leaving the place where she found the red metal she set up a stone for a mark here and there on the tops of the hills, so that if she ever came that way again she might be guided to the exact spot by these private marks.

She walked for many days more towards the south, and then saw some tipis which looked like those of her own people. Approaching them cautiously, so as not to be seen, she satisfied herself that the people living in the tipis belonged to her own tribe. She then entered one of the lodges, tired and hungry, and was well received. The occupants gave her food, and she then lay down and slept. When she awoke she found the women of the tipi examining the shining bracelet on her arm. They asked her where she had got it, and were told that she had made it herself from a piece of red metal picked up a long way off, but she said she would go with them to the place in the spring. When the winter had passed, a number of the men of the band proposed to go to the red metal mine, and when they started she accompanied them as guide. They traveled back in the direction in which she had come, and as they approached the place she recognized the private marks she had set up, but said nothing about them to the men.

They camped at the spot and gathered a number of pieces of the metal to take back with them, but before starting on the return journey they insulted her and treated her so badly that she refused to go back with them, but resolved to stay always at the mine in order to guard it. So she sat down upon it, and the men went away.

About ten years afterwards a second party of men came to the spot and found that about half of her body had sunk into the ground. Another ten years had passed before the Indians again visited the place. Only her head then remained above the surface. It was thirty or forty years after the first visit when the last party went there, and she had then sunk entirely out of sight, pressing the mine down beneath her. Since that time many have searched for the treasure, but none have found it, because it is buried.

The Man Who Called the Buffalo
(Pawnee)

This happened in the olden time before we had met the white people. Then the different bands lived in separate villages. The lodges were made of dirt. The Kit-ka-hahk'-i band went off on a winter hunt, roaming over the country, as they used to do, after buffalo. At this time they did not find the buffalo near. They scouted in all directions, but could discover no signs of them. It was a hard time of starvation. The children cried and the women cried; they had nothing at all to eat.

There was a person who looked at the children crying for something to eat, and it touched his heart. They were very poor, and he felt sorry for them. He said to the head chief: "Tell the chiefs and other head men to do what I tell them. My heart is sick on account of the suffering of the people. It may be that I can help them. Let a new lodge be set up outside the village for us to meet in. I will see if I can do anything to relieve the tribe." The chief said that it was well to do this, and he gave orders for it.

While they were preparing to build this lodge they would miss this man in the night. He would disappear like a wind, and go off a long way, and just as daylight came he would be there again. Sometimes, while sitting in his own lodge during the day, he would reach behind him, and bring out a small piece of buffalo meat, fat and lean, and would give it to some one, saying, "When you have had enough, save what is left, and give it to some one else." When he would give this small piece of meat to any one, the person would think, "This is not enough to satisfy my hunger;" but after eating until he was full, there was always enough left to give to some other person.

In those days it was the custom for the head chief of the tribe, once in a while, to mount his horse, and ride about through the village, talking to the people, and giving them good advice, and telling them that they ought to do what was right by each other. At this time the chief spoke to the people, and explained that this man was going to try to benefit the tribe. So the people made him many fine presents, otter skins and eagle feathers, and when they gave him these things each one said: "I give you this. It is for yourself. Try to help us." He thanked them for these presents, and when they were all gathered together he said: "Now you chiefs and head men of the tribe, and you people, you have done well to give me these things. I shall give them to that person who gives me that power, and who has taken pity on me. I shall let you starve yet four days. Then help will come."

During these four days, every day and night he disappeared, but would come back the same night. He would say to the people that he had been far off, where it would take a person three or four days to go, but he was always back the same night. When he got back on the fourth night, he told the people that the buffalo were near, that the next morning they would be but a little way off. He went up on the hill near the camp, and sacrificed some eagle feathers, and some blue beads, and some Indian tobacco, and then returned to the camp. Then he said to the people, "When that object comes to that place of sacrifice, do not interfere with it; do not turn it back. Let it go by. Just watch and see."

The next morning at daylight, all the people came out of their lodges to watch this hill, and the place where he had sacrificed. While they were looking, they saw a great buffalo bull come up over the hill to the place. He stood there for a short time and looked about, and then he walked on down the hill, and went galloping off past the village. Then this man spoke to the people and said, "There. That is what I meant. That is the leader of the buffalo; where he went the whole herd will follow."

He sent his servant to the chiefs to tell them to choose four boys, and let them go to the top of the hill where the bull had come over, and to look beyond it. The boys were sent, and ran to the top of the hill, and when they looked over beyond it they stopped, and then turned and came back running. They went to the chiefs' lodge and said to the chiefs, sitting there, "Beyond that place of sacrifice there is coming a whole herd of buffalo; many, many, crowding and pushing each other."

Then, as it used to be in the old times, as soon as the young men had told the chief that the buffalo were coming, the chief rode about the village, and told every one to get ready to chase them. He said to them besides: "Do not leave anything on the killing ground. Bring into the camp not only the meat and hides, but the heads and legs and all parts. Bring the best portions in first, and take them over to the new lodge, so that we may have a feast there." For so the man had directed.

Presently the buffalo came over the hill, and the people were ready, and they made a surround, and killed all that they could, and brought them home. Each man brought in his ribs and his young buffalo, and left them there at that lodge. The other parts they brought into the village, as he had directed. After they had brought in this meat, they went to the lodge, and stayed there four days and four nights, and had a great feast, roasting these ribs. The man told them that they would make four surrounds like this, and to get all the meat that they could. "But," he said, "in surrounding these buffalo you must see that all the meat is saved. Ti-ra'-wa does not like the people to waste the buffalo, and for that reason I advise you to make good use of all you kill." During the four nights they feasted, this man used to disappear each night.

On the night of the fourth day he said to the people: "Tomorrow the buffalo will come again, and you will make another surround. Be careful not to kill a yellow calf —a little one—that you will see with the herd, nor its mother." This was in winter, and yet the calf was the same color as a young calf born in the spring. They made the surround, and let the yellow calf and its mother go.

A good many men in the tribe saw that this man was great, and that he had done great things for the tribe, and they made him many presents, the best horses that they had. He thanked them, but he did not want to accept the presents. The tribe believed that he had done this wonderful thing,—had brought them buffalo,—and all the people wanted to do just what he told them to.

In the first two surrounds they killed many buffalo, and made much dried meat. All their sacks were full, and the dried meat was piled up out of doors. After the second surround, they feasted as before.

After four days, as they were going out to surround the buffalo the third time, the wind changed, and, before the people got near them, the buffalo smelled them and stampeded. While they were galloping away, the man ran up on to the top of the hill, to the place of sacrifice, carrying a pole, on which was tied the skin of a kit fox; and when he saw the buffalo running, and that the people could not catch them, he waved his pole, and called out *Ska-a-a-a!* and the buffalo turned right about, and charged back right through the people, and they killed many of them. He wished to show the people that he had the power over the buffalo.

After the third surround they had a great deal of meat, and he called the chiefs together and said, "Now, my chiefs, are you satisfied?" They said, "Yes, we are satisfied, and we are thankful to you for taking pity on us and helping us. It is through your power that the tribe has been saved from starving to death." He said: "You are to make one more surround, and that will be the end. I want you to get all you can. Kill as many as possible, for this will be the last of the buffalo this winter. Those presents that you have made to me, and that I did not wish to take, I give them back to you." Some of the people would not take back the presents, but insisted that he should keep them, and at last he said he would do so.

The fourth surround was made, and the people killed many buffalo and saved the meat. The night after this last surround he disappeared and drove the buffalo back. The next morning he told the people to look about, and tell him if they saw anything. They did so, but they could not see any buffalo.

The next day they moved camp, and went east toward their home. They had so much dried meat that they could not take it all at once, but had to come back and make two trips for it. When they moved below, going east, they saw no fresh meat, only dried meat; but sometimes, when this man would come in from his journeys, he would bring a piece of meat,—a little piece,—and he would divide it up among the people, and they would put it into the kettles and boil it, and everybody would eat, but they could not eat it all up. There would always be some left over. This man was so wonderful that he could change even the buffalo chips that you see on the prairie into meat. He would cover them up with his robe, and when he would take it off again, you would see there pounded buffalo meat and tallow (pemmican), *tŭp-o-haŕ ŭs.*

The man was not married; he was a young man, and by this time the people thought that he was one of the greatest men in the tribe, and they wanted him to marry. They went to one of the chiefs, and told him that they wanted him to be this man's father-in-law, for they wanted him to raise children, thinking that they might do something to benefit the tribe. They did not want that race to die out. The old people say that it would have been good if he had had children, but he had none. If he had, perhaps they would have had the same power as their father.

That person called the buffalo twice, and twice saved the tribe from a famine. The second time the suffering was great, and they held a council to ask him to help the tribe. They filled up the pipe, and held it out to him, asking him to take pity on the tribe. He took the pipe, and lighted it and smoked. He did it in the same way as the first time, and they made four surrounds, and got much meat.

When this man died, all the people mourned for him a long time. The chief would ride around the village and call out: "Now I am poor in mind on account of the death of this man, because he took pity on us and saved the tribe. Now he is gone and there is no one left like him."

This is a true and sacred story that belongs to the Kit-ka-hahk'-i band. It happened once long ago, and has been handed down from father to son in this band. The Skidi had a man who once called the buffalo, causing them to return when stampeded, as was done in this story.

SACRED OTTER

(Blackfoot)

Chill breezes had long forewarned the geese of the coming cold season, and the constant cry from above of "Honk, honk," told the Indians that the birds' migration was in progress.

The buffalo-hunters of the Blackfeet, an Algonquin tribe, were abroad with the object of procuring the thick robes and the rich meat which would keep them warm and provide good fare through the desolate winter moons. Sacred Otter had been lucky. Many buffaloes had fallen to him, and he was busily occupied in skinning them. But while the braves plied the knife quickly and deftly they heeded not the dun, lowering clouds heavy with tempest hanging like a black curtain over the northern horizon. Suddenly the clouds swooped down from their place in the heavens like a flight of black eagles, and with a roar the blizzard was upon them.

Sacred Otter and his son crouched beneath the carcass of a dead buffalo for shelter. But he knew that they would quickly perish unless they could find some better protection from the bitter wind. So he made a small tipi, or tent, out of the buffalo's hide, and both crawled inside. Against this crazy shelter the snow quickly gathered and drifted, so that soon the inmates of the tiny lodge sank into a comfortable drowse induced by the gentle warmth. As Sacred Otter slept he dreamed. Away in the distance he descried a great tipi, crowned with a color like the gold of sunlight, and painted with a cluster of stars symbolic of the North. The ruddy disc of the sun was pictured at the back, and to this was affixed the tail of the Sacred Buffalo. The skirts of the tipi were painted to represent ice, and on its side had been drawn four yellow legs with green claws, typical of the Thunder-bird. A buffalo in glaring red frowned above the door, and bunches of crow-feathers, with small bells attached, swung and tinkled in the breeze.

Sacred Otter, surprised at the unusual nature of the paintings, stood before the tipi lost in admiration of its decorations, when he was startled to hear a voice say:

"Who walks round my tipi? Come in—come in!"

Sacred Otter entered, and beheld a tall, white-haired man, clothed all in white, sitting at the back of the lodge, of which he was the sole occupant. Sacred Otter took a seat, but the owner of the tipi never looked his way, smoking on in stolid silence. Before him was an earthen altar, on which was laid juniper, as in the Sun ceremonial. His face was painted yellow, with a red line in the region of the mouth, and another across the eyes to the ears. Across his breast he wore a mink-skin, and round his waist small strips of otter-skin, to all of which bells were attached. For a long time he kept silence, but at length he laid down his black stone pipe and addressed Sacred Otter as follows:

"I am *Es-tonea-pesta,* the Lord of Cold Weather, and this, my dwelling, is the Snow-tipi, or Yellow Paint Lodge. I control and send the driving snow and biting winds from the Northland. You are here because I have taken pity upon you, and on your son who was caught in the blizzard with you. Take this Snow-tipi with its symbols and medicines. Take also this mink-skin tobacco-pouch, this black stone pipe, and my supernatural power. You must make a tipi similar to this on your return to camp."

The Lord of Cold Weather then minutely explained to Sacred Otter the symbols of which he must make use in painting the lodge, and gave him the songs and ceremonial connected with it. At this juncture Sacred Otter awoke. He observed that the storm had abated somewhat, and as soon as it grew fair enough he and his son crawled from their shelter and tramped home waist-high through the soft snow. Sacred Otter spent the long, cold nights in making a model of the Snow-tipi and painting it as he had been directed in his dream. He also collected the "medicines" necessary for the ceremonial, and in the spring, when new lodges were made, he built and painted the Snow-tipi.

The power of Sacred Otter waxed great because of his possession of the Snow-lodge which the Lord of Cold had vouchsafed to him in dream. Soon was it proved. Once more while hunting buffalo he and several companions were caught in a blizzard when many a weary mile from camp. They appealed to Sacred Otter to utilize the "medicine" of the Lord of Cold. Directing that several women and children who were with the party should be placed on sledges, and that the men should go in advance and break a passage through the snow for the horses, he took the mink tobacco-pouch and the black stone pipe he had received from the Cold-maker and commenced to smoke. He blew the smoke in the direction whence the storm came and prayed to the Lord of Cold to have pity on the people. Gradually the storm-clouds broke and cleared and on every side the blue sky was seen. The people hastened on, as they knew the blizzard was only being held back for a space. But their camp was at hand, and they soon reached it in safety.

Never again, however, would Sacred Otter use his mystic power. For he dreaded that he might offend the Lord of Cold. And who could afford to do that?

PAHUKATAWÁ
(Rees)

The following is a story of Pahukatawá as told by the Rees. The Pawnees started on the warpath, coming up toward the north. Pahukatawá was the leader. They got as far as the middle of the Black Hills, when a large party of the enemy came in sight, and rushed forward to attack them. Pahukatawá said to the people whom he was leading: "You go up on that hill there and I will stay here and fight them off." The others ran up on the high hill, but Pahukatawá remained below and fought the Cheyennes. After a long time they killed and scalped him, and cut off his arms and legs, and left him there and went away. While his people were still looking down from the hill, a cloud of fine white mist came down from the sky. It came lower and lower, until it reached the ground over the body, but it was only in that one place. After a time, the Pawnees came down from the hill and went to look for the body, but they could not find it, nor any part of it. The parts had come together, and had become alive, and Pahukatawá had gone away. They found the tracks where he had walked away, and they found a wet place where he had drunk, and the prints of his knees in the mud. Therefore they gave him that name *Pa-hu-ka-tawá,* Knee Print by the Water. Some claim that it was the night and the stars, the moon and thunder that made him strong to get up. His body is supposed to have gone up above.

MIK-A'PI
(Blackfoot)

It was in the valley of "It fell on them" Creek, near the mountains, that the Pikŭn'i were camped when Mik-a'pi went to war. It was far back, in the days of stone knives, long before the white people had come. This was the way it happened.

Early in the morning a band of buffalo were seen in the foot-hills of the mountains, and some hunters went out to get meat. Carefully they crawled along up the coulées and drew near to the herd; and, when they had come close to them, they began to shoot, and their arrows pierced many fat cows. But even while they were thus shooting, they were surprised by a war party of Snakes, and they began to run back toward the camp. There was one hunter, named Fox-eye, who was very brave. He called to the others to stop, saying: "They are many and we are few, but the Snakes are not brave. Let us stop and fight them." But the other hunters would not listen. "We have no shields," they said, "nor our war medicine. There are many of the enemy. Why should we foolishly die?"

They hurried on to camp, but Fox-eye would not turn back. He drew his arrows from the quiver, and prepared to fight. But, even as he placed an arrow, a Snake had crawled up by his side, unseen. In the still air, the Piegan heard the sharp twang of a bow string, but, before he could turn his head, the long, fine-pointed arrow pierced him through and through. The bow and arrows dropped from his hands, he swayed, and then fell forward on the grass, dead. But now the warriors came pouring from the camp to aid him. Too late! The Snakes quickly scalped their fallen enemy, scattered up the mountain, and were lost to sight.

Now Fox-eye had two wives, and their father and mother and all their near relations were dead. All Fox-eye's relatives, too, had long since gone to the Sand Hills. So these poor widows had no one to avenge them, and they mourned deeply for the husband so suddenly taken from them. Through the long days they sat on a near hill and mourned, and their mourning was very sad.

There was a young warrior named Mik-a'pi. Every morning he was awakened by the crying of these poor widows, and through the day his heart was touched by their wailing. Even when he went to rest, their mournful cries reached him through the darkness, and he could not sleep. So he sent his mother to them. "Tell them," he said, "that I wish to speak to them." When they had entered, they sat close by the doorway, and covered their heads.

"Kyi!" said Mik-a'pi. "For days and nights I have heard your mourning, and I too have silently mourned. My heart has been very sad. Your husband was my near friend, and now he is dead and no relations are left to avenge him. So now, I say, I will take the load from your hearts. I will avenge him. I will go to war and take many scalps, and when I return, they shall be yours. You shall paint your faces black, and we will all rejoice that Fox-eye is avenged."

When the people heard that Mik-a'pi was going to war, many warriors wished to join him, but he refused them; and when he had taken a medicine sweat, and got a medicine-pipe man to make medicine for him during his absence, he started from the camp one evening, just after sunset. It is only the foolish warrior who travels in the day; for other war parties may be out, or some camp-watcher sitting on a hill may see him from far off, and lay plans to destroy him. Mik-a'pi was not one of these. He was brave but cautious, and he had strong medicine. Some say that he was related to the ghosts, and that they helped him. Having now started to war against the Snakes, he traveled in hidden places, and at sunrise would climb a hill and look carefully in all directions, and during the long day would lie there, and watch, and take short sleeps.

Now, when Mik-a'pi had come to the Great Falls (of the Missouri), a heavy rain set in; and, seeing a hole in the rocks, he crawled in and lay down in the farther end to sleep. The rain did not cease, and when night came he could not travel because of the darkness and storm; so he lay down to sleep again. But soon he heard something coming into the cave toward him, and then he felt a hand laid on his breast, and he put out his hand and touched a person. Then Mik-a'pi put the palm of his hand on the person's breast and jerked it to and fro, and then he touched the person with the point of his finger, which, in the sign language, means, "Who are you?"

The strange person then took Mik-a'pi's hand, and made him feel of his own right hand. The thumb and all the fingers were closed except the forefinger, which was extended; and when Mik-a'pi touched it the person moved his hand forward with a zigzag motion, which means "Snake." Then Mik-a'pi was glad. Here had come to him one of the tribe he was seeking. But he thought it best to wait for daylight before attacking him. So, when the Snake in signs asked him who he was, he replied, by making the sign for paddling a canoe, that he was a Pend d'Oreille, or River person. For he knew that the Snakes and the Pend d'Oreilles were at peace.

Then they both lay down to sleep, but Mik-a'pi did not sleep. Through the long night he watched for the first dim light, so that he might kill his enemy. The Snake slept soundly; and just at daybreak Mik-a'pi quietly strung his bow, fitted an arrow, and, taking aim, sent the thin shaft through his enemy's heart. The Snake quivered, half rose up, and with a groan fell back dead. Then Mik-a'pi took his scalp and his bow and arrows, and also his bundle of moccasins; and as daylight had come, he went out of the cave and looked all about. No one was in sight. Probably the Snake, like himself, had gone alone to war. But, ever cautious, he traveled only a short distance, and waited for night before going on. The rain had ceased and the day was warm. He took a piece of dried meat and back fat from his pouch and ate them, and, after drinking from the river, he climbed up on a high rock wall and slept.

Now in his dream he fought with a strange people, and was wounded. He felt blood trickling from his wounds, and when he awoke, he knew that he had been warned to turn back. The signs also were bad. He saw an eagle rising with a snake, which dropped from its claws and escaped. The setting sun, too, was painted,—a sure warning to people that danger is near. But, in spite of all these things, Mik-a'pi determined to go on. He thought of the poor widows mourning and waiting for revenge. He thought of the glad welcome of the people, if he should return with many scalps; and he thought also of two young sisters, whom he wanted to marry. Surely, if he could return and bring the proofs of brave deeds, their parents would be glad to give them to him.

It was nearly night. The sun had already disappeared behind the sharp-pointed gray peaks. In the fading light the far-stretching prairie was turning dark. In a valley, sparsely timbered with quaking aspens and cotton-woods, stood a large camp. For a long distance up and down the river rose the smoke of many lodges. Seated on a little hill overlooking the valley, was a single person. With his robe drawn tightly around him, he sat there motionless, looking down on the prairie and valley below.

Slowly and silently something was crawling through the grass toward him. But he heard nothing. Still he gazed eastward, seeking to discover any enemy who might be approaching. Still the dark object crawled slowly onward. Now it was so close to him that it could almost touch him. The person thought he heard a sound, and started to turn round. Too late! Too late! A strong arm grasped him about the neck and covered his mouth. A long jagged knife was thrust into his breast again and again, and he died without a cry. Strange that in all that great camp no one should have seen him killed!

Still extended on the ground, the dark figure removed the scalp. Slowly he crawled back down the hill, and was lost in the gathering darkness. It was Mik-a'pi, and he had another Snake scalp tied to his belt. His heart was glad, yet he was not satisfied. Some nights had passed since the bad signs had warned him, yet he had succeeded. "One more," he said. "One more scalp I must have, and then I will go back." So he went far up on the mountain, and hid in some thick pines and slept.

When daylight came, he could see smoke rise as the women started their fires. He also saw many people rush up on the hill, where the dead watcher lay. He was too far off to hear their angry shouts and mournful cries, but he sung to himself a song of war and was happy.

Once more the sun went to his lodge behind the mountains, and as darkness came Mik-a'pi slowly descended the mountain and approached the camp. This was the time of danger. Behind each bush, or hidden in a bunch of the tall rye grass, some person might be watching to warn the camp of an approaching enemy. Slowly and like a snake, he crawled around the outskirts of the camp, listening and looking. He heard a cough and saw a movement of a bush. There was a Snake. Could he kill him and yet escape? He was close to him now. So he sat and waited, considering how to act. For a long time he sat there waiting. The moon rose and traveled high in the sky. The Seven Persons slowly swung around, and pointed downward. It was the middle of the night. Then the person in the bush stood up and stretched out his arms and yawned, for he was tired of watching, and thought that no danger was near; but as he stood thus, an arrow pierced his breast. He gave a loud yell and tried to run, but another arrow struck him and he fell.

At the sound the warriors rushed forth from the lodges and the outskirts of the camp; but as they came, Mik-a'pi tore the scalp from his fallen enemy, and started to run toward the river. Close behind him followed the Snakes. Arrows whizzed about him. One pierced his arm. He plucked it out. Another struck his leg, and he fell. Then a great shout arose from the Snakes. Their enemy was down. Now they would be revenged for two lately taken lives. But where Mik-a'pi fell was the verge of a high rock wall; below rushed the deep river, and even as they shouted, he rolled from the wall, and disappeared in the dark water far below. In vain they searched the shores and bars. They did not find him.

Mik-a'pi had sunk deep in the water. The current was swift, and when at last he rose to the surface, he was far below his pursuers. The arrow in his leg pained him, and with difficulty he crawled out on a sand-bar. Luckily the arrow was lance-shaped instead of barbed, so he managed to draw it out. Near by on the bar was a dry pine log, lodged there by the high spring water. This he managed to roll into the stream; and, partly resting on it, he again drifted down with the current. All night he floated down the river, and when morning came he was far from the camp of the Snakes. Benumbed with cold and stiff from the arrow wounds, he was glad to crawl out on the bank, and lie down in the warm sunshine. Soon he slept.

The sun was already in the middle when he awoke. His wounds were swollen and painful; yet he hobbled on for a time, until the pain became so great he could go no further, and he sat down, tired and discouraged.

"True the signs," he said. "How crazy I was to go against them! Useless now my bravery, for here I must stay and die. The widows will still mourn; and in their old age who will take care of my father and my mother? Pity me now, oh Sun! Help me, oh great Above Medicine Person! Look down on your wounded and suffering child. Help me to survive!"

What was that crackling in the brush near by? Was it the Snakes on his trail?

Mik-a'pi strung his bow and drew out his arrows. No; it was not a Snake. It was a bear. There he stood, a big grizzly bear, looking down at the wounded man. "What does my brother here?" he said. "Why does he pray to survive?"

"Look at my leg," said Mik-a'pi, "swollen and sore. Look at my wounded arm. I can hardly draw the bow. Far the home of my people, and my strength is gone. Surely here I must die, for I cannot travel and I have no food."

"Now courage, my brother," said the bear. "Now not faint heart, my brother, for I will help you, and you shall survive."

When he had said this, he lifted Mik-a'pi and carried him to a place of thick mud; and here he took great handfuls of the mud and plastered the wounds, and he sung a medicine song while putting on the mud. Then he carried Mik-a'pi to a place where were many sarvis berries, and broke off great branches of the fruit, and gave them to him, saying, "Eat, my brother, eat!" and he broke off more branches, full of large ripe berries, for him; but already Mik-a'pi was satisfied and could eat no more. Then said the bear, "Lie down, now, on my back, and hold tight by my hair, and we will travel on." And when Mik-a'pi had got on and was ready, he started off on a long swinging trot.

All through the night he traveled on without stopping. When morning came, they rested awhile, and ate more berries; and again the bear plastered his wounds with mud. In this way they traveled on, until, on the fourth day, they came close to the lodges of the Piku̇n'i; and the people saw them coming and wondered.

"Get off, my brother, get off," said the bear. "There are your people. I must leave you." And without another word, he turned and went off up the mountain.

All the people came out to meet the warrior, and they carried him to the lodge of his father. He untied the three scalps from his belt and gave them to the widows, saying: "You are revenged. I wipe away your tears." And every one rejoiced. All his female relations went through the camp, shouting his name and singing, and every one prepared for the scalp dance.

First came the widows. Their faces were painted black, and they carried the scalps tied on poles. Then came the medicine men, with their medicine pipes unwrapped; then the bands of the I-kun-uh'-kah-tsi, all dressed in war costume; then came the old men; and last the women and children. They all sang the war song and danced. They went all through the village in single file, stopping here and there to dance, and Mik-a'pi sat outside the lodge, and saw all the people dance by him. He forgot his pain and was proud, and although he could not dance, he sang with them.

Soon they made the Medicine Lodge, and, first of all the warriors, Mik-a'pi was chosen to cut the raw-hide which binds the poles, and as he cut the strands, he counted the coups he had made. He told of the enemies he had killed, and all the people shouted his name and praised him. The father of those two young sisters gave them to him. He was glad to have such a son-in-law. Long lived Mik-a'pi. Of all the great chiefs who have lived and died, he was the greatest. He did many other great and daring things. It must be true, as the old men have said, that he was helped by the ghosts, for no one can do such things without help from those fearful and unknown persons.

E-KŪS-KINI

(Blackfoot)

Many years ago there lived in the Blood camp a boy named Screech Owl (*A'-tsi-tsi*). He was rather a lonely boy, and did not care to go with other boys. He liked better to be by himself. Often he would go off alone, and stay out all night away from the camp. He used to pray to all kinds of birds and animals that he saw, and ask them to take pity on him and help him, saying that he wanted to be a warrior. He never used paint. He was a fine looking young man, and he thought it was foolish to use paint to make oneself good looking.

When Screech Owl was about fourteen years old, a large party of Blackfeet were starting to war against the Crees and the Assinaboines. The young man said to his father: "Father, with this war party many of my cousins are going. I think that now I am old enough to go to war, and I would like to join them." His father said, "My son, I am willing; you may go." So he joined the party.

His father gave his son his own war horse, a black horse with a white spot on its side—a very fast horse. He offered him arms, but the boy refused them all, except a little trapping axe. He said, "I think this hatchet will be all that I shall need." Just as they were about to start, his father gave the boy his own war headdress. This was not a war bonnet, but a plume made of small feathers, the feathers of thunder birds, for the thunder bird was his father's medicine. He said to the boy, "Now, my son, when you go into battle, put this plume in your head, and wear it as I have worn it."

The party started and traveled north-east, and at length they came to where Fort Pitt now stands, on the Saskatchewan River. When they had got down below Fort Pitt, they saw three riders, going out hunting. These men had not seen the war party. The Blackfeet started around the men, so as to head them off when they should run. When they saw the men, the Screech Owl got off his horse, and took off all his clothes, and put on his father's war plume, and began to ride around, singing his father's war song. The older warriors were getting ready for the attack, and when they saw this young boy acting in this way, they thought he was making fun of the older men, and they said: "Here, look at this boy! Has he no shame? He had better stay behind." When they got on their horses, they told him to stay behind, and they charged the Crees. But the boy, instead of staying behind, charged with them, and took the lead, for he had the best horse of all. He, a boy, was leading the war party, and still singing his war song.

The three Crees began to run, and the boy kept gaining on them. They did not want to separate, they kept together; and as the boy was getting closer and closer, the last one turned in his saddle and shot at the Screech Owl, but missed him. As the Cree fired, the boy whipped up his horse, and rode up beside the Cree and struck him with his little trapping axe, and knocked him off his horse. He paid no attention to the man that he had struck, but rode on to the next Cree. As he came up with him, the Cree raised his gun and fired, but just as he did so, the Blackfoot dropped down on the other side of his horse, and the ball passed over him. He straightened up on his horse, rode up by the Cree, and as he passed, knocked him off his horse with his axe. When he knocked the second Cree off his horse, the Blackfeet, who were following, whooped in triumph and to encourage him, shouting, *"A-wah-heh'"* (Take courage). The boy was still singing his father's war song.

By this time, the main body of the Blackfeet were catching up with him. He whipped his horse on both sides, and rode on after the third Cree, who was also whipping his horse as hard as he could, and trying to get away. Meantime, some of the Blackfeet had stopped to count coup on and scalp the two dead Crees, and to catch the two ponies. Screech Owl at last got near to the third Cree, who kept aiming his gun at him. The boy did not want to get too close, until the Cree had fired his gun, but he was gaining a little, and all the time was throwing himself from side to side on his horse, so as to make it harder for the Cree to hit him. When he had nearly overtaken the enemy, the Cree turned, raised his gun and fired; but the boy had thrown himself down behind his horse, and again the ball passed over him. He raised himself up on his horse, and rushed on the Cree, and struck him in the side of the body with his axe, and then again, and with the second blow, he knocked him off his horse.

The boy rode on a little further, stopped, and jumped off his horse, while the rest of the Blackfeet had come up and were killing the fallen man. He stood off to one side and watched them count coup on and scalp the dead.

The Blackfeet were much surprised at what the young man had done. After a little while, the leader decided that they would go back to the camp from which they had come. When he had returned from this war journey this young man's name was changed from A'-tsi-tsi to *E-kūs'-kini* (Low Horn). This was his first war path.

From that time on the name of E-kūs'-kini was often heard as that of one doing some great deed.

E-kūs'-kini started on his last war trail from the Blackfoot crossing (*Su-yoh-pah'-wah-ku*). He led a party of six Sarcees. He was the seventh man.

On the second day out, they came to the Red Deer's River. When they reached this river, they found it very high, so they built a raft to cross on. They camped on the other side. In crossing, most of their powder got wet. The next morning, when they awoke, E-kūs'-kini said: "Well, trouble is coming for us. We had better go back from here. We started on a wrong day. I saw in my sleep our bodies lying on the prairie, dead." Some of the young men said: "Oh well, we have started, we had better go on. Perhaps it is only a mistake. Let us go on and try to take some horses anyhow." E-kūs'-kini said: "Yes, that is very true. To go home is all foolishness; but remember that it is by your wish that we are going on." He wanted to go back, not on his own account, but for the sake of his young men—to save his followers.

From there they went on and made another camp, and the next morning he said to his young men: "Now I am sure. I have seen it for certain. Trouble is before us." They camped two nights at this place and dried some of their powder, but most of it was caked and spoilt. He said to his young men: "Here, let us use some sense about this. We have no ammunition. We cannot defend ourselves. Let us turn back from here." So they started across the country for their camp.

They crossed the Red Deer's River, and there camped again. The next morning E-kūs'-kini said: "I feel very uneasy to-day. Two of you go ahead on the trail and keep a close lookout. I am afraid that today we are going to see our enemy." Two of the young men went ahead, and when they had climbed to the top of a ridge and looked over it on to Sarvis Berry (*Saskatoon*) Creek, they came back and told E-kūs'-kini that they had seen a large camp of people over there, and that they thought it was the Piegans, Bloods, Blackfeet, and Sarcees, who had all moved over there together. Saskatoon Creek was about twenty miles from the Blackfoot camp. He said: "No, it cannot be our people. They said nothing about moving over here; it must be a war party. It is only a few days since we left, and there was then no talk of their leaving that camp. It cannot be they." The two young men said: "Yes, they are our people. There are too many of them for a war party. We think that the whole camp is there." They discussed this for some little time, E-kūs'-kini insisting that it could not be the Blackfoot camp, while the young men felt sure that it was. These two men said, "Well, we are going on into the camp now." Low Horn said: "Well, you may go. Tell my father that I will come into the camp tonight. I do not like to go in in the daytime, when I am not bringing back anything with me."

It was now late in the afternoon, and the two young men went ahead toward the camp, traveling on slowly. A little after sundown, they came down the hill on to the flat of the river, and saw there the camp. They walked down toward it, to the edge of the stream, and there met two women, who had come down after water. The men spoke to them in Sarcee, and said, "Where is the Sarcee camp?" The women did not understand them, so they spoke again, and asked the same question in Black-foot. Then these two women called out in the Cree language, "Here are two Black-feet, who have come here and are talking to us." When these men heard the women talk Cree, and saw what a mistake they had made, they turned and ran away up the creek. They ran up above camp a short distance, to a place where a few willow bushes were hanging over the stream, and pushing through these, they hid under the bank, and the willows above concealed them. The people in the camp came rushing out, and men ran up the creek, and down, and looked everywhere for the two enemies, but could find nothing of them.

Now when these people were running in all directions, hunting for these two men, E-kūs'-kini was coming down the valley slowly with the four other Sarcees. He saw some Indians coming toward him, and supposed that they were some of his own people, coming to meet him, with horses for him to ride. At length, when they were close to him, and E-kūs'-kini could see that they were the enemy, and were taking the covers off their guns, he jumped to one side and stood alone and began to sing his war song. He called out, "Children of the Crees, if you have come to try my manhood, do your best." In a moment or two he was surrounded, and they were shooting at him from all directions. He called out again, "People, you can't kill me here, but I will take my body to your camp, and there you shall kill me." So he advanced, fighting his way toward the Cree camp, but before he started, he killed two of the Crees there. His enemies kept coming up and clustering about him: some were on foot and some on horseback. They were thick about him on all sides, and they could not shoot much at him, for fear of killing their own people on the other side.

One of the Sarcees fell. E-kūs'-kini said to his men, *"A-wah-heh'"* (Take courage). "These people cannot kill us here. Where that patch of choke-cherry brush is, in the very center of their camp, we will go and take our stand." Another Sarcee fell, and now there were only three of them. E-kūs'-kini said to his remaining men: "Go straight to that patch of brush, and I will fight the enemy off in front and at the sides, and so will keep the way open for you. These people cannot kill us here. There are too many of their own people. If we can get to that brush, we will hurt them badly." All this time they were killing enemies, fighting bravely, and singing their war songs. At last they gained the patch of brush, and then with their knives they began to dig holes in the ground, and to throw up a shelter.

In the Cree camp was *Kŏm-in'-ă-kūs* (Round), the chief of the Crees, who could talk Blackfoot well. He called out: "E-kūs'-kini, there is a little ravine running out of that brush patch, which puts into the hills. Crawl out through that, and try to get away. It is not guarded." E-kūs'-kini replied: "No, Children of the Crees, I will not go. You must remember that it is E-kūs'-kini that you are fighting with—a man who has done much harm to your people. I am glad that I am here. I am sorry for only one thing; that is, that my ammunition is going to run out. Tomorrow you may kill me."

All night long the fight was kept up, the enemy shooting all the time, and all night long E-kūs'-kini sang his death song. Kŏm-in'-ă-kūs called to him several times: "E-kūs'-kini, you had better do what I tell you. Try to get away." But he shouted back, "No," and laughed at them. He said: "You have killed all my men. I am here alone, but you cannot kill me." Kŏm-in'-ă-kūs, the chief, said: "Well, if you are there at daylight in the morning, I will go into that brush and will catch you with my hands. I will be the man who will put an end to you." E-kūs'-kini said: "Kŏm-in'-ă-kūs, do not try to do that. If you do, you shall surely die." The patch of brush in which he had hidden had now been all shot away, cut off by the bullets of the enemy.

When day came, E-kūs'-kini called out: "Eh, Kŏm-in'-ă-kūs, it is broad daylight now. I have run out of ammunition. I have not another grain of powder in my horn. Now come and take me in your hands, as you said you would." Kŏm-in'-ă-kūs answered: "Yes, I said that I was the one who was going to catch you this morning. Now I am coming."

He took off all his clothes, and alone rushed for the breastworks. E-kūs'-kini's ammunition was all gone, but he still had one load in his gun, and his dagger. Kŏm-in'-ă-kūs came on with his gun at his shoulder, and E-kūs'-kini sat there with his gun in his hand, looking at the man who was coming toward him with the cocked gun pointed at him. He was singing his death song. As Kŏm-in'-ă-kūs got up close, and just as he was about to fire, E-kūs'-kini threw up his gun and fired, and the ball knocked off the Cree chief's forefinger, and going on, entered his right eye and came out at the temple, knocking the eye out. Kŏm-in′-ă-kūs went down, and his gun flew a long way.

When Kŏm-in′-ă-kūs fell, the whole camp shouted the war whoop, and cried out, "This is his last shot," and they all charged on him. They knew that he had no more ammunition.

The head warrior of the Crees was named Bunch of Lodges. He was the first man to jump inside the breastworks. As he sprang inside, E-kūs′-kini met him, and thrust his dagger through him, and killed him on the spot. Then, as the enemy threw themselves on him, and he began to feel the knives stuck into him from all sides, he gave a war whoop and laughed, and said, "Only now I begin to think that I am fighting." All the time he was cutting and stabbing, jumping backward and forward, and all the time laughing. When he was dead, there were fifteen dead Crees lying about the earthworks. E-kūs′-kini's body was cut into small pieces and scattered all over the country, so that he might not come to life again.

That morning, before it was daylight, the two Sarcees who had hidden in the willows left their hiding-place and made their way to the Blackfoot camp. When they got there, they told that when they had left the Cree camp E-kūs′-kini was surrounded, and the firing was terrible. When E-kūs′-kini's father heard this, he got on his horse and rode through the camp, calling out: "My boy is surrounded; let us turn out and go to help him. I have no doubt they are many tens to one, but he is powerful, and he may be fighting yet." No time was lost in getting ready, and soon a large party started for the Cree camp. When they came to the battle-ground, the camp had been moved a long time. The old man looked about, trying to gather up his son's body, but it was found only in small pieces, and not more than half of it could be gathered up.

After the fight was over, the Crees started on down to go to their own country. One day six Crees were traveling along on foot, scouting far ahead. As they were going down into a little ravine, a grizzly bear jumped up in front of them and ran after them. The bear overtook, and tore up, five of them, one after another. The sixth got away, and came home to camp. The Crees and the Blackfeet believe that this was the spirit of E-kūs′-kini, for thus he comes back. They think that he is still on the earth, but in a different shape.

When he was killed, he was still a boy, not married, only about twenty-four years old.

LITTLE WARRIOR
(Pawnee)

Most of the Pawnee heroes are so regarded because of victories, daring deeds, the coups they have counted and the horses they have stolen. The glory of Comanche Chief and of Lone Chief depends mainly on their bravery, rather than on the fact that they were peace-makers. Yet there should be room among these stories for the account of an educated Pawnee—a brave—who by his wise counsel to an Indian of a hostile tribe saved many lives, both of Indians and of white men.

Little Warrior was educated at a Western college, but has shown his bravery on the field of battle, and has sacrificed a scalp to Ti-ra'-wa.

In the year 1879, at the time of the Ute outbreak, after Major Thornburgh's command had been annihilated, Little Warrior was employed as a scout for the troops. On the headwaters of the Arkansas River he was one day scouting in advance of the command, in company with four white soldiers and four Indian scouts. One day, the party saw far off on the prairie an Indian, who showed a white flag, and came toward them. When he had come near to them, the soldiers proposed to kill him, and report that he was a Ute, one of the Indians that they were looking for. But Little Warrior said, "No. He has a white flag up, and it may be that he is carrying a dispatch, or, perhaps, he is a white man disguised as an Indian."

When the man had come close to them, they saw that he was dressed like a Comanche; he did not have the bristling fringe of hair over the forehead that the Utes wear, and his side locks were unbraided. Little Warrior asked him, by signs, if he was alone, to which he replied in the same language that he was alone. Then Little Warrior inquired who he was. The stranger made the sign for Comanche—a friendly tribe.

They took him into the camp, and after a while Little Warrior began to talk to him in Comanche. He could not understand a word of it.

Then the Pawnee said to him, "My friend, you are a Ute." The stranger acknowledged that he was.

Then Little Warrior talked to him, and gave him much good advice. He said, "My friend, you and I have the same skin, and what I tell you now is for your good. I speak to you as a friend, and what I say to you now is so that you may save your women and your children. It is of no use for you to try to fight the white people. I have been among them, and I know how many they are. They are like the grass. Even if you were to kill a hundred it would be nothing. It would be like burning up a few handfuls of prairie grass. There would be just as many left. If you try to fight them they will hunt you like a ghost. Wherever you go they will follow after you, and you will get no rest. The soldiers will be continually on your tracks. Even if you were to go up on top of a high mountain, where there was nothing but rocks, and where no one else could come, the soldiers would follow you, and get around you, and wait, and wait, even for fifty years. They would have plenty to eat, and they could wait until after you were dead. There is one white man who is the chief of all this country, and what he says must be done. It is no use to fight him.

"Now if you are wise you will go out and get all your people, and bring them in, on to the reservation, and give yourself up. It will be better for you in the end. I speak to you as a friend, because we are both the same color, and I hope that you will listen to my words."

The Ute said, "My friend, your words are good, and I thank you for the friendly advice you have given me. I will follow it and will agree to go away and bring in my people."

Little Warrior said, "How do you make a promise?"

The Ute said, "By raising the right hand to one above."

Little Warrior said, "That is the custom also among my people."

The Ute raised his hand and made the promise.

After he had been detained two or three weeks, he was allowed to go, and about a month afterward, he brought in the band of which he was chief, and surrendered. Through his influence afterward, the whole tribe came in and gave themselves up. He was grateful to Little Warrior for what he had done for him, and told him that if he ever came back into his country he would give him many ponies.

LONE CHIEF
(Pawnee)

Lone Chief was the son of the chief of the Kit-ke-hahk'-i band. His father died when the boy was very young, less than a year old. Until he was old enough to go to war, his mother had supported him by farming—raising corn, beans and pumpkins. She taught the boy many things, and advised him how to live and how to act so that he might be successful. She used to say to him, "You must trust always in Ti-ra'-wa. He made us, and through him we live. When you grow up, you must be a man. Be brave, and face whatever danger may meet you. Do not forget, when you look back to your young days, that I have raised you, and always supported you. You had no father to do it. Your father was a chief, but you must not think of that. Because he was a chief, it does not follow that you will be one. It is not the man who stays in the lodge that becomes great; it is the man who works, who sweats, who is always tired from going on the warpath."

Much good advice his mother gave him. She said, "When you get to be a man, remember that it is his ambition that makes the man. If you go on the warpath, do not turn around when you have gone part way, but go on as far as you were going, and then come back. If I should live to see you become a man, I want you to become a great man. I want you to think about the hard times we have been through. Take pity on people who are poor, because we have been poor, and people have taken pity on us. If I live to see you a man, and to go off on the warpath, I would not cry if I were to hear that you had been killed in battle. That is what makes a man: to fight and to be brave. I should be sorry to see you die from sickness. If you are killed, I would rather have you die in the open air, so that the birds of the air will eat your flesh, and the wind will breathe on you and blow over your bones. It is better to be killed in the open air than to be smothered in the earth. Love your friend and never desert him. If you see him surrounded by the enemy, do not run away. Go to him, and if you cannot save him, be killed together, and let your bones lie side by side. Be killed on a hill; high up. Your grandfather said it is not manly to be killed in a hollow. It is not a man who is talking to you, advising you. Heed my words, even if I am a woman."

The boy listened to these words, and he did not forget them.

In the year 1867 he enlisted in the Pawnee Scouts under Major Frank North, and served in L. H. North's company. He was always a good soldier, ready, willing and brave. At a fight near the Cheyenne Pass in 1867, he counted coup on a woman and a man, Arapahoes who had stolen some horses at Fort Laramie.

At this time the boy's name was *Wi-ti-ti le-shar'-uspi*, Running Chief. After he came back from this scout, he went on a war party of which Left Hand was the leader, and they went to the Osage country. He was no longer a servant, but a scout, a leading man in the party, one of those who went ahead as spies. He had good judgment and understood his duties. When they came to the Osage country, he was selected as one of the leaders of a small branch party to steal horses. His party took thirty head of horses. In the Osage country the young men were not allowed to take all the horses they could. On account of the few fords where they could cross the streams, they could not take a big herd, but only what they could ride and lead, and at the same time go fast. Across one river there was only one rocky ford, and over another stream with deep banks there was only one rocky ford where they could cross. Because they did not know this, in former times many Pawnees had been caught and killed in the Osage country: So now they took but few horses at a time, because these rivers were very deep and no one could cross them except at these rock fords. Out of the horses taken at this time Running Chief obtained one of the best and fastest ever known among the Pawnees—a cream-colored horse, long famous in the tribe. For his skillful leadership of this party he was given much credit.

After returning home—the same year—he led a party to go off on the warpath to the Cheyennes. He found a camp on the headwaters of the North Canadian, and his party took seven horses, but these horses looked thin and rough, and he was not satisfied with them; he was ashamed to go home with only these. He told his party to take them home, but that he was going off by himself to get some better ones. He had with him a friend, with whom he had grown up, and whom he loved. This young man was like a brother to Running Chief. These two went off together, and went to the Osage camp, and stayed about it for three nights, and then took five horses, the best in the camp. They took them back to the village. It was customary for the leading man in a party to make a sacrifice to Ti-ra'-wa. Running Chief did this, giving one horse to the chief priest. This sacrifice promoted him to be a warrior.

The next year he led a party again to the Osage country. He took some horses and brought them home. This same year (1868) a party started south. He was not the leader, but he went with them. They went to the Wichita, Comanche and Kiowa villages—they were all camped together—stole some horses and started back with them. Before they had gone very far Running Chief stopped and said he was going back. His friend was with the party, and when he found that Running Chief had resolved to go back he said, "I will stop here with you."

The two went back toward the village that they had just left, and climbed a hill that stood near it, and hid themselves there. They waited, watching, for they had not decided what they would do. The next day in the afternoon they began to get hungry, and they began to talk together. Running Chief said to his friend, "My brother, are you poor in your mind? Do you feel like doing some great thing—something that is very dangerous?"

His friend answered at once, "Yes, I am poor. I am ready. Why do you ask me?"

Running Chief thought a little while before he answered, and as he thought, all the pain and suffering of his life seemed to rise up before him, so that he could see it. He remembered how he had been a poor boy, supported by his mother, and all that they two had suffered together while he was yet a child. He remembered how his sister had been killed when he was a boy only ten years old, and how he had mourned for her, when her husband, who was jealous of her, had shot her through the body with an arrow and killed her. She was the only sister he had, and he had loved her. He felt that he was poor now, and that there was no hope of anything better for him, and he did not want to live any longer. After he had thought of all these things he said to his friend, "My life is not worth anything to me;" and then he told him of his bad feelings. Finally he said, "Now you go off and leave me here alone. I am tired of living, but you go home. You have relations who would mourn for you. I do not want you to lose your life on my account."

His friend answered him, "I will not go away from you. We have grown up together, and I will stick to you. Wherever you go I will go, and whatever you do I will do."

Then Running Chief meditated for a long time. He had not made up his mind what to do. He thought to himself, "This, my friend, will stay with me. I do not want to be the cause of his death." So he considered. Finally he said to his friend, "If I shall make up my mind to go to some place where there is great danger, I shall go."

His friend said, "I will go with you."

Running Chief thought again, and at last he said, "On account of my feelings I have decided to go into the camp of my enemies, and be eaten by their dogs."

The other man said, "Whatever you have determined on I also will do."

Then they jumped up out of the hole they were hiding in, and tied up their waists, and prepared to start. They were not very far from a trail which connected two villages, along which persons kept passing, and the Indians of these villages were all about them. When they jumped up to go toward the trail, they saw four or five persons passing at a little distance. When they saw these people, Running Chief called out to them, *"High—eigh,"* and made motions for them to come to him. He wanted to show his strong will, and that on account of his bad feelings he wished to have his troubles ended right there. He called to them twice, and each time the Indians stopped and looked at the Pawnees, and then went on. They did not know who it was that was calling them; perhaps they thought the Pawnees were two squaws.

The two young men went out to the trail and followed these persons toward the village. They went over a little hill, and as soon as they had come to the top and looked over it, they saw the village. On this side of it, and nearest to them were three lodges. At the foot of the hill was a river, which they must cross to come to these three lodges. When they came to the river, the friend asked, "Shall we take off our moccasins and leggings to cross?" Running Chief replied, "Why should I take off my moccasins and leggings when I know that my life is just going over a precipice? Let us go in as we are." So they crossed with moccasins and leggings on. The river was only half-leg deep.

Just as they reached the further bank, all on a sudden, it came over Running Chief what they were doing—that they were going to certain death. All his courage seemed to leave him, and he felt as if he had no bones in his body. Then for a moment he faltered; but he could not give up now. He felt that if he was a man he must go forward; he could not turn back. He stopped for an instant; and his friend looked at him, and said, "Come, let us hurry on. We are near the lodges." He stepped forward then, but his feet seemed to be heavy and to drag on the ground. He walked as if he were asleep.

There was no one about near at hand, and as they went forward Running Chief prayed with all his mind to Ti-ra′-wa that no one might come until they had reached the lodge, and had got inside. When they had got to within about one hundred yards of the lodge, a little boy came out, and began to play around the door, and when they were about fifty yards from him he saw them. As soon as he looked at them, he knew that they did not belong to the camp, and he gave a kind of a scream and darted into the lodge, but no one came out. The people within paid no attention to the boy. As they walked toward the lodges Running Chief seemed not to know where he was, but to be walking in a dream. He thought of nothing except his longing to get to this lodge.

They went to the largest of the three lodges. Running Chief raised the door and put his head in, and as he did so, it seemed as if his breath stopped. He went in and sat down far back in the lodge, opposite the entrance, and though his breath was stopped, his heart was beating like a drum. His friend had followed him in, and sat down beside him. Both had their bows in their hands, strung, and a sheaf of arrows.

When they entered the lodge, the man who was lying down at the back of the lodge uttered a loud exclamation, *"Woof,"* and then seemed struck dumb. A plate of corn mush had just been handed him, but he did not take it, and it sat there on the ground by him. One woman was just raising a buffalo horn spoon of mush to her mouth, but her hand stopped before reaching it, and she stared at them, holding the mush before her face. Another woman was ladling some mush into a plate, and she held the plate in one hand and the ladle above it, and looked at them without moving. They all seemed turned into stone.

As the two Pawnees sat there, Running Chief's breath suddenly came back to him. Before it had all been dark about him, as if he had been asleep; but now the clouds had cleared away, and he could see the road ahead of him. Now he felt a man, and brave. As he looked around him, and saw the man lying motionless, and one woman just ready to take a mouthful, and the other woman with the ladle held over the dish, he perceived that they could not move, they were so astonished.

At length the Wichita had come to his senses. He drew a long breath, and sat up, and for a while looked at the two Pawnees. Then he made some sign to them which they did not understand, but they guessed that he was trying to ask who they were.

Running Chief struck his breast, and said, *"Pi-ta'-da"* (Pawnee). As soon as the Wichita heard that he caught his breath, and heaved a long sigh. He did not know what to think of two Pawnees coming into his lodge. He could not think what it meant. He drew a long breath. He did not touch his plate of food, but motioned a woman to take it away. Presently he called to some one in the neighboring lodge. He was answered, and in a moment a man came in. He called again, and another entered, and the three looked for a long time at the two Pawnees. These were sitting motionless, but watching like two wildcats to see what was going to happen. Each had his bow and arrows by his side, and his knife inside his robe. At length the owner of the lodge spoke, and one of the men went out, and after a little they heard the sound of horses' hoofs coming, and they supposed some one was riding up. Every now and then Running Chief would touch his friend's knee with his own, as if to say, "Watch."

The owner of the lodge made a sign and pointed to the east and said *"Capitan."* At the same time he was dressing himself up, putting on a pair of officer's trousers and a uniform coat. Meantime the Pawnees heard the rattle of one saddle, and then of another. The Wichita chief put on his blanket, and his pistol belt around it, and then made signs for them to go out. He led the way, and the Pawnees followed. As they went, Running Chief touched his friend, as if to say, "Watch. They may shoot us as we go out." But when they looked out of the lodge, the Wichita was walking toward the horses, so there was no danger. He mounted a horse, and signed to Running Chief to get up behind him. Another man mounted the other horse, and the friend got up behind him.

As they rode toward the main village, it came into the mind of Running Chief to kill the man he was riding behind, and to ride away. There was where he had to fight his hardest battle. He was tempted to kill this man in front of him, but he was not overpowered by this temptation. He overcame it. He thought that perhaps he might be mounted on a poor horse, and even if he did kill this man and his friend the other, they might be on slow horses and be caught at once. Every little while he would look at his friend and roll his eyes, as if to say, "Watch on your side and I will watch on mine."

As he came near to the village, the Wichita warrior called out, and began to sing a song, and all at once the village was in an uproar. The men, women and children seemed to start up out of the ground, and the lodges poured forth their inmates. Running Chief felt that he was in danger, but he knew that he was not in as much danger as the man before him. He could take the pistol out of the belt that he had hold of and kill him, or he could use his own knife. The Wichita knew that he was in danger. He knew that he was in the power of the enemy.

After the Wichita had called out to the people that they had enemies with them, he kept on talking, saying, "Keep quiet. Do not do anything. Wait. Keep away from me and be still. I am in danger." They would not have listened to him, if it had not been that he was a leading man, and a brave warrior. The riders came to the largest lodge, which stood in the middle of the village. Here they stopped. When Running Chief got off the horse, he held tightly the belt of the Wichita, who dismounted; and they went together into the lodge of the Head Chief, and the others followed and went in, and all sat down opposite the door. All this time there was a hubbub outside. People were flying from their lodges to that of the Head Chief, and lifting up the edge of the lodge, and peeping under it at the Pawnees. They chattered to each other, and called out to those who were coming; all was noise and confusion.

The under chiefs came in one by one, until all were present. Then one of them made a speech, saying that it would be best to leave everything to the Head Chief, and that he should decide what ought to be done with these enemies. Then it was silent for a time, while the Chief was making up his mind what should be done; and during this silence Running Chief felt a touch on his shoulder, and looked behind him, and there was handed to him under the edge of the lodge a dish of meat. He took it and began to eat, and his companion also ate with him. After he had eaten a few mouthfuls, he took his arrows, which he had held in his hand, and put them in his quiver, and unstrung his bow and laid it aside, and his friend did the same.

Then the Chief stood up and spoke to those sitting there and said, "What can I do? They have eaten of my food. I cannot make war on people who have been eating with me." While he was saying this, Running Chief was again touched on the shoulder, and some one handed him a cup of water, and he drank; and the Chief, as he saw this, added, "and have also drunk of my water." He then turned and called to a certain man, who could speak Pawnee, and told him to ask these men if they were on the warpath. He asked them, "Are you on the warpath?" and they replied, "Yes, we are on the warpath."

Then said he, "What are you here for?"

Running Chief answered, "You have plenty of dogs. I am here that my body may be eaten by them."

When the Wichitas heard this they all made a sound, *Ah-h-h-h!* for they were surprised at his bravery. The Chief asked him, "Do you know anything about the horses that were missed last night?"

He said, "Yes."

"Where are they?" said the Head Chief.

Running Chief replied, "The party have gone off with them—Pawnees."

"Were you with them?"

"Yes, I was with them, and I stopped behind on purpose to come into your village."

The Head Chief then turned to the others and talked for a little while. He said, "See what a brave man this is. He had resolved to die. But he shall not die, because he has eaten our food and drunk of our water. Although we are enemies of this man's tribe, yet we are the same people with them, who have been apart for a long time. I cannot help it; my heart is touched by his talk and by their bravery. By their bravery they are safe." And all the Wichitas said *"Waugh."*

Then the Head Chief through the interpreter talked to Running Chief. He said, "Are you a chief?"

Running Chief replied, "No, I am not a chief; I am like a dog; I am poor."

The Head Chief said to him, "By your bravery you have saved yourselves. You shall have the road to your home made white before you. Let there not be one blood spot on it." Then he turned to those who were sitting about the lodge and said, "Now, my young men, do something for them."

A young man named Crazy Wolf stood up and spoke; and when he had finished, the interpreter said, "That man has given you a black horse, the best that he has."

Another young man on the other side of the lodge spoke, and the interpreter said, "He has given you a roan horse, the best that he has." Then all the Wichitas began to speak at once, and before they knew it, the Pawnees had ten head of horses, and robes and blankets, saddles, bridles, shields, spears and moccasins—many beautiful presents. So they were well provided.

The Head Chief again stood up and talked to the assembly, praising these Pawnees; and he stepped over to Running Chief and shook hands with him, and when he did so, Running Chief stood up and put his arms around the Chief and pressed him to his breast, and the Chief did the same to him, and when Running Chief had his arms around the Chief, the Chief trembled, and came near to crying. The Chief embraced the other Pawnee, and looked him in the face and said, "What brave men you are!"

The friend said, "What my friend stepped, that I stepped; I trod in his footprints; I had one mind with him."

As the Chief stepped back to his place he spoke through the interpreter, "Now you have eaten of my food and drunk of my water. Everything that I have is yours. My women and my children are yours. You are not a chief, but you are a chief." Then he spoke to the crowd and they all went away, leaving only the principal men in the lodge.

That afternoon the Pawnees were feasted everywhere, and had to eat till they were almost dead; and as they went about, all of their former sadness seemed to be swept away, and Running Chief felt like crying for joy.

While they were feasting, the man who had given the black horse went out, and caught it up, and painted it handsomely, and rode into the village, and put on it a silver bridle, and eagle feathers in its mane and tail, and when Running Chief was going from one lodge to another he met him, and jumped off the horse and said, "Brother, ride this." He gave him also a shield and a spear.

These Pawnees stayed two months with the Wichitas, and all their troubles seemed at an end. At length Running Chief called a council of the chiefs, and told them that now he wished to make ready to go home to his village. He thanked them for all that they had done for him, and said that now he would go. The chiefs said, "It is well. We are glad that you have been with us and visited us. Take the good news back to your tribe. Tell them that we are one people, though long separated. Let the road between our villages be made white. Let it no more show any spots of blood."

Running Chief thanked them and said, "I will go and take the good news to my people. I shall show them the presents you have made us, and tell them how well we have been treated. It may be that some of the chiefs of my tribe will wish to come down to visit you, as I have done." The Head Chief said, "Can I rely on your words, that I shall be visited?" Running Chief replied, "You can rely on them if I have to come alone to visit you again." The Chief got up and put his arms about him, and said, "I want to be visited. Let there be no more war between us. We are brothers; let us always be brothers." Then they gave him many more presents, and packed his horses, and six braves offered to go with him through the Cheyenne country. They went through in the night. Running Chief said afterward, "I could have stolen a lot of horses from the Cheyennes, but I thought, I will be coming back through this country and it is better not."

At the Pawnee village these two young men had been mourned by their relations as lost or dead. It was in the spring (March, 1869) when they reached home, and there was joy in the tribe when they came in with the presents. Running Chief was praised, and so was his friend. Both had been brave and had done great things.

Now Running Chief's name was changed from Wi-ti-ti le-shar'-uspi to *Skŭ'r-ar-a le-shar* (Lone Chief).

The following summer in August, at the close of the summer hunt, three hundred Pawnees, old men and young, under the leadership of Lone Chief, visited the Wichitas, who received them well, and gave them many horses. Lone Chief was not satisfied with the peace that he had made with the Wichitas. He also visited the Kiowas, and made peace, and was given by them eight fine horses. He also led his party to the Comanches, and visited them, and got many presents. In the fall the Pawnees returned to their village. Many of them fell sick on the way, and some died.

In the winter of 1869–70 Lone Chief and his friend led a war party against the Cheyennes. They took six hundred head of horses. The Cheyennes now tell us that in the seventy-five lodges of that camp there was not left a hoof. All night and all next day they ran the herd. Then Lone Chief said, "Let us not run the horses any longer, they will not come after us; they are afoot." When the party got on the north side of the Republican, on the table lands, a terrible storm of snow and wind came upon them, and they were nearly lost. For three days and three nights they lay in the storm. All were frozen, some losing toes and fingers. They survived, however, and brought in all their horses. Again Lone Chief sacrificed to Ti-ra'-wa. A second sacrifice is very unusual and a notable event.

COMANCHE CHIEF
(Pawnee)

M any years ago there lived in the Ski'-di village a young man, about sixteen years old. His name was *Kut-a'wi-kutz* (the hawk). At this time the Pawnees wore their hair in the ancient fashion, cut as the Osages wear theirs; the whole head was shaved except a roach running back from the forehead beyond the scalp lock.

A war party went off to the south and he joined them as a servant. They went a long way and a long way, traveling far, but they got no horses and came back. Afterward another party started off on the warpath, and he went with it. They traveled many days, going to the southwest, and at length they came to a camp, and hid themselves to wait until it was dark. It was a camp of the Comanches.

When night had come they all went into the camp to steal horses. This young man went to a lodge near which stood three horses, two spotted horses and one gray. They were tied near the door of the lodge, and from this he thought they must be fast, for the Indians usually tie up their best horses close to the lodge door, where they will be under their eyes as much as possible. He went to the lodge to cut the ropes, and just as he was about to do so he thought he heard some one inside. He stepped up close to the lodge, and looked in through a little opening between the door and the lodge, and saw a small fire burning, and on the other side of the fire was sitting a young girl, combing her long hair. The young man looked around the lodge to see who else was there, and saw only an old man and an old woman, and the firemaker. He cut the ropes of the two spotted horses standing outside, led the horses out of the camp, and met his companion. To him he said, "Now, brother, you take these horses and go to the hill where we were hiding today, and wait for me there. I have seen another fine spotted horse that I want to get; I will go back for it and will meet you before morning at that place."

He went back, as if to get the spotted horse, but returned to the lodge where the girl was. He went all around it, and looked at it carefully. He saw that there were feathers on the lodge, and rows of animal hoofs hanging down the sides, which rattled in the wind, and to one of the lodge-poles was tied a buffalo tail, which hung down. Then he went back to the door and looked in at the girl again. She had braided her hair and was sitting there by the fire. He stayed there a long time that night looking at her. Toward morning he went to look for his companion. When he met him he told him that some one had taken the spotted horse before he got to it; he could not find it. When the party all met next morning, they found that they had taken a lot of horses, and they started north to go home. They reached the Pawnee village, and every one was glad of their success.

After this, whenever this young man saw anything that was nice or pretty, such as medals, ear-rings, finger rings for women, beadwork leggings, bracelets, necklaces, wampum, beads—things that the Comanches did not have—he would give a pony for it. For one year he went on like this, gathering together these pretty things. When the year had gone by he had no horses left; he had given them all away to get these presents. He packed all these things up in a bundle, and then spoke one night to his friend, saying, "I intend to go off on the warpath again, and I would like to have you go with me; we two will go alone." His friend agreed to go.

Before the time came to start, other young men heard of it, and several joined them. There were eight of them in all. Kut-a'wi-kutz was the leader. He told his young men that they were going to a certain place where he knew there were lots of spotted horses to steal. They started out on foot. After traveling many days, they came to the place where the camp had been at the time he saw the girl. There was now no camp there.

They went on further, and at length came to a camp and hid themselves. When night came the leader told his men to remain where they were hiding, and he would go into the camp and see if there were any horses to take. He went through all the camp looking for the lodge in which he had seen the girl, but he did not find it. Then he went back to where the young men were hiding, and told them that this was not the camp they were looking for; that they did not have here the spotted horses that they wanted. In the camp of the year before there had been many spotted horses.

The young men did not understand this, and some of them did not like to leave this camp without taking any horses, but he was the leader and they did as he said. They left that camp and went on further.

After traveling some days they came to another camp, and hid themselves near it. When night came on Kut-a'wi-kutz said to his young men, "You stay here where you are hiding, and I will go into this camp and see if it is the one we are looking for." He went through the camp but did not find the lodge he sought. He returned to the hiding place, and told the party there that this was not the camp they were looking for, that the spotted horses were not there. They left the camp and went on.

When they had come close to the mountains they saw another camp. Kut-a'wi-kutz went into this camp alone, and when he had been through it, he went back to his party and told them that this was the camp they had been looking for. Then he sent the young men into the camp to steal horses, and he put on his fine leggings and moccasins that he had in his bundle, and painted himself and went with them. He took a horse and his friend took one. They met outside the village. He told his friend to get on his own horse and lead the other, and with the rest of the party to go off east from the camp to a certain place, and there to wait for him. "I have seen," he said, "another fine horse that I like, and I wish to go back and get it."

His friend looked sorrowfully at him and said, "Why are you all dressed up like this, and why is your face painted? What are you doing or what is in your mind? Perhaps you intend to do some great thing tonight that you do not want me, your friend, to know about. I have seen for a long time that you are hiding something from me."

Kut-a'wi-kutz caught his friend in his arms and hugged him and kissed him and said, "You are my friend; who is so near to me as you are? Go on as I have said, and if it turns out well I will tell you all. I will catch up with you before very long."

His friend said, "No, I will stay with you. I will not go on. I love you as a brother, and I will stay with you, and if you are going to do some great thing I will die with you."

When Kut-a'wi-kutz found that his friend was resolved to remain with him, he yielded and told him his secret. He said to him, "My brother, when we were on the warpath a year ago, and I took those two spotted horses, I heard a little noise in the lodge by which they were tied. I looked in and I saw there a girl sitting by the fire combing her hair. She was very pretty. When I took the spotted horses away, I could not put that girl out of my mind. I remembered her. Brother, when we went back home that girl was constantly in my mind. I could not forget her. I came this time on purpose to get her, even if it shall cost me my life. She is in this camp, and I have found the lodge where she lives."

His friend said, "My brother, whatever you say shall be done. I stay with you. You go into the camp. I will take the horses and go to that high rocky hill east of the camp, and will hide the horses there. When you are in the village I will be up in one of the trees on the top of the hill, looking down on the camp. If I hear shooting and see lots of people running to the lodge I will know that you are killed, and I will kill myself. I will not go home alone. If I do not see you by noon, I will kill myself."

Kut-a'wi-kutz said, "It is good. If I am successful I will go up there after you, and take you down into the camp."

They parted. The friend hid the horses and went up on the hill. Kut-a'wi-kutz went into the camp.

It was now the middle of the night. When he came to the lodge, he saw there was a fire in it. He did not go in at once; he wanted the fire to go out. He stayed around the lodge, and gradually the fire died down. It was dark. He went into the lodge. He was painted and finely dressed, and had his bundle with him. He took his moccasins off and his leggings, and hung them up over the girl's bed; then strings of beads, then five or six medals, bracelets, ear-bobs, beaded leggings, everything he had—his shirt. He took his blanket, and spread it over the bed where the girl was lying, stepped over the bed, and crept under his own blanket, and lay down by her side.

When he lay down she woke up, and found that there was some one lying by her, and she spoke to him, but he did not answer. He could not understand her, for he did not know Comanche. She talked for a long time, but he did not speak. Then she began to feel of him, and when she put her hands on his head—*Pi-ta'-da*—Pawnee —an enemy! Then she raised herself up, took a handful of grass from under the bed, spread the fire and put the grass on it. The fire blazed up and she saw him. Then she sprang up and took the top blanket, which was his, off the bed, and put it about her, and sat by the fire. She called her father and said, "Father get up; there is a man here."

The old man got up, and got his pipe and began smoking. This old man was the Head Chief of the Comanches. He called the servant, and told him to make a fire. The girl got up and went over to where her mother was lying and called her. The mother got up; and they all sat by the fire.

The old man smoked for a long time. Every now and then he would look at the bed to see who it could be that was lying there, and then he would look at all the things hanging up over the bed—at the medals and other things. He did not know what they were for, and he wondered. At length the old man told the servant to go and call the chiefs of the tribe, and tell them to come to his lodge.

Presently the chiefs came in one by one and sat down. When they had come there was still one brave who ought to have come that was not there. His name was Skin Shirt; the father wanted him. He sent for him three times. He sent word back to the chief to go on with the council, and that he would agree to whatever they decided. The fourth time he was sent for he came, and took a seat by the chief, the girl's father. This brave spoke to Kut-a'wi-kutz, and told him to get up, and take a seat among them. He did so. The girl was sitting on the other side of the fire. When he got up, he had to take the blanket that was left, which was the girl's. He put it around him, and sat down among them.

When the chiefs came in, there was among them a Pawnee who had been captured long ago and adopted by the Comanches, and was now himself a chief; he talked with Kut-a'wi-kutz and interpreted for him, telling him everything that was said as each one spoke.

After the young man had seated himself, the chief filled his pipe, and gave the pipe to his brave to decide what should be done with this enemy. The brave took the pipe, but he did not wish to decide, so he did not light it, but passed it on to another chief to decide. He passed it on to another, and he to another, and so it went until the pipe came back to the Head Chief. When he got it again, he asked Kut-a'wi-kutz, "Why have you come here this night and lain down in my lodge, you who are an enemy to my people? And why have you hung up in the lodge all these strange things which we see here? I do not understand it, and I wish to know your reasons."

The boy said to him, "A long time ago I came south on the warpath to steal horses. I traveled until I came to your camp. I saw three horses tied outside a lodge, two spotted horses and a gray. While I was cutting one of the ropes, I heard a little noise inside the lodge, and pushing aside the door I looked in, and saw that girl combing her hair. I stole the two spotted horses, and took them out of the camp, and gave them to a friend of mine, and came back to your lodge, and kept looking at the girl. I stayed there until she went to bed. For a long year I have been buying presents; beads and many other things, for I had made up my mind that I would go after this girl. I came down here to find her. I have been to where you were camped last year, and to two other camps that I discovered. She was not in these and I left them, and came on until I found the right camp. This is the fourth place. Now I am here. I made up my mind to do this thing, and if her relations do not like it they can do as they please. I would be happy to die on her account."

When he had spoken the old chief laughed. He said: "Those two spotted horses that you stole I did not care much about. The gray horse was the best one of the three, and you left him. I was glad that you did not take him. He was the best of all." Then for a little while there was silence in the lodge.

Then the chief, the girl's father, began to talk again; he said, "If I wanted to decide what should be done with this man, I would decide right now, but here is my brave, Skin Shirt, I want him to decide. If I were to decide, it would be against this man, but he has my daughter's blanket on, and she has his, and I do not want to decide. I pass the pipe to my brave, and want him to light it."

The brave said, "I want this chief next to me to decide," and he passed him the pipe, and so it went on around the circle until it came to the Head Chief again. He was just about to take it and decide the question, when they heard outside the lodge the noise made by some one coming, shouting and laughing; then the door was pushed aside and an old man came in, and as he passed the door he stumbled and fell on his knees. It was the girl's grandfather. He had been outside the lodge, listening.

The pipe was passed to the chief, and he gave it again to his brave to decide. While the brave was sitting there, holding the pipe, the old grandfather said, "Give me the pipe, if you men cannot decide, let me do it. In my time we did not do things this way. I never passed the pipe; I could always decide for myself."

Then Skin Shirt passed him the pipe, and he lit it and smoked. Then he said, "I do not wish to condemn to death a man who is wearing my granddaughter's blanket." The interpreter began to tell Kut-a'wi-kutz that the old man was going to decide in his favor, and that when he got through speaking he must get up and pass his hands over him, and thank him for taking pity on him, and so to all the others. The old man continued, "Now, chiefs, do not think hardly of what I am going to say, nor be dissatisfied with my decision. I am old. I have heard in my time that there is a tribe up north that is raising from the ground something that is long and white, and something that is round; and that these things are good to eat. Now, chiefs, before I die, I want to eat of these things, and I want my granddaughter to go and take her seat by this man, and for them to be man and wife. Since I was young we have been enemies, but now I want the two tribes to come together, join hands and be friends." And so it was decided.

The young man got up and passed his hands over the old man, and over the brave, and passed around the circle and blessed them all. The Pawnee, who was interpreter, now told him to get up, and get a medal and put it on the brave, and then another and put it on the chief, and so on until all the presents were gone. And he did so, and put on them the medals, and earrings, and strings of beads, and breast-plates of wampum, until each had something. And these things were new to them, and they felt proud to be wearing them, and thought how nice they looked.

By this time it was daylight, and it had got noised abroad through the camp that there was a Pawnee at the Head Chief's lodge, and all the people gathered there. They called out, "Bring him out; we want him out here." They crowded about the lodge, all the people, the old men and the women and the young men, so many that at last they pushed the lodge down. They shouted: "Let us have the Pawnee. Last night they stole many horses from us." The chiefs and braves got around the Pawnee, and kept the Comanches off from him, and protected him from the people. The Cheyennes were camped close by, near the hill southeast of the Comanches, and they, too, had heard that the Comanches had a Pawnee in the camp. They came over, and rode about in the crowd to try and get the Pawnee, and they rode over a Comanche or two, and knocked them down. So Skin Shirt got his bow and arrows, and jumped on his horse, and rode out and drove the Cheyennes away back to their camp again.

The Cheyennes saw that the Comanches did not want the Pawnee killed, so they sent a message inviting him over to a feast with them, intending to kill him, but Skin Shirt told them that he was married into the tribe. While the Cheyennes were parading round the Comanche camp, they were shooting off their guns in the air, just to make a noise. Now, the young Pawnee on the hill, who was watching the camp to see what would happen to his friend, saw the crowd and heard the shooting, and made up his mind that Kut-a'wi-kutz had been killed. So he took his knife, and put the handle against a tree and the point against his breast, and put his arms around the tree and hugged it, and the knife blade passed through his heart and he fell down and died.

In the afternoon when all the excitement had quieted down, the Cheyennes came over again to the Comanche camp, and invited the Pawnee and his wife to go to their village, and visit with them. Then Skin Shirt said, "All right, we will go." Three chiefs of the Comanches went ahead, the Pawnee followed with his wife, and Skin Shirt went behind. They went to the Cheyenne camp. The Cheyennes received them and made a great feast for them, and gave the Pawnee many horses. Then they went back to the Comanche camp. Kut-a'wi-kutz never went up to the hill until the next morning. Then he went, singing the song he had told his friend he would sing. He called to him, but there was no reply. He called again. It was all silent. He looked for his friend, and at last he found him there dead at the foot of the tree.

Kut-a'wi-kutz then stayed with the Comanches. The Cheyennes came north and east, and the Comanches went on west, nearer to the mountains. While the Pawnee was with the Comanches, they had several wars with the Utes, Lipans and Tonkaways. Kut-a'wi-kutz proved himself a brave man, and, as the son-in-law of the chief, he soon gained great influence, and was himself made a chief.

After some years the old man, his wife's grandfather, told the Pawnee that he thought it was time that he should eat some of those things that he had long wanted to eat that grew up north; that he was getting pretty old now. Kut-a'wi-kutz said, "It is time. We will go." So he had his horses packed, and with his immediate family and the old man, started north toward the Pawnee country. At this time he was called *Kut-a'wi-kutz-u si-ti'-da-rit,* which means "See! The Hawk." When going into battle he would ride straight out to strike his enemy, and the Comanches who were looking at him would say, "See! The Hawk." So that became his name.

They traveled a long time until they came to the Pawnee ground. As they were traveling along, they came to a field where were growing corn, beans and squashes. The Pawnee said to the old man, "Grandfather, look at that field. There are the things that you have desired to eat." He got off his horse and went into the field, and pulled some corn, some beans and some squashes, and took them to the old man, and gave them to him. The old man supposed they were to be eaten just as they were, and he tried to bite the squashes. This made the Pawnee laugh. When they came to the village, the Pawnees were very glad to see him who had been lost long ago. He told the people that he had brought these Indians to eat of the corn and other things; that they were his kinsfolk. He told them, too, about the young man who had killed himself. His relations went out into the fields, and gathered corn and beans and squashes, and cooked them for the Comanches.

They stayed there a long time at the Pawnee village. When they were getting ready to return, the Pawnees dried their corn, and gave a great deal of it to the Comanches, packing many horses with it for the Indians at home. Then the Comanches started south again, and some of the Pawnee young men, relations of Kut-a'wi-kutz, joined him, and went back with them. After they had returned to the Comanche camp, the old grandfather died, happy because he had eaten the things he wanted to eat.

Soon after this, Kut-a'wi-kutz started back to the Pawnee village, and some young men of the Comanches joined him. Some time after reaching the village he went south again, accompanied by some young Pawnees, but leaving most of the Comanches behind. He had arranged with the chiefs of the Pawnees that they should journey south, meet the Comanches on the plains and make peace. When he reached the Comanches, the whole village started north to visit the Pawnees, and met them on their way south. When they met, the two tribes made friends, smoked together, ate together, became friends.

After they had camped together for some time, some Comanches stayed in the Pawnee camp, and some Pawnees in the Comanche camp. Kut-a'wi-kutz was called by the Pawnees Comanche Chief. He would have remained with the Comanches, but when he went back with them his wife fell sick. The Comanche doctors could not help her, and he wanted to take her north to see the Pawnee doctors, but the Comanches would not let him. They kept him there, and his wife died. Then he was angry, for he thought if he had taken her north her life might have been saved.

So he left the Comanches, and went and lived with the Pawnees, and was known among them always as Comanche Chief, the Peace-Maker, because he made peace between the Pawnees and Comanches. He was chief of the Ski'-di band, and a progressive man of modern times. He sent his children East to school at Carlisle, PA.

Comanche Chief died September 9, 1888.

Assemō'ka[n]
(Mississagua)

Long ago there lived two brothers: one of them was a hunter; the other was Assemō'ka[n], who always stayed in the camp and did no hunting. One day Assemō'ka[n] thought he would go away on a journey somewhere or other, and he meant to tell his brother so, when he returned from hunting, but forgot about it. He forgot it this way two or three times. Finally he said: "I'll keep saying '*Gamā'dja! gamā'dja!*' (I'm going! I'm going!) over and over again until my brother comes." So he did this a long time. When his brother arrived he heard some one saying "*Gamā'dja! gamā'dja!*" He then saw his brother, who told him he was going away. "What do you mean?" said he to Assemō'ka[n]. "You would not go very far before you would meet with something to lead you astray." "Well! I'm going, anyway," said Assemō'ka[n], and he went off.

Before long he heard a noise,—the noise of trees lodged rubbing against one another. He thought it very nice, and said, "I want to be that, let me have that!" But the tree said: "Oh, no! I am not comfortable, it is a bad place to be in." For, whenever the wind came on, the tree had to squeak and make a noise, *ī-īū! ī-īū!* But Assemō'ka[n] would have it, and took the place of the tree. So the tree lay on Assemō'ka[n]'s breast, and when the wind came he had to cry out for the pain. But his brother knew all about it soon and came after him. "It's just as I told you," said he to Assemō'ka[n], and released him.

Assemō'ka[n] went on again. Soon he came to a river, where he saw a stick (*mītig*) on end in the mud, moving about with the current and making a noise. He thought this was nice, too, and so he took the place of the stick. His brother had to follow after him and take him out, but told him that he would not help him again.

Assemō′kaⁿ then went on farther and came to a village. Here all the people were dead except two children ($\bar{a}bin\bar{o}'dj\bar{i}yug$),—a little boy and a little girl. Assemō′kaⁿ asked what had happened to the people who were dead. The children, who were lamenting, told him that a wicked old woman and her daughter had killed them. The way she killed them was this. She had asked them to get for her the white loon that dwelt in the middle of sea. Not one of them was able to do this, so she killed them one after the other. The children told Assemō′kaⁿ that the old woman would come back soon to set them the same task, and that they would have to die also. But Assemō′kaⁿ caught the white loon, and gave it to the children. He told them to show it to the old woman when she came, and to ask her if she were able to get the chipmunk's horn. The old woman came and the children showed her the white loon, at which she was greatly surprised, and said it must have got there itself.

The children then asked her to get the chipmunk's horn. "You talk old-fashioned," said she to them, and threw down some deers' horns, pretending that it was the chipmunk's horn. As she could not perform the task, Assemō′kaⁿ killed her. He then made a little bow-and-arrows for the boy, and told him to shoot up in the air and to tell the dead people to rise. He shot into the air three times, and each time he said: *"Gĭbitchĭnō′nim ōnĭ′shkog!* (Get up, the arrow is going to fall on you)." The first time he shot the arrow into the air, the people stirred a little and began to gape, and after the third time they rose up.

TURTLE, GRASSHOPPER, AND SKUNK
(Cheyenne)

Three animals went on the warpath: the turtle, the grasshopper, and the skunk. On the way the grasshopper, in trying to jump a river, stuck in the mud with his legs, and could not go on. The skunk and the turtle continued on their way, and finally came to a large camp. At night they entered the chief's tent, and cut his throat. Next morning the deed was discovered, and the people started in pursuit. The skunk had escaped; but the turtle had crawled under a bucket; and in this hiding-place he was found. He was taken to a council, and it was decided to burn him. A fire was lit, and he was seized. The turtle knew what awaited him if he were put in the fire. So he ran toward the fire himself, as fast as he could go. The people at once thought that he was anxious to enter the fire in order to explode, or do them some other harm; so they quickly stopped him. Then they poured a little water on him, and he pretended to faint and be near death. When they brought a bucket of water, he seemed to try to run away from it. The people accordingly thought that he was afraid of water because he could easily be killed with it, and they all went to see him drowned in a lake, rejoicing over the fate in store for him. A warrior took him into the lake. As the turtle pretended to be trying to keep away from the water by catching the bushes and clinging to them, the people all shouted, but he knew that he was about to be saved. The warrior dragged him into deep water, and then suddenly the turtle bit him hard, dived with him, and held him under the water until he was drowned. The people stood about, weeping and howling and looking at the lake. At last they got wooden buckets and pails made of buffalo-intestine; everybody, even children, was to carry water, until the lake was dry. At last they came to the body of the warrior; he was scalped. But the turtle had escaped with the scalp, and reaching home, found the skunk, who had brought the chief's scalp with him. So the animals celebrated a scalp-dance.

COYOTE TALES
(Various)

COYOTE AND TURTLE
(Cheyenne)

The coyote was very hungry and looking for food. He could catch no rabbit, nor any bird, and could find nothing to eat. At last he met a hard-shelled prairie turtle. The coyote knew that he was unable to kill the turtle outright, but he tried to find some way to get him for his food. So the coyote said to him: "I am a great friend of the turtle people; and the turtles used to call me by the name of Turtle Chief, because I am a friend to the life of all turtles." In this way the coyote tried as hard as he could to succeed in killing him. The turtle said that his name was Medicine Turtle. The coyote said, "Well, turtle, we have had a good meeting as friends, and we must remember our meeting." When they were about to leave each other, the coyote thought he could kill the turtle. So he went to kiss him, and as he kissed him, he tried to bite him. But the turtle bit him, and the coyote ran off.

THE MAN AND THE COYOTE
(Cheyenne)

A man was traveling up along a river, carrying a bag. He met some ducks, who asked him what he had in the sack. He said, songs. Then they begged him to sing for them. At first he declared that he had no time to stop, but at last he consented, and the ducks all gathered about him. He pretended to be lame and leaned on a stick. Then he sang, and the ducks danced, and he told them to keep their eyes closed until he stopped singing. He sang: *tse mu^n makuyets* (your eyes will be red); therefore they were afraid of getting sore eyes, and did not look at him. He took his stick and hit them with it. As they danced, one duck did not feel its neighbors any longer, and at last opened its eyes, and saw the man hitting away, and a pile of dead ducks. So he cried out to the rest to escape, and all that were left flew away. Then the man rejoiced. He went to the shade of some trees, made a fire, and spitted and roasted his ducks. He also made a sausage of them, and this he laid in the ashes. Then he sang and danced for joy. A hungry coyote heard him and smelled the meat, and drew near. Overhead two trees were rubbing together, and making noise. The man said to them: "Stop fighting! Don't disturb me, for I am going to have a good dinner." The screeching continued. He went to the foot of the trees and again told them to stop. Finally he climbed up. The wind rose, and again the trees screeched. The man put his hand between them to hold them apart. Suddenly the wind fell, and his wrist was held fast. The coyote came nearer, wondering. The man ordered him to go away, and tried to conceal his hand that was caught. The coyote at last understood the situation and took a duck. "Yes, you may take one duck; that one at the end there," said the man. As the coyote took a second, the man called to him, "You may take another." Thus it went on, until all the ducks were eaten. The wind began to come again, the trees rubbed together, and the man's wrist hurt so much that he no longer thought of the coyote. The coyote meanwhile found the sausage and ate it. Then he filled it with ashes, put it back, and went away. At last the wind rose, and the man became free. "This is bad," he thought, "but it is lucky that he did not find the sausage." He took it out, bit into it, and the ashes flew into his eyes. He stumbled about, until he fell into the river. Then he washed his eyes out. Now he was angry. He followed the coyote's trail, and found him asleep, with distended belly. He determined to eat both ducks and coyote, but he thought: "If I choke him, I may bruise his meat; if I hit him on the head I may bruise and spoil his meat." While he was deliberating, the coyote jumped up and ran away. Again he followed him and found him asleep. He made a great fire, having decided to seize the coyote by his ears and tail, throw him into the fire, and roast him whole. He seized him, but as he threw him, the coyote jumped forward through the flames, and ran off, singed but safe. The man could not see him through the flames and thought he was in the fire. He waited until it burnt down; then he looked for the coyote and could not find him.

Bird Tales
(Various)

The Hunter and the Crow
(Cheyenne)

A hunter had killed a buffalo. A crow came flying to where he was butchering. When the man saw him, the crow said: "I am very hungry, and I have never eaten buffalo's eyes. I know very much about troubles of the eyes. Will you let me eat the buffalo's eyes, and as much meat as I wish?" The man said to the crow: "I will let you have all the meat you wish, and I will kill more buffalo for you, so that you can eat their eyes." The crow said: "I will go back after my family, and bring my wife and my young crows. And I will instruct you in my power concerning the eyes, so that you will have remedy if any one has trouble in his eyes." The man thought it would be good to learn this power, for his wife was blind on one eye, and the other was very weak. The crow came back with his family to where the man was cutting meat, and they ate. Then the crow and his wife proceeded to teach the man about the eyes. They told him to lie on his back, and close his eyes tight. Then both of them sat on his breast, and the crow began to sing. The medicine-song was: "I have great knowledge of troubles of the eyes." The man believed firmly in what the crow had said to him; but from the crow's teaching he at once lost both his eyes. He tried to go home, but was lost. At last he fell down a steep and deep place. He howled and cried out that he was in great trouble. So now there was only one eye in his family.

THE RAVEN
(Athabascan)

There once lived an old couple who wished to see their only daughter married to a rich man. When any one arrived at their camp, the old man sent his son down to the landing to see if the stranger was provided with the necessary bone beads upon his clothing, in order that he might be received according to his rank. One day the boy came running in, saying that some one had come whom he would like to have for a brother-in-law, for he had a great number of fine beads. The mother went down to the river bank, and saw a richly dressed stranger, whom she also thought would make a suitable husband for her daughter. She noticed that the shore was wet and muddy, so she procured some bark and tore it into strips for the stranger to walk upon. He was invited to enter their tipi and was seated next the girl. A dog was tied in the corner of the lodge, and the visitor said, "I cannot eat while that dog is in here;" so the woman, thinking the man must be a very great personage to be so particular, took the dog away into the forest and killed it. The next morning as she went for wood, she noticed that the earth around the body of the dog was marked with bird tracks, and that its eyes had been picked out. When she returned to the camp she told what she had seen, and insisted upon having all present take off their moccasins that she might see their feet, as she had heard of the Raven deceiving people by appearing in the human form. The stranger, who was really the Raven, took his moccasins off, and slipped them on so quickly that his feet were not noticed. The girl had promised to marry him, and he insisted upon having her go away with him at once, as he feared that his true character would be discovered. He arranged to return in a few days, and took his bride down to his canoe. As soon as they set off down the river it began to rain. The Raven was seated in front of the woman, who noticed that the falling rain was washing out something white from his back; this made her suspicious, and she determined to escape from the canoe. Reaching forward, she succeeded in tying the tail of the Raven's coat to a cross-bar of the canoe. She then asked to be set ashore for a minute, saying that she would come right back. He told her not to go far, but she started to run for home as soon as she got behind the trees. The Raven also tried to get ashore, but his tail was tied, and he could not succeed in his human form; so he resumed the form of the raven and cried out to the girl, "Once more I cheat you," then he caw-cawed and flew away.

When the girl reported this to her mother the old woman asked her what she meant, and the girl answered that the rich son-in-law was the Raven, who had come to them dressed in his own lime, which the rain had melted, and so exposed the trick.

The Raven was always cheating the people, so they took his beak away from him. After a time he went away up the river and made a raft which he loaded with moss, and came floating down to the camps upon it. He told the people that his head was sore where his beak had been torn off, and that he was lying in the moss to cool it. Then he went away for two or three days, and made several rafts; as the people saw these coming down the river, they thought that there were a large number of people upon the rafts, who were coming to help the Raven regain his beak; so they held a council and decided to send the beak away in the hands of a young girl, that she might take it to an old woman who lived all alone at some distance from the camp. The Raven concealed himself among them and heard their plans, so when the girl came back he went to the old woman, and told her that the girl wished to have the beak returned. The old woman suspected nothing and gave him his beak, which he put on and flew away, cawing with pleasure at his success. The supposed people that had been seen upon the rafts proved to be nothing but the tufts or hummocks of bog moss which are commonly known as *têtes de femmes*.

THE WOLF AND WOLVERINE
(Athabascan)

There was once a Wolverine who married a Wolf, and for some time he was very faithful in providing beaver for food. In the course of time he stayed longer upon his hunting trips, and brought home fewer beaver for his wife to cook. She reproached him for this, and he said that he had to go farther for beaver now, and that was why he was detained so long. His wife thought there was surely something wrong, and decided to watch him. One day, as he set out on one of his hunting trips in his canoe, she followed along the river bank under cover of the forest. At length she saw her husband go ashore with a beaver which he had killed, and with which he entered a tipi that stood by the riverside. When he went away again, the wife went into the camp and saw a Wildcat sitting before the kettle in which the beaver was cooking. She saw that her husband had been unfaithful, and determined to kill the Wildcat. She told the Cat to look into the kettle and she would see herself there; when the Wildcat looked into the kettle the Wolf pushed her in, so that her face was burned so severely that death resulted. The Wolf then dragged the Wildcat to the top of the bank overlooking the landing-place, and hid herself in the adjoining bushes. Her husband came back with more beavers, and as he came up the bank he said to the Wildcat which he saw above him, "Are you waiting for me? What are you laughing at me for?" for the shrivelled and grinning head appeared to be laughing. But when he saw that the Cat was dead, he exclaimed, "Ah, that is what the trouble is," and he began to weep. He stayed a long time at the camp, and finally carried the Wildcat away into the forest. At last he started for home, and his wife ran back in time to be at work carrying wood when he arrived. The Wolverine asked, "Why is there no fire?" "I have been out all day gathering wood," replied his wife; "why are you back so soon today?" "Because I have found a new place where there are plenty of beaver," said the Wolverine. But he was very sad and unhappy for some time afterward. "Why are you so different lately?" asked the Wolf. But he would not tell her, and hunted very faithfully and brought home many beavers, so that they lived very contentedly together ever afterward.

A STORY ABOUT 'POSSUM
(Sac and Fox)

Once upon a time, Mr. 'Possum was out hunting something to eat. He saw a farmer coming home from town. He pretended to be dead right in the road. So the farmer jumped out and threw him into the wagon and went on. The 'Possum threw the meat out of the wagon, got out himself and trotted off with it. He commenced to eat it, when Mr. Wolf came along, and asked him where and how he got it. The 'Possum told his story to the wolf. Said the Wolf, "Well, my friend, I must try it. I am very hungry." Sure enough, a farmer was coming, so he "played dead" in the middle of the road. When the farmer came and got out of the wagon, he got his axe and chopped the Wolf's head off. The Wolf thought he was going to put him into the wagon like the 'Possum, but he "got left," and an end was put to his life.

TCHAKABECH
(Ojibwa)

The parents of a child had been killed by a bear and a great hare, and the infant was adopted by a woman who called him her little brother, and gave him the name of Tchakabech. He always remained a child in size, but had prodigious strength. Trees served for arrows for his bow, and he killed the bear and hare which had destroyed his parents. Then he desired to do something more.

In short, this Tchakabech, wishing to go to heaven, mounted upon a tree; being almost at the top, he blew against this tree, which rose and increased at the blowing of this little dwarf; the higher he mounted the more he blew, and the more the tree kept rising and increasing, so that he arrived at last at the sky, where he found the most beautiful country in the world. Everything there was delightful; the earth was excellent and the trees beautiful. Having well observed everything, he came to bring back the news of all this to his sister, in order to induce her to ascend to the sky and remain there forever. He then descends by this tree, erecting in its branches cabins at certain distances, where he might lodge his sister in mounting again. His sister at first opposed him, but he represented the beauty of that country so forcibly to her that she resolved to surmount the difficulty of the way. She takes with her a little nephew of hers and climbs upon this tree, Tchakabech following, for the purpose of catching them if they fell. At each resting-place they always found their cabin made, which comforted them much. At last they arrived at the sky, and, in order that no one should follow them, this child broke off the end of the tree quite low down, so that no one could reach from there to heaven.

After having sufficiently admired the country, Tchakabech went away to stretch some bow-strings, or, as others call them, snares, hoping possibly to take some animal. The night departing while he was going to see to his snares, he saw them all on fire, and did not dare to approach. He returns to his sister and says to her: "My sister, I do not know what there is in my snares; I see only a great fire, which I do not dare to approach." His sister, suspecting what it was, says to him: "Ah, my brother, what a misfortune! Surely you must have taken the Sun in the snare. Go quickly to set him free. Perhaps, walking in the night, he has thrown himself into it without thinking." Tchakabech returned, much astonished, and, having well considered, found that in truth he had taken the Sun in a snare. He tried to free him, but did not dare to approach. By chance he met a little mouse, blew it, and made it become so great that he used it to slacken his snares and set the Sun free, who, finding himself at liberty, continued his course as usual. While he was caught in these snares, the day failed here upon the earth below.

A CHEYENNE BLANKET
(Pawnee)

The Cheyennes, like other Indians, do not speak to each other when they are away from the camp. If a man goes away from the village, and sits or stands by himself on the top of a hill, it is a sign that he wants to be alone; perhaps to meditate; perhaps to pray. No one speaks to him or goes near him.

Now, there was once a Pawnee boy, who went off on the warpath to the Cheyenne camp. In some way he had obtained a Cheyenne blanket. This Pawnee came close to the Cheyenne camp, and hid himself there to wait. About the middle of the afternoon, he left his hiding place, and walked to the top of the hill overlooking the village. He had his Cheyenne blanket wrapped about him and over his head, with only a little hole for his eyes. He stood there for an hour or two, looking over the Cheyenne camp.

They were coming in from buffalo hunting, and some were leading in the pack horses loaded down with meat. A man came along, riding a horse packed with meat, and leading another pack horse, and a black spotted horse that was his running horse. These running horses are ridden only on the chase or on war parties, and are well cared for. After being used they are taken down to the river and are washed and cleaned with care. When the boy saw this spotted horse, he thought to himself that this was the horse that he would take. When the man who was leading it reached his lodge, he dismounted and handed the ropes to his women, and went inside.

Then the Pawnee made up his mind what he would do. He started down the hill into the village, and walked straight to this lodge where the women were unloading the meat. He walked up to them, reached out his hand, and took the ropes of the spotted horse and one of the others. As he did so the women fell back. Probably they thought that this was some one of the relations of the owner, who was going to take the running horse down to the river to wash it. The Pawnee could not talk Cheyenne, but as he turned away he mumbled something—*m-m-m-m*—as if speaking in a low voice, and then walked down toward the river. As soon as he had gone down over the bank and was out of sight, he jumped on the spotted horse and rode into the brush, and pretty soon was away with two horses stolen out of the Cheyenne camp in broad daylight.

Rolling Head Tales
(Various)

The Children Who Ran from Their Mother: Version I
(Cheyenne)

Once there was a lonely lodge, where lived a man, his wife, and two children—a girl and a boy. In front of the lodge, not far off, was a great lake, and a plain trail leading from the lodge down to the shore where they used to go for water.

Every day the man used to go hunting, but before starting he would paint his woman red all over,—her face, her arms, and her whole body. But at night, when he returned, he would always find her clean—the paint all washed off.

When he started out to hunt, she would go for water, leaving the children alone in the lodge; when she returned with the water, the paint would all be gone, and her hair unbraided. She always managed to get back with her water just before her husband arrived. He never brought in any meat.

Her husband thought it strange that every day, when he returned at night, the paint that he had put on his wife in the morning had disappeared, but he asked her no questions. One day he said to his daughter, "What does your mother do every day? When I go out, I paint her, and when I get back, she has no paint on."

The girl replied, "Whenever you start out hunting, she goes for water, and she is usually gone for a long time."

The next day, before he started out, the man painted his wife as usual, and then took his bow and arrows, and went out of the lodge. But instead of going off in the direction in which he usually went to hunt, he went around and down to the shore of the lake, and dug a hole in the sand, and buried himself there, leaving a little place where he could look out. He was going to watch.

The man had not been long hidden when he saw his wife coming, carrying a bucket. When she had come near to the water's edge, she slipped off her dress, and unbraided her hair; and then walked on, and sat down close to the water, saying, "*Ná shū ēh'*, I am here." Soon the man saw the water begin to move, and a mih'ni rose from the water, and crawled out on the land, and crept up to the woman, and wrapped itself all about her, and licked off all the red paint that was on her body.

When the man saw this, he rose from his hiding-place, and rushed down to the pair, and cut the monster to pieces with his knife, and cut off his wife's head. The pieces of the monster crept and rolled back into the water—they were not seen again. The man cut off the woman's arms at the elbow, and her legs at the knees, and threw the pieces and her head into the water, saying, "Take your wife." Then he opened the body, and took out a side of her ribs. He skinned the side of ribs, and then returned to the lodge.

When he reached the lodge, he said, "Ah, my little children, I have had good luck; I have killed an antelope, and have brought back some of the meat. Where is your mother?"

The children answered him, "Our mother has gone to bring water."

"Well," he said, "since I killed my meat sooner than I thought, I brought it back to camp. Your mother will be here pretty soon. In the mean time, I will cook something for you to eat, and will then go out again." He cooked a kettle of meat, and took it out to the children, and they both ate. The little boy, who was the younger, said to his sister, "Sister, this tastes like mother;"—he was the last one that had suckled.

"Oh," said his sister, "keep still; this is antelope meat." After the children had eaten, the little girl saved some of the meat for her mother to eat when she returned.

The father got his moccasins and other things together, and started off, intending never to come back. He was going to look for the tribe.

After he had gone, the children were sitting in the lodge, the girl making moccasins and putting porcupine quills on them. As they sat there, they heard some one outside say, "I love my children, but they do not love me; they have eaten me."

The girl said to her brother, "Look out of the door, and see who is coming." The boy looked out, and then cried out, very much frightened, "Sister, here comes our mother's head."

"Shut the door," cried the girl. The little boy did so. The girl picked up her moccasins and her quills, red, white, and yellow, and rolled them up, and seized her root digger. Meantime the head had rolled against the door, and called out, "Daughter, open the door." The head would strike the door, and roll part way up the lodge, and then fall back again.

The girl and her brother ran to the door, pushed it open, and stood on one side of it. The head rolled into the lodge and clear across it to the back. The girl and boy sprang out, the girl closed the door, and both children ran away as fast as they could. As they ran, they heard the mother in the lodge, calling to them.

They ran, and they ran, and at last the boy called out to his sister, "Sister, I am tired out, I cannot run any longer." The girl took his robe, and carried it for him, and they still ran on.

At last, as they reached the top of the divide, they looked back, and there they could see the head coming, rolling along over the prairie. Somehow it had got out of the lodge. The children kept running, but at last the head had almost overtaken them. The little boy was frightened nearly to death, and was tired out.

The girl said, "This running is almost killing my brother. When I was a little girl, and playing, sometimes the prickly pears were so thick on the ground that I could not get through them." As she said this, she scattered behind her a handful of the yellow porcupine quills, and at once there was behind her a great bed of high prickly pears with great yellow thorns. The bed was strung out for a long way in both directions across the trail they had made.

When the head reached this place, it rolled up on the prickly pears, and tried to roll over them, but it kept getting caught in the thorns, and could not get through.

It kept trying and trying for a long time, and at last it did get loose from the thorns, and passed over. But by this time the girl and the boy had gone a long distance.

After they had gone a long way, they looked back, and again could see the head coming. Somehow it had got through. When the little boy saw the head again, it frightened him so that he almost fainted. He kept calling out, "Sister, I am tired out; I cannot run any longer."

When the girl heard him speak thus, she said, as she was running, "When I was a little girl, I often used to find the bullberry bushes very thick." As she said this, she threw behind her a handful of the white quills, and where they touched the ground there grew up a great grove of thick thorny bullberry bushes. This blocked the way, and the head stopped there for a long time, unable to pass through the bushes.

The children ran on and on, toward the place where the people had last been camped, but at length, as they looked back, they again saw the head coming.

The little boy called out, "Sister, I am tired out; I cannot run any longer." Again the girl threw quills behind—this time the red ones—and a great thicket of thorny rosebushes was formed, which stopped the head.

Again the children had gone a long way, but at last, once more, they saw the head coming, and the boy called out, "Sister, I am tired." Then the girl said, "When I was a little girl, playing, I often came to little ravines that I could not cross." She stopped, and drew the point of her root-digger over the ground in front of her, and made a little groove in the ground, and she placed the root-digger across this groove, and she and her brother walked over on the root-digger. When they had crossed over, the furrow became wider and wider and deeper and deeper, until it was a great chasm with cut walls, and at the bottom they could see a little water trickling.

"Now," said the girl, "we will run no longer; we will stay here."

"No, no," said the boy, "let us run."

"No," said the girl, "I will kill our mother here."

Presently the head came rolling up to the edge of the ravine, and stopped there, talking to the girl, and saying, "Daughter, where did you cross? Place your root-digger on the ground, so that I too may cross." The girl attempted to do so, but every time that she tried to, the boy pulled her back. At last she put it down, and the head began to roll over on the root-digger; but when it was half way across, the girl tipped the stick, and the head fell into the ravine, and the ravine closed on it.

After this, the children started on again to look for the people, and at last they found the camp, and drew near it. Before they had reached it, they could hear a man haranguing in the camp, and as they came nearer and nearer, they saw that it was their father. He was walking about the camp, calling out and saying that while he was out hunting, his two children had killed and eaten their mother, and that if the children came to the camp, they ought not to be allowed to enter it. When they heard this, the children were frightened; but still they went on into the camp. When they entered it, the people caught them, and tied their hands and feet, and the next day moved away, and left them there, tied.

In the camp there was an old, old dog who knew what had happened, and took pity on these children. That night she went into a lodge, and stole some sinew and a knife and an awl, and took them into a hole where she had her pups.

The next day, after the people had all gone, the children heard a dog howling, and presently they saw an old, old dog coming. She came to them, and said, "Grandchildren, I have come to take pity on you."

The girl said, "Untie me first, and I can untie my brother." So the old dog began to gnaw at the rawhide strings with which the girl's hands were tied. She had no teeth, and could not cut the cords, but they got wet, and began to slip, and the girl kept working her hands, and at last she got them free, and untied her legs, and then went and untied her brother. That evening they went about through the camp, picking up old moccasins to wear. Both children were crying, and the dog was crying, too. They sat on the hill near the camp, crying, for they had nothing to eat and no place to sleep in, and nothing to cover themselves with, and winter was coming on. They sat there, crying, with their heads hanging down; but the boy was looking about, and presently he said to his sister, "Sister, look at that wolf, it is coming right straight toward us."

"No," said the girl, "it is useless for me to look; I could not kill him by looking at him; we could not get him to eat."

"But look, sister," insisted the boy, "he is coming right up to us."

At last the girl looked, and when she looked at the wolf, it fell down dead. Then the dog brought the things that she had stolen, and with the knife they cut up the wolf, and from its skin they made a bed for the dog.

The children stayed in this camp, living well now, while the people in the main camp were starving. The children kept up a big fire day and night, and used big logs, so that it did not go out at all.

After they had eaten the wolf, they began to be hungry again. The girl was very unhappy, and one day she sat there, crying, the dog sitting by her, and the boy standing near looking about. Presently the little boy said, "Sister, look at that antelope coming."

"No," said the girl, "it is useless for me to look; looking will do no good."

"But look;" said the boy, "perhaps it will do as the wolf did." The girl looked, and it happened to the antelope as to the wolf—it fell down dead. They cut it up, and of its skin made a bed for themselves. They ate the flesh, and fed the old dog on the liver. The girl would chew pieces up fine for the dog, which had no teeth.

At last the antelope was all eaten, and again they grew hungry. Again the same thing happened. The boy saw a strange-looking animal coming—it was an elk, which fell dead before the girl's look. She stretched the elk hide, and they used it for a shelter. With the sinews the dog had stolen, they sewed their moccasins, and mended their clothing.

When the elk meat ran out, the same thing happened. A buffalo was seen by the boy coming straight to their shelter, and the girl killed it by a look. They cut up the meat, and used the hide to make them a larger and better shelter. They stayed here until winter came and snow began to fall. They had only these two hides for shelter.

One night, when the girl went to bed, she made a wish, saying, "I wish that I might see a lodge over there in that sheltered place in the morning. I could sleep there with my brother and the dog, and could have a bed in the back of the lodge. I could make him a bow and some arrows, so that he could kill the buffalo close to the camp when they gather here in bad weather to use this underbrush for a wind-break." She also wished that her brother might become a young man, and that they might have meat racks in the camp and meat on them.

In the morning, when the boy got up and looked out, he said, "Sister, there is our lodge over there now." It was in the very place the girl had wished. They moved their things over to it, and took the fire over. When the boy entered the lodge, he was a young man. That winter he killed many buffalo, and they had plenty of meat.

One night, as she was going to bed, the girl made another wish. She was talking to her brother when she made it. She said, "Brother, our father has treated us very badly. He has caused us to eat our mother, and he had us tied up and deserted by the people. He has treated us badly. I wish that we knew how to get word to the camp, and I wish that we had two bears that we could cause to eat our father."

Next morning, when the girl got up, she saw in the lodge, sitting on either side of the door, two bears. She spoke to them, and said, "Hello, my animals, arise and eat;" and then she gave them food. She went out to one of the meat racks, and pulled from some meat that was hanging there, a piece of bloody fat, and spoke to a raven that was sitting in a tree near by, saying, "Come here; I wish to send you on an errand." When the raven had flown to her, she said to it, "Go and look for the camp of my people, and fly about among the lodges, calling, and when the people come out and ask each other, 'what is that raven doing? and what is he carrying?' drop down this piece of fat where there is a crowd gathered, and tell them that the people you came from have great scaffolds of meat."

The raven took the piece of fat in his bill and flew away. He found the camp, and flew about calling and calling, and a number of men who were sitting about the camp began to say to each other, "What is that raven carrying?" The raven dropped the meat, and some one who picked it up said, "Why, it is fresh fat."

Then the raven said, "Those people whom you threw away are still in the old camp, and they have scaffolds of meat like this." Then the raven flew away, and went back to the girl, and told what he had done.

An old man began to walk through the camp, crying out to the people, and saying, "Those children that we threw away have plenty of meat; they are in the old camp, and now we must move back to it as quickly as we can." The people tore down their lodges, and packed up and started back. Some of the young men went ahead in little groups of threes and fours, and reached the children's camp before the others. When they arrived there, the girl fed them, and gave them meat to carry back to the main camp. All the trees about the lodge were covered with meat, and the buffalo hides were stacked up in great piles.

After a time the whole village came to the place, and camped not far from the children's lodge, and all the people began to come to the lodge to get food. The girl sent word to her father not to come until all the rest had come. When they had been supplied, he should come and take his time, and not eat in a hurry.

She said to the bears, "I am going to send for your food last. After that person gets here, and has eaten, as he goes out of the lodge, I will say, there is your food. When I say this, you shall eat him up."

In the evening, when the last one of the people was going out of the lodge, she said to him, "Tell the people not to come here any more; my father is coming now."

When the father came, they fed him, and he was glad. He said, "Oh, my children, you are living nicely here; you have plenty of meat and tongues and back fat." He did not eat everything that the girl had set before him; he said, "I will take all this home for my breakfast."

After he had gone out of the lodge to return to the camp, the girl said to the bears, "There is your food, eat him up." The bears sprang after the father, and pulled him down. He called to his daughter to take her animals off, but they killed him there, and began to drag him back to the lodge. The girl said to them, "Take him off somewhere else and eat him, and what you do not eat throw into the stream."

What the bears did not eat they threw in the creek, and then they washed their hands off, and no one ever knew what had become of the father. Since that time bears have eaten human flesh when they could.

The boy and the girl returned to the camp, and always afterward lived there well.

THE CHILDREN WHO RAN FROM THEIR MOTHER: VERSION II
(Cheyenne)

In a solitary tent lived a lone family,—a man, his wife, and two children. When the man went out hunting, he always painted his wife's face and body before he started in the morning. His wife went for water to a lake near by. She always went to the same place; and when she came to the lake, she took off her clothes, as if to bathe. Then a large snake rose out of the lake, after the woman had spoken to it and told it to appear. The snake asked her to come out to him, since her husband had gone away hunting. The woman did as the snake said. Every morning she went to the lake. Her husband brought back meat, and she and the children were glad. The man did not know what happened. He did not know that his wife went after water to the lake and met a large snake. But one day he asked her what made the paint come off her. She said that she took a bath. Next morning he started as if to hunt; but dug a hiding-place near the lake to see what his wife did. She came to the shore and called to the snake: "Come, I am waiting." Then he saw a big old snake rise from the water, and ask her if her husband had gone hunting. She answered: "Yes, I am coming." She took off her clothes and entered the lake, and the snake was soon around her. The man had watched them, and now, leaving his hiding place, he jumped on the snake, and with a large knife cut it in pieces and at last killed it. Then he caught his wife and killed her. He cut her up and took her meat home and gave it to his children. He cooked his wife, and the children unknowingly ate their mother. Then the man said to them: "Tell your mother when she comes home that I went to get more meat which I left hanging on a tree so that the wolves cannot reach it." And he went away. The younger child said: "Our mother is merely teasing us (by staying away)." But the older girl answered: "Do not say anything against our mother." Then their mother's head came rolling to them; and it said: "I am very sorry that my children have eaten me up." The two children ran away, but the head pursued them. At last they were worn out, but their mother's head still rolled after them. Then the older girl drew a line or mark on the ground and so deep a hole opened that the head could not cross. The younger girl was very hungry. She said to her sister: "Look at that deer." The older girl looked at the deer, and it fell down dead as if shot. So they ate of it. Then some one was kind to them and helped them, and they lived in a large lodge and had much food of various kinds to eat. Two large panthers and two large black bears guarded them against all wild animals and persons.

A camp of people was starving. Neither buffalo nor smaller game could be found. The people heard that the children had abundance of food of all kinds, and they all moved to them. When they arrived the children invited them, and the various companies came and ate with them. Finally they all went out again; only the children's father now stayed with them again. But they regretted what he had done to them. So they caused the lions to jump upon their father, and he was killed.

The Woman Who Ran After Her Children and Husband
(Blackfoot)

A long time ago, very far back, before any of these things had happened, or these stories had been told, there was a man who had a wife and two children. This man had no arrows nor bow, and no way to kill food for his family. They lived on roots and berries.

One night he had a dream, and the dream told him that if he would go out and get one of the large spider-webs, such as hang in the brush, and would take it and hang it on the trail of the animals where they passed, he would be helped, and would get plenty of food. He did this, and used to go to the place in the morning and find that the animals had stepped in this web, and their legs were tangled in it, and they would make no effort to get out. He would kill the animals with his stone axe, and would haul the meat to camp with the dog travois.

One day, when he got to the lodge, he found that his wife was perfuming herself with sweet pine, burned over the fire, and he suspected at once that she had a lover, for he had never seen her do this before. He said nothing. The next day he told his wife that he must set his spider-web farther off. He did so, and caught an animal, and brought part of the meat back to camp. The next morning he told his wife to go and bring in the meat that he had left over in the hills.

Now the woman thought that her husband was watching her, so when she started she went over the hill out of sight, and then stopped and looked back at the camp. As she peered through the grass, she saw her husband still sitting in the same place where he had been when she left him. She drew back and waited for a time, and then went out and looked a second time and saw him still sitting there. A third time she came back and looked, but he was still there, so she went off to get the meat.

The man at length got up and went to the crest of the hill and saw that his wife was gone. He spoke to his children, saying: "Children, do you ever go with your mother to gather wood?" They said: "No, we never go there." He asked: "Where does your mother go to get her wood?" They answered: "Over there in that large patch of dead timber is where she gets it."

The man went over to this big patch of timber, and found there a den of large rattlesnakes. One of these snakes was his wife's lover. He gathered up wood and made great piles of it and set them on fire. Then he went back to the camp and said to the children: "I have set fire to that timber, and your mother is going to be very angry. She will try to kill us. I will give you three things, and you must run away. For myself, I will wait here for her." He gave the children a stick, a stone, and a bunch of moss, and said: "If your mother runs after you, and you see that she is coming up to you, throw this stick behind you on your trail; and if she comes up with you again, throw the stone back. If that does not check her coming on, wet this moss, and wring out the water on your back trail. If you do as I tell you, your mother will not kill you nor me." The children started off, as he had told them to. Then he went out into the brush and got another spider web and hung it over the door of the lodge.

When the woman, a long way off, looked back and saw that her timber patch was all on fire she felt very sorry, and she ran back as hard as she could toward the lodge, angry, and feeling that she must do something. When she came to the lodge, she stooped to go in at the door, but got caught in the cobweb. She had one foot in the lodge, but the man was standing there ready, and he cut it off with his stone axe. She still struggled to get in, and at last put her head in, and he cut this off. When he had done this, the man ran out of the lodge and down the creek. His children had gone south. When the man ran down the creek, the woman's body followed him, while the head started after the children, rolling along the ground.

As they ran away the children kept looking behind them to see whether their mother was following, but they did not see her coming until the head was close to them. The older of the two, when he saw it, said: "Why, here is our mother's head coming right after us!" The head called out and said: "Yes, children, but there is no life for you." The boy quickly threw the stick behind him, as he had been told to do, and back from where the stick struck the ground it was all dense forest.

The children ran on, but soon they again saw behind them the head coming. The younger said: "Brother, our father said to throw the stone behind us if our mother was catching up. Throw it." The elder brother threw the stone, and when it struck the ground it made a high mountain from ocean to ocean,—from the north waters to the south waters. The woman could see no way to pass this wall, so she rolled along it till she came to a big water. Then the head turned and rolled back in the other direction until it came to another big water.

There was no way to pass over this mountain. As she was rolling along, presently she came to two rams feeding, and she said to them: "Open a passage for me through this mountain, so that I can overtake my children. They have passed over it, and I want to overtake them. If you will open a passage for me, I will marry the chief of the sheep." The rams took this word to the chief of the sheep, and he said: "Yes, butt a passage through the mountains for her." The sheep gathered and the rams began to butt the mountains. They knocked down rocks and peaks and cliffs and opened ravines, but it took a long time to butt a passage through the mountains. They butted, and butted, and butted till their horns were all worn down, but the pass was not yet open. All this time the head was rolling around very impatient, and at last it came to an ant-hill. It said to the ants: "Here, if you will finish the passage through those mountains, I will marry the chief ant." The chief of the ants called out all his people, and they went to work boring in the mountains. They bored a passage through the mountains south of the Dearborn River. This tunnel is still to be seen, and the rocks about it all bored and honeycombed by the ants. When they had finished the passage, the head rolled through and went rolling down the mountain on the other side.

The children were still running, and had now gone a long way, but after a long travel they could see the head rolling behind them. The younger one said to the older: "Brother, you must wet that moss;" and as they were running along they soaked it, and it was ready. When they saw that the head was catching up, they wrung out the bunch of moss on their trail behind them, and at once found that they were in a different land, and that behind them was a big water surrounding the country which they had just left. That is why this country is surrounded by water. The head rolled into this big water and was drowned.

When the children saw that the head was drowned, they gathered wood and made a large raft, binding the sticks together with willow bark, and at a place west of here, where the water is narrowest, they tried to sail back to the land that they had left. The wind was blowing from the west, and helped them, and they used sticks for paddles, and at last they reached the land.

When they had landed they traveled east through countries occupied by many different tribes of Indians, to get back to the land that they had left, and when they reached this country they found it occupied by a different people, the Snakes and the Crows. So the youngest boy said: "Let us separate. Here we are in a strange country and among a different people. You follow the foot of the mountains and go north, and I will follow the mountains south, and see what I can discover." So they separated, one going north and the other south.

One of these boys was very shrewd and the other very simple. The simple one went north to discover what he could and to make people. The smart boy is the one who made the white people in the south, and taught them how to make irons and many other things. This is why the whites are so smart. The simple boy who went north made the Blackfeet. Being ignorant, he could not teach them anything. He was known across the mountains as Left Hand, and in later years by the Blackfeet as Old Man (*Nápi*). The woman's body chased the father down the stream, and is still following him. The body of the woman is the moon, and the father is the sun. If she can catch him she will kill him, and it will be always night. If she does not catch him, it will be day and night as now.

THE SALT WITCH
(Unidentified)

A pillar of snowy salt once stood on the Nebraska plain, about forty miles above the point where the Saline flows into the Platte, and white men used to hear of it as the Salt Witch. An Indian tribe was for a long time quartered at the junction of the rivers, its chief a man of blood and muscle in whom his people gloried, but so fierce, withal, that nobody made a companion of him except his wife, who alone could check his tigerish rages.

In sooth, he loved her so well that on her death he became a recluse and shut himself within his lodge, refusing to see anybody. This mood endured with him so long that mutterings were heard in the tribe and there was talk of choosing another chief. Some of this talk he must have heard, for one morning he emerged in war-dress, and without a word to any one strode across the plain to westward. On returning a full month later he was more communicative and had something unusual to relate. He also proved his prowess by brandishing a belt of fresh scalps before the eyes of his warriors, and he had also brought a lump of salt.

He told them that after traveling far over the prairie he had thrown himself on the earth to sleep, when he was aroused by a wailing sound close by. In the light of a new moon he saw a hideous old woman brandishing a tomahawk over the head of a younger one, who was kneeling, begging for mercy, and trying to shake off the grip from her throat. The sight of the women, forty miles from the village, so surprised the chief that he ran toward them. The younger woman made a desperate effort to free herself, but in vain, as it seemed, for the hag wound her left hand in her hair while with the other she raised the axe and was about to strike.

At that moment the chief gained a view of the face of the younger woman—it was that of his dead wife. With a snarl of wrath he leaped upon the hag and buried his own hatchet in her brain, but before he could catch his wife in his arms the earth had opened and both women disappeared, but a pillar of salt stood where he had seen this thing. For years the Indians maintained that the column was under the custody of the Salt Witch, and when they went there to gather salt they would beat the ground with clubs, believing that each blow fell upon her person and kept her from working other evil.

BANSHEE OF THE BAD LANDS
(Ponka)

Hell, with the fires out," is what the Bad Lands of Dakota have been called. The fearless Western nomenclature fits the place. It is an ancient sea-bottom, with its clay strata worn by frost and flood into forms like pagodas, pyramids, and terraced cities. Labyrinthine cañons wind among these fantastic peaks, which are brilliant in color, but bleak, savage, and oppressive. Game courses over the castellated hills, rattlesnakes bask at the edge of the crater above burning coal seams, and wild men have made despairing stand here against advancing civilization. It may have been the white victim of a red man's jealousy that haunts the region of the butte called "Watch Dog," or it may have been an Indian woman who was killed there, but there is a banshee in the desert whose cries have chilled the blood that would not have cooled at the sight of a bear or panther. By moonlight, when the scenery is most suggestive and unearthly, and the noises of wolves and owls inspire uneasy feelings, the ghost is seen on a hill a mile south of the Watch Dog, her hair blowing, her arms tossing in strange gestures.

If war parties, emigrants, cowboys, hunters, any who for good or ill are going through this country, pass the haunted butte at night, the rocks are lighted with phosphor flashes and the banshee sweeps upon them. As if wishing to speak, or as if waiting a question that it has occurred to none to ask, she stands beside them in an attitude of appeal, but if asked what she wants she flings her arms aloft and with a shriek that echoes through the blasted gulches for a mile she disappears and an instant later is seen wringing her hands on her hill-top. Cattle will not graze near the haunted butte and the cowboys keep aloof from it, for the word has never been spoken that will solve the mystery of the region or quiet the unhappy banshee.

The creature has a companion, sometimes, in an unfleshed skeleton that trudges about the ash and clay and haunts the camps in a search for music. If he hears it he will sit outside the door and nod in time to it, while a violin left within his reach is eagerly seized and will be played on through half the night. The music is wondrous: now as soft as the stir of wind in the sage, anon as harsh as the cry of a wolf or startling as the stir of a rattler. As the east begins to brighten the music grows fainter, and when it is fairly light it has ceased altogether. But he who listens to it must on no account follow the player if the skeleton moves away, for not only will it lead him into rocky pitfalls, whence escape is hopeless, but when there the music will intoxicate, madden, and will finally charm his soul from his body.

THE HAND GAME
(Cheyenne)

A certain "ghost" had a body like a man's, but he had two faces, one looking forward and one backward. He was immensely large, and could almost step over the greatest rivers when he came to them while walking. He was a great hunter, for he could catch and take hold of the game. He found a tent standing by itself, in which lived a man with his family, including a handsome daughter. The ghost fell very much in love with the girl, and determined to supply the family with meat. Every morning before daylight he brought game to the tent. The man did not know who was so kind to them. He dug a hiding-place, and entered it while it was still dark. Then he saw the ghost come, bringing game. But he was very much afraid now, and after the ghost had gone, he started off to hide with his family. The ghost followed them, and came to their tent. But the man would not give him his daughter. They decided to play "hand-game" (hiding-button) for her. So they played for five nights. But the man won, so that the ghost lost both the girl and his meat.

Two Faces
(Cheyenne)

Nearly every night a child disappeared from a camp. A young man wondered who stole the babies. One dark night he said to himself: "I will watch tonight. I will watch every tent where the people are sleeping. If any one takes a child tonight, I may hear it cry out." So he watched the whole village, and looked outside. He found that the thief was Two-Faces, who had one face in front and one at the back of his head, so that he could look on both sides of him. The young man found him fast asleep. Near him were many dead babies that he had stolen. Most of them had their ears cut off, and Two-Faces had a long string of ears on a line, for he lived on human ears. The young man ran to the river and looked for shells. He gathered a great number of shells, which looked almost like human ears, and strung them, and bloodied them. Then he cut a piece of meat, and shaped it like an ear. When Two-Faces awoke, he saw a person sitting near him eating an ear. It was this young man eating the meat. Two-Faces asked him where he learned to eat ears. The man said to him: "I live on ears. I always steal children and cut off their ears. The only thing that I am afraid of is that if I eat salt, it will kill me." Then Two-Faces said: "I should at once die if any one beat a gourd and fat was thrown in the fire." When night came, they both went to the camp. The young man then told Two-Faces to wait for him; he would go ahead. Then he went to his friends and told them to prepare: he was bringing Two-Faces, who had stolen all the children. He directed that a gourd be beaten and fat meat thrown at the fire. So at last they succeeded in killing Two-Faces. Then he was burned.

The Snake-Wife
(Sioux)

A certain chief advised his son to travel. Idling, he pointed out, was not the way to qualify for chieftainship.

"When I was your age," said he, "I did not sit still. There was hard work to be done. And now look at me: I have become a great chief."

"I will go hunting, father," said the youth. So his father furnished him with good clothing, and had a horse saddled for him.

The young man went off on his expedition, and by and by fell in with some elk. Shooting at the largest beast, he wounded it but slightly, and as it dashed away he spurred his horse after it. In this manner they covered a considerable distance, till at length the hunter, worn out with thirst and fatigue, reined in his steed and dismounted. He wandered about in search of water till he was well-nigh spent, but after a time he came upon a spring, and immediately improvised a song of thanksgiving to the deity, Wakanda, who had permitted him to find it. His rejoicing was somewhat premature, however, for when he approached the spring a snake started up from it. The youth was badly scared, and retreated to a safe distance without drinking. It seemed as though he must die of thirst after all. Venturing to look back after a time, he saw that the snake had disappeared, and very cautiously he returned. Again the snake darted from the water, and the thirsty hunter was forced to flee. A third return to the spring had no happier results, but when his thirst drove him to a fourth attempt the youth found, instead of a snake, a very beautiful woman. She offered him a drink in a small cup, which she replenished as often as he emptied it. So struck was he by her grace and beauty that he promptly fell in love with her. When it was time for him to return home she gave him a ring, saying: "When you sit down to eat, place this ring on a seat and say, 'Come, let us eat,' and I will come to you."

Having bidden her farewell, the young man turned his steps homeward, and when he was once more among his kindred he asked that food might be placed before him. "Make haste," said he, "for I am very hungry."

Quickly they obeyed him, and set down a variety of dishes. When he was alone the youth drew the ring from his finger and laid it on a seat. "Come," he said, "let us eat."

Immediately the Snake-woman appeared and joined him at his meal. When she had eaten she vanished as mysteriously as she had come, and the disconsolate husband (for the youth had married her) went out of the lodge to seek her. Thinking she might be among the women of the village, he said to his father: "Let the women dance before me."

An old man was deputed to gather the women together, but not one of them so much as resembled the Snake-woman.

Again the youth sat down to eat, and repeated the formula which his wife had described to him. She ate with him as before, and vanished when the meal was over.

"Father," said the young man, "let the very young women dance before me."

But the Snake-woman was not found among them either.

Another fleeting visit from his wife induced the chief's son to make yet another attempt to find her in the community.

"Let the young girls dance," he said. Still the mysterious Snake-woman was not found.

One day a girl overheard voices in the youth's lodge, and, peering in, saw a beautiful woman sharing his meal. She told the news to the chief, and it soon became known that the chief's son was married to a beautiful stranger.

The youth, however, wished to marry a woman of his own tribe; but the maiden's father, having heard that the young man was already married, told his daughter that she was only being made fun of.

So the girl had nothing more to do with her wooer, who turned for consolation to his ring. He caused food to be brought, and placed the ring on a seat.

"Come," he said, "let us eat."

There was no response; the Snake-woman would not appear.

The youth was greatly disappointed, and made up his mind to go in search of his wife.

"I am going a-hunting," said he, and again his father gave him good clothes and saddled a horse for him.

When he reached the spot where the Snake-woman had first met him, he found her trail leading up to the spring, and beyond it on the other side. Still following the trail, he saw before him a very dilapidated lodge, at the door of which sat an old man in rags. The youth felt very sorry for the tattered old-fellow, and gave him his fine clothes, in exchange for which he received the other's rags.

"You think you are doing me a good turn," said the old man, "but it is I who am going to do you one. The woman you seek has gone over the Great Water. When you get to the other shore talk with the people you shall meet there, and if they do not obey you send them away."

In addition to the tattered garments, the old man gave him a hat, a sword, and a lame old horse.

At the edge of the Great Water the youth prepared to cross, while his companion seated himself on the shore, closed his eyes, and recited a spell. In a moment the young man found himself on the opposite shore. Here he found a lodge inhabited by two aged Thunder-men, who were apparently given to eating human beings. The young stranger made the discovery that his hat rendered him invisible, and he was able to move unseen among the creatures. Taking off his hat for a moment, he took the pipe from the lips of a Thunder-man and pressed it against the latter's hand.

"Oh," cried the Thunder-man, "I am burnt!"

But the youth had clapped on his hat and disappeared.

"It is not well," said the Thunder-man gravely. "A stranger has been here and we have let him escape. When our brother returns he will not believe us if we tell him the man has vanished."

Shortly after this another Thunder-man entered with the body of a man he had killed. When the brothers told him their story he was quite skeptical.

"If I had been here," said he, "I would not have let him escape."

As he spoke the youth snatched his pipe from him and pressed it against the back of his hand.

"Oh," said the Thunder-man, "I am burnt!"

"It was not I," said one brother.

"It was not I," said the other.

"It was I," said the youth, pulling off his hat and appearing among them. "What were you talking about among yourselves? Here I am. Do as you said."

But the Thunder-men were afraid.

"We were not speaking," they said, and the youth put on his hat and vanished.

"What will our brother say," cried the three in dismay, "when he hears that a man has been here and we have not killed him? Our brother will surely hate us."

In a few minutes another Thunder-man came into the lodge, carrying the body of a child. He was very angry when he heard that they had let a man escape.

The youth repeated his trick on the new-comer—appeared for a moment, then vanished again. The fifth and last of the brothers was also deceived in the same manner.

Seeing that the monsters were now thoroughly frightened, the young man took off his magic hat and talked with them.

"You do wrong," said he, "to eat men like this. You should eat buffaloes, not men. I am going away. When I come back I will visit you, and if you are eating buffaloes you shall remain, but if you are eating men I shall send you away."

The Thunder-men promised they would eat only buffaloes in future, and the young man went on his way to seek for the Snake-woman. When at last he came to the village where she dwelt he found she had married a man of another tribe, and in a great rage he swung the sword the magician had given him and slew her, and her husband, and the whole village, after which he returned the way he had come. When he reached the lodge of the Thunder-men he saw that they had not kept their promise to eat only buffaloes.

"I am going to send you above," he said. "Hitherto you have destroyed men, but when I have sent you away you shall give them cooling rain to keep them alive."

So he sent them above, where they became the thunder-clouds.

Proceeding on his journey, he again crossed the Great Water with a single stride, and related to the old wizard all that had happened.

"I have sent the Thunder-men above, because they would not stop eating men. Have I done well?"

"Very well."

"I have killed the whole village where the Snake-woman was, because she had taken another husband. Have I done well?"

"Very well. It was for that I gave you the sword."

The youth returned to his father, and married a very beautiful woman of his own village.

STORIES OF THE DEATH SWING
(Various)

THE WITCH OF PICTURED ROCKS
(Ojibwa)

On the Pictured Rocks of Lake Superior dwelt an Ojibway woman, a widow, who was cared for by a relative. This relative was a hunter, the husband of an agreeable wife, the father of two bright children. Being of a mean and jealous nature, the widow begrudged every kindness that the hunter showed to his wife—the skins he brought for her clothing, the moose's lip or other dainty that he saved for her; and one day, in a pretence of fine good-nature, the old woman offered to give the younger a swing in a vine pendent from a tree that overhung the lake.

The wife accepted, and, seating herself on the vine, was swayed to and fro, catching her breath, yet laughing as she swept out over the water. When the momentum was greatest the old woman cut the stem. A splash was heard—then all was silent. Returning to the lodge, the hag disguised herself in a dress of the missing woman, and sitting in a shadow, pretended to nurse the infant of the household. The hunter, returning, was a little surprised that his wife should keep her face from him, and more surprised that the old woman did not appear for her share of the food that he had brought; but after their meal he took his little ones to the lake, to enjoy the evening breeze, when the elder burst into tears, declaring that the woman in the lodge was not his mother, and that he feared his own mother was dead or lost.

The hunter hurled his spear into the earth and prayed that, if his wife were dead, her body might be found, so he could mourn over it and give it burial. Instantly a bolt of lightning came from a passing cloud and shot into the lake, while the thunder-peal that followed shook the stones he stood on. It also disturbed the water and presently something was seen rising through it. The man stepped into a thicket and watched. In a few moments a gull arose from the lake and flew to the spot where the children were seated. Around its body was a leather belt, embroidered with beads and quills, which the hunter recognized, and, advancing softly, he caught the bird—that changed at once into the missing woman. The family set forth toward home, and as they entered the lodge the witch—for such she was— looked up, with a start, then uttered a cry of despair. Bending low, she moved her arms in both imprecation and appeal. A moment later a black, ungainly bird flew from the wigwam and passed from sight among the trees. The witch never came back to plague them.

THE MALICIOUS MOTHER-IN-LAW
(Ojibwa)

An Ojibway or Chippeway legend tells of a hunter who was greatly devoted to his wife. As a proof of his affection he presented her with the most delicate morsels from the game he killed. This aroused the jealousy and envy of his mother, who lived with them, and who imagined that these little attentions should be paid to her, and not to the younger woman. The latter, quite unaware of her mother-in-law's attitude, cooked and ate the gifts her husband brought her. Being a woman of a gentle and agreeable disposition, who spent most of her time attending to her household duties and watching over her child and a little orphan boy whom she had adopted, she tried to make friends with the old dame, and was grieved and disappointed when the latter would not respond to her advances.

The mother-in-law nursed her grievance until it seemed of gigantic proportions. Her heart grew blacker and blacker against her son's wife, and at last she determined to kill her. For a time she could think of no way to put her evil intent into action, but finally she hit upon a plan.

One day she disappeared from the lodge, and returned after a space looking very happy and good-tempered. The younger woman was surprised and delighted at the alteration. This was an agreeably different person from the nagging, cross-grained old creature who had made her life a burden! The old woman repeatedly absented herself from her home after this, returning on each occasion with a pleased and contented smile on her wrinkled face. By and by the wife allowed her curiosity to get the better of her, and she asked the meaning of her mother-in-law's happiness.

"If you must know," replied the old woman, "I have made a beautiful swing down by the lake, and always when I swing on it I feel so well and happy that I cannot help smiling."

The young woman begged that she too might be allowed to enjoy the swing.

"Tomorrow you may accompany me," was the reply. But next day the old woman had some excuse, and so on, day after day, till the curiosity of her son's wife was very keen. Thus when the elder woman said one day, "Come with me, and I will take you to the swing. Tie up your baby and leave him in charge of the orphan," the other complied eagerly, and was ready in a moment to go with her mother-in-law.

When they reached the shores of the lake they found a lithe sapling which hung over the water.

"Here is my swing," said the old creature, and she cast aside her robe, fastened a thong to her waist and to the sapling, and swung far over the lake. She laughed so much and seemed to find the pastime so pleasant that her daughter-in-law was more anxious than ever to try it for herself.

"Let me tie the thong for you," said the old woman, when she had tired of swinging. Her companion threw off her robe and allowed the leather thong to be fastened round her waist. When all was ready she was commanded to swing. Out over the water she went fearlessly, but as she did so the jealous old mother-in-law cut the thong, and she fell into the lake.

The old creature, exulting over the success of her cruel scheme, dressed herself in her victim's clothes and returned to the lodge. But the baby cried and refused to be fed by her, and the orphan boy cried too, for the young woman had been almost a mother to him since his parents had died.

"Where is the baby's mother?" he asked, when some hours had passed and she did not return.

"At the swing," replied the old woman roughly.

When the hunter returned from the chase he brought with him, as usual, some morsels of game for his wife, and, never dreaming that the woman bending over the child might not be she, he gave them to her. The lodge was dark, for it was evening, and his mother wore the clothes of his wife and imitated her voice and movements, so that his error was not surprising. Greedily she seized the tender pieces of meat, and cooked and ate them.

The heart of the little orphan was so sore that he could not sleep. In the middle of the night he rose and went to look for his foster-mother. Down by the lake he found the swing with the thong cut, and he knew that she had been killed. Crying bitterly, he crept home to his couch, and in the morning told the hunter all that he had seen.

"Say nothing," said the chief, "but come with me to hunt, and in the evening return to the shores of the lake with the child, while I pray to Manitou that he may send me back my wife."

So they went off in search of game without a word to the old woman; nor did they stay to eat, but set out directly it was light. At sunset they made their way to the lake-side, the little orphan carrying the baby. Here the hunter blackened his face and prayed earnestly that the Great Manitou might send back his wife. While he prayed the orphan amused the child by singing quaint little songs; but at last the baby grew weary and hungry and began to cry.

Far in the lake his mother heard the sound, and skimmed over the water in the shape of a great white gull. When she touched the shore she became a woman again, and hugged the child to her heart's content. The orphan boy besought her to return to them.

"Alas!" said she, "I have fallen into the hands of the Water Manitou, and he has wound his silver tail about me, so that I never can escape."

As she spoke the little lad saw that her waist was encircled by a band of gleaming silver, one end of which was in the water. At length she declared that it was time for her to return to the home of the water-god, and after having exacted a promise from the boy that he would bring her baby there every day, she became a gull again and flew away. The hunter was informed of all that had passed, and straightway determined that he would be present on the following evening. All next day he fasted and besought the good-will of Manitou, and when the night began to fall he hid himself on the shore till his wife appeared. Hastily emerging from his concealment, the hunter poised his spear and struck the girdle with all his force. The silver band parted, and the woman was free to return home with her husband.

Overjoyed at her restoration, he led her gently to the lodge, where his mother was sitting by the fire. At the sight of her daughter-in-law, whom she thought she had drowned in the lake, she started up in such fear and astonishment that she tripped, overbalanced, and fell into the fire. Before they could pull her out the flames had risen to the smoke-hole, and when the fire died down no woman was there, but a great black bird, which rose slowly from the smoking embers, flew out of the lodge, and was never seen again.

As for the others, they lived long and happily, undisturbed by the jealousy and hatred of the malicious crone.

Malicious Medicine Man
(Cheyenne)

There was a great medicine-man, who was powerful and did injury, but who had a good daughter. He lived near a geyser, in an earth-lodge. Several young men lived with him, and went out hunting for him. He had great quantities of dried buffalo meat hanging all around his lodge. When meat was scarce in a village near by, he sent his young men to summon the people to him, and then he gave a feast to the various companies. Then this great man told the companies to dress, and dance before him. When the dance was almost over, he announced that he would pick out a young man to be his son-in-law. So he selected a young man, but after the marriage he sent the village away again. He was malicious, and did not treat his son-in-law rightly. Every night he had a fire, and slept close by his son-in-law and daughter. When they moved, he raised his head, and said: "Don't stir! Sleep!" When they talked, or even whispered, he made them be quiet, and ordered them to sleep. Even when they were outside, and spoke against him, he was so powerful that he knew it. The first morning he sent his son-in-law out to cut arrows. He told him that if he brought no smooth, straight sticks, he need not come back. The young man wandered through the woods, but he found only rough sticks, and he was discouraged, and tired, and cried. A person called to him, and asked him why he wept. The young man related his trouble, and the person told him to cut bulrushes of the right length. So he got as many bulrushes as he could carry, and they turned to smooth sticks. Then he went on up a mountain, and cried again. The birds heard him, and asked him why he cried. He said that he could not get the eagle-feathers that his father-in-law wanted for feathering the arrows. So the eagle shook himself, and feathers flew out, and he got as many as he could use. Then he returned, carrying the sticks and feathers. His father-in-law had four men who could make bows and arrows, and they began to make the arrows for him. Then he sent his son-in-law to get plums for the arrow-makers. It was nearly winter, and there was no fruit of any sort left, but he told him to get fresh plums, and bring none that were rotten or dried. He knew this was impossible. The young man took a bag, and went out, crying. Again a person asked him why he wept. The young man said it was because he was to get plums for the arrow-makers of his father-in-law. The person told him to go to a plum-bush, and that the tree would shake itself, and only fresh plums would fall from it. All this happened. When the great medicine-man saw his son-in-law returning well loaded, he was pleased and went to meet him. So they made the arrows, and ate the plums. Next morning the great man wanted to play at throwing arrows at a hoop with his son-in-law. They played near the geyser, and the medicine-man pushed his son-in-law into it. Only his bones came out again.

Three times the great man had selected a son-in-law, and all this had happened. His daughter did not like his acts; but even when she went far off to tell her husband of his danger, the great man could hear by the wind or the earth what she said. The fourth time he got a very fine young man for son-in-law. He sent him out to drive a buffalo of good age immediately in front of his house, so that he could shoot him with his new arrows. The son-in-law went far off, crying. Seven buffalo were about him, and one asked him what he wanted. The young man told him, but they said they were powerless against this great man, and told him to go farther south. He went on, and met four buffalo, who asked him what he wished. But they also were powerless, and sent him farther south. He went on and came to two buffalo. With them the same happened. As he again went on southward, he was so discouraged that he walked with his head down, and when he met a single buffalo, did not stop even when the bull asked him what he wished. Finally he turned around, and told his story. He was hopeless, for the great man could not be cut or burnt or wounded in any way. "He is like this rock," he said, and pointed to a large black stone. Then the buffalo said: "I will try on this whether I can do anything to him." He went off east, and charged against the stone, but did not injure it. He charged from the south, from the west, from the north—all vainly. The fifth time he went toward the northeast, and this time he broke a piece out of the rock. Then he told the young man to drive him toward his father-in-law's house. They arrived there, both seeming completely tired out; the buffalo pretended to be trying to escape, while the young man headed him off. At last, after a long chase, he drove him near his father-in-law's door. The medicine-man came out with his new arrows, and shot at the bull. When the arrows neared the buffalo, they turned to reeds again, and did not injure him; but to the medicine-man they appeared to enter the bull, and disappear in him. The bull staggered and seemed nearly dead, and the man approached him. The bull staggered farther and farther away from the house, leading the medicine-man with him, so that he might not escape. Then he turned, charged, and tossed him. As the man fell, he tossed him again and again, so that he never touched the ground. Thus he tossed him until he was completely bruised and unable to move. Then they put him in his lodge, covered him with brush and wood, and lit it. The flames burnt higher and higher, but they only heard the medicine-man inside the fire cursing and threatening them with death when he should come out. Then suddenly there were poppings, and explosions, and beads, diamonds, and precious stones flew out of the fire. They were afraid to touch these, for fear the man might then come to life again, and put them back into the fire. But the whites to whom some of them flew kept them, and thus became richer.

THE KILLING OF CLOUDY SKY
(Sioux)

In the Dakota camp on the bank of Spirit Lake, or Lake Calhoun, IA, lived Cloudy Sky, a medicine-man, who had been made repellent by age and accident, but who was feared because of his magic power. At eighty years of age he looked for a third wife, and chose the daughter of a warrior, his presents of blankets and calicoes to the parents winning their consent. The girl, *Harpstenah* (a common name for a third daughter among the Sioux), dreaded and hated this man, for it was rumored that he had killed his first wife and basely sold his second. When she learned what had been decided for her she rushed from the camp in tears and sat in a lonely spot near the lake to curse and lament unseen. As she sat there the waters were troubled. There was no wind, yet great waves were thrown up, and tumbled hissing on the shore. Presently came a wave higher than the rest, and a graceful form leaped from it, half shrouded in its own long hair.

"Do not tremble," said the visitant, for Harpstenah had hidden her face. "I am the daughter of Unktahe, the water god. In four days your parents will give you to Cloudy Sky, as his wife, though you love Red Deer. It is with you to wed the man you hate or the man you love. Cloudy Sky has offended the water spirits and we have resolved upon his death. If you will be our agent in destroying him, you shall marry Red Deer and live long and happily. The medicine-man wandered for years through the air with the thunder birds, flinging his deadly fire-spears at us, and it was for killing the son of Unktahe that he was last sent to earth, where he has already lived twice before. Kill him while he sleeps and we will reward you."

As Harpstenah went back to the village her prospective bridegroom ogled her as he sat smoking before his lodge, his face blackened and blanket torn in mourning for an enemy he had killed. She resolved to heed the appeal of the manitou. When

Red Deer heard how she had been promised to the old conjurer, he was filled with rage. Still, he became thoughtful and advised caution when she told him of the water spirit's counsel, for the dwellers in the lakes were, of all immortals, most deceitful, and had ever been enemies of the Dakotas. "I will do as I am bidden," she said, sternly. "Go away and visit the Tetons for a time. It is now the moon of strawberries" (June), "but in the moon when we gather wild rice" (September) "return and I will be your wife."

Red Deer obeyed, after finding that she would not elope with him, and with the announcement that he was going on a long hunt he took his leave of the village. Harpstenah made ready for the bridal and greeted her future husband with apparent pleasure and submissiveness. He gave a medicine feast in token of the removal of his mourning, and appeared in new clothing, greased and braided hair, and a white blanket decorated with a black band—the record of a slain enemy.

On the night before the wedding the girl creeps to his lodge, but hesitates when she sees his medicine-bag hanging beside the door—the medicine that has kept its owner from evil and is sacred from the touch of woman. As she lingers the night-breeze seems to bring a voice from the water: "Can a Dakota woman want courage when she is forced to marry the man she hates?"

She delays no longer. A knife-blade glitters for an instant in the moonlight—and Cloudy Sky is dead. Strange, is it not, that the thunder birds flap so heavily along the west at that moment and a peal of laughter sounds from the lake? She washes the blood from the blade, steals to her father's lodge, and pretends to sleep. In the morning she is loud in her grief when it is made known to her that the medicine-man was no more, and the doer of the deed is never discovered. In time her wan face gets its color and when the leaves begin to fall Red Deer returns and weds her.

They seem to be happy for a time, and have two sons who promise to be famous hunters, but consumption fastens on Red Deer and he dies far from the village. The sons are shot by enemies, and while their bodies are on their way to Harpstenah's lodge she, too, is stricken dead by lightning. The spirit of Cloudy Sky had rejoined the thunder birds, and the water manitou had promised falsely.

THE BUFFALO KEEPERS
(Cheyenne)

Far away there was a large camp-circle. Food was very scarce, and some persons had starved. One day one of the old men went about inquiring whether the people wanted to travel to a large lake, where ducks and game abounded. They moved camp, packing their goods on dogs. Two young men were sent ahead, but they returned with the news that they had found no game whatever. The children were all crying for food, and the misery was extreme. The people selected two strong young men able to travel four days without food, and told them that they must find something for the whole tribe, and bring back good news. The young men set out and traveled steadily for two days, until they were worn out and slept from the middle of the night until the morning star rose. Then they went on northward again. Finally they came near a large river, and beyond it they saw a blue mountain. The river was slow, smooth, wide, and sandy on both sides, but beyond it rose bluffs, and close behind these the mountain. The two scouts put their clothes on their heads, and entered the river. In the center, one of them got fast. He shouted that some powerful thing under water was taking him; and he asked his friend to tell his parents not to weep too much for him. The other man crossed in safety. Then his friend called to him to come back and touch him as a farewell. So the other went back into the river, and touched him. Then he went out again, and cried all day, wandering about. A person came to the top of the bank above the river, and asked him why he cried, and whether he could do anything for him. The young man replied that a powerful animal was holding fast his friend in the river, and pointed to him. The person who had come was powerful; he wore a wolfskin, painted red, on his back; it was tied around his neck and waist, so that he looked like a wolf; and he carried a large knife. He dived into the river, and the water moved and waved, and finally an immense snake with black horns came up, and he cut its throat. The man who had been held fast was already cold and stiff in his legs, but the two others dragged him off, and floated him ashore, and laid him in the sun. The rescuer told the other young man: "Go to the mountain, to its stone door, and tell your grandmother that I have killed the animal that I have been after so long." The young man ran to the foot of the mountain, stood before a flat stone door, and called as he had been told, telling the woman to bring a rope with her. The old woman was glad that the animal had at last been killed. The young man ran back, and was told by the man to help him butcher the snake; then they would carry his friend to his house. They dragged the snake on shore by its horns, and cut it in two, and then into many smaller pieces. They made many trips to the mountain, carrying the meat. Inside, the mountain was like the interior of a tipi, with tent-poles, beds, and so on. Then the young man carried his friend to the mountain, taking him on his back, and holding his hands. The woman made a sweat-house, and he was put into it. The woman told him to try to move. The second time they poured water on the hot rocks he moved a little, the third time more, and after the fourth time he was perfectly well. Then they went into the mountain, and the man told his daughter to cook food,—corn and buffalo meat. This was the first time the young men had seen the daughter, who was very handsome. They ate all the food given them, and were well satisfied. Then the woman asked them why they had come. They told her that they were looking for game for their starving people. The woman said: "It is well, you will have some-thing for your tribe." Then she asked them what kin they would be to the girl; whether they would be her brothers. While they conferred, she said that they could marry her. The other young man proposed to the one that had been fast that he should marry her; and the latter agreed. They were then all very grateful to each other, and the young man married the girl. The woman told her daughter to take the two young men to the herd of buffalo, and the girl showed them large herds of buffalo, and on the other side wide fields of corn. Then the woman told them to cross the river in the same place as before, and not to look backwards, and to rest four times on their way home. So they traveled for four days. Then an old man cried through the village that they were coming. All their relatives and many others came forward; but when they saw that there were three persons, they held somewhat aloof. They entered a tent, and the new husband told an old man to cry to the people to come to shake hands with his wife and embrace her. This was done, and then the young man said that he brought good news, and that that same night his wife's herd would come from the mountain. At night long strings of buffalo came, and the people heard them on all sides. Early in the morning they saw the buffalo, as far as they could look. It was announced that the dogs were not to disturb the game. Then the hunt commenced. The buffalo ran when pursued, but always came back. As many were killed as could be used, and there was abundance of meat. The chiefs gathered, and resolved that they were thankful to the girl for her kindness, and every family was to bring her a present, the best that they had; and they asked her to take the presents to her parents. So all gave to her, and she started back to her parents with her husband and his friend. When they arrived at the mountain, the man stood there, calling to his wife to come out, for their son-in-law had returned. She embraced the two young men from joy and gratitude. When they returned, the tribe was still hunting successfully, and they were again given presents to bring to the girl's parents. When they brought presents a second time, the man was still more grateful, and asked his daughter to take a few ears of corn to the tribe. But she, thinking that they had enough with the buffalo, was silent. When her parents asked her why she did not answer, she told them the reason. So they returned, after her parents had warned her not to feel sorry for any buffalo killed in her sight. Soon after, the children drove a young calf toward the village, and the boys shot at it, and it died in front of her tent. As she came out, she said to herself that she pitied the calf. But as she said it, the herd ran back toward the mountain, and nothing could be seen but dust. A crier went about, saying that presents must again be sent to the old man in the mountain. After prayer and with blessings, the two young men and the girl started once more. After four days they arrived. At once the old man told his daughter that she ought to have been careful. But he would not let them return to the tribe. The parents of the young men and their relatives felt lonely at the long absence, and went out alone to cry. But the young men never returned.

LOVERS
(Various)

CLOUD CATCHER AND THE MOON WOMAN
(Ojibwa)

H ere is the myth of Endymion and Diana, as told on the shores of Saginaw Bay, in Michigan, by Indians who never heard of Greeks. Cloud Catcher, a handsome youth of the Ojibways, offended his family by refusing to fast during the ceremony of his coming of age, and was put out of the paternal wigwam. It was so fine a night that the sky served him as well as a roof, and he had a boy's confidence in his ability to make a living, and something of fame and fortune, maybe. He dropped upon a tuft of moss to plan for his future, and drowsily noted the rising of the moon, in which he seemed to see a face. On awaking he found that it was not day, yet the darkness was half dispelled by light that rayed from a figure near him—the form of a lovely woman.

"Cloud Catcher, I have come for you," she said. And as she turned away he felt impelled to rise and follow. But, instead of walking, she began to move into the air with the flight of an eagle, and, endowed with a new power, he too ascended beside her. The earth was dim and vast below, stars blazed as they drew near them, yet the radiance of the woman seemed to dull their glory. Presently they passed through a gate of clouds and stood on a beautiful plain, with crystal ponds and brooks watering noble trees and leagues of flowery meadow; birds of brightest colors darted here and there, singing like flutes; the very stones were agate, jasper, and chalcedony. An immense lodge stood on the plain, and within were embroideries and ornaments, couches of rich furs, pipes and arms cut from jasper and tipped with silver. While the young man was gazing around him with delight, the brother of his guide appeared and reproved her, advising her to send the young man back to earth at once, but, as she flatly refused to do so, he gave a pipe and bow and arrows to Cloud Catcher, as a token of his consent to their marriage, and wished them happiness, which, in fact, they had.

This brother, who was commanding, tall, and so dazzling in his gold and silver ornaments that one could hardly look upon him, was abroad all day, while his sister was absent for a part of the night. He permitted Cloud Catcher to go with him on one of his daily walks, and as they crossed the lovely Sky Land they glanced down through open valley bottoms on the green earth below. The rapid pace they struck gave to Cloud Catcher an appetite and he asked if there were no game. "Patience," counseled his companion. On arriving at a spot where a large hole had been broken through the sky they reclined on mats, and the tall man loosing one of his silver ornaments flung it into a group of children playing before a lodge. One of the little ones fell and was carried within, amid lamentations. Then the villagers left their sports and labors and looked up at the sky. The tall man cried, in a voice of thunder, "Offer a sacrifice and the child shall be well again." A white dog was killed, roasted, and in a twinkling it shot up to the feet of Cloud Catcher, who, being empty, attacked it voraciously.

Many such walks and feasts came after, and the sights of earth and taste of meat filled the mortal with a longing to see his people again. He told his wife that he wanted to go back. She consented, after a time, saying, "Since you are better pleased with the cares, the ills, the labor, and the poverty of the world than with the comfort and abundance of Sky Land, you may return; but remember you are still my husband, and beware how you venture to take an earthly maiden for a wife."

She arose lightly, clasped Cloud Catcher by the wrist, and began to move with him through the air. The motion lulled him and he fell asleep, waking at the door of his father's lodge. His relatives gathered and gave him welcome, and he learned that he had been in the sky for a year. He took the privations of a hunter's and warrior's life less kindly than he thought to, and after a time he enlivened its monotony by taking to wife a bright-eyed girl of his tribe. In four days she was dead. The lesson was unheeded and he married again. Shortly after, he stepped from his lodge one evening and never came back. The woods were filled with a strange radiance on that night, and it is asserted that Cloud Catcher was taken back to the lodge of the Sun and Moon, and is now content to live in heaven.

THE STAR-MAIDEN
(Chippewa)

A pretty legend of the Chippeways, an Algonquin tribe, tells how Algon, a hunter, won for his bride the daughter of a star. While walking over the prairies he discovered a circular pathway, worn as if by the tread of many feet, though there were no foot-marks visible outside its bounds. The young hunter, who had never before encountered one of these "fairy rings," was filled with surprise at the discovery, and hid himself in the long grass to see whether an explanation might not be forthcoming. He had not long to wait. In a little while he heard the sound of music, so faint and sweet that it surpassed anything he had ever dreamed of. The strains grew fuller and richer, and as they seemed to come from above he turned his eyes toward the sky. Far in the blue he could see a tiny white speck like a floating cloud. Nearer and nearer it came, and the astonished hunter saw that it was no cloud, but a dainty osier car, in which were seated twelve beautiful maidens. The music he had heard was the sound of their voices as they sang strange and magical songs. Descending into the charmed ring, they danced around and around with such exquisite grace and abandon that it was a sheer delight to watch them. But after the first moments of dazzled surprise Algon had eyes only for the youngest of the group, a slight, vivacious creature, so fragile and delicate that it seemed to the stalwart hunter that a breath would blow her away.

He was, indeed, seized with a fierce passion for the dainty sprite, and he speedily decided to spring from the grass and carry her off. But the pretty creatures were too quick for him. The fairy of his choice skillfully eluded his grasp and rushed to the car. The others followed, and in a moment they were soaring up in the air, singing a sweet, unearthly song. The disconsolate hunter returned to his lodge, but try as he might he could not get the thought of the Star-maiden out of his head, and next day, long before the hour of the fairies' arrival, he lay in the grass awaiting the sweet sounds that would herald their approach. At length the car appeared. The twelve ethereal beings danced as before. Again Algon made a desperate attempt to seize the youngest, and again he was unsuccessful.

"Let us stay," said one of the Star-maidens. "Perhaps the mortal wishes to teach us his earthly dances." But the youngest sister would not hear of it, and they all rose out of sight in their osier basket.

Poor Algon returned home more unhappy than ever. All night he lay awake dreaming of the pretty, elusive creature who had wound a chain of gossamer round his heart and brain, and early in the morning he repaired to the enchanted spot. Casting about for some means of gaining his end, he came upon the hollow trunk of a tree in which a number of mice gamboled. With the aid of the charms in his "medicine"-bag he turned himself into one of these little animals, thinking the fair sisters would never pierce his disguise.

That day when the osier car descended its occupants alighted and danced merrily as they were wont in the magic circle, till the youngest saw the hollow tree-trunk (which had not been there on the previous day) and turned to fly. Her sisters laughed at her fears, and tried to reassure her by overturning the tree-trunk. The mice scampered in all directions, and were quickly pursued by the Star-maidens, who killed them all except Algon. The latter regained his own shape just as the youngest fairy raised her hand to strike him. Clasping her in his arms, he bore her to his village, while her frightened sisters ascended to their Star-country.

Arrived at his home, Algon married the maiden, and by his kindness and gentleness soon won her affection. However, her thoughts still dwelt on her own people, and though she indulged her sorrow only in secret, lest it should trouble her husband, she never ceased to lament her lost home.

One day while she was out with her little son she made a basket of osiers, like the one in which she had first come to earth. Gathering together some flowers and gifts for the Star-people, she took the child with her into the basket, sang the magical songs she still remembered, and soon floated up to her own country, where she was welcomed by the king, her father.

Algon's grief was bitter indeed when he found that his wife and child had left him. But he had no means of following them. Every day he would go to the magic circle on the prairie and give vent to his sorrow, but the years went past and there was no sign of his dear ones returning.

Meanwhile the woman and her son had almost forgotten Algon and the earth-country. However, when the boy grew old enough to hear the story he wished to go and see his father. His mother consented, and arranged to go with him. While they were preparing to descend the Star-people said:

"Bring Algon with you when you return, and ask him to bring some feature from every beast and bird he has killed in the chase."

Algon, who had latterly spent almost all his time at the charmed circle, was overjoyed to see his wife and son come back to him, and willingly agreed to go with them to the Star-country. He worked very hard to obtain a specimen of all the rare and curious birds and beasts in his land, and when at last he had gathered the relics—a claw of one, a feather of another, and so on—he piled them in the osier car, climbed in himself with his wife and boy, and set off to the Star-country.

The people there were delighted with the curious gifts Algon had brought them, and, being permitted by their king to take one apiece, they did so. Those who took a tail or a claw of any beast at once became the quadruped represented by the fragment, and those who took the wings of birds became birds themselves. Algon and his wife and son took the feathers of a white falcon and flew down to the prairies, where their descendants may still be seen.

The Chief's Daughter and the Orphan
(Sac and Fox)

Once there was an Indian village. The chief had one daughter. She was very pretty and a nice girl. All the boys admired her, but she would not marry any one. When a certain man was going on the war-path with some men and boys against another tribe, this girl made up her mind to go with them. So she asked her father. At first he was not willing, but she would not give up the idea, so he consented, and asked the head man of the party of men and boys that was going out. She went with them. She had on all a man wears and "packs." They traveled a good many days before they could find anybody. At last they found a village. Before they came to it, the boys used to cook something very nice and take it to her. This was the way they "sparked." If she didn't eat it, it was a sign that she didn't like them. So all the nice boys tried her in that way, but she wouldn't eat anything they cooked for her. But towards the last, an orphan boy (he was good, but not well-off as the rest were) cooked her something which she ate. All the other boys were surprised to see her eat what the poor boy had given her. This was on the way. This boy had a friend who stayed with him all the time (they were always together). The scouts saw the village, and all went to kill the people. When it was all over this boy never came back. The girl felt very bad when the poor boy was missing. She asked of his friend about him. The friend said that he had been killed. The people thought it could not be helped now that he was dead, and concluded to start for home next day. But they could not get the girl to go home with them. She stayed to look for the poor boy. She went toward the village to look for him. At night she got close to the village, and saw him, right in the middle of the village, at the chief's tent. There he was in the midst of a crowd, with his hands and feet tied. They were making him sing a song, or a kind of prayer, used in olden times when any one is going to be killed (his death-song). It made her feel very bad to see him in that way. About midnight she fixed up a stick and made it look like a baby. Then she went around the village and began singing for the "baby" she had made. In this way she put everybody to sleep, even those who were watching him. After they were all asleep, she went up to him and cut the strings that bound his hands and feet. She had an axe in her belt, with which she chopped one of the men's heads off. She then told the young man to hurry and go with her. But his limbs were so numb that she had to carry him on her back as far as the end of the village. They reached home all right. The people were all surprised, for they thought she was dead, and that he would never come back again. The boy's friend had not seen him killed. He had desired him to be killed so that he could have the girl. When the friend tried to take her home, she would not go, although he said the boy was killed, and there was no use in her acting that way, for he was dead and gone. He had cut the poor boy's bowstring, and of course he thought he was sure to be killed when caught. The poor boy's friend was very much ashamed when he saw him return. So the poor orphan married the chief's daughter.

The Keusca Elopement
(Dakota)

Keusca was a village of the Dakota Indians on the Wisconsin bluffs of the Mississippi eighteen hundred miles from its mouth. The name means, to overthrow, or set aside, for it was here that a tribal law was broken. Sacred Wind was a coquette of that village, for whose hand came many young fellows wooing with painted faces. For her they played the bone flute in the twilight, and in the games they danced and leaped their hardest and shot their farthest and truest when she was looking on. Though they amused her she cared not a jot for these suitors, keeping her love for the young brave named the Shield—and keeping it secret, for he was her cousin, and cousins might not wed. If a relative urged her to marry some young fellow for whom she had no liking, she would answer that if forced to do so she would fling herself into the river, and spoke of Winonah and Lovers' Leap.

She was afraid to wed the Shield, for the medicine-men had threatened all who dared to break the marriage laws with unearthly terrors; yet when the Shield had been absent for several weeks on the war-path she realized that life without his companionship was too hollow to be endured—and she admired him all the more when he returned with two scalps hanging at his belt. He renewed his wooing. He allayed her fears by assurances that he, too, was a medicine-man and could counteract the spells that wizards might cast on them. Then she no longer repressed the promptings of her heart, but yielded to his suit. They agreed to elope that night.

As they left the little clearing in the wood where their interview had taken place, a thicket stirred and a girl stole from it, looking intently at their retreating forms. The Swan, they had named her; but, with a flush in her dusky cheeks, her brows dark, her eyes glittering, she more recalled the vulture—for she, too, loved the Shield, and she had now seen and heard that her love was hopeless. That evening she alarmed the camp; she told the parents of Sacred Wind of the threatened violation of custom, and the father rose in anger to seek her. It was too late, for the flight had taken place. The Swan went to the river and rowed out in a canoe. From the middle of the stream she saw a speck on the water to the southward, and knew it to be Sacred Wind and her lover, henceforth husband. She watched until the speck faded in the twilight—then leaning over the side of the boat she capsized it, and passed from the view of men.

Flying Shadow and Track Maker
(Sioux)

The Chippewas and Sioux had come together at Fort Snelling to make merry and cement friendships. Flying Shadow was sad when the time came for the tribes to part, for Track Maker had won her heart, and no less strong than her love was the love he felt for her. But a Chippewa girl might not marry among the Sioux, and, if she did, the hand of every one would be against her should ever the tribes wage war upon each other, and war was nearer than either of them had expected. The

Chippewas left with feelings of good will, Flying Shadow concealing in her bosom the trinkets that testified to the love of Track Maker and sighing as she thought of the years that might elapse ere they met again.

Two renegade Chippewas, that had lingered behind the band, played the villain after this pleasant parting, for they killed a Sioux. Hardly was the news of this outrage received at the fort ere three hundred warriors were on the trail of their whilom guests and friends, all clamoring for revenge. Among them was Track Maker, for he could not, as a warrior, remain behind after his brother had been shot, and, while his heart sank within him as he thought of the gentle Flying Shadow, he marched in advance, and early in the morning the Chippewas were surprised between St. Anthony's Falls and Rum River, where they had camped without fear, being alike ignorant and innocent of the murder for which so many were to be punished.

The Sioux fell upon them and cut down all alike—men, women, and children. In the midst of the carnage Track Maker comes face to face with Flying Shadow, and with a cry of gladness she throws herself into his arms. But there is no refuge there. Gladly as he would save her, he knows too well that the thirst for blood will not be sated until every member of that band is dead. He folds her to his bosom for an instant, looks into her eyes with tenderness—then bowing his head he passes on and never glances back. It is enough. She falls insensible, and a savage, rushing upon her, tears the scalp from her head.

The Sioux win a hundred scalps and celebrate their victory with dance and song. Track Maker has returned with more scalps than any, and the maidens welcome him as a hero, but he keeps gravely apart from all, and has no share in the feasting and merry-making. Ever the trusting, pleading, wondering face of Flying Shadow comes before him. It looks out at him in the face of the deer he is about to kill. He sees it in the river, the leaves, the clouds. It rises before him in dreams. The elder people say he is bewitched, but he will have none of their curatives. When war breaks out he is the first to go, the first to open battle. Rushing among his enemies he lays about him with his axe until he falls, pierced with a hundred spears and arrows. It is the fate he has courted, and as he falls his face is lighted with a smile.

A Lover Rejected
(Dakota)

A game of lacrosse was played by Indian girls on the ice near the present Fort Snelling, one winter day, and the victorious trophies were awarded to Wenonah, sister of the chief, to the discomfiture of Harpstenah, her opponent, an ill-favored woman, neglected by her tribe, and jealous of Wenonah's beauty and popularity. This defeat, added to some fancied slights, was almost more than she could bear, and during the contest she had been cut in the head by one of the rackets—an accident that she falsely attributed to her adversary in the game. She had an opportunity of proving her hatred, for directly that it was known how Wenonah had refused to marry Red Cloud, a stalwart boaster, openly preferring a younger warrior of the tribe, the ill-thinking Harpstenah sought out the disappointed suitor, who sat moodily apart, and thus advised him, "Tomorrow is the Feast of Virgins, when all who are pure will sit at meat together. Wenonah will be there. Has she the right to be? Have you not seen how shamelessly she favors your rival's suit? Among the Dakotas to accuse is to condemn, and the girl who is accused at the Virgins' Feast is disgraced forever. She has shown for Red Cloud nothing but contempt. If he shows no anger at it the girls will laugh at him."

With this she turned away and left Red Cloud to his meditations. Wenonah, at the door of her brother's wigwam, looked into the north and saw the stars grow pale through streams of electric fire. "The Woman of the North warns us of coming evil," muttered the chief. "Some danger is near. Fire on the lights!" And a volley of musketry sent a shock through the still air.

"They shine for me," said Wenonah, sadly. "For I shall soon join our father, mother, and sister in the land of spirits. Before the leaves fell I sat beside the Father of Waters and saw a manitou rise among the waves. It said that my sisters in the sunset world were calling to me and I must soon go to them." The chief tried to laugh away her fancies and comforted her as well as he might, then leading her to the wigwam he urged her to sleep.

Next day is the Virgins' Feast and Wenonah is among those who sit in the ring, dressed in their gayest. None who are conscious of a fault may share in the feast; nor, if one were exposed and expelled, might any interpose to ask for mercy; yet a groan of surprise and horror goes through the company when Red Cloud, stalking up to the circle, seizes the girl roughly by the shoulder and orders her away. No use to deny or appeal. An Indian warrior would not be so treacherous or unjust as to act in this way unless he had proofs. Without a word she enters the adjacent wood, draws her knife, and strikes it to her heart. With summer came the fever, and it ravaged through the band, laying low the infant and the counselor. Red Cloud was the first to die, and as he was borne away Harpstenah lifted her wasted form and followed him with dimming eyes, then cried, "He is dead. He hated Wenonah because she slighted him. I hated her because she was happy. I told him to denounce her. But she was innocent."

BLACK HAWK AND MEDICINE-WOMAN
(Cheyenne)

A man named Black Hawk had married Medicine-woman, and had a child called Stone-walker. Medicine-woman was very handsome to see, and as fine as the sun; and the child was pretty, too. Medicine-woman was a great help to her husband and very kind to him. She used to embroider all his robes and moccasins. But Black Hawk was desirous of another woman. He thought his wife would not know of this. But one day she discovered his love-affair. She became so angry that she ran off with her child. They went on a hill, and stayed there until they were turned to stone, just as they were sitting in grief. Black Hawk found out that they had been turned to stone; and then he, too, wished to become stone. He cried at the place until he died. Many Cheyennes have passed the Woman and Child turned to stone. It is in the Rocky Mountains.

A Husband's Betrayal
(Dakota)

Several of the Dakotas, who had been in camp near the site of St. Paul, left their families and friends, when the hunting season opened, and went into the north. On their arrival at another village of their tribe, they stayed to rest for a little, and one of the men used the time to ill advantage, as it fell out, for he conceived an attachment for a girl of this northern family, and on his way southward he wedded her and took her home with him. Proper enough to do, if he had not been married already. The first wife knew that any warrior might take a second, if he could support both; but the woman was stronger than the savage in her nature, and when her husband came back, with a red-cheeked woman walking beside him, she felt that she should never know his love again. The man was all attention to the young wife, whether the tribe tarried or traveled. When they shifted camp the elder walked or rowed behind with her boy, a likely lad of ten or twelve.

It was when they were returning down the river after a successful hunt that the whole company was obliged to make a carry around the quick water near the head of St. Anthony's Falls. While the others were packing the boats and goods for transportation by hand to the foot of the cataract, the forsaken wife chose a moment when none were watching to embark with her boy in one of the canoes. Rowing out to an island, she put on all her ornaments, and dressed the lad in beads and feathers as if he were a warrior. Her husband, finding her absent from the party, looked anxiously about for some time, and was horrified to see her put out from the island into the rapid current. She had placed the child high in the boat, and was rowing with a steady stroke down the stream. He called and beckoned franticly. She did not seem to hear him, nor did she turn her head when the others joined their cries to his. For a moment those who listened heard her death-song, then the yeasty flood hid them from sight, and the husband on the shore fell to the earth with a wail of anguish.

"White-Man" Stories
(Various)

White-Man and Coyote
(Cheyenne)

White-man was traveling. He caught some rabbits, made a fire, and cooked them. When he had had enough, but there was still much left, the coyote came limping along. He was hungry, and asked for something to eat. White-man refused to give him anything. The coyote said he was starving. Then White-man proposed to run him a race for the food. They started off, and the coyote suddenly lost his lameness. He ran far ahead of White-man, came in, and ate all the rabbits before the other came back. Then he went off. Now he felt sleepy from his good meal, and lay down. White-man followed his tracks, and found him. He thought: "If I hit his head, I will spoil it;" and so on of the different parts of his body. Finally he decided to roast him whole, as then no portion of him would be bruised. So he made a fire. The coyote, only feigning sleep, was ready to escape. He only waited to see what White-man would do. White-man seized him to put him on the fire. But suddenly the coyote was out of his hands, jumped over the fire at one bound, and was off.

White-Man and His Lost Eyes
(Cheyenne)

There was a man that could send his eyes out of his head, on the limb of a tree, and call them back again, by saying *naexansts hinnicistaniwââ* (eyes hang upon a branch). White-man saw him doing this, and came to him crying; he wanted to learn this too. The man taught him, but warned him not to do it more than four times in one day. White-man went off along the river. When he came to the highest tree he could see, he sent his eyes to the top. Then he called them back. He thought he could do this as often as he wished, disregarding the warning. The fifth time his eyes remained fastened to the limb. All day he called, but the eyes began to swell and spoil, and flies gathered on them. White-man grew tired and lay down, facing his eyes, still calling for them, though they never came; and he cried. At night he was half asleep, when a mouse ran over him. He closed his lids that the mice would not see he was blind, and lay still, in order to catch one. At last one sat on his breast. He kept quiet to let it become used to him, and the mouse went on his face, trying to cut his hair for its nest. Then it licked his tears, but let its tail hang in his mouth. He closed it, and caught the mouse. He seized it tightly, and made it guide him, telling him of his misfortune. The mouse said it could see the eyes, and they had swelled to an enormous size. It offered to climb the tree and get them for him, but White-man would not let it go. It tried to wriggle free, but he held it fast. Then the mouse asked on what condition he would release it, and White-man said, only if it gave him one of its eyes. So it gave him one, and he could see again, and let the mouse go. But the small eye was far back in his socket, and he could not see very well with it. A buffalo was grazing near by, and as White-man stood near him crying, he looked on and wondered. White-man said: "Here is a buffalo, who has the power to help me in my trouble." So the buffalo asked him what he wanted. White-man told him he had lost his eye and needed one. The buffalo took out one of his and put it in White-man's head. Now White-man could see far again. But the eye did not fit the socket; most of it was outside. The other was far inside. Thus he remained.

White-Man and His Pointed Leg
(Cheyenne)

There was a man whose leg was pointed, so that by running and jumping against trees he could stick in them. By saying naiwa-toutawa, he brought himself back to the ground. On a hot day he would stick himself against a tree for greater shade and coolness. However, he could not do this trick more than four times. Once while he was doing this, *Vihuk* (White-man) came to him, crying, and said: "Brother, sharpen my leg!" The man replied: "That is not very hard. I can sharpen your leg." White man stood on a large log, and the other, with an axe, sharpened his leg, telling him to hold still bravely. The pain caused the tears to come from his eyes. When the man had sharpened his leg, he told him to do the trick only four times a day, and to keep count in order not to exceed this number. White-man went down toward the river, singing. Near the bank was a large tree; toward this he ran, then jumped and stuck in it. Then he called himself back to the ground. Again he jumped, this time against another tree; but now he counted one, thinking in this way to get the better of the other man. The third time, he counted two. The fourth time, birds and animals stood by, and he was proud to show his ability, and jumped high, and pushed his leg in up to the knee. Then coyotes, wolves, and other animals came to see him; some of them asked how he came to know the trick, and begged him to teach it to them, so they could stick to trees at night. He was still prouder now, and for the fifth time he ran and jumped as high as he could, and half his thigh entered the tree. Then he counted four. Then he called to get to the ground again. But he stuck. He called out all day; he tried to send the animals to the man who had taught him. He was fast in the tree for many days, until he starved to death.

White-Man Who Wished to Be a Buffalo
(Cheyenne)

It was spring, and the grass was green along the riverside, and all over the land. A buffalo bull was having a fine time eating the fresh grass, while a white man near by had a hard time to make his living. Day after day he watched the bull and wished to be a buffalo. So one day he approached him and stood near him, and cried, thinking that if he were a buffalo he would enjoy himself all his life, and all winter he would have a good robe on him, and he would not have to pay for his clothing and food. The buffalo looked at him and said to him: "What can I do for you?" But the man continued to cry, and answered that he wanted to be a buffalo. The bull told him not to be afraid, and to stand at a little distance away. Then he charged at the man four times, and the man was not afraid of him, because he wished to become a buffalo. At the fourth charge the man turned into a buffalo, and then the bull taught him how to live. But at once the white man thought he could make money by teaching his friends to become buffalo. But a white man, whom he approached, ran away from him in fear.

In another version White-man is hunted after he has become a buffalo. He tries to tell the hunters that he is a man, but cannot, and is shot.

WHITE-MAN AND MÁTCEIT
(Cheyenne)

Mátceit (Little-man) was a poor orphan boy. An old woman took care of him, and they lived at a large camp. It was winter, snow was on the ground, buffalo were scarce, and the people were nearly starved. One day Mátceit told his grandmother to make him a bow and arrows. These are ordinarily made by men, but she did the best she could, and made him a bow and arrows. Then he told her to make him a wheel used for the buffalo game. She cried, and asked him where he expected her to get the hide that was necessary. He told her to soak a parflêche bag, and when it was soft to cut a string from it, and then paint it. She did this. When the hoop was finished, he sat on the bed, and she at the door; he told her to roll the wheel, saying to him: "There is a buffalo calf." When she said this, he shot the wheel through the heart (the central interstice), and there sat a buffalo calf, swaying and dying. The old woman skinned it, cut and dried the meat, and stretched the skin. He told her to save the fat as salve for his sore eyes. Next morning he told his grandmother to roll the wheel again, and this time he shot a grown calf. She packed away the first meat, and hung up what they had just got. Next morning he shot a fat cow in the same way, and the old woman was still prouder of him. The meat she hid in a hole, the refuse she threw into a bush, where the snow covered it. Meanwhile the rest of the camp were starving, and cooking hides and saddles for food. On the fourth day the boy shot a very fat well-aged cow. All the meat of this his grandmother dried, and of the marrow she made sausage, and of the bones soup.

Their tent was apart, off on one side of the village. The principal chief had two daughters, of whom the youngest was very pretty. The boy was in love with her; but his belly was large, his legs short, his eyes sore and running; and every one called him Little-man. Now he told his grandmother to go to the principal chief, taking with her some fat in a piece of gut; and when going away, to drop it, as if by accident, so that it would be seen. If the chief asked her about it, she should say it was salve for his eyes. She did accordingly, and the starving chief and his family asked for some of the fat. She gave him all, saying that she had more; and the chief was pleased. She came home and told the boy what had happened. Next day he sent her to buy the youngest girl for him, taking a part of their meat to the principal chief. The chief asked her how she obtained the meat, and she said that the boy had the power to make game. So the chief gave his daughter, and a large tent was put up for Mátceit, and everything made ready for him to come at night.

Almost all the young men of the camp were in love with the chief's daughters, and even the younger girl was marriageable; but the boy was too young to marry. Her friends made fun of her, saying that her son went to sleep with her. She was also ashamed of the ugliness and sore eyes of her husband. At the same time White-man married the elder daughter, but he was given no tent, and slept in the same lodge as the boy. White-man told his wife to give the boy a separate vessel of water, as he did not want to use the same one with him. The boy heard this, and observed the ridicule of himself, and felt sorry. That night he became different: he was a young man, clean, with long dark hair, yellow skin, and bright eyes. Every one heard of his change and wondered. Now his sister-in-law tried to get him to drink of White-man's water, but he paid no attention to her. At night, when he coughed, bright shining colors came out of his mouth, and the two women saw it. White-man saw it too, and wondered. Next night, he went out to the cooking-place and got two brands. When he coughed, he hit the two sticks together, so that the sparks flew. But the boy and his wife continued to sleep. And in the morning it was found that White-man's blanket was burned, his wife's lip scarred, and himself burned on the cheek.

Before daylight, the boy got up and went eastward. He gathered buffalo chips, and piled them on himself, so that they appeared as if they were a string of buffalo going south before the wind. Finally the sun rose, and he sent his wife to tell her father that there was a herd of buffalo. The chief cried out that his son-in-law had seen buffalo. The starving people prepared hastily. They went east, on a high hill, and then on the next hill, and there they saw a long line of buffalo. They headed them off, and killed every one. They butchered them, ate the raw meat, rejoiced, cried, and sang about what Little-man had done and the great help he had been to the tribe. The boy went by all the buffalo, pretending to take the best parts and put them in his shirt; but he only took hair. He went to his father-in-law, threw down the hair, and it turned to ribs, tongues, and all the best pieces. He went out again with his wife, and a red-bird flew up and sat on his wife's head, and occasionally on his, and sang, and fluttered about. All saw this and wondered, especially White-man. The next day the very same thing happened. The buffalo were killed, and from their hair the boy made hides, pieces of meat, or whatever he wished. White-man also got hair from the buffalo, in imitation of Mátceit, and he and his wife went home without carrying any meat, but with a great mass of hair. He had caught a red-headed woodpecker, and tied it with a string to his wife's hair. But the woodpecker sat on her head and pecked at it. When they arrived home, he told his wife to order his mother-in-law to prepare the hides and the meat; but all the hair remained hair. The older sister was in love with her brother-in-law. One day he touched her on the skin of her shoulder, and his fingers, which were colored, left colored marks there. She was proud of this, and tore her dress open, to show the marks to every one, until her shoulder froze. That night the boy coughed again. Then White-man also coughed, and struck his brands. A spark fell into his eye, and one into his wife's, so that their eyes spoiled and turned white.

White-Man and the Boy
(Cheyenne)

There was a great camp, facing toward the sun (east). In the tent farthest on the right there lived a young girl. One morning she was missing. Every sunrise a girl was missing from the camp. An old man went around, inquiring who was gone. The village became frightened, and suddenly moved that very morning. They were so hasty that they left an old woman, forgetting her in their panic. When she was left behind, she looked for food and water for herself, but she had none and could find none. She went down to the river and drank. Looking up the river she saw something rolling or floating down, shining like looking-glass. She sat on the bank, watching; it came close, then dived under in deep water. A boy about eight years old came out of the river. He was rough and needy-looking, and his eyes were sore. "Grandmother," he said, "why are you sitting here?" She told him why the village had moved and how she had been left behind. He said he would follow the tracks which led to where the girls had been taken. She tried to dissuade him, but he was determined. Going back to the camp, they went to the sleeping-places of the lost girls, and he found a mouse trail. He said he was about to set out. The old woman asked him to provide for her, as else she might starve. He told her to make a round tent of willows at the edge of the river. Then he asked for a large knife, but the old woman said she had none. He went over the camp-site, looking, and succeeded in finding a hide-scraper. Then he told the old woman to make him bow and arrows, and she did so. Then he told her to say to him: "Two yearling heifers are near you." He shot into the ground, and there was a heifer-buffalo bleeding to death from her mouth. So the old woman butchered and dressed it. The boy told her to await his return, and set out. He followed the trail until it went under water; he dived in, and came out on the other side of the river. He found a plain path now, and it continued to grow plainer, until it was a hard, level road. He walked fast, making a terrible noise, as if something big was rolling along. A man came to meet the person making this noise. This man it was who had taken the girls, and the path was his trail; he had a large iron sword. He said "If I had known you were only a little boy, I should not have come out; but I thought some one great was coming to rescue the girls. I can knock you down with my fist." The boy answered that he could knock him down. The man said: "You cannot be as strong as this large tree," and he hit a tree once with his sword, and it fell over. The boy reached into his pocket and took out a square book, and asked the man if he had so powerful a book. By looking into it one could see all the various kinds of animals, and plants too, all living, and moving. So the man proposed that they should be great friends. The boy agreed, and then he exchanged his book for the sword; but he insisted on having the sword handed to him first. Then they went toward the man's tent. He was two-faced; and he walked ahead. The boy wanted to strike him with the sword, but whenever he raised it, the man said, "Don't hit me with the sword." But when the man looked sideways, the boy cut him in two across the middle. Then he took back his book and threw away the sword. He went on, and again he met a person, like the preceding, and also with a sword. The same happened, except that this man, to show his power, did not cut down a tree, but cut the earth in two, splitting it like ice. Again the boy showed his book, and again they exchanged. He killed this man in the same way, and took back his book and left the sword. Then he came near a tent, standing alone. One of the girls came out to get water. He went to meet her. He turned into a young man, bright in appearance, with quilled leggings and robe, and a quiver made of panther skin, and otter fur around his hair. When he met the girl, she was frightened, for she did not know that he had killed the two persons. She told him to run away, for many men who were on the warpath were killed and plundered here. She said that in the tent there were an old man and an old woman, and that she brought water for them whenever they were thirsty. If a leaf or stick floated on the water, they threw it in her face. The young man said to the girl: "I will go with you and fight for you. Put a bunch of weeds into the bucket. If they say anything, throw the water in the old woman's face, and run out to me." She did so, and the old man pursued her with a large tomahawk. The boy had a large cedar whistle. This he blew, and all the people of his tribe came out. The old man knocked them down, but the boy continued whistling, and more and more people came, until they killed the old man. Then the old woman came out with a toma-hawk, and she was killed in the same way. Then the boy made a sweat-tent, and put in it the skulls of all that had been killed here previously. The girl heated rocks, and every time water was poured on them, the skulls moved; the last (fourth) time the people came out alive. They were of many different tribes. The young man told them to find their property and return each to his people. Then he started with the girl, turning into a rough boy again. He took his book and opened it; and there was a house, with food, tables as the white people have them, and two chairs. After eating, he closed the book, and the house was gone. Finally he came to the place at which he had emerged from the river, and there he lived in a house of sod. He saw three persons coming up the river. They were the girl's parents, and her brother White-man. White-man ran ahead, looking for the girl; then he went back, telling his parents that he had found his sister, but that an ugly boy was her husband. They all came in. They did not like their son-in-law, he was so ugly. White-man went fishing with his brother-in-law, in deep water. When a fish caught on his bait, he got the boy to take his line, and then shoved him in. The boy walked along in the river. He came to where a great camp stood, facing east. Here he got out of the water, and went into an old woman's tent. With her lived an orphan boy, of his own age, who was much surprised to see him. The boy was hungry, but they could give him nothing to eat, and he slept. The orphan boy asked him if he had any news; then he told him of his own rescue of the girl as he would tell the exploit of another person. Then the orphan told him that every morning a beautiful red eagle flew along, almost touching the tent-poles. Whoever killed the eagle was to marry the prettiest girl in the village. Both determined to try, as they might have good luck. The girl offered was the younger daughter of the same man that had lost the other girl; he wanted the eagle to hang at his tent-door, to show that he was a great chief. In the morning the eagle came; all shot at him but missed. The boys told their grandmother to open the tipi top, as they were going to try to shoot. They shot, and the eagle fell right into the tent. All ran in to find out who had done it, and the old man came with his daughter; but when he saw the two orphan boys, he took the eagle and kept the girl. But the boy kept a small bunch of the eagle's feathers. There were two fish in the river, one of silver, one of gold; when they turned in the water, their reflection shone so brightly that they could not be seen. The old man offered his daughter to whoever should catch one of the fish. The young men all fished, but the fish only looked at the bait. The boys used a sinew without a hook, but with a large chunk of meat. The golden fish passed by all the baits and bit theirs. The boy told his companion to hide it if they caught it, as the man might take it away from them. They caught it, and there was a great light in the prairie, so that every one ran to see who had caught the fish. The orphan told that his friend had caught it. The old man came, but he said he did not want so ugly a son-in-law. He took the fish, but the boy kept a piece of skin from it. As all came and stood by, the girl he had rescued was there, and she noticed her husband. At night she ran off to his tent again. When she had thus disappeared again, the chief, her father, told the men to make search for her. White-man knew that this boy was the same one that he had pushed into the water, and suspected where she was. At night he peeped into the tent and saw her, and reported to his father. Then his father caused an old man to announce that all men were to come to urinate and defecate over the boy's tent. This was done. White-man climbed up on the tent-poles, and dropped excrement down on his brother-in-law.

The boy told his friend that next morning the women who went out to dig prairie-turnips would be murdered. So it happened. The camp prepared to go to war. The boy told his wife to get a horse from his father-in-law so that he could fight. When the chief saw his daughter, he made her stop, and stand off, and tell her purpose. Then he told her "Take that white one;" but it was a pig. When they went to battle, they crossed a creek. Here the pig stuck in the mud. The boy tried all day, apparently, to get it out, while the others fought. But somehow he got a good white horse. He, too, now became a bright young man with a war-bonnet, otterskin, and eagle tail-feathers on his spear, while his clothes were all beaded. He rode right among the enemy, killed seven with his spear, and drove the rest away. Then he ran back and got on his pig. When the people returned, they saw him still there, ridiculed him, and threw mud at him. They tried to find out who had ridden into the battle; but they could not. That night the boy made the same prediction to his friend as before. Everything happened as on the preceding day, except that he was given a black and white pig, and rode a black and white painted horse in the fight. The third time he had a black horse. Now it was agreed that the horse of this unknown should be cut on the buttock, so that he might be recognized. The fourth day the boy rode a bay painted horse. White-man rode the same kind of horse as the boy, and when the fight was over, he rode down to the creek and cut his horse, and wounded himself a little. So they thought that it was White-man, and he married the girl, though she was his own sister. Next morning the boy came into camp, handsome, finely dressed, with feathers on his spear, otterskin, and so on. All saw him coming and ran up. He got off and led his horse, for it was quite lame. The people spread blankets to carry him, but he walked. His wife ran out to meet him and took his arms from him. The people cleaned the place they had soiled. So they found that White-man was an impostor. Four men seized him by the hands and legs, to throw him into deep water. He was strong and resisted, but at last they dragged him to the bank and threw him in. They could see the fish eating him, until only bones were left. Then the chief wanted his daughter and his son-in-law to leave the old woman's dirty place and to live with him, and even prepared a tipi for him. But they refused. The boy took out his book, and they had a house. But the boy felt bad about his treatment. That night he blew his whistle, and white men came out, and at daylight they killed the whole tribe. (This shows that the whites have more power than the Indians.)

WHITE-MAN BEING HUNGRY
(Cheyenne)

White-man was traveling, with nothing to eat. He came to a large lake, on which he saw numbers of birds. At the edge of the pond was a prairie-dog town; the inhabitants were sitting up, all of them fat. White-man was very hungry, and very anxious to catch some of these animals, but he knew he could not get to them. So he went off into a hollow, and thought out a plan. He got a stick, peeled off the bark, and painted it. He also painted a pretty buffalo horn that he found, and stuck it on the end of the stick. This he pretended was powerful against disease. He went back to the lake, and said: "Great danger and sickness are coming behind me, but whoever comes up to touch this stick will be safe." The birds believed this, and all asked to be allowed to touch the horn. He told them to follow him to an open place. Then he went to the prairie-dog village, and said the same that he said to the ducks, so their leader told all the prairie-dogs to follow him, with their whole families. White-man ordered them to shut their holes tight, on account of the danger. They worked hard and did this. Then they all followed him—prairie-dogs, ducks, geese, and other birds—while he led the way to an open plain, carrying his horn so that all could see it. Then he stuck the pole in the ground. In a circle around it he placed the prairie-dogs, around them the ducks, then the geese, and inside the cranes. Inside of all he put the white-nosed ducks. He told them to shut their eyes, as they would get red eyes if they looked. He would sing powerful songs, and dance among them, but they were not to look or move until he told them to. Then he commenced to sing. With a pole he knocked down and killed the dancers, meanwhile singing: "Your eyes will turn red, your backs will become twisted, your necks will be twisted, if you look." At the end was a white-nosed duck; as White-man came near him, he was trying to touch his neighbors, but could not. At last he opened his eyes and saw one of his friends being knocked down and others lying dead. He cried out, and the rest of the birds flew away. But since then that duck has had a red eye and crooked back and neck. The man went to the river, built a fire, and made sausages of his meat. Near him were two great willows; the wind waved them, they rubbed together, and made a noise. White-man spoke to them, telling them not to fight, for he was very hungry. Finally he climbed up. "My brothers must not fight." He held them apart, putting his hand between them; the wind stopped, and he was fast. The coyote smelled the meat and came. White-man told him he need not come around. He called him names and ridiculed his shape: he had a sharp nose, he was too slim. He told him to go about his own business; he said that he himself had climbed up in order to be cooler in the shade. The coyote came close; then he knew that White-man was fast. Then the man said to the coyote: "Brother, eat half, and I will eat half." While the coyote ate his meat, White-man reviled him, but he spoke kindly to the tree. The coyote looked at the fire, and there he saw a fine sausage, of fat and heart. He ate it. Then he covered it up again, and ran off, but as he was full he was soon tired and went to sleep. The wind rose, and the man was once more free. Very angry, he climbed down. He saw only the sausage. "It is good that he did not eat all," he said. He bit in the center of it, and got his mouth full of ashes. This made him still angrier. He followed the coyote's tracks, and found him. "If I hit him with a club, I might spoil his flesh by bruising it," he thought. So he made a tent of weeds around and over the coyote, intending to burn him alive. He lit the brush. When the fire became high, the coyote jumped out. Again he followed his tracks and found him. Three times this same thing happened. The fourth time he determined that he would catch the coyote by the hind legs. He seized him thus, and tried to scare the coyote to death by shouting. He nearly succeeded. But the coyote defecated over his clothes, into his mouth, and into his eyes. White-man could see the coyote no longer, let him go, and the coyote ran off. But White-man vomited to death.

PART III

TALES FROM THE SOUTHWEST REGION

CHAPTER 12

CREATION AND NATURE MYTHS

ZUÑI CREATION MYTH
(Zuñi)

T he mythologies of the Red Man are infinitely more rich in creative and deluge myths than those of any other race in the two hemispheres. Tales which deal with the origin of man are exceedingly frequent, and exhibit every phase of the type of creative story. Although many of these are similar to European and Asiatic myths of the same class, others show great originality, and strikingly present to our minds the characteristics of American aboriginal thought.

The creation-myths of the various Indian tribes differ as much from one another as do those of Europe and Asia. In some we find the great gods molding the universe, in others we find them merely discovering it. Still others lead their people from subterranean depths to the upper earth. In many Indian myths we find the world produced by the All-Father sun, who thickens the clouds into water, which becomes the sea. In the Zuñi record of creation *Awonawilona,* the creator, fecundates the sea with his own flesh, and hatches it with his own heat. From this green scums are formed, which become the fourfold mother Earth and the all-covering father Sky, from whom sprang all creatures. Then from the nethermost of the four caves of the world the seed of men and the creatures took form and grew; even as with eggs in warm places worms quickly form and appear, and, growing, soon burst their shells and there emerge, as may happen, birds, tadpoles, or serpents: so man and all creatures grew manifoldly and multiplied in many kinds. Thus did the lowermost world-cave become overfilled with living things, full of unfinished creatures, crawling like reptiles over one another in black darkness, thickly crowding together and treading one on another, one spitting on another and doing other indecency, in such manner that the murmurings and lamentations became loud, and many amidst the growing confusion sought to escape, growing wiser and more manlike. Then Po-shai-an-K'ia, the foremost and the wisest of men, arising from the nethermost sea, came among men and the living things, and pitying them, obtained egress from that first world-cave through such a dark and narrow path that some seeing somewhat, crowding after, could not follow him, so eager mightily did they strive one with another. Alone then did Po-shai-an-K'ia come from one cave to another into this world, then island-like, lying amidst the world-waters, vast, wet, and unstable. He sought and found the Sun-Father, and besought him to deliver the men and the creatures from that nethermost world.

CREATION OF THE WORLD
(Apache)

W hen the world was formed, there were twelve (12) Gods; these were called *Natzonlit;* and there were twelve others,—*Nadagonyit,*—who assisted the first twelve.

Then there were twelve others—the *Kudindiye*—inferior to both the others.

There were twelve (12) *black* Winds, the *Iltchí,* and twelve Heavens, *Yâ-désish;* twelve (12) Suns, *Chígo-na-áy;* twelve (12) Moons, *Klégo-na-áy;* and the earth was divided into twelve (12) parts.

Now all these Gods came together, and one of them, *Iltchí-dishísh* (Black Wind), made the world as it now is. *Ilchí-duklíj,* the Green or Blue Wind, stayed by him while he made the world.

Then *Iltchí-lezóc,* Yellow Wind, gave light to the world. *Iltchí-lokáy,* the White Wind, improved on this light. Then came the Child of the Dawn, *Ikâ-eshkín,* bringing fruits for the support of people. He threw out water upon the world; it became a fog, and, descending upon the land, made all to grow, and fruits, trees, etc., came forth in the four quarters of the earth.

The earth when first formed was a perfectly flat plain, but the Black Wind came along with his horns, and, bending his head, ripped open the earth and made ravines and cañons.

Then the Black Wind sent down on earth a piece of limestone *(Tzês-payé),* and the Sun sent one of his rays down upon it, and it conceived and brought forth a little white stone,—a pebble.

Then came another ray, and the rock brought forth a stone of "mal pais" (lava), called *Tze-ji.* Then the Sun shone on the two little rocks. Each rock brought forth a pair of human beings; they were the first human beings, and were of a gray color.

The great stone then brought forth a stone for grinding meal. Then the Sun cast his rays on the west part of the earth *(Guzanutli),* which brought forth a man, who was *Tu-vá-dis-chí-ni,* the Child of the Water.

When Tu-vá-dis-chí-ni was born he had not the appearance of a man, but the Black Wind came down again and gave him all his parts,—eyes, hair, nose, etc.

Then the Sun ordered the Black Wind to split open the head and fingers of Tu-vá-dis-chí-ni, and from these wounds sprang all the nations of the earth.

Then the Sun ordered his servant to prepare arms for Tu-vá-dis-chí-ni, and he gave him a bow and arrows of iron *(sic)*, and the bow had a cord of iron *(sic)*.

Then Tu-vá-dis-chí-ni made a mark and fired at it, but, as he did so, he fell dead *(i.e.* he swooned). Soon he came to, and addressed the Sun: "My father! This arm you have had made for me is no good." Then the Sun made for him a *carrizal (i.e.* reedswamp), and told him to make his own arms.

The Sun and Moon used to rise together in those days, and they met and spoke together on the earth; and they formed an *Eltin,* or mulberry-tree. *("Eltin"* in Apache means both mulberry and bow. The mulberry plays an important part in the domestic economy of the Apaches; the branches are made into bows, and the small twigs are used in the fabrication of baskets.) Then the Sun and the Black Wind came out and found a black glass, *Dolguíni* (Obsidian), and stuck it in the shoulders of Tu-vá-dis-chí-ni. (That is, they tipped his arrows with it, and placed them in the quiver which he bore on his shoulder.)

Then there came out a stag *(Pi-nal-té,* the elk) and *Bû* (owl), and the *Kâ-chu* (the Jack-rabbit).

Tu-vá-dis-chí-ni killed them all.

Up to this time Tu-vá-dis-chí-ni had no clothes and no place in which to sleep, but the Sun caused to spring up on the earth a sweet, soft grass, upon which he reclined, and by which he was lulled to sleep.

Then the Sun told the Black Wind to go and stay in a field of sacaton (the coarse bunch-grass of the Southwest). From this came forth a multitude of people, and not only people but grasses of all kinds,—grama, and all other kinds.

The Sun arose again and cast another ray upon the earth; the Pine-tree sprang forth, and with it the Piñon tree.

The Sun and Moon consulted together again and formed a mesquite tree, and upon the branches they hung bunches of mesquite beans. Then they formed a grove of the Spanish Bayonet; they then made a grove of the Prickly Pear, and filled both these with fruit.

Then the Sun, Moon, Black Wind, Yellow Wind, and all the other Gods held a council and decided to create many fruits, the Acorn, Mescal, Manzanita, and the Sunflower *(Nâdinlít).*

After this, all the *Kân* (Gods) held a council and decided to make a cloud, from which they scattered the water which now refreshes the earth.

Then the Sun sent his son, Tu-vá-dis-chí-ni, and scattered over the earth all kinds of birds, every moving thing, such as snakes, rabbits, hares, deer, etc. He sent his son to put all these on the earth.

After providing all these things, then the Sun placed the Apaches on the earth.

Then Tu-vá-dis-chí-ni gave the Apaches a bow of mulberry and an arrow of reed, and told them to go and live off the rabbits and game.

The Sun, Moon, Winds, and all living things consulted together and decided upon what things the Apaches should live, and upon them they are living to this day.

Then Tu-vá-dis-chí-ni placed in proper positions in this part of the earth all the fruits and other foods for the Apaches, and also the materials, mulberry, etc., from which the squaws should make the baskets in which to gather them.

And then he taught them how to make houses, and ollas or pots *(Izá)*, of mud *(Jôsh-Klísh)* in which to bake them.

Then the Bear and Coyote made a bet.

The Bear bet it was always to be Night and never to be Dawn; the Coyote won the bet.

Then the Sun made two mountain ranges, one full of fruits, flowers, and grasses, the other barren and rocky. He asked the Apaches "Which one do you want?" They chose the beautiful range, so from that day they have lived on the fruits and seeds of the mountains; while the barren-looking hills given to the whites have furnished cattle, horses, etc., in plenty.

On this flowery hill all the Indians united, and to this day they lament that they did not take the other hill.

They had no farming implements of any kind, no axes, no hoes, spades, or anything else for sowing or reaping.

The Coyote and Squirrel then met; the latter was going along in the upper branches of a tall pine-tree, and was dragging along behind him a fagot of burning cedar-bark, which fell to the ground.

The Coyote seized it and ran away and set fire to the world, and from that the Indians got fire. The Coyote taught them to rub the Cedar and Palmilla *(Yucca)* together to make fire.

How the Cave People Found Dry Land on the Earth
(Zuñi)

I n the old days all men lived in caves in the center of the earth. There were four caves, one over the other. Men first lived in the lowest cave. It was dark. There was no light, and the cave was crowded. All men were full of sorrow.

The Holder of the Paths of Life, the Sun-father, heard the people cry. He created two children for himself, and they fell to the earth to help the cave people.

The Sun-father gave his two children eternal youth. He gave them power to do things as he would do them. He gave them gifts. One gift was a painted bow that reached from one end of the sky to the farther end. It was the rainbow. He gave them an arrow of fire. It was the lightning. He gave them a great shield like his own. The shield was a net of cotton cords on a hoop of wood, and the last gift, a great magic war knife of flint, was fastened to the center of the shield.

After the two children had cut the face of the earth with the stone war knife, they rode on the magic shield to the lowest cave where men lived. There they lived with mankind as leaders.

The priests prayed to the Sun-children for help in the darkness. The Sun-children led mankind into the second cave; it was still all darkness. Men asked the priests to pray for more help. They came to the Sun-children, and the people were led into the third world or cave.

This was a larger world than the other two. It was like twilight in this cave, but at first all thought that they had reached the blazing sun, it was so light.

After a thousand years this cave became crowded. Men sought the priests and prayed them to find some way to help them.

The two Sun-children cut their way through the cave above them, and led the people out upon the earth. It was only a small island, for all the rest was water.

Men covered their faces with their hands, for the light made them blind. They fell down and tried to hide in the sand, they were so hot. The people were taught to make clothing of yucca fiber. Their eyes were like owls' eyes, and they covered them with their hands till they were strong.

The Sun-children led the people over the quaking earth to the east, where the Sun-father had his home.

The Sun-children were told to dry the earth. They put the magic shield upon the earth and laid the rainbow upon it. They put arrows of lightning to the north, south, east, and west, and the arrows crossed each other. The older brother shot with an arrow the lightning arrows where they crossed upon the rainbow.

Thlu-tchu! the lightning arrows shot toward every point. Fire rolled over the face of the earth. The earth was dried when the fire storm was over.

The earth was then full of great beasts that had lived in the water. The Sun-children shot the beasts with their arrows; then the beasts became stone. The people were free to go on the earth wherever they wanted to go.

Thus the people were led out of the deep caves; thus the land became dry, and men came to live on the earth.

CREATION OF SUMMER AND WINTER
(Acoma)

The oldest tradition of the people of Acoma and Laguna indicates that they lived on some island; that their homes were destroyed by tidal waves, earthquakes, and red-hot stones from the sky. They fled and landed on a low, swampy coast. From here they migrated to the northwest, and wherever they made a long stay they built a "White City" *(Kush-kut-ret)*.

The fifth White City was built somewhere in southern Colorado or northern New Mexico. The people were obliged to leave it on account of cold, drought, and famine.

The first governor of Acoma had a daughter named Co-chin-ne-na-ko; she was the wife of *Shakok,* the spirit of Winter. After he came to live with them the seasons grew colder, colder; the snow and ice stayed longer; the corn would no longer mature; and the people were compelled to live on cactus leaves *(E-mash-chu)* and other wild plants.

One day Co-chin-ne-na-ko went out to gather cactus leaves and burn off the thorns so that she could take them home for food. She had a leaf singed and was eating it, when upon looking up she saw a young man coming towards her. He had on a yellow shirt, woven of corn silk, a belt, and a tall pointed hat; green leggings made of the green moss which grows in the springs and ponds, and moccasins beautifully embroidered with flowers and butterflies. In his hand he carried an ear of green corn. He came up and saluted her. She replied. Then he asked her what she was eating. She told him that the people were almost starved; that no corn would grow; and that they were all compelled to live on cactus leaves.

"Here," he said, "take this ear of corn and eat it, and I will go and bring you an armful to take home with you." He started and was soon out of sight, going towards the south. In a very short time, however, he returned, bringing a large bundle of green corn *(ken-utch)*, which he laid at her feet. Co-chin-ne-na-ko asked him where he had found the corn, and if it grew near by. He replied that he had brought it from his home, far to the south, where the corn grows and the flowers bloom all the year. "Oh, how I would like to see your country; will you not take me with you to your home?" she said. "Your husband, Shakok, the Spirit of Winter, would be angry if I should take you away," he said. Said she, "I do not love him, he is cold; ever since he came here no corn will grow, no flowers will bloom, and the people are compelled to live on prickly-pear leaves."

"Well," said he, "take the bundle of corn home with you and do not throw any of the husks outside of the door; then come tomorrow and I will bring you more. I will meet you here." Then, bidding her farewell, he left again for his home in the south. Co-chin-ne-na-ko took the bundle of corn he had given her and started to go home to the town. She had not gone far when she met her sisters, for becoming alarmed at her long stay they had come out to look for her. They were very much surprised on seeing her with an armful of green corn instead of cactus leaves. Co-chin-ne-na-ko told them how the young man had come to her and brought the corn. So they helped her carry it home. When they arrived their father and mother were wonderfully surprised, but pleased to see them bringing big ears of green corn instead of cactus leaves. They asked Co-chin-ne-na-ko where she had found it, and she told them, as she had already told her sisters, that a young man, whom she minutely described, had brought her the corn, and had asked her to meet him at the same place on the following day, and that he would accompany her home. "It is Miochin," said her father; "it is Miochin." "It is surely Miochin," said her mother. "Bring him home with you by all means." The next day Co-chin-ne-na-ko went to the place where she had met Miochin, for he really was *Miochin,* the Spirit of Summer. He was already there waiting for her. He had big bundles of corn.

Between them they carried it to the town, and there was enough to feed all the people of Acoma, and Miochin was welcomed at the house of the governor. In the evening, as was his custom, *Shakok,* the Spirit of Winter, and husband of Co-chin-ne-na-ko, returned from the north where he spent the days playing with the north wind, and with the snow and sleet and hail. He came in a blinding storm of snow, sleet, and hail.

On reaching the town he knew that Miochin was there, and called out to him, "Ha, Miochin, are you here?" Miochin advanced to meet him. "Ha, Miochin, now I will destroy you." "Ha, Shakok, I will destroy you," answered Miochin. Shakok stopped, and as Miochin advanced towards him the snow and hail melted and the fierce wind turned to a summer breeze. Shakok was covered with frost, icicles hung all about him, but as Miochin advanced towards him the frost melted, the icicles dropped off, and his clothing was revealed. It was made of dry bleached rushes *(Ska-ra-ska-ru-ka)*. Shakok said, "I will not fight you now, but will meet you here in four days from now and fight you till one or the other is beaten. The winner shall have Co-chin-ne-na-ko." With that Shakok left in a rage.

The wind again roared and shook the very walls, but the people were warm in their houses. Miochin was there. Next day he left for his home in the south. Arriving there he made preparations for the meeting with Shakok. He first sent an eagle to his friend Yat-chum-me Moot, who lived in the west, asking him to come and help him in his fight with Shakok. Then he called all the birds, insects, and four-legged animals that live in summer lands. All these he called to help him. The bat *(Pick-le-ke)* was his advance guard and his shield, as the tough skin of the bat could best withstand the sleet and hail that Shakok would throw at him. On the third day Yat-chum-me kindled his fires, and heated the thin flat stones that he was named after. Then big black clouds of smoke rolled up from the south and covered the sky. When Shakok left he went to the north and called to him all the winter birds and the four-legged animals of the winter lands. He called these all to come and help him in the coming battle. The magpie *(Shro-ak-ah)* was his shield and advance guard. On the morning of the fourth day the two enemies could be seen coming. In the north the black storm clouds of winter, with snow, sleet, and hail were bringing Shakok to the battle. In the south, Yat-chum-me piled more wood on his fires and great puffs of steam and smoke arose and formed into clouds. These were coming fast towards Acoma, and the place where the fight was to take place, and were bringing Miochin, the Spirit of Summer. The thick smoke of Yat-chum-me's fires blackened all the animals Miochin had with him, and that is why the animals in the south are black or brown. Forked blazes of lightning shot out of the clouds that were bringing Miochin. Each came fast. Shakok from the north; Miochin from the south. At last they reached the town, and the flashes from the clouds singed the feathers and hair on the birds and animals that came with Shakok, turning them white; that is the reason why all the animals and birds that live in the north are white, or have some white about them. Shakok and Miochin were now close together. From the north Shakok threw snow-flakes, sleet, and hail that hissed through the air a blinding storm. In the south the big black clouds rolled along, and from Yat-chum-me's fires still rose up great puffs of smoke and steam that heated the air and melted Shakok's snow and sleet and hail, and compelled him to fall back. At last Shakok called for a truce. Miochin agreed, and the winds stopped and the snow and rain ceased falling.

They met at the wall of Acoma, and Shakok said, "I am defeated; you are the winner; Co-chin-ne-na-ko is yours." Then they agreed that Shakok should rule during half of the year, and Miochin during the other half, and that neither should trouble the other thereafter.

Ever since then one half of the year has been cold and the other half warm.

CHAPTER 13

GODS AND GODDESSES

AWONAWILONA
(Zuñi)

e have already alluded in the Zuñi creation-myth to the native deity *Awonawilona*. This god stands out as one of the most perfect examples of deity in its constructive aspect to be found in the mythologies of America. He seems in some measure to be identified with the sun, and from the remote allusions regarding him and the manner in which he is spoken of as an architect of the universe we gather that he was not exactly in close touch with mankind.

GODDESS OF SALT
(Zuñi)

Between Zuñi and Pescado is a steep mesa, or table-land, with fantastic rocks weathered into tower- and roof-like prominences on its sides, while near it is a high natural monument of stone. Say the Zuñis: The goddess of salt was so troubled by the people who lived near her domain on the sea-shore, and who took away her snowy treasures without offering any sacrifice in return, that she forsook the ocean and went to live in the mountains far away. Whenever she stopped beside a pool to rest she made it salt, and she wandered so long about the great basins of the West that much of the water in them is bitter, and the yield of salt from the larger lake near Zuñi brings into the Zuñi treasury large tolls from other tribes that draw from it.

Here she met the turquoise god, who fell in love with her at sight, and wooed so warmly that she accepted and married him. For a time they lived happily, but when the people learned that the goddess had concealed herself among the mountains of New Mexico they followed her to that land and troubled her again until she declared that she would leave their view forever. She entered this mesa, breaking her way through a high wall of sandstone as she did so. The arched portal through which she passed is plainly visible. As she went through, one of her plumes was broken off, and falling into the valley it tipped upon its stem and became the monument that is seen there. The god of turquoise followed his wife, and his footsteps may be traced in outcrops of pale-blue stone.

THE BLACK GOD
(Navajo)

It is long since the Navahoes went to war; but in former days when they fought their enemies they often suffered from war diseases. Their young men know nothing of this. One who killed an enemy by striking him in the chest would get disease in the chest; one who killed his enemy by striking on the head would get disease of the head, and one who killed by wounding in the abdomen would get disease of that part.

Thus it came to pass that, in the ancient days, when the war-gods *Nayénĕzgani* and *To'badzĭstsíni* had killed many of the Alien Gods, they got war diseases in many parts of their bodies. They suffered much and became so weak that they could not walk. Their friends tried all the remedies they could think of, but for a long time no cure was found.

At length some one said: "There is one dwelling at *Tse'zĭndiaí* (Black Standing Rock) named *Dóntso* (an insect) who knows of one who can cure war disease." So the people lay in wait for *Dóntso* and caught him. "Who is it that can cure the war disease?" they asked. "I dare not tell," said *Dóntso;* "it is one whom I fear, who does not like to have his power known." But the people persisted and persuaded and threatened till at last *Dóntso* said: "It is *Hastsézĭni* (Black God), the owner of all fire. But never let him know it was I who revealed the secret, for I fear his vengeance."

On hearing this, the people got a sacred buckskin, filled it with jeweled baskets, precious stones, shells, feathers, and all the treasures the gods most prize, and sent the bundle by a messenger to *Hastsézĭni*. When the messenger entered the house of the fire-god he found the latter lying on the ground with his back to the fire—a favorite attitude of his. The messenger presented his bundle and delivered his message; but the fire-god only said, "Begone! Go home and take your bundle with you."

The messenger returned to his people and told the result of his errand. They filled another sacred buckskin with precious things and sent him back with two bundles as a present to Black God; but the latter never rose from the ground or took his back from the fire. He dismissed the messenger again with angry words. Once more the messenger was sent back with three bundles and again with four bundles of goods tied up in sacred buckskins; but the god only bade him begone, as he had done before. When he returned to his people he found them singing.

Now *Dóntso* appeared before them and asked them what they had offered the fire-god. They told him, and added: "We have offered him great pay for his medicine, but he refuses to aid us, and sends our messenger away with angry words." "He is not like other gods," said *Dóntso;* "he is surly and exclusive. Few of the holy ones ever visit him, and he rarely visits any one. He cares nothing for your sacred buckskins, your baskets of turquoise and white shell, your abalone and rock crystal. All he wants is a smoke, but his cigarette must be made in a very particular way." And then he told them how to make the cigarette sacred to *Hastsézĭni*. But he made the people all pledge secrecy. He lived with the fire-god, and thus he came to know how the cigarette should be made and how it should be given to the god.

Three messengers now went to *Hastsézĭni*. Two remained outside, and one went in to deliver the cigarette, and thus he gave it: He carried it from the right foot of the god, up along his body, over his forehead, down his left side, and laid it on his left instep. Shading his eyes with his hand, the god gazed at the cigarette on his instep. He picked it up, examined it on all sides, and said angrily: "Who taught you to make this cigarette? No one knows how to make it but *Hastíniazi* (Little Old Man) and *Dóntso*. One of these must have taught you." The messenger replied: "I made it myself according to my own thoughts. No one taught me. *Dóntso* dwells above you and watches you day and night; he never leaves you." *Hastsézĭni* examined the cigarette again, inhaled its odor four times, and said: *"Láa!* It is well! This is my cigarette. Stay you and show me the way I must travel. Let the other messengers go home in advance. I shall get there on the morning of the third day." But they begged him to start that night. He bade the messengers who went in advance to kill a deer with two prongs on each horn, and to boil it all for a feast. When they returned to their home, they told what *Hastsézĭni* had said to them, and the people got all things ready as he had directed.

Next morning the Black God left his home, went about half way to Nayénězgani's house, and camped for the night. Many people came to his camp and held a dance there. There were birds among them, for in those days birds were people. And because of this occurrence now, in our day, when *Hastsézĭni* camps at night on his way to the medicine-lodge, the people go to his camp and hold a dance.

On the morning after this dance, all left for the house of sickness and got there at sunset. Before they arrived they began to shout and to whoop. The Navahoes in these days shout and whoop, and they call this shouting *altsĭtse*. A party from Nayénězgani's house, when they heard the shouting, went out to meet the returning party, and they had a mock battle, in which *Hastsézĭni's* party seemed victorious. Such a mock battle is held today in the rites.

When *Hastsézĭni* and his party arrived at the lodge there was a feast of the venison. Then the ailing gods said they wished to go out of the lodge. Previously, for many days they had to be carried out; but now they were only helped to rise, and they walked out unaided. The people who came with *Hastsézĭni* now went out and began to sing. The Black God was there; he had not yet entered the lodge. But when the people came out he joined them, and when they returned to the lodge he entered with them.

They now burned materials and made two kinds of mixed charcoal. The first was made of pine bark and willow. The second was composed of five ingredients, namely: *tsĭldĭlgĭsi* (a composite plant, *Guitierrezia euthamiae*), *tlo'nastázi* (a grama-grass, *Bouteloua hirsuta*), *tsé'aze,* or rock-medicine (undetermined), a feather dropped from a live crow, and a feather dropped from a live buzzard. They made four bracelets for the patients, each out of three small yucca leaves plaited together. Then they prepared for each seven sacred strings called *wolthád,* such as are now used by the shamans, and are so tied to a part that with a single pull they come loose. They pounded together cedar leaves and a plant called *thágiitsin* and made of these a cold infusion. All present drank of this infusion, and the patients washed their bodies with a portion of it. They applied the *wolthád* to different parts of the patients' bodies, proceeding from below upwards, viz: feet, knees, hands, and head. While they were tying these, the Black God entered and song was begun. When the singing was half done, the patients and all present drank again of the cold infusion, and the patients washed their bodies with the residue. Assistants next touched each of the ailing gods with black paint made of the second charcoal, on the soles, the palms, on each side of the chest, on each side of the back, over the shoulder-blade, and painted the throat. They greased the bodies of the gods with a big lump of sacred fat, and over this coating of grease they rubbed the first charcoal until the bodies looked as black as that of *Hastsézĭni* himself. But they painted the faces with grease and red ochre, and they spotted each cheek in three places with specular iron ore. They put on each a garment called *kátaha hástsé* (worn diagonally like a sash); they tied on the yucca bracelets, and tied a downy eagle-feather, plucked from a live eagle, to each head. The two who painted the patients got for a fee four buckskins each. They placed gopher manure in the moccasins of the ailing gods, and then put the moccasins on. They put strings of beads around their necks. They gave to each a bag of medicine, out of the mouth of which stuck the bill of a crow. They began to sing, and sent the *tantési* (patients) forth from the lodge.

The patients went to a place where lay the scalp of an enemy on which ashes had been sprinkled. Each picked the scalp four times with the crow's bill from his medicine-bag. Then they went to a distance from the lodge and "inhaled the sun." They did not then return to the medicine-lodge, but each went, as he was instructed, to his home, where a mixture of *gles* (white earth) and water was already prepared for him. Each dipped his hand into this, and marked on the shins, thighs, and other parts of his body the impress of his open hand in white. They partook of corn pollen, the first food they had eaten during the day, and they arose and walked around, happily restored. It was beautiful above them. It was beautiful below them. It was beautiful before them. It was beautiful behind them. It was beautiful all around them.

At sundown *Hastsézĭni* left for his home, and the war-gods went back to the medicine-lodge. The people sang all night, and beat the basket-drum. As was done to the gods then, so would they do today, if one among them got the war-disease.

ADVENTURES OF THE TWIN-GODS
(Various)

THE TWIN GODS AND HÄKI SUTO
(Zuñi)

H äki Suto, or Foretop Knot, he whose hair was done up over his forehead like a
quail's crest, lived among the great cliffs of the north long ago, when the world
was new. He was a giant, so tall that men called him *Lo Ikwithltchunona,* or the
Cloud-swallower. A devourer of men was he,—men were his meat—yea, and a
drinker of their very substance was he, for the cloud-breaths of the beloved gods,
and souls of the dead, whence descend rains, even these were his drink. Wherefore
the People of the Cliffs sought to slay him, and hero after hero perished thuswise.
Wherefore, too, snow ceased in the north and the west; rain ceased in the south
and the east; the mists of the mountains above were drunk up; the waters of the
valleys below were dried up; corn withered in the fields; men hungered and died in
the cliffs.

Then came the Twin Gods of War, *Áhaiyúta* and *Mátsailéma,* who in play staked
the lives of foes and fierce creatures. "Lo! it is not well with our children, men," said
they. "Let us destroy this *Häki Suto,* the swallower of clouds," said they.

They were walking along the trail which leads southward to the Smooth-rocks-
descending.

"O, grandchildren, where be ye wending?" said a little, little quavering voice.
They looked,—the younger, then the elder. There on the tip of a grass-stalk, waving
her banner of down-stuff, stood their grandmother, Spinner of Meshes.

"The Spider! Our Grandmother Spider!" cried one of the gods to the other. "Ho!
grandmother, was that you calling?" shouted they to her.

"Yea, children; where wend ye this noon-day?"

"A-warring we are going," said they. "Look now!

> "No beads for to broider your awning
> Have fallen this many a morning."

"Aha, wait ye! Whom ye seek, verily I know him well," said the Spider-woman.

> "Like a tree fallen down from the mountain
> He lies by the side of the cliff-trail
> And feigns to sleep there, yet is wary.
> I will sew up his eyes with my down-cords.
> Then come ye and smite him, grandchildren."

She ran ahead. There lay Häki Suto, his legs over the trail where men journeyed.
Great, like the trunks and branches of pine trees cast down by a wind-storm, were

his legs arching over the path-way, and when some one chanced to come by, the giant would call out: "Good morning!" and bid him "pass right along under." "I am old and rheumatic," he would continue, oh, so politely! "Do not mind my rudeness, therefore; run right along under; never fear, run right along under!" But when the hunter tried to pass, *kúutsu!* Häki Suto would snatch him up and cast him over the cliff to be eaten by the young Forehead-cresters.

The Spider stepped never so lightly, and climbed up behind his great ear, and then busily wove at her web, to and fro, up and down, and in and out of his eyelashes she busily plied at her web.

"Pesk the birds and buzz creatures!" growled the giant, twitching this way and that his eyebrows, which tickled; but he would not stir,—for he heard the War-gods coming, and thought them fat hunters and needs must feign sleepy.

And these? Ha! ha! They begin to sing, as was their fearless wont sometimes. Häki Suto never looked, but yawned and drawled as they came near, and nearer. "Never mind, my children, pass right along under, pass right along under; I am lame and tired this morning," said he.

Áhaiyúta ran to the left. Mátsailéma ran to the right. Häki Suto sprang up to catch them, but his eyes were so blinded with cobwebs that he missed them and feigned to fall, crying: "Ouch! my poor back! my poor back! Pass right along under, my children, it was only a crick in my back. Ouch! Oh, my poor back!" But they whacked him over the head and stomach till he stiffened and died. Then shouting *"So ho!"* they shoved him over the cliff.

The Navahos say that the grandmother tied him there by the hair—by his topknot—where you see the white streaks on the pillar, so *they* say; but it's the birds that streak the pillar, and *this* is the way. When Häki Suto fell, his feet drave far into the sands, and the Storm-gods rushed in to the aid of their children, the War-gods, and drifted his blood-bedrenched carcass all over with sand, whence he dried and hardened to stone. When the young ones saw him falling, they forthwith flocked up to devour him, making loud clamor. But the Twain, seeing this, made after them too and twisted the necks of all save only the tallest (who was caught in the sands with his father) and flung them aloft to the winds, whereby one became instantly the Owl, who twists her head wholly around whensoever she pleases, and stares as though frightened and strangled; and another the Falcon became, who perches and nests to this day on the crest of his sand-covered father, the Giant Cloud-drinker. And the Falcons cry ever and ever " 'Tis father; O father!" *("Tí-tätchu ya-tätchu.")*

But, fearing that never again would the waters refreshen their cañons, our ancients who dwelt in the cliffs fled away to the southward and eastward—all save those who had perished aforetime; they are dead in their homes in the cliff-towns, dried, like their cornstalks that died when the rain stopped long, long ago, when all things were new.

THE TALE
(Zuñi)

N ow, the Twain Little-ones, *Áhaiyúta* and *Mátsailéma*, were ever seeking scenes of contention; for what was deathly and dreadful to others was lively and delightful to them; so that cries of distress were ever their calls of invitation, as to a feast or dance is the call of a priest to us.

On a day when the world was quiet, they were sitting by the side of a deep pool. They heard curious sounds coming up through the waters, as though the bubbles were made by moans of the waters affrighted.

"Uh!" cried the elder. "What is that?"

The younger brother turned his ear to the ground and listened.

"There is trouble down there, dire trouble, for the people of the Underworld are shrieking war-cries like daft warriors and wailing like murder-mourners. What can be the matter? Let us descend and see!"

"Just so!" said Áhaiyúta.

Then they covered their heads with their cord-shields—turned upside down—and shut their eyes and stepped into the deep pool.

"Now we are in the dark," said they, "like the dark down there. Well, then, by means of the dark let us go down"—for they had wondrous power, had those Twain; the magic of in-knowing-how thought had they.

Down, like light through dark places, they went; dry through the waters; straight toward that village in the Underworld.

"Whew! the poor wretches are already dead," cried they, "and rotting"—for their noses were sooner accustomed to the dark than their eyes, which they now opened.

"We might as well have spared ourselves the coming, and stayed above," said Áhaiyúta.

"Nay, not so," said Mátsailéma. "Let us go on and see how they lived, even if they are dead."

"Very well," said the elder; and as they fared toward the village they could see quite plainly now, for they had made it dark (to themselves) by shutting their eyes in the daylight above, so now they made it light (to themselves) by opening their eyes in the darkness below and simply looking,—it was their way, you know.

"Well, well!" said Mátsailéma, as they came nearer and the stench doubled. "Look at the village; it is full of people; the more they smell of carrion the more they seem alive!"

"Yes, by the chut of an arrow!" exclaimed Áhaiyúta. "But look here! It is food we smell—cooked food, all thrown away, as we throw away bones and corn-cobs because they are too hard to eat and profitless withal. What, now, can be the meaning of this?"

"What, indeed! Who can know save by knowing," replied the younger brother. "Come, let us lie low and watch."

So they went very quietly close to the village, crouched down, and peered in. Some people inside were about to eat. They took fine food steaming hot from the cooking-pots and placed it low down in wide trenchers; then they gathered around and sipped in the steam and savor with every appearance of satisfaction; but they were as chary of touching the food or of letting the food touch them as though it were the vilest of refuse.

"Did you see that?" queried the younger brother. "By the delight of death, but—"

"Hist!" cried the elder. "If they are people of that sort, feeding upon the savor of food, then they will hear the suggestions of sounds better than the sounds themselves, and the very demon fathers would not know how to fare with such people, or to fight them, either!"

Hah! But already the people had heard! They set up a clamor of war, swarming out to seek the enemy, as well they might, for who would think favorably of a sneaking stranger under the shade of a house-wall watching the food of another? Why, dogs growl even at their own offspring for the like of that!

"Where? Who? What is it?" cried the people, rushing hither and thither like ants in a shower. "Hah! There they are! There! Quick!" cried they, pointing to the Twain, who were cutting away to the nearest hillock. And immediately they fell to singing their war-cry.

> "Ha-a! Sús-ki!
> Ó-ma-ta
> Há-wi-mo-o!
> Ó-ma-ta,
> Ó-ma-ta Há-wi-mo!"

sang they as they ran headlong toward the Two, and then they began shouting:

"Tread them both into the ground! Smite them both! Fan them out! *Ho-o! Ha-a! Há-wi-mo-o ó-ma-ta!*"

But the Twain laughed and quickly drew their arrows and loosed them amongst the crowd. *P'it! tsok!* sang the arrows through and through the people, but never a one fell.

"Why, how now is this?" cried the elder brother.

"We'll club them, then!" said Mátsailéma, and he whiffed out his war-club and sprang to meet the foremost whom he pummeled well and sorely over the head and shoulders. Yet the man was only confused (he was too soft and unstable to be hurt); but another, rushing in at one side, was hit by one of the shield-feathers and fell to the ground like smoke driven down under a hawk's wing.

"Hold, brother, I have it! Hold!" cried Áhaiyúta. Then he snatched up a bunch of dry plume-grass and leaped forward. *Swish!* Two ways he swept the faces and breasts of the pursuers. Lo! right and left they fell like bees in a rainstorm, and quickly sued for mercy, screeching and running at the mere sight of the grass-straws.

"You fools!" cried the brothers. "Why, then, did ye set upon us? We came for to help you and were merely looking ahead as becomes strangers in strange places, when, lo! you come running out like a mess of mad flies with your *'Ha-a sús-ki-ó-ma-*

ta!' Call us coyote-sneaks, do you? But there! Rest fearless! We hunger; give us to eat."

So they led the Twain into the court within the town and quickly brought steaming food for them.

They sat down and began to blow the food to cool it, whereupon the people cried out in dismay: "Hold! Hold, ye heedless strangers; do not waste precious food like that! For shame!"

"Waste food? Ha! This is the way *we* eat!" said they, and clutching up huge morsels they crammed their mouths full and bolted them almost whole.

The people were so horrified and sickened at sight of this, that some of them sweated furiously,—which was their way of spewing—whilst others, stouter of thought, cried: "Hold! hold! Ye will die; ye will surely sicken and die if the stuff do but touch ye!"

"Ho! ho!" cried the Twain, eating more lustily than ever. "Eat thus and harden yourselves, you poor, soft things, you!"

Just then there was a great commotion. Everyone rushed to the shelter of the walls and houses, shouting to them to leave off and follow quickly.

"What is it?" asked they, looking up and all around.

"Woe, woe! The gods are angry with us this day, and blowing arrows at us. They will kill you both! Hurry!" A big puff of wind was blowing over, scattering slivers and straws before it; that was all!

"Brother," said the elder, "this will not do. These people must be hardened and be taught to eat. But let us take a little sleep first, then we will look to this."

They propped themselves up against a wall, set their shields in front of them, and fell asleep. Not long after they awakened suddenly. Those strange people were trying to drag them out to bury them, but were afraid to touch them now, for they thought them dead stuff, more dead than alive.

The younger brother punched the elder with his elbow, and both pretended to gasp, then kept very still. The people succeeded at last in rolling them out of the court like spoiling bodies, and were about to mingle them with the refuse when they suddenly let go and set up a great wail, shouting "War! Murder!"

"How now?" cried the Twain, jumping up. Whereupon the people stared and chattered in greater fright than ever at seeing the dead seemingly come to life!

"What's the matter, you fool people?"

"Akaa kaa," cried a flock of jays.

"Hear that!" said the villagers. "Hear that, and ask what's the matter! The jays are coming; whoever they light on dies—run you two! *Aii!* Murder!" And they left off their standing as though chased by demons. On one or two of the hindmost some jays alighted. They fell dead as though struck by lightning!

"Why, see that!" cried the elder brother—"these people die if only birds alight on them!"

"Hold on, there!" said the younger brother. "Look here, you fearsome things!" So they pulled hairs from some scalp-locks they had, and made snares of them, and whenever the jays flew at them they caught them with the nooses until they had caught every one. Then they pinched them dead and took them into the town and roasted them. "This is the way," said they, as they ate the jays by morsels.

And the people crowded around and shouted: "Look! look! why, they eat the very enemy—say nothing of refuse!" And although they dreaded the couple, they became very conciliatory and gave them a fit place to bide in.

The very next day there was another alarm. The Two ran out to learn what was the matter. For a long time they could see nothing, but at last they met some people fleeing into the town. Chasing after them was a cooking-pot with earrings of onions. It was boiling furiously and belching forth hot wind and steam and spluttering mush in every direction. If ever so little of the mush hit the people they fell over and died.

"He!" cried the Twain;

"Té-k'ya-thla-k'ya
Í-ta-wa-k'ya
Äsh'-she-shu-kwa!

—As if food-stuff were made to make people afraid!" Whereupon they twitched the earrings off the pot and ate them up with all the mush that was in the pot, which they forthwith kicked to pieces vigorously.

Then the people crowded still closer around them, wondering to one another that they could vanquish all enemies by eating them with such impunity, and they begged the Twain to teach them how to do it. So they gathered a great council of the villagers, and when they found that these poor people were only half finished, . . . they cut vents in them (such as were not afraid to let them), . . . and made them eat solid food, by means of which they were hardened and became men of meat then and there, instead of having to get killed after the manner of the fearful, and others of their kind beforetime, in order to ascend to the daylight and take their places in men born of men.

And for this reason, behold! a new-born child may eat only of wind-stuff until his cord of viewless sustenance has been severed, and then only by sucking milk or soft food first and with much distress.

Behold! And we may now see why, like newborn children are the very aged; childish withal—*á-ya-vwi;*—not only toothless, too, but also sure to die of diarrhea if they eat ever so little save the soft parts and broths of cooked food. For are not the babes new-come from the Shi-u-na world; and are not the aged about to enter the Shi-po-lo-a world, where cooked food unconsumed is never heeded by the fully dead?

THE STEALING OF THE THUNDER-STONE
(Zuñi)

Á haiyúta and Mátsailéma, with their grandmother, lived where now stands the ancient Middle Place of Sacrifice on Thunder Mountain.

One day they went out hunting prairie-dogs, and while they were running about from one prairie-dog village to another, it began to rain, which made the trail slippery and the ground muddy, so that the boys became a little wrathful. Then they sat down and cursed the rain for a brief space. Off in the south it thundered until the earth trembled, and the lightning-shafts flew about the red-bordered clouds until the two brothers were nearly blinded with the beholding of it. Presently the younger brother smoothed his brow, and jumped up with an exclamation somewhat profane, and cried out: "Elder brother, let us go to the Land of Everlasting Summer and steal from the gods in council their thunder and lightning. I think it would be fine fun to do that sort of thing we have just been looking at and listening to."

The elder brother was somewhat more cautious; still, on the whole, he liked the idea. So he said: "Let us take our prairie-dogs home to the grandmother, that she shall have something to eat meanwhile, and we will think about going tomorrow morning."

The next morning, bright and early, they started out. In vain the old grandmother called rather crossly after them: "Where are you going now?" She could get no satisfaction, for she knew they lied when they called back: "Oh, we are only going to hunt more prairie-dogs." It is true that they skulked round in the plains about Thunder Mountain a little while, as if looking for prairie-dogs. Then, picking up their wondrously swift heels, they sped away toward that beautiful country of the corals, the Land of Everlasting Summer.

At last,—it may be in the mountains of that country, which are said to glow like shells of the sea or the clouds of the sunset,—they came to the House of the Beloved Gods themselves. And that red house was a wondrous terrace, rising wall after wall, and step after step, like a high mountain, grand and stately; and the walls were so smooth and high that the skill and power of the little War-gods availed them nothing; they could not get in.

"What shall we do?" asked the younger brother.

"Go home," said the elder, "and mind our own affairs."

"Oh, no," urged the younger; "I have it, elder brother. Let us hunt up our grandfather, the Centipede."

"Good!" replied the elder. "A happy thought is that of yours, my brother younger."

Forthwith they laid down their bows and quivers of mountain-lion skin, their shields, and other things, and set about turning over all the flat stones they could find. Presently, lifting one with their united strength, they found under it the very old fellow they sought. He doubled himself, and covered his eyes from the sharpness of the daylight. He did not much like being thus disturbed, even by his grandchildren, the War-gods, in the middle of his noonday nap, and was by no means polite to them. But they prodded him a little in the side, and said: "Now, grandfather, look here! We are in difficulty, and there is no one in the wide world who can help us out as you will."

The old Centipede was naturally flattered. He unrolled himself and viewed them with a look which he intended to be extremely reproachful and belittling. "Ah, my grandchildren," said he, "what are you up to now? Are you trying to get yourselves into trouble, as usual? No doubt of it! I will help you all I can; but the consequences be on your own heads!"

"That's right, grandfather, that's right! No one in the world could help us as you can," said one of them. "The fact is, we want to get hold of the thunder-stone and the lightning-shaft which the Rain-gods up there in the tremendous house keep and guard so carefully, we understand. Now, in the first place, we cannot get up the wall; in the second place, if we did, we would probably have a fuss with them in trying to steal these things. Therefore, we want you to help us, if you will."

"With all my heart, my boys! But I should advise you to run along home to your grandmother, and let these things alone."

"Oh, pshaw, nonsense! We are only going to play a little while with the thunder and lightning."

"All right," replied the old Worm; "sit here and wait for me." He wriggled himself and stirred about, and his countless legs were more countless than ever with rapid motions as he ran toward the walls of that stately terrace. A vine could not have run up more closely, nor a bird more rapidly; for if one foot slipped, another held on; so the old Centipede wriggled himself up the sides and over the roof, down into the great skyhole; and, scorning the ladder, which he feared might creak, he went along, head-downward, on the ceiling to the end of the room over the altar, ran down the side, and approached that most forbidden of places, the altar of the gods themselves. The beloved gods, in silent majesty, were sitting there with their heads bowed in meditation so deep that they heard not the faint scuffle of the Centipede's feet as he wound himself down into the altar and stole the thunder-stone. He took it in his mouth—which was larger than the mouths of Centipedes are now— and carried it silently, weighty as it was, up the way he had come, over the roof, down the wall, and back to the flat stone where he made his home, and where, hardly able to contain themselves with impatience, the two youthful gods were awaiting him.

"Here he comes!" cried the younger brother, "and he's got it! By my war-bonnet, he's got it!"

The old grandfather threw the stone down. It began to sound, but Áhaiyúta grabbed it, and, as it were, throttled its world-stirring speech. "Good! good!" he cried to the grandfather; "thank you, old grandfather, thank you!"

"Hold on!" cried the younger brother; "you didn't bring both. What can we do with the one without the other?"

"Shut up!" cried the old Worm. "I know what I am about!" And before they could say any more he was off again. Ere long he returned, carrying the shaft of lightning, with its blue, shimmering point, in his mouth.

"Good!" cried the War-gods. And the younger brother caught up the lightning, and almost forgot his weapons, which, however, he did stop to take up, and started on a full run for Thunder Mountain, followed by his more deliberate, but equally interested elder brother, who brought along the thunder-stone, which he found a somewhat heavier burden than he had supposed.

It was not long, you may well imagine, so powerful were these Gods of War, ere they reached the home of their grandmother on the top of Thunder Mountain.

They had carefully concealed the thunder-stone and the shaft of lightning meanwhile, and had taken care to provide themselves with a few prairie-dogs by way of deception.

Still, in majestic revelry, unmoved, and apparently unwitting of what had taken place, sat the Rain-gods in their home in the mountains of Summerland.

Not long after they arrived, the young gods began to grow curious and anxious to try their new playthings. They poked one another considerably, and whispered a great deal, so that their grandmother began to suspect they were about to play some rash joke or other, and presently she espied the point of lightning gleaming under Mátsailéma's dirty jacket.

"Demons and corpses!" she cried. "By the moon! You have stolen the thunderstone and lightning-shaft from the Gods of Rain themselves! Go this instant and return them, and never do such a thing again!" she cried, with the utmost severity; and, making a quick step for the fireplace, she picked up a poker with which to belabor their backs, when they whisked out of the room and into another. They slammed the door in their grandmother's face and braced it, and, clearing away a lot of rubbish that was lying around the rear room, they established themselves in one end, and, nodding and winking at one another, cried out: "Now, then!" The younger let go the lightning-shaft; the elder rolled the thunder-stone. The lightning hissed through the air, and far out into the sky, and returned. The thunder-stone rolled and rumbled until it shook the foundations of the mountain. "Glorious fun!" cried the boys, rubbing their thighs in ecstasy of delight. "Do it again!" And again they sent forth the lightning and rolled the thunder-stone.

And now the gods in Summerland arose in their majesty and breathed upon the skies; and the winds rose, and the rains fell like rivers from the clouds, centering their violence upon the roof of the poor old grandmother's house. Heedlessly those reckless wretches kept on playing the thunder-stone and lightning-shaft without the slightest regard to the tremendous commotion they were raising all through the skies and all over Thunder Mountain; but nowhere else as above the house where their poor old grandmother lived fell the torrent of the rain, and there alone, of course, burst the lightning and rolled the thunder.

Soon the water poured through the roof of the house; but, move the things as the old grandmother would, she could not keep them dry; scold the boys as she would, she could not make them desist. No, they would only go on with their play more violently than ever, exclaiming: "What has she to say, anyway? It won't hurt her to get a good ducking, and this is fun!" By-and-by the waters rose so high that they extinguished the fire. Soon they rose still higher, so that the War-gods had to paddle around half submerged. Still they kept rolling the thunder-stone and shooting the lightning. The old grandmother scolded harder and harder, but after awhile desisted and climbed to the top of the fireplace, whence, after recovering from her exertion, she began again. But the boys heeded her not, only saying: "Let her yell! Let her scold! This is fun!" At last they began to take the old grandmother's scolding as a matter of course, and allowed nothing but the water to interrupt their pastime. It rose so high, finally, that they were near drowning. Then they climbed to the roof, but still they kept on.

"By the bones of the dead! why did we not think to come here before? 'Tis ten times as fine up here. See him shoot!" cried one to the other, as the lightning sped through the sky, ever returning.

"Hear it mutter and roll!" cried the other, as the thunder bellowed and grumbled.

But no sooner had the Two begun their sport on the roof, than the rain fell in one vast sheet all about them; and it was not long ere the house was so full that the old grandmother—locked in as she was—bobbed her poor pate on the rafters in trying to keep it above the water. She gulped water, and gasped, coughed, strangled, and shrieked to no purpose.

"What a fuss our old grandmother is making, to be sure!" cried the boys. And they kept on, until, forsooth, the water had completely filled the room, and the grandmother's cries gurgled away and ceased. Finally, the thunder-stone grew so terrific, and the lightning so hot and unmanageable, that the boys, drawing a long breath and thinking with immense satisfaction of the fun they had had, possibly also influenced as to the safety of the house, which was beginning to totter, flung the thunder-stone and the lightning-shaft into the sky, where, rattling and flashing away, they finally disappeared over the mountains in the south.

Then the clouds rolled away and the sun shone out, and the boys, wet to the skin, tired in good earnest, and hungry as well, looked around. "Goodness! the water is running out of the windows of our house! This is a pretty mess we are in! Grandmother! Grandmother!" they shouted. "Open the door, and let us in!" But the old grandmother had piped her last, and never a sound came except that of flowing water. They sat themselves down on the roof, and waited for the water to get lower. Then they climbed down, and pounded open the door, and the water came out with a rush, and out with a rush, too, their poor old grandmother,—her eyes staring, her hair all mopped and muddied, and her fingers and legs as stiff as cedar sticks.

"Oh, ye gods! ye gods!" the two boys exclaimed; "we have killed our own grandmother—poor old grandmother, who scolded us so hard and loved us so much! Let us bury her here in front of the door, as soon as the water has run away."

So, as soon as it became dry enough, there they buried her; and in less than four days a strange plant grew up on that spot, and on its little branches, amid its bright green leaves, hung long, pointed pods of fruit, as red as the fire on the breast of the red-bird.

"It is well," said the boys, as they stood one day looking at this plant. "Let us scatter the seeds abroad, that men may find and plant them. It seems it was not without good cause that in the abandonment to our sport we killed our old grandmother, for out of her heart there sprung a plant into the fruits of which, as it were, has flowed the color as well as the fire of her scolding tongue; and, if we have lost our grandmother, whom we loved much, but who loved us more, men have gained a new food, which, though it burn them, shall please them more than did the heat of her discourse please us. Poor old grandmother! Men will little dream when they eat peppers that the seed of them first arose from the fiery heart of the grandmother of Áhaiyúta and Mátsailéma."

Thereupon the two seized the pods and crushed them between their hands, with an exclamation of pleasure at the brisk odor they gave forth. They cast the seeds abroad, which seeds here and there took root; and the plants which sprang from them being found by men, were esteemed good and were cultivated, as they are to this day in the pepper gardens of Zuñi.

Ever since this time you hear that mountain wherein lived the gods with their grandmother called Thunder Mountain; and often, indeed, to this day, the lightning flashes and the thunder plays over its brows and the rain falls there most frequently.

It is said by some that the two boys, when asked how they stole the lightning-shaft and the thunderstone, told on their poor old grandfather, the Centipede. The beloved Gods of the Rain gave him the lightning-shaft to handle in another way, and it so burned and shriveled him that he became small, as you can see by looking at any of his numerous descendants, who are not only small but appear like a well-toasted bit of buckskin, fringed at the edges.

THE GAMBLING GOD
(Moqui)

Down in the cañon of Chaco, NM, stands a building evidently coeval with those of the cliff-dwellers, that is still in good preservation and is called the Broad House. When *Noqoilpi,* the gambling god, came on earth he strayed into this cañon, and, finding the Moquis a prosperous people, he envied them and resolved to win their property. To do that he laid off a race-track at the bottom of the ravine and challenged them to meet him there in games of chance and strength and skill. They accepted his challenge, and, as he could turn luck to his own side, he soon won not their property alone, but their women and children, and, finally, some of the men themselves.

In his greed he had acquired more than he wanted, and as the captives were a burden to him he offered to make a partial restoration if the people would build this house for him. They did so and he gave up some of the men and women. The other gods looked with disapproval on this performance, however, and they agreed to give the wind god power to defeat him, for, now that he had secured his house, he had gone to gambling again. The wind god, in disguise as a Moqui, issued a challenge, and the animals agreed to help him.

When the contest in tree-pulling took place the wind god pulled up a large tree while Noqoilpi was unable to stir a smaller one. That was because the beavers had cut the roots of the larger. In the ball contest Noqoilpi drove the ball nearly to the bounds, but the wind god sent his far beyond, for wrapped loosely in it was a bird that freed itself before touching the ground and flew away. In brief, Noqoilpi was beaten at every point and the remaining captives left him, with jeers, and returned to their people.

The gambler cursed and raged until the wind god seized him, fitted him to a bow, like an arrow, and shot him into the sky. He flew far out of sight, and presently came to the long row of stone houses where the man lives who carries the moon. He pitied the gambler and made new animals and people for him and let him down to the earth in old Mexico, the moon people becoming Mexicans. He returned to his old haunts and came northward, building towns along the Rio Grande until he had passed the site of Santa Fé, when his people urged him to go back, and after his return they made him their god—*Nakai Cigini.*

CHAPTER 14

CORE BELIEFS

THE SUN-CHILDREN
(Zuñi)

The Zuñi philosophy of the fetish is given in the "Tale of the Two Sun-Children" as follows: Now that the surface of the earth was hardened even the animals of prey, powerful and like the fathers (gods) themselves, would have devoured the children of men, and the two thought it was not well that they should all be permitted to live, for, said they, "Alike the children of men and the children of the animals of prey multiply themselves. The animals of prey are provided with talons and teeth; men are but poor, the finished beings of earth, therefore the weaker." Whenever they came across the pathway of one of these animals, were he a great mountain lion or but a mere mole, they struck him with the fire of lightning which they carried on their magic shields. *Thlu!* and instantly he was shriveled and turned into stone. Then said they to the animals that they had changed into stone, "That ye may not be evil unto man, but that ye may be a great good unto them, have we changed you into rock everlasting. By the magic breath of prey, by the heart that shall endure for ever within you, shall ye be made to serve instead of to devour mankind." Thus was the surface of the earth hardened and scorched, and many of all kinds of beings changed to stone. Thus, too, it happens that we find here and there throughout the world their forms, sometimes large, like the beings themselves, sometimes shriveled and distorted, and we often see among the rocks the forms of many beings that live no longer, which shows us that all was different in the "days of the new." Of these petrifactions, which are, of course, mere concretions or strangely shaped rock-forms, the Zuñi say: "Whomsoever of us may be met with the light of such great good-fortune may see them, and should treasure them for the sake of the sacred (magic) power which was given them in the days of the new."

Sun-God Ceremony
(Hopi)

A man who personated the Sun-god donned the characteristic mask and dressed near the sun shrine at Walla, northeast of the pueblos, and after certain preliminaries at this shrine, led by the Katcina chief, proceeded up the trail to the pueblos, first Hano, from which he proceeded to Sichomovi and Walpi, visiting the kivas and houses of all the principal chiefs in these three villages.

As the personator of the Sun-god walked through the pueblos he imitated the gait and general manner of an old man, using a staff for support as he proceeded from one room to another, and performed the following rites at each kiva. Having approached the hatchway of one of these rooms he leaned down, and drew a vertical mark with sacred-meal on the inside of the entrance, opposite the ladder. Turning to the east he made solemn inclinations of his body, bending backward and bowing forward, uttering at the same time a low, falsetto growl. He then turned to the kiva entrance and made similar obeisances, calling in the same voice; two or three of the principal men responded by coming up the kiva ladder, each bearing a handful of prayer-meal, and a feather-string which he placed in the hand of the Sun-god, at the same time saying a low, inaudible prayer.

At the houses of the chiefs the personator performed similar acts having the same import. Advancing to the doorway, he rubbed a handful of meal on the house wall, at the left of the doorway, making a vertical mark about the height of his chest. He then turned to face the rising sun, and made six silent inclinations of his body, uttering the falsetto calls, holding his staff before him at arm's length. Turning again to the doorway he bowed his body four times, and made the same calls.

The chief man or woman emerged from the house and placed in the hand of the personator a handful of prayer-meal and stringed-feather, saying at the same time a low prayer. In return for which the Sun-god handed him a few bean sprouts.

All the prayer offerings which the Sun-god had received in this circuit of the towns were later deposited in a sun-shrine, and the personator returned to the kiva, where he disrobed; the mask was carried to the house of the Katcina chief in whose custody it is kept, and to whom it is said to belong.

The above actions admit of the following explanations: The personator of the Sun-god enters the pueblos from the east at or near sunrise, receiving at each house the prayers of the inmates symbolized by the meal which each chief places in his hand, receiving in return sprouted beans symbolically representing the gifts for which they pray. The inclinations and obeisances with the accompanying calls may be theoretically interpreted as signs to his beneficent followers, the clan-ancients, and the bows to the doorways, gestures indicating the houses that he wishes them to enter, bringing blessing. The whole performance is a "prayer by signatures," or a pantomimic representation in which the desires of the Hopi are expressed by symbols and symbolic actions. The priests ask the Sky-god to aid them, and he answers in a symbolic way for himself and his followers, the ancients of clans.

The representation of the departure of the clan-ancients is not less dramatic than that of their advent; in it they are conducted or led away by a personage with symbols which are characteristic of another god.

THE DEPARTURE OF THE CLAN-ANCIENTS
(Hopi)

The representation of the departure of the clan-ancients, as stated above, occurs in July. Their leader is called *Eototo,* the germ god, who is ruler of the underworld, back to which habitation he leads the personators of the dead. On his head Eototo wears a closely fitting cloth bag, without decoration, but with simple openings pierced for eyes and mouth. The gorgeous headdress of the Sun-god is absent; in its place he wears a sprig of green tied to the top of this bag. He carries a planting-stick, a symbol of growth, and wears leggings not unlike those of the Sun-god.

The representation of the departure of the clan-ancients occurred at sunrise on the morning following the last day of a nine days' festival, and was performed by four men, three of whom were masked to represent clan-ancients, and one to personate their leader, Eototo.

The performance of these actors, just before leaving the pueblo, was as follows. Each stood at one of the four sides of the kiva entrance, where symbols of rain-clouds had previously been drawn with meal on the ground, which the masked men faced, looking down the hatchway.

A man stood on a ladder so that the top of his head protruded out of the entrance into the chamber below, and from this position threw pinches of meal outside, making several attempts to strike with it the garments of Eototo, who, when he saw the meal, laid on the symbol of the rain-cloud before him a black stick and a small annulet made of leaves.

These were so placed as to be beyond the reach of the man within the room, who again threw pinches of meal at Eototo. In response, the latter raised the two objects and moved them nearer the entrance. Again prayer-meal was thrown out of the room at the god, who again raised the two objects, and advanced them within reach of the man who carried them into the room below.

The chief in the kiva cast meal at the three other masked men representing clan-ancients, and received from them similar black sticks and annulets, after which all marched around the hatchway of the kiva, returning to their former position.

The chief then cast meal at Eototo and his three companions, this time praying for rain, and they in turn poured water into a bowl held at the four sides of the kiva entrance. This prayer was followed by others for food, in response to which small imitation cakes were thrown into the room.

These performances are interpreted as follows: They represent prayers and answers to the same by signatures. The meal carries the wish of the priest, the sticks and annulets symbolize growth of crops; the water poured into the bowl typifies falling rain; and the miniature cakes, food.

The final act in the departure of the clan-ancients and their leader was as follows: The chief having emerged from the room, led the procession from the plaza to their symbolic home, a shrine to the west of the town, all the spectators casting meal (praying) towards the masked men as they passed out of the town. They went down the west trail, because the entrance to the underworld, the home of the beings personated, is situated in the west where the sun sets. The masked men, having deposited their prayer emblems in this shrine, disrobed, for they then ceased to personate the gods, as the dramatization had ended. We are especially concerned with the identity of Eototo. What god does he represent?

The conductor of the clan-ancients from the pueblo, in this annual celebration of their departure, has symbolic resemblances to a being called *Masauû,* who is often personated as the ruler of the realm of the dead and god of fire; but Masauû, like Eototo, sometimes plays the role of Germ-god, as described in the pages which immediately follow.

Impersonating Masauû
(Hopi)

M any personations of Masauû have been witnessed but in most of these he is represented as a god of death or fire. A ceremony in which he appears in the role of a planting-god was witnessed on one of the nights of the great Powamû festival. He is at all times much feared and reverenced, and on the night in which he was personated there was a profound hush in all the pueblos on the East Mesa. Few men and no women or children at that time ventured out of doors, and all said that it was an occasion of great solemnity to them when this god was personated in their kivas, an event not celebrated every year. On the night of this performance, the leading men of the pueblos were seated in a circle about the fireplace. Every one who is a witness of the personation of the "old god" must not omit the preliminary formal smoke.

Seated with the chiefs around the fireplace, it was noted that many other men besides the chiefs were in the room busily occupied in decorating their bodies, painting their cheeks with daubs of white kaolin, and tying yucca fiber on their legs. These men later personated the so-called *Maswik Katcinas,* a kind of escort accompanying Masauû from place to place. Although they wore no distinctive masks or other paraphernalia, they were said to represent both male and female Katcinas. They constituted a chorus, performing dances and singing excellent songs. When these men were ready they stood in line on three sides of the kiva, singing and dancing, as Moume came down the ladder bringing the mask of Massauû, which with reverence he laid back of the fireplace within the circle of the chiefs. In general appearance this object resembled a large human skull, but on nearer inspection it was found to be a hollow gourd rudely painted, punctured with round holes for eyes and mouth. The edge of the orifice, through which the head was inserted, was notched, and the gourd had been broken and repaired in several places. It had no decorations or appendages, but its surface was daubed with black paint.

When it had been put on the floor before the fireplace the chiefs solemnly smoked, reverentially taking it in their hands in turn, and puffing great clouds of smoke over it. They also prayed very fervently, in sequence, addressing their prayers in all instances directly to the object. In the same bundle with the mask, Moume brought also two basket plaques, two planting-sticks, and two old blankets, all of which he laid on the floor in front of the fireplace.

These objects having been deposited on the floor and the fervent prayers to the mask having ceased, Sakwistiwa proceeded to paint the latter by squirting upon it from his mouth a pigment made of ground black shale mixed with spittle, sprinkling also upon it a little glistening iron oxide. No other color and no feathers were added to this archaic object; but while it was being painted all sang a fine solemn song. Each of the Maswik Katcinas then laid a feathered string in one of the basket trays on the floor near the gourd, as his personal prayer for benefits desired, and then all filed out of the room. At their departure the man who was to personate Masauû put the gourd on his head, and prepared for the rites which occur in the other kivas. The subsequent events took place in the Moñ-kiva, and were repeated in all the secret rooms in Walpi on the same night. Pautiwa, chief of the warrior society, personated Masauû, and was assisted in preparation by Sakwistiwa, who tied a yucca fiber garter on his legs, and adjusted the gourd to his head. In a few moments he was ready to join the escort which had preceded him. Many people gathered in the chamber below to witness the advent of the god; all the spectators sitting on the raised floor of the room, north and east of the ladder, but the chiefs squatted by the fireplace, in which sputtered a flickering flame of greasewood.

Soon the chorus began to file down the ladder and arrange themselves in line on the three sides of the kiva. As each of these personages entered, Naka, the Katcina chief, dropped on his left shoulder a pinch of meal, symbol of a prayer. The last man of the line asked, as he stepped from the rung of the ladder upon the floor, if they were welcome, and all present responded that they were. It was observed that they bore many cow-bells, which they immediately began to rattle, at the same time dancing a solemn step. In the midst of this dance the personator of Masauû came down the ladder, as one would stairs, not as ordinarily, facing the ladder, and without a word slipped behind the row of dancers passing to the back of the room, ultimately making his way between two of the chorus to the space near the fireplace. He was followed by an unmasked man who had black marks painted on his cheeks, and carried a planting-stick in his hand. This man sat by the side of Masauû and imitated his actions, but his true function seemed to be to guide his comrade in the dark from one place to another.

Masauû facing the fireplace assumed the posture of a man planting. He held a planting-dibble and a basket-tray in his hands, while over his shoulders was thrown an old blanket. Yucca fiber garters were tied on his legs, and he was barefoot. The most striking object in his appearance was the old glistening gourd, painted black. Nothing was said by any one as the two personators took their position, but continued the song and dance, which began before they came. Finally they ceased and the chorus filed out, each saying, "good-night" as he left the room, but the last of their number, who carried a bundle on his back, announced that at planting a few months hence there would be a more extended dramatization of the god at a place called Maski, the home of Masauû, near the trail to the Middle Mesa. This ceremony, thus formally announced, was later performed, but the author was unable to witness it on account of his absence from the pueblo.

After the departure of the chorus, the two figures remained seated, and all the men, preceded by their chiefs, pressed forward with their feather emblems, each in turn saying his prayer to the masked being, and depositing his feather in the basket plaque. Masauû made no response to these appeals, which were in a low voice, inaudible to any but the god, and soon went out, followed by his companion. Meanwhile the chorus, who has preceded him, awaited his arrival, huddled on the hatch of the adjacent kiva, and subsequently the same ceremony was repeated that night in all the sacred rooms of Walpi, but not in Sitcomovi and Hano. The closing exercises, or those in the last room, took place about midnight.

In the ceremony described above we have a personation of a being not in the role of a god of fire or ruler of the underworld, home of the dead, but of a Germ-god, the same as Eototo, who in the departure festival leads the ancients to their home, the realm of the dead.

From what has been written it is evident that there is yearly performed in one Hopi pueblo, and probably in four others, two festivals, or elaborate dramatizations of the arrival and departure of the gods. In the personnel of each there is a masked man their leader known in the advent drama as the Sun-god; in the exit, the Germ-god. The shape of the mask of the former, its radiating feathers and horsehair, represents the sun's disk; the head-covering of the latter, a simple bag or gourd without ornament, a fitting symbol of the underworld. In their objective symbolism these two personations have little in common, and yet theoretically there is good evidence to regard them as variants of the same being, the magic power of the sky, the genitor of men, animals, and plants; one designated by the mask of the sun; the other, the ruler of the underworld, home of the ancients, the old Fire-god or Germ-god, male parent of all beings.

At present, most clans have ceased to observe their festivals *in extenso,* having curtailed them, and in this reduction lost all save the personation and totemic symbols of their ancients and their Sky-god. They still personate their Sky-god, but as a subordinate being, which still preserves enough symbolism to betray its celestial origin.

While there is no other group of clans on the East Mesa which preserve the drama of the advent and departure of the Sky-god in as unmodified a form as the Katcina clan and its relatives, there are others in which enough of the dramatic element exists to show that the same general plan was followed in them. One of these occurs in Sichomovi, a small pueblo of the East Mesa. The dramatization of the advent of the clan-ancients conducted by a Sun or Sky-god, called *Pautiwa,* takes place in that pueblo in January, and is called the *Pamüti.*

FESTIVAL OF THE PAMÜTI
(Zuñi)

The pueblo, Sichomovi, is mainly inhabited by clans of Tiwa and Tanoan extraction, which, however, have long since lost their languages. The predominating clan is called the Asa, which is represented by kindred at Zuñi. The Zuñi kinship of this clan dates to a time when in its migration it lived for many years at that pueblo. So that even now the Zuñis sometimes speak of *Sichomovi* as a "Zuñi pueblo among the Mokis," on account of the kinship of Asa clans in the two pueblos.

The festival of the Pamüti is a Sichomovi dramatization of the return of clan-ancients, most of which bear Zuñi names, controlled by the Asa clan. In it there appears a personation of the Sky-god whose acts resemble those of the Sun personation already described. While the author reserves a complete description of the Pamüti to another article, he here considers the personation of the Sun-god Pautiwa, which particularly concerns the reader of this article.

In this festival all the participants march into the pueblo in solemn procession from a distant house in the plain, led by this personator of the Sun-god, who, a few days previous to this celebration, had visited all the kivas and houses of the foremost clans, but in a much less formal way than Ahüla, as already described.

Passing from the representation by personations of the advent of totemic ancients of Asa and other clans, we come to a consideration of such clans as no longer celebrate, *in extenso,* festivals of advent and departure of their ancients, although still retaining knowledge of the symbols which characterize their ancients, and, in several instances, their Sun or Sky-god. The festival of such clans, formerly as extensive and elaborate as those above mentioned, has been worn down to a simple dance in which their ancients are represented, but the personator of their Sun-god has become one of many subordinate masked persons in festivals not their own, like Powamû, and Pamüti. The names of these personations have been changed, their identity is practically lost, but their symbolism is not changed, and its design enables us to determine with fair certainty whom they represent, even if name and action give no clue to their identity. Superficially they are simply masked men; in reality they are personations of Sun-gods of clans which have died out or lost prominence.

WINTER SOLSTICE DRAMATIZATION
(Hopi)

From the type of dramatization and sun personation adopted in the Katcina cultus let us pass to another somewhat different but essentially the same, that of the Rain Cloud and those related clans which came to Tusayan from the south. A similar dramatic representation of the return and departure of the Sky-god or Sun-god occurs here as in the Katcina festivals.

Among these southern clans this being is symbolized by a Bird-Snake personation, who is represented in the kiva at the Winter Solstice ceremony at Walpi. In this drama he appears as a man "made up" to imitate a bird, and the actions he performs symbolize a bird.

In more elaborated dramatizations in which the Sky-god of kindred southern clans represent the epiphany of their celestial father we find the Sky-god personated as at Oraibi, by a man wearing a star on his head and bearing the sun disk in his hand. The star or cross on the head of this personation is a Sky-god symbol which sometimes hangs before altars to represent the same god here personated by a man.

In the public dramatization of the advent and possibly the departure of the Sky-god of these clans we find a considerable variation as compared with that of the Katcina clans already described.

In one variant a masked representation of the Sun or Sky-god with two maidens, cultus heroine and Earth-goddess, appear in the pueblo of Walpi at sunrise, and in answer to prayers present to the women, heads of all the clans, ears of seed-corn symbolizing abundant harvests. They do not visit the houses and there receive prayers from the chiefs, giving in return sprouts of beans, as does Ahüla in Powamû, but the heads of households come to the personation of the Sky-god, and pray to him, receiving corn-ears in response. The proceedings in both instances have the same symbolic meaning, a sign prayer, and answers to the same.

PERSONATION OF A SKY-GOD WIELDING LIGHTNING
(Hopi)

There is an instructive act in the great mystery-play of the Hopi, called the Palülükoñti, which gives an idea of the symbolism of another form of a Sun-god personation, as well as that of the lightning. In this act a masked man representing Shalako stands in the middle of the kiva before the spectators holding an effigy of the Plumed Snake which he causes to coil about his body and head and to dart into the air. The means by which the movement is effected is at first not apparent, but closer examination reveals a false arm hanging at the actor's side in place of his real arm which is inserted in the body of the effigy imparting to it its deceptive movements.

This act represents the Sky-god wielding the lightning; the former represented as Shalako, the latter as the Plumed Snake.

In another episode of this remarkable mystery-play effigies of the Great Serpent are thrust through openings closed by disks with Sun symbols. These effigies are made to knock over a symbolic cornfield. The meaning of this drama is apparent. The serpent effigies represent the lightning and the rains and winds which accompany it. They are made to emerge from the Sun symbols representing the Sky-god, whose servants they are or from whom their power comes. They knock over the hills of corn, representing how the floods and winds destroy the works of the farmer. The final part of this episode is also dramatic and symbolic; a man personating the Earth-goddess Hahaiwüqti, wife of the Sky-god, symbolically prays to the angry serpents, symbols of his power,—in other words, prays to the god to cease afflicting man and destroying the fields of the farmers by means of his agent the lightning. In both these acts the personation of the lightning is controlled by the Sun or Sky-god; the lightning, once regarded an attribute, has become a special personation controlled by the Sky-god.

Now this Great Serpent conception or personation of lightning has powers which naturally grew up in the mind from analogical reasoning. Certain kinds of rain accompany the lightning; therefore, reasons primitive man, one causes the other; the lightning causes rain, or, put in another way, the Great Serpent brings the rain. Hence the Sky-god through his agent is a powerful rain-god, and symbols of the lightning in form of zigzag designs are constant on Hopi rain altars.

The Underworld
(Zuñi)

It seems—so the words of the grandfathers say—that in the Underworld were many strange things and beings, even villages of men, long ago. But the people of those villages were unborn-made,—more like the ghosts of the dead than ourselves, yet more like ourselves than are the ghosts of the dead, for as the dead are more finished of being than we are, they were less so, as smoke, being hazy, is less fine than mist, which is filmy; or as green corn, though raw, is soft like cooked corn which is done (like the dead), and as both are softer than ripe corn which, though raw, is hardened by age (as we are of meat).

And also, these people were, you see, dead in a way, in that they had not yet begun to live, that is, as we live, in the daylight fashion.

And so, it would seem, partly like ourselves, they had bodies, and partly like the dead they had no bodies, for being unfinished they were unfixed. And whereas the dead are like the wind, and take form from within of their own wills *(yän'te-tseman)*, these people were really like the smoke, taking form from without of the outward touching of things, even as growing and unripe grains and fruits do.

Well, in consequence, it was passing strange what a state they were in! Bethink ye! Their persons were much the reverse of our own, for wherein we are hard, they were soft—pliable. Wherein we are most completed, they were most unfinished; for not having even the organs of digestion, whereby we fare lustily, food in its solidity was to them destructive, whereas to us it is sustaining. When, therefore, they would eat, they dreaded most the food itself, taking thought not to touch it, and merely absorbing the mist thereof. As fishes fare chiefly on water, and birds on air, so these people ate by gulping down the steam and savor of their cooked things whilst cooking or still hot; then they threw the real food away, forsooth!

CHAPTER 15

TRIBAL ORIGINS

THE COMING OF THE NAVAJOS
(Navajo)

Many fantastic accounts of the origin of man are found among the red tribes. The Onondagas say that the Indians are made from red earth and the white men from sea-foam. Flesh-making clay is seen in the precipitous bank in the ravine west of Onondaga Valley, where at night the fairies—"little fellows"—sport and slide. Among others, the Noah legend finds a parallel. Several tribes claim to have emerged from the interior of the earth. The Oneidas point to a hill near the falls of Oswego River, NY, as their birthplace; the Wichitas rose from the rocks about Red River; the Creeks from a knoll in the valley of Big Black River in the Natchez country, where dwelt the Master of Breath; the Aztecs were one of seven tribes that came out from the seven caverns of Aztlan, or Place of the Heron; and the Navajos believe that they emerged at a place known to them in the Navajo Mountains.

In the underworld the Navajos were happy, for they had everything that they could wish: there was no excess of heat or cold, trees and flowers grew everywhere, and the day was marked by a bright cloud that arose in the east, while a black cloud that came out of the west made the night. Here they lived for centuries, and might have been there to this day had not one of the tribe found an opening in the earth that led to some place unknown. He told of it to the whole tribe. They set off up the passage to see where it led, and after long and weary climbing the surface was reached. Pleased with the novelty of their surroundings, they settled here, but on the fourth day after their arrival their queen disappeared.

Their search for her was unavailing until some of the men came to the mouth of the tunnel by which they had reached the upper land, when, looking down, they saw their queen combing her long, black locks. She told them that she was dead and that her people could go to her only after death, but that they would be happy in their old home. With that the earth shut together and the place has never since been open to the eye of mortals. Soon came the cannibal giants who ravaged the desert lands and destroyed all of the tribe but four families, these having found a refuge in a deep cañon of the Navajo Mountains. From their retreat they could see a beam of light shining from one of the hills above them, and on ascending to the place they found a beautiful girl babe.

This child grew to womanhood under their care, and her charms attracted the great manitou that rides on a white horse and carries the sun for a shield. He wooed and married her, and their children slew the giants that had destroyed the Navajos. After a time the manitou carried his wife to his floating palace in the western water, which has since been her home. To her the prayers of the people are addressed, and twelve immortals bear their petitions to her throne.

Origin of the Apaches
(Apache)

In the underworld, *Uⁿ-gó-ya-yĕn-ni,* there was no sun, moon, or light of any kind, except that emanating from large eagle feathers which the people carried about with them. This method of lighting proved unsatisfactory, and the head men of the tribe gathered in council to devise some plan for lighting the world more brightly. One of the chiefs suggested that they make a sun and a moon. A great disk of yellow paint was made upon the ground, and then placed in the sky. Although this miniature creation was too small to give much light, it was allowed to make one circuit of the heavens ere it was taken down and made larger. Four times the sun set and rose, and four times it was enlarged, before it was "as large as the earth and gave plenty of light." In the underworld dwelt a wizard and a witch, who were much incensed at man's presumption, and made such attempts to destroy the new luminaries that both the sun and the moon fled from the lower world, leaving it again in darkness, and made their escape to this earth, where they have never been molested, so that, until the present time, they continue to shine by night and by day. The loss of the sun and moon brought the people together, that they might take council concerning the means of restoring the lost light. Long they danced and sang, and made medicine. At length it was decided that they should go in search of the sun. The Indian medicine-men caused four mountains to spring up, which grew by night with great noise, and rested by day. The mountains increased in size until the fourth night, when they nearly reached the sky. Four boys were sent to seek the cause of the failure of the mountains to reach the opening in the sky, *ha-ná-za-ä,* through which the sun and moon had disappeared. The boys followed the tracks of two girls who had caused the mountains to stop growing, until they reached some burrows in the side of the mountain, where all trace of the two females disappeared. When their story was told to the people, the medicine-men said, "You who have injured us shall be transformed into rabbits, that you may be of some use to mankind; your bodies shall be eaten," and the rabbit has been used for food by the human race down to the present day.

All then journeyed to the tops of the mountains, where a ladder was built which reached the aperture in the sky or roof of the underworld. The badger was then sent out to explore the earth above; the messenger soon returned, and reported water everywhere except around the margin of the opening. The legs of the badger were covered with mud, which accounts for their dark color at the present day. Four days later, the turkey was sent to see if the waters had subsided. The turkey reported no land yet to be seen above. As the turkey came in contact with the foam of the flood surrounding the opening, his tail became wet and heavy; in shaking this he scattered filmy drops upon his wings, and that is why the feathers of the turkey to the present day present an iridescent play of colors. Then the Wind came to the anxious people and said, "If you will ask me to help you, I will drive back the water for you." Thus the first prayers came to be addressed to the Wind, which yet remains a powerful deity. When the Wind had rolled back the waters to the limits of the present ocean, the Indians began to ascend the ladder; four times the ladder broke with them, and four times it was replaced by a new one. All the people reached the new world except one old woman, too old and infirm to climb the ladder, who said to them: "I do not wish to leave the land of my youth. Go your way and leave me here; you will come back to join me when you die. You have forgotten one thing; you will soon discover what it is." For four days after their emergence no one could sleep; then the people remembered the warning of the old woman, and two boys were sent down to the underworld to learn what it was that had been forgotten. The old woman said in reply to their question, "You forgot to take lice with you; without them you cannot sleep." She took two black ones from her hair and two white ones from her body, saying, "These will be all you will need, for they will increase night and day." So it has happened that the Apaches sleep well to this day because they harbor these parasites upon their bodies.

So well had the Wind performed his task of drying up the waters, that none remained for the people to drink; but prayers addressed to that deity were answered by the appearance of the present springs and rivers. The few lakes that occur in the Apache country are remnants of the primeval ocean. All the inhabitants of the earth were then Apaches, but the Cheyennes and Utes were soon created from willows. The supreme god, *Yi-ná-yĕs-gŏⁿ-i,* directed the people westward; as they journeyed, small parties became separated, and settled by the wayside. These were given different names and languages.

ORIGIN OF THE WICHITA
(Wichita)

In the times at the beginning, there was no sun, no moon, no stars, nor did the earth exist as it does now. Time passed on and Darkness only lived. With the lapse of time came a woman, Watsikatsia, made after the form of the man Darkness. The woman found an ear of corn in front of her, while before Darkness was placed an arrow. They did not know what these objects were nor where they came from, but they knew that they were for their use. The woman wondered what the ear of corn was for, and Darkness, by the gift of Man-Never-Known-on-Earth, was able to tell her that the corn was for her to eat. Then Darkness wondered what the arrow was for, and the woman, by aid from the same power, was able to tell him that with the arrow he was to kill game.

The time now arrived when Man-Never-Known-on-Earth promised them that he would make more people. So a village soon sprang into existence with many families. And according to the wish of Man-Never-Known-on-Earth a certain person was to be chief, and his name was to be Boy-Chief. Man-Never-Known-on-Earth also decreed that the name of the village should be Wandering-Village, which meant that the people should not travel on their feet, as people do now, but should wander like spirits,—they could think of a distant point and be there at once. After a while Darkness and the woman (Watsikatsia) began to wonder why so many things had happened? why there were so many people? For there were crowds and crowds of people. There were so many people that Darkness told them to scatter, to divide into parties and go off in different directions. After this, Darkness began to get power to foretell things. Once he told Watsikatsia everything,—that he was about to go to a certain being over there,—Man-Never-Known-on-Earth. When he was ready to go he reached down at his left side and with his right hand and brought up a ball. Then he reached down with his left hand at his right side and brought up a belt. Then he reached down in front, touched the ball to the belt and brought up a shinny stick. He took the ball, tossed it up and struck it with the stick. As the ball flew he went with it. Thus he went on towards the place for which he had set out and where he expected to find Man-Never-Known-on-Earth. Now Man-Never-Known-on-Earth had great power and knew that this man was coming to pay him a visit. (The object of this man's visit was that power be given him so that there should be light on the face of the earth.) Again he tossed the ball, struck it and traveled through space with it, but he was not there yet. So he knew that he could not depend on the ball. Then he took his bow and arrow, which he had brought with him, shot the arrow and flew with it. This he did a second, third, and fourth time, but he had not yet arrived. Still he knew that he had to get there. Then he remembered that he could run. So he made one long run and stopped to rest. Then he ran again, and a third and fourth time. He had now made twelve trials and knew that he was near the place of his journey.

Now he came across a grass lodge and he knew that some one lived there. Before he got right at the lodge, he heard somebody speaking to him,—telling him the object of his journey: for Man-with-Great-Power-to-Foretell lived there. Darkness at once asked for something to eat. Man-with-Great-Power-to-Foretell asked him inside the lodge. When Darkness entered he saw light; for the lodge was filled with bright light. As he had come on a long journey he was very tired and hungry, and again asked for food. So Man-with-Great-Power-to-Foretell reached down behind him and brought up four grains of corn. Darkness began eating, and the four grains were more than he could eat, so full did they make him. Then they began to talk and Man-with-Great-Power-to-Foretell said to Darkness: "Man-Never-Known-on-Earth has made me also; the time is coming nearer; it will not be long until we are able to go around everywhere." So after they had stayed there in the grass lodge a long time, they went outside and faced east.

Man-with-Great-Power-to-Foretell then told Darkness to look,—and there was water almost as far as they could see. On the opposite bank they saw a man. This man told them to make haste and cut a stick. Then he said to them: "There are three animals in the water traveling towards you. Do not kill the first or the second, but kill the third, which is half black and half white." Then Man-with-Great-Power-to-Foretell said: "We are not quite ready;" for he was just making his arrows. Then the man said: "Hurry and make your arrows!" Man-with-Great-Power-to-Foretell replied: "We are about ready; we have the bow, arrows, and sinew, but the arrows are not quite dry." Man-with-Great-Power-to-Foretell again cried out: "We are about ready; we have fixed the sinew." Again the man called to them to hurry. Then Man-with-Great-Power-to-Foretell said: "We are about to feather the arrows." The man again called to them to hurry. Man-with-Great-Power-to-Foretell replied: "We are ready now; we are ready to draw the arrows, for we have trimmed the feathers." While they were working they saw the three animals draw closer. Again the man called out: "Don't shoot the first or the second, but kill the third, which is half black and half white." Then he said: "They are closer to you. I go now. I will never be here any more. When you go back, tell your people that there will be such a word as *Hosaiisida* (Last-Star-after-Light) and that I will appear from time to time." After he had spoken, they looked, but the man was gone; they looked higher and saw him as a star of bright light, for he was Young-Star, or the morning star. It now grew a little lighter and they saw the three animals still closer to them, and they saw that they were deer and that they were standing on the water. Then Man-with-Great-Power-to-Foretell shouted, and the first deer jumped up on the bank to the south of the place where they stood, and it was black; then the second deer jumped up, it was white; then the half black and half white deer jumped up on the bank, and Man-with-Great-Power-to-Foretell shot it on its side. Man-with-Great-Power-to-Foretell now told Darkness that that was the power given to man, that when you go after game such weapons would be used. Then he added: "I will not be on earth much longer, but I will be seen at times." Darkness now looked, but Man-with-Great-Power-to-Foretell was gone; he looked toward the east and there he saw him as the sun; and his name was Sun-God. Then it became light and they knew that the first deer was night, the second day, and the third, which they had killed, was day and night, and that henceforth there was to be day and night. These three deer became the three stars which we see every night in the west.

When these things had happened, Darkness turned and faced the west. All was bright with light now. He began his journey back to the point from which he had set out. As he went he traveled very fast; for he now had power to travel very fast. Indeed, so rapidly did he travel that he arrived home early that day. When he got home he found all kinds of people, but they did not know him and asked him who he was. As he also knew no one, he asked where he could go for shelter. He was told to go to the west edge of the village, where he would find a large lodge belonging to Boy-Chief. So Darkness went there for shelter. He asked Boy-Chief how many more villages there were like that one. Boy-Chief replied that in the south there was one with a chief named Wolf-Robe, who had great power like Man-with-Great-Power-to-Foretell. Then Boy-Chief asked Darkness where he had been, and he replied that he had been to a certain place where he had met Man-with-Great-Power-to-Foretell and Young-Star. Then Darkness asked Boy-Chief to assemble every one in the village in order that they might hear what he had to say. Boy-Chief called for all to come, and a great crowd gathered about the lodge. Boy-Chief then announced that all were present and asked him what he had to say. Then Darkness told them that he and his woman were the first beings created and that Man-Never-Known-on-Earth had given them power to carry out his work, and that they were going to do it. "Therefore," added Darkness, "I have come before you again, to tell you that after I have done this work for you I will have to leave you." After he had said this he commanded all the people to return to their homes and tell everything he had said.

Then he started on his journey to the south village and soon arrived. Again he asked where he could find shelter, and was told as before to go to a certain place at the edge of the village, where he would find the headman, who would treat him well. He went to that house and met the chief, who asked him what he had to say. He replied that he had something to say, and asked the chief to assemble all his people. So some one was sent around to tell the people of the village to gather at the chief's place. Now before Darkness had arrived in this village three people had predicted his arrival, for they had great power in those days; so they were not surprised when he came. The crowd came and he told them they were to have such a game as shinny ball. He reached down with his right hand on his left side and produced a ball, and then reached down on his right side with his left hand and brought up a shinny stick. These he showed the people and told them they were for their use. Then he commanded the people to gather just outside the village at about evening time, and then he set the time for play. They went as he told them. When they were all there he tossed the ball toward the north and traveled with it. It went a long ways. When it lit he picked it up and struck it with the stick and drove the ball back south, then said that the point where he stood when he struck the ball would be called "flowing water" (the goal). Then he took the ball, tossed it, went with it, and again struck it southward. Where it hit was the second "flowing water," or goal. Between these two goals or bases was level ground, and in both directions as far as you could see. Then he divided the men into two parties, and placed one at each goal. Between these two parties and in the center of the field he placed two men, one from each of the two parties. He gave one man the ball and told him to toss it up. As the ball was tossed he told the other man to strike it towards the south. He did so and drove the ball towards his opponents on the south. Now they played, and the north side drove the ball to the south goal and won. They then changed goals and the other side won. Then Darkness said that they had played enough.

Before the shinny ball game began, Darkness had asked that a lodge be emptied and cleaned out. It was now late in the afternoon. He now entered the lodge, but first told the people to go to their homes, that the times were drawing near when things would change, for the powers which had been given to people were increasing, "and now," he said finally, "I go. I am to leave you, but I am also to be seen." He made his final appearance, the people went to their homes and he entered the prepared lodge, and when he appeared again it was to bring light into darkness.

By this time the power which Man-Never-Known-on-Earth had first given people had developed and the people were very powerful, but they used their power for bad purposes.

The first woman, Watsikatsia, now appeared in this village and asked for shelter. She was told to go to a certain place, but she was warned that the chief had greatly changed and that now he was an enemy to his visitors. She replied that she had great powers, given her by Man-Never-Known-on-Earth, that she could do anything. Her informant told her that she would arrive in the morning. She would find some one inquiring for her who wanted her to go on a journey with him. The next morning she arrived at the lodge of the chief, and shortly after she went after water, when she heard some one inquiring for her. This was a man who was acting for, or the servant of Without-Good-Power, son of Wolf-Robe. Now Without-Good-Power was a very bad man, while his father was just as good as ever, and had never abused the power which Man-Never-Known-on-Earth had given him. This servant of Without-Good-Power now told her to get ready to travel, as Without-Good-Power was going to war, and she must go along. Without-Good-Power now started and a great crowd followed. He told his followers that he was not going very far, only to a place called Eyes-like-Mountains, which stood in the water. After they had gone a short way Without-Good-Power ordered the people to stop for a while so that he could make a sacrifice, by offering his pipe to every one to smoke. While he was doing this, with his followers sitting around him in a circle, there appeared on his right side and on his left side a bow. All at once these two bows turned into two snakes and began to fight each other. Then Without-Good-Power asked the people to interpret the meaning of this event. A certain man spoke up and said it meant thus and so. Then Without-Good-Power said that his interpretation was wrong and he got up and went where the man was and killed him with a club. Then the woman spoke up and said that Without-Good-Power's powers were great, but were not all beneficial to the people, for Without-Good-Power had killed people before this time when they had failed to interpret properly. She now said, "the meaning of what has just happened is that the village which we have left is being attacked by a certain kind of enemy." After she had made this interpretation, all the people turned back to go home.

When they had arrived the woman called all the women together and told them that everywhere she went she had certain great powers, and that the last place where she had been was Place-where-Corn-is-Raised. Then she told the women that power would be given to them, so that they could kill many animals for food, that after taking the hide off all they had to do was to take the hide by one side, shake it, and it would be a robe; that they should take the bark from the trees, save it, sprinkle it on the robe from end to end, and that power would be given them to take up anything and pack it on their back. She also said that the time was coming when certain of their powers would be cut off and all would be just ordinary people; also that she would soon no longer appear as she was, but in a different form. Soon after that she was changed into a bird with bright red feathers; for she had had red hair.

It had now come to pass that, after all these things had happened, Wolf-Robe, the chief of the south village, was an old man, and nearly everything went wrong,—the people were no longer good. Wolf-Robe had told them to go ahead and do as they pleased.

Now there was a certain wise man living north of Wolf-Robe, who spoke out and said that this condition could not last, and that there would soon appear a man, by the name of Howling-Boy, who would do things. He also said that the people were not living naturally, that they were exercising too much supernatural power, and that there were certain people who considered themselves greater than Man-Never-Known-on-Earth. In addition to Howling-Boy, who was to appear, another man would appear, whose name was to be Heard-Crying-in-His-Mother's-Womb (although people thought that what they heard crying was a knife which the woman carried at her side). Now the wise man advised the chief, Wolf-Robe, to select all his men who were capable of traveling fast to go out to look for these two men who were to appear. Wolf-Robe selected only four, two of the number being brothers, and they started, one in each direction, to hunt for the two men, and also to tell other people to look for them and to go to the village. People began to come in from far and wide. Finally it was announced that all were in the village. Then a certain man appeared and gave his name as Howling-Boy, and presently the other man, Heard-Crying-in-His-Mother's-Womb, appeared. The latter told the chief that he had great power, and enumerated what he could do. The chief admitted that he was a man of great power. Heard-Crying-in-His-Mother's-Womb then said, "I always have known what you have in your mind. Now say what you have in your mind, for it is best for the people to hear what you have to say in my presence." The chief then talked and said that there were too many people who were bad, who used too much unnatural power; that he ordered all such people to be destroyed; and that he left the performance of this task to Howling-Boy and Heard-Crying-in-His-Mother's-Womb. He also added that his son was a bad man and that he could not account for it, as he himself was a good man and did not practise so much power as did his son. Howling-Boy then announced that he would delegate his share of the killing of bad people to Heard-Crying-in-His-Mother's-Womb. So Heard-Crying-in-His-Mother's-Womb accepted the task in accordance with the chief's orders. Heard-Crying-in-His-Mother's-Womb now arose, saying that he would begin his work at once, and that the chief's son would be the first to be destroyed. So he took his bow, found the chief's son and destroyed him, tearing him to pieces. Then he went on with his work of killing the bad people, shouting before he got to each one, so that his victim would get excited and could not move or do anything. As he encountered each, he also would tell what great powers he had, and that the people thought they had greater powers than anybody else. He also would tell them that Man-Never-Known-on-Earth had given them great powers, but that they had not acted as he wanted them to.

Next he went to a lodge where there was a large family, the father of which had a head with two faces; this man he killed, telling him if he ever lived again he would have less power.

Then he went to another man, whose name was Haitskaria, and who was a creature like an alligator and who burnt the ground over which he traveled. He told Haitskaria that he was there to destroy him, and that if he ever lived again he would have less power.

Then he went to another lodge, where he met a family of Mountain-Lions, consisting of father and mother and two children. He told them he had come to destroy them, that they had lived a bad life. They begged him not to carry out his orders, but to let them live and continue the possession of their power. But he told them he would have to carry out his order, and that if they came to life again they would have less power.

Then he went on to the mountains where there was a cave. As he approached he hallooed and saw a great crowd of Scalped or Bloody-Head people. When he drew near they ran into the cave. He went to the opening and told them that power had been given him to destroy them because they were bad; that he would have to carry out the order which had been given him by the chief; that they thought they had greater powers than any living being, and that they abused them. Finally one of the men came from the cave and asked what right he had to say and do these things. In reply he told him that a Creator had given them this power so that they might be great, but that they had gone beyond this power. Then he began to kill them, and left only two, a man and a woman.

Then, having done his work, he returned to the village, where he told the chief that he had destroyed the meanest and most powerful creatures. He added, "Now I have fulfilled your orders, and now I want to find out what you have in your mind." The chief then announced that every one would be changed into another form, that there would be many human beings, but he advised that every one do as he pleased; that is, if any wished to change into animals they might do so. After Wolf-Robe had made this announcement, he told the people that he had made his choice and had decided to become an animal. So he went on his way, taking with him his walking stick and robe and leaving his other possessions behind, and journeyed to the nearest body of water. There he went down into the water, dived, and after coming up he went out on the other side a wolf.

Then Heard-Crying-in-His-Mother's-Womb said that something charmed him to the water, drew him towards it. So he went to the water, although he did not want to go, dived to the bottom and saw a woman whose name was Woman-in-Water-Never-Seen. As he did not want to stay there he came to the surface, spouted water up in the air and went up and away with it, and became Weather (that is, lightning, rain, etc.).

After he had disappeared, all the people got vessels, went to the water, filled them, and carried water home to their families. Then some of them put water on their fires, and as the steam ascended up in the air they went with it and so became birds; other beings went their way to the woods, prairies, and mountains and became various kinds of animals, while the remainder of the people lived on in the same place.

Without-Good-Power was among these people who remained, and he still had great powers. He announced that he would continue to live with the people. His powers were especially great in doctoring,—so great that he could by a simple command change any person into another form. Thus if he saw any of his enemies coming around his lodge he would command them to stop and then they would vanish,—sometimes he would change them into wood. Then he decided to give a new name to the group of people who lived about and he changed the name from Okaitshideia (Village) to Katskara (Village).

Then Without-Good-Power went on to a place where there was an earth lodge, which he entered. Within he put his hand to the wall of the lodge and it left the imprint of his hand in color, and wherever he touched the wall there was the imprint in a different color. Now the owner of the lodge knew that Without-Good-Power had great powers, among them that of changing people into different forms, so when Without-Good-Power shouted, the man ran out and started north, but he was changed into a bird, Gtataikwa (its name coming from its peculiar cry—just as if some one were going to strike it). Still another man ran out of the lodge and started north, but he was changed into a star (not the morning star).

Time passed on and the people remembered how things used to be. A certain young man, Every-Direction, went out on an expedition with twelve men. Time passed on and they did not return till about spring. The people wondered why they were gone so long. In the village at the northeast corner lived an old man and an old woman, who had a little orphaned grandson whose name was Of-Unknown-Parents. This boy finally went into the center of the village and told the people that the thirteen who had gone on the expedition were no longer alive, but had gone into the ground, and that no one of them would return. Then Of-Unknown-Parents said that some hunters should go out for two days and look for a certain place where there would be some people coming out of the ground, enough to form a village. When it was night the boy went to bed, but before he went to sleep he heard some one calling him. He arose and went out on the northwest side of the lodge. There he saw some one standing who told Of-Unknown-Parents that he was mistaken, that his prophecy would not come true. He also told Of-Unknown-Parents that his father had sent him down to appear before him and tell him this; that a year hence something would happen, which would be done by his father, and that he would appear to him again.

Now at that time the chief's wife, who had a son among the thirteen which had disappeared, was confined and brought forth four children shaped like dogs. When one day old, they had grown, and when three days old they had grown so fast that they played with the children. But they were mean and ran over the children. When they were grown up, the chief was tired of them and got people to carry them off to the west, as he did not like them. But on the way the dogs, who were now very large, swallowed up the people who were taking them away, and none of the people ever returned. As time went on, other people would go out where these monstrous creatures lived, but they had such long necks that they would reach out and get them and swallow them. So the people finally got excited and moved the village. The older people talked much and said that although the Creator had made everything it seemed that he had also made monsters to destroy every one, and that if things went on in this way more bad things would be done. Time passed on and the people would not go to the west for fear of the monsters. So the chief selected four men to visit the place of the old village, but they returned safe.

Now the old man and woman and their grandson, Of-Unknown-Parents, had been left at the old village. One night the person who had formerly appeared to the boy again visited him. He said: "At noon, go to a certain place due north of here and I will appear to you." The next day at noon the boy went to a hill in the north where he had been told to go, and there he saw this person. He called the boy to him and told him that his father did not like the way things were going and that he would have to destroy everything. Then he told the boy to return to the village and tell the people that they were to be destroyed, that if they did not believe him, to repeat the message. Then Of-Unknown-Parents said his father was tired of the monsters and that he wished to destroy them. The person then told the boy he must do certain things: that he must get the twelve longest canes he could find, fasten them together, and give them to a certain woman (Spider-Woman) who lived in the village; that he must tell this woman to get her servant (Mouse-Woman) to go about and get a big lot of corn of all colors and bring it to her master; that when this was done he must put the canes in the ground up to five joints; that after this four days would elapse and at the end of that time to be on the lookout for something to happen, for something would come from the north. He also said that there was a certain thing in the water that would destroy the four monsters, and that now it was time for him to depart.

Now the boy returned to the village and told the chief what was to happen, but the chief would not believe him. Then he went to the Spider-Woman and told her as he had been commanded. She was pleased to hear the story and was willing to do whatever the boy told her to do. After the people had heard the news some would not believe, especially the people who wished to live longer. But many believed the boy's story. Spider-Woman now got the twelve long canes and sent her servant out to get whatever seeds she could find. She got seeds of corn, beans, pumpkins, watermelons, and seeds of every kind which she could find. Then Spider-Woman first filled some of the joints with corn seed and closed the cane up, then she put in some pumpkin seed and closed it up, and so on, filling the canes with all the seeds.

When night came, Of-Unknown-Parents returned to Spider-Woman and asked her what she had done. She told him that she had done everything except to put the canes in the ground. So Of-Unknown-Parents told her to take the rib of a buffalo and dig a hole in the ground. She did so, and said there was one thing more to be done, and that was to raise the canes and put them in the ground up to the fifth joint. Of-Unknown-Parents said that he would attend to that. So he went away for a little while and returned. Then he commanded a small whirlwind to blow, and it raised the canes right up, and Spider-Woman and Of-Unknown-Parents placed them in the hole up to the fifth joint as they had been commanded.

The time was now come for something to happen. At noon they looked north and saw something like a wind blowing, but it was the fowls of the air all headed south. After they had passed came the animals, the buffalo first, then the deer, and so on.

When the people saw these things they were excited. A little later they looked north and saw great floods of water coming very fast, and they saw the thing which was to destroy the four monsters. It was a great turtle which had broken out of the water and was headed toward the monsters. On it came, and went under their feet, where it stopped. On came the great floods of water. So Spider-Woman, who had helped Of-Unknown-Parents put up the canes, now began climbing at the bottom and soon reached the top of the twelve canes. Then she let down a rope and drew her husband to the top, and then let down the rope and drew up the boy to the top, and then drew up Mouse-Woman. She now made a place on the top with a good shelter, but so made that the water would leak through.

The time was now late in the evening and the water was to the tops of the lodges in the village. The monsters could hardly stand still, it was so slippery. Late in the evening it was more difficult for them to stand still, and one said to the other three: "My brothers, my legs are giving out, and I will have to fall. I will fall that way (north) and when the time comes in later generations that direction will be called 'North.' "

The next day the backs of these monsters could only just be seen, and one of them said to the other two: "Brothers, do the best you can; I have to fall; my legs are giving out; I will fall in that direction (east), and in later times people will call that direction 'Point-Where-Sun-Rises.' " On the next day the water was higher and the people on the canes were getting uneasy. The water was now up to the necks of the two monsters. The one said to the other: "Brother, you are the youngest of us four; you will have to get along the best you can; I am going to fall; I am giving out; the direction I am going to fall is that way (south), and by later generations it will be called 'South.' " The fourth day of the flood came. The fourth monster had to hold his head back to keep the water out of his face. He said that he could tell nobody what was going to happen, as his three brothers had perished, but that he would have to fall towards that point where the sun goes down, and it would be called "West."

From that time it was twelve days more before the flood passed on. Nothing could be seen, no village, no people, only some water and a little earth. The ground was all soft. At this time everything was still. There was no wind. But a certain person appeared who came from above, of the name of Man-Going-All-Around, who had power to dry all slime. He appeared from the northeast direction and was headed southwest. While on his way he saw something like a shadow shining on the ground. He wondered what it was and thought he had better go over to see. When he got over to the place he saw something on the ground, shaped like a human being. Examining it closely he saw that it was molded like a woman.

Man-Going-All-Around went on in another direction. Time passed and he went all around and again came to the same place where he had seen the form of a woman in earth. He now saw that the upper half of the image, as it lay at full length on its back, was alive, and that the lower half was still mud. Then he saw further that the woman had given birth to a child (Standing-Sweet-Grass) which was nursing on her breast. After seeing this he went on again on his journey. Then came a bird, a dove, and it saw something on the ground; it went to see what was there. When it got near it lighted on the ground and saw the woman sitting up on the ground with the child in her lap. The dove had a piece of grass in its mouth.

In the mean time Man-Going-All-Around had passed on over a place where he thought he heard some one beating a drum. Then he returned a third time to the woman, told her to rise and accompany him. He took her to the place where he had heard the noise of drums. He went in with Shadow-Woman and the child and saw that he was in a room shaped like a beaver's lodge, and that it was deep down under the water. The name of the lodge was Place-of-Beavers or Beavers'-Lodge. When he entered the room he saw many people sitting about. He also saw a young man lying on a bed. Then he told the woman that she was to live with this man who was on the bed, and the man accepted the offer.

After Shadow-Woman had lived in the lodge with the man for five days, her child (Standing-Sweet-Grass) had grown rapidly and was now a boy and could talk. The boy said to his mother: "I am going to begin my work. When I begin this work I want you to keep continent till I finish my work." At this time his mother told him that he was the son of no man on earth, but of Man-Above.

The next day Standing-Sweet-Grass went out in a northwest direction. After he had gone on a while, he stopped, facing the northwest. Then he turned towards the east and saw the same man (Man-Going-All-Around) who had taken him and his mother into the lodge. This man now discovered the place where the people were on top of the canes. All this time it had been still and there had been no wind; only where he went was there wind. Having reached the spot where the canes stood, he was told by Spider-Woman, who was on top of the canes, to look out for the boy, Of-Unknown-Parents, who was coming down the rope. So Spider-Woman let down the rope with the boy on the end of it. When Of-Unknown-Parents was down, he was told to command the wind to blow from the north, east, south, and west, into the ground. Then the canes began to go down toward the west, and it was found that the water had sunk as far as the fourth joint of the canes, so that they lacked but one more joint of reaching the bottom. When they were all down the boy from the Place-of-Beavers told them to go with him to his home, saying that there were many people there. Then they set out, carrying the canes with them, Spider-Woman holding the canes at the middle, with Mouse-Woman at one end and Of-Unknown-Parents at the other.

When they arrived at the Place-of-Beavers they all went in, except Standing-Sweet-Grass, and saw crowds of people, birds, and animals. Having entered, Shadow-Woman got up and went to the strangers and told them that she was glad to see them. They replied that it was a fact that she was glad to see them, for they had some things for her. Then they opened the canes and divided the seeds, the men putting them in wrappers. Then all the seeds were given to Shadow-Woman for her use in beginning her life. Standing-Sweet-Grass, Shadow-Woman's son, now came down into the lodge to see what they had. After he had seen everything he said it was time for everybody to lie down and go to sleep.

Early the next day after all had awoke, Standing-Sweet-Grass got up and had a talk with his mother. He told her that the seeds had been given her by these people for her use, and for the use of all when they should increase in numbers, and that she should distribute them so that they would always be in use. He himself, he said, had to go on with his work.

So he started on a journey, going south. He commanded the trees to grow and they grew; he commanded the water to flow and it flowed, as he had commanded. After the great flood of waters there were many forms left in the mud,—these he commanded to change into hills and mountains. He commanded the wild animals to roam over the prairies and through the forests. When he had done these things he returned to his mother and told her to remember what he had said to her, that everything must be straight with her while he was doing his work. Then he commanded the birds to leave the Beaver-Lodge, saying that hereafter human beings would sometimes need to use them for food, etc. When he had given this command, the birds all left the lodge, saying first they wished to go near him. So when they left they all gathered around him. The boy told them that his mother had not obeyed him and had therefore done him wrong, hence he would not return to her, but would go to his father, the Man-Above. While the birds were still around him the boy put them in a trance and when they came to they realized that the boy had disappeared, but where he had stood they saw a little bunch of standing sweet-grass.

After all this had happened, Shadow-Woman, the mother of Standing-Sweet-Grass, and her husband moved out of the Place-of-Beavers and erected a lodge of their own. Soon the woman became pregnant and a little later she gave birth to a child which was a girl. In those times everything grew very rapidly and soon the girl could move about. Time passed on and Shadow-Woman soon gave birth to another child which was a boy, so that they had now a girl and a boy.

Time passed on and the boy asked his mother if they could not put up another and a better lodge, so that they might have more room. The mother said yes; so the boy and his sister went and got some mud, blood, and sand, mixed them and molded them into an axe, that was to be used in cutting the timber. Then the husband of Shadow-Woman had killed a buffalo while hunting and had brought in the four shoulder blades,—they were to be used in digging. With these tools the boy and girl went to work and built a house,—a dug-out. They all moved in to the new lodge and the boy and girl married and they soon had a girl baby and then again very soon they had a boy baby. In the mean time, Shadow-Woman had given birth to another boy, and the children all grew very fast. Then the first pair of children, which were married, said to their mother that they ought to make another and a larger house. This they did, and they moved into it, and the boy's wife was now pregnant again. Time passed on and the boy was now a man, but he was mean and abused his father and mother. Finally the mother told him that it was not right for him to act this way. She also said that the time was about come when she (Shadow-Woman) and her husband would have to go to some place else. By this time the second girl and second boy of Shadow-Woman were married. They decided to build still another house, into which this couple moved. They now had made pottery to boil meat in, while the newly married couple had brought in a stone with which they were to make a corn grinder.

Time passed on and everything grew rapidly, and soon Shadow-Woman gave birth to a third girl, and soon to a third boy, and then they grew rapidly, were soon married, and the second couple built a lodge for them. The time now came when the old people called all their children and grandchildren to their lodge, saying to them that they had something to say to them. The mother, when they were all together, told her children that there was some person (above) who had made them and who had given them power; that she was the mother of another son (Standing-Sweet-Grass) who had disappeared; that only by believing that the Man-Above had given them these things could they rely on getting everything. Now in those times it was always the case that the oldest children were the meanest and the youngest the smartest, hence the oldest daughter and the oldest son did not seem to pay any attention to what the mother said.

Time passed on and the three families increased and the three lodges became crowded. So the children, as they married, moved out and built new lodges for themselves. The oldest son kept on abusing his mother and she had grown more and more tired of this treatment and she decided to move away off. When she had come to this decision, her husband said that he would go with her. So they started on a journey and went due north. After they had gone a long distance they stopped, and Shadow-Woman asked her husband to what place he wanted to go. He started on alone and went in a northwest direction, where he became Clearness-after-a-Rain. Then Shadow-Woman went alone on her way toward the north, where she disappeared and became Rain-Woman.

Time passed on and there was now a large village of the descendants of these people, for they had increased and increased. There were now three head men: the first chief was named Boy-Chief; the second chief was named Coup-Sticks, for he had two red painted sticks which he used after any brave act; the third chief was named Everywhere-Always-Brave, for in attacks on enemies he had been very brave, had done everything, and had gone every place. The village itself where all these people lived was called Village-by-Side-of-Big-Elm-Tree. Now, if since the time of that village seven men had each lived one hundred years and each man had been born on the day of the death of the other, the seventh man would be alive now and if he should live one hundred years, at his death it would be seven hundred years since the time of the Village-by-Side-of-Big-Elm-Tree.

Time passed on, and this village was attacked by enemies (Apache). In the fight, one of the chiefs killed a chief of the enemy. After the fight they found that of their own people no one was killed and that the enemy had lost one. So the chief invited all his people around the big elm-tree, and gave out four drums, two on each side, and they had a Victory dance. When the dance began it happened that there were so many people around the tree and the drums were making so much noise that the elm-tree began to shake and quiver, and the people saw that the tree was enjoying itself and taking part in the dance. As they danced the women would get partners to dance with.

After this dance the chiefs came together in council, and said that they ought to go and look for another place to live in instead of the old place, so they invited everybody to be present, and when the people had all arrived they told them what they had decided to do. This decision was then announced to all the people. Then they moved under the leadership of Boy-Chief. At those times all had to pack their belongings on their back. Thus they journeyed on and came to a place where they built new houses, and the new village they called Perched-upon-a-Mountain. The people would make journeys to their old homes to fetch things they had left behind.

At the time of the new village there was a big band of people living very near them and called Pawnees. Time went on and matters progressed as usual; they raised their crops, and the men hunted game. The men used to go out in a party, and when they came to buffalo or other game they would make a surround, for they had no horses, and their weapons were stone-pointed arrows and stone knives.

Now of the two big bands (Wichita and Pawnee) there were five chiefs, two of them being Pawnee. They all came together in council, and, in talking over matters, they decided that the time had come for the two bands to depart from each other. One band was to travel northward (the Pawnee), while their own band (the Wichita) with three chiefs was to travel southward.

It was spring, and the band (Wichita) kept traveling toward the south. On their way they would stop a little while, but still they went south, looking over the country to spy out the best place for their homes. But they returned to the place where there were some mountains (Perched-Upon-a-Mountain). It was now about the middle of hot weather. They found that the Pawnee chiefs with their band had gone on to the north. Then they invited all the people about them and told them that they had selected a fine place for their new homes and that soon they would move thither. Finally they all began to move, packing things on their backs and on dog travois. It took a long time to get to the place. When they got there they called their village Village-on-North-Slope-with-Wind-from-the-North.

A little while after they had settled here, enemies began to appear: the Apache would come from the southwest, and the Osage from the northeast. Now there was living at the time an old man who was always giving good advice to the men, especially to the young men, telling them what was right, and the best ways to do things. So now he announced to the young men that there would be a race on the following morning. The next morning he started off for the race, in a northeasterly direction, taking with him all the young men who wished to run. Arriving at the starting-place, the old man told them that the Man-Above had given them all their power; that these races were for exercise, to make them strong; that they were never to eat anything before the race. Then the time came for the start. They all ran a little way, then they turned and went back to the old man. They did this three times and at the fourth time the race began in earnest. At the end of the race all the young men were told by the old man to go to the nearest stream, dive in the water, and drink a lot of water and vomit it all up again. This was the rule of the race.

The village had now been founded about one year, and they raised a crop to sustain them. They now decided to move camp again. So they packed their things on their backs and on the dog travois and set out on a journey, crossing a river, and went on to a place which the three chiefs had selected for them. They halted at the bend of the river, where the river had a long straight course toward the east. At night it seemed as if the moon were traveling on the water. Sometimes the river was dry and it had a sandy bed, and then it seemed as though the moon were coming along on the sand. So they named the place Moon-Coming-on-Sand. At this place there was good protection from the enemy and they lived there a long time, forgetting their desire to move on to a better place. The old chiefs had ordered the people to make dug-out lodges, and they were secure from the enemy. By this time the three old chiefs had grown very old, and were so feeble that they had to be led around. Also by this time the chiefs had grown sons who had become head men in their fathers' places. But the tribe had not yet arrived at the place in the high mountains (Wichita Mountains) which the old man had chosen. And now the three old chiefs, Coup-Sticks, Boy-Chief, and Everywhere-Always-Brave, died of old age.

Time passed on, and one of the young chiefs said it was time to continue their journey to the place which their fathers had selected for their homes. They now set out again toward the south, but on the way, at a certain place on a rocky ford of the river (near Chilocco) the son of old Coup-Sticks separated from the other two young chiefs and with his band drifted toward the east and made a new settlement near the mouth of Black Bear creek. The other two chiefs with their bands continued their journey and stopped at a place known as High-Hills-Extending-into-River (near the Red Hills at Watonga).

They did not stay there long, and soon moved south again. This time they started down in two bands, for there were so many of them. One band settled on top of the hills, and their village was called Highland Village (head of McCusky Canyon), while the other band settled at Lowland Village. When they were all settled, the people used to go out on hunting trips, and often they would look toward the southwest where they could see the mountains (Wichita) and they would often say among themselves, "those mountains have been selected for our home." So they called the mountains "Our Mountains," and they often wondered what was over there. Now at this time there was a certain woman who had heard much about the mountains and she wanted to move there, but she died of old age.

At that time there was off to the east of the village a lake and in the middle of the lake was an island with large cottonwood trees on it. In a tree was a nest of bald eagles. The men were always going out hunting, and one day a young man went off that way to hunt. He stopped at the edge of the lake and heard some kind of noise up in the air. He looked up and saw an eagle rapidly descending; it lit on a tree on the island. Then the eagle spoke to the young man, telling him not to go back home but to stay there, as he had some power he wanted to give him. When it was late in the evening the eagle came down from the nest and requested the young man to come up close to where he was, that he must not be afraid, for the water was shallow. So the young man waded over to the island and went up close to the eagle, from which he received power. The eagle asked the young man if he had seen him descend, whereupon the young man replied that he had, and the eagle told him that this was the way he always looked out for his prey and that this was the power that he had given him. He also said that if at any time any one should kill a bald eagle he should go and take it to the right side of the wind and take out the eagle's wing-bone and make of it a whistle for his use; but he was forbidden to kill the eagle himself.

After saying this, the eagle continued: that he was, of course, one of the fowls of the air, but that once he had been a human being having great powers; that he would give him these powers, though less marked in degree than those which he himself possessed; that he would be useful to him during his life. The eagle also told the young man that he could not say that he should live forever, but that some day he would have to die; that these powers were good until death; that they were of use in doctoring. The eagle also told the young man that he would give him power to start up a dance, which would be for the people, to be called the deer dance.

Then the eagle said, "Come closer," whereupon he blew breath in the young man's mouth, giving him power with which to make himself useful while on expeditions and while doctoring or in dancing. The young man now took his quiver and returned home and went to bed.

While sleeping, he dreamed that some one was talking to him; he did not know who it was, or where he was, but he heard a confirmation that the eagle had given to him power, that it was for his own good, and that it would make him a useful man. On awaking, the young man at first thought that some one had actually spoken to him, but it was only a dream.

After this, time passed on, and the head man of Lowland Village sent for some man from Highland Village to come down to his camp, telling them that he wanted to move to the point south and west, which he had selected. Four men were selected to go down to the Lowland Village chief. They were told on arriving that he wanted to go at once to this spot, that if at any time they should get ready, they would find him there, and that as the country was becoming familiar to all hunters they all would know the way. The time came when this chief set out with his party for the spot which he had chosen, where they finally arrived, finding that a place had been selected for their home, and they named the place Place-of-Rock-Extending-over-Water (at the west end of the Wichita range). Now on the day of the departure of this party, a second party, ignorant of the plans of the first party, set out for the same place. After the first party had arrived in their new home, the man who had received the power from the eagle bade the people to allow him to make his sacrifice to the eagle by taking his pipe, and thus taking possession of the country. The second party now made their appearance, coming to the very same spot selected by the first party. The time was now come for the young man to make his offering. Calling upon all, men, women, and children, to arrange themselves in a line from north to south, facing the east, and to sit upon the ground; this done, he passed in front of the line and received from them a small buffalo robe which he placed upon the ground. He then took out of his bundle tobacco seeds and filled his pipe. When the first man made his offering to the above, it meant that they asked the Man-Above to let the people have no trouble, and that they might live without experiencing hard times. By puffing smoke to the south he meant to ask of the South star, which has power to care for a person while out on an expedition, that their people, while out on the expedition, might be under his care and always return home safe. By puffing smoke to the north he meant to ask the North star to watch over their children, that they might grow and be without sickness. By puffing smoke to the east he was making an offering to the Sun, that the people whenever traveling might be in his care.

After these things had come to pass, the people announced that they had seen everything that had been done, that now all the people, especially the women, could go out and stake out their homes in security.

CHAPTER 16

TRIBAL HISTORY AND TRIBAL CUSTOMS

ORIGIN OF ANIMALS
(Apache)

When the Apaches emerged from the underworld, *Uⁿ-go'-ya-yĕn-ni,* they traveled southward on foot for four days. They had no other food than the seeds of the two plants, *k'atl'-tai-ĭ,* and *k'atl'-tai-il-tsu-yɒ,* from which they made a sort of flour by grinding between stones. When they camped for the fourth time, one of the tipis, called *ka-ge-gŏⁿ-has-ka-ĭn-de-yĕ,* stood somewhat apart from the others. While the owner and his wife were absent from this lodge, a Raven brought a bow and a quiver of arrows, and hung them upon the lodge poles. The children within took down the quiver, and found some meat in it; they ate this, and at once became very fat. When the mother returned, she saw the grease on the hands and cheeks of the children, and was told how the it-tsil'-te had been obtained. The woman hastened to her husband with the tale. Marvelling at the appearance of the children, the people gathered to await the reappearance of the Raven which subsisted upon such remarkable food. When the Raven found the it-tsil'-te had been stolen from the quiver, he flew away toward the eastward; his destination was a mountain just beyond the range of vision of the Indians. A bat, however, followed the flight of the Raven, and informed them where the Raven had alighted. That night, a council of the whole tribe was held, and it was decided that they should go to the home of the Raven, and try to obtain from him the food which had wrought such a miraculous change in those who had partaken of it. At the end of four days they came to a place where a large number of logs were lying in irregular heaps. Many ravens were seen, but they avoided the Indians, and no information could be obtained from them. At one point they discovered a great circle of ashes where the ravens were accustomed to cook their meals. Again a council was held, and they talked over the problem of how to spy upon the ravens, and learn whence they obtained the precious animal food. That night the medicine-men transformed a boy into a puppy, and concealed him in the bushes near the camp. After the Indians had departed, next morning the ravens came, as is their habit, to examine the abandoned camp. One of the young ravens found the puppy, and was so pleased with it that he exclaimed, *"Ci-chĭn-ni-ja-ta"* ("This shall be my puppy"). When he carried home his prize his parents told him to throw it away. He begged permission to keep it, but agreed to give it up if the puppy winked when a splinter of burning wood was waved before its eyes. As the puppy possessed much more than canine intelligence, it stared during the test without the quiver of an eyelid. So the young raven won consent to keep the puppy, which he placed under his own blanket, where it remained until evening. At sunset the puppy peeped from his cover, and saw an old raven brush aside the ashes of the fireplace, and take up a large flat stone which disclosed an opening beneath; through this he disappeared, but arose again with a buffalo, which was killed and eaten by the ravens.

For four days the puppy remained at the camp of the ravens, and each evening he saw a buffalo brought up from the depths and devoured. Satisfied that he had discovered the source from which the ravens derived their food, the puppy resumed the form of a boy on the morning of the fifth day, and, with a white eagle feather in one hand and a black one in the other, descended through the opening beneath the fireplace, as he had seen the ravens do. In the underworld in which he found himself he saw four buffaloes. He placed the white eagle-feather in the mouth of the nearest Buffalo, and commanded it to follow him, but the Buffalo told him to go on to the last of the four and take it. This the boy tried to do, but the fourth Buffalo sent him back to the first, in whose mouth the boy again thrust the feather, declaring it to be the king of animals. He then returned to the world above, followed by all the animals at present upon the surface of the earth, except those specially created later, such, for example, as the horse and aquatic animals. As the large herd of animals passed through the hole, one of the ravens awoke, and hastened to clap down the stone covering the opening, but he was too late to prevent their escape. Seeing that they had passed from his control into that of man, he exclaimed, "When you kill any of these animals you must at least leave their eyes for me."

Attended by the troop of beasts of many species, the boy followed the track made by the departing Apaches. On the site of their first camp he found a firestick or poker, *gos-se-na'-it-tsi,* of which he inquired, "When did my people leave here?" "Three days ago," was the reply. At the next camping-place was an abandoned ladder, *has'-ai-ĭ,* of which he asked, "When did my people leave here?" "Two days ago," replied the ladder. Continuing his journey the boy soon reached the third camping-place, where he questioned a second firestick, and learned that the people had been gone but one day. At the fourth camp another ladder answered his question, with the news that the Indians had left there that morning. That evening he overtook them and entered the camp, the herd of animals following him like a flock of sheep. One old woman who lived in a brush lodge became vexed at the deer which ate the covering of her rude shelter. Snatching up a stick from the fire, she struck the deer over the nose, to which the white ashes adhered, causing the white mark which we see on the nose of that animal at the present time. "Hereafter you shall avoid mankind; your nose will tell you when you are near them," said she. Thus terminated the brief period of harmony between man and the beast: they left the camp at once, going farther each day, until on the fourth they disappeared from sight. That night the Apaches prayed for the return of the animals, that they might use them for food, and that is why animals approach nearer the camps now at night than at any other time. They never come very close, because the old woman told them to be guided by their noses and avoid the Indians.

Origin of Fire
(Apache)

At that early day the trees could talk, but the people could not burn them, as they were without fire. Fire was at length obtained through the instrumentality of the Fox. One day Fox went to visit the geese, *tĕtl,* whose cry he wished to learn. They promised to teach him, but it would be necessary for him to accompany them in their flights, in order to receive instruction. They gave him wings with which to fly, but cautioned him not to open his eyes while using them. When the geese rose in flight Fox flew with them. As darkness came on, they passed over the enclosure where the fireflies, *ko-na-tcic'ᴅ,* lived. Some gleams from their flickering fires penetrated the eyelids of Fox, causing him to open his eyes. His wings at once failed to support him, and he fell within the walls of the corral in which were pitched the tents of the fireflies. Two flies went to see the fallen Fox, who gave each a necklace of juniper berries, *kotl'-te-i-tsᴅ,* to induce them to tell him where he could pass the wall which surrounded them. The fireflies showed Fox a cedar-tree which would bend down at command and assist any one to pass over the wall. In the evening Fox went to the spring where the fireflies obtained water, and found colored earths suitable for paint, with which he gave himself a coat of white. Returning to the camp, he told the fireflies that they ought to have a feast; they should dance and make merry, and he would give them a new musical instrument. They agreed to his proposal, and gathered wood for a great camp-fire, which they ignited by their own glow. Before the ceremonies began, Fox tied shreds of cedar bark to his tail, and then made a drum, the first ever constructed, which he beat for some time. Tired of beating the drum, he gave it to one of the fireflies and moved nearer the fire, into which he thrust his tail, in opposition to the advice of those about him, who said it would surely burn. "I am a medicine-man," said Fox, "and my tail will not burn." However, he kept a close watch upon it, and when the bark was burning well he said, "It is too warm for me here; stand aside and let me go where it is cooler." Fox ran away with tail blazing, followed by the fireflies, who cried, "Stop, you do not know the road; come back." Straight to the cedar-tree Fox ran, and called, "Bend down to me, my tree, bend down." The tree lifted him out of the enclosure, and on he ran, still pursued by the fireflies. As he passed along, the brush and wood on either side was ignited by the sparks which fell from the burning cedar, and fire was widely spread over the earth. Fox became fatigued from running, and gave the firebrand to the hawk, *i-tsatl'-tsu-i,* which carried it on, and finally delivered it to the brown crane, *tsi-nĕs-tso'-i.* This bird flew far southward, but not so far but that one tree was not reached, and it will not burn to this day. (No name for such a tree among the Jicarilla Apaches.) The fireflies pursued Fox to his burrow and informed him that, as punishment for having stolen fire from them and spread it abroad over the land, he should never be permitted to use it himself.

ORIGIN OF CORN
(Apache)

A n Apache who was an inveterate gambler had a small tame turkey, which followed its master about everywhere. One day the Turkey told him that the people were tired of supporting him, as he gambled until he lost everything that they in charity gave him. They had decided to give him one more stock of supplies, and if he made away with that he should be killed. Knowing that he could not resist the temptation to gamble if he had any property in his possession, he decided to leave the tribe before their wrath should overtake him. The next day he began to chop down a tree from which to build a boat. The Woodpecker, *Tsitl-ka-ta,* commanded him not to cut the tree; the woodpeckers must do that for him. They also cut out the inside of the trunk, so that he could get into the cylinder, after which the spider sealed him in by making a web over each end. The woodpeckers carried the log, thus prepared, to the Rio Grande River, and threw it in. The faithful Turkey followed along the shore. In the whirlpool above San Juan the log left the main current, and spun round and round until the Turkey pushed it on into the channel again. Farther down the river the log caught in the rocks in an upright position above a fall, but the Turkey again started it on its journey. At the pueblo of Isleta, the boys hauled out the log with others for fuel. The Turkey rescued the log and placed it in the water, and again, at another pueblo far down the river, the log was returned to the stream. Far to the southward the log drifted out of the channel into a grove of cottonwoods. The man came out of the log and found a large quantity of duck feathers lying about. That night he had no blanket in which to sleep, so he covered himself with duck feathers. He killed a duck, and with the sinews of its legs made a bowstring. After he landed, the Turkey soon overtook him, and they remained there for four days. During this time the man cleared a small space and levelled it. "Why do you clear this place?" said the Turkey; "if you wish to plant something you must make a larger field." Then the Turkey ran toward the east, and the field was extended in that direction: toward the south, the west, and the north he ran, until the field was large enough. Then he ran into the field from the east side, and the black corn lay behind him; from the south side, and the blue corn appeared; from the west, and the yellow corn was made; from the north, and the seeds of every kind of cereal and vegetable lay upon the ground. The Turkey told the man to plant all these seeds in rows. In four days the growing plants appeared. The Turkey helped his master tend the crops, and in four more days everything was ripe. Then the man took an ear of corn and roasted it, and found it good.

THE MOQUI SNAKE DANCE
(Moqui)

M uch has been written regarding the Moqui Snake Dance and the work, meaning and influence of their secret orders. But the half has never been told and much more will of necessity be written before the reading public has any well defined ideas of the story of this ancient race or the historical value of their traditions. The seemingly awful orgies of the Snake Dance alone, which is but a demonstrative feature of their religion, has been frequently described by gifted writers who have been permitted to witness it, as that particular portion of their ceremonials is of a public character and therefore can be seen by all who will take the trouble to journey to their villages at the proper time.

But to the student and the thinker who has learned to look beneath for ideas, who cares for the philosophy of a people rather than their ceremonials, the Moqui customs present a field of research as yet but scarcely entered upon, and, what is more disheartening, the difficulties to be overcome are so great that none but those deeply interested will attempt to surmount them.

There are seven villages located on three different mesas known as the East, Middle and West Mesas. There are three villages on each the East and Middle, and one on the West Mesa. The political government of the villages is strictly under the United States Indian agent's direction, as he appoints the different chiefs of the villages, and all the peculiar customs talked and written about pertain entirely to the religion of the people with which the government has made no effort to interfere.

The tribe is divided into different gens, of which it is believed there are about twenty-three. The priests hold their religious offices solely by virtue of the gens to which they belong, and their dignified positions are attained through what might be called a system of royalty.

The ruling officer of the Antelope gens is an aged chief, very deaf and well along toward the day when he will be gathered to his fathers. He bears the euphonious title of Wi-ki, the letter "i" being pronounced like the letter "e" in English, the same as in the Spanish language. Wi-ki is by birth a member of the Snake gens.

Another peculiarity in the tribal customs is that no man can marry in the same gens to which he belongs, and the children of the marriage all belong to the gens of the mother. The secret orders of the different gens are carefully guarded so that the members of each may know nothing of the councils of the others. They are especially guarded from the white man, not so much for the fear of the white man's use of the information for their own purposes as for fear the white men will divulge their information to native members of other gens, thus disorganizing tribal relations.

The lodge room in the Moqui tongue is called "Kiva." Each gens has its kiva and the Snake chief and wi-ki, who is by birth a Snake, are the only two of that gens who have access to the Antelope kiva.

Another restriction placed on the relationship of the gens is that a member of the Antelope kiva can never become a chief of the Snake gens, though he may become a priest of that order.

Though the doctor is bound by solemn oaths not to give away the secrets of his kiva, he gives some valuable and interesting points relative to their customs that are not necessarily of a secret nature. For instance, their secret work and their religious theories are founded on astronomical deductions, of which more will be said later. Their lodge room is constructed in conformity with the cardinal points of the compass as religiously as is the lodge room of the Masons, with this difference: Owing to the fact that they take their observations in the summer time when the sun is farthest north, their north is thirty degrees west of north as calculated by white men. Their tradition also is that the race originally came from the underworld and emerged through a hole in the ground, which is believed to be in the Grand Canyon of the Colorado. Their lodge room, therefore, is north and south, and north is to them what the east is to a Mason.

The northeast of the cardinal points is always left open, the idea being that the path of life is from the southwest to the northeast and that after death the spirit passes out in that direction. Baptism, consecration, etc., are but mileposts along the road of those who follow faithfully this royal path of life.

Their story of the creation is similar to that of the white man. God had a son, who is called Esaw-uh, who killed a virgin and the body of the virgin lay four days in the grave. In line with this tradition their pottery and decorative work very frequently are adorned by four parallel lines symbolical of this event. As to the creation of material things, while God was thus engaged His son told Him to scatter all to the four winds of heaven, which suggestion being acted upon, the seeds, grasses, flowers, etc., were scattered promiscuously over the earth and even the heavenly bodies were distributed throughout the firmament seemingly with lack of order or plan.

The Snake ceremonies are, concisely stated, a series of prayers for general prosperity, including special requests for an ample supply of rain and an increase of population as well as an increase of wealth. Though they may appear to be, and in many respects are, an ignorant race, it is nevertheless proved beyond peradventure that they have a considerable knowledge of astronomy or astrology. This is the more remarkable when it is remembered that they have no instruments with which to aid them in the interpretation of the stories of the stars. The Snake ceremonials do not begin on the same day each year, but the date is fixed annually by an astronomical deduction in which figures the relationship between Orion, Pleiades and the Milky Way. This is a fact that has not been noted by previous investigators. Just what this relationship is, or the peculiar auspicious situation of these heavenly bodies desired, the doctor is at present unable to determine, and is now engaged in making calculations in the hope of ascertaining by rules how this date is annually fixed. One thing, however, seems to be apparent. That is that the native priests desire as propitious an occasion as possible on which to offer their prayers, believing, reasonably, that they will be of more practical effect.

The stars are watched faithfully during the summer season and when the proper time arrives the observation is taken by the chiefs between the hours of 12 and 2 o'clock in the morning, and the date of the Snake Dance is then set twenty days thereafter. The next night after the setting of the date of the dance a priest named Han-yi, in the capacity of town crier, goes on the housetop and makes public announcement of the date.

WHY THE APACHE EATS NO FISH
(Apache)

Many individuals when put the question, "Do Apaches eat fish?" would answer "No!" with a shrug of disgust. When I asked them why, some merely said, "No good!" and one said, "All same water,"—meaning, that fish were as tasteless and useless for food as that liquid.

The traditional version was that there came five or six years when Apaches could not get enough to eat. Deer and antelope were very scarce, because there were too many to hunt them. The wise men said, "We must make a big war and kill many people, so that the other can live." But first came a big powwow. All the mountain Indians went on a visit to the river Indians and had a big talk. "Then they made a big swear." The mountain Indians agreed not to eat any fish, and the river Indians agreed not to eat deer. "So, after that, every one had enough."

Now it is a fact that the Mohave and Yuma Indians who dwell on the Colorado River subsist entirely on fish and vegetables and kill no deer; the same story was current among the members of that tribe. He also stated that, there were a number of Apaches living side by side with the Mohaves, and that the former could never be persuaded to taste fish, though the latter subsisted on a fish diet almost exclusively.

While the Indians themselves accept the above explanation, it does not seem a plausible one. There must have been, in the distant and long-forgotten past of this tribe, some event or experience of a most startling character—something more impressive than a mere verbal agreement—to have stamped this custom so indelibly into their nature. And, since the Apache abides by no other agreements or promises, it is almost inconceivable that, merely on account of a promise made by his forefathers, he should continue to refrain from the favorite food of his neighbors. I venture to suggest that this is an ethnological fact that may lead to the discovery of the source whence this tribe, differing as it does from every other on the continent, derived their origin.

WHY THE ZUNI EATS NO FISH
(Zuñi)

The Zuñis, like the Navahoes, will not, under any circumstances, eat fish or any other water animal. The reason is this: Abiding in a desert land, where water is scarce, they regard it as especially sacred; hence all things really or apparently belonging to it, and in particular all creatures living in it, are sacred or deified. But, in the case of the fishes, they eat water, chew it, and are therefore, since they also breathe water and the currents or breaths of water, especially tabooed. The Zuñi name for the Isletas is *Kyas-i-ta(w)-kwe,* Fish Cannibals, because they ate fish formerly. The Keres share the Tinneh and Zuñi taboo, but do not know.

Amongst the Zuñis, a primary mode of classifying animals, with reference to their sacredness, is according to their relationship to water. Thus the animals of prey are, except in hunting and war, less sacred than game animals, and water animals are, in matters of peace, health, and life-making, the most sacred of all. Now these degrees of sacredness of the three classes of animals are strictly correlated to their observed ways of taking water. The animals of prey lap water; the game animals suck or sip it; the water animals gulp it; while fish not only drink water, but, as their name implies, also breathe and even prepare and "eat" it, as we do sweet food.

There is a further reason why, with the Zuñis, fish are, in common with certain water snakes, sacred above all other creatures of the water: In that country fishes live only in living springs, or in rivers perennially fed by springs. It is this which distinguishes them from such rain-water gods as tadpoles and frogs, and it is this which causes the Zuñis to believe that the water of springs (the water of life *par excellence*) belongs to the fish; they can pray it up from the depths of the underworld, as tadpoles and water-fowl can pray it down from the skies.

Under these circumstances, the eating of fish seems to the Zuñis no less than cannibalism, and is followed by the direst consequences, chief among which is madness,—that kind of madness the first symptoms of which are incessant gasping and swallowing,—or the giddiness which comes from gazing down into swift-flowing waters, and is considered so fatal to reproduction that pregnant women must be guarded from the sight of moving water, fish, and water-reptiles, no less than from fierce and fearful things.

THE SWASTIKA
(Zuñi)

What is its significance? Its origin, and where is it used and understood? These questions are asked and answered very often in these days of interest in things Indian. The symbol stares at you from the carvings of the Alaskan, the blankets of the Navajo, the baskets of the Pima and the pottery of the Zuñi, in reality nearly universal is its use among the North American Indians. It has a significance to all these people and each tribe has for it a new use and meaning. To the Navajo it is a symbol of good luck and a calendar, it denoting to him the four seasons. He looks to the north and in the Polar Constellation finds his calendar. Four times during the year, at midnight can be seen the sign that since 4000 B.C. has been the symbol of so many races. The Polar star is the center and the Constellation of Ursa Major forming the four arms or branches, make a complete swastika. The Pima Indian reads it as the history of his race, once so powerful, and dwelling by the big water, evidently the Mississippi, ruled over by a wise and great chief who, being desirous of giving the best possible government to his people sent four of his sub chiefs, one east, one west, one north and one south, with orders to travel far and not return until a race of people were found whose government was better than their own. Should such a one be found then with all haste return and report, and if possible bring ambassadors from the fortunate people that he might learn of them. The four arms are the chiefs in their journey and the center of home. The coming of the white man was heralded as a return of a chief with the ambassadors and orders were given to treat them with great kindness. They realized their error after sampling the white man's government. The Zuñis looked upon it as a sign of pleasure or an event cross marking some occurrence of more than usual interest. It is also the primary symbol in every Buddhist shrine and as the ancients were great astronomers and worshipped the planets as it has great religious significance among the followers of Budda. Whatever the true meaning, there is no doubt about its growing popularity as an ornament and a pretty little swastika in beaten silver, gold, or even copper makes a charm that surely will bring good luck to the wearer. Much could be written about this symbol and its full meaning and still be in doubt.

Disposing the Dead
(Comanche)

The ways of disposing of the Indian dead are many. In some places ground sepulture is common; in others, the corpses are placed in trees. South Americans mummified their dead, and cremation was not unknown. Enemies gave no thought to those that they had slain, after plucking off their scalps as trophies, though they sometimes added the indignity of mutilation in killing.

Sachem's Head, near Guilford, CT, is so named because Uncas cut a Pequot's head off and placed it in the crotch of an oak that grew there. It remained withering for years. It was to save the body of Polan from such a fate, after the fight on Sebago Lake in 1756, that his brothers placed it under the root of a sturdy young beech that they had pried out of the ground. He was laid in the hollow in his wardress, with silver cross on his breast and bow and arrows in his hand; then, the weight on the trunk being released, the sapling sprang back to its place and afterward rose to a commanding height, fitly marking the Indian's tomb. Chief Blackbird, of the Omahas, was buried, in accordance with his wish, on the summit of a bluff near the upper Missouri, on the back of his favorite horse, fully equipped for travel, with the scalps that he had taken hung to the bridle.

When a Comanche dies he is buried on the western side of the camp, that his soul may follow the setting sun into the spirit world the speedier. His bow, arrows, and valuables are interred with him, and his best pony is killed at the grave that he may appear among his fellows in the happy hunting-grounds mounted and equipped. An old Comanche who died near Fort Sill was without relatives and poor, so his tribe thought that any kind of a horse would do for him to range upon the fields of paradise. They killed a spavined old plug and left him. Two weeks from that time the late unlamented galloped into a camp of the Wichitas on the back of a lop-eared, bob-tailed, sheep-necked, ring-boned horse, with ribs like a grate, and said he wanted his dinner. Having secured a piece of meat, formally presented to him on the end of a lodge-pole, he offered himself to the view of his own people, alarming them by his glaring eyes and sunken cheeks, and told them that he had come back to haunt them for a stingy, inconsiderate lot, because the gate-keeper of heaven had refused to admit him on so ill-conditioned a mount. The camp broke up in dismay. Wichitas and Comanches journeyed, en masse, to Fort Sill for protection, and since then they have sacrificed the best horses in their possession when an unfriended one journeyed to the spirit world.

LEGEND OF SUPERSTITION MOUNTAIN
(Toltec)

Centuries ago, when Toltec civilization had extended over Arizona, and perhaps over the whole West, the valleys were occupied by large towns—the towns whose ruins are now known as the City of Ovens, City of Stones, and City of the Dead. The people worked at trades and arts that had been practiced by their ancestors before the pyramids were built in Egypt. Montezuma had come to the throne of Mexico, and the Aztecs were a subject people; Europe had discovered America and forgotten it, and in America the arrival of Europeans was recalled only in traditions. But, like other nations, the Toltecs became a prey to self-confidence, to luxury, to wastefulness, and to deadening superstitions. Already the fierce tribes of the North were lurking on the confines of their country in a faith of speedy conquest, and at times it seemed as if the elements were against them.

The villagers were returning from the fields, one day, when the entire region was smitten by an earthquake. Houses trembled, rumblings were heard, people fell in trying to reach the streets, and reservoirs burst, wasting their contents on the fevered soil. A sacrifice was offered. Then came a second shock, and another mortal was offered in oblation. As the earth still heaved and the earthquake demon muttered underground, the king gave his daughter to the priests, that his people might be spared, though he wrung his hands and beat his brow as he saw her led away and knew that in an hour her blood would stream from the altar.

The girl walked firmly to the cave where the altar was erected—a cave in Superstition Mountains. She knelt and closed her eyes as the officiating priest uttered a prayer, and, gripping his knife of jade stone, plunged it into her heart. She fell without a struggle. And now, the end.

Hardly had the innocent blood drained out and the fires been lighted to consume the body, when a pall of cloud came sweeping across the heavens; a hot wind surged over the ground, laden with dust and smoke; the storm-struck earth writhed anew beneath pelting thunder-bolts; no tremor this time, but an upheaval that rent the rocks and flung the cities down. It was an hour of darkness and terror. Roars of thunder mingled with the more awful bellowing beneath; crash on crash told that houses and temples were falling in vast ruin; the mountainsides were loosened and the rush of avalanches added to the din; the air was thick, and through the clouds the people groped their way toward the fields; rivers broke from their confines and laid waste farms and gardens! The gods had indeed abandoned them, and the spirit of the king's daughter took its flight in company with thousands of souls in whose behalf she had suffered uselessly.

The king was crushed beneath his palace-roof and the sacerdotal executioner perished in a fall of rock. The survivors fled in panic and the Ishmaelite tribes on their frontier entered their kingdom and pillaged it of all abandoned wealth. The cities never were rebuilt and were rediscovered but a few years ago, when the maiden's skeleton was also found. Nor does any Indian cross Superstition Mountains without a sense of apprehension.

LEGEND OF DEATH VALLEY
(Unidentified)

In the southern part of California, near the Arizona line, is the famous Death Valley—a tract of arid, alkaline plain hemmed in by steep mountains and lying below the level of the sea. For years it was believed that no human being could cross that desert and live, for horses sink to their knees in drifts of soda dust; there is no water, though the traveler requires much drink; and the heat is terrific. Animals that die in the neighborhood mummify, but do not decay, and it is surmised that the remains of many a thoughtless or ignorant prospector lie bleached in the plain. On the east side of Dead Mountain are points of whitened rock that at a distance look like sheeted figures, and these, the Indians say, are the ghosts of their brethren.

In the heart of this desert is said to be the ruin of a pueblo, or village, though the shape and size of it suggest that it was made for a few persons rather than for a tribe or family. Long ago, the tale runs, this place of horrors was a fair and fertile kingdom, ruled by a beautiful but capricious queen. She ordered her subjects to build her a mansion that should surpass those of her neighbors, the Aztecs, and they worked for years to make one worthy of her, dragging the stones and timbers for miles. Fearing lest age, accident, or illness should forbid her to see the ending of her dream, she ordered so many of her subjects to assist that her tribe was reduced to practical slavery.

In her haste and heartlessness she commanded her own daughter to join the bearers of burdens, and when the toilers flagged in step in the noonday heat she strode among them and lashed their naked backs. As royalty was sacred, they did not complain, but when she struck her daughter the girl turned, threw down her load of stone, and solemnly cursed her mother and her kingdom; then, overcome by heat and weariness, she sank to the earth and died. Vain the regrets and lamentations of the queen. The sun came out with blinding heat and light, vegetation withered, animals disappeared, streams and wells dried up, and at last the wretched woman gave up her life on a bed of fever, with no hand to soothe her dying moments, for her people, too, were dead. The palace, half-completed, stands in the midst of this desolation, and sometimes it seems to lift into view of those at a distance in the shifting mirage that plays along the horizon.

LEGEND OF SPIDER TOWER
(Zuñi)

In Dead Man's Cañon—a deep gorge that is lateral to the once populated valley of the Rio de Chelly, AZ—stands a stark spire of weathered sandstone, its top rising eight hundred feet above its base in a sheer uplift. Centuries ago an inhabitant of one of the cave villages was surprised by hostiles while hunting in this region, and was chased by them into this cañon. As he ran he looked vainly from side to side in the hope of securing a hiding-place, but succor came from a source that was least expected, for on approaching this enormous obelisk, with strength well-nigh exhausted, he saw a silken cord hanging from a notch at its top. Hastily knotting the end about his waist, that it might not fall within reach of his pursuers, he climbed up, setting his feet into roughnesses of the stone, and advancing, hand over hand, until he had reached the summit, where he stayed, drinking dew and feeding on eagles' eggs, until his enemies went away, for they could not reach him with their arrows, defended as he was by points of rock. The foemen having gone, he safely descended by the cord and reached his home. This help had come from a friendly spider who saw his plight from her perch at the top of the spire, and, weaving a web of extra thickness, she made one end fast to a jag of rock while the other fell within his grasp—for she, like all other of the brute tribe, liked the gentle cave-dwellers better than the remorseless hunters. Hence the name of the Spider Tower.

LEGEND OF TISHOMINGO
(Tishomingo)

In the country about Tishomingo, Indian Territory, troubles are foretold by a battle of unseen men in the air. Whenever the sound of conflict is heard it is an indication that many dead will lie in the fields, for it heralds battle, starvation, or pestilence. The powerful nation that lived here once was completely annihilated by an opposing tribe, and in the valley in the western part of the Territory there are mounds where hundreds of men lie buried. Spirits occupy the valley, and to the eyes of the red men they are still seen, at times, continuing the fight.

In May, 1892, the last demonstration was made in the hearing of John Willis, a United States marshal, who was hunting horse-thieves. He was belated one night and entered the vale of mounds, for he had no scruples against sleeping there. He had not, in fact, ever heard that the region was haunted. The snorting of his horse in the middle of the night awoke him and he sprang to his feet, thinking that savages, outlaws, or, at least, coyotes had disturbed the animal. Although there was a good moon, he could see nothing moving on the plain. Yet the sounds that filled the air were like the noise of an army, only a trifle subdued, as if they were borne on the passing of a wind. The rush of hoofs and of feet, the striking of blows, the fall of bodies could be heard, and for nearly an hour these fell rumors went across the earth. At last the horse became so frantic that Willis saddled him and rode away, and as he reached the edge of the valley the sounds were heard going into the distance. Not until he reached a settlement did he learn of the spell that rested on the place.

THE DIVISION OF TWO TRIBES
(Shoshone)

When white men first penetrated the Western wilderness of America they found the tribes of Shoshone and Comanche at odds, and it is a legend of the springs of Manitou that their differences began there. This "Saratoga of the West," nestling in a hollow of the foot-hills in the shadow of the noble peak of Pike, was in old days common meeting-ground for several families of red men. Councils were held in safety there, for no Indian dared provoke the wrath of the manitou whose breath sparkled in the "medicine waters." None? Yes, one. For, centuries ago a Shoshone and a Comanche stopped here on their return from a hunt to drink. The Shoshone had been successful; the Comanche was empty handed and ill tempered, jealous of the other's skill and fortune. Flinging down the fat deer that he was bearing homeward on his shoulders, the Shoshone bent over the spring of sweet water, and, after pouring a handful of it on the ground, as a libation to the spirit of the place, he put his lips to the surface. It needed but faint pretext for his companion to begin a quarrel, and he did so in this fashion: "Why does a stranger drink at the spring-head when one of the owners of the fountain contents himself with its overflow? How does a Shoshone dare to drink above me?"

The other replied, "The Great Spirit places the water at the spring that his children may drink it undefiled. I am Ausaqua, chief of Shoshones, and I drink at the head-water. Shoshone and Comanche are brothers. Let them drink together."

"No. The Shoshone pays tribute to the Comanche, and Wacomish leads that nation to war. He is chief of the Shoshone as he is of his own people."

"Wacomish lies. His tongue is forked, like the snake's. His heart is black. When the Great Spirit made his children he said not to one, 'Drink here,' and to another, 'Drink there,' but gave water that all might drink."

The other made no answer, but as Ausaqua stooped toward the bubbling surface Wacomish crept behind him, flung himself against the hunter, forced his head beneath the water, and held him there until he was drowned. As he pulled the dead body from the spring the water became agitated, and from the bubbles arose a vapor that gradually assumed the form of a venerable Indian, with long white locks, in whom the murderer recognized Waukauga, father of the Shoshone and Comanche nation, and a man whose heroism and goodness made his name revered in both these tribes. The face of the patriarch was dark with wrath, and he cried, in terrible tones, "Accursed of my race! This day thou hast severed the mightiest nation in the world. The blood of the brave Shoshone appeals for vengeance. May the water of thy tribe be rank and bitter in their throats."

Then, whirling up an elk-horn club, he brought it full on the head of the wretched man, who cringed before him. The murderer's head was burst open and he tumbled lifeless into the spring, that to this day is nauseous, while, to perpetuate the memory of Ausaqua, the manitou smote a neighboring rock, and from it gushed a fountain of delicious water. The bodies were found, and the partisans of both the hunters began on that day a long and destructive warfare, in which other tribes became involved until mountaineers were arrayed against plainsmen through all that region.

STORIES OF THE INDIAN MESSIAH
(Various)

THE INDIAN MESSIAH
(Sanpoels)

The promise of the return to earth of various benign spirits has caused much trouble among the red men, and incidentally to the white men who are the objects of their fanatic dislike. The New Mexicans believed that when the Emperor Montezuma was about to leave the earth he planted a tree and bade them watch it, for when it fell he would come back in glory and lead them to victory, wealth, and power. The watch was kept in secret on account of the determination of the Spaniards to break up all fealty to tribal heroes and traditions. As late as 1781 they executed a sentence of death on a descendant of the Peruvian Incas for declaring his royal origin. When Montezuma's tree fell the people gathered on the house-tops to watch the east—in vain, for the white man was there. In 1883 the Sanpoels, a small tribe in Washington, were stirred by the teaching of an old chief, who told them that the wicked would soon be destroyed, and that the Great Spirit had ordered him to build an ark for his people. The remains of this vessel, two hundred and eighty-eight feet long, are still to be seen near one of the tributaries of the Columbia.

A frenzy swept over the West in 1890, inspiring the Indians by promise of the coming of one of superhuman power, who was generally believed to be Hiawatha, to threaten the destruction of the white population, since it had been foretold that the Messiah would drive the white men from their land. Early in the summer of that year it was reported that the Messiah had appeared in the north, and the chiefs of many tribes went to Dakota, as the magi did to Bethlehem, to learn if this were true. Sitting Bull, the Sioux chief, told them, in assembly, that it was so, and declared that he had seen the new Christ while hunting in the Shoshone Mountains. One evening he lost his way and was impelled by a strange feeling to follow a star that moved before him. At daybreak it paused over a beautiful valley, and, weary with his walk, he sank on a bed of moss. As he sat there throngs of Indian warriors appeared and began a spirit dance, led by chiefs who had long been dead. Presently a voice spoke in his ear, and turning he saw a strange man dressed in white. The man said he was the same Christ who had come into the world nineteen hundred years before to save white men, and that now he would save the red men by driving out the whites. The Indians were to dance the ghost-dance, or spirit dance, until the new moon, when the globe would shiver, the wind would blow, and the white soldiers and their horses would sink into the earth. The Messiah showed to Sitting Bull the nail-wounds in his hands and feet and the spear-stab in his side. When night came on the form in white had disappeared—and, returning, the old chief taught the ghost-dance to his people.

ABOUT THE MESSIAH
(Cheyenne)

DEAR FRIENDS—one and all. Don't force your and others' minds on this letter, but resist it and keep your minds from it. I simply want to tell you just what I learned from Mr. Porcupine, Big Beaver, and I am sorry to say from one of them, a cousin of mine, Ridge Walker, son of Beaver Claws. I expect many of you are wishing to know, and perhaps many of you have already heard about it. I have met them face to face, and have questioned them personally when I met them; and so I learned from them some of their Messiah ideas. I try to make an account of just what I have learned from these three persons.

In the fall of the year 1890, they say, they first heard of this new Christ, at the Arapaho and Shoshone Agency, Wyoming Territory. When they and other Cheyennes of Tongue River went on a visit to said tribes in the autumn of 1890, an Arapaho Indian named Sage, who had been to the southwestern country in 1888, told them that a new Christ had arisen for the Indians; he said where he could be found and explained his doctrine to them. Farther on, Porcupine said that he and the other Cheyennes were much interested, and determined to see the Messiah, but as all could not go so far, nine of these Cheyennes were sent back to Tongue River Agency to tell the people what they had heard. Porcupine and several of the Cheyennes went on. When they arrived in Utah, they received large accessions to their caravan, Indians joining them *en route* at the different points, and so at last their meeting took place at Walker Lake, to hear the new Christ speak. There were many people present, including women and children.

Then Mr. Porcupine says to the Messiah: "I and my people have been living in ignorance until I went and found out the truth." He sat with his head bowed all the time, and after a while he arose and said he was very glad to see his children: "I have sent for you and I am glad that you have come, and I am going to talk to you after a while about our relations who are dead and gone. My children, I want you to listen to all I have to say, and I will teach you how to dance a dance, and I want you to dance it; get ready for the dance, and then when the dance is over I will talk to you."

He was dressed in a white coat with stripes; the rest of his dress was that of a white man's, except that he had on a pair of moccasins. And then we commenced to dance, everybody joining in with the Christ, singing while we danced. We danced till late in the night, and he said we had danced enough. And in the morning after breakfast we went in the circle and spread grass over it on the ground, the Christ standing in the midst of us, and told us that he was going away on that day and that he would be back next morning and talk to us.

In the night, when I first saw him I thought he was an Indian; but the next day, when I could see him better, he looked different; he was not so dark as an Indian, nor so light as a white man. He had no beard or whiskers, but very heavy eyebrows; he was a good-looking man, and we were crowded up very close.

We had been told that nobody was to talk; and even if a thing was whispered, the Christ would know it. I heard that Christ had been crucified, and I looked to see, and I saw a scar on his wrist and one on his face and he seemed to be the man. I could not see his feet.

He would talk to us all day. On that evening we were all assembled again to part with him. When we assembled he began to sing, and he commenced to tremble all over violently for a while, and then sat down; and we danced all on that night, the Christ lying beside us apparently dead. The next morning we went to our breakfast; the Christ was with us again. After breakfast four heralds went around and called out that the Christ was back with us, and wanted talk with us; and so the circle was made again; they assembled and Christ came amongst them and sat down. He said they were to listen to him while he talked to us. "I am the man who made everything you see around you. I am not lying to my children. I made this earth and everything on it. I have been to Heaven and seen your dead friends, and seen my father and mother. In the beginning, after God made the earth, they sent me back to teach the people; and when I came back on the earth, the people were afraid of me and treated me badly. This is what they have done to me (showing his scars). I did not try to defend myself, and I found my children were bad, so I went back to Heaven and left them; and in so many years I would come back and see to my children, and at the end of this time I was sent back to teach them. My father told me that the earth is getting old and worn out, and the people getting bad, and that I was to renew everything as it used to be, and make it better; and he said all our dead were to be resurrected and they were all to come back to the earth, and that the earth was too small for them and us; he would do away with heaven and make the earth large enough to contain us all; and that we must tell all the people we meet about these things.

He spoke to us about fighting, and said that was bad and we must keep from it; that the earth was to be all good hereafter; that we must be friends with one another. He said that in the fall of the year the youth of all the good people would be renewed, so that nobody would be more than forty years old. The youth of every one would be renewed in the spring. He said if we were all good he would send people among us who could heal all our wounds and sickness by mere touch, and that we could live forever.

This is what I have witnessed, and many other things wonderful which I cannot describe. Please don't follow the ideas of that man. He is not the Christ. No man in the world can see God at any time. Even the angels of God cannot.

Chapter 17

Tribal Legends

Djo-na-aì-yì-ĭ ⁿ
(Apache)

In the early days, animals and birds of monstrous size preyed upon the people; the giant Elk, the Eagle, and others devoured men, women, and children, until the gods were petitioned for relief. A deliverer was sent to them in the person of Djo-na-aì'-yì-ĭⁿ, the son of the old woman who lives in the West and the second wife of the Sun. She divided her time between the Sun and the Waterfall, and by the latter bore a second son, named Ko-ba-tcis'-tci-ni, who remained with his mother while his brother went forth to battle with the enemies of mankind. In four days Djo-na-aì'-yì-ĭⁿ grew to manhood, then he asked his mother where the Elk lived. She told him that the Elk was in a great desert far to the southward. She gave him arrows with which to kill the Elk. In four steps he reached the distant desert where the Elk was lying. Djo-na-aì'-yì-ĭⁿ cautiously observed the position of the Elk from behind a hill. The Elk was lying on an open plain, where no trees or bushes were to be found that might serve to shelter Djo-na-aì'-yì-ĭⁿ from view while he approached. While he was looking at the Elk, with dried grass before his face, the Lizard, *Mai-cu-i-ti-tce-tcĕ,* said to him, "What are you doing, my friend?" Djo-na-aì'-yì-ĭⁿ explained his mission, whereupon the Lizard suggested that he clothe himself in the garments of the Lizard, in which he could approach the Elk in safety. Djo-na-aì'-yì-ĭⁿ tried four times before he succeeded in getting into the coat of the Lizard. Next the Gopher, *Mi-i-ni-li,* came to him with the question, "What are you doing here, my friend?" When Djo-na-aì'-yì-ĭⁿ told the Gopher of his intention, the latter promised to aid him. The Gopher thought it advisable to reconnoitre by burrowing his way underground to the Elk. Djo-na-aì'-yì-ĭⁿ watched the progress of the Gopher as that animal threw out fresh heaps of earth on his way. At length the Gopher came to the surface underneath the Elk, whose giant heart was beating like a mighty hammer. He then proceeded to gnaw the hair from about the heart of the Elk. "What are you doing?" said the Elk. "I am cutting a few hairs for my little ones, they are now lying on the bare ground," replied the Gopher, who continued until the magic coat of the Elk was all cut away from about the heart of the Elk. Then he returned to Djo-na-ai'-yi-ī^{n}, and told the latter to go through the hole which he had made and shoot the Elk. Four times the Son of the Sun tried to enter the hole before he succeeded. When he reached the Elk, he saw the great heart beating above him, and easily pierced it with his arrows; four times his bow was drawn before he turned to escape through the tunnel which the Gopher had been preparing for him. This hole extended far to the eastward, but the Elk soon discovered it, and, thrusting his antler into it, followed in pursuit. The Elk ploughed up the earth with such violence that the present mountains were formed, which extend from east to west. The black spider closed the hole with a strong web, but the Elk broke through it and ran southward, forming the mountain chains which trend north and south. In the south the Elk was checked by the web of the blue spider, in the west by that of the yellow spider, while in the north the web of the many-colored spider resisted his attacks until he fell dying from exhaustion and wounds. Djo-na-ai'-yi-ī^{n} made a coat from the hide of the Elk, gave the front quarters to the Gopher, the hind quarters to the Lizard, and carried home the antlers. He found that the results of his adventures were not unknown to his mother, who had spent the time during his absence in singing, and watching a roll of cedar bark which sank into the earth or rose in the air as danger approached or receded from Djo-na-ai'-yi-ī^{n}, her son.

Djo-na-ai'-yi-ī^{n} next desired to kill the great Eagle, I-tsa. His mother directed him to seek the Eagle in the west. In four strides he reached the home of the Eagle, an inaccessible rock, on which was the nest, containing two young eaglets. His ear told him to stand facing the east when the next morning the Eagle swooped down upon him and tried to carry him off. The talons of the Eagle failed to penetrate the hard elk-skin by which he was covered. "Turn to the south," said the ear, and again the Eagle came, and was again unsuccessful. Djo-na-ai'-yi-ī^{n} faced each of the four points in this manner, and again faced toward the east; whereupon the Eagle succeeded in fastening its talons in the lacing on the front of the coat of the supposed man, who was carried to the nest above and thrown down before the young eagles, with the invitation to pick his eyes out. As they were about to do this, Djo-na-ai'-yi-ī^{n} gave a warning hiss, at which the young ones cried, "He is living yet." "Oh, no," replied the old Eagle; "that is only the rush of air from his body through the holes made by my talons." Without stopping to verify this, the Eagle flew away. Djo-na-ai'-yi-ī^{n} threw some of the blood of the Elk which he had brought with him to the young ones, and asked them when their mother returned. "In the afternoon when it rains," they answered. When the mother Eagle came with the shower of rain in the afternoon, he stood in readiness with one of the Elk antlers in his hand. As the bird alighted with a man in her talons, Djo-na-ai'-yi-ī^{n} struck her upon the back with the antler, killing her instantly. Going back to the nest, he asked the young eagles when their father returned. "Our father comes home when the wind blows and brings rain just before sunset," they said. The male Eagle came at the appointed time, carrying a woman with a crying infant upon her back. Mother and babe were dropped from a height upon the rock and killed. With the second antler of the Elk, Djo-na-ai'-yi-ĭ^n avenged their death, and ended the career of the eagles by striking the Eagle upon the back and killing him. The wing of this eagle was of enormous size; the bones were as large as a man's arm; fragments of this wing are still preserved at Taos. Djo-na-ai'-yi-ĭ^n struck the young eagles upon the head, saying, "You shall never grow any larger." Thus deprived of their strength and power to injure mankind, the eagles relinquished their sovereignty with the parting curse of rheumatism, which they bestowed upon the human race.

Djo-na-ai'-yi-ĭ^n could discover no way by which he could descend from the rock, until at length he saw an old female Bat, Tca-na'-mi-ĭ^n, on the plain below. At first she pretended not to hear his calls for help; then she flew up with the inquiry, "How did you get here?" Djo-na-ai'-yi-ĭ^n told how he had killed the eagles. "I will give you all the feathers you may desire if you will help me to escape," concluded he. The old Bat carried her basket, ilt-tsai-ĭ-zĭs, by a slender spider's thread. He was afraid to trust himself in such a small basket suspended by a thread, but she reassured him, saying: "I have packed mountain sheep in this basket, and the strap has never broken. Do not look while we are descending; keep your eyes shut as tight as you can." He began to open his eyes once during the descent, but she warned him in time to avoid mishap. They went to the foot of the rock where the old Eagles lay. Djo-na-ai'-yi-ĭ^n filled her basket with feathers, but told her not to go out on the plains, where there are many small birds. Forgetting this admonition, she was soon among the small birds, who robbed the old Bat of all her feathers. This accounts for the plumage of the small bird klo'-kĭn, which somewhat resembles the color of the tail and wing feathers of the bald eagle. The Bat returned four times for a supply of feathers, but the fifth time she asked to have her basket filled, Djo-na-ai'-yi-ĭ^n was vexed. "You cannot take care of your feathers, so you shall never have any. This old skin on your basket is good enough for you." "Very well," said the Bat, resignedly, "I deserve to lose them, for I never could take care of those feathers."

WEKSALAHOS
(Wichita)

There was a time when some people lived in a village, and some out by themselves. There was a poor boy by the name of *Weksalahos* (The-Boy-who-Urinates-in-Bed), who lived in the village with his grandfather and grandmother, and they were poor. The village was headed by a chief, whose name was Young-Man-Chief.

It was the habit of Weksalahos to run about the village picking up things to eat that had been thrown away by the people. This is the way this poor boy got his food. At times he would go to some one who was pounding corn into meal, and sometimes, when people felt like it, they would give the poor boy some meal, hence he was often called "Boy-who-Ate-from-the-Corn-Mill." The boy's folks were of what we would call a low class of people. The poor boy had a buffalo robe which he wore while going around the village, so there were people, among whom was *Kedox* (Coyote) in particular, who disliked Weksalahos' folks, and abused them. Kedox would sometimes go to their home and urinate on their lodge. Because they were poor, this is the way they were treated by some people.

Young-Man-Chief had a father, mother, and four sisters in the village, and this chief was always out on the war-path. He had a good many followers who were always ready to go along with him whenever he felt like going out on the war-path.

It happened that Young-Man-Chief announced to the people that he wanted to send out a large war-party which he had formed, and that they would leave in a few days. It must be remembered that there was always a large body of men who would go out with such a war-party. So he set out with the war-party, went toward the south, and they traveled all that day; they stopped early in the evening.

Just as they were going out on the war-path, Weksalahos said to his grandmother, "Grandmother, I want to go with the war-party;" but the old man said, "Why do you want to go?" The old woman said, "I am afraid you would be a cause to hold the people back should you go, for I know they would have to wait for you or, if you should stay with the crowd, some of them might get tired of you and kill you." When the appointed time came for the war-party to set out, they left their wives at home, and were all equipped for war, and all started at the same time.

After all had started, Weksalahos, against his grandfather's and grandmother's wish, set out to go along with the party. When the people stopped for a night's rest, some of the men happened to look back whence they had come, and they saw some one coming. The people began to ask one another who this man might be. But when he came nearer, he began to get smaller and smaller, and when he was close, they found that it was Weksalahos. Some of the men tried to coax him to go back, for the men would travel fast, and he might not stay with the crowd, and might delay them. Weksalahos turned back, but did not go far, and stayed all night somewhere else, instead of going clear back home. Next morning they started again, and Weksalahos got up and followed them. In the evening, when they stopped, they saw him coming again, and as he was now far from home, the chief warrior asked him to come to the camp; but some of them thought he had better go back, especially Kedox, who abused him in every way he could.

During this day the chief had already sent out spies to see if they could find the enemy. Late that evening, after they had camped, the spies came in and told the chief that they had found the enemy's village. The chief was then asked to announce whatever he thought best to be done. So in reply he said: "These surely must be the ones I am after; early in the morning everybody must be ready to make the attack." All then traveled the rest of the night, Weksalahos in the midst of them. About daylight they came to the enemy's village.

All the warriors now began to dress themselves in their war costumes, and the poor boy Weksalahos was asked to remain with the things that they left, such as buffalo robes and other things that they did not need while making their attack. As soon as all had left to go before the village, and while everybody at the village was asleep, Weksalahos made his way to the creek, and dived into the water; he changed himself to a man, and when he came out he had a war-bonnet on his head such as no one else had. When the war-party made their charge, there was seen going before them a man whom no one knew; but they noticed that he was a better runner and warrior too than the rest, and his war-bonnet was entirely different from any one's else; and the only war weapon he had was a war-club. Weksalahos was the first one to begin the fighting, and going through the village, he went around the other way, without meeting any one, to the creek, dived again, came out of the water the same as he always was,—a poor boy,—and went back where he had been told to remain.

Then the warriors returned, some having scalps and some having prisoners captive. Finally, the head warrior of the village was brought to the war-party, and delivered to the chief.

All then turned back toward home. While on the way the men cut stick to hang their scalps on, and so Weksalahos had some one cut him a stick to hang the scalp on which the chief had given him, to carry it, according to custom. He then had it painted with red paint which they called *"dathqyets."* Some painted theirs black, using the ashes of burnt grass. They traveled all that day, and finally darkness came, and all camped for a night's rest.

It was the custom, when stopping for a night's rest, to sit up a while, and have conversation among themselves, consulting about things they had seen. When they had done this, the chief warrior asked who the man was whom he had seen in the lead while making the attack, running faster than he himself, and whose war-bonnet was entirely different from any one's else. All said they did not know who the man was. When they had said this, Kedox spoke and said, "Who else could you have expected to have done the first of the fighting but me? It was I who did all that before any one could reach the village; I was there first." But it was known that Kedox would once in a while tell the truth, and at other times would lie; and in these times, of such people it was said that they had two tongues, one telling the truth, and the other telling the untrue. Every one knew that Kedox was in the midst of the crowd when they all ran towards the village and when they made the attack; so they did not believe him at all.

After these things, every one went to sleep with the expectation of getting home the next day. Every one's mind was excited by what had occurred during the attack —*i.e.* that some one had got ahead of others in the attack—and guessing who the man was that did the first fighting.

On the next morning all started for home, and late the following day, when they were near their homes, according to custom, they sent some one on ahead to show the people at home that their warriors would enter the village victorious. After the man had signaled, the people knew that their warriors were coming and got ready for them to come in. So the warriors entered the village in triumphant way.

They were met by a great multitude of their people, and dances were at once begun, lasting all night long, and this is the way the people spent their time when any of their warriors came home victorious. Weksalahos met his grandfather and grandmother, and delivered the scalp to them, which they thought to be the great-est thing that had ever occurred to them through their grandchild; so they danced like the other people.

Since Weksalahos went to war, every one of the people began to think lots of his folks, and would give them things to eat, and Weksalahos' grandmother could then dance in front of each of the greatest warriors, praising them as any other woman would. It was the custom for people to give away things, especially the young men who had been with the war-party to give to their parents; so when the parents went around their places, they would get presents from them, such things as robes, meat and other food, such as corn.

After a while Young-Man-Chief announced to his warriors that he was going to send out another war-party, and told them that he wanted to appoint a certain day on which to start. So everybody was ready and looked for that day to come.

Weksalahos again asked his folks to allow him to go with the war-party; and this time they allowed him to go, for they knew that since he had been successful once, he would get along well again, and they knew that when he should come back from war, they would be very well treated.

When the time came to start on the war-path, they all started, and with this war-party Weksalahos volunteered to go along. They traveled all that day, and camped early, so they could send out spies. All day they had been headed toward the south. They sent out spies to see if there were any enemies near to them that they wanted to attack. When they camped, beside sending out spies, they also sent out hunters to hunt for some game, so they could have some meat for food. Late that day the hunters came with deer that they had killed and some turkeys. They cooked some meat for their supper, and after they had cooked it, they all ate their meal. Weksalahos always ate after all the rest had eaten and were through. According to custom, while out on the war-path, the men sat up late, waiting for the spies to come in. So that night all sat up talking about what to do when attacking their enemies.

About midnight the spies came. It was a rule that when spies came in, they should whoop, and say, *"Sahgiwáris"* ("I am sure of it"). When the spies came, the men formed in a circle, and the spies went around the circle once. Then the men asked them what they had seen. Some reported the enemy were Gusseyos. Others told the chief or head warrior that when they left the crowd they traveled to such and such a place, looking out for the enemy, and of course told all about how they traveled and what sort of places they had seen; they had seen a village, and the village was there if they wished to attack it. The chief was then asked what he wanted to do about what had been reported by his two men who were serving under him, so the rest of the men would know what they were to do. The chief then said to his warriors that when the war-party was formed, he had intended to attack the first enemies he should find. So when this news was brought to him, he informed his men that this was the enemy he was after, and that early next morning they would make an attack. He then asked his men to get ready to start that night.

They all started, heading toward the point where the enemies were seen by spies. Weksalahos was in the midst of the crowd, and had heard every word that was said regarding the attack they were to make. They traveled all that night, expecting to get to the enemy's village before the next morning. About daylight they entered the edge of the village.

The chief told his men to dress themselves, and get ready. When everybody was ready, the chief told Weksalahos to remain at the place where they had left all the robes. When all had started toward the village, Weksalahos went to the creek, dived in the water, and came out just as he had done on a similar occasion with the first war-party he had gone out with. As all were running toward the village, there was in the lead of all a man whom no one knew, and he was the one they had seen on making their attack in the previous war-party. This was Weksalahos again, but he would not show himself to the people, but went ahead of everybody, and did the first fighting. Before any one could reach the village, he went right through and came around the other way, without letting any one see him. He let the remainder of the warriors do the rest, and returned to the place where he had been stationed, first having gone to the creek again, the same as he had done on the previous occasion. Finally, the rest of the warriors came about the place where they had left their things for Weksalahos to look after while they went out to war. When the rest of the warriors came, the head warrior gave Weksalahos a scalp again. Of course the others had scalps, and some had people whom they had taken captive. So this was the second scalp Weksalahos got from the chief.

All then turned back, and Weksalahos, before starting, hired a man to cut him a stick for his scalp, to hang it on. He then had it painted red like the first stick he had ordered. They traveled all that day and at night camped, for it was a long way to their village. The following day the men went out to hunt for meat, and at night the party stopped for a night's rest. The men came in with deer meat and turkey. Whenever the men came in from a hunt, there were other men who did the cooking; so part of the men in the camp cooked for them.

After meals Weksalahos, being but a small boy, had to get into bed early; he was the first one to go to bed. The rest of the men stayed up until late at night, and commenced to talk about the unknown man whom they had seen go ahead of them when making an attack; then they asked one another if there was any one in the crowd that always went ahead of everybody else, and if there was, to speak out; and if there was anybody who knew who it was, he should tell; for the man who had done this would receive a big offer to become a chief over every one of the existing chiefs. But there was no sign of any one who knew who this man was. Kedox was the only man who said it was he. But the people knew that while making the attack Kedox had been in the midst of the crowd, and had nothing to show that it was he; but he would say, "Who else could you people suspect it to be; you know that I am the only great warrior you have." But the other men would say, "I don't believe Kedox." They knew that he was always wanting to appear braver and better than every one else. So no one knew who this man was that went in the lead to the attack. Since no one could be found who could tell who the man was, they went to bed.

Early the next morning, after eating their meal, they all began to move out and travel on their way back to their homes, going faster than ever, by a straight trail, instead of going around by the way they had come. They all aimed to get home the following day, and continued to travel that day until late in the evening. They sent out a man ahead to give the home people a signal, so that they would know of their coming. The only man who could do this was Gusseyos, who was the fastest traveler. So while the rest of the men traveled slowly, Gusseyos went ahead to inform the village.

Late in the evening the people at home saw a man appearing at a place called *"Naasaquadowini"* ("Place-where-Warriors-give-Signals-on-their-Way-Home-from-War"). Now the people began to know of their warriors coming home victorious. Late in the evening the warriors all got home, Weksalahos being the last one to come. But the people and his folks received him in good manner.

In the evening the people who had been at home began to dance the scalp dances, continuing all night, in honor of their brave warriors. Weksalahos and his folks also had the same kind of a time as the rest of the people were having. The old woman would join in the dance, and early in the morning, it being the custom, the old women sang and went around to every tipi, singing about a certain person who had been in the battle and what heroic deeds he had done; and at this time the women were given presents of all kinds. The songs they sang were called *"Garhi-ikawilaeh,"* as they are also nowadays. The women were heard whenever any war-party returned from war.

It was then the custom that whenever any one sent out a war-party, the person who was sending it looked for the return of his victorious warriors. Then, as now, when any one wished to become a great warrior or a chief, he sought to perform brave deeds. This is how Weksalahos was planning to become a prominent man.

The dancers were still going on the same as usual, until everything quieted down, and the great fun was over.

Weksalahos, while at home, went around the village, picking up things to eat; but there was a time when some boys of his age met him, and abused him, after which he cried all the way back to his home. The poor boy was kind-hearted; he would never fight back, but would endure whatever the boys did to him.

Again Young-Man-Chief announced to his warriors that he was going to send out another war-party. Weksalahos was then going around the village, and when he heard of this, he turned back to his home, and told his folks about the war-party that was soon to be sent out. Weksalahos was glad to hear of this, because this is the way he got his fun. So he remained at home, waiting for the time to come. He asked his grandmother to make him a pair of moccasins. About the time these moccasins were finished, all got notice that the man was about to start out on the great war expedition. So this was to be the third time that Weksalahos was to go on the war-path.

When the appointed day came, all started at the same time, and the poor boy Weksalahos was again in the midst of the party. While on the road, Kedox saw him again, and tried to make him go back to the village, for he saw that Weksalahos was always treated well by the chief warrior, and because the chief always gave him a scalp. But the chief said that Weksalahos should be allowed to go with them, and at this time the chief began to suspect Weksalahos to be the unknown man they had always seen when making their attacks. So Kedox let him alone.

After traveling all that day, some men were sent out to hunt a little for something to eat; the rest of the men went on until late that evening. They camped and waited for the other men to come in, and after dark the hunters came in with deer meat they had killed. Then war smoke ceremonies were performed. Part of the men were commanded to cook the meat, and after all had eaten their meal, they sat up for a while, telling about what they were to do when meeting their enemies; then they went to bed.

On the next day, after eating their breakfast, they started on their way again, and traveled all day; they sent out spies, and selected a certain place where they would meet them the following day on their return. So the main party went on, taking a straight road, and the spies went ahead of them. On the following day the main party camped at a certain place they had selected to meet the spies. About dark there came some hunters that they had sent out to hunt for food. When the fire was made, the smoke ceremony was performed, and after this was over, the men who are called "servants" commenced to do the cooking for the rest of the warriors. After the cooking was done, they all began to look for the return of the spies, anxious to hear the news. Of course they had to sit up until their return. While the rest of the men were sitting up, the chief warrior sent out men to look for the spies. About midnight some of the spies returned, but they had failed to hear anything about their enemies' camp. Finally all returned except one. This man was still absent; but finally, when everybody was in, he came. He was never known to fail to carry out whatever he undertook to do. On his arrival the men were as quiet as they could be, all expecting to hear about what he had seen. According to custom, he was well received. He of course had to go through the performance that a spy had to do on his return from spying.

The spy was now asked to tell the story of his trip. He informed the warriors of what he had seen. He said that when making that trip, he traveled around a large creek in search of the enemy's village, and while on the creek he came to a high point; that he saw the village of the enemy. This was the end of his story. He then told them that the enemies were there, and that he supposed that this was their permanent home, leaving the consideration of the whole thing to the chief warrior and his men.

So the two men who were serving under the chief both asked their head warrior if these were the ones he wanted to go after. The chief then gave his orders to the two men who were serving under him to announce to the warriors that this was what he would do,—that on the same night he would start off, so he might attack the enemy early in the morning. The opinion of the chief regarding the returns was announced to the warriors. So the other warriors were then satisfied to learn what opinion the chief had about this. After this announcement the warriors were told to get ready to make the trip to the enemy's village. They all started on this trip that same night, and continued the rest of the night, and reached the village early in the morning.

The chief now told his men to get ready to make the attack; and Weksalahos to remain where they left all their things. As soon as they had started, Weksalahos left the things that were under his care and went to the creek to change his form, and dived in the water as he had done before, so that he might not be recognized while making the attack. The chief was always known to be the fastest runner, so that he was always in the lead; but when Weksalahos made his appearance, he always got ahead of the chief warrior, and was the first one to enter the village, dressed the same way as previously, wearing a war-bonnet that was not like that of any one else; and when he entered the village, he went through, killing the enemies just as they were getting out of their lodges, and going through the village, he went around the other way to prevent anybody seeing him, went to the creek, and dived in the water, and changed himself, the same as he had always done. Then he went to the place where he was told to remain until they all returned.

After the poor boy arrived at the place, he got his buffalo robe, and put it on; and when the warriors came to the place, he saw some with prisoners whom they had captured, and some with scalps to deliver to their wives and the old women who would come to meet them on their return. When the chief arrived, poor Weksalahos knew that he would get a scalp, for the chief was the man that always gave him a scalp. As soon as the chief arrived, he gave the boy a scalp, which was the third one given him.

As soon as all the warriors arrived, they turned back and traveled toward home, and took the straightest route in order to get home the next day. Weksalahos, while on the way, asked a certain man whom he knew would do whatever he asked him to do, to cut him a stick and paint it red, so he could hang his scalp on it. This was done for him while they were all traveling. At night they camped to rest. In the evening the men whose business it was to hunt came in with deer meat, and the men who cooked prepared the meat for all. When the meat was done, they ate, and when they were through eating, some of the men said among themselves that they were tired, and retired to sleep. Some of the other men sat up, and began to talk about the man who always appeared when making an attack, and told who they thought it was; but no one ever knew who this man was, for they never saw him after the battle. After failing to find out who he was, they all went to sleep.

The next morning, after they had eaten their breakfast, they began to travel home again. They traveled all that day, and in the afternoon they sent a man on ahead to give the signal of their coming, and to give the news of the victory, and about the man who had appeared in the lead and then left them. Then they traveled on until evening, when they entered their village, and were met by many of the older folks.

After they had entered the village, and darkness came, the big ceremony began. They danced all night, continuing till morning. Weksalahos delivered to his grandmother the scalp that was given him by the chief. She then participated in the dancing with the people in honor of the warriors.

Weksalahos then began his old ways, going around the village to the ash piles, and eating the waste parched corn that he found. It was his habit to go around the village for food.

Long after this the chief again announced that a war-party was going to go out. He appointed a certain time to start. Weksalahos had a habit of being around about the village, and heard of this announcement, went straight on to his home, and told his folks what had been said. He said he wanted to go again. So day after day he looked for the appointed day. Some time afterward the chief announced that he wanted to start out the next day. Weksalahos retired to bed that night, and lay awake nearly all night, waiting for the next day to come.

When morning came, all started out at the same time, and there was Weksalahos in the midst of the warriors. They traveled all that day until late in the afternoon, and the hunters went out to hunt for food, and when they camped the hunters began to come in with the deer meat and some buffalo meat. When all these things were done, the smoke ceremony was performed under the directions of the head warrior by the two men who were serving under him as leading warriors. Then they cooked. When the cooking was all done, the food was first offered to the main warrior; then, after he had eaten, the food was eaten by all. After the eating was over, some went to sleep, and some of the men sat up part of the night.

Next morning, while the men were cooking their breakfast, the chief warrior announced to his warriors that on the following day, when traveling, spies should be sent out to spy, and that the following day he should select a certain place where they should meet the spies on their return. About this time the cooking was done, and it remained for them to eat their breakfast. After breakfast they started out to where they supposed they could find the enemy. In the afternoon of that day the spies were sent out to look for the enemy's village.

They continued their journey all that day until late in the evening, when they stopped to wait for the spies and hunters. About dark the hunters came, and the spies also, one after another. The spies had failed to locate the enemy, and the hunters returned, some with game and some without anything. After the return of the spies the smoke ceremony was performed, and they began to cook meat enough to go all around. They then ate, sat up and waited for the remaining spy, for there was still one out. Late that night he came in, having succeeded in locating the enemy. He reported to the head warrior what he had seen while out spying. After telling all about the location of the village, how fast he had to travel, and what a hard time he had had, having nothing to eat, and tired as he could be, he was given something to eat. While this spy was eating, the chief warrior announced to his warriors that early on the next morning he wanted to make the attack on the enemy; that they should get ready to start out that night in order to make the attack early next morning. While this spy was resting, the rest of the men were getting ready.

As soon as the man who was eating got through, they began to set out on the trip. They continued for the rest of the night, until next morning, when they reached the enemy's village. Weksalahos was of course in the midst of the party. When they were near to the village, the chief warrior ordered his men to get ready for the attack, and Weksalahos to remain with the things that they had left behind.

When these men started towards the village, Weksalahos left the things, and went straight to the creek in haste, dived in the water, changed himself, went on ahead of everybody, and made the attack first. So just when everybody made a run towards the village, the chief warrior being in the lead, because he was a faster runner than any of the other men, he saw the same man that they had always seen before making an attack, and who attracted everybody's attention, as they wondered who he was. This unknown man entered the village long before any of the rest of the men had reached it, and already excited the enemy, some leaving their lodges without their weapons, and killed those who thought to kill him. He went through the whole village, and came around the other way without letting any one see him or meet him. So while the rest of the warriors were fighting, Weksalahos turned back to the creek, dived, and turned himself into a small boy again; then he went back to the place he was told to remain at till the rest of the warriors came back from battle.

Later that morning the warriors came, as they had always done when going out on the war-path. Some of the men had captives along with them, and some had scalps, and had already cut sticks on which to hang the scalps. Finally there came the leading warrior, who gave a scalp to Weksalahos, this being the fourth one he had received from the same man, and this the fourth time he had been with the war-party. Weksalahos then had some one to cut him a stick like the rest of them had, to put the scalp on.

In the morning all turned back for their homes. They continued their journey all that day, taking a straight route. This was hard traveling. So Weksalahos had to fall behind the rest of the men; but since the chief warrior had made some kind of friendly terms with him, he stayed behind, in order to protect him from the enemy, as he was afraid they would pursue them. So some of the men who knew their business, while traveling, went one way to hunt for their food for the night, while the other men traveled on and on, until darkness overtook them, and they camped for the night, waiting for the other men to come in from the hunt. So the rest of the men, who had camped, built fires in order to be ready for the hunters coming in with their meat. Finally the hunters came with their deer, turkeys, and buffalo meat, and men, being men ready for this, commenced to cook the meat for the whole party. When this was done, they commenced to eat their food. After the eating was done, the men set the prairie on fire, to show the people at home that they were victorious. At night the burning prairie could be seen a long way. As we now know, when we see a prairie fire a long way off, it looks like gold in the sky at night. After all this was done, they all retired to sleep a full night this time.

On the next morning a fog appeared at the village, this being weather for a warrior who has great powers in sending out war-parties. During each of the four times that Weksalahos had been with the war-party this fog had occurred at the home village.

In the morning, after they had eaten their breakfast, they started for their homes again, making their journey faster than ever. But Weksalahos would stay with the crowd. In the afternoon they sent Gusseyos on ahead to show some sign of their coming. The place he was sent to was called "Place-where-Warriors-give-Signals-on-their-Way-Home-from-War." This was a little high point where a person would be seen by everybody; and after this signal was given to the people, they would shout out. So on the following day the man they had sent out ahead reached the high point, going forward a short distance, then back again, and so on, about four times, so that when the people saw his movements, they knew that their warriors were coming home victorious.

In the evening the warriors entered the village with their captives and scalps. As we know that Weksalahos was in the midst of the party, he delivered his fourth scalp to his grandmother. After they had arrived, the dances at once began, continuing the whole night long. Early in the morning the old women went from one lodge to another, singing about the warriors who were in the war-party that was sent out and had returned. In the crowd of women was Weksalahos' grandmother, and when night came, the dances went on as usual. At this time, Weksalahos would visit the chief pretty often, and there he would get something to eat and take it home to his grandfather and grandmother.

Later on, while Weksalahos was home one night, he asked his grandmother to go to the chief and ask for his oldest sister, saying that Light-of-the-Prairie-Fire-Set-the-Evening-after-Battle-Signal-of-Victory-to-the-Home-People wanted to marry her. But the old woman refused, and said she didn't think the young woman would accept him. But he kept on coaxing the old woman to go and try. So she went on to the chief's lodge, and entered. She saw a great big crowd of men in the lodge, sitting up, and was asked by the chief to tell why she had come so late. She said Light-of-the-Prairie-Fire-Set-the-Evening-after-Battle-Signal-of-Victory-to-the-Home-People sent her to ask if his oldest sister could be married to him. As soon as she said this, the chief's sister quickly replied, saying that it didn't make any difference who he was, she would not accept him, and the old woman was chased out by Kedox, who was then a servant for the chief. On her return to her own lodge, she told what the young woman had said. Again Weksalahos coaxed her to go back again and say that Fog-that-Comes-in-the-Village-Sign-of-Absent-War-party's-Victory-on-Way-Home wanted to marry his oldest sister. So the old woman returned to the chief's lodge, and when she had entered the chief asked her to tell why she had come. She again said that Fog-that-Comes-in-the-Village-Sign-of-Absent-War-party's-Victory-on-Way-Home was wanting to marry his oldest sister. As soon as she had said this, the chief's sister replied that she had told the old woman it didn't make any difference who he was, she would not accept him, and the old woman was again chased out of the lodge by Kedox, for he himself was always wanting that same chance, and he wished for the time to come when she would accept him instead of some one else.

The old woman returned to her lodge, and told Weksalahos that the girl had refused again, and said she didn't think any one would accept him, especially as he was so dirty and small. But again Weksalahos coaxed her to go back and tell the chief that Person-who-would-bring-Captives-Alive wanted to marry his oldest sister, and that she had been sent by the same man as before. So she turned back to the chief's lodge, and when she had entered the chief asked her why she had come. She said that Person-who-would-bring-Captives-Alive had sent her to ask if there could be any arrangement made for his oldest sister to marry him. As she said this, the young woman again quickly spoke, saying it didn't make any difference who he was, she would never accept him, and the old woman was again chased out by Kedox, who said, "Who could ever have that old stinking thing for a husband!"

When she returned, she told Weksalahos what the girl had said, and that she had refused him. But Weksalahos again coaxed his grandmother to try once more, and this time to say that Man-having-four-Buffalo sent her to ask if he could not marry the chief's oldest sister. So she again turned back to the chief's lodge, and on entering the chief asked her to tell why she had come. This time Kedox was very near chasing her out before she had a chance to say why she had come. So she told the chief that Man-having-four-Buffalo had told her to ask him if he could marry his oldest sister. Just then, when she had said this, the young woman again said that it didn't make any difference who he was, she would never accept him. Then, before the old woman was chased out, the chief spoke to her, saying: "I regret that my sister has refused so many times, but if that fellow can accept my youngest sister for his wife, he may have her." The old woman returned to her lodge, and told about this young woman again refusing, and how the chief had offered his youngest sister to Weksalahos for a wife. So Weksalahos said to his grandmother that he knew he could get one of the chief's sisters any how, whether he got the oldest one or not. Then Weksalahos was satisfied.

As soon as he was told of this, he at once started for the chief's lodge to become the chief's brother-in-law. While everybody was sitting up, he entered the lodge, and was asked to pass on to his future wife's bed. Then, while these men were sitting up, Weksalahos and his wife went to bed, and those who sat up heard Weksalahos urinating on the bed.

Then all the men went out to their homes to sleep, and on the next morning the mother of Weksalahos' wife had to hang out the robes to dry. After eating his breakfast, he went to his home instead of staying at the chief's place; and from this time on, when night came, he would go to his wife's lodge. His wife was the ugliest one of the four sisters; she had great sores under her chin.

Some time afterwards the people heard that buffalo were seen near the village, and so the men all went down to drive them closer to the village, and after driving them closer, the men surrounded the buffalo and killed all of them. This was the way the people of those times killed buffalo. This was during the daytime, so Weksalahos was then at home.

Weksalahos at once asked his grandmother to go to the place where the men were butchering the buffalo and get him a tongue, but the old woman refused and said that some one might cut her hand, but he kept on asking her, and finally she got up and said, "I am sure that some one will hurt me." But Weksalahos said to her, "Grandmother, you go on and do as I tell you." She then went to the place where they were butchering, and when she arrived she tried to pull the head to one side and cut the tongue. Then came Kedox, and cut her on her face and wrist, and told her to go back home, and never do that again. So she cried and went home; and when she entered her lodge, there was Weksalahos. She said to him, "Now you see what Kedox did on your account!"

Now Weksalahos said to his grandmother that time after time they had been abused by many people, and that he had endured everything that anybody had done to them; that from time to time he had thought he would always live a poor boy, but that the time had come when he must make himself known to the people, so that any one as poor as he was might in time become a man, and some time a chief. So at this very time, when his grandmother was bleeding, he stepped out to the creek, and did as he had done while on the war-path. He went to the creek, dived in the water, and came out with the appearance he had had in making attacks on the enemy, and from this time on he never changed his appearance again.

Weksalahos went straight to the place where the people were butchering, and when the people saw him they knew that it was the same man that they had seen when making attacks on the enemy; he had come again. He was dressed the same as when with the war-party. When the people saw him, they went toward him to meet him. He then asked who had cut his grandmother's face and wrist. The crowd then yelled and said it was Kedox that had done the cutting. Then everybody began to say to one another, "That's the man that we always saw in time of war." So Weksalahos told Kedox that he would not be killed; but if he wanted to pay him for so much injury as he had done his people, he could do so.

While the crowd was there, Weksalahos made a long talk to them regarding his boyhood, saying that never in his life as a boy had he done any harm to any one, nor had he ever got mad at any one; when they abused him, he endured it; but now he had decided to show himself out to the world just as he had done while on the war-path; that it was his business, when out with a war-party, to lead them from danger from time to time when a chief warrior would attack his enemies, and there were times when he would first enter the village, and draw the enemies out, so they would be without their weapons; that now the time had come when he had got tired of all the abuse offered himself and his folks.

So all the people who were butchering the buffalo came around the place where Weksalahos was to see him and to hear him. The rest of the chiefs at once had meat taken to Weksalahos' place, and Weksalahos ordered the people not to kill Kedox, but to pack some of the meat to his place. Weksalahos then had these men give Kedox a heavy load, while he took a bow-string for rope, and tied the meat together, then put the string into Kedox's mouth, and started him off at once to his lodge. Kedox was in front of Weksalahos, and when Kedox would stop to rest, Weksalahos would punch him with the flint point of an arrow. So he hurt Kedox so much that he had no chance to rest. Kedox was then about to split in two, for the box-string was small, and it cut his mouth farther back than the mouths of human beings; so the only thing to save him from being split in two was to hurry to Weksalahos' place.

Weksalahos went on ahead of everybody, for he knew that the men would do the rest of the work for him, and he went on to his home. On entering the lodge, the old woman told him that there were better places where strangers were received, and she also told him that she was poor; for she did not know who he was. But finally he told his grandmother that he was Weksalahos, or Boy-who-ate-from-the-Corn-Mill. He told her how he had got tired of the way they had been treated by the people who were their enemies. After making himself known to his grandmother, he went on to his wife's place, and on entering, called her to go with him. The three sisters began to talk about him. They said among themselves, "I wonder if that is Weksalahos."

After Weksalahos and his wife left the lodge, they went straight on to the creek, and when they reached it, Weksalahos bade his wife get in the water and dive once. After she dived, she came out of the water, her features changed, and she was better looking. They then turned back to his wife's home, and on their entering the people saw how both of them had changed to be better looking. So it came to pass that the three sisters began to like Weksalahos.

The chief of the village now got several women to sew up several tanned buffalo hides for tipis for Weksalahos' use. This work was to be done immediately.

The following day Weksalahos went back to his grandmother's to heal up the wounds that she had received when going after the tongue for him. To heal her, he used his breath. He blew on the wounds, and they were healed. That night, after he had revealed himself, he and his wife lived with his wife's folks.

The next day the chief called forth his men, and when the people had come around the place, they asked why he had called them forth. Then he announced to his people that they knew about his brother-in-law, who, with his folks, was poor and was living with them; that he wanted the men to go after the boy's old folks, taking robes along, with four men to each robe, so that they could carry the old folks to their new home that had been built by the people; but the men were hired to go to this place. He then announced again the way Weksalahos had done things on the war-path; that he wanted him to be a great chief, over himself, for Weksalahos was a great warrior, having greater powers than any one else; that he was to be leader in everything, such as sending out hunting or war parties.

The old folks were brought to their new home, and everybody thought a great deal of them. Whenever any one returned from hunting, the meat was brought to Weksalahos' folks, and Weksalahos lived well, for he was over the chief in powers. When Weksalahos was living with his wife, her three sisters wished they had accepted him when he had asked to marry the oldest; and the oldest one was worse off than the next two, for she wished that she had Weksalahos for a husband.

The time came when Weksalahos decided to form a large party of men to go out on the war-path. As soon as he had told his brother-in-law that he wanted to send out this party, he had his servant announce it. This kind of an announcement was always made by a man who was selected, who would go through the village, talking and telling all about what had been said. So the man selected made it known to every one in the village that all who wished to go with the war-party should be ready in a certain length of time, which was two days. Weksalahos wanted to go out on this expedition. This news then spread out among the other warriors, for everybody was anxious to see the way Weksalahos would do; for at other times, when he had gone with the war-party, he had been seen as a poor boy, and had remained where they had left their things. So when the time came, early that morning, there was a fog; this was the kind of weather that happened for all great warriors who had great powers.

On the following day the warriors started out under the leadership of Weksalahos and his brother-in-law, Young-Man-Chief. There were a great many warriors who always followed Young-Man-Chief on any war-party, and since another great warrior had joined him, there were many more who followed them on this occasion. So they traveled all that day, and in the evening some of the men went away to hunt for game, for the warriors to eat to give them strength. The rest of the men went on until late that day, and camped. The men built their fires. They had to build two fires, one being for the smoke ceremony and the other for cooking. Here the men waited for the hunters to come in. Finally, late that night, the hunters came in, one after another, with meat of all kinds, some having turkeys, some deer meat, and some with buffalo meat.

It was a rule that before the smoke ceremony was performed every one should be present. So after the men were in, the smoke ceremony was performed. Before doing this, Weksalahos told his warriors to watch the place where the ashes from the pipe were emptied. So the men all had their eyes fixed on the man who was going through the smoke performance, and when he emptied the pipe during this performance, everybody had to be pretty silent, for this was the rule. So after this was done, some of the men spoke out and said that where the ashes were emptied they saw a scalp. Then Weksalahos told them this was to foretell what was to happen, and it indicated they were to defeat their enemies, causing them to lose a great many of their men; that when sending out war-parties, these things always happened when he who had great powers in sending out war-parties was to be successful.

After these performances were over, all the men went to bed on the ground. The next morning all of the men woke up, and the smoke ceremony was repeated; then the cooking was begun, and when it was all ready, the main warrior was first offered food to eat, and then all the rest of the men commenced to eat.

When this was over, all again started on the journey. They were of course headed towards the south. They traveled all that day until late in the evening. Some hunters were sent out to hunt while the rest of the men took a straight course. Late in the evening they again camped, the men built fires again, and waited for the hunters to come, who finally came, one after another, with their game that they had killed, all excepting one man. They then of course did some things that were necessary, such as the smoke ceremony and the cooking. It was then a custom that after one day's traveling all the men who were out on the war-path hunting and spying were to be regarded in the same way. After all had eaten, they waited for the man who was still out. Finally, about midnight, he came, and reported that he had found the enemy's village. After he had told all, it was referred to Weksalahos as to what he thought about it, that he might tell what he thought was best to be done. So he announced to his men that that was all he could wish any man to report, and that it was all right to start off that same night, to be ready to attack the enemy at their homes early in the morning. While they were getting ready, the man who had brought the news was given something to eat. After he got through, all started on their way to the enemy's village, and so they traveled all the rest of the night, until early next morning, when they reached the enemy's village.

All stopped and got ready, and this time all the men knew who would be the first one to reach the village. This was before any of the enemies got out of their lodges. Then all were ready, and made the attack. Of course Weksalahos reached the village first; he was in the lead of all when they ran towards their sleeping enemies. After they had waked the enemies, and some of them had stepped out, Weksalahos and the chief warrior did the first fighting, and the remainder of the men did the rest. Then all turned back to the place where they had left their things.

After all the men had arrived at the place, they at once turned back to their homes. Now everybody had a scalp, and some had a prisoner. This time Weksalahos had a scalp of his own instead of some one having to give him one. They traveled the rest of the day, and took the straightest route. The men did not have to wait for Weksalahos any more, for he traveled faster than they. About evening some of the men went hunting, and before leaving, the crowd were notified where they were to meet the rest of the men when they should come back. Late on that day all stopped to camp and waited for the men to come in from the hunt. It was Weksalahos' rule that whatever was done while on the way should be done the same as though they were at home, instead of carrying on smoke ceremonies. So the fires were built in the common way, and that night they set the prairie on fire, so the people at home would see that their warriors were coming home from war victorious. Finally the hunters came in, one after another, with meat. After their arrival the men who were at the camp did the cooking, then they ate their supper, and some of the men sat up part of the night, talking about what they had done during the entire battle. Finally they went to sleep, and on the next morning there was a thick fog, and on that day they started for their homes. Weksalahos did not have to be waited for this time.

In the afternoon they sent a man on ahead to spread the news to the people. So this man whom they had sent on ahead had to travel faster than the crowd, and the crowd kept on traveling until late that evening, when they reached their home village.

They were met by the people as victors. As soon as they arrived, when the people met them, it being the custom, the warriors presented their scalps to the women, and those who were married presented scalps to their wives. After these things were done, dances of all kinds began in honor of the warriors, the dancing continuing all night long. The women folks came every morning to sing for Weksalahos songs called "victories." These songs were heard when any warrior came home victorious.

Weksalahos was now coming to be a great chief among his people. So this first war-party he had sent out was the beginning of his life as a great warrior; instead of going to his brother-in-law, the men would come and visit Weksalahos at night and stay all day long. From this time on he sent out war-parties at all times, and always came home victorious. After he had showed all these things to these people, he made some of the warriors famous, giving his powers to some men whom he thought most of.

When the proper time came, Weksalahos called forth all the men whom he had led to war, and whom he had gained battles for. When all had come, they asked him to say to his people whatever he had to say. So these were his words: "I have long been with you people, and in the early part of my life I lived a poor boy; I went from one place to another, begging for food to eat, and in those times I had a hard time to get along with the people, but to show them how kind I was I endured all the troubles that they made for me and my folks; the time came when I made up my mind to be somebody; I showed myself by going to war, and made the warriors famous through the influence of my powers; I made myself known to the people, was made a great chief and warrior among you; now I have left my powers to you; I want now to leave you, and there will be times in the future that I will help the one who uses my powers the way I used them, in sending out war-parties." This he said, referring to some whom he had made to become great warriors, and to whom he had left his powers. All these things he left to the world for future generations.

So Weksalahos was going to leave his people, and be something else, and all those who wished to do so could. He then in the presence of everybody ascended into the sky, where he still exists as what we call *"Hossilaariwa"* ("Shooting Star").

In the early days this star was often seen in the early morning when men went out on the war-path; and whenever the shooting star came to the earth, it would leave a great big hole in the ground, and there would grow from the stone brushes that pipe-stems are made from; and when this occurred in connection with some of the warriors, it would indicate victory for him, and if the place was found, some of the leading warriors would cut the pipe-stem for their own use from the brush that grew there.

So the village remained under the lead of the former chief, but some became changed in form, though most remained human beings. War-parties were still carried on by the people, and sometimes, of course, the warriors would get aid from Weksalahos, the star shooting out in the direction the war-party was going; then they would of course know they had received aid from him, and then at the same time some of the men had his powers. Weksalahos was also known by the name of "Sign-to-the-People-that-their-Warriors-were-about-to-Return."

The Sacred Hunter
(Zuñi)

Once, long, long ago, at Háwikuh, there lived a maiden most beautiful. In her earlier years her father, who was a great priest, had devoted her to sacred things, and therefore he kept her always in the house secure from the gaze of all men, and thus she grew.

She was so beautiful that when the Sun looked down along one of the straight beams of his own light, if one of those beams chanced to pass through a chink in the roof, the sky-hole, or the windows of the upper part of the maiden's room, he beheld her and wondered at her rare beauty, unable to compare it with anything he saw in his great journeys round about the worlds. Thus, as the maiden grew apace and became a young woman, the Sun loved her exceedingly, and as time went on he became so enamored of her that he descended to earth and entered on one of his own beams of light into her apartment, so that suddenly, while she was sitting one noon-day weaving pretty baskets, there stood before her a glorious youth, gloriously dressed. It was the Sun-father. He looked upon her gently and lovingly; she looked upon him not fearfully: and so it came about that she loved him and he loved her, and he won her to be his wife. And many were the days in which he visited her and dwelt with her for a space at noon-time; but as she was alone mostly, or as she kept sitting weaving her trays when any one of the family entered her apartment, no one suspected this.

Now, as she knew that she had been devoted to sacred things, and that if she explained how it was that she was a mother she would not be believed, she was greatly exercised in mind and heart. She therefore decided that when her child was born she would put it away from her.

When the time came, the child one night was born. She carefully wrapped the little baby boy in some soft cotton-wool, and in the middle of the night stole out softly over the roof-tops, and, silently descending, laid the child on the sheltered side of a heap of refuse near the little stream that flows by Háwikuh, in the valley below. Then, mourning as a mother will mourn for her offspring, she returned to her room and lay herself down, poor thing, to rest.

As daylight was breaking in the east, and the hills and the valleys were coming forth one after another from the shadows of night, a Deer with her two little brightly-speckled fawns descended from the hills to the south across the valley, with ears and eyes alert, and stopped at the stream to drink. While drinking they were startled by an infant's cry, and, looking up, they saw dust and cotton-wool and other things flying about in the air, almost as if a little whirlwind were blowing on the site of the refuse-heap where the child had been laid. It was the child, who, waking and finding itself alone, hungry, and cold, was crying and throwing its little hands about.

"Bless my delight!" cried the Deer to her fawns. "I have this day found a waif, a child, and though it be human it shall be mine; for, see, my children, I love you so much that surely I could love another."

Thereupon she approached the little infant, and breathed her warm breath upon it and caressed it until it became quiet, and then after wrapping about it the cotton-wool, she gently lifted it on her broad horns, and, turning, carried it steadily away toward the south, followed on either side by her children, who kept crying out *"Neh! neh!"* in their delight.

The home of this old Deer and her little ones, where all her children had been born for years, was south of Háwikuh, in the valley that turns off among the ledges of rocks near the little spring called Póshaan. There, in the shelter of a clump of piñon and cedar trees, was a soft and warm retreat, winter and summer, and this was the lair of the Deer and her young.

The Deer was no less delighted than surprised next morning to find that the infant had grown apace, for she had suckled it with her own milk, and that before the declining of the sun it was already creeping about. And greater was her surprise and delight, as day succeeded day, to find that the child grew even more swiftly than grow the children of the Deer. Behold! on the evening of the fourth day it was running about and playing with its foster brother and sister. Nor was it slow of foot, even as compared with those little Deer. Behold! yet greater cause for wonder, on the eighth day it was a youth fair to look upon—looking upon itself and seeing that it had no clothing, and wondering why it was not clothed, like its brother and sister, in soft warm hair with pretty spots upon it.

As time went on, this little foster-child of the Deer (it must always be remembered that it was the offspring of the Sun-father himself), in playing with his brother and sister, and in his runnings about, grew wondrously strong, and even swifter of foot than the Deer themselves, and learned the language of the Deer and all their ways.

When he had become perfected in all that a Deer should know, the Deer-mother led him forth into the wilds and made him acquainted with the great herd to which she belonged. They were exceedingly happy with this addition to their number; much they loved him, and so sagacious was the youth that he soon became the leader of the Deer of the Háwikuh country.

When these Deer and the Antelopes were out on the mesas ranging to and fro, there at their head ran the swift youth. The soles of his feet became as hard as the hoofs of the Deer, the skin of his person strong and dark, the hair of his head long and waving and as soft as the hair on the sides of the Deer themselves.

It chanced one morning, late that summer, that the uncle of the maiden who had cast away her child went out hunting, and he took his way southward past Póshaan, the lair of the Deer-mother and her foster-child. As he traversed the borders of the great mesas that lie beyond, he saw a vast herd of Deer gathered, as people gather in council. They were quiet and seemed to be listening intently to some one in their midst. The hunter stole along carefully on hands and knees, twisting himself among the bushes until he came nearer; and what was his wonder when he beheld, in the midst of the Deer, a splendid youth, broad of shoulder, tall and strong of limb, sitting nude and graceful on the ground, and the old Deer and the young seemed to be paying attention to what he was saying. The hunter rubbed his eyes and looked again; and again he looked, shading his eyes with his hands. Then he elevated himself to peer yet more closely, and the sharp eyes of the youth discovered him. With a shout he lifted himself to his feet and sped away like the wind, followed by the whole herd, their hoofs thundering, and soon they were all out of sight.

The hunter dropped his bow and stood there musing; then picking it up, he turned himself about and ran toward Háwikuh as fast as he could. When he arrived he related to the father of the girl what he had seen. The old priest summoned his hunters and warriors and bade the uncle repeat the story. Many there were who said: "You have seen an apparition, and of evil omen to your family, alas! alas!"

"No," said he, "I looked, and again I looked, and yet again, and again, and I avow to you that what I saw was as plain and as mortal as the Deer themselves."

Convinced at last, the council decided to form a grand hunt, and word was given from the house-tops that on the fourth day from that day a hunt should be undertaken—that the southern mesa should be surrounded, and that the people should gather in from all sides and encompass the herd there, in order that this wonderful youth should not escape being seen, or possibly captured.

Now, when the Deer had gone to a safe distance they slackened their pace and called to their leader not to fear. And the old foster-mother of the youth for the first time related to him, as she had related to them long ago, that he was the child of mortals, telling how she had found him.

The youth sat with his head bowed, thinking of these things. Then he raised his head proudly, and said: "What though I be the child of mortals, they have not loved me: they have cast me from their midst, therefore will I be faithful to thee alone."

But the old Deer-mother said to him: "Hush, my child! Thou art but a mortal, and though thou might'st live on the roots of the trees and the bushes and plants that mature in autumn, yet surely in the winter time thou could'st not live, for my supply of milk will be withholden, and the fruits and the nuts will all be gone."

And the older members of that large herd gathered round and repeated what she had been saying. And they said: "We are aware that we shall be hunted now, as is the invariable custom when our herd has been discovered, on the fourth day from the day on which we were first seen. Amongst the people who come there will be, no doubt, those who will seek you; and you must not endeavor to escape. Even we ourselves are accustomed to give up our lives to the brave hunters among this people, for many of them are sacred of thought, sacred of heart, and make due sacrifices unto us, that our lives in other form may be spared unceasingly."

A splendid Deer rose from the midst of the herd, and, coming forward, laid his cheek on the cheek of the boy, and said: "Yet we love you, but we must now part from you. And, in order that you may be like unto other mortals, only exceeding them, accompany me to the Land of the Souls of Men, where sit in council the Gods of the Sacred Dance and Drama, the Gods of the Spirit World."

To all this the youth, being convinced, agreed. And on that same day the Deer who had spoken set forward, the swift youth running by his side, toward the Lake of the Dead. On and on they sped, and as night was falling they came to the borders of that lake, and the lights were shining over its middle and the Gardens of the Sacred Dance. And the old Drama-woman and the old Drama-man were walking on its shores, back and forth, calling across to each other.

As the Deer neared the shore of the lake, he turned and said to his companion: "Step in boldly with me. Ladders of rushes will rise to receive you, and down underneath the waters into the great Halls of the Dead and of the Sacred Dance we will be borne gently and swiftly."

Then they stepped into the lake. Brighter and lighter it grew. Great ladders of rushes and flags lifted themselves from the water, and upon them the Deer and his companion were borne downward into halls of splendor, lighted by many lights and fires. And in the largest chamber the gods were sitting in council silently. *Páutiwa,* the Sun-priest of the Sacred Drama (*Kâkâ*), *Shúlawitsi* (the God of Fire), with his torch of ever-living flame, and many others were there; and when the strangers arrived they greeted and were greeted, and were given a place in the light of the central fire. And in through the doors of the west and the north and the east and the south filed long rows of sacred dancers, those who had passed through the Lake of the Dead, clad in cotton mantles, white as the daylight, finely embroidered, decked with many a treasure shell and turquoise stone. These performed their sacred rites, to the delight of the gods and the wonder of the Deer and his foster-brother.

And when the dancers had retired, Páutiwa, the Sun-priest of the Sacred Dance, arose, and said: "What would'st thou?"—though he knew full well beforehand.

"What would'st thou, oh, Deer of the forest mesas, with thy companion, thy foster-brother; for not thinking of nothing would one visit the home of the *Kâkâ.*"

Then the Deer lifted his head and told his story.

"It is well," said the gods.

"Appear, my faithful one," said Páutiwa to Shúlawitsi. And Shúlawitsi appeared and waved his flame around the youth, so that he became convinced of his mortal origin and of his dependence upon food prepared by fire. Then the gods who speak the speech of men gathered around and breathed upon the youth, and touched to his lips moisture from their own mouths, and touched the portals of his ears with oil from their own ears, and thus was the youth made acquainted with both the speech and the understanding of the speech of mortal man. Then the gods called out, and there were brought before them fine garments of white cotton embroidered in many colors, rare necklaces of sacred shell with many turquoises and coral-like stones and shells strung in their midst, and all that the most beautifully clad of our ancients could have glorified their appearance with. Such things they brought forth, and, making them into a bundle, laid them at the feet of the youth. Then they said: "Oh, youth, oh, brother and father, since thou art the child of the Sun, who is the father of us all, go forth with thy foster-brother to thy last meeting-place with him and with his people; and when on the day after the morrow hunters shall gather from around thy country, some of ye, oh, Deer," said he, turning to the Deer, "yield thyselves up that ye may die as must thy kind ever continue to die, for the sake of this thy brother."

"I will lead them," simply replied the Deer. "Thanks."

And Páutiwa continued: "Here full soon wilt thou be gathered in our midst, or with the winds and the mists of the air at night-time wilt sport, ever-living. Go ye forth, then, carrying this bundle, and, as ye best know how, prepare this our father and child for his reception among men. And, O son and father," continued the priest-god, turning to the youth, "Fear not! Happy wilt thou be in the days to come, and treasured among men. Hence thy birth. Return with the Deer and do as thou art told to do. Thy uncle, leading his priest-youths, will be foremost in the hunt. He will pursue thee and thy foster-mother. Lead him far away; and when thou hast so led him, cease running and turn and wait, and peacefully go home whither he guides thee."

The sounds of the Sacred Dance came in from the outer apartments, and the youth and the Deer, taking their bundle, departed. More quickly than they had come they sped away; and on the morning when the hunters of Háwikuh were setting forth, the Deer gathered themselves in a vast herd on the southern mesa, and they circled about the youth and instructed him how to unloose the bundle he had brought. Then closer and closer came the Deer to the youth and bade him stand in his nakedness, and they ran swiftly about him, breathing fierce, moist breaths until hot steam enveloped him and bathed him from head to foot, so that he was purified, and his skin was softened, and his hair hung down in a smooth yet waving mass at the back of his head. Then the youth put on the costume, one article after another, he having seen them worn by the Gods of the Sacred Dance, and by the dancers; and into his hair at the back, under the band which he placed round his temples, he thrust the glowing feathers of the macaw which had been given him. Then, seeing that there was still one article left,—a little string of conical shells,—he asked what that was for; and the Deer told him to tie it about his knee.

The Deer gathered around him once more, and the old chief said: "Who among ye are willing to die?" And, as if it were a festive occasion to which they were going, many a fine Deer bounded forth, striving for the place of those who were to die, until a large number were gathered, fearless and ready. Then the Deer began to move.

Soon there was an alarm. In the north and the west and the south and the east there was cause for alarm. And the Deer began to scatter, and then to assemble and scatter again. At last the hunters with drawn bows came running in, and soon their arrows were flying in the midst of those who were devoted, and Deer after Deer fell, pierced to the heart or other vital part.

At last but few were left,—amongst them the kind old Deer-mother and her two children; and, taking the lead, the glorious youth, although encumbered by his new dress, sped forth with them. They ran and ran, the fleetest of the tribe of Háwikuh pursuing them; but all save the uncle and his brave sons were soon left far behind. The youth's foster-brother was soon slain, and the youth, growing angry, turned about; then bethinking himself of the words of the gods, he sped away again. So his foster-sister, too, was killed; but he kept on, his old mother alone running behind him. At last the uncle and his sons overtook the old mother, and they merely caught her and turned her away, saying: "Faithful to the last she has been to this youth." Then they renewed the chase for the youth; and he at last, pretending weariness, faced about and stood like a stag at bay. As soon as they approached, he dropped his arms and lowered his head. Then he said: "Oh, my uncle" (for the gods had told who would find him)—"Oh, my uncle, what wouldst thou? Thou hast killed my brothers and sisters; what wouldst thou with me?"

The old man stopped and gazed at the youth in wonder and admiration of his fine appearance and beautiful apparel. Then he said: "Why dost thou call me uncle?"

"Because, verily," replied the youth, "thou art my uncle, and thy niece, my maiden-mother, gave birth to me and cast me away upon a dust-heap; and then my noble Deer found me and nourished me and cherished me."

The uncle and his sons gazed still with wonder. Then they thought they saw in the youth's clear eyes and his soft, oval face a likeness to the mother, and they said: "Verily, this which he says is true." Then they turned about and took him by the hands gently and led him toward Háwikuh, while one of them sped forward to test the truth of his utterances.

When the messenger arrived at Háwikuh he took his way straight to the house of the priest, and told him what he had heard. The priest in anger summoned the maiden.

"Oh, my child," said he, "hast thou done this thing which we are told thou hast done?" And he related what he had been told.

"Nay, no such thing have I done," said she.

"Yea, but thou hast, oh, unnatural mother! And who was the father?" demanded the old priest with great severity.

Then the maiden, thinking of her Sun-lover, bowed her head in her lap and rocked herself to and fro, and cried sorely. And then she said: "Yea, it is true; so true that I feared thy wrath, oh, my father! I feared thy shame, oh, my mother! and what could I do?" Then she told of her lover, the Sun,—with tears she told it, and she cried out: "Bring back my child that I may nurse him and love but him alone, and see him the father of children!"

By this time the hunters arrived, some bringing game, but others bringing in their midst this wondrous youth, on whom each man and maiden in Háwikuh gazed with delight and admiration.

They took him to the home of his priest-grandfather; and as though he knew the way he entered the apartment of his mother, and she, rising and opening wide her arms, threw herself on his breast and cried and cried. And he laid his hand on her head, and said: "Oh, mother, weep not, for I have come to thee, and I will cherish thee."

So was the foster-child of the Deer restored to his mother and his people.

Wondrously wise in the ways of the Deer and their language was he—so much so that, seeing them, he understood them. This youth made little ado of hunting, for he knew that he could pay those rites and attentions to the Deer that were most acceptable, and made them glad of death at the hand of the hunter. And ere long, so great was his knowledge and success, and his preciousness in the eyes of the Master of Life, that by his will and his arm alone the tribe of Háwikuh was fed and was clad in buckskins.

A rare and beautiful maiden he married, and most happy was he with her.

It was his custom to go forth early in the morning, when the Deer came down to drink or stretch themselves and walk abroad and crop the grass; and, taking his bow and quiver of arrows, he would go to a distant mesa, and, calling the Deer around him, and following them as swiftly as they ran, he would strike them down in great numbers, and, returning, say to his people: "Go and bring in my game, giving me only parts of what I have slain and taking the rest yourselves."

So you can readily see how he and his people became the greatest people of Háwikuh. Nor is it marvelous that the sorcerers of that tribe should have grown envious of his prosperity, and sought to diminish it in many ways, wherein they failed.

At last one night the Master of Sorcerers in secret places raised his voice and cried: *"Weh-h-h-h! Weh-h-h-h-h!"* And round about him presently gathered all the sorcerers of the place, and they entered into a deep cavern, large and lighted by green, glowing fires, and there, staring at each other, they devised means to destroy this splendid youth, the child of the Sun.

One of their number stood forth and said: "I will destroy him in his own vocation. He is a hunter, and the Coyote loves well to follow the hunter." His words were received with acclamation, and the youth who had offered himself sped forth in the night to prepare, by incantation and with his infernal appliances, a disguise for himself.

On the next morning, when the youth went forth to hunt, an old Coyote sneaked behind him after he reached the mesas, and, following stealthily, waited his throwing down of the Deer; and when the youth had called and killed a number of Deer and sat down to rest on a fallen tree, the Coyote sneaked into sight. The youth, looking at him, merely thought: "He seeks the blood of my slain Deer," and he went on with his prayers and sacrifices to the dead of the Deer. But soon, stiffening his limbs, the Coyote swiftly scudded across the open, and, with a puff from his mouth and nostrils like a sneeze toward the youth, threw himself against him and arose a man,—the same man who had offered his services in the council of the wizards—while the poor youth, falling over, ran away, a human being still in heart and mind, but in form a coyote.

Off to the southward he wandered, his tail dragging in the dust; and growing hungry he had naught to eat; and cold on the sides of the mesas he passed the night, and on the following morning wandered still, until at last, very hungry, he was fain even to nip the blades of grass and eat the berries of the juniper. Thus he became ill and worn; and one night as he was seeking a warm place to lay him down and die, he saw a little red light glowing from the top of a hillock. Toward this light he took his way, and when he came near he saw that it was shining up through the sky-hole of someone's house. He peered over the edge and saw an old Badger with his grizzly wife, sitting before a fire, not in the form of a badger but in the form of a little man, his badger-skin hanging beside him.

Then the youth said to himself: "I will cast myself down into their house, thus showing them my miserable condition." And as he tried to step down the ladder, he fell, *teng,* on the floor before them.

The Badgers were disgusted. They grabbed the Coyote, and hauling him up the ladder, threw him into the plain, where, *toonoo,* he fell far away and swooned from loss of breath. When he recovered his thoughts he again turned toward the glowing sky-hole, and, crawling feebly back, threw himself down into the room again. Again he was thrown out, but this time the Badger said: "It is marvelously strange that this Coyote, the miserable fellow, should insist on coming back, and coming back."

"I have heard," said the little old Badger-woman, "that our glorious beloved youth of Háwikuh was changed some time ago into a Coyote. It may be he. Let us see when he comes again if it be he. For the love of mercy, let us see!"

Ere long the youth again tried to clamber down the ladder, and fell with a thud on the floor before them. A long time he lay there senseless, but at last opened his eyes and looked about. The Badgers eagerly asked if he were the same who had been changed into a Coyote, or condemned to inhabit the form of one. The youth could only move his head in acquiescence.

Then the Badgers hastily gathered an emetic and set it to boil, and when ready they poured the fluid down the throat of the seeming Coyote, and tenderly held him and pitied him. Then they laid him before the fire to warm him. Then the old Badger, looking about in some of his burrows, found a sacred rock crystal, and heating it to glowing heat in the fire, he seared the palms of the youth's hands, the soles of his feet, and the crown of his head, repeating incantations as he performed this last operation, whereupon the skin burst and fell off, and the youth, haggard and lean, lay before them. They nourished him as best they could, and, when well recovered, sent him home to join his people again and render them happy. Clad in his own fine garments, happy of countenance and handsome as before, and, according to his regular custom, bearing a Deer on his back, returned the youth to his people, and there he lived most happily.

It is because this youth lived so long with the Deer and became acquainted with their every way and their every word, and taught all that he knew to his children and to others whom he took into his friendship, that we have today a class of men—the Sacred Hunters—who surpassingly understand the ways and the language of the Deer.

HÉASAILUHTIWA
(Zuñi)

In very ancient times, there lived at Tâ'ia, below the Zuñi Mountains, an old *shiwani* or priest-chief, who had a young son named *Héasailuhtiwa* ("Metal-hand"), famed throughout the land of the Zuñis for his success in hunting.

When very young, this lad had said to his parents: "My old ones, let me go away from the home of my fathers and dwell by myself."

"Why do you, a young boy, wish to go and dwell by yourself, my son? Know you not that you would fare but badly, for you are careless and forgetful? No, no! remain with us, that we may care for you."

But the boy answered: "Why should I fare badly? Can I not hunt my own game and roast the meat over the fire? It is because you never care to have me go forth alone that I wish to live by myself, for I long to travel far and hunt deer in the mountains of many countries: yet whenever I start forth you call me back, and it is painful to my longing thoughts thus to be held back when I would go forward."

It was not until the lad had spoken thus again and again, and once more, that the parents sadly yielded to his wish. They insisted, however, much to the boy's displeasure, that his younger sister, Waíasialuhtitsa, should go with him, only to look after his house, and to remind him here and there, at times, of his forgetfulness. So the brother and sister chose the lofty rooms of a high house in the upper part of the pueblo and lived there.

The boy each day went out hunting and failed not each time to bring in slain animals, while the sister cooked for him and looked after the house. Yet, although the boy was a great hunter, he never sacrificed to the Deer he had slain, nor to the Gods of Prey who delight in aiding the hunter who renews them; for the lad was forgetful and careless of all things.

One day he went forth over the mountain toward the north, until he came to the Waters of the Bear. There he started up a huge Buck, and, finding the trail, followed it far toward the northward. Yet, although swift of foot, the youth could not overtake the running Deer, and thus it happened that he went on and on, past mesas, valleys, and mountains, until he came to the brink of a great river which flows westwardly from the north. On the banks of this great river grew forests of cotton-wood, and into the thickets of these forests led the trail, straight toward the river bank. Just as the young man was about to follow the track to the bank, he thought he saw under a large tree in the midst of the thickets the form of the Deer, so, bending very low, he ran around close to the bank, and came up between the river and the thicket.

As he guardedly approached the tree, his eyes now following the track, now glancing up, he discovered a richly dressed, handsome young man, who called out to him: "How art thou these days, and whither art thou going?"

The young man straightened up, and quickly drawing his breath, replied: "I am hunting a Deer whose tracks I have followed all the way from the Waters of the Bear."

"Indeed!" exclaimed the stranger, "and where has thy Deer gone?"

"I know not," replied the youth, "for here are his tracks." Then he observed that they led to the place where the stranger was sitting, and the latter at the same time remarked:

"I am the Deer, and it was as I would have it that I enticed thee hither."

"Hai-í!" exclaimed the young man.

"Aye," continued the stranger. "Alas! alas! thou forgetful one! Thou hast day after day chased my children over the plains and slain them; thou hast made thyself happy of their flesh, and of their flesh added unto thine own meat and that of thy kindred; but, alas! thou hast been forgetful and careless, and not once hast thou given unto their souls the comfort of that which they yearn for and need. Yet hast thou had good fortune in the chase. At last the Sun-father has listened to the supplications of my children and commanded that I bring thee here, and here have I brought thee. Listen! The Sun-father commands that thou shalt visit him in his house at the western end of the world, and these are his instructions."

"Indeed! Well, I suppose it must be, and it is well!" exclaimed the young man.

"And," continued the Deer-being, "thou must hasten home and call thy father. Tell him to summon his *Pithlan Shíwani* (Priest of the Bow, or Warrior) and command him that he shall instruct his children to repair to the rooms of sacred things and prepare plumed prayer-sticks for the Sun-father, the Moon-mother, and the Great Ocean, and red plumes of sacrifice for the Beings of Prey; that fully they must prepare everything, for thou, their child and father, shalt visit the home of the Sun-father, and in payment for thy forgetfulness and carelessness shalt render him, and the Moon-mother, and the Beings of the Great Ocean, plumes of sacrifice. Hasten home, and tell thy father these things. Then tell thy sister to prepare sweetened meal of parched corn to serve as the food of thy journey, and pollen of the flowers of corn; and ask thy mother to prepare great quantities of new cotton, and, making all these things into bundles, thou must summon some of thy relatives, and come to this tree on the fourth day from this day. Make haste, for thou art swift of foot, and tell all these things to thy father; he will understand thee, for is he not a priest-chief? Hast thou knives of flint?"

"Yes," said the young man, "my father has many."

"Select from them two," said the Deer-being—"a large one and a smaller one; and when thou hast returned to this place, cut down with the larger knife yonder great tree, and with the smaller knife hollow it out. Leave the large end entire, and for the smaller end thou must make a round door, and around the inside of the smaller end cut a notch that shall be like a terrace toward the outside, but shall slope from within that thou mayest close it from the inside with the round door; then pad the inside with cotton, and make in the bottom a padding thicker than the rest; but leave space that thou mayest lie thy length, or sit up and eat. And in the top cut a hole larger inside than out, that thou mayest close it from the inside with a plug of wood. Then when thou hast placed the sweetened meal of parched corn inside, and the plumed prayer-sticks and the sacred pollen of corn-flowers, then enter thyself and close the door in the end and the hole in the top that thy people may roll thee into the river. Thou wilt meet strange beings on thy way. Choose from amongst them whom thou shalt have as a companion, and proceed, as thy companion shall direct, to the great mountain where the Sun enters. Haste and tell thy father these things." And ere the youth could say, "Be it well," and, "I will," the Deer-being had vanished, and he lifted up his face and started swiftly for the home of his fathers.

At sunset the sister looked forth from her high house-top, but nowhere could she see her brother coming. She turned at last to enter, thinking and saying to her breast: "Alas! what did we not think and guess of his carelessness." But just as the country was growing dim in the darkness, the young man ran breathlessly in, and, greeting his sister, sat down in the doorway.

The sister wondered that he had no deer or other game, but placed a meal before him, and, when he had done, herself ate. But the young man remained silent until she had finished, then he said: "Younger sister, I am weary and would sit here; do you go and call father, for I would speak to him of many things."

So the sister cleared away the food and ran to summon the father. Soon she returned with the old man, who, sighing, *"Ha hua!"* from the effort of climbing, greeted his son and sat down, looking all about the room for the fresh deer-meat; but, seeing none, he asked: "What and wherefore hast thou summoned me, my son?"

"It is this," replied the son, and he related all that had been told him by the Deer-being, describing the magnificent dress, the turquoise and shell ear-rings, necklaces, and wristlets of the handsome stranger.

"Certainly," replied the father. "It is well; for as the Sun-father hath directed the Deer-being, thus must it be done."

Then he forthwith went away and commanded his Priest of the Bow, who, mounting to the top-most house, directed the elders and priests of the tribe, saying:

> "Ye, our children, listen!
> Ye I will this day inform,
> Our child, our father,
> He of the strong hand,
> He who so hunts the Deer,
> Goes unto the Sunset world,
> Goes, our Sun-father to greet;
> Gather at the sacred houses,

Bring thy prayer-sticks, twines, and feathers,
And prepare for him,—
For the Sun-father,
For the Moon-mother,
For the Great Ocean,
For the Prey-beings, plumes and treasures.
Hasten, hasten, ye our children, in the morning!"

So the people gathered in the *kiwetsiwe* and sacred houses next morning and began to make prayer-plumes, while the sister of the young man and her relatives made sweet parched cornmeal and gathered pollen. Toward evening all was completed. The young man summoned his relatives, and chose his four uncles to accompany him. Then he spread enough cotton-wool out to cover the floor, and, gathering it up, made it into a small bundle. The sweet meal filled a large sack of buckskin, and he took also a little sack of sacred red paint and the black warrior paint with little shining particles in it. Then he bade farewell to his lamenting people and rested for the evening journey.

Next morning, escorted by priests, the young man, arrayed in garments of embroidered white cotton and carrying his plumes in his arms, started out of the town, and, accompanied only by his four uncles, set out over the mountains. On the third day they reached the forest on the bank of the great river and encamped.

Then the young man left the camp of his uncles and went alone into the forest, and, choosing the greatest tree he could find, hacked midway through it with his great flint knife. The next day he cut the other half and felled it, when he found it partly hollow. So with his little knife he began to cut it as he had been directed, and made the round door for it and the hole through the top. With his bundle of cotton he padded it everywhere inside until it was thickly coated and soft, and he made a bed on the bottom as thick as himself.

When all was ready and he had placed his food and plumes inside, he called his uncles and showed them the hollow log. "In this," said he, "I am to journey to the western home of our Sun-father. When I have entered and closed the round door tightly and put the plug into the upper hole securely, do ye, never thinking of me, roll the log over and over to the high brink of the river, and, never regarding consequences, push it into the water."

Then it was that the uncles all lamented and tried to dissuade him; but he persisted, and they bade him "Go," as forever, "for," said they, "could one think of journeying even to the end of the earth and across the waters that embrace the world without perishing?"

Then, hastily embracing each of them, the young man entered his log, and, securely fastening the door from the inside, and the plug, called out (they heard but faintly), *"Kesi!"* which means "All is ready."

Sorrowfully and gently they rolled the log over and over to the high river bank, and, hesitating a moment, pushed it off with anxious eyes and closed mouths into the river. Eagerly they watched it as it tumbled end-over-end and down into the water with a great splash, and disappeared under the waves, which rolled one after another across to the opposite banks of the river. But for a long time they saw nothing of it. After a while, far off, speeding on toward the Western Waters of the World, they saw the log rocking along on the rushing waters until it passed out of sight, and they sadly turned toward their homes under the Mountains of the South.

When the log had ceased rocking and plunging, the young man cautiously drew out the plug, and, finding that no water flowed in, peered out. A ray of sunlight slanted in, and by that he knew it was not yet midday, and he could see a round piece of sky and clouds through the hole. By-and-by the ray of sunlight came straight down, and then after a while slanted the other way, and finally toward evening it ceased to shine in, and then the youth took out some of his meal and ate his supper. When after a while he could see the stars, and later the Hanging Lines (the sword-belt of Orion), he knew it was time to rest, so he lay down to sleep.

Thus, day after day, he traveled until he knew he was out on the Great Waters of the World, for no longer did his log strike against anything or whirl around, nor could he see, through the chink, leaves of overhanging trees, nor rocks and banks of earth. On the tenth morning, when he looked up through the hole, he saw that the clouds did not move, and wondering at this, kicked at his log, but it would not move. Then he peered out as far as he could and saw rocks and trees. When he tried to rock his log, it remained firm, so he determined to open the door at the end.

Now, in reality, his log had been cast high up on the shore of a great mountain that rose out of the waters; and this mountain was the home of the Rattlesnakes. A Rattlesnake maiden was roaming along the shore just as the young man was about to open the door of his log. She espied the curious vessel, and said to herself in thought: "What may this be? Ah, yes, and who? Ah, yes, the mortal who was to come; it must be he!" Whereupon she hastened to the shore and tapped on the log.

"Art thou come?" she asked.

"Aye," replied the youth. "Who may you be, and where am I?"

"You are landed on the Island of the Rattlesnakes, and I am one of them. The other side of the mountain here is where our village is. Come out and go with me, for my old ones have expected you long."

"Is it dry, surely?" asked the young man.

"Why, yes! Here you are high above the waters."

Thereupon the young man opened from the inside his door, and peered out. Surely enough, there he was high among the rocks and sands. Then he looked at the Rattlesnake maiden, and scarcely believed she was what she called herself, for she was a most beautiful young woman, and like a daughter of men. Yet around her waist—she was dressed in cotton mantles—was girt a rattlesnake-skin which was open at the breast and on the crown of the head.

"Come with me," said the maiden; and she led the way over the mountain and across to a deep valley, where terrible Serpents writhed and gleamed in the sunlight so thickly that they seemed, with their hissing and rattling, like a dry mat shaken by the wind. The youth drew back in horror, but the maiden said: "Fear not; they will neither harm you nor frighten you more, for they are my people." Whereupon she commanded them to fall back and make a pathway for the young man and herself; and they tamely obeyed her commands. Through the opening thus made they passed down to a cavern, on entering which they found a great room. There were great numbers of Rattlesnake people, old and young, gathered in council, for they knew of the coming of the young man. Around the walls of their houses were many pegs and racks with serpent skins hanging on them—skins like the one the young girl wore as a girdle. The elders arose and greeted the youth, saying: "Our child and our father, comest thou, comest thou happily these many days?"

"Aye, happily," replied the youth.

And after a feast of strange food had been placed before the young man, and he had eaten a little, the elders said to him: "Knowest thou whither thou goest, that the way is long and fearful, and to mortals unknown, and that it will be but to meet with poverty that thou journeyest alone? Therefore have we assembled to await thy coming and in order that thou shouldst journey preciously, we have decided to ask thee to choose from amongst us whom thou shalt have for a companion."

"It is well, my fathers," said the young man, and, casting his eyes about the council to find which face should be kindest to him, he chose the maiden, and said: "Let it be this one, for she found me and loved me in that she gently and without fear brought me into your presence."

And the girl said: "It is well, and I will go."

Instantly the grave and dignified elders, the happy-faced youths and maidens, the kind-eyed matrons, all reached up for their serpent skins, and, passing them over their persons,—lo! in the time of the telling of it, the whole place was filled with writhing and hissing Serpents and the din of their rattles. In horror the young man stood against the wall like a hollow stalk, and the Serpent maiden, going to each of the members of the council, extracted from each a single fang, which she wrapped together in a piece of fabric, until she had a great bundle. Then she passed her hand over her person, and lo! she became a beautiful human maiden again, holding in her hand a rattlesnake skin. Then taking up the bundle of fangs, she said to the young man: "Come, for I know the way and will guide you,"—and the young man followed her to the shore where his log lay.

"Now," said she, "wait while I fix this log anew, that it may be well," and she bored many little holes all over the log, and into these holes she inserted the crooked fangs, so that they all stood slanting toward the rear, like the spines on the back of a porcupine.

When she had done this, she said: "First I will enter, for there may not be room for two, and in order that I may make myself like the space I enter, I will lay on my dress again. Do you, when I have entered, enter also, and with your feet kick the log down to the shore waters, when you must quickly close the door and the waters will take us abroad upon themselves."

In an instant she had passed into her serpent form again and crawled into the log. The young man did as he was bidden, and as he closed the door a wave bore them gently out upon the waters. Then, as the young man turned to look upon his companion coiled so near him, he drew back in horror.

"Why do you fear?" asked the Rattlesnake.

"I know not, but I fear you; perhaps, though you speak gently, you will, when I sleep, bite me and devour my flesh, and it is with thoughts of this that I have fear."

"Ah, no!" replied the maiden, "but, that you may not fear, I will change myself." And so saying, she took off her skin, and, opening the upper part of the door, hung the skin on the fangs outside.

Finally, toward noon-time, the youth prepared his meal food, and placing some before the maiden, asked her to eat.

"Ah, no! alas, I know not the food of mortals. Have you not with you the yellow dust of the corn-flower?"

"Aye, that I have," said the young man, and producing a bag, opened it and asked the girl: "How shall I feed it to you?"

"Scatter it upon the cotton, and by my knowledge I will gather it."

Then the young man scattered a great quantity on the cotton, wondering how the girl would gather it up. But the maiden opened the door, and taking down the skin changed herself to a serpent, and passing to and fro over the pollen, received it all within her scales. Then she resumed her human form again and hung the skin up as before.

Thus they floated until they came to the great forks of the Mighty Waters of the World, and their floating log was guided into the southern branch. And on they floated toward the westward for four months from the time when the uncles had thrown him into the river.

One day the maiden said to the youth: "We are nearing our journey's end, and, as I know the way, I will guide you. Hold yourself hard and ready, for the waters will cast our house high upon the shores of the mountain wherein the Sun enters, and these shores are inaccessible because so smooth."

Then the log was cast high above the slippery bank, and when the waters receded there it remained, for the fangs grappled it fast.

Then said the maiden: "Let us now go out. Fear not for your craft, for the fangs will hold it fast; it matters little how high the waves may roll, or how steep and slippery the bank."

Then, taking in his arms the sacred plumes which his people had prepared for him, he followed the girl far up to the doorway in the Mountain of the Sea. Out of it grew a great ladder of giant rushes, by the side of which stood an enormous basket-tray. Very fast approached the Sun, and soon the Sun-father descended the ladder, and the two voyagers followed down. They were gently greeted by a kind old woman, the grandmother of the Sun, and were given seats at one side of a great and wonderfully beautiful room.

Then the Sun-father approached some pegs in the wall and from them suspended his bow and quiver, and his bright sun-shield, and his wonderful traveling dress. Behold! there stood, kindly smiling before the youth and maiden, the most magnificent and gentle of beings in the world—the Sun-father.

Then the Sun-father greeted them, and, turning to a great package which he had brought in, opened it and disclosed thousands of shell beads, red and white, and thousands more of brilliant turquoises. These he poured into the great tray at the doorside, and gave them to the grandmother, who forthwith began to sort them with great rapidity. But, ere she had done, the Sun-father took them from her; part of them he took out with unerring judgment and cast them abroad into the great waters as we cast sacred prayer-meal. The others he brought below and gave them to the grandmother for safe-keeping.

Then he turned once more to the youth and the maiden, and said to the former: "So thou hast come, my child, even as I commanded. It is well, and I am thankful." Then, in a stern and louder voice, which yet sounded like the voice of a father, he asked: "Hast thou brought with thee that whereby we are made happy with our children?"

And the young man said: "Aye, I have."

"It is well; and if it be well, then shalt thou precious be; for knowest thou not that I recognize the really good from the evil,—even of the thoughts of men,—and that I know the prayer and sacrifice that is meant, from the words and treasures of those who do but lie in addressing them to me, and speak and act as children in a joke? Behold the treasure which I brought with me from the cities of mankind today! Some of them I cherished preciously, for they are the gifts to me of good hearts and I treasure them that I may return them in good fortune and blessing to those who gave them. But some thou sawest I cast abroad into the great waters that they may again be gathered up and presented to me; for they were the gifts of double and foolish hearts, and as such cannot be treasured by me nor returned unto those who gave them. Bring forth, my child, the plumes and gifts thou hast brought. Thy mother dwelleth in the next room, and when she appeareth in this, thou shalt with thine own hand present to her thy sacrifice."

So the youth, bowing his head, unwrapped his bundle and laid before the Sun-father the plumes he had brought. And the Sun-father took them and breathed upon them and upon the youth, and said: "Thanks, this day. Thou hast straightened thy crooked thoughts."

And when the beautiful Mother of Men, the Moon-mother—the wife of the Sun-father—appeared, the boy placed before her the plumes he had brought, and she, too, breathed upon them, and said: "Thanks, this day," even as the Sun-father had.

Then the Sun-father turned to the youth and said: "Thou shalt join me in my journey round the world, that thou mayest see the towns and nations of mankind— my children; that thou mayest realize how many are my children. Four days shalt thou join me in my journeyings, and then shalt thou return to the home of thy fathers."

And the young man said: "It is well!" but he turned his eyes to the maiden.

"Fear not, my child," added the Father, "she shall sit preciously in my house until we have returned."

And after they had feasted, the Sun-father again enrobed himself, and the youth he dressed in appearance as he himself was dressed. Then, taking the sun-dress from the wall, he led the way down through the four great apartments of the world, and came out into the Lower Country of the Earth.

Behold! as they entered that great world, it was filled with snow and cold below, and the tracks of men led out over great white plains, and as they passed the cities of these nether countries people strange to see were clearing away the snow from their housetops and doorways.

And so they journeyed to the other House of the Sun, and, passing up through the four great rooms, entered the home of the aunts of the Sun-father; and here, too, the young man presented plumes of prayer and sacrifice to the inmates, and received their thanks and blessings.

Again they started together on their journey; and behold! as they came out into the World of Daylight, the skies below them were filled with the rain of summer-time.

Across the great world they journeyed, and they saw city after city of men, and many tribes of strange peoples. Here they were engaged in wars and in wasting the lives of one another; there they were dying of famine and disease; and more of misery and poverty than of happiness saw the young man among the nations of men. "For," said the Sun-father, "these be, alas! my children, who waste their lives in foolishness, or slay one another in useless anger; yet they are brothers to one another, and I am the father of all."

Thus journeyed they four days; and each evening when they returned to the home where the Sun-father enters, he gave to his grandmother the great package of treasure which his children among men had sacrificed to him, and each day he cast the treasures of the bad and double-hearted into the great waters.

On the fourth day, when they had entered the western home of the Sun-father, said the latter to the youth: "Thy task is meted out and finished; thou shalt now return unto the home of thy fathers—my children below the mountains of Shíwina. How many days, thinkest thou, shalt thou journey?"

"Many days more than ten," replied the youth with a sigh.

"Ah! no, my child," said the Sun-father. "Listen; thou shalt in one day reach the banks of the river whence thou camest. Listen! Thou shalt take this, my shaft of strong lightning; thou shalt grasp its neck with firm hands, and as thou extendest it, it will stretch out far to thy front and draw thee more swiftly than the arrow's flight through the water. Take with thee this quiver of unerring arrows, and this strong bow, that by their will thou mayest seek life; but forget not thy sacrifices nor that they are to be made with true word and a faithful heart. Take also with thee thy guide and companion, the Rattlesnake maiden. When thou hast arrived at the shore of the country of her people, let go the lightning, and it will land thee high. On the morrow I will journey slowly, that ere I be done rising thou mayest reach the home of the maiden. There thou must stop but briefly, for thy fathers, the Rattle-tailed Serpents, will instruct thee, and to their counsel thou must pay strict heed, for thus only will it be well. Thou shalt present to them the plumes of the Prey-beings thou bringest, and when thou hast presented these, thou must continue thy journey. Rest thou until the morrow, and early as the light speed hence toward the home of thy fathers. May all days find ye, children, happy." With this, the Sun-father, scarce listening to the prayers and thanks of the youth and maiden, vanished below.

Thus, when morning approached, the youth and the maiden entered the hollow house and closed it. Scarce did the youth grasp the lightning when, drawn by the bright shaft, the log shot far out into the great waters and was skimming, too fast to be seen, toward the home of the Rattle-tailed Serpents.

And the Sun had but just climbed above the mountains of this world of daylight when the little tube was thrown high above the banks of the great island whither they were journeying.

Then the youth and the maiden again entered the council of the Rattlesnakes, and when they saw the shining black paint on his face they asked that they too might paint their faces like his own; but they painted their cheeks awkwardly, as to this day may be seen; for all rattlesnakes are painted unevenly in the face. Then the young man presented to each the plumes he had brought, and told the elders that he would return with their maiden to the home of his father.

"Be it well, that it may be well," they replied; and they thanked him with delight for the treasure-plumes he had bestowed upon them.

"Go ye happily all days," said the elders. "Listen, child, and father, to our words of advice. But a little while, and thou wilt reach the bank whence thou started. Let go the shaft of lightning, and, behold, the tube thou hast journeyed with will plunge far down into the river. Then shalt thou journey with this our maiden three days. Care not to embrace her, for if thou doest this, it will not be well. Journey ye preciously, our children, and may ye be happy one with the other."

So again they entered their hollow log, and, before entering, the maiden placed her rattlesnake skin as before on the fangs. With incredible swiftness the lightning drew them up the great surging river to the banks where the cottonwood forests grow, and when the lad pressed the shaft it landed them high among the forest trees above the steep bank. Then the youth pressed the lightning-shaft with all his might, and the log was dashed into the great river. While yet he gazed at the bounding log, behold! the fangs which the maiden had fixed into it turned to living serpents; hence today, throughout the whole great world, from the Land of Summer to the Waters of Sunset, are found the Rattlesnakes and their children.

Then the young man journeyed with the maiden southward; and on the way, with the bow and arrows the Sun-father had given him, he killed game, that they might have meat to eat. Nor did he forget the commandments of his Sun-father. At night he built a fire in a forest of piñons, and made a bower for the maiden near to it; but she could not sit there, for she feared the fire, and its light pained her eyes. Nor could she eat at first of the food he cooked for her, but only tasted a few mouthfuls of it. Then the young man made a bed for her under the trees, and told her to rest peacefully, for he would guard her through the night.

And thus they journeyed and rested until the fourth day, when at evening they entered the town under the mountains of Shíwina and were happily welcomed by the father, sister, and relatives of the young man. Blessed by the old priest-chief, the youth and the maiden dwelt with the younger sister Waíasialuhtitsa, in the high house of the upper part of the town. And the boy was as before a mighty hunter, and the maiden at last grew used to the food and ways of mortals.

After they had thus lived together for a long time, there were born of the maiden two children, twins.

Wonderful to relate, these children grew to the power of wandering, in a single day and night; and hence, when they appeared suddenly on the housetops and in the plazas, people said to one another:

"Who are these strange people, and whence came they?"—and talked much after the manner of our foolish people. And the other little children in the town beat them and quarrelled with them, as strange children are apt to do with strange children. And when the twins ran in to their mother, crying and complaining, the poor young woman was saddened; so she said to the father when he returned from hunting in the evening:

"Ah! 'their father,' it is not well that we remain longer here. No, alas! I must return to the country of my fathers, and take with me these little ones," and, although the father prayed her not, she said only: "It must be," and he was forced to consent.

Then for four days the Rattlesnake woman instructed him in the prayers and chants of her people, and she took him forth and showed him the medicines whereby the bite of her fathers might be assuaged, and how to prepare them. Again and again the young man urged her not to leave him, saying: "The way is long and filled with dangers. How, alas! will you reach it in safety?"

"Fear not," said she; "go with me only to the shore of the great river, and my fathers will come to meet me and take me home."

Sadly, on the last morning, the father accompanied his wife and children to the forests of the great river. There she said he must not follow; but as he embraced them he cried out:

"Ah, alas! my beautiful wife, my beloved children, flesh of my flesh, how shall I not follow ye?"

Then his wife answered: "Fear not, nor trouble thyself with sad thoughts. Whither we go thou canst not follow, for thou eatest cooked food—(thou art a mortal); but soon thy fathers and mine will come for thee, and thou wilt follow us, never to return." Then she turned from him with the little children and was seen no more, and the young man silently returned to his home below the mountains of Shíwina.

It happened here and there in time that young men of his tribe were bitten by rattlesnakes; but the young man had only to suck their wounds, and apply his medicines, and sing his incantations and prayers, to cure them. Whenever this happened, he breathed the sacred breath upon them, and enjoined them to secrecy of the rituals and chants he taught them, save only to such as they should choose and teach the practice of their prayers.

Thus he had cured and taught eight, when one day he ascended the mountains for wood. There, alone in the forest, he was met and bitten by his fathers. Although he slowly and painfully crawled home, long ere he reached his town he was so swollen that the eight whom he had instructed tried in vain to cure him, and, bidding them cherish as a precious gift the knowledge of his beloved wife, he died.

Immediately his fathers met his breath and being and took them to the home of the Maiden of the Rattlesnakes and of his lost children. Need we ask why he was not cured by his disciples?

Thus it was in the days of the ancients, and hence today there are men amongst us to whom the dread bite of the rattlesnake need cause no sad thoughts,—the *Tchi Kialikwe* (Society of the Rattlesnakes).

Coyote Stories
(Various)

The Coyote Who Killed the Demon Síuiuki
(Zuñi)

It was very long ago, in the days of the ancients.

There stood a village in the cañon south of Thunder Mountain where the Gods of Prey all lived with their sisters and mothers: the Mountain Lion, the great Black Bear, the Wildcat, the Gray Wolf, the Eagle, and even the Mole—all the Gods of Prey lived there together with their mothers and sisters. Day after day they went out hunting, for hunting was their business of life, and they were great hunters.

Now, right up on the edge of Thunder Mountain there lived a spotted Demon, named Síuiuki, and whenever the people of the towns round about went hunting, he lay in wait for them and ate them up.

After a long while the Gods of Prey grew discontented, and they said to one another: "What in the world can we do? None of the children of men ever make sacrifices to us, for, whenever our children among men go out hunting, this Demon who lives on the top of Thunder Mountain destroys them and eats them up. What in the world can be done?"

"It would be a good thing if we could kill him," said some of them.

Now, just down below the house of the Demon, in Wolf Cañon, lived a Coyote, and he had found out where the Gods of Prey lived, and whenever he wanted a feast of sinew and gristle, he went below their houses and gnawed at the bones that they had thrown away, and thus it happened that when the gods were talking together in this way he was near their doorway gnawing a bone, and he heard all they said.

"Yes," said one or two of the others, "and if anybody will go and kill Síuiuki, we will give him our sister to marry."

"Aha!" said the Coyote to himself. "Ha, ha!"—and he dropped the bone he was gnawing and cut off for home as fast as ever he could.

Next morning, bright and early, he began to dig into the side of the cañon below the Demon's home, and after he had dug a great hollow in the side of the arroyo, he rolled a heavy stone into it, and found another, which he placed beside it. Then he brought a great many leg-bones of deer and antelope. Then he found a large bowl and put a lot of yellow medicine-fluid in it, and placed it beside the rock. He then sat down and began to crack the leg-bones with the two stones he had brought there.

The old Demon was not in the habit of rising very early, but when he arose that morning he came out and sat down on the edge of the cliff; there the Coyote was, battering away at the bones and pretending to bathe his own lips with the medicine-fluid.

"I wonder what in the world that little sneak is doing down there," said the old Demon. So he put on his war-badge and took his bow and arrows, as though he were going out to hunt, and started down to where the Coyote was.

"Hello!" said the Coyote, "how did you pass the night?"

"What in the world are you doing here?" asked the Demon.

"Why, don't you know?" replied the Coyote. "This is the way I train myself for running, so as to catch the deer; I can run faster than any deer in the country. With my medicine, here, I take the swiftness out of these bones."

"Is it possible?" said the old Demon.

"Of course it is," said the Coyote. "There is no deer that can run away from me."

"Will you show me?" said the Demon, eagerly.

"Why, yes, of course I will; and then we will go hunting together."

"Good, good!" said the old Demon. "I have a hard time catching deer and antelope."

"Well, now, you sit down right over there and watch me," said the Coyote, "and I will show you all about it."

So he laid his left leg over the rock, and then slyly took an antelope bone and laid it by the side of it. Then he picked up a large stone and struck it as hard as ever he could against the bone. Whack! went the stone, and it split the bone into splinters; and the Coyote pretended that it was the bone of his own leg.

"Aye! Ah! Oh!" exclaimed he. "But then it will get well!" Still crying "Oh! Ah!" he splashed the leg with the medicine-water and rubbed it. "Didn't I tell you?" said he, "it is all right now." And then away he went and ran like lightning round and round on the plain below, and rushed back again. "Didn't I tell you so?" said he.

"Fury! what a runner it makes out of you," said the old Demon, and his eyes stuck out more than ever. "Let me try it now."

"Hold on, hold on," said the Coyote; "I have not half finished yet."

So he repeated the experiment with his other leg, and made great ado, as if it hurt him more than ever. But, pretending to cure himself with the medicine-water, he ran round and round on the plain below so fast that he fairly left a streak of dust behind him.

"Why, indeed, you are one of the fastest runners I ever saw!" said the Demon, rubbing his eyes.

Then the Coyote repeated the experiment first with his left paw and then with his right; and the last time he ran more swiftly than before.

"Why, do you mean to say that if I do that I can run as fast as you do?" said the Demon.

"Certainly," replied the Coyote. "But it will hurt you."

"Ho! who cares for a little hurt?" said the Demon.

"Oh! but it hurts terribly," said the Coyote, "and I am afraid you won't have the pluck to go through with it."

"Do you think I am a baby?" said the old Demon, getting up,—"or a woman, that I should be afraid to pound my legs and arms?"

"Well, I only thought I'd tell you how much it hurts," said the Coyote; "but if you want to try it yourself, why, go ahead. There's one thing certain: when you make yourself as swift as I am, there's no deer in all the country that can get away from us two."

"What shall I do?" said the Demon.

"You just sit right down there, and I'll show you how," said the Coyote. So the Demon sat down by the rock.

"There, now, you just lay your leg right over that stone and take the other rock and strike your leg just as hard as you can; and as soon as you have done, bathe it in the medicine-water. Then do just the same way to the other."

"All right," said the Demon. So he laid his leg over the rock, and picking up the other stone, brought it down with might and main across his thigh—so hard, indeed, that he crushed the bone into splinters.

"Oh, my! Oh, my! what shall I do?" shouted the Demon.

"Be patient, be patient; it will get well," said the Coyote, and he splashed it with the medicine-fluid.

Then, picking up the stone again, the Demon hit the other thigh even harder, from pain.

"It will get well, my friend; it will get well," shouted the Coyote; and he splashed more of the medicine-water on the two wounded legs.

Then the Demon picked up the stone once more, and, laying his left arm across the other stone, pounded that also until it was broken.

"Hold on; let me bathe it for you," said the Coyote. "Does it hurt? Oh, well, it will get well. Just wait until you have doctored the other arm, and then in a few minutes you will be all right."

"Oh, dear! Oh, dear!" groaned the Demon. "How in the world can I doctor the other arm, for my left arm is broken?"

"Lay it across the rock, my friend," said the Coyote, "and I'll doctor it for you."

So the Demon did as he was bidden, and the Coyote brought the stone down with might and main against his arm. "Have patience, my friend, have patience," said he, as he bathed the injured limb with more of the medicine-water. But the Demon only groaned and howled, and rolled over and over in the dust with pain.

"Ha, ha!" laughed the Coyote, as he keeled a somersault over the rocks and ran off over the plain. "How do you feel now, old man?"

"But it hurts! It hurts!" cried the Demon. "I shall never get well; it will kill me!"

"Of course it will," laughed the Coyote. "That's just what I wanted it to do, you old fool!"

So the old Demon lay down and died from sheer pain.

Then the Coyote took the Demon's knife from him, and, cutting open his breast, tore out his heart, wind-pipe, and all. Then, stealing the war-badge that the Demon had worn, he cut away as fast as ever he could for the home of the Prey-gods. Before noon he neared their house, and, just as he ran up into the plaza in front of it, the youngest sister of the Prey-gods came out to hang up some meat to dry. Now, her brothers had all gone hunting; not one of them was at home.

"I say, wife," said the Coyote. "Wife! Wife!"

"Humph!" said the girl. "Impertinent scoundrel! I wonder where he is and who he is that has the impudence to call me his wife, when he knows that I have never been married!"

"Wife! Wife!" shouted the Coyote again.

"Away with you, you shameless rascal!" cried the girl, in indignation. Then she looked around and spied the Coyote sitting there on the ash-heap, with his nose in the air, as though he were the biggest fellow in the world.

"Clear out, you wretch!" cried the girl.

"Softly, softly," replied the Coyote. "Do you remember what your brothers said last night?"

"What was that?" said the girl.

"Why, whoever would kill the speckled Demon, they declared, should have you for his wife."

"Well, what of that?" said the girl.

"Oh, nothing," replied the Coyote, "only I've killed him!" And, holding up the Demon's heart and war-badge, he stuck his nose in the air again.

So the poor girl said not a word, but sat there until the Coyote called out: "I say, wife, come down and take me up; I can't climb the ladders."

So the poor girl went down the ladder, took her foul-smelling husband in her arms, and climbed up with him.

"Now, take me in with you," said the Coyote. So she did as she was bidden. Then she was about to mix some dough, but the Coyote kept getting in her way.

"Get out of the way a minute, won't you?" said the girl, "until I cook something for you."

"I want you to come and sit down with me," said the Coyote, "and let me kiss you, for you know you are my wife, now." So the poor girl had to submit to the ill-smelling creature's embraces.

Presently along came her brother, the Gray Wolf, but he was a very good-natured sort of fellow; so he received the Coyote pleasantly. Then along came the Bear, with a big antelope over his shoulder; but he didn't say anything, for he was a lazy, good-natured fellow. Then presently the other brothers came in, one by one; but the Mountain Lion was so late in returning that they began to look anxiously out for him. When they saw him coming from the north with more meat and more game than all the others together had brought, he was evidently not in good humor, for as he approached the house he exclaimed, with a howl: *"Hu-hu-ya!"*

"There he goes again," said the brothers and sisters, all in a chorus. "Always out of temper with something."

"Hu-hu-ya!" exclaimed the Mountain Lion again, louder than before. And, as he mounted the ladder, he exclaimed for a third time: *"Hu-hu-ya!"* and, throwing his meat down, entered swearing and growling until his brothers were ashamed of him, and told him he had better behave himself.

"Come and eat," said the sister, as she brought a bowl of meat and put it on the floor.

"Hu-hu-ya!" again exclaimed the Mountain Lion, as he came nearer and sat down

to eat. "What in the world is the matter with you, sister? You smell just like a Coyote. *Hu-hu-ya!*"

"Have you no more decency than to come home and scold your sister in that way?" exclaimed the Wolf. "I'm disgusted with you."

"*Hu-hu-ya!*" reiterated the Mountain Lion.

Now, when the Coyote had heard the Mountain Lion coming, he had sneaked off into a corner; but he stuck his sharp nose out, and the Mountain Lion espied it. "*Hu-hu-ya!*" said he. "Sling that bad-smelling beast out of the house! Kick him out!" cried the old man, with a growl. So the sister, fearing that her brother would eat her husband up, took the Coyote in her arms and carried him into another room.

"Now, stay there and keep still, for brother is very cross; but then he is always cross if things don't go right," she said.

So when evening came her brothers began to discuss where they would go hunting the next day; and the Coyote, who was listening at the door, heard them. So he called out: "Wife! Wife!"

"*Shom-me!*" remarked old Long Tail. "Shut up, you dirty whelp." And as the sister arose to go to see what her husband wanted, the Mountain Lion remarked: "You had better sling that foul-smelling cub of yours over the roof."

No sooner had the girl entered than the Coyote began to brag what a runner he was, and to cut around at a great rate.

"*Shom-me!*" exclaimed the Mountain Lion again. "A Coyote always will make a Coyote of himself, foul-smelling wretch! *Hu-hu-ya!*"

"Shut up, and behave yourself!" cried the Wolf. "Don't you know any better than to talk about your brother-in-law in that way?" But neither the Coyote nor the girl could sleep that night for the growlings and roarings of their big brother, the Long Tail.

When the brothers began to prepare for the hunt the next morning, out came the Coyote all ready to accompany them. "You, you?" said the Mountain Lion. "You going to hunt with us? You conceited sneak!"

"Let him go if he wants to," said the Wolf.

"*Hu-hu-ya!* Fine company!" remarked the Mountain Lion. "If you fellows want to walk with him, you may. There's one thing certain, I'll not be seen in his company," and away strode the old fellow, lashing his tail and growling as he went. So the Coyote, taking a luncheon of dried meat that his wife put up for him, sneaked along behind with his tail dragging in the dust. Finally they all reached the mountain where they intended to hunt, and soon the Mountain Lion and the Bear started out to drive in a herd of antelope that they had scented in the distance. Presently along rushed the leaders of the herd.

"Now, then, I'll show your cross old brother whether I can hunt or not," cried the Coyote, and away he rushed right into the herd of antelope and deer before anyone could restrain him. Of course he made a Coyote of himself, and away went the deer in all directions. Nevertheless, the brothers, who were great hunters, succeeded in catching a few of them; and, just as they sat down to lunch, the Mountain Lion returned with a big elk on his shoulders.

"Where is our sweet-scented brother-in-law?" he asked.

"Nobody knows," replied they. "He rushed off after the deer and antelope, and that was the last of him."

"Of course the beast will make a Coyote of himself. But he can go till he can go no longer, for all I care," added the Mountain Lion, as he sat down to eat.

Presently along came the Coyote.

"Where's your game, my fine hunter?" asked the Mountain Lion.

"They all got away from me," whined the Coyote.

"Of course they did, you fool!" sneered the Mountain Lion. "The best thing that you can do is to go home and see your wife. Here, take this meat to sister," said he, slinging him a haunch of venison.

"Where's the road?" asked the Coyote.

"Well," said the Wolf, "follow that path right over there until you come to where it forks; then be sure to take the right-hand trail, for if you follow the left-hand trail it will lead you away from home and into trouble."

"Which trail did you say?" cried the Coyote.

"Shom-me!" again exclaimed the Mountain Lion.

"Oh, yes," hastily added the Coyote; "the right-hand trail. No, the left-hand trail."

"Just what you might expect," growled the Mountain Lion. "Already the fool has forgotten what you told him. Well, as for me, he can go on the left-hand trail if he wants to, and the farther he goes the better."

"Now, be sure and take the right-hand trail," called the Wolf, as the Coyote started.

"I know, I know," cried the Coyote; and away he went with his heavy haunch of venison slung over his shoulder. After a while he came to the fork in the trail. "Let me see," said he, "it's the left-hand trail, it seems to me. No, the right-hand trail. Well, I declare, I've forgotten! Perhaps it is the right-hand trail, and maybe it is the left-hand trail. Yes, it is the left-hand trail. Now I'm certain." And, picking up his haunch of venison, away he trotted along the left-hand trail. Presently he came to a steep cliff and began to climb it. But he had no sooner reached the middle than a lot of Chimney-swallows began to fly around his head and pick at his eyes, and slap him on the nose with their wings.

"Oh, dear! oh, dear!" exclaimed the Coyote. "Aye! aye!" and he bobbed his head from side to side to dodge the Swallows, until he missed his footing, and down he tumbled, heels over head,—meat, Coyote, and all,—until he struck a great pile of rocks below, and was dashed to pieces.

That was the end of the Coyote.

Now, the brothers went on hunting again. Then, one by one, they returned home. As before, the Mountain Lion came in last of all. He smelt all about the room. "Whew!" exclaimed he. "It still smells here as if twenty Coyotes had been around. But it seems to me that our fine brother-in-law isn't anywhere about."

"No," responded the rest, with troubled looks on their faces. "Nobody has seen anything of him yet."

"Shom—m-m!" remarked the Mountain Lion again. "Didn't I tell you, brothers, that he was a fool and would forget your directions? I say I told you that before he started. Well, for my part, I hope the beast has gone so far that he will never return," and with that he ate his supper.

When supper was over, the sister said: "Come, brothers, let's go and hunt for my husband."

At first the Mountain Lion growled and swore a great deal; but at last he consented to go. When they came to where the trails forked, there were the tracks of the Coyote on the left-hand trail.

"The idiot!" exclaimed the Mountain Lion. "I hope he has fallen off the cliff and broken every bone in his body!"

When at last the party reached the mountain, sure enough, there lay the body of the Coyote, with not a whole bone in him except his head.

"Good enough for you," growled the Mountain Lion, as he picked up a great stone and, *tu-um!* threw it down with all his strength upon the head of the Coyote.

That's what happened a great while ago. And for that reason whenever a Coyote sees a bait of meat inside of a stone deadfall he is sure to stick his nose in and get his head smashed for his pains.

The Coyote and the Burrowing-Owls
(Zuñi)

You may know the country that lies south of the valley in which our town stands. You travel along the trail which winds round the hill the ancients called *Ishana-tak'yapon,*—which means the Hill of Grease, for the rocks sometimes shine in the light of the sun at evening, and it is said that strange things occurred there in the days of the ancients, which makes them thus to shine, while rocks of the kind in other places do not,—you travel on up this trail, crossing over the arroyos and foot-hills of the great mesa called Middle Mountain, until you come to the foot of the cliffs. Then you climb up back and forth, winding round and round, until you reach the top of the mountain, which is as flat as the floor of a house, merely being here and there traversed by small valleys covered with piñon and cedar, and threaded by trails made not only by the feet of the Zuñis but by deer and other animals. And so you go on and on, until, hardly knowing it, you have descended from the top of Middle Mountain, and found yourself in a wide plain covered with grass, and here and there clumps of trees. Beyond this valley is an elevated sandy plain, rather sunken in the middle, so that when it rains the water filters down into the soil of the depressed portion (which is wide enough to be a country in itself) and nourishes the grasses there; so that most of the year they grow green and sweet.

Now, a long, long time ago, in this valley or basin there lived a village of Prairie-dogs, on fairly peaceable terms with Rattlesnakes, Adders, Chameleons, Horned-toads, and Burrowing-owls. With the Owls they were especially friendly, looking at them as creatures of great gravity and sanctity. For this reason these Prairie-dogs and their companions never disturbed the councils or ceremonies of the Burrow-ing-owls, but treated them most respectfully, keeping at a distance from them when their dances were going on.

It chanced one day that the Burrowing-owls were having a great dance all to themselves, rather early in the morning. The dance they were engaged in was one peculiarly prized by them, requiring no little dexterity in its execution. Each dancer, young man or maiden, carried upon his or her head a bowl of foam, and though their legs were crooked and their motions disjointed, they danced to the whistling of some and the clapping beaks of others, in perfect unison, and with such dexterity that they never spilled a speck of the foam on their sleek mantles of dun-black feather-work.

It chanced this morning of the Foam-dance that a Coyote was nosing about for Grasshoppers and Prairie-dogs. So quite naturally he was prowling around the by-streets in the borders of the Prairie-dog town. His house where he lived with his old grandmother stood back to the westward, just over the elevations that bounded Sunken Country, among the rocks. He heard the click-clack of the musicians and their shrill, funny little song:

> "I yami hota utchu tchapikya,
> Tokos! tokos! tokos! tokos!"

So he pricked up his ears, and lifting his tail, trotted forward toward the level place between the hillocks and doorways of the village, where the Owls were dancing in a row. He looked at them with great curiosity, squatting on his haunches, the more composedly to observe them. Indeed, he became so much interested and amused by their shambling motions and clever evolutions, that he could no longer contain his curiosity. So he stepped forward, with a smirk and a nod toward the old master of ceremonies, and said: "My father, how are you and your children these many days?"

"Contented and happy," replied the old Owl, turning his attention to the dancing again.

"Yes, but I observe you are dancing," said the Coyote. "A very fine dance, upon my word! Charming! Charming! And why should you be dancing if you were not contented and happy, to be sure?"

"We are dancing," responded the Owl, "both for our pleasure and for the good of the town."

"True, true," replied the Coyote; "but what's that which looks like foam these dancers are carrying on their heads, and why do they dance in so limping a fashion?"

"You see, my friend," said the Owl, turning toward the Coyote, "we hold this to be a very sacred performance—very sacred indeed. Being such, these my children are initiated and so trained in the mysteries of the sacred society of which this is a custom that they can do very strange things in the observance of our ceremonies. You ask what it is that looks like foam they are balancing on their heads. Look more closely, friend. Do you not observe that it is their own grandmothers' heads they have on, the feathers turned white with age?"

"By my eyes!" exclaimed the Coyote, blinking and twitching his whiskers; "it seems so."

"And you ask also why they limp as they dance," said the Owl. "Now, this limp is essential to the proper performance of our dance—so essential, in fact, that in order to attain to it these my children go through the pain of having their legs broken. Instead of losing by this, they gain in a great many ways. Good luck always follows them. They are quite as spry as they were before, and enjoy, moreover, the distinction of performing a dance which no other people or creatures in the world are capable of!"

"Dust and devils!" ejaculated the Coyote. "This is passing strange. A most admirable dance, upon my word! Why, every bristle on my body keeps time to the music and their steps! Look here, my friend, don't you think that I could learn that dance?"

"Well," replied the old Owl; "it is rather hard to learn, and you haven't been initiated, you know; but, still, if you are determined that you would like to join the dance—by the way, have you a grandmother?"

"Yes, and a fine old woman she is," said he, twitching his mouth in the direction of his house. "She lives there with me. I dare say she is looking after my breakfast now."

"Very well," continued the old Owl, "if you care to join in our dance, fulfill the conditions, and I think we can receive you into our order." And he added, aside: "The silly fool; the sneaking, impertinent wretch! I will teach him to be sticking that sharp nose of his into other people's affairs!"

"All right! All right!" cried the Coyote, excitedly. "Will it last long?"

"Until the sun is so bright that it hurts our eyes," said the Owl; "a long time yet."

"All right! All right! I'll be back in a little while," said the Coyote; and, switching his tail into the air, away he ran toward his home. When he came to the house, he saw his old grandmother on the roof, which was a rock beside his hole, gathering fur from some skins which he had brought home, to make up a bed for the Coyote's family.

"Ha, my blessed grandmother!" said the Coyote, "by means of your aid, what a fine thing I shall be able to do!"

The old woman was singing to herself when the Coyote dashed up to the roof where she was sitting, and, catching up a convenient leg-bone, whacked her over the pate and sawed her head off with the teeth of a deer. All bloody and soft as it was, he clapped it on his own head and raised himself on his hind-legs, bracing his tail against the ground, and letting his paws drop with the toes outspread, to imitate as nearly as possible the drooping wings of the dancing Owls. He found that it worked very well; so, descending with the head in one paw and a stone in the other, he found a convenient sharp-edged rock, and, laying his legs across it, hit them a tremendous crack with the stone, which broke them, to be sure, into splinters.

"Beloved Powers! Oh!" howled the Coyote. "Oh-o-o-o-o! the dance may be a fine thing, but the initiation is anything else!"

However, with his faith unabated, he shook himself together and got up to walk. But he could walk only with his paws; his hind-legs dragged helplessly behind him. Nevertheless, with great pain, and getting weaker and weaker every step of the way, he made what haste he could back to the Prairie-dog town, his poor old grandmother's head slung over his shoulders.

When he approached the dancers,—for they were still dancing,—they pretended to be greatly delighted with their proselyte, and greeted him, notwithstanding his rueful countenance, with many congratulatory epithets, mingled with very proper and warm expressions of welcome. The Coyote looked sick and groaned occasionally and kept looking around at his feet, as though he would like to lick them. But the old Owl extended his wing and cautioned him not to interfere with the working power of faith in this essential observance, and invited him (with a *hem* that very much resembled a suppressed giggle), to join in their dance. The Coyote smirked and bowed and tried to stand up gracefully on his stumps, but fell over, his grandmother's head rolling around in the dirt. He picked up the grisly head, clapped it on his crown again and raised himself, and with many a howl, which he tried in vain to check, began to prance around; but ere long tumbled over again. The Burrowing-owls were filled with such merriment at his discomfiture that they laughed until they spilled the foam all down their backs and bosoms; and, with a parting fling at the Coyote which gave him to understand that he had made a fine fool of himself, and would know better than to pry into other people's business next time, skipped away to a safe distance from him.

Then, seeing how he had been tricked, the Coyote fell to howling and clapping his thighs; and, catching sight of his poor grandmother's head, all bloody and begrimed with dirt, he cried out in grief and anger: "Alas! alas! that it should have come to this! You little devils! I'll be even with you! I'll smoke you out of your holes."

"What will you smoke us out with?" tauntingly asked the Burrowing-owls.

"Ha! you'll find out. With yucca!"

"O! O! ha! ha!" laughed the Owls. "That is our succotash!"

"Ah, well! I'll smoke you out!" yelled the Coyote, stung by their taunts.

"What with?" cried the Owls.

"Grease-weed."

"He, ha! ho, ho! We make our mush-stew of that!"

"Ha! but I'll smoke you out, nevertheless, you little beasts!"

"What with? What with?" shouted the Owls.

"Yellow-top weeds," said he.

"Ha, ha! All right; smoke away! We make our sweet gruel with that, you fool!"

"I'll fix you! I'll smoke you out! I'll suffocate the very last one of you!"

"What with? What with?" shouted the Owls, skipping around on their crooked feet.

"Pitch-pine," snarled the Coyote.

This frightened the Owls, for pitch-pine, even to this day, is sickening to them. Away they plunged into their holes, pell-mell.

Then the Coyote looked at his poor old grandmother's begrimed and bloody head, and cried out—just as Coyotes do now at sunset, I suppose—"Oh, my poor, poor grandmother! So this is what they have caused me to do to you!" And, tormented both by his grief and his pain, he took up the head of his grandmother and crawled back as best he could to his house.

When he arrived there he managed to climb up to the roof, where her body lay stiff. He chafed her legs and sides, and washed the blood and dirt from her head, and got a bit of sinew, and sewed her head to her body as carefully as he could and as hastily. Then he opened her mouth, and, putting his muzzle to it, blew into her throat, in the hope of resuscitating her; but the wind only leaked out from the holes in her neck, and she gave no signs of animation. Then the Coyote mixed some pap of fine toasted meal and water and poured it down her throat, addressing her with vehement expressions of regret at what he had done, and apology and solicitation that she should not mind, as he didn't mean it, and imploring her to revive. But the pap only trickled out between the stitches in her neck, and she grew colder and stiffer all the while; so that at last the Coyote gave it up, and, moaning, he betook himself to a near clump of piñon trees, intent upon vengeance and designing to gather pitch with which to smoke the Owls to death. But, weakened by his injuries, and filled with grief and shame and mortification, when he got there he could only lie down.

He was so engrossed in howling and thinking of his woes and pains that a Horned-toad, who saw him, and who hated him because of the insults he had frequently suffered from him and his kind, crawled into the throat of the beast without his noticing it. Presently the little creature struck up a song:

> "Tsakina muuu-ki
> Iyami Kushina tsoiyakya
> Aisiwaiki muki, muki,
> Muuu ka!"

"Ah-a-a-a-a," the Coyote was groaning. But when he heard this song, apparently far off, and yet so near, he felt very strangely inside, so he thought and no doubt wondered if it were the song of some musician. At any rate, he lifted his head and looked all around, but hearing nothing, lay down again and bemoaned his fate.

Then the Horned-toad sang again. This time the Coyote called out immediately, and the Horned-toad answered: "Here I am." But look as he would, the Coyote could not find the Toad. So he listened for the song again, and heard it, and asked who it was that was singing. The Horned-toad replied that it was he. But still the Coyote could not find him. A fourth time the Horned-toad sang, and the Coyote began to suspect that it was under him. So he lifted himself to see; and one of the spines on the Horned-toad's neck pricked him, and at the same time the little fellow called out: "Here I am, you idiot, inside of you! I came upon you here, and being a medicine-man of some prominence, I thought I would explore your vitals and see what was the matter."

"By the souls of my ancestors!" exclaimed the Coyote, "be careful what you do in there!"

The Horned-toad replied by laying his hand on the Coyote's liver, and exclaiming: "What is this I feel?"

"Where?" said the Coyote.

"Down here."

"Merciful daylight! it is my liver, without which no one can have solidity of any kind, or a proper vitality. Be very careful not to injure that; if you do, I shall die at once, and what will become of my poor wife and children?"

Then the Horned-toad climbed up to the stomach of the Coyote. "What is this, my friend?" said he, feeling the sides of the Coyote's food-bag.

"What is it like?" asked the Coyote.

"Wrinkled," said the Horned-toad, "and filled with a fearful mess of stuff!"

"Oh! mercy! mercy! good daylight! My precious friend, be very careful! That is the very source of my being—my stomach itself!"

"Very well," said the Horned-toad. Then he moved on somewhat farther and touched the heart of the Coyote, which startled him fearfully. "What is this?" cried the Horned-toad.

"Mercy, mercy! what are you doing?" exclaimed the Coyote.

"Nothing—feeling of your vitals," was the reply. "What is it?"

"Oh, what is it like?" said the Coyote.

"Shaped like a pine-nut," said the Horned-toad, "as nearly as I can make out; it keeps leaping so."

"Leaping, is it?" howled the Coyote. "Mercy! my friend, get away from there! That is the very heart of my being, the thread that ties my existence, the home of my emotions, and my knowledge of daylight. Go away from there, do, I pray you! If you should scratch it ever so little, it would be the death of me, and what would my wife and children do?"

"Hey!" said the Horned-toad, "you wouldn't be apt to insult me and my people any more if I touched you up there a little, would you?" And he hooked one of his horns into the Coyote's heart. The Coyote gave one gasp, straightened out his limbs, and expired.

"Ha, ha! you villain! Thus would you have done to me, had you found the chance; thus unto you"—saying which he found his way out and sought the nearest water-pocket he could find.

So you see from this, which took place in the days of the ancients, it may be inferred that the instinct of meddling with everything that did not concern him, and making a universal nuisance of himself, and desiring to imitate everything that he sees, ready to jump into any trap that is laid for him, is a confirmed instinct with the Coyote, for those are precisely his characteristics today.

Furthermore, Coyotes never insult Horned-toads nowadays, and they keep clear of Burrowing-owls. And ever since then the Burrowing-owls have been speckled with gray and white all over their backs and bosoms, because their ancestors spilled foam over themselves in laughing at the silliness of the Coyote.

THE COYOTES AND THE CHILDREN OF THE SACRED DANCE
(Zuñi)

In the times of the ancients, when people lived in various places about the valley of Zuñi where ruins now stand, it is said that an old Coyote lived in Cedar Cañon with his family, which included a fine litter of pups. It is also said that at this time there lived on the crest of Thunder Mountain, back of the broad rock column or pinnacle which guards its western portion, one of the gods of the Sacred Drama Dance (*Kâkâ*), named K'yámakwe, with his children, many in number and altogether like himself.

One day the old Coyote of Cedar Cañon went out hunting, and as he was prowling around among the sage-bushes below Thunder Mountain, he heard the clang and rattle and the shrill cries of the K'yámakwe. He pricked up his ears, stuck his nose into the air, sniffed about and looked all around, and presently discovered the K'yámakwe children running rapidly back and forth on the very edge of the mountain.

"Delight of my senses, what pretty creatures they are! Good for me!" he piped, in a jovial voice. "I am the finder of children. I must capture the little fellows tomorrow, and bring them up as Coyotes ought to be brought up. Aren't they handsome, though?"

All this he said to himself, in a fit of conceit, with his nose in the air (presumptuous cur!), planning to steal the children of a god! He hunted no more that day, but ran home as fast as he could, and, arriving there, he said: "Wife! Wife! O wife! I have discovered a number of the prettiest waifs one ever saw. They are children of the *Kâkâ,* but what matters that? They are there, running back and forth and clanging their rattles along the very edge of Thunder Mountain. I mean to steal them tomorrow, every one of them, and bring them here!"

"Mercy on us!" exclaimed the old Coyote's wife. "There are children enough and to spare already. What in the world can we do with all of them, you fool?"

"But they are pretty," said the Coyote. "Immensely fine! Every Coyote in the country would envy us the possession of them!"

"But you say they are many," continued the wife.

"Well, yes, a good many," said the Coyote.

"Well, why not divide them among our associated clans?" suggested the old woman. "You never can capture them alone; it is rare enough that you capture *anything* alone, leave out the children of the K'yámakwe. Get your relatives to help you, and divide the children amongst them."

"Well, now, come to think of it, it is a good plan," said the Coyote, with his nose on his neck. "If I get up this expedition I'll be a big chief, won't I? Hurrah! Here's for it!" he shouted; and, switching his tail in the face of his wife, he shot out of the hole and ran away to a high rock, where, squatting down with a most important air and his nose lifted high, he cried out:

> *"Au hii lâ-â-â-â!*
> *Su Homaya-kwe!*
> *Su Kemaya-kwe!*
> *Su Ayalla-kwe!*
> *Su Kutsuku-kwe!*

> [Listen ye all!
> Coyotes of the Cedar-cañon tribe!
> Coyotes of the Sunflower-stalk-plain tribe!

Coyotes of the Lifted-stone-mountain tribe!
Coyotes of the Place-of-rock-gullies tribe!]

I have instructions for you this day. I have found waif children many—of the K'yámakwe, the young. I would steal the waif-children many, of the K'yámakwe, the young. I would steal them tomorrow, that they may be adopted of us. I would have your aid in the stealing of the K'yámakwe young. Listen ye all, and tomorrow gather in council. Thus much I instruct ye:

"Coyotes of the Cedar-cañon tribe!
Coyotes of the Sunflower-stalk-plain tribe!
Coyotes of the Lifted-stone-mountain tribe!
Coyotes of the Place-of-rock-gullies tribe!"

It was growing dark, and immediately from all quarters, in dark places under the cañons and arroyos, issued answering howls and howls. You should have seen that crowd of Coyotes the next morning, large and small, old and young,—all four tribes gathered together in the plain below Thunder Mountain!

When they had all assembled, the Coyote who had made the discovery mounted an ant-hill, sat down, and, lifting his paw, was about to give directions with the air of a chief when an ant bit him. He lost his dignity, but resumed it again on the top of a neighboring rock. Again he stuck his nose into the air and his paw out, and with ridiculous assumption informed the Coyotes that he was chief of them all and that they would do well to pay attention to his directions. He then showed himself much more skillful than you might have expected. As you know, the cliff of Thunder Mountain is very steep, especially that part back of the two standing rocks. Well, this was the direction of the Coyote:

"One of you shall place himself at the base of the mountain; another shall climb over him, and the first one shall grasp his tail; and another over them, and his tail shall be grasped by the second, and so on until the top is reached. Hang tight, my friends, every one of you, and every one fall in line. Eructate thoroughly before you do so. If you do not, we may be in a pretty mess; for, supposing that any one along the line should hiccough, he would lose his hold, and down we would all fall!"

So the Coyotes all at once began to curve their necks and swell themselves up and strain and wriggle and belch wind as much as possible. Then all fell into a line and grabbed each other's tails, and thus they extended themselves in a long string up the very face of Thunder Mountain. A ridiculous little pup was at one end and a good, strong, grizzled old fellow—no other than the chief of the party—at the other.

"Souls of my ancestors! Hang tight, my friends! Hang tight! Hang tight!" said he, when, suddenly, one near the top, in the agitation of the moment, began to sneeze, lost his hold, and down the whole string, hundreds of them, fell, and were completely flattened out among the rocks.

The warrior of the *Kâkâ*—he of the Long Horn, with frightful, staring eyes, and visage blue with rage,—bow and war-club in hand, was hastening from the sacred lake in the west to rescue the children of the K'yámakwe. When he arrived they had been rescued already, so, after storming around a little and mauling such of the Coyotes as were not quite dead, he set to skin them all.

And ever since then you will observe that the dancers of the Long Horn have blue faces, and whenever they arrive in our pueblo wear collars of coyote-skin about their necks. That is the way they got them. Before that they had no collars. It is presumable that that is the reason why they bellow so and have such hoarse voices, having previously taken cold, every one of them, for the want of fur collars.

THE COYOTE AND THE BEETLE
(Zuñi)

In remote times, after the ancients were settled at Middle Ant Hill, a little thing occurred which will explain a great deal.

You have doubtless seen Tip-beetles. They run around on smooth, hard patches of ground in spring time and early summer, kicking their heels into the air and thrusting their heads into any crack or hole they find.

Well, in ancient times, on the pathway leading around to Fat Mountain, there was one of these Beetles running about in all directions in the sunshine, when a Coyote came trotting along. He pricked up his ears, lowered his nose, arched his neck, and stuck out his paw toward the Beetle. "Ha!" said he, "I shall bite you!"

The Beetle immediately stuck his head down close to the ground, and, lifting one of his antennae deprecatingly, exclaimed: "Hold on! Hold on, friend! Wait a bit, for the love of mercy! I hear something very strange down below here!"

"Humph!" replied the Coyote. "What do you hear?"

"Hush! hush!" cried the Beetle, with his head still to the ground. "Listen!"

So the Coyote drew back and listened most attentively. By-and-by the Beetle lifted himself with a long sigh of relief.

"Okwe!" exclaimed the Coyote. "What was going on?"

"The Good Soul save us!" exclaimed the Beetle, with a shake of his head. "I heard them saying down there that tomorrow they would chase away and thoroughly chastise everybody who defiled the public trails of this country, and they are making ready as fast as they can!"

"Souls of my ancestors!" cried the Coyote. "I have been loitering along this trail this very morning, and have defiled it repeatedly. I'll cut!" And away he ran as fast as he could go.

The Beetle, in pure exuberance of spirits, turned somersaults and stuck his head in the sand until it was quite turned.

Thus did the Beetle in the days of the ancients save himself from being bitten. Consequently the Tip-beetle has that strange habit of kicking his heels into the air and sticking his head in the sand.

THE TWO BLIND OLD WOMEN
(Jicarilla Apache)

Two old women were once cooking a pot of mush which two mischievous boys were trying to steal. Both were blind, so one sat on each side of the fire, and they kept their sticks waving back and forth above the pot, to prevent any one from taking advantage of their blindness and removing the vessel or its contents. The boys found an empty pot, which they substituted for the one on the fire. Finding that the pot now had an empty ring when struck by their sticks, the old women concluded that the water had boiled away, and the mush must be sufficiently cooked. "Let us smoke while it cools," said one. "Very well," said the other, and they began to smoke alternately the single pipe in their possession: as they smoked they kept the sticks waving to and fro above the empty vessel. The boys took the pipe from the hand of one old woman as she was passing it to the other. "You are smoking all the time," said the second woman. "I gave you the pipe long ago," said the first. "You did not," said the second. Just then the boys struck the first woman in the mouth, and she, thinking it was the other woman, struck her companion, who, of course, retaliated, and they proceeded to belabor one another with their staves. When they were tired of fighting they went to eat their mush; each thought the other had eaten it, which set them to fighting again.

THE OLD BEGGAR
(Jicarilla Apache)

There was once an old Apache who went begging from camp to camp every evening. His wife tried to reform the old beggar by playing a trick upon him. One night during his absence she fetched a bleached horse's pelvis into the tipi, and painted it so that it somewhat resembled a face. The old man came home about midnight, and beheld, as he thought, the head of a monster glaring at him in the bright moonlight from the door of the lodge. Twice the woman held up the pelvis, when he turned in terror-stricken flight, calling, "Help, help! Something has killed my woman. Bring spears, bring arrows!" With a spear he cautiously lifted the side of the tipi, but his wife threw out the bone at the back, and he could not discover the cause of the apparition.

The next night he went out to beg again. He found plenty of buffalo meat at one of the lodges, some of which was given him to carry home. There were several horses lying outside the lodge, and the old man mistook one of them for a log, and jumped upon its back. The frightened horse rose under him, and soon succeeded in bucking him off. As the Indians came out of the tipi to investigate the cause of the stampede of the ponies, the old man said, "I told you long ago to break this horse, and now I must do it myself!" Thus avoiding, in some measure, their ridicule, he groped about until he found his meat again, and then hastened home.

The next morning he decided to move his camp. His family formed a large party, and he wished to precede them on the march. His sons were alarmed, and told him that the Cheyennes would kill and scalp him. "Oh, no," said he, "nobody will attack a warrior like me," and he walked on ahead of the others. His three sons painted their faces black and white, so that they were no longer recognizable, and then ran around in front of their father. As they ran toward him he shot all his arrows, but was too frightened to shoot straight. The young men caught him; one ran his fingernail around his scalp, while another placed a fresh buffalo's heart on the old man's head. The blood from the heart ran down his face, and he thought he was scalped. His sons allowed him to go back toward the party; on the way he came to a river, where he stooped to drink, and saw the reflected image of the raw flesh upon his head. He was then sure that he had been scalped, and sat down to die. His sons made signs to him to cross the river and go back. Again frightened by their gestures, he ran until he reached the women, who all laughed at his story of being scalped by the Cheyennes. The sons had explained the joke to their mother, and when the old man appealed to his wife for sympathy she only laughed at him, as he sat and shook with fear before her. At last they pulled off the strange head-covering, and a fresh burst of ridicule of the "brave warrior" followed.

THE OLD MAN
(Jicarilla Apache)

There was once an old man who was very fond of beaver meat. He hunted and killed beaver so frequently that his son remonstrated with him, telling him that some misfortune would surely overtake him as a punishment for his persecution of the sagacious animals, which were then endowed with the magic powers of the medicine-men. The old man did not heed the warning, but continued to kill beaver nearly every day. Again the son said, "If you kill them, they will soon catch and kill you." Not long afterward the old man saw a beaver enter a hole in the bank; disregarding his son's advice, he plunged head foremost into the burrow to catch the animal. The son saw him enter the hole, and went in after him. Catching the old man by the heels, he pushed him farther in. Thinking another beaver had attacked him, the old man was at first too frightened to move, then he cried for mercy. "Let me go, Beaver, and I will give you my knife." He threw his knife back toward the entrance, but received no reply to his entreaty. "Let me go, Beaver, and I will give you my awl." Again no answer. "Let me go, and I will give you my arrows." The young man took the articles as they were handed to him, and hastened away without making himself known.

When the old man returned to the tipi, he said nothing of his adventures, and his son asked no questions. As soon as the old man left the tipi, the son replaced the knife and other articles in his father's fire-bag. "Where is your knife?" said the son when the old man returned. "I gave it to the beaver to induce them to let me escape with my life." "I told you they would catch you," said the son.

The old man never hunted beaver again.

THE STONE-SHIELDS
(Cherokee)

In ancient times there lived among the Cherokees two strange beings,—monsters of human form, resembling Cherokees in appearance. These two monsters, a man and a woman, lived in a cave. They were called *Nayunu'wi* (Stone-shields, or Stone-jackets), or *Uilata* (sharp, pointed), because they had sharp-pointed steel (?) hands.

These monsters killed children, and sometimes adults. As they dressed like Cherokees, and spoke their language, it was difficult to distinguish them from this people.

The man generally killed hunters and other people who were alone and far from home, by attacking them. The woman used tricks to procure her victims. She came to the houses, kindly offering her services, offering to nurse children, and do similar things.

As soon as she had a child in her arms, she ran away with it, until she was out of hearing, and pierced the brain of the child with her steel hand, then took the liver from the body and disappeared. The Nayunu'wi appear to have lived on the livers of their victims.

The older Cherokees, long tired of the ravages of these monsters, held a council to determine the best way of killing the Uilata. At last they resolved to kill them with arrows, not knowing that the Uilata were stone clad. As soon as they saw an opportunity to attack the woman, they shot their arrows at her with all their might, but they were very much astonished to see that the arrows did not take the slightest effect.

Then a topknot-bird, which was perched on the branch of a tree close by, said to the warriors: "In the heart, in the heart!"

The Cherokees shot their arrows at the spot where they supposed the heart to be, but no better than before did they succeed in killing the monster.

At last a jay appeared, and said to the warriors: "In the hand, in the hand!"

They shot the monster's hand, and it dropped dead. At the moment it fell its stone jacket broke into pieces. The people gathered the fragments, and kept them as sacred amulets, for luck in war, in hunting, and in love.

The man-monster disappeared; according to tradition, it went north.

The Cherokees possess also a legend about flying monsters, having the form of falcons. These caught and killed especially children. They were slain by a brave man, whose little and only son had been captured by them. He followed them to their cave, where they kept their young, and killed the latter. Thereafter the old falcons disappeared forever.

THE HORNED SNAKES
(Cherokee)

In ancient times there lived great snakes, glittering as the sun, and having two horns on the head. To see one of these snakes was certain death. They possessed such power of fascination, that whoever tried to make his escape, ran toward the snake and was devoured.

Only great hunters who had made medicine especially for this purpose could kill these snakes. It was always necessary to shoot them in the seventh stripe of their skins.

The last of these snakes was killed by a Shawnee Indian, who was a prisoner among the Cherokees. They had promised him freedom if he could find and kill the snake.

He hunted for the snake during several days, in caves, and over wild mountains, and found it at last high up on the mountains of Tennessee.

The Shawnee kindled a great fire of pine cones, in the form of a large circle, and then walked up to the snake.

As soon as it saw the hunter, the snake slowly raised its head, but the Shawnee shouted, "Freedom or death!" and shot his arrow through the seventh stripe of the snake's skin; then turning quickly, he jumped within the circle of the fire, where he was safe. At this moment a stream of poison poured down from the mouth of the snake, but the fire stopped it. So the Shawnee had regained his liberty.

Four days afterwards the Cherokees went to the spot where the snake had been killed, and gathered fragments of bone and scales of the snake's skin. These they kept carefully, as they believed the pieces would bring them good luck in love, the chase, and war.

On the spot where the snake had been killed, a lake formed, the water of which was black. In the water of this lake the Cherokee women used to dip the twigs with which they made their baskets.

CANNIBAL STORIES
(Various)

THE BROTHER WHO WAS EATEN
(Ute)

A man lived on a rock with his two grandsons. He told the boys, "You had better go hunting and bring something to eat. I am hungry. Go to the hills, sit on the top, and watch in all directions; then you may find something." Then the boys went off and watched in the brush. An elk came straight towards them. One of them said, "I see an elk. Let us kill it." The other said, "My older brother, let us run away. I am afraid." The older said, "No. Sit still. It is an elk. I shall shoot it, as our grandfather directed." The other one said, "No. I am afraid."

When the older was nearly ready to shoot, his younger brother fled, crying, "Let us run away. I am frightened." Then the elk started back. The older one said, "What is it? Are you crazy? I was nearly ready to shoot that elk." The younger said, "I was frightened; but I know now that it is an elk. Let us go after it; it cannot have gone far."

When they got near the elk again, the younger brother wanted to shoot at it. The older brother wanted him to stay behind, but did not persuade him. When they were ready to shoot, the younger again ran off shouting, and the elk escaped. The older brother upbraided him; he nearly struck him. The younger said, "I was afraid that it would jump on me. I became frightened." Again he persuaded the older to take him with him. When they approached the elk another time, he again persuaded his older brother to allow him to shoot, saying, that if one of them missed, the other could still try to hit it. But the same thing happened as before. Then the older brother again became angry and reviled the younger. It was now sunset, but once again the younger persuaded the older to go after the elk; so they went around ahead of it. Then the older tied the arms and the legs of the younger, and tied up his mouth. The elk came close. The younger one began to emit smothered screams. Then the older brother hurriedly shot. He killed the elk. The younger was tossing about, trying to scream and to flee. "Are you crazy? I have killed the elk," said the older. "Have you really killed it?" asked the younger. Then he loosened his younger brother and showed him the elk. The younger said, "What kind of a deer is that?" The older said, "It is an elk. Hurry! Get some brush for a fire. Let us skin it and go home quickly. There may be bad persons about here." The younger said, "I will get some presently." Then the older said, "What is the matter with you? Get some brush so that we can go home." "I will get some presently," said the younger. Again the older said to him, "Make a fire quickly. I will roast some meat and eat it, then I will go home. Be quick!" "No. Presently. I want to rest now," said the younger. He would not help his older brother. So that one alone skinned the game and cooked some of the meat. Then he said, "Let us go home now. There may be bad things about. I am frightened." The younger said, "No. I am afraid to go. I cannot go home. Let us stay here for the night; there is nothing bad about here." Then the older urged him no more. He said, "Let us sleep in a cedar. Make a bed." The younger one agreed and made a bed in the top of the cedar, after they had buried the meat. Then they slept. In the middle of the night the younger one said, "I am hungry. I will go down to eat." The older said to him, "What is the matter with you? Eat tomorrow, sleep now." But the younger one insisted on going down to eat. Finally his older brother said, "Very well." Then the younger brother went down, made a large fire, and cooked a whole shoulder of the elk. He began to eat. Then there were cries from far off from all directions. The boy said, "What is it? Is anyone approaching? Come here! we will eat." The older brother remained in the cedar.

Then some one came to the opposite side of the fire. He was a large, long man. The younger brother said, "Come, my friend, eat; I have good food; sit down there." There was no answer. "Here is something to eat," said the boy, holding it out to him. The person did not take it. He did not answer even when he was repeatedly spoken to. Then the boy hit him on the head and knocked him down. Coming closer, he then stood by his head, whereupon the man reached out and caught him with a violent grip, in scroto. "Oh! Oh! Let me go!" cried the boy. The man continued to hold him. "Do not hold me. Oh! Oh! You hurt me. Let me go. My older brother, come to help me. This man is holding me." But his older brother was angry and did not come down. The man squeezed him harder, while the boy groaned. Then he walked off with him. The older brother heard his cries growing faint; then he ceased to hear them on account of the distance.

In the morning he came down from the tree. Crying, he followed the tracks. He saw that they led to a lake and right down into it. He could go no farther. Going back and taking the elk-meat, he went home and told his grandfather. (The story here makes him repeat what has been told.) His grandfather said to him, "We will go tomorrow to see that place." Then they went to the lake and watched it. Then the old man said, "Wait here while I go down, following the tracks." He was away until noon. Then he came up, bringing a dead man, and laid him down. He said, "This is the man that killed your brother. Deep down I killed him." Again he went into the lake and stayed until nearly sunset. Then he came up with another. "This is the man that killed your brother," he said. "I entered his house and killed him. Now open his mouth and look at his teeth." The boy saw a little meat between the teeth. His grandfather said to him, "Take a stick and pick out the meat from his teeth." The boy did so and made a little pile of it. Then the old man told him to cut open the dead man. When he had done so, he asked him, "Do you see any bones or other parts? Pick them out." The boy did as he was told, and then did the same to the other man. They put the meat and bones into a hollow stone and carried it home. They left it standing outside, a short distance from the tent. Then they slept. Early in the morning his grandfather said, "He is shouting, *'Wuwu-wuwu!'* Do you hear him?" "Yes," said the older brother. They answered with a shout. Then he came. "Well, my older brother," he said. He had arisen from the meat.

THE CANNIBAL AND HIS TWO WIVES
(Ute)

There was a very large man. He had a big head, a protruding belly, and long feet. He had two wives. They had nothing to eat but ground grass-seed. They lived alone, where they saw no one. There was not even game to hunt. The man said to his wives, "Let us go Eastward again. I am tired of eating this grass-seed. I am tired of seeing no tracks, and of seeing no game; therefore I wish to go East." The next day they moved away. Seeing a mountain, they went up it, then down the other side. They saw a spring and camped there, staying the next day. The man said, "Stay here. I will go on and hunt."

He found the tracks of a man, a woman, and two children. Coming back he said, "I saw the tracks of four persons. I shall go and look for them; perhaps we shall see them living somewhere." Then he went with his wives to where he had seen the tracks. There they saw two antelopes. "Kill them. I am hungry," said one of the women to him. "No, they belong to him (they are his horses)," said the man. They followed the tracks and again camped at a spring. Then the man left the two women after saying to them, "I will go after that man and kill him. I want to eat him. I shall bring him back, and you also will like to eat him." Then he went, watching closely. He saw the man, and shot him. Then he shot the woman and choked the children. He returned to his women and said, "Let us go there. I have killed them all. We will go to butcher them." So they skinned the man and woman. Then he told one of his wives to skin the boy neatly and carefully. The meat they dried, hanging it up. They stayed there two days. The man ate all the meat. He ate the bones of the feet and everything else, throwing nothing away. Then he said, "Stay here; I will travel about to see if I can find anything. I will take the skin of that boy with me."

He ascended a mountain, he peered over the top, but saw nothing. Then he raised his head higher, and saw a tent, with two women and a man near it. He took the stuffed skin of the boy, held it up, and moved it about. The second time he did so, the man saw it, and said to the women, "A boy is up there. Did you see him? I will go up to him." The cannibal laid the stuffed skin down and hid in the bushes. The man came up and said to the boy, "Who are you? Get up. Can you not sit up?" The cannibal drew his bow and shot the man. He ran a short way, fell, and died. Then the cannibal went on another hill, and did the same there. He held the boy in front of a cedar and made him wave his hand. "Did you see that boy? He is over there," said a young man, who was with the women. He went up the hill. The cannibal laid the boy down, and shot this one, as he had shot the other. Thus he had killed two men. Then he showed the boy in another place; but the women did not come to him. "We will both stay here and wait until the men come," they said. Then the cannibal made a circuit to the other side of the tent. He approached it and again showed the skin. One of the women saw the boy, and called to him, "Who are you? What tribe are you?" But the man only lowered the boy out of sight, and then made him appear to look again. But the women did not come to him; therefore he left the hide lying and approached the tent from another side. He came up to the women. "Where is your husband?" he asked. They said to him, "He went there after a boy. A young man also went away after that one and has not come back; perhaps the boy was only playing." Then he shot both of the women, one after the other. Taking the stuffed hide, he went back to his tent. He told his wives, "I have killed four pieces of game. Let us remove there." Then they went there and lived in that tent. He said to his women, "Skin this woman well and tan her hide; make it your dress. After three nights, I will go to hunt again." Then they skinned her. They tanned the skin; they made it stiff and crackling. One of them used it for a dress. The cannibal ate one of the men. He put the head into the fire to roast. "Gather the bones and get the marrow," he said. Soon the women were fat from eating grease and marrow.

After the man had slept three times, he said, "I will kill another one for you now. You stay here and I will go hunting." Then he went away, taking the boy's skin. He saw an old man, a woman, and a girl. On the top of the hill, he showed them the boy. The old man said, "I see a boy there. I will go to see what kind of a boy is there." So he went up and was shot. Again the man showed the boy in another place. The old woman said, "Let us go to see who the boy is. Perhaps some one is living on the other side of the hill now." Then they both went there. The man put down the stuffed skin and hid behind some cedars. He shot both of the women. Then he went to their tent, but he found no one else there; he had killed all. He went home and told his women. They all went there. He said to them, "Skin this woman, and make a dress of her. I will skin this old man. I think I like his skin for my blanket." So they skinned them and dried the meat. "Now tan that skin," he said to one of the women. Then she made it stiff. Then he said, "Remain here. I will hunt again."

Again he went, carrying the boy's skin. He went far and found no one. In the middle of the day he became tired. He went to a spring and drank, and lay down with the stuffed hide beside him. He slept. Two men came to drink. They found him with the stuffed skin of the boy. They spoke to each other, and knew that he was a bad man. They fled. Then he shot at them and killed one. The other one escaped. The cannibal went home and said, "I killed one at the spring; let us go there. One of them escaped." The women cried. "Why do you cry?" he asked. "They said, "Because you let him escape. I want him." "Oh!" he said. "I will get him later." The other man fled. He said to the people, "I saw a bad person. He has a big belly, a big head, and big feet. I saw that he had the skin of a boy. He is bad." Then they removed to another camp and told those persons there. These also were afraid, and removed to another place. Thus all went away, being much afraid. Only in one camp there remained a young man and his mother. All the others fled. His mother said to him, "Let us flee, my son. He is a bad person; he will kill us." He said to her, "No, we will stay here. I want to talk to that one; I think he is my friend." His mother was much frightened, and continued to tell him to go away. After a while he said to her, "Now, mother, get water in a large basket." They lived on a slate hill. On the rock he made a small lake with the water that she brought. Ten times she brought him water, and he poured it in. Then he told his mother to grind a basketful of seeds and to cook them. She did this. She was much frightened. "I am afraid," she said. "I will run away." He said to her, "No, my mother, do not fear him. Let him come. He will not hurt you. Go and set fire to that cedar so that he will see the smoke, and come to visit us." The man saw it and told his wives. "Some one is over there. I saw smoke." They said to him, "Good, you will kill him." He said to them, "I will go there now; perhaps there are many people. I will stay there one night; perhaps I will kill ten. If I do not come back after one night, you must come after me."

Then he traveled fast. He went on a hill and peered over. The young man was looking for him and saw him. "Look, mother, there is that man," he said. "Oh, my son, I will run away," said she. Then the cannibal raised the stuffed skin. The young man cried out, "Why do you do that? Come here, you." So that one left the skin and went there. His mother said, "He is coming now. Let us run." "No," said the young man. She ran a short distance. He called to her, "Come back, my mother. Let him come. Give him this food." Then she came back to him, shaking. Now the cannibal arrived there. The young man went to him quickly and said, "Well, my friend," and took his hand. "Sit down there," he said to him; and the man with the large belly sat down there. "Are you hungry?" he asked him. "Yes," he said. "What do wish? Do you want meat or something else?" he said to him. "Anything," said the man. "Very well. Do you like this food? It is already cooked," said the young man. Then he gave him a basketful. That one drank it all. "Have you finished?" he asked the man. He said, "No." Then he gave him another basketful. Again the man drank this off. The young man said to him, "Where do you live? Where is your tent? What is your purpose in coming here?" The man said to him, "I live far away. I came here with no purpose." The young man said to him, "Stay here one night. We will talk together." But that one wished to go back home. The young man said, "Do you wish to urinate or defecate?" "No," said the man. "When you wish it, do so there," said the young man to him. After a little while the man said, "I am full now. I must defecate." The young man said to him, "Very well. Come. I made a lake over there by urinating." The cannibal said, "Where shall I urinate?" "Here," said the young man. Then he said, "I have a pretty eagle here on this cliff. Do you wish to see it?" Then the large-bellied one lay down and looked over the jutting cliff to see the eagle. The young man threw him down into the lake. He swam around and around. All about him the rock was steep. He could not get out. The young man watched him. Soon he began to be tired. He went down. Then he came up again; he was nearly dead. At last he drowned.

The next day the young man stayed at home. He said to his mother, "Where is your rope? What did you do with it? I wish to pull that man out." "No. He is a bad man," she said to him. But he said, "Give me the rope. I will do what is good." She gave him the rope. He went down to the water and tied the legs and the hands of the man. Then he pulled him up. He butchered him, skinned him, and told his mother to dry the meat. "Why do you do this?" she said. He said to her, "I think his women will come. We will give them his meat to eat and go outside. We will watch what they do." Then he put the head under the fire in order to cook it. He laid down two large, fat pieces ready cooked. Then he went away behind a rock and watched. He saw two women come. They saw the meat hanging to dry, and saw the cooked meat lying there. They sat down and ate it greedily, laughing. One of them said to the other, "Perhaps my husband went to kill the others. He has already killed a fat one." Soon they had finished. One of them saw the head covered up in the fire. She said, "See the head. Let us eat it." Then they took it out. "I want part of it," said the other. Then they cut it in two. They ate it, laughing. One said, "My husband cooks well." Then one said, "I am sleepy." The other one said she was sleepy; so they went to sleep. The young man watched them. One began to sleep lightly. Then she awoke. She said, "Get up, my sister! My heart is bad, it hits me hard. I think I ate the flesh of my husband." The other one said, "Yes, I also feel bad. I do not know what is the trouble. I think the same as you think." Now they both cried. The young man had been watching them. Now he came and they saw him. He said, "What is the matter with you? Why do you not eat this meat hanging here? Your husband has gone away hunting." They said to each other, "Perhaps he killed our husband." Then he said to them, "Yes, I killed your husband. He is a bad man. I will kill you also." "No, do not kill me," they cried. He said, "No, I will certainly kill you." "Do not kill me," they said. Again he said, "No, I will kill you." Then he shot them. He killed them both. He said, "That one has killed many persons, but now he is gone.

He is killed. People will not do thus any more. They will be friends and will not eat each other. That one was insane."

LOVERS
(Various)

KÓLOWISSI AND THE MAIDEN
(Zuñi)

In the times of our forefathers, under Thunder Mountain was a village called *K'iákime* ("Home of the Eagles"). It is now in ruins; the roofs are gone, the ladders have decayed, the hearths grown cold. But when it was all still perfect, and, as it were, new, there lived in this village a maiden, the daughter of the priest-chief. She was beautiful, but possessed of this peculiarity of character: There was a sacred spring of water at the foot of the terrace whereon stood the town. We now call it the Pool of the Apaches; but then it was sacred to *Kólowissi* (the Serpent of the Sea). Now, at this spring the girl displayed her peculiarity, which was that of a passion for neatness and cleanliness of person and clothing. She could not endure the slightest speck or particle of dust or dirt upon her clothes or person, and so she spent most of her time in washing all the things she used and in bathing herself in the waters of this spring.

Now, these waters, being sacred to the Serpent of the Sea, should not have been defiled in this way. As might have been expected, Kólowissi became troubled and angry at the sacrilege committed in the sacred waters by the maiden, and he said: "Why does this maiden defile the sacred waters of my spring with the dirt of her apparel and the dun of her person? I must see to this." So he devised a plan by which to prevent the sacrilege and to punish its author.

When the maiden came again to the spring, what should she behold but a beautiful little child seated amidst the waters, splashing them, cooing and smiling. It was the Sea Serpent, wearing the semblance of a child,—for a god may assume any form at its pleasure, you know. There sat the child, laughing and playing in the water. The girl looked around in all directions—north, south, east, and west—but could see no one, nor any traces of persons who might have brought hither the beautiful little child. She said to herself: "I wonder whose child this may be! It would seem to be that of some unkind and cruel mother, who has deserted it and left it here to perish. And the poor little child does not yet know that it is left all alone. Poor little thing! I will take it in my arms and care for it."

The maiden then talked softly to the young child, and took it in her arms, and hastened with it up the hill to her house, and, climbing up the ladder, carried the child in her arms into the room where she slept.

Her peculiarity of character, her dislike of all dirt or dust, led her to dwell apart from the rest of her family, in a room by herself above all of the other apartments.

She was so pleased with the child that when she had got him into her room she sat down on the floor and played with him, laughing at his pranks and smiling into his face; and he answered her in baby fashion with cooings and smiles of his own, so that her heart became very happy and loving. So it happened that thus was she engaged for a long while and utterly unmindful of the lapse of time.

Meanwhile, the younger sisters had prepared the meal, and were awaiting the return of the elder sister.

"Where, I wonder, can she be?" one of them asked.

"She is probably down at the spring," said the old father; "she is bathing and washing her clothes, as usual, of course! Run down and call her."

But the younger sister, on going, could find no trace of her at the spring. So she climbed the ladder to the private room of this elder sister, and there found her, as has been told, playing with the little child. She hastened back to inform her father of what she had seen. But the old man sat silent and thoughtful. He knew that the waters of the spring were sacred. When the rest of the family were excited, and ran to behold the pretty prodigy, he cried out, therefore: "Come back! come back! Why do you make fools of yourselves? Do you suppose any mother would leave her own child in the waters of this or any other spring? There is something more of meaning than seems in all this."

When they again went and called the maiden to come down to the meal spread for her, she could not be induced to leave the child.

"See! it is as you might expect," said the father. "A woman will not leave a child on any inducement; how much less her own."

The child at length grew sleepy. The maiden placed it on a bed, and, growing sleepy herself, at length lay by its side and fell asleep. Her sleep was genuine, but the sleep of the child was feigned. The child became elongated by degrees, as it were, fulfilling some horrible dream, and soon appeared as an enormous Serpent that coiled itself around and around the room until it was full of scaly, gleaming circles. Then, placing its head near the head of the maiden, the great Serpent surrounded her with its coils, taking finally its own tail in its mouth.

The night passed, and in the morning when the breakfast was prepared, and yet the maiden did not descend, and the younger sisters became impatient at the delay, the old man said: "Now that she has the child to play with, she will care little for aught else. That is enough to occupy the entire attention of any woman."

But the little sister ran up to the room and called. Receiving no answer, she tried to open the door; she could not move it, because the Serpent's coils filled the room and pressed against it. She pushed the door with all her might, but it could not be moved. She again and again called her sister's name, but no response came. Beginning now to be frightened, she ran to the skyhole over the room in which she had left the others and cried out for help. They hastily joined her,—all save the old father,—and together were able to press the door sufficiently to get a glimpse of the great scales and folds of the Serpent. Then the women all ran screaming to the old father. The old man, priest and sage as he was, quieted them with these words: "I expected as much as this from the first report which you gave me. It was impossible, as I then said, that a woman should be so foolish as to leave her child playing even near the waters of the spring. But it is not impossible, it seems, that one should be so foolish as to take into her arms a child found as this one was."

Thereupon he walked out of the house, deliberately and thoughtful, angry in his mind against his eldest daughter. Ascending to her room, he pushed against the door and called to the Serpent of the Sea: "Oh, Kólowissi! It is I, who speak to thee, O Serpent of the Sea; I, thy priest. Let, I pray thee, let my child come to me again, and I will make atonement for her errors. Release her, though she has been so foolish, for she is thine, absolutely thine. But let her return once more to us that we may make atonement to thee more amply." So prayed the priest to the Serpent of the Sea.

When he had done this the great Serpent loosened his coils, and as he did so the whole building shook violently, and all the villagers became aware of the event, and trembled with fear.

The maiden at once awoke and cried piteously to her father for help.

"Come and release me, oh, my father! Come and release me!" she cried.

As the coils loosened she found herself able to rise. No sooner had she done this than the great Serpent bent the folds of his large coils nearest the doorway upward so that they formed an arch. Under this, filled with terror, the girl passed. She was almost stunned with the dread din of the monster's scales rasping past one another with a noise like the sound of flints trodden under the feet of a rapid runner, and once away from the writhing mass of coils, the poor maiden ran like a frightened deer out of the doorway, down the ladder and into the room below, casting herself on the breast of her mother.

But the priest still remained praying to the Serpent; and he ended his prayer as he had begun it, saying: "It shall be even as I have said; she shall be thine!"

He then went away and called the two warrior priest-chiefs of the town, and these called together all the other priests in sacred council. Then they performed the solemn ceremonies of the sacred rites—preparing plumes, prayer-wands, and offerings of treasure.

After four days of labor, these things they arranged and consecrated to the Serpent of the Sea. On that morning the old priest called his daughter and told her she must make ready to take these sacrifices and yield them up, even with herself, —most precious of them all,—to the great Serpent of the Sea; that she must yield up also all thoughts of her people and home forever, and go hence to the house of the great Serpent of the Sea, even in the Waters of the World. "For it seems," said he, "to have been your desire to do thus, as manifested by your actions. You used even the sacred water for profane purposes; now this that I have told you is inevitable. Come; the time when you must prepare yourself to depart is near at hand."

She went forth from the home of her childhood with sad cries, clinging to the neck of her mother and shivering with terror. In the plaza, amidst the lamentations of all the people, they dressed her in her sacred cotton robes of ceremonial, embroidered elaborately, and adorned her with earrings, bracelets, beads,—many beautiful, precious things. They painted her cheeks with red spots as if for a dance; they made a road of sacred meal toward the Door of the Serpent of the Sea—a distant spring in our land known to this day as the Doorway to the Serpent of the Sea—four steps toward this spring did they mark in sacred terraces on the ground at the western way of the plaza. And when they had finished the sacred road, the old priest, who never shed one tear, although all the villagers wept sore,—for the maiden was very beautiful,—instructed his daughter to go forth on the terraced road, and, standing there, call the Serpent to come to her.

Then the door opened, and the Serpent descended from the high room where he was coiled, and, without using ladders, let his head and breast down to the ground in great undulations. He placed his head on the shoulder of the maiden, and the word was given—the word: "It is time"—and the maiden slowly started toward the west, cowering beneath her burden; but whenever she staggered with fear and weariness and was like to wander from the way, the Serpent gently pushed her onward and straightened her course.

Thus they went toward the river trail and in it, on and over the Mountain of the Red Paint; yet still the Serpent was not all uncoiled from the maiden's room in the house, but continued to crawl forth until they were past the mountain—when the last of his length came forth. Here he began to draw himself together again and to assume a new shape. So that ere long his serpent form contracted, until, lifting his head from the maiden's shoulder, he stood up, in form a beautiful youth in sacred gala attire! He placed the scales of his serpent form, now small, under his flowing mantle, and called out to the maiden in a hoarse, hissing voice: "Let us speak one to the other. Are you tired, girl?" Yet she never moved her head, but plodded on with her eyes cast down.

"Are you weary, poor maiden?"—then he said in a gentler voice, as he arose erect and fell a little behind her, and wrapped his scales more closely in his blanket —and he was now such a splendid and brave hero, so magnificently dressed! And he repeated, in a still softer voice: "Are you still weary, poor maiden?"

At first she dared not look around, though the voice, so changed, sounded so far behind her and thrilled her wonderfully with its kindness. Yet she still felt the weight on her shoulder, the weight of that dreaded Serpent's head; for you know after one has carried a heavy burden on his shoulder or back, if it be removed he does not at once know that it is taken away; it seems still to oppress and pain him. So it was with her; but at length she turned around a little and saw a young man—a brave and handsome young man.

"May I walk by your side?" said he, catching her eye. "Why do you not speak with me?"

"I am filled with fear and sadness and shame," said she.

"Why?" asked he. "What do you fear?"

"Because I came with a fearful creature forth from my home, and he rested his head upon my shoulder, and even now I feel his presence there," said she, lifting her hand to the place where his head had rested, even still fearing that it might be there.

"But I came all the way with you," said he, "and I saw no such creature as you describe."

Upon this she stopped and turned back and looked again at him, and said: "You came all the way? I wonder where this fearful being has gone!"

He smiled, and replied: "I know where he has gone."

"Ah, youth and friend, will he now leave me in peace," said she, "and let me return to the home of my people?"

"No," replied he, "because he thinks very much of you."

"Why not? Where is he?"

"He is here," said the youth, smiling, and laying his hand on his own heart. "I am he."

"You are he?" cried the maiden. Then she looked at him again, and would not believe him.

"Yea, my maiden, I am he!" said he. And he drew forth from under his flowing mantle the shrivelled serpent scales, and showed them as proofs of his word. It was wonderful and beautiful to the maiden to see that he was thus, a gentle being; and she looked at him long.

Then he said: "Yes, I am he. I love you, my maiden! Will you not haply come forth and dwell with me? Yes, you will go with me, and dwell with me, and I will dwell with you, and I will love you. I dwell not now, but ever, in all the Waters of the World, and in each particular water. In all and each you will dwell with me forever, and we will love each other."

Behold! As they journeyed on, the maiden quite forgot that she had been sad; she forgot her old home, and followed and descended with him into the Doorway of the Serpent of the Sea and dwelt with him ever after.

The Marriage Test
(Zūñi)

In the days of the ancients, long, long ago, there lived in our town, which was then called the Middle Ant Hill of the World, a proud maiden, very pretty and very attractive, the daughter of one of the richest men among our people. She had every possession a Zuñi maiden could wish for,—blankets and mantles, embroidered dresses and sashes, buckskins and moccasins, turquoise earrings and shell neck-laces, bracelets so many you could not count them. She had her father and mother, brothers and sisters, all of whom she loved very much. Why, therefore, should she care for anything else?

There was only one thing to trouble her. Behold! it came of much possession, for she had large corn-fields, so large and so many that those who planted and worked them for her could not look after them properly, and no sooner had the corn ears become full and sweet with the milk of their being than all sorts of animals broke into those fields and pulled down the corn-stalks and ate up the sweet ears of corn. Now, how to remove this difficulty the poor girl did not know.

Yes, now that I think of it, there was another thing that troubled her very much, fully as much as did the corn-pests,—pests of another kind, however, for there wasn't an unmarried young man in all the valley of our ancients who was not running mad over the charms of this girl. Besides all that, not a few of them had an eye on so many possessions, and thought her home wouldn't be an uncomfortable place to live in. So they never gave the poor girl any peace, but hung round her house, and came to visit her father so constantly that at last she determined to put the two pests together and call them one, and thereby get rid, if possible, of one or the other. So, when these young men were very importunate, she would say to them, "Look you! if any one of you will go to my cornfields, and destroy or scare away, so that they will never come back again, the pests that eat up my corn, him I will marry and cherish, for I shall respect his ability and ingenuity."

The young men tried and tried, but it was of no use. Before long, everybody knew of this singular proposition.

There was a young fellow who lived in one of the outer towns, the poorest of the poor among our people; and not only that, but he was so ugly that no woman would ever look at him without laughing.

Now, there are two kinds of laugh with women. One of them is a very good sort of thing, and makes young men feel happy and conceited. The other kind is some-what heartier, but makes young men feel depressed and very humble. It need not be asked which kind was laughed by the women when they saw this ugly, ragged, miserable-looking young man. He had bright twinkling eyes, however, and that means more than all else sometimes.

Now, this young man came to hear of what was going on. He had no present to offer the girl, but he admired her as much as—yes, a good deal more than—if he had been the handsomest young man of his time. So just in the way that he was he went to the house of this girl one evening. He was received politely, and it was noticeable to the old folks that the girl seemed rather to like him,—just as it is noticeable to you and me today that what people have they prize less than what they have not. The girl placed a tray of bread before the young man and bade him eat; and after he had done, he looked around with his twinkling little eyes. And the old man said, "Let us smoke together." And so they smoked.

By-and-by the old man asked if he were not thinking of something in coming to the house of a stranger. And the young man replied, it was very true; he had thoughts, though he felt ashamed to say it, but he even wished to be accepted as a suitor for his daughter.

The father referred the matter to the girl, and she said she would be very well satisfied; then she took the young man aside and spoke a few words to him,—in fact, told him what were the conditions of his becoming her accepted husband. He smiled, and said he would certainly try to the best of his ability, but this was a very hard thing she asked.

"I know it is," said the girl; "that is why I ask it."

Now, the young man left the house forthwith. The next day he very quietly went down into the corn-fields belonging to the girl, and over toward the northern mesa, for that is where her corn-fields were—lucky being! He dug a great deep pit with a sharp stick and a bone shovel. Now, when he had dug it—very smooth at the sides and top it was—he went to the mountain and got some poles, placing them across the hole, and over these poles he spread earth, and set up corn-stalks just as though no hole had been dug there; then he put some exceedingly tempting bait, plenty of it, over the center of these poles, which were so weak that nobody, however light of foot, could walk over them without breaking through.

Night came on, and you could hear the Coyotes begin to sing; and the whole army of pests—Bears, Badgers, Gophers, all sorts of creatures, as they came down slowly, each one in his own way, from the mountain. The Coyotes first came into the field, being swift of foot; and one of them, nosing around and keeping a sharp lookout for watchers, happened to espy those wonderfully tempting morsels that lay over the hole.

"Ha!" said he (Coyotes don't think much what they are doing), and he gave a leap, when in he went—sticks, dirt, bait, and all—to the bottom of the hole. He picked himself up and rubbed the sand out of his eyes, then began to jump and jump, trying to get out; but it was of no use, and he set up a most doleful howl.

He had just stopped for breath, when a Bear came along. "What in the name of all the devils and witches are you howling so for?" said he. "Where are you?"

The Coyote swallowed his whimpers immediately, set himself up in a careless attitude, and cried out: "Broadfoot, lucky, lucky, lucky fellow! Did you hear me singing? I am the happiest creature on the face of the earth, or rather under it."

"What about? I shouldn't think you were happy, to judge from your howling."

"Why! Mercy on me!" cried the Coyote, "I was singing for joy."

"How's that?" asked the Bear.

"Why," said the Coyote, "I came along here this evening and by the merest accident fell into this hole. And what do you suppose I found down here? Green-corn, meat, sweet-stuff, and everything a corn-eater could wish for. The only thing I lacked to complete my happiness was someone to enjoy the meal with me. Jump in! —it isn't very deep—and fall to, friend. We'll have a jolly good night of it."

So the old Bear looked down, drew back a minute, hesitated, and then jumped in. When the Bear got down there, the Coyote laid himself back, slapped his thighs, and laughed and laughed and laughed. "Now, get out if you can," said he to the Bear. "You and I are in a pretty mess. I fell in here by accident, it is true, but I would give my teeth and eyes if I could get out again!"

The Bear came very near eating him up, but the Coyote whispered something in his ear. "Good!" yelled the Bear. "Ha! ha! ha! Excellent idea! Let us sing together. Let them come!"

So they laughed and sang and feasted until they attracted almost every corn-pest in the fields to the spot to see what they were doing. "Keep away, my friends," cried out the Coyote. "No such luck for you. We got here first. Our spoils!"

"Can't I come?" "Can't I come?" cried out one after another.

"Well, yes,—no,—there may not be enough for you all." "Come on, though; come on! who cares?"—cried out the old Bear. And they rushed in so fast that very soon the pit-hole was almost full of them, scrambling to get ahead of one another, and before they knew their predicament they were already in it. The Coyote laughed, shuffled around, and screamed at the top of his voice; he climbed up over his grandfather the Bear, scrambled through the others, which were snarling and bit-ing each other, and, knowing what he was about, skipped over their backs, out of the hole, and ran away laughing as hard as he could.

Now, the next morning down to the corn-field came the young man. Drawing near to the pit he heard a tremendous racket, and going to the edge and peering in he saw that it was half filled with the pests which had been destroying the corn of the maiden,—every kind of creature that had ever meddled with the corn-fields of man, there they were in that deep pit; some of them all tired out, waiting for "the end of their daylight," others still jumping and crawling and falling in their efforts to get out.

"Good! good! my friends," cried the young man. "You must be cold; I'll warm you up a little." So he gathered a quantity of dry wood and threw it into the pit. "Be patient! be patient!" said he. "I hope I don't hurt any of you. It will be all over in a few minutes." Then he lighted the wood and burned the rascals all up. But he noticed the Coyote was not there. "What does it matter?" said he. "One kind of pest a man can fight, but not many."

So he went back to the house of the girl and reported to her what he had done. She was so pleased she hardly knew how to express her gratitude, but said to the young man with a smile on her face and a twinkle in her eye, "Are you quite sure they were all there?"

"Why, they were all there except the Coyote," said the young man; "but I must tell you the truth, and somehow he got out or didn't get in."

"Who cares for a Coyote!" said the girl. "I would much rather marry a man with some ingenuity about him than have all the Coyotes in the world to kill." Where upon she accepted this very ugly but ingenious young man; and it is notable that ever since then pretty girls care very little how their husbands look, being pretty enough themselves for both. But they like to have them able to think and guess at a way of getting along occasionally. Furthermore, what does a rich girl care for a rich young man? Ever since then, even to this day, as you know, rich girls almost invariably pick out poor young men for their husbands, and rich young men are sure to take a fancy to poor girls.

Thus it was in the days of the ancients. The Coyote got out of the trap that was set for him by the ugly young man. That is the reason why coyotes are so much more abundant than any other corn-pests in the land of Zuñi, and do what you will, they are sure to get away with some of your corn, anyhow.

ACANTOW AND MANETABEE
(Ute)

Acantow, one of the chiefs of his tribe, usually placed his lodge beside the spring that bubbled from a thicket of wild roses in the place where Rosita, CO, stands today. He left his wife—*Manetabee* (Rosebud)—in the lodge while he went across the mountains to attend a council, and was gone four sleeps. On his return he found neither wife nor lodge, but footprints and hoofprints in the ground showed to his keen eye that it was the Arapahoes who had been there.

Getting on their trail he rode over it furiously, and at night had reached Oak Cañon, along which he traveled until he saw the gleam of a small fire ahead. A squall was coming up, and the noise of it might have enabled him to gallop fairly into the group that he saw huddled about the glow; but it is not in the nature of an Indian to do that, and, tying his horse, he crawled forward.

There were fifteen of the Arapahoes, and they were gambling to decide the ownership of Manetabee, who sat bound beneath a willow near them. So engrossed were the savages in the contest that the snake-like approach of Acantow was unnoticed until he had cut the thongs that bound Manetabee's wrists and ankles—she did not cry out, for she had expected rescue—and both had imperceptibly slid away from them. Then, with a yell, one of the gamblers pointed to the receding forms, and straightway the fifteen made an onset.

Swinging his wife lightly to his shoulders Acantow set off at a run and he had almost reached his horse when his foot caught in a root and he fell headlong. The pursuers were almost upon him when the storm burst in fury. A flood of fire rushed from the clouds and struck the earth with an appalling roar. Trees were snapped, rocks were splintered, and a whirlwind passed. Acantow was nearly insensible for a time—then he felt the touch of the Rosebud's hand on his cheek, and together they arose and looked about them. A huge block of riven granite lay in the cañon, dripping blood. Their enemies were not to be seen.

"The trail is gone," said Acantow. "Manitou has broken it, that the Arapahoes may never cross it more. He would not allow them to take you. Let us thank the Manitou." So they went back to where the spring burst amid the rose-bushes.

Ta-in-ga-ro and Zecana
(Unidentified)

A mong the sandstone columns of the Colorado foot-hills stood the lodge of *Ta-in-ga-ro* (First Falling Thunder). Though swift in the chase and brave in battle, he seldom went abroad with neighboring tribes, for he was happy in the society of his wife, *Zecana* (The Bird). To sell beaver- and wild sheep-skins he often went with her to a post on the New Mexico frontier, and it was while at this fort that a Spanish trader saw the pretty Zecana, and, determining to win her, sent the Indian on a mission into the heart of the mountains, with a promise that she should rest securely at the settlement until his return.

On his way Ta-in-ga-ro stopped at the spring in Manitou, and after drinking he cast beads and wampum into the well in oblation to its deity. The offering was flung out by the bubbling water, and as he stared, distressed at this unwelcome omen, a picture formed on the surface—the anguished features of Zecana. He ran to his horse, galloped away, and paused neither for rest nor food till he had reached the post. The Spaniard was gone. Turning, then, to the foot-hills, he urged his jaded horse toward his cabin, and arrived, one bright morning, flushed with joy to see his wife before his door and to hear her singing. When he spoke she looked up carelessly and resumed her song. She did not know him. Reason was gone.

It was his cry of rage and grief, when, from her babbling, Ta-in-ga-ro learned of the Spaniard's treachery, that brought the wandering mind back for an instant. Looking at her husband with a strange surprise and pain, she plucked the knife from his belt. Before he could realize her purpose she had thrust it into her heart and had fallen dead at his feet. For hours he stood there in stupefaction, but the stolid Indian nature soon resumed its sway. Setting his lodge in order and feeding his horse, he wrapped Zecana's body in a buffalo-skin, then slept through the night in sheer exhaustion. Two nights afterward the Indian stood in the shadow of a room in the trading fort and watched the Spaniard as he lay asleep. Nobody knew how he passed the guard.

In the small hours the traitor was roused by the strain of a belt across his mouth, and leaping up to fling it off, he felt the tug of a lariat at his throat. His struggles were useless. In a few moments he was bound hand and foot. Lifting some strips of bark from the low roof, Ta-in-ga-ro pushed the Spaniard through the aperture and lowered him to the ground, outside the enclosure of which the house formed part. Then, at the embers of a fire he kindled an arrow wrapped in the down of cotton-wood and shot it into a haystack in the court. In the smoke and confusion thus made, his own escape was unseen, save by a guardsman drowsily pacing his beat outside the square of buildings. The sentinel would have given the alarm, had not the Indian pounced on him like a panther and laid him dead with a knife-stroke.

Catching up the Spaniard, the Indian tied him to the back of a horse and set off beside him. Thus they journeyed until they came to his lodge, where he released the trader from his horse and fed him, but kept his hands and legs hard bound, and paid no attention to his questions and his appeals for liberty. Tying a strong and half-trained horse at his door, Ta-in-ga-ro placed a wooden saddle on him, cut off the Spaniard's clothes, and put him astride of the beast. After he had fastened him into his seat with deer-skin thongs, he took Zecana's corpse from its wrapping and tied it to his prisoner, face to face.

Then, loosing the horse, which was plunging and snorting to be rid of his burden, he saw him rush off on the limitless desert, and followed on his own strong steed. At first the Spaniard fainted; on recovering he struggled to get free, but his struggles only brought him closer to the ghastly thing before him. Noon-day heat covered him with sweat and blood dripped from the wales that the cords cut in his flesh. At night he froze uncovered in the chill air, and, if for an instant his eyes closed in sleep, a curse, yelled into his ear, awoke him. Ta-in-ga-ro gave him drink from time to time, but never food, and so they rode for days. At last hunger over-bore his loathing, and sinking his teeth into the dead flesh before him he feasted like a ghoul.

Still they rode, Ta-in-ga-ro never far from his victim, on whose sufferings he gloated, until a gibbering cry told him that the Spaniard had gone mad. Then, and not till then, he drew rein and watched the horse with its dead and maniac riders until they disappeared in the yellow void. He turned away, but nevermore sought his home. To and fro, through the brush, the sand, the alkali of the plains, go the ghost riders, forever.

PART IV

TALES FROM COASTAL CALIFORNIA & THE NORTHWEST REGION

CHAPTER 18

CREATION AND NATURE MYTHS

THE CREATION
(Salishan, Boas)

T he Chief above made the earth. It was small at first, and he let it increase in size. He continued to enlarge it, and rolled it out until it was very large. Then he covered it with a white dust, which became the soil. He made three worlds, one above another,—the sky world, the earth we live on, and the underworld. All are connected by a pole or tree which passes through the middle of each. Then he created the animals. At last he made a man, who, however, was also a wolf. From this man's tail he made a woman. These were the first people. They were called *"Tai'en"* by the old people, who knew the story well, and they were the ancestors of all the Indians.

ORIGIN OF THE EARTH AND PEOPLE
(Salishan, Boas)

T he Chief (or God) made seven worlds, of which the earth is the central one. There are three worlds above, and three below. Maybe the first priests or white people told us this, but some of us believe it now. When the Chief made the earth, he stretched it out with its head to the west, therefore the west is the head of the earth. Heaven, or the place of the dead, is in that direction, and the great rivers all flow westward. West is the direction the souls take. Some say they follow the course the waters take. Perhaps in the beginning the earth was a woman. Some Indians say so, and state that the Chief stretched her body across the world (probably the water), and that she lay with her feet east and her head west. He transformed her into the earth we live on, and he made the first Indians out of her flesh (which is the soil). Thus the first Indians were made by him from balls of red earth or mud, and this is why we are reddish-colored. Other races were made from soil of different colors. Afterwards some of these different races met at certain points and intermingled, and thus the intermediate shades of color have arisen. As red earth is more nearly related to gold and copper than other kinds of earth, therefore the Indians are nearer to gold, and finer than other races.

OLD-ONE
(Salishan, Boas)

Old-One, or Chief, made the earth out of a woman, and said she would be the mother of all the people. Thus the earth was once a human being, and she is alive yet; but she has been transformed, and we cannot see her in the same way we can see a person. Nevertheless she has legs, arms, head, heart, flesh, bones, and blood. The soil is her flesh; the trees and vegetation are her hair; the rocks, her bones; and the wind is her breath. She lies spread out, and we live on her. She shivers and contracts when cold, and expands and perspires when hot. When she moves, we have an earthquake. Old-One, after transforming her, took some of her flesh and rolled it into balls, as people do with mud or clay. These he transformed into the beings of the ancient world, who were people, and yet at the same time animals.

These beings had some of the characteristics that animals have now, and in some respects acted like animals. In form, some were like animals, while others more nearly resembled people. Some could fly like birds, and others could swim like fishes. All had greater powers, and were more cunning, than either animals or people. They were not well-balanced. Each had great powers in certain ways, but was weak and helpless in other ways. Thus each was exceedingly wise in some things, and exceedingly foolish in others. They all had the gift of speech. As a rule, they were selfish, and there was much trouble among them. Some were cannibals, and lived by eating one another. Some did this knowingly, while others did it through ignorance. They knew that they had to live by hunting, but did not know which beings were people, and which deer. They thought people were deer, and preyed on them.

Some people lived on the earth at the same time. They had all the characteristics that Indians have now, but they were more ignorant. Deer also were on the earth at that time, and were real animals as now. People hunted them. They were never people or semi-human ancients, like the ancestors of most animals. Some people say that moose and caribou were also animals, although stories are told of the last three as though they were ancients or semi-human.

Old-One made each ball of mud a little different from the others, and rolled them over and over. He shaped them, and made them alive. The last balls of mud he made were almost all alike, and different from any of the preceding ones. They were formed like Indians, and he called them men. He blew on them, and they became alive. They were Indians, but were ignorant, and knew no arts. They were the most helpless of all things created; and the cannibals and others preyed on them particularly. The people and animals were made male and female, so that they might breed. Thus everything living sprang from the earth; and when we look around, we see everywhere parts of our mother.

How Old Man Above Created the World
(Shasta)

Long, long ago, when the world was so new that even the stars were dark, it was very, very flat. *Chareya,* Old Man Above, could not see through the dark to the new, flat earth. Neither could he step down to it because it was so far below him. With a large stone he bored a hole in the sky. Then through the hole he pushed down masses of ice and snow, until a great pyramid rose from the plain. Old Man Above climbed down through the hole he had made in the sky, stepping from cloud to cloud, until he could put his foot on top the mass of ice and snow. Then with one long step he reached the earth.

The sun shone through the hole in the sky and began to melt the ice and snow. It made holes in the ice and snow. When it was soft, Chareya bored with his finger into the earth, here and there, and planted the first trees. Streams from the melting snow watered the new trees and made them grow. Then he gathered the leaves which fell from the trees and blew upon them. They became birds. He took a stick and broke it into pieces. Out of the small end he made fishes and placed them in the mountain streams. Of the middle of the stick, he made all the animals except the grizzly bear. From the big end of the stick came the grizzly bear, who was made master of all. Grizzly was large and strong and cunning. When the earth was new he walked upon two feet and carried a large club. So strong was Grizzly that Old Man Above feared the creature he had made. Therefore, so that he might be safe, Chareya hollowed out the pyramid of ice and snow as a tipi. There he lived for thousands of snows. The Indians knew he lived there because they could see the smoke curling from the smoke hole of his tipi. When the pale-face came, Old Man Above went away. There is no longer any smoke from the smoke hole. White men call the tipi Mount Shasta.

The Golden Age
(Tinne)

Long ago the world was only a great sheet of water. There was no land. There were no people. Only the Thunder Bird lived. The beating of its wings was thunder. Its glance was lightning. Then the Thunder Bird flew down and touched the water. Thus the earth arose. Then the Thunder Bird flew down again and touched the earth. Thus the animals were created. Thus Thunder Bird created all living things except people. Dog was the ancestor of the Tinne.

Then Thunder Bird gave to the Tinne a sacred arrow. This arrow was never to be used or lost. Thus the Tinne, because of the sacred arrow, never died. Men wore out their throats with eating. Men lived so long their feet wore out from walking. Thus the Tinne were happy. Then they disobeyed Thunder Bird. They used the sacred arrow, therefore Arrow flew away. Thus the Tinne now die as do other Indians.

CHAPTER 19

GODS AND GODDESSES

AS'AI'YAHAL
(Tillamook)

As'ai'yahaʟ lived far up the country. A long time ago he traveled all over the world. He came down the river and arrived at Natā'hts. There he gathered clams and mussels; he made a fire and roasted them. When he opened them he found that there were two animals in each shell. After he had roasted them he began to eat, and found very soon that he had enough. He grew very angry and said, "Henceforth there shall be only one animal in each shell."

He traveled on and came to Tillamook. There he found an enormous bay at the mouth of the river. Then he went up the river and crossed it near its headwaters, as he had no canoe and was unable to cross it where it was deep. He met a number of women who were digging roots. He asked, "What are you doing there?" They replied, "We are digging roots." He said, "I do not like that." He took the roots away and sent them to Clatsop, and ever since that time there have been no roots at Tillamook, while at Clatsop they are very plentiful. He descended to the beach and said, "Henceforth you shall gather clams at ebb tide. When the water rises you shall carry them home, and you shall quarrel about them." It happened as he said. He gave the women the Tillamook language.

He went on and came to a river which was full of salmon, who were clapping their hands (fins). He took one of them, threw it ashore, stepped on it and flattened it. It became a flounder, and ever since that time flounders have been plentiful in Tillamook River, while there have been no salmon.

Then he went on and came to two women, who were carrying gamass. He wished to eat some roots, and asked, "What are you carrying there?" They replied, "We are carrying gamass roots." He asked them to give him some. They complied and gave him some roots. He liked them very much and wanted some more, but the women did not give him any more. He went on and said, "I will frighten them, and they will give me more." He cut off his membrum virile, and cut it into three pieces, which he transformed into dogs. Then he approached the women from another side, carrying his dogs. As soon as he came near the women the dogs wanted to creep under their clothes. He said, "What do you carry there?" They replied, "We carry gamass roots." He asked them for some, and they complied with his request. He left them and again approached them from another side and in another shape, accompanied by his three dogs, which again wanted to creep under the women's clothes. Then the women thought, "It is As'ai′yahaʟ. He is cheating us," and they thought of playing him a trick. After a while a man approached them again with three dogs, and asked them what they were carrying, and they replied, "Gamass roots." He asked them for some, and they gave him what they were carrying in their baskets. They told him not to open the baskets until he should reach a place where it was perfectly calm. He followed their directions and carried the basket to a place which was well sheltered. He sat down under dense bushes, opened the baskets, intending to eat the gamass roots, but when he opened them a swarm of bumble bees flew out and stung him all over his body. Then he grew angry and resolved to kill the women who had played him the trick. He pursued them, killed them, and took away all the roots which they carried. Then he went down the river and destroyed all the gamass roots he found on his way.

Finally he reached a small river which was full of salmon. He thought, "I am hungry, I will catch some salmon." He caught one and fastened it in a split stick, and roasted it over the fire. While it was roasting he lay down, covered his eyes with his left hand, and patted his breast with his right hand, humming a song. When he looked up he found the salmon dancing to his song. Then he lay down again, patted his breast, covered his eyes, and continued to sing. When he looked up the salmon was gone. Then he got angry and thought, "How foolishly I have behaved! I am very hungry and have nothing to eat."

He rose and went down to Clatsop, where he found salmon. He caught one and threw it ashore. It flopped its tail. He transfixed it with a stick, but it still flopped its tail. Then he took some sand, put it on its eyes and face, and thus killed it. He said, "When my children come to be grown up, they shall kill salmon in the same way by putting sand on their eyes." Therefore the Clatsop kill the salmon by putting sand on their eyes. Then he made a large fire, intending to roast his salmon. After having eaten, he wanted to cross Columbia River. As he had no canoe he went up the river, and when he came to a shallow place he tried to ford it; he took his blankets under his arms. When As'ai′yahaʟ began to ford the river and found the water very deep and cold, he thought he would deceive the people. He kicked a rock up so that it fell into the river, where it still stands, while he himself disappeared. The rock is pointed out as As'ai′yahaʟ turned into stone. But he himself traveled on. After having crossed the river he felt very cold, and lay down with his back upward basking in the sun. He fell asleep. Thus he was found by five panthers, who tied up his hair and fastened ugly things to his head. When he awoke he was thirsty, and went at once to a brook to drink. When he bent down to the water he saw his own image and became frightened, thinking it was the image of some enemy who wanted to kill him, and ran away. He ran a whole day, until he was too tired to run any longer. Then he went to touch his head, and discovered what had happened. "Oh!" he said, "am I frightened at myself? Who may have done that to me?" But he was not quite sure whether he had actually been frightened by his own image. He went to the brook and shook his head to see if the image shook its head, too. When he discovered that it did shake its head, he was sure that he had run away from himself. Then he set out to find the man who had played him the trick. After a while he came to the five panthers. They were fast asleep. He pulled their ears long and tied their hair up. He said: "Henceforth you shall be panthers and not men." When they awoke they were all so frightened at seeing their own images that they ran up the mountains into the woods.

He traveled on and met a boy, who appeared to be three years old, sleeping quietly, his hand covering his face. As'ai'yahaʟ thought, "I will kill that boy." He intended to lift his hand in order to strike him, but was unable to lift it. Then he wanted to strike him with a stick, but was unable to lift his arm. He tried to throw a stone, but was unable to lift it; neither could he lift a club with which he wanted to break the boy's head. The latter slept on quietly. When As'ai'yahaʟ was tired out by his attempts to kill the boy, the latter turned round and suddenly became a very strong man, who said, "Who is doing this? I will kill him. Tell me my name instantly or I will kill you." As'ai'yahaʟ said quickly, "Your name is Arrow." "No," said the boy. As'ai'yahaʟ said, "Your name is Four Arrows." "No," said the boy, "that is my brother's name." As'ai'yahaʟ cried, "Your name is Taxä'ha." "Yes," said the boy, "that is my name," and he took As'ai'yahaʟ to his house and made him his slave. He prided himself at having As'ai'yahaʟ for a slave. He kept him for some time and finally set him free.

As'ai'yahaʟ traveled on and came to another place, where he found three old women. He had been warned not to go near this place, as the women were said to be cannibals. He, however, desired to visit them, and going there he carried a large stone along, so heavy that he was hardly able to lift it. When he met the women he threw the stone right among them, and one of them jumped at it and tried to devour it. It was too large and it stuck in her mouth. Then he walked down to the women, transformed them into rocks, and said, "Henceforth you shall not be cannibals, but stones, and remain here as long as the world lasts. Children shall play here, and you shall not be able to do them harm. People shall camp here when they travel up and down the river, and you shall protect them." They were transformed into rocks with large caves in which travelers camp.

He traveled on and came to a house in which he saw people lying around the fire. He asked them, "What is the matter? Are you sick?" "No," they replied; "we are starving. The East Wind wants to kill us. The river, sea, and beach are frozen over, and we cannot get any food." Then he said, "Can't you make the wind stop, so that you may obtain food?" Then he went out of the house and down to the river, which was completely frozen over. It was so slippery that he was hardly able to stand on the ice. He went up the river to meet the East Wind and to conquer him. While he went on, mucus flew out of his nose and froze at once, because it was so cold. When he came near the house of the East Wind, he took up some pieces of ice, which he threw into the river, saying, "Henceforth it shall not be as cold as it is now. Winter shall be a little cold, but not very much so. You shall become herring." The ice was at once transformed into herrings. Every piece became a herring and swam down the river.

As'ai'yahaʟ went on and finally arrived at the house of the East Wind. He entered, sat down, and whistled. His whole face was covered with frozen mucus. He did not go near the fire, and his whole body was trembling with cold. He said, however, "I feel so warm I cannot go near the fire. I am perspiring," and he told the East Wind that he came from a house where they were drying herrings. The East Wind said, "Don't say so. It is winter now. There will be no herring for a long time to come." As'ai'yahaʟ replied, "Don't you believe me? There are plenty of herrings outside." He went out and took an icicle, which he warmed at the fire. "Look how quickly it boils," he said to the East Wind, while actually the ice was melting. Thus he made the East Wind believe that he held a herring in his hand. Then the East Wind ceased to blow, the ice began to melt, and the people had plenty of food.

Up to that time it had been winter all through the year, but As'ai'yahaʟ made summer and winter alternate.

Then he went back to the people whom he had helped. "Rise and catch herring, and when you have enough tell your wives to pick berries, and you may hunt elk and deer." Then they rose and did as he had told them, and they lived happy lives.

He traveled on, and came to a place on the seacoast, where he saw a stranded whale, but he had no knife to cut it with. Near by there was a house from which a little smoke was rising. He entered and saw two men sitting one on each side of the fire. One of them was Nctāle̅′qsɛn (flint nose), the other Taʟe̅′qtɛn (copper for making arrow-points). He thought, "I wish they would fight." As soon as he had thought so, they began to fight. Whenever Nctāle̅′qsɛn hit Taʟe̅′qtɛn's nose the latter was bent in; and when Taʟe̅′qtɛn hit Nctāle̅′qsɛn's nose, chips of flint would fly from it.

Then As'ai'yahaʟ picked up the fragments and said, "Stop fighting; there is a large whale on the beach." He picked out three good flint knives, and went out to cut the blubber of the whale. He traveled on and met an old woman who carried a basket of gamass. He asked, "Where are you going?" She replied, "I am carrying this gamass to the old men in that house." As'ai'yahaʟ replied, "That is good; they are just now engaged carving a whale." Then the old woman ran down to the shore as fast as she could, sharpening her knife. She wanted to have some of the whale meat, too.

As'ai'yahaʟ was carrying a quiver filled with arrows. Whenever he desired to amuse himself, he took the arrows out of his quiver, broke them to pieces, and threw them down. At once they were transformed into men, who began to sing and dance. On the following morning, when he opened his quiver, they all resumed the shape of arrows and jumped into the quiver.

He came to a place called Ntsɛä′nixil, on Siletz River. There he transformed himself, his wife and his child, into rocks, which are seen up to this day. The head of the man and the breasts of the woman are easily recognized. He is standing between the two other rocks. His life returned to the country of the salmon, of which he is the master.

The Yaquina tell that As'ai'yahaʟ transformed himself into a dry tree at Yaquina Bay, and that his life returned from there to the salmon country. The Alsea and Yaquina, when passing this tree, shot an arrow at it. It is quite full of arrows.

As'ai'yahaʟ made all the rocks, rivers, and cascades while traveling all over the world. Finally he returned to the country of the salmon, whence he came.

CHAPTER 20

CORE BELIEFS

THE DOCTRINE OF SOULS AND OF DISEASE
(Chinook)

When a person is sick, the seers go and visit the ghosts. Three or four are sent. One who has a powerful guardian spirit goes first; another one who has a powerful guardian spirit goes last; the less powerful ones goes in the middle. They go to search for the soul of the sick chief. Their guardian spirits go to the country of the ghosts. When their road becomes dangerous, the first one sings his song. When danger approaches from the rear, the last one sings his song. They begin their ceremonies in the evening, and when the morning star rises they reach the soul of the sick person. They take it and return. Sometimes i takes them two nights to find the soul. As soon as they return it the patient recovers.

Sometimes, when the guardian spirits of these seers pursue the soul, they see that it has taken the trail leading to the left hand, and they say he must die. If it has taken the trail to the right he will get well.

Now the guardian spirits arrive at the hole where the ghosts use to drink. If the soul of the sick one has drunk of the water in that hole he cannot recover; even if all the conjurers attempt to heal him, they cannot do so. When they find a soul that has drunk of this water, they take it and return to the country of the living. At first the soul is large, but as they approach the country of the Indians it becomes smaller, and the people who know the art of healing say: "Perhaps he will die tomorrow." On the next day they try to give him his soul. It has become too small for his body and does not fill it. Then the patient dies.

When the guardian spirits of the seers go to the country of the ghosts, and see that the soul of the patient is far from their town and that he has not taken any food, they say, "We shall heal him, because he has not partaken of any food." Then they take the soul and return with it. Even if the patient is very sick he will recover.

When the ghosts take away a soul, its owner faints at once. Then the seers are paid and their guardian spirits pursue the ghosts. The soul which has been taken away sees the ghosts. Part of them he knows, and part of them he does not know; only those who died a short time ago he recognizes. When the guardian spirits meet the soul, they turn it round and the patient recovers at once.

When the ghosts carry away the soul of a person, and there are no seers to recover the soul, the sick one must die.

When the guardian spirits of the seers pursue the soul and it has entered the house of the ghosts, they cannot recover it and the sick one must die; then the guardian spirits cry.

When they see a horse in the country of the ghosts and they do not take it back, it must die; also if they see a man there who is apparently well, and they do not take back his soul, he must die. When they see a canoe and they do not bring it back, it will be broken.

The conjurers in their incantations use a manikin made of wood and cedar bark. When a conjurer wants to make use of this manikin he gives it to a person who has no guardian spirit, who shakes it for him, and they two go to the country of the ghosts. Then the man who carries the manikin sees the country of the ghosts, the manikin carrying him.

Each person has two souls, a large one and a small one. When a person falls sick the lesser soul leaves his body. When the conjurers catch it again and return it to him he will recover.

The guardian spirits of the conjurers, when pursuing the souls, go toward sunset. When they return with the soul they go toward sunrise. If the face of the conjurer should be turned in the opposite direction, he must die.

When a chief dies his soul goes to the beach; only the most powerful conjurers know where to find it and can bring it back.

When a sick person is to die, it is always high water, and the guardian spirits move slowly. If he is to recover, it is always low water.

When the guardian spirits find a soul it is visible, but after they have taken it nothing is to be seen, and they say that they have taken it away. When they try to take the soul of a person who is to die, the soul resembles fire, and sparks fall down. They try in vain to gather them up, and the conjurer says: "You will die." When the patient will recover, the soul feels light; when he will die, it feels heavy.

The ghosts watch the souls which they have taken away; then the conjurer sends off his guardian spirit in the shape of a deer. The ghosts pursue it and leave the soul alone. They forget it. Thus the conjurer deceives them and takes the soul away.

When a person is angry with another, he engages a seer to watch for his enemy. If he finds him asleep he takes out his soul, which he hides in a graveyard, under the house, or in rotten wood. Then the person falls sick. His friends pay a conjurer to look for his soul. He says: "Somebody has taken it away." He looks for it and finds it where it has been hidden. If the soul is still unhurt, the sick one will recover. If the conjurer's guardian spirit has eaten of it, he must die.

Sometimes a conjurer is paid a high price secretly to take away the soul of a person. Sometimes he is given dentalia, sometimes he is given a woman; then indeed he takes away the soul. Sometimes he takes both souls of the person, who in this case cannot recover. When the relatives of the sick one learn about it they kill the conjurer. If they do not kill him he must pay a blood-fine.

When a conjurer wants to kill a person, he shoots, in a supernatural way, diseases at his enemy. Sometimes he is paid secretly for doing so. When the relatives learn about it they kill the conjurer. When a supernatural disease is found in a sick person, a good conjurer is paid to take it out. He finds five such diseases and one rope. Then the sick one recovers. When the disease goes right through the conjurer's enemy he must die.

As soon as it is discovered that a person is shot, his friends endeavor to take out the disease. The conjurer clasps his hands so that the thumb of the right hand is held by the fingers of the left. He catches the disease in his hands. It tries to escape, and when the thumb of the right hand comes out of the clasped hands the disease has escaped. While he holds the disease in his hands, five people take hold of him, two at his legs, two at his arms, and one at his back. They lift him; then a kettle is placed near the fire and filled with water. They try to bring the conjurer to the water, but the spirit of the disease resists. When he escapes, the men fall down, because the resisting spirit suddenly gives way. Sometimes they succeed in carrying the conjurer to the water. Then the disease-spirit is put into the water. When it gets cold it loses its power. Then they look at it. Sometimes they see that the spirit is made of claws of a wolf or of a bird; and sometimes of the bone of a dead person, which is carved in the form of a man. If the spirit has killed five people, then there are three cuts on one of its arms and two on the other. If it has killed eight persons, there are five cuts on one arm and three on the other. If it has killed ten people, there are five cuts on each arm. Sometimes, when they bring the conjurer to the kettle and he puts his hands into it, the kettle bursts, and they must get another one. When the conjurer gets tired, he asks another one to strike his hands with a rattle. Then the other one strikes the hands, in which the disease-spirit is held, with a rattle. He rubs the disease-spirit under water until it gets soft. While taking it out of the body of the sick person his hands become very hot. As last he takes out the rope. Sometimes there is only one rope, sometimes there are several, in the sick person. Two conjurers take hold of it, one at each end. Then they ask somebody to cut it. If the person who cuts it has no guardian spirit, he cuts through between the hands, but does not strike anything. If, however, the person has a guardian spirit, he cuts between the hands of the conjurer with a small knife, and at once blood is seen to flow.

When a long rope is put into a man, he will fall sick after a long time; if a short rope is taken he will fall sick after a short time.

CHAPTER 21

TRIBAL ORIGINS

A SABOBA ORIGIN-MYTH
(Saboba)

Before the Saboba came here they lived far, far away in the land that is in the heart of the Setting Sun. But Siwash, the great God, told Uuyot, their warrior captain, that they must come away from this land and sail away and away in a direction that he would give. Under Uuyot's orders they built big boats and then with Siwash himself leading them, and with Uuyot as captain, they launched these into the ocean and rowed away from the shore. There was no light on the ocean. Everything was covered with a dark fog, and it was only by singing as they rowed that the boats were enabled to keep together.

It was still dark and foggy when the boats landed on the shores of this land, and they groped about in the darkness, wondering why they had been brought hither. Then, suddenly, the heavens opened, and lightnings flashed and thunders roared and rains fell, and a great earthquake shook all the earth. Indeed, all the elements of the earth, ocean, and heaven, seemed to be mixed up together, and, with terror in their hearts and silence on their tongues, the people stood still awaiting what would happen further. Though no voice had spoken they knew something was going to happen, and they were breathless in their anxiety to know what it was.

Then they turned to Uuyot and asked him what the raging of the elements meant. Gently he calmed their fears and bade them be silent and wait. As they waited, a terrible clap of thunder rent the very heavens, and the vivid lightnings revealed the frightened people huddling together as a pack of sheep. But Uuyot stood alone, brave and fearless, facing the storm and daring the anger of Those Above. With a loud voice he cried out *"Wit-i-a-ko!"* which signified "Who's there? What do you want?"

But there was no response. The heavens were silent! the earth was silent! The ocean was silent! All nature was silent!

Then with a voice full of tremulous sadness and loving yearning for his people Uuyot said: "My children, my own sons and daughters, something is wanted of us by Those Above. What it is I know not. Let us gather together and bring 'pivat,' and with it make the big smoke and then dance and dance until we are told what is wanted." So the people brought pivat—a native tobacco that grows in Southern California—and Uuyot brought the big ceremonial pipe which he had made out of rock, and he soon made the big smoke and blew the smoke up into the heavens while he urged the people to dance. They danced hour after hour until they grew tired, and Uuyot smoked all the time, but still he urged them to dance.

Then he called out again to Those Above, *"Wit-i-a-ko!"* but still could obtain no response. This made him sad and disconsolate, and when the people saw Uuyot despondent and downhearted they became panic-stricken, and ceased to dance, and began to cling around him for comfort and protection. But poor Uuyot had none to give. He himself was saddest and most forsaken of all, and he got up and bade the people leave him alone, as he wished to walk to and fro by himself. Then he made the people smoke and dance, and when they rested they knelt in a circle and prayed. But he walked away by himself, feeling keenly the refusal of Those Above to speak to him. His heart was deeply wounded.

But as the people prayed and danced and sang, a gentle light came stealing into the sky from the far, far east. Little by little the darkness was driven away. First the light was gray, then yellow, then white, and at last the glistening brilliancy of the sun filled all the land and covered the sky with glory. The sun had arisen for the first time, and in its light and warmth the people knew they had the favor of Those Above, and they were contented.

But when Siwash, the God of Earth looked around, and saw everything revealed by the sun, he was discontented, for the earth was bare and level and monotonous, and there was nothing to cheer the sight. So he took some of the people and of them he made high mountains, and of some, smaller mountains. Of some he made rivers and creeks, and lakes and waterfalls, and of others, coyotes, foxes, deer, antelopes, bears, squirrels, porcupines, and all the other animals. Then he made out of the other people all the different kinds of snakes and reptiles and insects and birds and fishes. Then he wanted trees and plants and flowers and he turned some of the people into these things. Of every man or woman that he seized he made something according to its value.

When he was done he had used up so many people he was scared. So he set to work and made a new lot of people, some to live here, some to live there, and some to live everywhere. And he gave to each family its own language and tongue and its own place to live, and he told them where to live and the sad distress that would come upon them if they mixed up their tongues by intermarriage. Each family was to live in its own place, and while all the different families were to be friendly and live as brothers, tied together by kinship, amity, and concord, there was to be no mixing of bloods.

Thus were settled the original inhabitants on the coast of southern California by Siwash, the God of the Earth, and under the captaincy of Uuyot.

But at length the time came when Uuyot must die. His work on the earth was ended and Those Above told him he must prepare to leave his earthly friends and children. He was told to go up into the San Bernardino Mountains, into a small valley there, and lie down in a certain spot to await his end. He died peacefully and calmly, as one who went to sleep. He was beloved of the Gods above and Siwash, the God of Earth, so that no pain came to him to make his death distressful.

As soon as he was dead the ants came and ate all the flesh from his bones. But the spirit messengers of Those Above looked after him and they buried him so that the mark of his burying place could never be wiped out. The powers of evil might strive, but this place would always remain clearly shown. A lake of water soon covered the place of his burial, and it assumed the shape of a colossal human being. It was the shape of Uuyot, and from that day to this it has remained there. It has been seen by all the people of all the ages, and will never be wiped out of existence. The legs and outstretched arms, as well as the great body, are distinctly to be seen, and even now, in the Great Bear Valley Lake, which is the site of Uuyot's burial, the eyes of the clear-seeing man may witness the interesting sight.

But it was not all at once that the people could see that Uuyot was buried in this spot. Before they knew it as a fact they sat in a great circle around the place. They sat and wept and wailed and mourned for Uuyot. They made their faces black and then they cut off their hair to show their deep sorrow, and they sat and waited, and wept and wailed, until Those Above showed them the buried body of their great leader and captain.

And to this day the places where that great circle of people sat may be seen. The marks of their bodies are left in the ground and they will remain there forever, or so long as the body of Uuyot is to be seen.

THE DIEGUEÑOS
(Diegueño)

T he Diegueños have been classified as belonging to the Yuman family of Turner and Brinton. They make part of the Mission Indians of San Diego County, CA, in which are also included fragments of Shoshonean tribes, akin to the Nahuatlan peoples of Southern Mexico. It would not be surprising to find in the folklore of the Shoshonean tribes traces of Aztec influence; but if the Diegueños belong to another family, a rather curious problem is presented by relics of tribal mythology related by old Cinon Duro, the last chief of the Diegueños, since they seem to suggest by internal evidence relations with primitive Aztec tradition.

CHAPTER 22

TRIBAL HISTORY AND TRIBAL CUSTOMS

THE SUN AND THE MOON
(Athapascan)

There was once a large village, where there lived a family of four boys, with their younger sister, making five children. And, as the story goes, the girl refused to marry when she grew up, even though many suitors came from a distance as well as from her own village.

And, as she continued to refuse them, by and by the men and women of her set were all married off. At that time, there was no sun and moon, and the earth was in a kind of twilight.

So this woman lived on, though the strangers no longer came, and her own mates took no further notice of her, being married already.

At length, one night, some one came and scratched her head while she was asleep. "There are no strangers in the village," thought she. "Who can this be?" Nevertheless, she spoke with him. Every night this man who spoke with her did the same thing, and finally he became as her husband. "But who can it be," she thought. "Every one in the village is married, except my older brother, and there are no strangers here. I will tie a feather in his hair, and when they leave the kashime, I will go and see who it is that has his hair tied." "Come," said she, "leave me and go to the kashime. Come! You must have some sleep, and I am sleepy, too." So she spoke after she had tied the feather in his hair, and he left her and went to the kashime, while she lay awake, thinking.

When it began to grow light, she went out and stood at the door of their house, and saw the men coming out, according to their custom, but none of them had the feather in his hair. Suddenly her older brother rushed out. She looked, and there was the feather. The blood rushed to her face, and everything grew dark; then she was overcome with anger. At daylight she brought in (from her cache) her best parka, a beautiful one which had never been worn. Berries also, and deer-fat she brought, without a word, and did not even answer her mother when she spoke to her.

Then, when she had made the fire, she bathed herself, and attired herself in her beautiful parka and her moccasins (as for a journey). Then she took the frozen food (which she had prepared) and put it into her brother's bowl, and taking her housewife's knife, she reached down within her parka and cut off her breasts and put them upon the frozen food, and thrust an awl into each, and went with it to the kashime.

Inside the door, she straightened herself up. Yonder, on the opposite side of the room, sat her brother. She set the dish down by him. "There is no doubt that it was you who did it," she said; "I thought surely it must be some one else. A pestilence will break out upon all mankind for what you have done."

She left the kashime, and yonder, in the east, she went up in the sky as the sun. Then her brother drew on his parka and moccasins also, but in his haste he left off one of them. "My sister has escaped me," he thought; and he too, going after her, became the moon.

And we do not look at the sun, because we sympathize with her shame.

ORIGIN OF FIRE
(Various)

HOW BEAVER STOLE FIRE
(Nez Percés)

L ong ago there were no people in the world. Animals and trees talked just as men do now. They also walked about. Now in those days, Pine Trees had the secret of fire. They would tell no one else. No one could have a fire, no matter how cold it was, unless he were a Pine. One winter it was so cold the animals almost froze to death. Then they called a council. They wanted to steal fire from Pine Trees.

Now on Grande Ronde River, Pine Trees were holding also a great council. They had built a large fire to warm themselves. Guards were put around the fire to keep off all animals. But Beaver hid under the bank, near the fire, before the guards took their places, so they did not see him. After a while a live coal rolled down the bank near Beaver. He hid it in his breast and ran away. Pine Trees started after him. When Pine Trees caught up near him, Beaver dodged from side to side. Other times he ran straight ahead. That is why Grande Ronde River winds from side to side in some places. In other places it is straight.

When they had run a long way, Pine Trees grew tired. They stopped on the river banks. So many stopped there, and so close together, that even today hunters can hardly get through the trees. A few kept on after Beaver and stopped here and there. These also remain here and there on the river bank.

A few Pine Trees kept close after Beaver. So did Cedar. Cedar said, "I will run to the top of that hill. I will see how far ahead he is." So Cedar ran to the top of the hill. Beaver was far ahead. He was just diving into Big Snake River where Grande Ronde joins it. Beaver swam across Big Snake River and gave fire to Willows on the opposite bank. Farther on he gave fire to Birches and to other trees. So these woods have fire in them. Ever since then animals and Indians can get fire from these woods by rubbing two pieces together.

Cedar still stands all alone on the very top of the hill. He is very old. His top is dead. The chase was a long one. You can see that because there are no other cedars within a hundred miles of him. Old men of the tribes point him out to the children. They say, "There is Old Cedar. He stands just where he stopped when he chased Beaver."

How Dog Stole Fire
(Achomawi)

Pine-Marten stole the two wives of Hawk-Man. Hawk-Man grew very angry, and at once put on his shaman's ornaments and began to dance and to sing, *"Ketj ketja winino, ketj ketja winino."*

At once it began to rain. Only Weasel noticed it and spoke of it. All night it poured. The water rose higher and higher until it ran in at the door. "Tell them to go back, these two women! That Hawk-Man will kill us, he will drown us."

But Pine-Marten said nothing until morning. Then he said, "I do not like this. Where is a brave man? I want him to go and kill Hawk-Man."

So a man got up and went over, taking a knife and a shield. Hawk-Man was dancing harder and harder, and at every leap his head came up through the smoke hole. The man crept nearer and nearer, and finally struck Hawk-Man. He cut off his head. At once the rain stopped and the clouds cleared away, and the water sank. Then people said, "If a shaman is bad, we will kill him. That is how it shall be." Then they went off to hunt.

After Hawk-Man had been killed and the waters had sunk again, people found that the fires were put out all over the world. Nothing could be cooked. For a time they did not trouble about it, but in a few days they began to talk about it. They sent Owl to Shasta to look out all over the world and see if he could find any trace of fire. Owl took a feather blanket and went. Lizard watched him go and told the people how he was getting on. After a long while, when Owl did not come back, people thought he was dead. But Lizard said, "Sh! I can see him." Owl got to the top at last, very tired and wet with sweat. He looked all around. Twice he looked to the west and there saw smoke coming from a sweat house. After a while Owl came down from the mountain and told the people what he had seen.

Next morning all got ready and went off to the west, to where the smoke had been seen. Every one had a cedar-bark torch. Dog had some punk hidden in his ear. Late in the evening they arrived at the lodge and asked to be allowed to warm their hands. Dog held his ear down and fire caught in the punk. Then every one thrust their torches into the fire and ran. The people in the lodge were angry and struck at them as they ran off. Coyote's fire gave out first, then the fire of one after another gave out until all the torches were out. The people who owned the fire had made it rain and this put out the torches. No one knew that Dog had fire. They got home and were much troubled, for they thought the fire had all been lost. Dog was laughing and said, "I am sweating." Coyote got angry at this and said, "Hit him! Put him out!"

Then Dog said to Fox, "Look in my ear." When he did so, he saw the fire. He took out the punk, made fire from it, and so people got fire again.

ORIGIN OF AMPHIBIANS
(Athapascan)

A young man was once paddling along and it seemed as though he were listening for something. He turned his head this way and that, and listened. "Surely, some one is singing; I believe it is a woman singing." *"Y-xa-n-na,"* she said, as the story goes. He quickly went ashore. A beautiful woman, with long hair, stood upon the beach. She was washing her hair in the swift water and singing. Going up unperceived, he caught her by the waist. "I'm not human, I'm not human," she shrieked. The man shut his eyes as she struggled, and opened them only to find that he was holding a Birch which had fallen toward the water with its branches in the current.

In a passion he paddled off in his canoe. Again he paddles as though listening, and turns his head this way and that. "Surely," he thinks, "there is some one singing again. It sounds like a woman. The same thing over again. Good enough," he thinks. "I wonder whether it is a sure-enough woman this time, that's making this noise." Peeking under the bushes, again he saw some one who was singing. *"A-ha-yu-ha-ha,"* she said, so they say. He went ashore. Such a beautiful woman, girded with a deer-tooth belt, stripping off willow bark. He caught her by the waist. "I'm not human, I'm not human," she screamed. He gave her a push. "You act as if you were human, making so much noise with your songs," said he, while she bounded away in the shape of a rabbit. Angrily he went off. Again he listened, and heard a sound of people shouting at play. Going toward them and getting out of his canoe, he went under the bushes. What a crowd of people playing ball upon the beach! What fine men and women both! He crouched down in the grass and looked out. Thinks he, "If they throw a woman upon me I will catch her." They pushed one upon him, and he quickly jumped up and caught her. "I'm not human, I'm not human," said the woman, struggling to get away. He pushed her away. It was only a Brant that ran off, screaming. The players, too, turned into geese, and off they flew. Angrily the man went off again in his canoe, and again he listened. He heard a chattering of men's voices, and went ashore. Keeping back from the open, he went toward the speakers, under the bushes. There was a pond, where there were many men in the water, one of whom was shamaning. The shaman was a huge old fellow, in a parka made of otter skin. He was saying: "It seems that this is the place where you will perish." But they replied, "We choose to live here in spite of what you tell us."

The young man leaped out, and leaving the shelter of the grass he rushed to the side of the shaman. The shaman became an otter and dived into the pond and swam away, and all the rest took to the water in the form of animals: mink, musk-rat, divers, and loons, and swam to the bottom, where they remained, while the hero of the story became a hawk and flew away.

ORIGIN OF WITCHCRAFT
(Tlingit)

In the early days of Indian life there lived a young man who was a good hunter, and he had a very pretty young wife and a son, both of whom filled his heart with love. Their lives were happy as the flowers' until one day the wife, while gathering wood in the forest, met the son of the chief, with whom she fell in love at the first glance. After this she met him every night by appointment on the seashore or in the woods. As days went on she feigned sickness, and calling her husband to her side, told him that she saw the spirits of her old friends coming to take her away, and that soon she would die and leave him, but made him promise not to burn her, but to put her body in a large box and place it in the gravehouse. That day she apparently died, when her last wish was carried out, and she was deposited in the small gravehouse in rear of the house. Night came on, and while the great feast (that it is customary with the Tlingit to give in honor of the dead) was being celebrated the chief's son went to the grave and assisted her to escape, and led her to his father's house, where she lived with him as his wife, but known only to his family. During the daytime she remained within doors, going out only under the shelter of darkness.

Many a winter evening the lonely hunter, sitting in his house with his little boy, would think about his dead wife, and all his heart would break out in tears. One day, returning from hunting and finding no fire, he sent his little boy into the chief's house to ask for some live coals to start his fire with. Upon entering the chief's house the little boy surprised his mother sitting by the fire. She saw him and immediately covered her face, but too late to prevent recognition. The boy went home and told his father that he had seen his mother, but his father told him to be quiet. He, however, insisted upon it, so that in the end the father's suspicions were aroused, and in the evening he stole softly to the chief's house, and looking through a chink discovered his wife sitting with her lover by the fire.

Upon returning home he sat down to think how best to avenge this great wrong, and concluded to possess himself of a witch spirit; so the following night he took himself to the deadhouse and slept by a corpse, but the spirit did not come to him; he next killed a dog, and skinning it, slept one night in its skin, but again failed. Then he took a dead shaman's skull from the deadhouse and used it to drink out of, and the next morning, going out, he suddenly fell down on the skull in a trance, and upon waking up the witch spirit had come to him, and he went home happy. Upon the coming of night he returned to the shamans' graves, and there met many spirits of men and lovely maidens who danced and played with him, and every night afterwards he visited them and learned more and more of witchcraft.

After a while he took the bones of the dead shaman and made them into a necklace, which he put on. Then he killed a dog and made a blanket of its skin; then he took two shaman skulls, and filling them with pebbles, made rattles of them (all of these articles are used by the shamans in cases of witchcraft). He continued visiting the graves, associating with spirits and witches, and learned more and more daily, until he was able to fly, when he took the two skull rattles into his hands and flew to the chief's house. Upon reaching the smoke-hole he shook the rattles, and put every one in a sound sleep. Then he entered the house and saw his wife asleep in the arms of her lover. The next morning he went out and played; the people came out of their houses and all said, 'We slept very sound last night.' He afterwards went out into the woods and cut a small pole, which he sharpened at one end to a fine point; and the next night, when all were asleep, he flew down the smoke-hole of the chief's house and drove the sharpened stake through his faithless wife, killing her instantly, without noise. The next morning she was found dead, but no one knew who had killed her.

Now the hunter determined to give the witch spirit to his little boy, so that he could work any charm. He took the hand of an old dead shaman and hung it around the child's neck, and the little boy fell down in a trance, and the witch spirit came to him; then he went with his father every night to play with the spirits. The hunter now proposed to avenge himself on the chief's son. He instructed his little boy to watch his enemy and to secure his spittle, cut off a piece of his blanket, or wipe up his tracks; and with this and other material he made a small human figure, which he put inside a dead shaman, and as the image rotted, so sickness came to the chief's son, and as the image decayed, so the chief's son grew weaker and weaker until death came upon him. Then the hunter initiated his family into the mysteries of witchcraft, and it was thus that the witches originated.

THE FIRST TOTEM POLE
(Kwakiutl)

Once there was a chief who had never had a dance. All the other chiefs had big dances, but Wakiash none. Therefore Wakiash was unhappy. He thought for a long while about the dance. Then he went up into the mountains to fast. Four days he fasted. On the fourth day he fell asleep. Then something fell on his breast. It was a green frog. Frog said, "Wake up." Then Wakiash woke up. He looked about to see where he was. Frog said, "You are on Raven's back. Raven will fly around the world with you."

So Raven flew. Raven flew all around the world. Raven showed Wakiash everything in the world. On the fourth day, Raven flew past a house with a totem pole in front of it. Wakiash could hear singing in the house. Wakiash wished he could take the totem pole and the house with him. Now Frog knew what Wakiash was thinking. Frog told Raven. Raven stopped and Frog told Wakiash to hide behind the door. Frog said, "When they dance, jump out into the room."

The people in the house began to dance. They were animal people. But they could not sing or dance. One said, "Something is the matter. Some one is near us."

Chief said, "Let one who can run faster than the flames go around the house and see."

So Mouse went. Mouse could go anywhere, even into a box. Now Mouse looked like a woman; she had taken off her animal clothes. Mouse ran out, but Wakiash caught her.

Wakiash said, "Wait. I will give you something." So he gave her a piece of mountain goat's fat. Wakiash said to Mouse, "I want the totem pole and the house. I want the dances and the songs."

Mouse said, "Wait until I come again."

Mouse went back into the house. She said, "I could find nobody." So the animal people tried again to dance. They tried three times. Each time, Chief sent Mouse out to see if some one was near. Each time, Mouse talked with Wakiash. The third time Mouse said, "When they begin to dance, jump into the room."

So the animal people began to dance. Then Wakiash sprang into the room. The dancers were ashamed. They had taken off their animal clothes and looked like men. So the animal people were silent. Then Mouse said, "What does this man want?" Now Wakiash wanted the totem pole and the house. He wanted the dances and the songs. Mouse knew what Wakiash was thinking. Mouse told the animal people.

Chief said, "Let the man sit down. We will show him how to dance." So they danced. Then Chief asked Wakiash what kind of a dance he would like to choose. They were using masks for the dance. Wakiash wanted the Echo mask, and the Little Man mask,—the little man who talks, talks, and quarrels with others. Mouse told the people what Wakiash was thinking.

Then Chief said, "You can take the totem pole and the house also. You can take the masks and dances, for one dance." Then Chief folded up the house very small. He put it in a dancer's headdress. Chief said, "When you reach home, throw down this bundle. The house will unfold and you can give a dance."

Then Wakiash went back to Raven. Wakiash climbed on Raven's back and went to sleep. When he awoke, Raven and Frog were gone. Wakiash was alone. It was night and the tribe was asleep. Then Wakiash threw down the bundle. Behold! the house and totem pole were there. The whale painted on the house was blowing. The animals on the totem pole were making noises. At once the tribe woke up. They came to see Wakiash. Wakiash found he had been gone four years instead of four days.

Then Wakiash gave a great dance. He taught the people the songs. Echo came to the dance. He repeated all the sounds they made. When they finished the dance, behold! the house was gone. It went back to the animal people. Thus all the chiefs were ashamed because Wakiash had the best dance.

Then Wakiash made out of wood a house and another totem pole. They called it *Kalakuyuwish,* "the pole that holds up the sky."

THE CHILTHCAT BLANKET
(Chilthcat)

M any generations ago there lived a very beautiful woman, named Tsihooskwal-laam, who had chosen to live far away from her tribespeople in the mountain wilderness of the great Chilthcat country.

Tsihooskwallaam had many admirers among her own tribespeople, who would have married her, but Tsihooskwallaam preferred to live a secluded life from her own tribespeople.

She selected as a place to live in an unknown lake far away from the haunts of men, believing that her people would never find her, and there she settled down to study the art and craft of weaving blankets. The outlet of the lake was a stream in which there were many rapids and falls, and which was frequented by salmon, which made their way to the lake.

The salmon sought many times to find Tsihooskwallaam, and when they found her she asked them as a special favor to help her by not telling anyone of her new *illahee* (home). When the salmon returned to the salt chuck (water), they told of Tsihooskwallaam's new home and the great chief and his son set out with all possible speed, after preparing their war canoe and providing themselves with *muck-a-muck* (eatables) and many *skookum* (strong) river men, to find her. Travel-ing according to the direction the salmon had given them, they arrived at the lake, and the chief, whose name was Num-Kil-slas, proposed to Tsihooskwallaam that she marry his son Gunnuckets, to which she consented, providing the chief and his son would agree to remain with her and never leave the premises during her life; to which they agreed. After the marriage and feast, they settled down to work on blankets. They asked Tsihooskwallaam where she obtained the material for making these blankets, and she answered that she hunted mountain goats in the moun-tains, from which she derived the material; the next day at *tenas sun* (daybreak) she would take Gunnuckets with her, where he could hunt the mountain sheep for her. Now Tsihooskwallaam's house was very large, being built of big timber forty to sixty feet in length and finely decorated inside with many beautiful woods, such as were unknown to the people of her tribe. Gunnuckets and his father, Num-Kil-slas, were very envious, and being bad at heart, began to plan how to steal all the woman's blankets and belongings. Gunnuckets told his father to take stock of what there was in the premises, and arrange it all in bundles so that between them they could take it during his wife's absence. The next day while Tsihooskwallaam and her husband had gone hunting sheep in the mountains, Num-Kil-slas took stock of all there was on the premises, and arranged everything in bundles so that he and his son could carry everything away when the opportunity offered. Meanwhile Gunnuckets made an excuse to his wife for returning to the house alone, and upon his arrival at the house both he and his father turned to their original characters.

Num-Kil-slas became a raven and Gunnuckets a martin. The raven took many bundles of valuable blankets in his beak, while the martin took all he possibly could carry in his jaws, and they started with great speed to carry away all they could. At night Tsihooskwallaam returned to the house and found she had been deceived by her husband and his father, and how they had stolen all her valuables, but the loss of the valuables did not worry her as much as the knowledge of being exposed to her tribespeople. She wandered away into the woods thinking that she might possibly overtake them and regain her possessions and valuables, but she failed in her efforts, and died from grief.

Num-Kil-slas and Gunnuckets reached their destination with all the blankets and valuables and distributed them as a *Cutlas Potlach* (free gift) to all the people of the Chilthcat tribe, after which the people learned to make these wonderful blankets which are used up to the present time, only by chiefs in their dances and during tribal ceremonies of the Chilthcat Indians.

THE VOYAGER OF THE WHULGE
(Siwash)

Like the ancient Greeks, the Siwash of the Northwest invest the unseen world with spiritual intelligence. Every tree has a soul; the forests were peopled with good and evil genii, the latter receiving oblation at the devil-dances, for it was not worth while to appease those already good; and the mountains are the home of tamanouses, or guardian spirits, that sometimes fight together—as, when the spirits of Mount Tacoma engaged with those of Mount Hood, fire and melted stone burst from their peaks, their bellowing was heard afar, and some of the rocks flung by Tacoma fell short, blocking the Columbia about the Dalles.

Across these fantastic reports of older time there come echoes of a later instruction, adapted and blended into native legend so that the point of division cannot be indicated. Such is that of the mysterious voyager of the Whulge—the Siwash name for the sound that takes the name of Puget from one of Vancouver's officers. Across this body of water the stranger came in a copper canoe that borrowed the glories of the morning. When he had landed and sent for all the red men, far and near, he addressed to them a doctrine that provoked expressions of contempt—a doctrine of love.

To fight and steal no more, to give of their goods to men in need, to forgive their enemies,—they could not understand such things. He promised—this radiant stranger—to those who lived right, eternal life on seas and hills more fair than these of earth, but they did not heed him. At last, wearying of his talk, they dragged him to a tree and nailed him fast to it, with pegs through his hands and feet, and jeered and danced about him, as they did about their victims in the devil-dance, until his head fell on his breast and his life went out.

A great storm, with thunderings and earthquakes! They took the body down and would have buried it, but, lo! it arose to its feet, as the sun burst forth, and resumed its preaching. Then they took the voyager's word for truth and never harmed him more, while they grew less warlike as each year went by until, of all Indians, they were most peaceable.

WHAT BEFELL THE SLAVE-SEEKERS
(Haidah)

From time immemorial until the year 1875, or perhaps even later, every native tribe on the northwest coast of America not only used to keep slaves, but often made raids on other tribes, especially on those with whom they were not on friendly terms, and kidnapped all persons on whom they could lay their hands, in order to obtain slaves for domestic use and also for selling to others.

Early in the present century, a large party of these Haidahs embarked in one of their large canoes, which hold from twenty-five to thirty warriors, for the purpose of making a raid on the Kittamats, a tribe living opposite the Queen Charlotte's Islands, on the mainland of British Columbia, upon the north arm of Gardner's Canal. Though their absence was prolonged, their wives and relatives, who expected them to be absent from five to six weeks, were not greatly disturbed. When weeks turned into months, their friends became alarmed, and strong search parties were sent forth in all directions. After visiting many islands, and seeking far and wide, these tired of the fruitless search, and gave up the wanderers as lost.

The slave-raiders had intended to go to Kittamat. Had the search proceeded thither, such a course, under the existing conditions, would have been equivalent to a declaration of war. Pride and ignorance of the languages of their neighbors were the principal cause of the wars and ill-feeling between the various nations: for example, some ill-timed joke would, through ignorance on the part of the members of another tribe, be construed into an insult, which their pride would not allow to go unpunished. On other parts of this coast the traders found it necessary to create a trade language or jargon. It stimulated friendly intercourse between tribes, by enabling them to converse with each other, whence sworn foes became lasting friends; and when meeting at any of the Hudson Bay Company's trading-posts, they would converse for hours of relatives who disappeared and never were heard of again. A few years ago the Haidahs and their ancient foes, the Kittamats, met and settled old feuds in a friendly manner. Among other topics, the conversation turned on the raid mentioned, when the following facts were elicited:—

A long while ago, a large party of Kittamats were on a hunting and fishing expedition, and, having reached a little island, in which there was a good harbor, they hauled up their canoes. One of the party, during their stay, happening to go into the long grass and the bushes, found concealed a large canoe. This they hastily launched and departed, taking the canoe and everything in it away with them, well knowing it to be a Haidah canoe, and that its owners in all probability were not far off. When they reached home they told how they had taken the canoe, and left the Haidahs to perish. Some time after, when they thought that the party on the island would be in a starving condition, and consequently glad to accept any terms, a large party of Kittamats went to look for them. Sailing cautiously around the island, they were seen by the Haidahs, who gladly hailed them. Going on shore, the latter presented a pitiable appearance, and seemed ready to accept anything in preference to death from starvation. The Kittamats demanded what they were doing there. In answer they said they came to hunt, and that in their absence their canoe had been stolen, and they expressed their desire to get away. The visitors told them to come on board, and they would see what could be done.

These terms the sufferers disliked, but there was no choice. As soon as all were aboard, sail was made by their captors for the Kittamat village, where all the prisoners were made slaves. Some were kept for a time in the village, while others were sold to distant tribes; and, at the time of the interview, nothing was known, even to their captors, as to the whereabouts of any of them, if alive. So much is certain, that none of them ever returned to their native village. And thus it happened that the slave-raiders were themselves made slaves.

Chapter 23

Tribal Legends

Ithenhiela
(Chippwyan)

Naba-Cha, or the Big Man, was one of the most enormous men who ever lived. His wigwam was made of three hundred skins of the largest caribou that could be killed on the vast plains far to the northward. It had taken the bark of six huge birch-trees to make the onogan from which he daily ate his meals. And it took one whole moose, or two caribou, or fifty partridges, to feed him each day. Famous indeed was Naba-Cha throughout the whole North Country, and many were the expeditions of war he had made into distant lands to the north, east, south, and west. He had traveled northward to the mouth of the Big Water to fight the Snow Men or Eskimo, eastward across the Great Lake of Many Slaves to the country of the Yellow Knives, where he had seen the pure copper shining in the sands of mighty rivers, southward away on to the great plains to the country of the Crees, where there were so many large animals,—but westward he had never ventured far, because in that direction it was said that a bigger man than Naba-Cha dwelt. Now Naba-Cha was not only big, but he was also cruel and wicked, especially to a young Wood-Cree boy whom he had brought back from the South once when on the warpath, and who had neither father nor mother nor sister nor brother to help fight. *Ithenhiela,* the Caribou-Footed, as the boy was called, had, however, one great friend at the wigwam of Naba-Cha. This was Hottah, the two-year-old moose, the cleverest of all the northern animals. Truly he was clever, for he had traveled all the distance from the mouth of the Too-Cha-Tes to the wigwam of Naba-Cha in three days, and this was very far indeed. Now Hottah had long thought of a plan by which he might help Ithenhiela. He knew that far to the westward, much beyond where Naba-Cha had ever gone, flowed another river almost as great as Too-Cha-

Tes, and that safety for a hunted man or beast lay on its farther side, because there dwelt *Nesnabi,* the Good Man.

One day Hottah came to Ithenhiela, and said to him, "We will go away. You get a stone, a clod of earth, a piece of moss, and a branch of a tree, and we shall escape from the cruel Naba-Cha." Ithenhiela got what he was told to get, and soon they were ready to be off. Hottah took Ithenhiela upon his back, and before long they were out on the great plains which lie many days beyond the Too-Cha-Tes. Hardly had they started when they saw coming behind them Naba-Cha on his great caribou. Then said Hottah, "Fling out behind you your clod of earth." Hottah did so, and immediately there rose up behind them, and between them and Naba-Cha, great hills of earth so wide and so high that it was many days before Naba-Cha again came in sight. And during this time Ithenhiela ate the ripened berries, while Hottah chewed the sweet grass which grew beyond the hills.

When Naba-Cha once more appeared in sight, Ithenhiela flung out behind him the piece of moss, and a great muskeg-swamp lay behind them. And for days the great man and his caribou floundered in the thick sphagnum. Meanwhile, on and on towards the country of the Setting Sun passed Hottah and Ithenhiela. And when once more Naba-Cha appeared, Ithenhiela dropped the stone, and great indeed were the high rocky hills which intervened between them and Naba-Cha. Up to the very clouds rose the hills, white with snow, and magnificent, such as had never been seen before. Long was it before the fugitives again saw Naba-Cha and the great caribou, and far had they gone towards the West before Ithenhiela had to throw the branch of the tree from him. Then arose a great and mighty forest of which the trees were so thick that Naba-Cha could not pass between them, and had to cut his way through, while the caribou was left behind because his horns had stuck in the branches, and he could not pass on. All this delay helped Ithenhiela; and when he once more saw the cruel Naba-Cha, he and his moose-friend had already crossed the Great Western River which they had tried so hard to reach. Away into the Northwest wound Tes-Yukon, through the high rocky hills to the northward, foaming as it flowed. Soon came Naba-Cha to the other side of the Tes-Yukon, and called aloud, "Help me, Hottah, across this mighty river. Help me to reach the country that lies beyond, and I shall do no harm to Ithenhiela." Then across for him went Hottah; and as he brought him back across the great Tes-Yukon, he overturned him, and down he swept through the swirling rapids of the river, and was lost. This was the last of the wicked Naba-Cha.

Then came Hottah to Ithenhiela standing upon the bank, and, turning to him, he said, "Ithenhiela, I must leave you now, and return whence I came. Go you and follow this great river, and soon you will come to a great tipi. This is the home of *Nesnabi,* the Good Man. Great indeed is he, and far has he traveled, into our country to the eastward, among the golden rivers lost in mountains to the southward, to the great water which has no ending to the westward, and to the silent plains, all snow-covered, to the northward, where live the Snow-Men. He, like Naba-Cha, is big, but he is not cruel, and harms no one. He will aid you." Then departed Ithenhiela, and following the bends of the great Tes-Yukon through the high spruce forest, he came to the wigwam of Nesnabi, who stood silent beside his home. "Whence have you come, young man," said he, "and where are you going?" At this, up spoke Ithenhiela, "Great Chief, I have come from far. I have neither father nor mother nor brother nor sister. My home was with my own people away in the South Country, and there I lived happily until the coming of Naba-Cha, who took me away with him to the cruel North Country, where the snow lasts long in winter, by the sweeping waters of the Too-Cha-Tes. Hard indeed was Naba-Cha to me, and many a season passed I in misery with him, until I came away with Hottah, the two-year-old moose who brought me to your country, O Great Nesnabi, and but now has he left me." To this answered the kind Nesnabi, "Ithenhiela, I have long known that you would come to me. Stay with me as long as you like, but if at the end of the week you wish to journey away, I will then prepare you for your journey farther into the West Country."

Thus it was that Ithenhiela stayed at the wigwam of Nesnabi; but when the week was done, he came to his protector, and said to him, "I must now leave you, and travel farther. Give me that preparation for my journey that you have promised me." Then took Nesnabi seven arrows from his wigwam, and said to him, "This is enough to help you, Ithenhiela, but should you shoot at any bird or beast in a spruce-tree and the arrow stick in the branches, take you care that you go not after it, for if you do, surely something will happen to you." Hardly had Ithenhiela left the good Nesnabi, when he saw a squirrel in the branches of a red spruce-tree, and, raising his bow, he shot an arrow at it. Down fell the squirrel, but the arrow lodged in the branches. At once, Ithenhiela, forgetting what Nesnabi had told him, started to climb after the arrow. As he mounted, the arrow went up, too. Up, up, they went, until at last they came to the sky, and the arrow passed through, and he after it.

Great was Ithenhiela's surprise when he entered the Sky Country. It was so different from what he had expected. He had imagined a glorious country, where the sun always shone, and where herds of musk oxen, caribou, and moose roamed at large in plenty, with many of his own people camped in large wigwams here and there. But instead, the air was damp, dreary, and cold; no trees or flowers grew; no herds of animals ran on the silent plains; the smoke of no wigwam greeted his anxious eyes; the war-whoop or hunting-cry of no Indian of his own people was heard; only, far in the distance against the sky shimmered a great white mass, like a pile of snow, when the sun shines upon it in the early summer. Towards this great white thing ran a winding path from the very spot where Ithenhiela stood. "I will follow it," thought he, "and see what I come to, and find out what lies in that blazing wigwam over there. As he passed along, he met an old woman who said to him, "Who are you, and where are you going?" "I have come from far," said Ithenhiela. "I am the Caribou-Footed. Can you tell me who lives over there in that big white wigwam?" "Ah," said Capoteka, "I know you, Ithenhiela. Long have I thought you would come here. But you have done wrong; this is no country for man. In that great wigwam over there lives Hatempka; and unhappy is he because he has lost his belt of medicine, and until he gets it again, no one will be happy in the Sky Country. The belt is at the tipi of the two blind women who live far beyond the wigwam which shines so white, and no one can get it from them. Whoever finds it, and gets it from the bad blind women, will have the daughter of Hatempka, the beautiful Etanda, for his wife." Off then started Ithenhiela, and, traveling hard, soon came he to the home of the two old blind women. And as he entered the wigwam, he saw hanging upon the side the belt of Hatempka, and many indeed were the skulls which hung about it, for many had gone to seek the belt, but none had returned. The blind women bade him welcome, and said to him, "When you leave, Ithenhiela, tell us, so that we may bid you good-by." Now Ithenhiela had noticed that each of the two old women had behind her back a knife of copper, long and sharp. "Ah!" thought he, "when I leave, they mean to kill me," for one sat on either side of the door in readiness, "but I shall fool them." In one part of the wigwam lay a muskamoot (or bag) of bones and feathers. To this he tied a string, which he pulled over the pole above the door. Then said he, "I am going now, blind women. Remember I am old and fat, and when I leave, I make much noise." At this he pulled the string, and towards the door passed the bag of bones and feathers. Immediately the two old blind women stabbed; but striking only feathers, the long knives passed through them into each other, and both were killed. Then took Ithenhiela the belt of medicine, and went he unto the shining white home of Hatempka, and said to him, "Great chief, be you happy now, I have brought to you your healing belt. Give me now my wife, your daughter, the beautiful Etanda, that I may leave you." Then said Hatempka, "Oh! much pleased am I, Ithenhiela. You have saved my people. Now shall the sun shine again. Now shall musk oxen, caribou, moose, and bear live once more in our country. Again shall we see the smoke of many wigwams. Once more shall we hear the voice of many hunters. Take you now my daughter, the fair Etanda, but leave me not. Stay with me, and be a great man after me." So Ithenhiela remained at the shining white home of Hatempka.

THE THUNDER-BIRD
(Tillamook)

Once upon a time there was a man who lived at Slab Creek. One day he went up the creek to spear salmon. When he started out the sun was shining, but soon dark clouds came up and it began to thunder and to rain. Then it cleared up again, but soon a new shower came on and he was unable to secure a single fish. He became angry and said, "What is that great thing that always darkens the water and prevents me from seeing the fish?" He went on and came to a tall spruce-tree in which a large hole had been burned by lightning. He looked into it and discovered a little boy. When he looked closer he saw the boy coming out. As soon as he had stepped out of the hole he began to grow, and soon reached a height taller than the spruce-tree; his skin was covered with feathers. Then he said, "Now you see how tall I am. Don't look at me; I am the one whom you have scolded."

Then the speaker, who was no other than the Thunderer, took the man's salmon spear and blanket. He leaned the spear against the tree and hung the blanket on to it. He took the man under his armpits and flew with him towards the sky. When they reached a considerable height the man almost fell from under the Thunderer's armpits, and the latter descended again and allowed him to regain his strength. He thought: "Where shall I put him in order to prevent his falling down?" He said, "When we reach a great height, close your eyes, so that the strong wind which prevails up there will do you no harm." Then he flew up again and ascended in large circles. Each flapping of his wings was a peal of thunder, and when the noise ceased the man knew that they had arrived at the Thunderer's home and he opened his eyes. On the following day the Thunderer told him to go and catch salmon. The man went to the beach but did not see any salmon, while many whales were swimming about. Then he went back to the house and said, "I do not see any salmon, but many whales are swimming about."

"Those are the fish I was speaking of," replied the Thunderer. "They are our food. Catch a few!" The man replied, "They are too large, and I cannot catch them."

They went out and the man saw that the people were catching whales in the same way as he was accustomed to catch salmon. The Thunderer told him to stand aside, as he himself was preparing to catch whales. He caught the largest one and carried it up to a large cave which was near by, and when he had deposited it there the whale flapped its tail and jumped about, violently shaking the mountain, so that it was impossible to stand upon it.

One day the man went up the river and saw many fish swimming in it. He thought, "I am tired of whale meat and wish I could have some fish." He went back to the house and spoke to the Thunderer, "Grandfather, I have found many fish, and I want to catch them." He made a fish spear, which he showed to the Thunderer. The latter looked at it, but found it so small that he was hardly able to feel it. It slipped under his finger-nail, and he was unable to find it again. The man said, "How large are your nails! They are just like the crack of a log," and the old grandfather laughed.

The man made a new spear and went fishing salmon. Before he went the old man said, "Don't catch more than you are able to eat. You may take four or five." "I cannot even eat one." Then the grandfather laughed again and said, "If I should eat one hundred I should not have enough."

The man went out, caught one salmon, and brought it home. He was going to split it, but was unable to find a knife small enough for cutting the fish.

Then the Thunderer split a rock, as he thought, into very small pieces, but the smallest of these was so large that the man was unable to lift it. Then the Thunderer broke it into still smaller pieces, and said, "I fear I have spoilt it, for it has become dust so fine that I cannot take hold of it." The man went out, but even then the smallest piece was so large that he was unable to lift it. After the Thunderer had broken it again and the man had selected the smallest piece, he said, "It is still too large, but I think I must try to make use of it. Then the Thunderer told him how to cut the fish. He followed his commands and cut the fish, as the people of the Thunderer were accustomed to do.

He roasted it and ate it, but was unable to eat all. Then his grandfather laughed and said, "Put it aside and go to sleep. When you awake you will be able to eat more." When the man awoke and wanted to continue to eat the fish it was gone. It had returned to the river from which he had taken it. He took his spear and went down the river to catch another salmon. There he saw one half of a fish swimming about. It was the one he had been eating. He caught it, roasted it, and finished eating it. The next day he caught another fish, and when he had eaten half of it and went to sleep he tied the rest to a pole in order to prevent its returning to the river. But when he awoke he found that it had returned to the river. He had burned one side of the head of this salmon, and the next day on going to the river he saw the same salmon swimming about. It had taken some grass into its mouth and covered one side of its face, as it was ashamed to show how badly it was burned. The Thunderer said, "Don't burn the salmon when you roast them, for they do not like it. They might take revenge upon you."

The next day the Thunderer again went whaling, and the man asked him to be allowed to accompany him, as he wished to witness the spectacle. The Thunderer granted his request, but when he came home in the evening he found that the man was badly hurt. He had been unable to stand on his feet when the whale was shaking the mountain, and was hurt by falling trees and stones. But on the following day he asked once more to be allowed to accompany the Thunderer. He tied himself to a tree, but when the Thunderer came back in the evening to fetch him he found him again badly hurt, as he had been knocked about by the swinging trees.

Meanwhile the relatives of the man had been searching for him for over a year. They had gone up Slab Creek, where they found his spear and blanket leaning against a large spruce-tree. They did not know what had become of him. They believed him to be dead, and his wife mourned for him.

One day while he was staying with the Thunderer he thought of his wives and children and longed to return. He said to himself: "Oh, my children, are you still alive? There is no one to provide for you, and I am afraid you are dead." The Thunderer knew his thoughts and said, "Do not worry, your wives are quite well. One of them has married again. I will take you back tomorrow." What the Thunderer called the next day was actually the next year.

The following day he took him under his armpits and put him back at the foot of the spruce-tree, from where he had taken him, and then flew back home. The man believed that he had been away only four days, but it had been four years. He did not go to his house, but stayed in the woods near by. There his son found him. He asked the boy, "Who are you? is your father at home?" The boy replied, believing him to be a stranger, "No, I have no father; he was lost four years ago. For a long time they looked for him, and finally they found his clothes and his salmon spear." Then the man said, "I am your father. The Thunderer took me up to the sky, and I have returned." Then he inquired after his wives, and the boy replied, "Mother is well, and all my brothers have grown up and are also well. Your other wife has married again, but mother remained true to you." Then the man sent him to call his wife. The boy ran home and said, "Mother! father is in the woods." His mother did not believe him, and whipped him for speaking about his father. Then the boy went out crying. He said to his father, "Mother did not believe me." The man gave him a piece of whale meat and said, "Take this to your mother; I brought it from where I have been." The boy obeyed, and took the whale meat to his mother, who said, "I will go with you, but if he is not your father I shall beat you." She accompanied her son and found her husband. He returned with her into the house, and she invited the whole tribe. The man danced and became a great shaman. For ten days he danced, and the people feasted. Then he told them where he had been and what he had seen, and said that whenever they wanted to have a whale he would get one.

After some time the Thunderer came back and took him up once more and he stayed for ten years with him. Then he came home and lived with his people.

One day he went elk-hunting, and came to a small lake, where he found a small canoe. When crossing the lake he heard a voice calling him from out of the water, and on looking down he saw a hole in the bottom, and a human being in it, which called him. He jumped overboard, went to the bottom of the lake and stayed with the supernatural being for ten years. Then the latter sent him out in company of the beaver to gather some skunk-cabbage. They followed a trail and came to a parting of the roads. The man did not know where they were going. Then the beaver asked him: "Do you know where we are going? This trail is Nestucka River, which we are now descending." They followed the trail to its end, where they found a large cave, from which the man emerged to the open air, while the beaver returned to the lake. At the entrance of the cave the man flung down two skunk-cabbages which he had found, and ascended the mountain. Ever since that time two stems of skunk-cabbage have been growing at the entrance of the cave.

His two sons found him on the summit of the rock. They took him home and invited the whole tribe. He danced and became the greatest shaman among his people. When a person died he was able to bring back his soul and restore him to life.

A RIP VAN WINKLE
(Siwash)

Many moons before the Siwashes used iron or gold or silver a strange thing happened. It must be true, for it is told by the old men to the boys to this day. White people do not always believe it.

There lived a great Siwash hunter in the land in the west near the great river full of salmon, where it comes into the sea. His arrows gave him much meat; his great canoe and his spear gave him much fish. He had very many strings of shell money; the Siwash people call it hiaqua.

No one ever loved hiaqua as much as this great hunter loved it. He had many strings of it around his neck. He was rich; but when he waited in the trees in the forest for the elk or the deer to come that he might shoot them, he was always counting the shells on these strings.

He would say to himself: "I shall have more hiaqua than the great chief. I shall have more than two chiefs."

When the great forest was very still his tamanous would come to him. It was like an elk, and it would talk with him. He waited at the foot of the great white snow mountain for the elk to come.

The great mountain is called Mount Tacoma. This was the home of the Great

Tamanous, who puts only good thoughts into the hearts of all people; when the hunter sat long in the tree and looked at the mountain he was ashamed in his heart.

The Great Tamanous, who is the Good Great Spirit, seemed to ask him, "Where did you get it, that last string of hiaqua?"

And he had to say: "I tore some of the shells from the faces of helpless squaws; from their noses and from their lips. I paid them for the shells with elk meat so dry that they cannot eat it. I know they are starving, but they could see; they did not have to take the meat. They could eat leaves and berries. I know there are no berries, but they could go on the long trail and find some."

"The squaws and children were very weak with hunger," said the Great Tamanous to his heart.

The hunter was much ashamed; in the tree by the mountain he would be ashamed, but he never gave back the hiaqua. It was good and he wanted more.

One day he went up the side of Mount Tacoma. His own tamanous came to him while he waited; the white elk talked to the hunter's spirit. The tamanous said:

"You are not wise. You are like the mouth of a great fish. You have great hunger, but it is all for hiaqua. Your shoulders are covered with heavy strings of hiaqua. You have taken the shells from the nose and lips of your own squaw. You sell her elk meat, and she is starving like the other women. You will not feed her with the elk meat you will get today. I will send her meat. I am sent by the Great Tamanous. Listen! I will give you hiaqua enough to fill your heart."

Then the tamanous, the spirit of the great elk from which his band was descended, told the hunter a secret. The tamanous told him of a place on the great white mountain where was much hidden hiaqua. If the hunter would seek it and obey, he should have enough to satisfy him.

The hunter went back to his village. He told his squaw he was going on a long hunt. He took many deerskins from his tent, and when it was very dark he went away.

He made his camp that night at the foot of Mount Tacoma. He could not sleep; he could not wait; he saw the sun rise from the top of the mountain; he had no fear. His tamanous had said he would be with him.

The hunter stood on a great rock on the top of the mountain and looked down; at his feet was a wide hole; he could not shoot his arrow across it. The hole was white with snow, except that in the middle was a wide black lake; across the lake he saw the three great rocks he had been told to find.

The hunter walked on the crackling snow until he reached these three rocks. He knew them, for they were the ones his tamanous had told him to find.

The first rock was shaped like the head of a salmon; the second was like the good camass root, which all Siwashes eat; the third rock was the same as an elk. It was his tamanous: it would take care of him; he was safe.

The hunter dropped his pack of deerskin on the ground before the elk. He opened it and took out a great elk-horn pick, and began to dig in the sand.

He struck one blow in the sand. Four otters rose out of the black lake and came and sat at the north of him. He struck the second blow. Four more otters came and sat at the south of him. He struck the third blow. Four more great otters came and sat at the west.

The sun was bright in the east. It was watching him. No otters came and sat at the east. These were all the guards for the place where the Great Tamanous kept his hiaqua. They did not hurt the hunter, and he did not see them, for he was thinking only of hiaqua.

When the sun was over his head he put down his pick. He ate a bit of dried elk meat and took his pick again. He struck a rock; it broke very quickly. He lifted up a piece of the rock and saw a great cave full of shell money, full of hiaqua.

The hunter put in his hand and played with the shells. He lifted up strings of it, for it was strung on elk sinews. He threw the strings around his neck. He worked fast, for the sun was moving to the west, and he knew he must go. He was strong, but he had a great load. The sun was too fast for him.

He stood up and ran, but he did not throw one string over the elk head, nor over the camass root, nor over the rock like a salmon. He turned his back on the great otters. He did not offer them one string, not one shell; he forgot his promise to the Great Tamanous. He did not obey.

He ran on with his great load of hiaqua. He reached the white snow on the side of the great pit; then all the otters jumped into the black lake and lashed it into white foam with their bodies and tails. A black mist came over the mountain; the storm winds came. The Great Tamanous was in the storm.

The winds blew the hunter from one side of the wide hole to the other side. He had his hands on his money and did not lose one string. The water helped the winds to throw him back to the great rock on the top of the mountain. The hunter did not let the otters get one hiaqua.

He heard two voices in the thunder; one was the Great Tamanous. He heard the tamanous of all the mountain scream to him in the wind; he heard them laugh.

His body was like a leaf, as the winds blew him and tossed him from one rock to another. They did not break a string; they did not take his hiaqua. He did not give them one shell.

The night was two days long; he broke one string and threw it away to the winds. They laughed. He threw another string to the thunder voices. The thunder was heavier than before. He threw away every string of hiaqua; then his body dropped on the ground on the side of the mountain, and he went to sleep.

When his eyes came open he was hungry; he dug some camass root, and made a pipe and smoked. His bones were not broken, but his joints made a noise like a paddle on the edge of a canoe. His hair was like a blanket on his back; it lay on the ground while he was smoking.

"The Great Tamanous has done this," said the hunter. He looked at the white mountain, and his heart was full of peace.

"I have no hiaqua. It is all given back to the Great Tamanous. I am well. I have no hunger for it. I will go home."

He found the trail overgrown with tall trees.

"Tamanous has done it," he said.

The people in his village did not know him. He asked for his wife, and they pointed to an old squaw, wrinkled and with her face bent to her knees. She knew him and pointed to his hair.

"Tamanous," he said.

"There is the little papoose," she said. The papoose was a man with white hair.

"He is your son and my son," said the old squaw.

The hunter looked in the water. "I have slept for many moons," he said.

He became a great medicine man, for he was wise. He taught the Siwash nation many things. He taught them to keep their promises. He told them not to forget the Great Tamanous whose home is on the white mountain.

Txäxä'

(Tillamook)

There lived a man in Nestucka who used to rise early every morning. One day when he came down to the beach he saw a large whale stranded. He ran back to the house to call the people, crying, "Don't sleep any longer. I have found a whale; let us carve it." They jumped up, but were unable to reach the whale, as the flood tide was coming in, and they were obliged to wait for low water. While they stood on the beach a man with his five sons from Natā'hts, named Txäxä', came and asked the man who had found the whale, "Will you allow me and my sons to cut off a bit of the tail for our dinner?" The man did not reply, because he did not wish them to share in the whale. Then the old man got angry and said to his sons, "Let us go back. We will take the whale along."

They turned around, and all at once the whale began to swim along the beach, following them. Then the Nestucka ran after them, and asked the old man, "Please don't do that; share the whale with us." They, however, would not listen, but went on.

The old man asked his guardian spirit where the whale would go ashore. The spirit replied, "It will strand at the place where you will find a large log of drift-wood." And when they came to Natā'hts they saw a large log on the shore. There they stopped, and on the following morning the man climbed up a small hill to look out. He saw the whale lying on the beach. He went back to the camp and told his sons that the whale had stranded; then they began to cut it up. They invited all the Neē'lim, Tillamook, and Natā'hts to join them. After this, whenever a whale was seen off the shore, he sent out his guardian spirit (his supernatural power), who caught the whale as a net would catch it, and through this means he caused all the whales to strand on his beach, and at no other place.

Once the Natā'hts challenged the Tillamook to a game of ball, the prize being a whale. The Tillamook accepted the challenge, as they never had a chance to get whale meat. They staked stores of roots and berries against the whale. When they were playing the old man put on his sea-otter cap and stood behind the players. He had painted his face red, white, and blue, and he talked as loud as he could the whole day, making the ball afraid of him. Therefore it never came near him, and the Tillamook were unable to win the game. They were beaten and lost their stake.

When they were beaten Txäxä' made them a present of whale meat. The following year they played again, and the Tillamook were beaten once more. Then they began to fight, and in the struggle Txäxä' was killed. The people began to cry when they saw that Txäxä' was killed. They put him into a canoe, which was paddled by six men, and went down the river. They came to the house where his mother was roasting clams, while his father was sitting idly by the fire. The people cried, "Your son has been shot through the heart."

The old man saw them coming, but he did not stir. He asked his wife, "Are the clams soon done?"

Now the canoe arrived, the men jumped ashore, and went up to the old man and said, "Your son has been killed." The old man merely turned his head and said, "Come up here and eat clams with us." Then the man who carried the message said, "The old man does not mind at all that his son has been killed. He invites us to eat clams with him." They went up, and, when they were eating, the old man joked with them and was very merry. When they had finished eating he said, "Let us go down and look at the body."

They went down; the old man shook his son and asked, "What is the matter, Paint-face? Three colors are on your face. Arise and purify the inside of your body." Then the dead one awoke, opened his eyes, and asked, "Is the tide coming in?" The old man replied, "No; it is still ebb-tide." Txäxä' replied, "Then I am dead. If it had been flood tide I should have returned to life." Then his father said, "Take him to Red-water Creek and call all the people from both sides of the river. Take this kettle and a small stick." When all had assembled he told them to stand on both sides of the river, and ordered two men to make a dam across the water. He told them, "He shall lie down. Then you must sing and beat time on the kettle. He will rise and vomit into it, and you must pour what he has vomited into the water where it is deepest."

They did as he had ordered. When they began to sing and to beat time, Txäxä' arose and vomited blood into the kettle. They threw it into the water where it was deepest, opened the dam, and let it run down the river. The kettle was quite full of blood. Twice he vomited and filled the kettle with blood. Then he took the arrow-point that had killed him out of his mouth, and was as well as before.

The people returned to the village, and now he caused a heavy thunderstorm to rise, which split the trees of the forest and killed many of the Tillamook. Then he sent some of his people to the village of the Tillamook and challenged them to another game of ball. The latter were singing and dancing because they believed they had killed Txäxä'. After they had been challenged again, they sent two old men to see what the Natā'hts were doing. When these messengers arrived at Natā'hts, they saw Txäxä' practicing with his ball. At first they would not believe their own eyes. But when approaching nearer, they saw that their enemy was still alive. They returned to Tillamook and said: "Are you not ashamed to dance and sing? He whom you killed is alive and playing ball." Then the people took off their fine garments and threw them into the fire.

WOMEN REBELS AND WOMEN WHO "SHINE"
(Various)

THE WOMAN WHO MARRIED THE MOONLIGHT
(Athapascan)

There was once a couple who lived by themselves. They had a house and a cache and the man occupied himself in hunting.

He hunted martens both with traps and with the arrow.

One day he said, "I believe I will go to my marten traps;" but the woman did not want to let him go. "No," said she, "please don't. Stay here today; there may be strangers coming." But the man answered, "Who is there to come? There's nobody at all. There are no tracks but mine;" and he put on his gear and left the house. Meanwhile the woman wept as she sat sewing at home.

At noon, yonder, outside the door, she heard some one knocking the snow from his boots, and a man came in, but it was not her husband.

The woman drew her hair down over her face so as to cover it, then put food into a bowl, meat and fat, and handed it to him. "Have something to eat," she said. "I am not hungry," said he; "it is for you that I came here; go with me." And when she refused he gave her a beautiful necklace of seed beads, and hung them about her neck and went out.

Meanwhile she had made a fire and cooked food, expecting her husband; for she thought, "When he comes he will be hungry." At length he returned, and after they had eaten he fixed the curtain over the smoke-hole and they went to bed. When she undressed, her husband saw the great necklace of beads. He broke out in anger, "Who gave them to you, if no one has been here?" And taking a great maul, he broke them to pieces, and putting them upon a shovel he threw them out at the smoke-hole, and lay down again.

Thereupon the woman began to cry. "Come," said her husband, "go outside and cry; there is no sleep to be had here;" and she went out crying. The moon was shining, but she stood where no light fell upon her, and where the moon shone she looked for (him). See! There in the moonlight is that man. He laughs as he stands looking at her in the moonlight. Then he went to her and came close to her. "What say you?" said he. "Why," she said, "he pounded up the beads and threw them out at the smoke-hole."

So up to the top of the house went the man, and took up the beautiful beads whole, as they were before, and put them upon the woman's neck, and took her and went out into the moonlight.

Meanwhile, her husband roused himself up, and went out to find that his wife was gone. All around the place he went, but found only his own tracks, for the stranger had left none. He kindled a fire, and burned his parka and his own hair and his back, and went away as a wolverine.

The Girl Who Married the Moon
(Unidentified)

Two girls, cousins, lived in a large village; and those evenings when the moon was out they went to the beach to play. Claiming the moon as their husband, they spent the night in gazing and making love to him. For shelter they had a propped-up bidarka (large skin boat), and in the course of the night they changed their positions several times, so as to be face to face with the moon. If on their return to their homes in the morning their parents questioned their whereabouts, they replied that they watched the moon till he passed from sight. Many of the people heard them remark on different occasions that they loved the moon, and wished they, too, were moons.

One evening, in company with other young people, they amused themselves on the beach. Night coming on, the others returned to their homes, but these two remained. When during the night the moon withdrew from sight, one of the girls complained: "Why does the moon hide himself so suddenly? I like to play with him, and have light." "I, too," said the other. Although they thought it was close on to morning, and that the moon had vanished for the night, it was yet midnight with the moon behind the clouds.

Up to this time they had not noticed their disheveled hair, and when they now began to put it in order, they were startled by hearing a noise close to them, followed immediately by a young man. He looked at them for a moment, and then said: "You have been professing love for me since a long time. I have watched and observed you, and know you love me, therefore have I come for you. But as my work is hard, I can take only one of you, the more patient one." As each claimed superiority in that virtue, he said, "I will decide this point myself; I will take both of you. Now close your eyes, and keep them closed." So saying, he grabbed each by the hair, and the next moment they were rushing through the air. The patience of one was soon exhausted, and, on peeping, she dropped down, down, down, leaving her hair behind her in his hands. In the morning she found herself near the bidarka, from which she had parted not long since. The other girl, however, kept her eyes closed, and in the morning found herself in a comfortable barrabara, the home of the moon. There as his wife she lived for a time, apparently happy in loving him. Generally he slept during the day, and was out during the night; but frequently he went away in the morning and returned in the evening; at other times he left in the middle of day, and when he returned, it was night. His irregular going-out and coming-in puzzled her much; but he never offered to explain to her where he went and what he did in his absence.

This silence and indifference piqued her not a little. She bore it as long as she could, and then called him to account.

"You go out every day, every evening, every morning, and every night. Where do you go? What do you do? Who knows the kind of people you associate with, while I am left here behind."

"I do not associate with the people here, for there are none of my kind here," said he. "I have work to do, and cannot hang around you all the time."

"If it is so hard, why don't you take me with you to help you sometimes," she asked.

"I have too much hard work to be bothered with you," he replied. "I brought you up here because I had no rest when you were down there. You and your lovely cousin were always staring and staring at me. No matter where I looked, your grins always met me. Now stop being foolish and wishing to go with me; for you cannot help me. Stay home, and be a good girl."

"You don't expect me to stay home all the time," she said, weeping. "If I cannot go with you, may I not go out by myself occasionally?"

"Yes, go anywhere you like, except in the two barrabaras yonder. In the corner of each there is a curtain, under which you must on no account look." Saying this, he left the barrabara, and that night he looked paler than usual.

Shortly after she went out for a walk; and although she went far and in different directions, she could see no people and only the three barrabaras aforementioned. Short trails there were many. Some of them she followed, and in each case stumbled on a man stretched out face down. It gave her much pleasure to kick them, which she invariably did. On being so disturbed, each would turn on her his one bright sparkling eye, and cry out: "Why do you kick me? I am working and am busy." She kicked them till she was tired and then started home.

The two barrabaras were on her way, and of course, she had to look in. With the exception of a curtain in the corner, the first barrabara was bare. She could not resist the desire to look under the curtain, and when she did so, she beheld a half-moon, a quarter of a moon, and a small piece of a moon. In the second barrabara, she found a full moon, one almost full, and another more than half full. After thinking it over, she could see no harm in trying one on just to see how well it would become her. The one almost full pleased her best, so she put it on one side of her face, and there it stuck. Notwithstanding she cried, *"Äi, Äi, Y-ä-h', Äi, Äi, Yäh',"* tugged, and pulled it would not come off. Fearing her husband would arrive on the scene, she hastened home, threw herself on the bed, and covered up her face.

There he found her on his return, complaining that her face was paining her. He, however, suspected the real cause, and went out to investigate. On his return, he questioned her about the missing moon. "Yes," she admitted; "I tried it on just for fun; and now I cannot take it off." She expected him to fly into a rage, but he did nothing of the kind. Going up to her, he pulled it off gently.

Seeing him in such unusual good humor, she related to him the adventures of the day, especially the sport she had with the one-eyed people scattered over the sky.

"They are stars," he said reprovingly.

When she had concluded, he said to her: "Since of your own free will you put on this moon, wear it from now on, and help me in my hard work. I will begin the month, and go the rounds until the full moon; after that you will start in, and finish out the month, while I rest." To this arrangement she consented, and ever since then the two have shared the hard work between them.

THE GIRL WHO MARRIED A STAR
(Aleut)

The chief of a very large village had an only daughter whom he never permitted to go outside of her barrabara. Two servant girls were at her beck and call, and they attended to her wants.

One lovely summer day, the earth and sky being clear and blue, the air inspiriting, she felt herself irresistibly drawn to the window by the glad sunshine peeping through it, by the joyful shouts of those outside, and by the plaintive notes of the golden-crowned sparrow: and as she stood there, seeing and not seeing, she thought of her own sad life, and wondered why the pleasures of the other people were closed to her. She stood there a long time, and when she turned away, there were tears in her eyes. Her servants were watching her; on noticing it, she sent them away, one for fresh water, and the other after sweet roots. At their departure her imagination and feelings took again control of her. Her past life stood out before her very distinctly, and she groaned when she thought of the numerous proposals of marriage she had received during the last year; for nearly every day one or more men from the neighboring villages came to ask her in marriage from her father. He was unwilling to part with her, especially against her consent; and she, with her very limited knowledge of men and their ways, thought marriage strange and foolish, and rejected all offers.

With this subject in her mind, she was interrupted by her servants, who were sent by her father to announce to her that a bidarka with two young men had just arrived to seek her in marriage.

"Oh! why should I marry? Go, and say to them that I have no desire to marry. I am content to live as I am. Here it is warm. Why should I marry when I am not even allowed to go outside?"

One of the servants took the liberty of suggesting that, "One of the fellows is very young and handsome, the other not quite so. You had better marry now."

"If he pleases you, marry him. I am satisfied and warm here; and why should I marry?" she curtly replied.

"They are waiting for you," the other servant said, "and you may come outside if you like."

"Go, bring me the water and roots, and tell them I will not marry." Saying this, she pushed them outside, and, throwing herself on the bed, had a good cry. When the servants returned with roots and water, they found her in such a state that they feared she was ill. They questioned and tried to pacify her, but she paid no attention to them. "What have we done to you that you should be angry with us. It is not our fault that you please all men, and they desire to marry you. If your father finds out your present condition, he will punish us," etc.

In the evening she said to the girls, "Go, sleep in the adjoining barrabara; if I need you, I will call you." When they had filled the stone lamp, fixed her bed, and in other ways arranged for her comfort during the night, they went out.

Unable to sleep, the girl sat up, making sinew thread; and about midnight she heard some one cutting the intestine window, and a man's voice calling softly,—

"*Chit! chit! chit! chit!* look this way." She did not, and went on with her work.

"*Chit! chit! chit! chit!* just look at me once," he pleadingly called. If she heard him, she took no notice of him.

"*Chit! chit! chit! chit!* look at me just once." For the third time she heard the tempter's call. This time she looked up, and beheld a very handsome young man, with a face as white as hers, and she asked him, "Why do you ask me to look at you?"

"Come here quick! I wish to marry you," he whispered.

"What for?"

"Come quick! I am going to marry you. Why spend your days and nights in loneliness here. Come with me and see the world," he coaxingly said.

Without more ado she obeyed, and with the aid of her lover escaped through the window, and hurried down to the beach. There a bidarka and her lover's friend were awaiting them, and after stowing her away in the bidarka, they paddled off.

It was daylight when they landed, and she was taken to a nice clean barrabara. Here she lived three days, and during that time she was by turns the wife of both. On the morning of the fourth day she was led to a large, open, cold barrabara, and tied up there. It was in the fall of the year, and the cold wind blew through it, and made her shiver with cold. Her food consisted of bare bones. In this cruel and sure way the men hoped to be rid of her.

The second morning of her imprisonment, and while the men were away hunting, the girl, cold and hungry, heard some one approaching. *"Tuck, tuck, tuck, tuck,"* it sounded as it drew nearer and nearer until it ceased in the entrance. She raised up the leather door, and a very old, shrunken, shriveled, and toothless woman, bearing a platter of hot meat, entered and said: "I have brought you some meat, for I know you are hungry. Eat fast." The girl, being very hungry, ate as fast as she could, but still not fast enough to please the old woman, who continued hurrying her to eat still faster. "Eat faster—they will soon appear—why did you marry them—faster still—they are almost here," she said almost in one breath. When the girl had done eating, the woman cleaned her teeth, so that no sign of food should be left on the premises, and hastily snatching up her platter, disappeared as mysteriously as she appeared. *"Tuck, tuck, tuck, tuck,"* floated back faintly, and died out altogether.

The old woman did not go too quickly; for the men appeared very soon after. "Still she lives; she does not even change color. Somewhat tougher than her predecessors," they laughingly remarked, and left her. A little later they brought her bones; and the girl went at them as if she were famishing. Noticing that the girl was not the worse from her treatment, and suspecting something was wrong, the men commenced to watch. They would go out a short distance from the shore, and then come right back, and conceal themselves. But during their brief absence the old woman appeared and fed the girl. For several days this spying continued.

Very early one morning, just after the men had gone out in their bidarka, the old woman came, with meat, and speaking rapidly, said, "Eat fast—why did you come here—they have starved many girls before you. If you do not wish to die, come with me. I have a son who desires to marry, but cannot get a wife. This is the last time I come to you—the men have discovered, are aware of my visits. If you come with me, the men shall never find you"—

"I will go with you," interrupted the girl.

In a twinkle the old woman unbound her, and set her in a large basket, which she put on her back. "Now close your eyes tight, and don't open them till I tell you," cautioned the old woman. As they began to move, the girl felt the cold air while they buzzed and whizzed through it. Tiring of keeping her eyes closed, she opened them just a little. *"Äi, Äi, Y-ä-h,"* screamed the old woman, "close them, or we will fall in the water." The noise and whir of the air, as they rushed through it, was so annoying that she began to unclose her eyes for the second time. "Don't open them now; we will soon arrive, and then you may look," pleaded the woman.

When they came to a standstill, the girl found herself in front of a large bar-rabara. The interior was cozy and clean. A cheerful fire was burning, over which were several pots with seal and duck meat. Spreading out a mat in the front part of the room, the old woman begged the girl to be seated; then she brought her a new pair of torbarsars and a sea-otter parka. While the girl was dressing, the old woman ran outside for a moment, and on her return said to the girl: "Don't be scared when you see my son; although his appearance is terrifying, yet he is very harmless." This news had a pensive effect on the girl, for she wondered what she had got into. To distract her from her gloomy thoughts, the old woman placed food, and talked to the girl. Pretty soon she went out again, and hurried back, announcing, "Here comes my son." The girl, already half-frightened, kept her eyes on the doorway, and when, of a sudden, a lot of willow twigs darkened it, she fell back, screaming, *"Äi, Äi, Y-ä-h! Äi, Äi, Y-ä-h!"* The old woman hastened to her, trying to calm her. "Don't be alarmed," she said; "this is my son; these are some of his hair." She stared at him, doubting her own eyes; for he was one-sided. That side, however, was complete, and had all its members in the usual place, except the eye, which was in the forehead, and shone very brilliantly.

"Look at the wife I brought you," the mother called the son's attention to the girl. He turned his one eye on her, and, from the way it winked and sparkled, he was well pleased. Probably because he was embarrassed, or perhaps he thought it wise to leave the two women to themselves for a time, he left the room. When he returned, a little later, with seals and several kinds of ducks, he found the bride looking more cheerful. The marriage was not delayed at all. In the course of a very short time a child was born, a boy, who was the perfect image of his father, and "just as pretty," as the grandmother said. There was happiness and no lack of cheering light in the family, especially when pretty, one-sided baby awoke and opened his little wee sparkling eye. Mamma, as was natural, vowed it was the brightest baby she had ever seen, and it had more expression in its one eye than other babies had in their two eyes and face together, to which statement grand-mother readily agreed.

Although a bride of several months, the girl had not yet become well acquainted with her husband and his strange body, as is shown from the following incident:

One night being stormy, the husband did not go out as usual, and during the night he asked his wife to scratch his moss-covered head, in which his hair, the twigs, were rooted. Telling him to keep his eye open, so she could see, she commenced the operation with the twigs first. In doing so, she disturbed a mouse, which ran and hid in its hole in the moss. *"Äi, Äi, Y-ä-h!"* she shrieked, and dropped his head; "there are mice in your head."

"Oh, no!" he declared, "they are mere fleas."

A year had passed since the happy marriage between the son of the sky and the daughter of the earth took place. The one-sided result of this marriage began to grow and become strong. Motherhood brought with it the desire to see her own parents once more. Permission to do this was granted, and the mother-in-law set about making a basket in which to send her down. When it was done, she called the young mother to the fireplace, around which were four flat rocks, and said: "Raise these rocks, and try and find your father's village." Darkness of night was in the first one; the rosy tints of dawn were visible in the second; a grand sunset filled the third; and in the fourth she recognized the village of her father, wrapped in midday splendor. Then she seated herself in the basket, to which a rope was tied; but, before lowering her, the mother-in-law gave her some advice: "Close your eyes tight, and don't open them, for if you do you will fall. Should you meet with an obstacle on the way, stamp your foot, and it will disappear. A second obstacle may impede your progress; do likewise, and it too will vanish. When for the third time the basket stops, unclose your eyes, and you will find yourself in the home of your childhood. If it does not please you down there, seat yourself in the basket again, pull on the rope, and I will draw you up."

Placing the child in her arms, the old woman lowered away, and after encountering the enumerated obstacles, the young woman saw in front her native village. To the barrabara of her father she directed her footsteps, and, as she drew near, she noticed a grave close by. For when she disappeared so suddenly, her parents, thinking her dead, made a grave for her, probably to take her place (?). She went in, and when the people there saw her with the queer-looking child in her arms, they ran pell-mell out of there, thinking she returned from the land of the dead.

This reception brought tears to her eyes, and, realizing for the first time the great gulf that separated her from her earthly relatives, and that her real home now was with the father of her child, she walked back to the basket, gave the signal, and a little later was welcomed by her mother-in-law and husband, from whom she parted no more, and with whom she is living to this day.

Her husband is a star. At sunrise each morning he goes to sleep for a few hours; after that he hunts ducks, seals, and other sea animals. If, on his return in the evening, it is cloudy and stormy, he spends the night at home with his family; but if it is clear, he stretches himself out on the sky, and observes the doings of the world below, as any one who takes the trouble to look up can see.

The Girl Who Defeated the Shaman
(Unidentified)

A terrible misfortune befell the people of a very large village. Of all the hunters that left the village not one ever came back, nor was it known what became of them. In that village lived a very beautiful girl, who loved and was beloved by a brave young hunter and joyfully consented to become his wife; but the parents objecting, the marriage never came off. The disappointed lover decided to drown his grief in hunting, and, although cautioned by the old men, insisted on going and went. A week, a month, passed, and when he did not return, he was given up as lost. Not so the girl; she could not believe him dead, and concluded to go and search for him.

Secretly she made preparations, and one night, when all the other villagers were sleeping, stole out quietly, and, taking her father's one-hatch bidarka and *kamalayka* (waterproof shirt made of intestines), started off. After going some distance from the village, she ceased paddling, closed her eyes, and began to sing. She sang a verse, then opened her eyes, and on noticing that the bidarka was drifting with the current, shut her eyes again and continued singing. At the end of the second verse, she looked about again, and, seeing the bidarka drifting as before, only faster, closed her eyes and sang a long time. When she looked around the next time, the bidarka was going very, very fast. Becoming alarmed, she tried unsuccessfully to change its course. The speed of the boat increased each moment; and soon she heard the mighty roar of falling waters. Her life without her lover was not worth living, so closing her eyes, she resigned herself to her fate and awaited death. Very swiftly the boat rushed now; the roaring waters became dreadful; and her heart almost stopped beating when she felt herself going down, down, down, and suddenly coming to a standstill. She was not hurt, but could neither come out nor move. The bidarka was fast.

Dawn was approaching as she lay there, wondering what would become of her and what became of her lover. When it was broad daylight, she saw a bidarka, with one man in it, coming toward her. On coming closer, the man exclaimed, "Ha! Ha! I have another victim," and placed a bow and arrow, having a two-edged knife on the end, near him for immediate use. But as he came a little nearer, he put back his weapons, saying to himself, "Seems to me that is a woman. No, it cannot be," he added a moment later, and picked up his bow and arrow again, only to replace them, and crying out, "If you are a woman, speak up, and I will not kill you; for I do not kill women." She assured him that she was a woman, and he came and took her out of the bidarka, seated her in his, and paddled off with her.

Reaching his home, a small barrabara, and occupied by him alone, she noticed many human heads; and in one, not yet badly decomposed, she recognized her lover's. She did not say a word, but swore vengeance. The man told her that he would have her for his wife, and ordered her to cook something for him to eat, which she did of deer and seal meat. At bedtime, he pointed to a corner of the barrabara, telling her to lie there, while he slept in the opposite corner. Although this arrangement seemed queer to her, she obeyed without questioning.

The following morning he led her to a little small barrabara, and showed her a number of headless human bodies. "These," said he, "I do not eat; but I have three sisters, living some distance from here, who eat human flesh only. It is for them that I killed these people. Each day I take one of these bodies to a different sister." He then lifted up a corpse, and, taking his bow and arrow, walked off. The girl followed him to the place where the road forked. One path led to the right, another to the left, and the third continued straight before her. Noticing which he took, she returned to the barrabara, and busied herself the rest of the day, removing two of the posts from one of the walls, and digging an underground passage out. All the dirt she removed and dumped into the sea, and cunningly concealed the passage. Towards evening she cooked supper, and when he returned, they ate it in silence and then retired; she in her corner and he in his.

After breakfast the next morning, he carried away another corpse. She, taking the bow and arrow which he left behind, followed him secretly. Where the road divided, he took the path to the left, while she followed the one in the middle. After keeping it for a while, she cut across to the left path, and by hurrying managed to reach the home of his sister and kill her before he came there. From there she ran to the homes of the other sisters, killing them, and then back to the barrabara. He, coming to his sister's, and finding her dead, hastened to the homes of the other sisters, and finding them dead also, suspected the criminal, and determined to kill her.

She was sitting on the barrabara when he came. "You killed my sisters and I will kill you," he cried. He rushed for his bow and arrow, but they were not in their places, and when he discovered them in her hands, he began begging them of her, promising to do her no harm. At first she refused, but he pleaded and promised until she, trusting in his promises, gave them to him. As soon as he had them, he shouted, "Now you shall die," and shot at her. But she, dropping through the smoke hole, was out of sight before the arrow could reach her; and while he was looking for the arrow, she crawled out through the underground passage, and perched herself anew on the barrabara. This sudden appearance was a mystery to him, since the door was closed. Again and again he shot at her, and each time she disappeared and appeared in the same mysterious manner. At last, seeing that he could not hurt her, he said, "Since I cannot kill you, take these, and kill me."

"I do not want to kill you," she said. "But I am afraid that you will kill me some day, when you think of my doings."

He swore never to hurt her, and she came down. They ate supper, and retired in the usual manner; but as he was about to fall asleep, she moved close to him, and commenced talking to him, keeping him awake the whole night. Five days and nights she tortured him in this way, giving him no opportunity to sleep. On the sixth day, in spite of all that she could do, he fell into a deep sleep. Although she pulled and pinched him, he could not be aroused. She then brought a block of wood from outside, and, placing it under his neck, cut his head off with a knife which she stole from one of his sisters.

In his bidarka she put his bow and arrow and knife, and, seating herself in it, started on her homeward journey by way of the falls. But the falls were there no more; for they existed through the evil power of the man, who was a shaman; and when he died, his influence ceased; the river flowed smoothly and steadily in the old channel. Her bidarka she found drifted on the beach, and after repairing and placing his weapons in it, paddled away, and in good time came home.

When the people of the village learned her adventures, and that she killed the shaman, they rejoiced exceedingly. The old men decreed that the shaman's weapons, which the girl had brought along, should be thrown on the garbage pile, where they would be polluted.

The Two Sisters
(Tillamook)

There were two sisters who were playing in front of their house. They made a small hut and lay down in it to sleep. During the night they awoke, and saw the stars in the sky. One of the sisters said: "Do you see that white star? I will have him for my husband. You take that red star." They joked and laughed on this proposition, and finally went to sleep again. While they were sleeping two men entered their hut. One of them wore a white blanket, the other wore a red blanket. The latter married the elder sister, while the former took the younger for his wife. They removed them from the house into the sky. They were the two stars of whom the girls had been speaking. When the sisters awoke and saw the strange men by their sides, they did not know where they were.

On the following morning their mother called them to come to breakfast. When she did not receive an answer, she grew angry and went to call the girls. Then she saw that they had disappeared. During the night a boy had heard how the girls had been talking about the stars, and thus the people were led to suppose that the stars had abducted the girls. The stars go out every night with bow and arrows hunting cariboos. Then they look through the holes in the sky and see what is going on on earth.

The two stars who had married the girls also went out every night, and brought home many cariboos. The young women skinned and carved them. They made gloves, shoes, and dresses from the skins. They cut long thongs from the skins of others, cutting spirally around their bodies. They hid the clothing and the thongs carefully from their husbands. There was no water, no cloud, and no rain in the sky, and they were always suffering thirst. They had nothing to eat but meat. Therefore they longed to return to their own country. When they had prepared a sufficient number of thongs and of cloths they made ready to escape. One day, when their husbands had started on a long hunting expedition, they went to the hole in the sky. They tied stones to one end of a thong and let it down towards the earth. When one thong was paid out they tied a new one to the end of the first, and thus they continued from morning to night. The one woman brought the cloths and the thongs from their hiding-place, while the other let them down. Finally, after four days, they felt the rope striking the ground. They could not see the earth because it was hidden by smoke. They shook the thong and it fell a little farther, but finally it seemed to have reached the ground. At least they felt that it was held by something. Now they tied two pairs of sticks together, one being on each side of the rope. They put on four suits of clothing, four pairs of shoes, and four pairs of gloves. The elder sister stepped on one pair of sticks and they began to glide down, the sticks acting as a brake. The rope swung to and fro, and the sister who had remained behind gradually lost sight of her. Finally the young woman reached the end of the rope and found herself on the top of a tall tree. Her clothing and her gloves were almost worn through by friction. Then she shook the rope, and upon this signal her sister began to slide down in the same manner. She came down very much quicker, because her sister was holding the end of the rope. Looking upward, she beheld a small dot in the air. It was coming nearer and increased in size. Soon she recognized her sister, who finally reached the top of the tree. There they were on the top of a tall spruce-tree, and there was no way of getting down. They broke off some branches, and made a bed in the tree. The elder sister, before starting, had tied an additional piece of thong around her waist, thinking that she might use it in case the long rope should not have reached the ground. She untied it, and fastened it on to the long rope, but still it was not long enough.

After a while, the young women saw a number of men passing the foot of the tree. They were armed with bows and arrows, and were on snowshoes. They recognized the wolf, the bear, and many other animals. They called to them, asking them to help them down, but they passed by without paying attention to their entreaties. The next morning they saw another man approaching the tree. They recognized the fisher. They called him, and he at once climbed the tree. The young women asked him to carry them down, but he demanded that they should first marry him. The elder one said: "I will do so, but first carry me down." The fisher finally agreed and carried her down. When they arrived at the foot of the tree, she demanded from him that he should first carry down her youngest sister. Reluctantly he was compelled to do so. Then he demanded from the youngest sister that she should marry him. She said: "I will do so, but carry me down first." He took her down. When he insisted upon his former demand, the elder sister said: "We are almost starved; first bring us some food." He went away and soon returned, carrying a bear that he had killed. During his absence the young women had lighted a fire. He wanted to roast the bear meat, but they said they wished to eat it boiled. Then the fisher made a basket of bark, and placed stones into the fire, which he intended to use to boil water in the basket. Meanwhile the young women had hidden a few pieces of meat under their blankets, and now they pretended to go to fetch water in which to boil the meat. As soon as they were out of sight they ran away down the mountains. After a while the eldest sister flung a piece of meat at a tree, asking it to whistle. They went on, and again she threw a piece of meat at a tree, asking it to talk. In this manner she continued to give meat to all the trees.

When the young women did not return, the fisher followed them to the brook, where they had gone to fetch water. He discovered their tracks, and saw that they had escaped. He pursued them. Soon he came to the tree which they had asked to whistle. It did so when the fisher went past. Then he thought they were on the tree, climbed it, and searched for them. When he did not find them, he continued his pursuit. He came to the second tree, which spoke when he went past. Again he thought the young women might be on the tree. He climbed up, but did not find them. Thus he lost so much time that they made good their escape.

Towards evening they reached a deep cañon. They walked along its edge, and soon they were discovered by the grizzly bear, who was residing here. He wanted to marry them, and they did not dare to refuse. But they said: "First go and bring us something to eat. We are almost starving." While the bear was away hunting, the girls built a platform over the steep precipice of the cañon. It overhung the abyss, and was held in place by two ropes which were tied to a tree that grew near the edges of the cañon. Its outer edge was supported by two slanting poles which leaned against a ledge a short distance down the precipice. When the bear came back, he found them apparently asleep on this platform. He did not bring any meat; he had only roots and berries. The young women said that they could not eat that kind of food, and demanded that he should go hunting again. It had grown dark, however, and the bear proposed to go out on the following morning. They lay down on the platform, and the young women induced the bear to lie near the edge, while they lay down near the tree to which the platform was tied. They kept away from the bear, promising to marry him after he should have obtained food for them. Early in the morning, when the grizzly bear was fast asleep, they arose without disturbing him, cut the ties with which the platform was fastened to the tree, and it tipped over, casting the bear into the abyss.

The young women traveled on, and for a whole month they did not fall in with a soul. Then, one day, they discovered tracks of snowshoes, and soon they found the hut of a woman who had given birth to a child. They entered, and recognized one of their friends. They stayed with her for a short time, and when the young mother was ready to return to the village, they sent her on in order to inform their relatives of their return. She went to the mother of the two lost girls, and told her that they were waiting in the woods, but she would not believe the news. The young mother returned to her friends and told them that their mother would not believe that they had come back. Then they gave her as a token a skin hat that was decorated with stars. She took it to the village and showed it to the mother of the two young women. Then she began to think that there might be some truth in the report, and went out to look. There she saw and recognized her daughters. At that time all the men were out hunting. The women on hearing of the return of the two lost girls went out to see them, and they told of their adventures. Then they climbed two trees, tied their skin belts to the branches, and hanged themselves.

COYOTE TALES
(Various)

THE COYOTE GOD
(Unidentified)

Among the people of the far west, the Californians and Chinooks, an outstanding deity is, strangely enough, the Coyote. But whereas among the Chinooks he was thought to be a benign being, the Maidu and other Californian tribes pictured him as mischievous, cunning, and destructive. Kodoyanpe, the Maidu creator, discovered the world along with Coyote, and with his aid rendered it habitable for mankind. The pair fashioned men out of small wooden images, as the gods of the Kiche of Central America are related to have done in the myth in the *Popol Vuh*. But the mannikins proved unsuitable to their purpose, and they turned them into animals. Kodoyanpe's intentions were beneficent, and as matters appeared to be going but ill, he concluded that Coyote was at the bottom of the mischief. In this he was correct, and on consideration he resolved to destroy Coyote. On the side of the disturber was a formidable array of monsters and other evil agencies. But Kodoyanpe received powerful assistance from a being called the Conqueror, who rid the universe of many monsters and wicked spirits which might have proved unfriendly to the life of man, as yet unborn. The combat raged fiercely over a protracted period, but at last the beneficent Kodoyanpe was defeated by the crafty Coyote. Kodoyanpe had buried many of the wooden mannikins whom he had at first created, and they now sprang from their places and became the Indian race.

This is, of course, a day-and-night or light-and-darkness myth. Kodoyanpe is the sun, the spirit of day, who after a diurnal struggle with the forces of darkness flies toward the west for refuge. Coyote is the spirit of night, typified by an animal of nocturnal habits which slinks forth from its den as the shades of dusk fall on the land. We find a similar conception in Egyptian mythology, where Anubis, the jackal-headed, swallows his father Osiris, the brilliant god of day, as the night swallows up the sun.

Another version of the Coyote myth current in California describes how in the beginning there was only the primeval waste of waters, upon which Kodoyanpe and Coyote dropped in a canoe. Coyote willed that the surf beneath them should become sand.

Coyote was coming. He came to Got'at. There he met a heavy surf. He was afraid that he might be drifted away, and went up to the spruce-trees. He stayed there a long time. Then he took some sand and threw it upon that surf: "This shall be a prairie and no surf. The future generations shall walk on this prairie!" Thus Clatsop became a prairie. The surf became a prairie.

But among other tribes as well as among the Chinooks Italapas, the Coyote, is a beneficent deity. Thus in the myths of the Shushwap and Kutenai Indians of British Columbia he figures as the creative agency, and in the folk-tales of the Ashochimi of California he appears after the deluge and plants in the earth the feathers of various birds, which according to their color become the several Indian tribes.

THE NAMING OF CREATION
(Nez Percé)

Coyote was chief of all the animals. Now, he told them that the tribes of men were coming near, one and all. Everything he told them came true. Then he said, "Tomorrow the people will come out of the ground. I will name them and they will spread out."

Then he named them; he named them until he had named them all. And the people came out, but Coyote had no name for himself. Many people came out. Then he named himself Coyote. Thus came people,—not we alone, but all people.

COYOTE AND THE PEND D'OREILLE CHIEF
(Flathead)

Coyote and Fox were traveling together and they were coming up from below. When they got to where Spokane Falls now is, Coyote said to Fox, "I believe I'll get married. I'll take one of the Pend d'Oreille women for my wife."

So he went to see the chief of the Pend d'Oreilles about getting one of the women for a wife. The chief was not willing to let his women intermarry with other tribes, so he told Coyote he could not have any of the Pend d'Oreille women for a wife.

Coyote said, "Now I'll put falls right here in the river, so the Salmon cannot get past them." That is how Spokane Falls were made.

COYOTE KILLS THE GIANT
(Flathead)

Coyote came on up to Ravalli. There he met an Old Woman, who was camped close to where Ravalli Station is now. The Old Woman said to Coyote, "Where are you going?"

"Oh," said Coyote, "I am going to travel all over the world."

"Well," said the Old Woman, "you had better go back from here."

"Why should I go back from here?" asked Coyote.

"Because there is a Giant in this valley who kills every one that goes through," replied the Old Woman.

"Well," said Coyote, "I will fight with him and kill him."

Then Coyote started on the trail again. He saw a great big tamarack-tree growing on the hillside, and he pulled it up and threw it over his shoulder and went on his way. He said to himself, "I'll choke that giant with this tamarack-tree. That's what I'll do."

Pretty soon he saw a woman that was nearly dead. "What is the matter with you?" asked Coyote. "Are you sick?"

The woman said, "No, I am not sick."

Coyote said, "I am going to choke the Giant with this tamarack-tree."

The woman said, "You might as well throw that stick away. Don't you know that you are already in the Giant's belly?"

Then Coyote threw the tamarack against the hillside, and it can be seen close to Arlee, a little station on the Northern Pacific Railroad. It stuck against the hillside and grew. All of what is now Jacko Valley was filled by the Giant's belly.

Coyote went on from there and he saw lots of people lying around. Some of them were dead, and some were pretty nearly dead. "What is the matter with you people?" asked Coyote.

They all said, "We are starving to death."

Coyote said, "What makes you starve? There is plenty to eat in here, lots of meat and fat."

Then Coyote cut chunks of grease from the sides of the Giant and fed them to the people, who got better. And then Coyote said, "Now, all of you people get ready to run out. I am going to cut the Giant's heart. When I start to cut you must all run out at O'Keef's Canyon or over at Ravalli."

The Giant's heart was the rounded cluster of mountains north of Flathead Agency, and there are marks on the side which show the place that Coyote cut with his stone knife.

Coyote began to cut the Giant's heart with his stone knife. Pretty soon the Giant said, "Please, Coyote, let me alone. You go out. I don't want you to stay in here. You can go out."

Coyote said, "No, I won't go out. I am going to stay right here. I'm going to kill you."

Then he started to cut the Giant's heart. He cut the Giant's heart off and then ran out. The Giant was dying, and his jaws began to close. Woodtick was the last to come out. The Giant's jaws were just closing down on him when Coyote caught him and pulled him out.

"Well," said Coyote, "you will always be flat. I can't help it now. You must be flat." That is the reason Woodtick is so flat.

COYOTE AND THE TWO SHELLS
(Flathead)

Coyote went on down to where Missoula now is. Coyote was walking along between Lolo and Fort Missoula when he heard some one call his name. He stopped and looked around, but he couldn't see any one. Then he started on a little trot, and he heard his name called again. He stopped and looked right through the trees, and there, by the side of the river, he saw two women sitting down.

He went across the river and up the hillside to where the women were sitting. When he got close to them he thought he would marry them, because they were good-looking women. So he went and sat down between them.

When he got between them they stood up and went dancing down the hill to the river. When they got close to the river, Coyote said, "Wait, I want to take off my clothes." Coyote had nice clothes on, all beaded and trimmed in shells. He was a great chief.

The women said, "No, we don't want to wait; we will have a nice time dancing." They danced right on into the river, and they pushed Coyote down and drowned him.

Some time after that, his partner, Fox, was around the river looking for something to eat. He looked down in the river and saw something lying at the bottom. "Why," said he, "that is my partner, Coyote," and he pulled him out, and jumped over him, and Coyote came to life again.

"Oh, my," said Coyote, "I have slept too long."

Fox told him, "You were not asleep; you were dead. What for did you go near those women? You had no business near them anyhow."

Coyote said, "Now, I'll go back there and I'll kill them both."

Coyote went back and climbed half way up the hill. Then he set fire to the grass. The women started to run, but they couldn't get away. Both of them were burned to death.

They were Shells, and the reason the side of a shell is black is because they were burned that time.

Coyote Kills Another Giant
(Flathead)

Coyote started to go up to Stevensville. Between Corvallis and Stevensville there is a very sharp Butte. The Giant lay on top of that Butte. Coyote had a little black squirrel for a dog. He called him One Ear. The Giant had Grizzly Bear for his dog. Grizzly Bear killed all the people that passed through the valley. He never missed one.

At the foot of the hill Coyote saw a little camp of Mice. He said to them, "What will you take to dig a little hole for me from the bottom of this hill up to where the Giant is? I want to go up under the ground. It is the only way I can get up."

The Mice said, "Give us some camas and blackberries and we will dig the hole." Then Coyote gave them some camas and blackberries, and they began to dig. They dug and dug until the hole reached from the foot of the hill to the top. It came right up to where the Giant lay.

Coyote went in about noon. He crawled through the little hole, and pretty soon he came out right under the Giant's belly, where the hole ended.

The Giant was very much surprised. "Where did you come from?" he said.

Coyote said, "Are you blind that you didn't see me come?"

"Which way did you come?" asked the Giant.

"I came right across the prairie," answered Coyote.

"I didn't see you," said the Giant. "I've been watching everywhere all day, and I didn't see any one come."

Coyote said again, "Are you blind that you didn't see me? You must have been asleep. That is the reason you didn't see me."

Just then the dogs began to growl at each other. Coyote said to the Giant, "You had better stop your dog. My dog will kill him if you don't."

The Giant said, "You had better stop your dog. My dog will swallow him."

Then the two dogs began to fight. One Ear ran under Grizzly Bear and cut his belly open with his sharp pointed ear. Grizzly Bear fell down dead.

Coyote said, "I told you to stop your dog. Now he is killed."

Then they sat down and began to talk. Coyote made a wish, and whatever he wished always came true. He wished there were lots of horses and women and men down at the foot of the hill. Pretty soon he could see the people and horses moving down there. The Giant didn't see them yet.

Coyote said, "I thought you had good eyes?"

The Giant said, "Of course I have good eyes. I can see everything."

Coyote answered, "You say you have good eyes. Can you see the Indians moving over there? You didn't see them yet?"

The Giant looked very carefully and he saw the Indians moving. He was ashamed that he didn't see them before.

"Now," said Coyote, "let us be partners. We will kill all these people."

"All right," answered the Giant.

"Now we will go after them," said Coyote. "We will go down to the foot of the hill."

They started down the hill, and when they were half way down the Giant was very tired.

"Give me your knife," said Coyote. "I will carry it for you. It is too heavy for you, and you are already very tired." So the Giant gave Coyote his knife. Then they started on.

When they got to the bottom of the hill the Giant said, "I am not going any farther than this. I am played out."

Coyote said, "Give me your bow and arrows. I will carry them for you." The Giant gave his bow and arrows to Coyote. Then he had nothing at all to fight with.

As soon as Coyote got the bow and arrows he began to jump and yell. "Now we'll start war right here," he said.

"Let me go free, Coyote," begged the Giant. "I won't kill any more people. I'll be good friends with everybody if you'll let me go."

"No," said Coyote. "I am going to kill you now. Today is your last day."

Then he commenced to shoot, and soon he killed the Giant.

Coyote and the Crying Baby
(Flathead)

From there Coyote went on to a place called Sleeping Child. As he was going through the woods he saw a child in its cradle-board leaned up against a pine-tree. The baby was crying and crying just as hard as it could cry. Coyote called for the baby's mother, but he could get no answer. He called again and again for the mother to come and take her baby. But the mother didn't come.

Then he took the baby to quiet it, and he said, "I know how I'll stop your crying."

He put his finger in the baby's mouth for it to suck. The baby sucked a while, and when Coyote took his finger out of the baby's mouth there was nothing left but the bones.

He put in another finger and another, until there was nothing left of all his fingers but the bones. Then his hand, then the arm, the other hand, the other arm, his feet, his legs, all of him, and then there was nothing of Coyote but the bones.

In a few weeks Fox came along that way, and he saw the bones of Coyote lying on the ground. He jumped over them, and Coyote came to life again.

Coyote said, "I have slept a long time."

Fox said, "You were not asleep. You were dead. What for did you go near that baby? It is one of the Killing People. That is the way it kills every one that goes through these woods."

Coyote said, "It kept on crying so hard that I put my finger in its mouth. It felt pretty good, so I put in another and another until it was all of me. Give me a knife and I will go back and kill that baby." So Coyote went back and killed the baby.

Coyote and the Woman
(Flathead)

Coyote went on across the river. As he was going up the mountain-side he heard the dogs barking furiously. He looked to see what they were barking at, and he saw a Mountain Sheep running ahead as fast as it could.

On the top of a high steep cliff stood a Woman, who kept holloaing to Coyote to come on and kill the Mountain Sheep, to shoot him quick before he got away.

Coyote went around the mountain-side, and came up where the Woman was. The Mountain Sheep was right in among a pile of rocks. The Woman kept showing Coyote where to stand when he shot the Mountain Sheep, but she kept behind him all the time.

When they got very close to the edge of the cliff, she was showing him how to aim, and then all at once she pushed him over the edge. Coyote fell down, down into the middle of the river, and lay there dead.

About a month after that, his partner Fox was fishing in the river, and he saw something white at the bottom. He looked again and saw that it was the bones of his partner. He fished him out of the river, jumped over him, and Coyote came to life again.

Fox said, "What have you been doing again?" Coyote told him about the Mountain Sheep and the Woman that had pushed him over the cliff.

Fox said, "Go back on the same trail and play blind. Get the Woman to go in front of you to show you the way, and when you are at the edge of the cliff, push her over and kill her."

Coyote went back over the same trail, and he played blind for the Woman to lead him and show him how to shoot straight. He kept her in front of him, and every once in a while he would open one eye just a little bit to see if they were near the edge of the cliff. When they were close to the edge, Coyote pushed her over and she got killed. This happened between Grandstell and Darvy.

The Medicine Trees
(Flathead)

Coyote took to the trail again, and went up to Medicine Trees between Ross's Hole and Darvy. Coyote was going down the mountain-side, and a big Mountain Sheep ran after him. There were big trees standing at the bottom of the mountain.

Coyote ran and the Mountain Sheep ran after him. Then all at once Coyote ran out to one side. The Mountain Sheep ran on down the mountain and right into the big trees at the bottom. One of his horns stuck in the side of the big tree. It is away up high now and can be seen quite plainly.

Every time the Indians go by there, they give earrings or beaded moccasins or anything they happen to have to that horn, because it is big medicine. That is why the trees are called Medicine Trees.

Coyote and Rock
(Flathead)

Coyote and Fox went to a place called Ross's Hole. Coyote had a very fine new blanket. As they went along they saw a very nice big smooth round Rock. Coyote thought it was a very nice Rock.

He said, "I think you are a very nice Rock. You're the nicest Rock I have ever seen. I guess I'll give you my blanket to keep you warm." So Coyote gave the blanket to Rock.

Then Coyote and Fox went on their way. Pretty soon it began to thunder and lightning. Coyote and Fox went under a tree for shelter. Now Coyote had no blanket to keep the rain off his nice beaded clothing, and he was afraid his clothes would get spoiled.

He told Fox to go back and get the blanket from Rock. Fox went and asked Rock for the blanket, but Rock said, "No." Then Fox came back, and told Coyote.

Coyote said, "Go back and ask Rock if I can't please have the blanket for a little while. I'll give it back to him again after the rain is over."

Fox went back and asked Rock again, but Rock said, "No, he can't have it. I want it myself." Then Fox went back and told Coyote what Rock had said.

"Well," said Coyote, "he is awful mean. I think he might let me have the blanket for just a little while. He never had a blanket before. What for should I work hard and get a blanket just to let him keep it? I'll not do it. I'll take my own blanket." So Coyote went back and jerked the blanket away from Rock.

Then all at once it cleared up. Coyote and Fox sat down to smoke. While they were smoking, they heard a crushing, crashing noise. They looked up and saw Rock come rolling toward them as hard as he could. They jumped, and ran down the hill as fast as they could run. Rock was going awful fast, and going down the hill he got pretty close to them. Fox jumped into a hole in the side of the Hill and Rock just touched the tip of his tail as he went by. That is what made the tip of a Fox's tail white.

Coyote went on down the hill, jumped into the river, and swam through and came up on the other side. He saw Rock go into the river and thought he would sink to the bottom, but Rock swam through all right, came up on the other side, and went after Coyote. Then Coyote ran for the thick timber. When he got to the middle of the thick woods, he lay down and went to sleep. Pretty soon he woke up, and heard the trees crashing and crackling, then he knew Rock was after him yet.

Coyote jumped up, and ran for the prairie. Rock came on after him on the prairie. Coyote saw a big Bear, and Bear said to Coyote, "I'll save you." Pretty soon Bear and Rock came together and Bear lay dead.

Then Coyote saw a big Buffalo, and Buffalo said to Coyote, "I'll save you." Rock passed on, he struck the big Buffalo, and Buffalo lay dead.

Coyote ran on till he came to where two Old Women were standing, who had stone hatchets in their hands. They said to Coyote, "We'll save you." Coyote ran in between them, and Rock came right after him. Coyote heard the Old Women strike Rock with their hatchets. He turned and saw Rock lying on the ground, all broken to pieces.

Then Coyote noticed that he was in a big camp. Pretty soon he heard the Old Women say, "He looks nice and fat. We'll have something good for our supper now. Let us eat him right away." Coyote sat and studied. When Coyote wished for anything it always came to pass. So he wished that all the water would dry up.

After he had made the wish, he said, "I am very thirsty. I wish you would let me get a good drink of water."

The Old Women said, "There is plenty of water here. You may have a drink." But when they looked in the pails they found that every one was empty, and all the little streams close by were dry.

Coyote said, "I know where there is a creek that has water in it. I will go and get some water for you." He took the pails and started off. When he got out of sight he ran away. The Old Women waited for him a long time. Then they began to blame each other for letting him go. At last they quarreled and killed each other.

Coyote in the Buffalo Country
(Flathead)

Coyote traveled on from there. After a while he had nothing to eat. He was pretty nearly starved. He went into a tipi about noon and lay down to rest. He was very weak because he had had nothing to eat for a long time.

He heard some one holloa, but he couldn't see any one. Then some one called again, and after he had looked carefully for some time he saw Eagle a long ways off.

Eagle told him that far away from there was a very rich country where there were plenty of Buffalo all the time. "I am going there," said Eagle, "but you can't go, you're too poor."

Then Coyote got mad. He said, "I can go any place I want to. I am going to go there." Coyote started out, and in fifteen days he got there. The place is on the Missouri River, not far from Great Falls. There was a big camp of people at this place. Bear was their chief. The people did not like Bear at all. When they killed lots of Buffalo, Chief Bear would always take the best pieces for himself, all the good meat, and the nice chunks of fat.

Coyote wanted to be chief himself, so he went out and killed a big Buffalo and stripped off all the fat. Then he cut the meat in strips and hung it up to dry. After that he built a big fire and heated some stones red hot.

Chief Bear found out that Coyote had killed a Buffalo, and he came to look at the meat. "This is nice meat," said Bear, "I'll take this."

Coyote said, "I saved some fat for you." Then Coyote took one of the red hot stones, and put plenty of fat around it. Then he shoved it into Bear's mouth. This killed Bear, and then they made Coyote chief.

Bear had been a great Medicine Man, and whenever he wished for anything it always came to pass. It was Bear who had caused the Buffalo to stay around in that country all the time, so when Coyote became chief all the Buffalo went away. In ten days the people were starving. Every one said, "Coyote is no good of a chief."

Coyote went out to hunt for Buffalo. He was all alone, and he hunted for five days, but he couldn't find any Buffalo at all. He was ashamed to go back to the people without anything, and so he kept right on.

In a little while Coyote met Wolf.

"Where are you going?" said Wolf.

"I am going to travel all over the world," answered Coyote.

Wolf went on ahead, and pretty soon Coyote heard a wagon coming after him. He looked around and saw that the wagon was full of meat. Coyote lay down by the side of the road, and pretended he was dead. The driver stopped his horses. "This is pretty good fur," said he. So he threw Coyote into the wagon and went on.

Coyote ate and ate all the meat he could hold. Then he jumped off the wagon, and ran away. Pretty soon he met Wolf again.

"Well," said Wolf, "you look fat. Where did you get the meat?"

Coyote told him that he had played dead and lay on the roadside. The driver picked him up, threw him into the wagon, and drove on. "Now," said Coyote, "he picked me up for my fur, and your fur is much finer than mine; he'll take you quicker than he did me."

Wolf lay down on the road, and pretended he was dead. Pretty soon the wagon came along. The driver stopped his horses and jumped out. "Ha, ha," he said, "Wolf looks as if he were dead, but I'll see this time." So he took a big club and hit Wolf on the head, and then right away he hit him another lick.

Wolf was pretty nearly killed. He jumped and ran away as fast as he could. He was awfully mad at Coyote. He said, "I know Coyote did this on purpose. I'll kill Coyote, that's what I'll do."

Wolf ran, and Coyote ran. After a while, Wolf overtook Coyote. "I'm going to kill you," said Wolf, "that's what I'm going to do to you. What for did you play that trick on me? I am going to kill you right now."

Coyote said, "Wait, I have something to say to you. Wait till I have said it. Then you can kill me after that."

"All right," said Wolf, "what is it?"

"Well," said Coyote, "there are only two of us. It isn't fair for us to fight alone. Let us get others to fight with us. Then it will be like one tribe fighting another. Let us get some other fellows to fight with us, and let us fight fair."

"All right," said Wolf.

Wolf went in one direction, and Coyote in another. Wolf saw a Bear, and he said to Bear, "Come with me and fight against Coyote."

"I will," said Bear. So Wolf and Bear went on together. In a little while they met Bore. Wolf said to Bore, "Come with us and fight against Coyote." "All right," said Bore. So they took Bore along. Then there were three in this party, Wolf, Bear, and Bore.

Coyote had gone the other way, and he had Cat and Dog in his party. Coyote and Wolf had agreed to meet at Butte. Coyote had said, "If you get there first, wait for me, and if I get there first I'll wait for you."

Wolf and his party got there first, and they waited for Coyote and his party to come up. Pretty soon Bear looked out and said, "I see Coyote and his party coming. He has Cat and Dog." "Yes," said Bore, "and Coyote is a brave man, but we'll do the best we can."

Coyote was all dressed up,—nice beaded moccasins and everything very fine. Coyote was a great chief. Then Coyote and his party came up, and the two crowds fought. Coyote killed all of his enemies. Then he went on alone.

Coyote and Fox Separate
(Flathead)

Coyote kept on alone till he met Fox, his partner. They went on together till they came to the White Man's camp. They had had nothing to eat for a long time, and they were both very hungry.

Fox said to Coyote, "You play dead and I'll take you to the White Man and sell you for a sack of sugar. Then, when the White Man cuts the strings that tie your feet, you must jump up and run away."

Coyote agreed to this plan. Fox took him and sold him to the White Man for a sack of sugar. He took the sack of sugar and went away. The White Man took his knife and began to skin Coyote's legs. Coyote yelled and tore, and finally he broke the strings that held his feet together, and ran away. He was awfully mad at Fox, and he said, "If I find my partner I will kill him sure."

After a while he met Fox and he said, "Where is the sugar? I want my share of the sugar."

Fox said, "Why didn't you come right away? I was so hungry I ate it all up."

Fox said, "I am going back now. I am not going any farther."

Coyote said, "I am going to keep right on."

So they parted there. Fox went back and Coyote went on alone.

COYOTE AND LITTLE PIG
(Flathead)

Coyote kept on alone for a while. When he was tired of traveling he built himself a little house and stayed in it for a while. Then he started out again. When he had been traveling for some time, he came to a place where the road divides.

The three Pigs had come there before Coyote, and each had taken a different road. They went out to find homes for themselves. When they parted, they said they would come back every month and see each other.

They found nice homes, but Coyote came after them. He killed the oldest brother, then the next oldest, and then he was looking for the youngest brother, Little Pig. Little Pig was the smartest of them all.

After a while, Coyote came to where Little Pig lived, and he said, "Hello! Little Pig."

Little Pig said, "Hello!" But he kept the door of his house closed tight. He had a very nice place.

"Let me in," said Coyote.

"Who is it?" said Little Pig.

"It's me," said Coyote.

"Well, who is me?" said Little Pig.

"It's Coyote, and I want to come in."

"You go away, Coyote," said Little Pig. "I don't want you here."

Little Pig was pretty smart. Coyote thought, "He's pretty smart, but I'll fool him, I'll kill him yet." Then he said,—

"Little Pig, don't you know there is a nice garden about half a mile from here,— cabbage and potatoes and everything in it?"

Coyote wished for the garden, and it was there. The next morning Little Pig got up early, and went to the garden and helped himself to everything.

The next morning, when Coyote got to the garden, he looked at all the things. He saw that Little Pig had been there and helped himself to everything and then gone away. He looked around and saw Little Pig down the road about half a mile. He ran and Little Pig ran. Little Pig got into the house first and locked the door and wouldn't let Coyote in.

Coyote knocked at the door, and said, "Little Pig, let me in. I have tobacco and kin-i-kin-ic. We will smoke together."

"No," said Little Pig, "I don't smoke. I don't want your tobacco and kin-i-kin-ic. I won't let you in. You want to kill me."

Then Coyote went away. That night he came back and knocked at the door. "Let me in," said Coyote.

"Who's there?" said Little Pig.

"It's me," said Coyote, "I don't want to hurt you. I want to help you. Let me in."

"Who are you?" asked Little Pig.

"I am Coyote."

"Go away, Coyote. I don't want you here."

"I want to tell you something," said Coyote.

"Well, what is it?" said Little Pig.

"About half a mile from here is a nice big orchard, and all kinds of fruit in it."

"All right," said Little Pig. "Tomorrow morning I will go there and get me what I want."

Coyote wished for an orchard to be there, and it was there. Early the next morning he got up and went to the orchard. When Coyote got there, Little Pig was up in a tree gathering apples. He was pretty badly scared when he saw Coyote.

Coyote said, "What have you got there? Some nice big apples?"

"Yes," said Little Pig. "I have some nice big apples. Don't you want me to throw you one?"

"Yes," said Coyote. "Throw me a nice big apple."

Little Pig took a big apple and threw it just as hard as he could. Coyote tried to catch it, but he couldn't. It hit him in the eye and knocked him down. Little Pig jumped down from the apple-tree and ran as fast as he could. Coyote jumped up and ran after him, but Little Pig got in the house first, and he locked the door on Coyote.

Coyote knocked and knocked, but Little Pig wouldn't let him in. Coyote said, "I'll come down the chimney."

"All right, come down the chimney, if you think you can," said Little Pig.

Little Pig began to build a fire. Coyote came down the chimney, and fell into the fire, and was burned to death. Fox was not there to step over him, and so he never came to life again, and that was the end of Coyote.

PANTHER TALES
(Various)

THE PANTHERS AND THE WOLVES
(Tillamook)

There were five wolves who lived on one side of the river, and on the other side of the river lived five panthers who had a wildcat for their servant. It was his duty to look after the fire while they went out hunting. Whenever his masters had left the house in order to hunt, he climbed up the vine-maples that stood near the house, and jumped from tree to tree. He stole pieces of grease out of the boxes and ate them on the trees. Therefore the wood of the vine-maple is oily when it burns.

When he got tired of playing about he returned to the house to look after the fire, which, however, had meanwhile gone out. Then he crossed the river and stole fire from the wolves, who had each a fire burning in their house. He took one of these and returned home. When he came to the river he did not know how to carry the fire across. First he put it on his head, but the fire burnt him. Finally he put it on the tip of his tail and so carried it across. He had hardly reached the house and started a new fire when the panthers returned, each carrying what he had shot.

When the wolves returned, and found that one of their fires had been stolen, they said, "Who has stolen our fire? We will kill him."

The panthers heard what had happened, and said to the wildcat, "Certainly you have done it. Why did you allow our fire to go out?" He replied, "No, I kept a large fire all day." Then the panthers sent the wildcat to see what the wolves were doing. He returned saying, "One of the wolves is just about to swim across the river." After a little while they sent him again, and he returned, saying, "Now he is in the middle of the river;" and when he had been sent the third time he came back, saying: "He has reached the bank of the river." Then the panthers gave the wildcat a knife, and covered him with a dish, saying, "When we call, you jump forth from under the dish and stab the wolf." Soon the latter came, and they fought for a long time. When they grew tired and feared to succumb, they called for the wildcat, who jumped forth, danced about, and sang, "Where shall I stab him? In his toe-nail or in his fingernail?" The panther cried, "If you dance any longer, he will kill me. Stab him in his lap." He obeyed and killed the wolf.

After a while another wolf came over to see what had become of his brother. Again the panthers covered the wildcat with a dish, and when they were unable to withstand the wolf any longer they called him. He jumped forth and stabbed the wolf. Then the third wolf went down to the water and called to his brother to come across.

The panthers cried, "Come across and we will show them to you. We will give you some flesh," meaning that of the wolves. The third wolf swam across, and fought with the panthers, and he, too, was killed by the wildcat. The fourth wolf shared the same fate. When the fifth one got ready to swim across, the blue jay told him not to go, because the panthers had killed all his brothers, and they would kill him, too. Then he ran away into the woods.

The Panther and the Man
(Tillamook)

Once upon a time there was a panther who was a great hunter. He lived in his house all alone. Every time he came back from hunting he found that his fire had gone out, and he wished to have a companion. He took a flint arrow-head which had been broken, wrapped it in leaves, and put it aside, saying, "I wish you were a man who would look after my fire."

On the following day he went hunting, and when he returned he noticed that the arrow-head did not lie in the same position in which he had left it. Then he wished again it would change into a man. On the following day he went hunting, and did not return until the following morning. Again he found that the arrow-head had changed its place, and he thought, "I am sure it will become a man."

On the following day he went hunting. At night he returned, carrying a deer on his shoulder. He threw it down at the side of the door, and on entering the house he saw an extremely homely person with a large head, sitting near the fire. Then he was afraid. The person said, "Why are you afraid? My name is Tcatc'ē'wiqsō. You yourself have wished for me."

Then the panther went to look for his arrow-head and found it was gone. Now he believed that the stranger was the arrow-head which had assumed the shape of a man. After this the two lived together and Tcatc'ē'wiqsō looked after the fire. One day a girl came by who carried a basket full of roots. Tcatc'ē'wiqsō asked her to come in, took away her basket, and concealed her under the roots which she had brought. He wished to marry her. When the panther came back he saw the roots which the girl had carried, and asked Tcatc'ē'wiqsō where he had obtained them. The latter replied, "There are plenty of roots near here, and I dug them myself when you were out hunting." He boiled them and gave some to the panther and to the four wildcats that had come home with him.

Whenever the panther was out Tcatc'ē'wiqsō greased his hair in order to make it soft, and put on his best clothes to please the girl. The girl wished to escape from the place where Tcatc'ē'wiqsō had concealed her, as she did not like him. She pulled one hair from her head and tied it around one of the roots, hoping the men would find it. Tcatc'ē'wiqsō boiled the roots and gave them to the panther when he returned at night. He ate of it and soon found the hair. He said, "There is a woman's hair." "No," said Tcatc'ē'wiqsō; "it is a hair of my head. If it is pulled, it grows very long." The panthers, the wildcats, and Tcatc'ē'wiqsō had quite long hair, but even the longest was only half as long as the one found among the roots.

After supper the panther and the wildcats played about the house, the cats hiding, and the panther running after them. Whenever they went near the roots Tcatc'ē'wiqsō cried, "Don't go near there, else you will spoil my roots."

The panther grew suspicious and told one of the wildcats to peep under the roots when running about. Then he found the girl. The panther resolved to take her from Tcatc'ē'wiqsō. The next day he went hunting again and killed an elk. When returning at night he pretended to have hurt his foot. He said to Tcatc'ē'wiqsō, "I have hurt my foot and have been unable to bring home the elk's head. Will you please go and fetch it?" Before returning, however, he had bewitched the elk's head, and ordered it to roll down the hill whenever Tcatc'ē'wiqsō had carried it up. Tcatc'ē'wiqsō went out, loaded the elk head on his shoulder, and turned homeward. As soon as he had climbed the first hill the elk head rolled down, and he had to go and carry it up again; but all his endeavors were to no purpose, the elk head rolled down as often as he had carried it up. Finally he grew impatient, and was about to return home, when the head said, "Tcatc'ē'wiqsō! my eyes are fat and good to eat." Then he resolved to try once more, but met with no better success, and finally he gave it up and went home. When he arrived he found that the panther had gone, and taken the girl with him.

The panther had ordered the wildcats to stay at home and to detain Tcatc'ē'wiqsō. One of them said, "Tcatc'ē'wiqsō, they have taken your wife from you." When he heard this he was very angry and cried, "I will eat you when I catch you." He jumped towards one of the wildcats, intending to bite it, but it had made its escape and Tcatc'ē'wiqsō bit only dirt. He tried to catch another one, but with no better results. Then the cats ran away, and he was unable to catch them. He followed them, dancing while he was running. Then he said, "I want to make the distance shorter." He took up the trail which he was following and pulled it, hoping to shorten by this means the distance between himself and the fugitives; but although he thought he had the trail in his hands, he did not hold anything. The wildcats teased and detained him continually, but finally he succeeded in catching and killing them. Then he caught the panther also. He killed him and took away the woman. When they passed by the body of the wildcats and of the panther, she took up their blood, taking care not to leave any on the ground, and put it into her basket, and when they came to a river she told Tcatc'ē'wiqsō to go and fetch some fuel. When he had gone she took the basket, threw all the blood into the river, and the panther and the wildcats came to life at once and swam ashore. They spoke to the woman and said, "Do you love your husband? He is ugly and nobody can understand him. The only thing he can say is 'lam.' We will throw him into the river and kill him."

But she would not permit them to do so. She traveled on with her husband and took him to her father, the East Wind. Her father resolved at once to kill him. He made a large fire and threw stones into it. When they were red-hot he carried them into his sweathouse, covered the entrance with skins, and went in there to sweat. After a short while he came out of the house, and the stones were found to be as cold as ice. Then he asked Tcatc'ē'wiqsō to go into the sweat-house. He threw stones into the fire, and when they were red-hot they were put into the sweat-house. Tcatc'ē'wiqsō entered it, and they closed it. After a while he cried: "Open the door, it is too hot for me!" But they kept it closed. Soon they heard a noise like the cracking of heated stones, and when they opened the door they found the sweat-lodge full of flint. The East Wind was glad to have obtained a plentiful supply of material for arrow-heads.

BIRD TALES
(Various)

BLUE JAY
(Chinook)

Another mischievous deity of the Chinooks and other western peoples is Blue Jay. He is a turbulent braggart, schemer, and mischief-maker. He is the very clown of gods, and invariably in trouble himself if he is not manufacturing it for others. He has the shape of a jay-bird, which was given him by the Supernatural People because he lost to them in an archery contest. They placed a curse upon him, telling him the note he used as a bird would gain an unenviable notoriety as a bad omen. Blue Jay has an elder brother, the Robin, who is continually upbraiding him for his mischievous conduct in sententious phraseology. The story of the many tricks and pranks played by Blue Jay, not only on the long-suffering members of his tribe, but also upon the denizens of the supernatural world, must have afforded intense amusement around many an Indian camp-fire. Even the proverbial gravity of the Red Man could scarcely hold out against the comical adventures of this American Owlglass.

The Blue Jay's Sister
(Chinook)

The ghosts wanted to buy a wife. They bought Blue Jay's sister, Ioi. They came in the evening, and on the following morning Ioi had disappeared. After one year her brother said, "I am going to search for her." He asked all the trees, "Where do people go after death?" He asked all the birds, but they did not answer him. Finally he said to his wedge, "Where do people go after death?" The wedge said, "Pay me and I will tell you." He paid him and the wedge took him along. They arrived at a large town. The last house of the town was very large, and he saw smoke rising only from this house. There he found his elder sister, who, when she saw him, said, "Where did you come from; are you dead?" "No, I am not dead; the wedge brought me here." He opened all the houses, and saw that they were full of bones. He saw a skull and bones close to his sister, and he asked her, "What are you going to do with that skull?" She replied, "That is your brother-in-law." When it grew dark the bones became alive. He asked, "Where did these people come from?" She replied, "Do you think they are people? They are ghosts." After some time the sister said to him, "Go with these people fishing with a dip-net." He went with a young boy. The people always spoke in very low tones, and he did not understand them. His sister wanted him also to speak in low tones, but when they were going in their canoe he heard a canoe coming down the river and people singing. He joined their song, and at once the boy was transformed into a skeleton. He stopped singing and then the boy became alive again. Whenever Blue Jay spoke in loud tones, the boy became transformed into a skeleton. Then the story goes on to tell how they caught leaves and branches in the dip-net, which were the trout and salmon of the ghosts. Blue Jay amused himself by shouting repeatedly, and thus transforming the ghosts into skeletons, which revived as soon as he was quiet. At another time they went whaling, and the whale of the ghosts is described as a log with very thick bark. One day Blue Jay amused himself by putting skulls of adults on the skeletons of children, and vice versa. Therefore the ghosts began to dislike him, and asked his sister to send him back. Their canoes are described as full of holes and covered with moss.

Blue Jay is sent back by his sister, and in returning dies, because he does not follow her instructions. Then he is taken to the country of the ghosts, and now the ghosts, their canoes, their whales, and their fish, appear to him as real men, new canoes, and real fish.

Big Bird Story
(Athapascan)

Big Bird was a widow of a famous chief who lived with her son and beautiful daughter on the banks of a large stream. Her great ambition was to secure a rich husband for her daughter, suitable to her birth. So she told her little boy to go to the bank of the river, and to watch unceasingly to see if he could discover anybody passing suitable for a son-in-law. One day the boy ran to his mother, and with a face beaming with joy told her there was somebody passing, whom he at least would like for a brother-in-law. Big Bird was delighted and immediately took some bark, and went down to the river to meet the expected bridegroom, whom she was pleased to see was magnificently dressed in a white skin costume covered with shell-like beads. Walking before him, she put pieces of bark on the ground all the way to her camp for him to step on. There she and her daughter, having prepared a meal of unusual splendor, set it before their guest. It happened there was an old dog in the camp, and the man said he could not eat until the animal was removed. Big Bird, wishing to show her new son-in-law every hospitality, complied with his request, and, taking the dog out, killed him, and left him in the bush. The man then ate his supper, and they all went to sleep.

Next morning Big Bird got up to make a fire, but, finding no wood in the tipi, went out to get some, and was surprised to see the dog lying with his eyes removed, with his flesh pecked all over, and with the footprints of a three-toed animal all around him. On going back to the camp, she told them all to take off their shoes to see who had only three toes. They all did so, save the stranger who told her that it was a thing he never did. However, Big Bird kept begging him to remove them, telling him she had a pair of new moccasins for him, which would exactly match his handsome costume. Evidently his vanity was at last touched, and he consented, and, while taking them off, said *"kinno, kinno"* (look! look!) and quickly put them on again. The boy then called out, "He has only three toes." The stranger denied this, and said, "I did it so quickly that you imagine I have only three toes, but you are mistaken."

After breakfast he told his wife that he wanted to go for his clothes which were at his camp some distance up stream, and that he wished her to accompany him. Thinking her husband's conduct rather strange, she at first objected, but, on hearing of the numerous gew-gaws at his camp, at last consented to go. So they got into their canoe, and started off, the man sitting in the bow, and the woman in the stern. They had not proceeded far up stream, when rain began to fall heavily, and the girl soon noticed that the rain was washing the shining white stuff off her husband's back, and then black feathers began to appear. "Ah," she thought to herself, "I have married a crow." When he was not looking, she tied his tail, now grown to visible proportions, to the bar of the canoe, whereat he turned around, and asked her what she was doing. She replied, "Your coat is so fine I am working with the beads." "Oh," said he, "I see I have married an industrious wife," and resumed his paddling. She then tried to find an excuse to make her escape, and told him that the point they were just passing was a famous locality for wild duck eggs, and that she would like to go ashore and hunt some for his supper. He readily consented, and as soon as she got ashore, she ran up the bank, and disappeared into the forest. The crow tried to get out to follow her; but as his tail was tied to the canoe, this was impossible, and he contented himself with calling out after her, "Caw, caw; once more I have tricked you people." He then leisurely preceeded to untie his tail, and flew off ready for another escapade.

The Raven
(Kodiak Island)

Light was not so universal formerly as now. Its cheering influences were then cast over one village only; and even there it depended on the caprices of the chief, who regulated and guarded it jealously. All other villages lived in darkness, although aware of the existence of light in that village. They made many attempts to get possession of it: some, after a few efforts, gave up in despair; others, not so easily discouraged, continued a longer time with the same empty result; and one village, owing to the persistent character of its chief, would never own itself defeated, and persevered in spite of past failures.

Here, in the village hall, the people gathered daily to discuss the all-important question of light, and concluded to call for volunteers to go in quest of it. To the fortunate one the following reward was held out—eternal glory, and the hand of the chief's beautiful and favorite daughter. Considering the inducements, there were no lack of volunteers at first, but, as none of these returned, not even to tell the story of the failure, the list became small and smaller, and after a time weeks would pass without any one offering himself. What became of these eager seekers after light was a mystery. It was generally supposed that some dropped by the wayside, and the others, on reaching the land of light, and finding the task too arduous, decided to remain there always rather than go back without light.

The chief, however, was undaunted, and continued calling the meetings and for volunteers regularly. At one of these the raven was present. He listened attentively to all the speeches, and heard the chief's call for volunteers, and when a considerable time had elapsed without any one indicatnig his desire to go, he rose and addressed the assembly. Sad to say, his speech has been lost in the dark ages, except the last and memorable words: "I will bring you light." This was followed by such loud peals of laughter and mocking hoots that the building almost shook. The chief, who was deep in thought during the raven's harangue, was aroused from his revery by this sudden outburst of laughter, and inquired the cause of it. With much derision the speech and boasts of the raven were repeated to him. Although he may have had as little faith in the words of the raven as the others, he was yet too wise a man to let any opportunity, no matter how slim, of obtaining light—the great object of his life—go by unembraced. Instead of joining in the laughter, he mildly reproved his followers, and then addressing himself to the raven, congratulated him on his noble resolution, encouraged him to persevere, and ended by reminding him of the prize that awaited him whose efforts should be crowned with success.

With this the meeting dissolved. The raven, satisfied with the present and rejoicing in the future, flew home to make ready for the expedition. Joyfully he related the events of the day to his grandmother, a woman. *"Caw! caw! caw!* Grandmother, tomorrow I start after the light; and on my return with it I shall marry the chief's beautiful daughter and become famous. Make all things ready, for I leave early in the morning. *Caw! caw! caw!"*

"Ai-Ai-Yah!" she exclaimed. "Better ones than you have tried and failed, and how

will you, a raven, get it? Why do you want to marry? Who will marry such a one as you? You smell too strong."

This was too much for him. "You old hag!" he screamed with rage. "Who is asking your opinion or advice? How does my smell concern you? You will not sleep with me. To spite you I will marry, and the chief's daughter at that. Even if I am a raven, I will do what I promise; and you do what I tell you, or you will be sorry."

She was sorry there and then, for he went at her with claws and bill till she begged for mercy, and promised to be more considerate in the future.

Early the next morning he left the village, and after several days of flight in the darkness it lightened up faintly. The farther he went, the lighter it became; and when he reached the village, the light was so strong that it almost blinded him. It was a large and cheerful village; the chief's large barrabara, where the lights were kept, was in the center. Close by was a spring of water, and there the raven alighted and eyed sharply the women as they came for water. Not noticing the chief's daughter among them, he began to wish that she would appear. A moment later he saw her coming towards him; and when she had dipped out some water, he murmured, "I wish she would drink some of it." The words had barely been said when she bent over to drink. Instantly he changed himself into a tiny piece of down, and, unnoticed, she gulped it down with the water.

She conceived, and in due time gave birth to a son, a raven. Being the first child of an only child, he was fondled and nursed tenderly. The chief was especially devoted to him, and loved him even more than his daughter. He was indulged and humored in all his wishes. Whatever he saw he called for; whatever he called for had to be given to him; and if it was not given him immediately, he cawed, cried, pestered, clawed, and pecked until he got it. In this manner he handled everything on the premises that might possibly contain the lights, except three little caskets on an out of the way shelf. These he noticed one day, and asked for them. The chief was asleep, and as no one else dared touch them, the request was denied. But he would have them, and he commenced such a cawing, scratching, and hawing that the chief awoke. Not waiting to learn the cause of all this disturbance, he shouted angrily, "O, give him anything he wants, and shut him up!" and went to sleep again.

The caskets were handed him, and he opened them one by one. In the first was night; the second contained the moon and stars; and in the third the sun was shining. He looked at them awhile, and then thrust them aside as worthless. But a few days later, when no one was about, he flew upon the shelf, grasped the two boxes containing the precious lights, and flew out with them. Some of the people outside noticed him, and raised the cry: "A raven flew out of the chief's barrabara with two boxes in his mouth!" When the chief discovered his loss, the raven was miles away.

He flew many days; and each day it grew darker and darker until he was in darkness altogether. After suffering some hardships he arrived in the village, reported himself to the chief, and requested that the people be called together. When all were assembled, he addressed them, congratulated them, reminded them of the last meeting, the promises made, and concluded by saying: "I have brought you light." In the presence of all he opened one of the caskets, and instantly the moon and stars were visible in the sky. The people and chief were almost wild with joy; and the latter kept his promise, and bestowed on him his favorite daughter.

On the morrow the raven called on his father-in-law, and asked what he had to offer for a still better light than even the moon and stars. "My other daughter," replied the chief. "Call the people, and you shall have it," said the raven. If the villagers were wild with joy on seeing the moon and stars, imagine their emotions on beholding for the first time the sun. Since that memorable day the sun, moon, and stars have illuminated the whole world. The crow married the two daughters of the chief, with whom he is living very happily to this day.

THE CROW'S DISAPPOINTMENT
(Athapascan)

O nce upon a time, when the crow was a man, he was paddling along abreast of a mountain, with his stomach calling for dinner. As he paddled, suddenly he saw a stake set at the edge of the water. He paddled alongside to examine it. There was a fishnet tied to it. Surely enough it was full of fish, and he put them into his canoe. In front of him and at his back they lay. Those in front of him he eats raw, and fills himself.

"*A-ha-ha,*" he thinks, "I am satisfied; thanks," thinks he, "I am satisfied;" and he took his paddle and went on. All day he paddled. All at once he saw another stake set. Surely enough, there was another net tied. Again he examined it, and was surprised to find it full of fish. Taking these he put them into his canoe, in front of him, and behind him, and part of those in front of him he ate raw. "*A-ha-ha,*" thinks he; "thanks, I am satisfied." Then he looked around, and upward as well, and saw a house; a beautiful house. Outside the house were hanging dried whitefish. Then he went into the house and looked around, but saw nobody. Inside the house there were dried whitefish, too, and berries. But see! on this side is somebody's place; there are beautiful parkas too, and fine mats and workbags. "Where is she?" thought he, and crossed the room again to go out. From over at the door he took a look outside. He looked, and saw a path going up the mountain. He started off, and rushed eagerly upward. He reached the top and looked around. There beside the path were berries in plenty, and baskets with berries in them. He went here and there looking for the owner. All at once there was a beautiful woman picking berries. He went to her and caught her by the shoulder. "Come," said he, "come along; let's go to your house," said he. But she was not willing. "I don't want to," said she. "You see I'm picking berries. By and by I will do as you say," said she; but he held her shoulder fast. "Come along now," said he. Then she grew angry. "What a brute!" said she. "You better go down to my house by yourself," said she. Finally the woman said, angrily, "Very well, live with me down at my house." She tied up her berries, and they put them on their backs; the woman as well as the crow. "Come now," said the woman, "take off your load and put it down where you are, and I will dance for you." Then she sung:—

Ikna, ikna, akcaito
Ikna, ikna, akcaito
Akcai tcugun hugu
Unu yavwugan he.
m m m.

"Now it is your turn," said she. "I want to see you. You dance for me, too," said she. "Yes," said he. He hopped about, singing:—

Tlikin gaqahl, tlik, tlik;
Tlikin gaqahl, tlik, tlik.

"Your song doesn't suit me," said she. "Shut your eyes;" and with a "Ctiq" she dived down between his legs, having turned into a squirrel. She reached her house and slammed to the door, while he climbed upon the roof and peered down through the smoke-hole.

The woman angrily threw up a ladleful of hot ashes into his eyes, so that they were scalded and turned white.

OWL AND RAVEN
(Eskimo)

Owl and Raven were close friends. One day Raven made a new dress, dappled black and white, for Owl. Owl, in return, made for Raven a pair of whalebone boots and then began to make for her a white dress. When Owl wanted to fit the dress, Raven hopped about and would not sit still. Owl became very angry and said, "If I fly over you with a blubber lamp, don't jump." Raven continued to hop about. At last Owl became very angry and emptied the blubber lamp over the new white dress. Raven cried, *"Qaq! Qaq!"* Ever since that day Raven has been black all over.

THE RAVEN AND HIS GRANDMOTHER
(Unidentified)

In a *barrabara* (native home), at the end of a large village, lived an old woman with her grandson, a raven. The two lived apart from the other villagers, for they were disliked by them. When the men returned from fishing for cod, and the raven would come and beg a fish, they would never give him one. But when all had left the beach, he would come and pick up any sick fish or refuse that may have been left there. On this he and his grandmother lived.

One winter was very severe. Hunting was impossible; food became scarce to starvation, and even the chief had but little left. One day he (chief) called all his people together, and urged them to make an effort to obtain food, or all would starve. He also announced that he desired his son to marry, and that the bride would be selected from the village girls, who were requested to wash and dress up for the occasion. For a time hunger was forgotten; and in a short time the girls, dressed and looking their best, were lined up under the critical eye of the chief, who selected one of the fairest for his son. A feast of all the eatables the chief had followed; the village was merry for a short time, and then starved again.

The raven perched on a pole outside, observed and listened attentively to all that passed, and after the feast flew home, and said to his grandmother, "Grandmother, I too want to marry." She made no reply; and he went about his duties, gathering food for his little home, which he did each day by flying along the beach, and picking up a dead fish or a bird. He gathered more than enough for two, while in the village the hunger was keener each day. When the famine was at its worst, the raven came to the chief, and asked, "Chief, what will you give me, if I bring you food?"

The chief looked at him a while, and answered, "You shall have my oldest daughter for a wife." No other reward would have pleased him better; he flew away in a joyful mood, and said to his grandmother: "Clean out the barrabara. Make everything ready. I am going to get food for the people, and marry the chief's oldest daughter."

"*Äi, Äi, Y-ä-h!* You are not going to marry. Our barrabara is small and dirty. Where will you put your wife?"

"*Caw! Caw! Caw!* Never mind. Do as I say," he screamed, at the same time pecking her.

Early next morning he flew away, and later in the day appeared with a bundle of "*yukelah*" (dried salmon) in his talons. "Come with me to the chief's house, grandmother," he called to her. He handed the fish over to the chief, and received the daughter in exchange. Telling his grandmother to bring the bride home, he preceded them, and cleared out of the barrabara all the straw and bedding. When the two women arrived, they found an empty barrabara, and the old woman began to scold him:—

"What are you doing? Why are you throwing out everything?"

"I am cleaning house," was his curt reply.

When the time for retiring came, the raven spread out one wing, and asked his bride to lie on it, and then covered her with the other. She spent a miserable and sleepless night in that position. The odor of his body and the breath of his mouth almost smothered her, and she determined to leave him in the morning. But in the morning she decided to stay and try and bear it. During the day she was cheerless and worried, and when the raven offered her food, she would not eat it. On the second night he again invited her to lay her head on his breast, and seek rest in his arms, but she cried and would not; and only after much threatening did he prevail on her to comply with his wish. The second night was not better than the first, and early in the morning she stole away from him and went back to her father, telling him everything.

On awaking and finding his wife gone, the raven inquired of his grandmother whether she knew aught of her whereabouts. She assured him that she did not. "Go, then," he said, "to the chief, and bring her back." She feared him, and did his bidding. When she came to the chief's house, and as soon as she put her foot into it, she was pushed out. This she reported to the raven on her return.

The summer passed, followed by a hard winter and famine. As in the winter before, the raven and his grandmother had plenty, but the others suffered greatly for lack of food. With the return of the hard times, the grandson's thoughts turned to love. This time it was a girl, young and beautiful, at the other end of the village. When he mentioned the subject and girl to his grandmother, and asked her to "go and bring the girl here—I want to marry her," she was quite indignant, and told him what she thought about it.

"*Äi, Äi, Y-ä-h!* Are you going to marry again? Your first wife could not live with you, because you smell so strong. The girls do not wish to marry you."

"*Caw! Caw! Caw!* Never mind the smell! Never mind the smell! Go—do as I say." To impress his commands and secure obedience he continued pecking her until she was glad to go. While she was gone, he was very restless and anxious. He hopped about the barrabara and near-by hillocks, straining his eyes for a sight of the expected bride. At last he saw them coming, his grandmother accompanied by the girl. Hurriedly he began cleaning out the barrabara, throwing out not only the straw, but bedding, baskets, and all. The old woman on her return scolded him, but he paid no attention to it.

The young bride, like her predecessor, was enfolded tightly in his wings, and like her predecessor had a wretched and sleepless night, but determined to endure it if possible; for with him she would have enough to eat, at least. The second night was as bad as the first, but she stayed on, and concluded to do so until spring. On the third day the raven, seeing that she was still with him, said to the old woman: "Tomorrow I will go and get a big, fat whale. While I am gone, make a belt and a pair of *torbarsars* (native shoes) for my wife."

"*Äi, Äi, Y-ä-h!* How will you bring a whale? The hunters cannot kill one, and how will you do it?"

"*Caw! Caw! Caw!* Be quiet, and do what I tell you: make the belt and torbarsars. I will do what I say," he angrily exclaimed, also using his more effective method of silencing her.

Before dawn next morning the raven flew away over the sea. In his absence the old woman was busily engaged making the things for the young bride, who was watching and talking to her. About midday they espied him flying toward the shore, carrying a whale. The grandmother started the fire, and the young woman tucked up her *parka* (native dress), belted it with the new belt, put on the new torbarsars, sharpened the stone knife, and went to the beach to meet her husband. As he drew near, he cried: "Grandmother, go into the village, and call the people; tell them I have brought a big, fat whale." She ran as hard as she could, and told the joyful news. The half-dead village all of a sudden became alive. Some began sharpening their knives, others to dress; but most of them ran just as they were and with such knives as they had, to the beach where the whale was. His importance was not lost on the raven, who hopped up and down the whale's back, viewing the scene of carnage and gorging below him. Every now and then he would take out a pebble from the tool bag which he had about him, and after a seeming consultation put it back. When the chief or any of his relatives came near, he drove them off, and they had to satisfy themselves with watching and feasting with their eyes from the distance, while the others were reveling in fat and even carrying off the blubber to their homes. (Later, in the village, the people shared with the chief.)

The raven's first wife, the chief's daughter, had a son by him, a little raven. She had it in her arms on this occasion, and walked in front of the raven where he would have to notice her. "Here is your child, look at it," she called. But he acted as if he heard not. She called several times, and continued forcing the baby before his eyes until he said, "Come nearer, nearer still;" and when quite close to him, he turned around and excreted on them, almost covering up the child. She turned away, and left him without a word.

Death was the result of the feast. A part of the people ate so much fat on the spot that they died soon after; the rest had eaten so much and filled their barrabaras so full of blubber that during the night they suffocated. In the whole village only three were left, the raven, his wife, and his grandmother, and there they live to this day.

WAR WITH THE SKY PEOPLE
(Salishan, Boas)

O nce upon a time the people wanted to make war on the Sky people. Grizzly-Bear, who was chief, called all the people together to shoot arrows at the sky. Each animal and bird shot, but all the arrows fell short. The Fish, Snakes, and Toads also tried. At last only Chickadee (or Wren?) was left, and no one expected that he could hit the sky. Coyote said he did not need to try, when he himself had failed. However, Chickadee's arrow hit the sky. The others all shot in turn again, and Chickadee shot an arrow which stuck in the nock of the first one. They kept on shooting until a chain of arrows had been made which reached the ground. On this they climbed to the sky. Grizzly-Bear and Black-Bear only remained. They quarreled as to who should climb next. Black-Bear said Grizzly was too heavy and would break the ladder. They chased each other around the ladder, and finally knocked it down. Meanwhile the people who had reached the sky had attacked the people there, and had been defeated. They fled; and when the first ones reached the hole in the sky, they descended one after another. When they reached half way down, they found the lower part gone, and hesitated to drop so far. Meanwhile the people crowded so thickly on the ladder above, that their weight broke it, and they all fell down. Those left above threw themselves down, and killed or hurt themselves, while the remainder were killed by the Sky people. The Fish, who had no wings, fared worst. Sucker broke all his bones.

XÎ′LGŌ
(Tillamook)

T here was an old woman named Xî′lgō, and an old man who lived far up Nestucka River. The old man lived a little farther up than the woman. He had no wife, and she had no husband. The old woman said, "I will go and try to find some children." She went down to the shore and sat down near a small lake, where she knew children used to go bathing. While she sat there waiting, two brothers and their sister came to the shore and began to play. After a while they took a bath, returned to the shore, and fell asleep. Then Xî'lgō, who carried a basket on her back, took one of the boys first, the girl next, and finally the other boy, threw them into her basket, and carried them away. After a while the boy who lay in the bottom of the basket, and whose name was Taxuxcā, awoke, and, on finding where he was, scratched a hole in the bottom of the basket, through which he escaped. He ran away, and for fear jumped into the sea, where he has lived ever since that time.

Xî'lgō did not notice his escape. When she reached home, she took the children out of the basket. They awoke, and did not know where they were. She led them into her house, and gave them a place to sleep. On the following morning she said, "If you wish anything to eat, you must go to an old man who lives farther up the river, and who has a salmon-trap which is full every morning; there are both small and large fish in it." The children went, and saw the old man roasting salmon which he had fastened in a split stick and placed near the fire. He asked them what they wanted, "Do you want to eat salmon?" and they replied, "Yes, we are hungry, and we came here to eat. Xî'lgō sent us here."

When they had eaten, they said to the old man, "Tell us something," and he told them a tale and gave them many instructions. Then they returned. They found the old woman near the fire, where she was heating stones. She asked the children, "Did the old man tell you a story?" and they replied, "Yes; he told us many a tale, and gave us many instructions." Then she took the stones off the fire, placed skunk-cabbage leaves on top of the stones, and covered them with grass. When the skunk-cabbage was done, she ate it. Then she said, "You must go to the old man tomorrow morning and take him some skunk-cabbage; he will give you salmon in return." The children obeyed, and took some skunk-cabbage to him; he gave them salmon in return, and told them stories. When the children returned, Xî'lgō asked them, "Did he tell you stories?" When she heard that the old man had done so, she became angry, took her knife, and said, "I will kill him." She went and lay down with the old man. After a while she returned and said, "I have killed him." Then the children thought, "Where shall we get anything to eat if the old man is dead?"

Xî'lgō sang all the afternoon until late in the evening. On the following day she rose early and went out to get some skunk-cabbage. She returned before the children awoke and cooked it. She told them to take some of it to the old man. They thought, "Didn't she kill him yesterday? She told us that he was dead." Xî'lgō knew their thoughts at once, and said, "Where would you find anything to eat if I had killed him?"

Then the children went and found him roasting salmon as usual. He gave them some to eat, and when they were done he told them a story. On their return, Xî'lgō asked at once, "Did he tell you stories?" "Yes," they replied, "he told us a story." Then the old woman grew very angry. She took a long knife and said she would kill the old man. First they heard them talking for a long time. Then it became quiet. Again Xî'lgō lay down with the old man. Before going back she pulled her hair over her face, then she went back singing, "I have killed him; I have killed the old man. He spoke evil of me."

Early the next morning she rose and went out to get some skunk-cabbage. She returned before the children were awake, and cooked it. She told the children to take some of it to the old man. They thought, "Didn't she kill him yesterday? She told us she had done so." Xî′lgō knew their thoughts at once, and said, "Where would you find anything to eat if I had killed him?" Then the children went and found the old man roasting salmon as usual. He gave them something to eat. Then the children said, "We have enough," and asked him to tell them something. The old man said, "What shall I tell you? She is fooling you; she is fooling you." Then the children thought, "How is she fooling us?" They returned, and Xî′lgō asked them, "What did he tell you? Did he tell you stories?" "Yes," they replied, "he told us stories." Xî′lgō began to cry. "And what did he tell you? He has always abused my father." Then she took a knife and went out, saying that she was going to kill the old man. When she left, the children were playing with shells. They arranged them in couples as husbands and wives. They saw her leaving, and they thought, "Did she say she was going to kill the old man? We will go and see what she is doing, and how she is fooling us." They took the shells along, except one couple, and followed her to the house of the old man. They heard the old couple whispering together. They went to a chink in the wall, through which they peeped, and they saw them lying down and talking. Xî′lgō cried at once, "How that tickles! I feel some one is looking at me." She wanted to jump up, but the old man said, "Oh, don't be in a hurry."

The children ran away at once. When Xî′lgō came back to her home, she did not find them. She saw only one pair of shells, which they had left. Then she said, "When you have grown up, you shall live as husband and wife."

The children went on and came to Clatsop, where they built a house. When the house was completed, the boy said to the girl, "Stay in that corner of the house, and I will stay in the one diagonally opposite." At night, when he was asleep, he heard the girl saying, "It is dripping here." Then the boy said, "Put your bed in the other far corner." The girl did so, and after a short time she said, "It is dripping here." Then the boy said, "Move your bed a little more this way, to the middle of the long side of the house." After a short time she said again, "It is dripping here," and he told her, "Come here to this side." After a short time the girl said again, "It is dripping here," and then he called her, and they lay down together. In due time she gave birth to a boy. The father and his son used to sleep on the roof of the house.

After a while Xî′lgō began to pursue the children, the old man following her. One day, when the young mother had gone picking berries, Xî′lgō reached Columbia River, at a place opposite to where the house stood. She saw the man and the boy sleeping on the roof. She called them to take her across. The man did not hear her, and finally she became angry and said, "I wish you were dead." Then she returned homeward.

The man died, blood pouring from his mouth. At the time of sunset the boy awoke and began to cry. By this time his mother returned, and heard her child crying. She called her husband. "Don't you hear our child crying? Come take him down." As he did not stir, she went up to the roof and saw the blood. She turned the body over and found that her brother was dead. Then she took her son on her back, crying, "What shall I do?" She thought, "I will set fire to the house and burn myself." She gave her boy to a woman who lived close by, set fire to the house at one corner, and jumped into the flames.

After the fire had burned down, the woman who had taken care of the boy went and took a bone of the wrist of the woman and one rib of the man. She made a ball of the former and a bat of the latter for the boy to play with. She kept them at home until he was able to walk.

One day, when he was playing with his ball, he happened to hit a girl who was standing by. She cried and said, "You have made me sick with your mother's and father's bones." Then the boy thought, "Are these my father's and mother's bones?" Crying, he went into the house of the woman who took care of him, and said, "A girl abused me, saying that those were my mother's and father's bones." Then the woman became very angry, and whipped the girl until she began to cry. She cried so long that her nose became thin and pointed. The boy grew up, always thinking of his father and mother. He asked the old woman, "Who has killed my father and mother?" She said, "They who killed them live very far off, but if you want to go there I will help you." He wished to go, and the woman said, "A girl must go with you."

They selected a girl, and gave her a fine sea-otter skin to wear. The woman said, "Try to walk underground." She did so, assuming the shape of a mole. Then she told the boy, "Try to fly." He put a feather under his arm and flew away in the shape of an eagle. Then the two went to find Xí′lgō.

When they were gone he told the girl, "When we reach a town I will fly in front of the houses, and the people will come forth, then you must go underground and steal all the dentalia you can get hold of." When they came to a village he assumed the shape of an eagle. The people were all assembled in one house. One man who happened to go out saw the eagle, and called the people, saying, "See what is coming there!" They rushed out, and among them was an old woman, who was no other than Xí′lgō. Meanwhile, the girl had assumed the shape of a mole, who had gained access to the houses by passing underground. She stole all the dentalia she could lay her hands on. When Xí′lgō came out of the house, the eagle rushed down and took her up. Her hat fell down when he lifted her up, but he took her out to the ocean, where he tore her to pieces.

Then he joined the girl again, and they traveled on. Soon they came to another town. Again the people rushed out of the house in order to see the eagle, and last of all there came an old woman, who was no other than Xí′lgō. The young man was surprised to see her still alive. He took her, carried her far out into the ocean, and tore her to pieces. When he took her up, her hat fell down.

He returned and met the girl, and they traveled on and met the Blue Jay, who asked them, "What are you going to do with the old woman?" The young man replied, "I want to kill her. Do you know how I can accomplish it?" The Blue Jay did not reply, and they left him. After a while they came to a town, and again the people came out to see the eagle, and last among them an old woman, who was no other than Xí′lgō. Once more he took her up and tore her to pieces far out in the ocean, and her hat fell to the ground as he lifted her up. He returned and met the girl, and when they were traveling on they again met the Blue Jay, who asked them what they were going to do with the old woman. The young man replied, "I want to kill her." Then the Blue Jay said, "You must not take her body, but take her hat. You will find a small, long thing in the top of her hat. That is her heart. You must tear that and throw it into the sea, then she will be dead." He followed this advice, and thus succeeded in killing the old woman.

In every town where they had been the girl had obtained dentalia, which they divided among themselves and returned home.

The Weeping Woman
(Salishan, Boas)

Chatalem lured away hunters by her beautiful, sad wailing. She always kept at a distance from them, so that they could not see her. They followed her until they perished.

One brave hunter followed the stream to its source. Then he camped and built a sweat-house. Every morning at dawn he heated rocks and took a bath. One morning, when he came back to his tent, he saw a beautiful woman sitting in the doorway. He fell in love with her, and made up his mind to ask her to remain. However, as he approached, she rose and floated away like a cloud, wailing. He was strongly tempted to follow her, but he turned and went the other way.

Later on, she came to him when he had killed a deer. He heard her voice, but did not see her. He thought of her often. He also thought of his wife and children whom he had left at home, and tried to forget her.

One day in mid-winter he slept soundly. When he awoke, she was cooking for him. Then for the first time he saw her back. She carried a child with its head down. She told him she had come to keep him company. When he left for home, she told him to come back alone, and promised to meet him at the entrance of the forest.

In the fall of the year he prepared to go hunting. His wife wished to accompany him. At first he refused her request; but when she insisted, he told her that she might go as far as the forest.

The next year she desired to accompany him again. As before, he refused her request, but she insisted. She went as far as the forest, but then she would not return. She followed him and heard a wailing-sound. She asked him what it was, but he would not tell her. Then came a high wind and a terrible storm. The man's mortal wife was killed. This made the hunter angry, and he returned at once to his own people, and did not go back to the weeping woman.

The Ghosts of Murdered Wives
(Mariposan)

Once a man lived with his wife up the cañon. She was a handsome woman and he loved her much. One time they quarreled and she died from his beating. He was sorry and cried aloud. He found no comfort. He ate nothing, and lay down beside her grave. He lay there continually for three days and three nights fasting. During the fourth night he was crying for her to come back to him. As the great star stood overhead he felt the ground tremble and saw the earth moving on her grave. The clods rolled back and she arose and stood brushing from herself every speck of dust until she was clean. He stared, but was silent (a man dies instantly when speaking to a ghost). She started away. She went swiftly down toward *Tóxil* (the point of sunset) and he ran after her weeping. She often turned and warned him back, declaring that she was bound for the *Tïb'-ïk-nïtc,* the home of the dead. He still pursued her for four days and four nights when they reached Tó-lït, a great roaring water. She mounted a bridge, slender and fragile like a spider's web, and began to cross over. He cried aloud with beseeching gestures. She turned. She pitied him. She stretched a hand toward him, and he felt strong and comforted. He sprang upon the bridge, but she would not suffer his touch. They crossed on Tcé-laul in this manner. Tcé-laul is long, very long, but the spirits of the good cross it easily; the bad fall off and turn into *ëp'ïs* (pike fish), who must swim back to feed the living. The man saw a great land, a rich land, a warm, fruitful land, and people from all the world. He saw all kinds of different peoples, and they lived peaceably together, for there was plenty for all. The woman told him to observe closely; for he must return and tell all to his people before he died on the fourth day. He did so. She took him back across Tcé-laul and he ran home. He told all to his kin people and died on the fourth day as predicted.

Another Mariposan rendition, is as follows:—

A certain man had a beautiful wife and he loved her. One time they quarreled, and he killed her unintentionally. He grieved over it greatly, and lay by her grave three nights and three days. In the fourth night he saw the ground heave up, and she was pushed upon the surface. She was loaded with all her burial gifts. She bade him not to follow her, but he sprang up and ran with her towards *Xó-cum* (the north). They ran a long distance until they came to Hó-hŏ, a tumbling, furious river. He cried out to her, but she ran out upon a very long, flimsy bridge *(tá-la-mûtc),* upon which no human can balance. He fell to the sand shrieking. Then she turned and beckoned him on, but would not touch him. His living scent was too strong. She guided him safely over the bridge, and the other shore was all dark. She said, "Wait a while and there will be light." Then great blue and red fires flashed up and went out again. They lighted up everything, and he saw a great country. He saw many kinds of people. He saw his dead relatives and friends. He saw a long line of little babies moving silently back across the bridge. They were coming here to our women. He had time to see everything in that land before the woman took him over the bridge again. She bade him tell his people all the wonders and then return to her on the third day. He ran back and called his tribe together and related all he had seen. He finished telling it and died.

THE ISLAND OF DEATH
(Salishan, Boas)

There was once a camp by a river. Among the people there was a handsome man, who was a brave warrior and a great hunter. He had two children. His wife was beautiful, and he loved her dearly. One day he met a very plain maiden. She attracted him. He took her for his wife, and put her in another tent. He took most of his meat to her.

Then the first wife and his children grew hungry. The younger child cried. Then the mother sent her son to his father for meat. The boy went to the tent and stood in the doorway. When his father asked him what he wanted, he said that they were hungry. He was sent back without any food, and the new wife laughed.

The boy returned, and told his mother that he had been rebuffed and scolded, and that his father's new wife had laughed at him. His mother listened to his words, took a deer's antler, and whittled three sharp bones out of it. With two of these she killed her children while they were asleep. The last one she drove into her own breast.

In the morning the grandmother of the children came with food, and found them dead. She raised a wail, and the people came to see what had happened. Then the father was grieved. He took his bow and arrows and left the camp.

He crossed the plain, and came to a river in which was a large island. He saw canoes and camps on it, but he did not see any signs of life. He became sleepy. One tent on the island was open. A woman came out, boarded a canoe, and paddled across. He recognized his first wife, who took him across. They landed, and she pulled the canoe up on shore. She took him into the large tent. Inside there were only skeletons. He saw his children's skeletons. Then he saw that his wife too was a skeleton. He looked at himself, and he saw that he had no flesh. He had crossed the River of Death.

CANNIBAL STORIES
(Various)

THE XŪDĒLÊ
(Tillamook)

The Xūdēlê are cannibals. They are very lean. Their noses are turned up and their eyebrows run upward. Their faces look almost like those of dogs. They wear small axes in their belts, with which they kill men. They take the scent of men like dogs.

One day the Xūdēlê had gone hunting man. They found the tracks of a hunter who was on the mountains. He saw them coming, and tried to escape. When he came near a snow-field that terminated abruptly at a precipice, he cut steps into it and climbed down. Half way down he found a small rock shelter, where he stayed.

He resolved to make an attempt to kill his pursuers by a ruse. He built a fire and roasted a porcupine that he had caught. The Xūdēlê saw the smoke and smelled the roasting meat. When they came to the snow-field it had grown dark. They shouted down: "Where are you? Let us have some of your meat!" The Ts'ɛts'ā'ut shouted back: "You must slide down this snow-field, then you will find me. I invite you to take part in my meal!" Then the Xūdēlê began to slide down the snow-field one after the other, and were precipitated into the abyss. Finally only one of their number was left. He did not dare to slide down, and shouted: "Where are all my friends?" The man replied: "They are all here." But the Xūdēlê could not be induced to slide down. He cut steps into the snow, and climbed down as the man had done. Finally he reached the man. When he did not see his friends, he asked what had become of them, and the man told him that they had all perished because they had slid past his shelter. Now the Xūdēlê, who did not dare to attack the man single-handed, offered to gamble with him, and said they would stake their lives. The Ts'ɛts'ā'ut refused. He had employed the time while the Xūdēlê were sliding down the snow-field to make a heavy club, which he had placed near his fire. While he was talking with the Xūdēlê he watched his opportunity, and slew him with his club. Then he returned to his village and told what had happened. The people were afraid that the friends of the Xūdēlê might come to look for them, and moved to another place.

At another time a man had gone out hunting. It was in summer. He discovered a vast number of Xūdēlê coming right up to him, so that he could not escape. There happened to be a swamp close to the trail which he was following. He jumped into the mud and lay down, keeping motionless. He looked just like a log. He extended his arms, so that they looked like limbs of a tree. The Xūdēlê came, and one after the other passed him without noticing him. Finally, one of their number noticed the resemblance of the supposed log to a human figure. He raised his axe, and was about to strike him. But since the man did not wince, he concluded that it was nothing but a log and passed on. When all had passed, the man jumped up and ran on the nearest way to his village. There he told the chief that the Xūdēlê were coming. He called a council, and they resolved what to do. They killed a number of dogs and cut them up, skin and bone and intestines. Then they pounded flint to dust, mixed it with the meat, and made a soup of it. When the Xūdēlê came, they invited them to the chief's house and set the soup before them. Before they began eating, a little boy happened to walk past a Xūdēlê, who seized him, tore out his arms and legs, and ate him. The Ts'ɛts'ā'ut did not dare to remonstrate. Now the Xūdēlê began to eat. Soon the effects of the poison—the pounded stone—began to be felt. They acted as though they were drunk, and some of them fell dead. Then the Ts'ɛts'ā'ut took up their clubs and killed them one and all.

The Xūdēlê put up traps for catching men on the trails which they travel on their snowshoes. They cover a stick with moss and snow, which is so arranged that it catches in the snowshoe of the traveler. A few feet in front of this stick is another, sharp-pointed stick, put into the ground point upward. When the snowshoes catch in the first stick, the traveler falls forward on to the pointed stick, which pierces him. One day a hunter was passing over a trail. He saw a small irregularity of the snow, and discovered that it was the trap of a Xūdēlê. He intended to go on, when he saw the Xūdēlê to whom the trap belonged. As he was unable to make his escape, he tried a stratagem. He struck his nose so that it bled and smeared his chest with blood. Then he lay down on the pointed stick of the trap. The Xūdēlê approached, and when he saw the man, he smiled and said: "Again my trap has caught something for me." He took the man off the stick, put him into his bag, and, after having reset his trap, turned to go home. The man was very heavy, and he had to put down his load from time to time. Then the man blew the air out of his compressed lips, thus imitating the noise of escaping gases. The Xūdēlê said: "He must have been in my trap for a long time, for the body is decomposing already; the gases are escaping." When he arrived at home he threw the body down near the fireplace. The man glanced around furtively, and, saw stores of dried human flesh in the house. There was a black woman in the house, and three children were playing near the fire. The Xūdēlê went to fetch his knife in order to skin and carve the man, and he sent his wife for water. The man saw an axe lying near the fire, and when the Xūdēlê turned his back he jumped up, seized it, and split the head of his captor. The Xūdēlê cried: *"Sxinadlê, asidlê,"* and died. (It is said that the Xūdēlê always utter this cry, which is unintelligible to the Ts'ɛts'ā'ut, at the time of their death.) When the children saw their father dying they ran out of the house, assumed the shape of martens, and ran up a tree. The man threw the body of the Xūdēlê into the fire. Then he went out of the hut to kill the woman, whom he met carrying a basket of water. He split her stomach with his axe. Then two minks jumped out of her and ran into the water. She died and he burnt her body. When he returned to his country he told what he had seen. Therefore we know that the martens and minks descend from the Xūdēlê.

BAQBAKUĀLANUSĪ'UAĒ
(Kwakiutl)

O nce upon a time there lived a man who had four sons. His name was Noaχaua. One day the sons were going to hunt mountain goat. Before they started Noaχaua said: "When you will reach a house from which a reddish smoke is rising, do not enter it, for it is the home of Baqbakuālanusī'uaē, the cannibal." The sons promised to obey, and started on their expedition.

After a while they saw a house from the roof of which black smoke was rising. It was the abode of the black bear. They proceeded, and after a short while they found another house, from which white smoke was rising. They entered, and saw that it was the home of the mountain goat. Having rested, they proceeded, and at last they saw a house from which reddish smoke was rising. They stopped and spoke unto each other: "Shall we pass by this house? Let us enter and see who lives in it!" This they did, and found a woman who was rocking her baby. Opposite her sat a boy with an enormously large head. The four brothers stepped up to the fire, and sat down on a box. In doing so the eldest one hurt his leg, and blood dripped from it. The boy with the large head nudged his mother and whispered: "Oh, mother, how I should like to lick that blood!" When his mother told him not to do it he scratched his head, and soon began, notwithstanding her command, to wipe off the blood and to lick it from his finger. Then the eldest brother nudged the youngest one and said: "Oh, I think father was right. I wish we had followed his advice." Meanwhile the boy licked up the blood more and more eagerly.

The eldest of the brothers mustered courage. He took an arrow from his quiver and shot it through the door of the house. Then he told his youngest brother to go and fetch the arrow. He obeyed, but as soon as he had left the house he ran away towards his home. After a little while the eldest of the brothers took another arrow from his quiver and shot it through the door of the house. He told the next brother to fetch it, and he also made his escape. When he had shot a third arrow, the third brother escaped. Then the boy with the large head began to cry, for he was afraid of the eldest of the brothers. The woman asked: "Where have your brothers gone? I hope they will be back soon." "Oh, yes," answered the young man; "they have only gone to fetch my arrows." Saying so, he took another arrow from his quiver and shot it through the door of the house. Then he went himself to fetch it. As soon as he had left the house he followed his brothers. After a short while, when nobody returned, the old hag knew that her guests had escaped. She stepped to the door and cried: "Baqbakuālanusī'uaē, come, oh come! I have allowed our good dinner to run away." Baqbakuālanusī'uaē, although he was far away, heard her, and quickly approached, crying: *"Ham, ham, ham!"* (that is, to eat, to eat, to eat). The four brothers heard him approaching, and ran as fast as their legs would carry them. The eldest happened to carry a whetstone, a comb, and some fish grease, which he used as an unction for his hair. When Baqbakuālanusī'uaē had almost reached them, he threw the whetstone behind him, and lo! it was transformed into a steep mountain, which compelled the pursuer to go round about it. But soon he came again near the fugitives. Now the young man poured out behind him the hair-oil, which was transformed into a large lake. While the pursuer had to go around it the young men gained a good start on him. When he had almost reached them for the third time, the eldest of the brothers threw behind him his comb, which was transformed into a thicket of young trees, which Baqbakuālanusī'uaē was unable to penetrate. Before he could pass around it the young men had reached their father's house. They knocked at the door, and asked their father to let them enter at once, as Baqbakuālanusī'uaē was again heard approaching. Hardly had they entered and the door was again bolted, when their pursuer arrived and knocked at the door, demanding entrance.

Noaχaua killed a dog, carved it, and collected its blood in a dish. Then he called Baqbakuālanusī'uaē to come to a small hole in the wall of the house, gave him the dish, and said: "This is the blood of my sons. Take it and carry it home to your wife. I invite you to a feast to-night, and be sure to come with your wife and your children. You may feast upon my sons." Baqbakuālanusī'uaē was delighted, and promised to come.

As soon as he had gone, Tsō'ēna, Noaχaua's wife, dug a deep pit near the fire, and made the latter blaze up. She put stones into it, which she threw into the pit as soon as they were red-hot. They concealed the pit by spanning a skin in front of it. These preparations were hardly finished when Baqbakuālanusī'uaē arrived in his boat, accompanied by his wife and his three children. One of these he left at the boat as a watchman, while the others went into the house.

Then Tsō'ēna made them sit down close by the fire, their backs turned toward the skin which concealed the pit. When Baqbakuālanusī'uaē had settled down comfortably, and the meat was boiling in the large wooden kettle, he said: "Noaχaua, you know how everything happened in the beginning of the world. Tell me what you know." Noaχaua replied: "I shall tell you this;" and beating the time with his dancing-stick he sang:—

> What of olden times,
> what of olden times
> shall I tell you of olden times
> my grandchildren?
>
> You of olden times,
> you of olden times
> cloud lay on the mountain.

When he had sung this spell twice, Baqbakuālanusī'uaē and his family began to slumber, and when he had sung it four times they slept sound and fast. Now Noaχaua and Tsō'ēna removed the skin and plunged them headlong into the pit. Twice Baqbakuālanusī'uaē cried: *"Ham, ham!"* then he was dead. When all were dead, Noaχaua tied a rope round their bodies, and pulled them out of the pit. The old cannibal's body he cut into pieces, which he threw in all directions, singing:—

> In course of time,
> Baqbakuālanusī'uaē,
> you will pursue the men.

They were transformed into mosquitoes. The boy who had remained in the boat made his escape, and lives since that time in the woods.

THE CANNIBAL DANCES
(Tsimpcian)

O nce upon a time a man went mountain-goat hunting. On the mountains he met a white bear, and pursued it. After a long time he got near enough to fly his arrow and hit him in the side. The bear continued to run away from the hunter and at last he came to a steep rock, which opened and let him enter. After a short while a man came out of the rock and invited the hunter to follow him. In the mountain he found a large house, and he was led to a seat at the right hand of the entrance. He saw four groups of people in the house. In one corner were the Mē'itla; in the second the Nō'otlam, who devoured dogs; in the third the Wihalait', the cannibals; and in the fourth the Cimhalai'det. The Mē'itla and the Cimhalai'det were in great fear of the other two groups. Three days the hunter stayed in the mountain, the three days were, however, three years for those living on earth. Then the man sent him back, and told him to do in his village as he had seen the people doing in the mountain. He was conveyed home, and on awaking found himself on the top of a tree. He saw the people of the village, and slid down from the tree on his back. He made a rush upon a man and devoured him; then he killed another one and tore him to pieces. At last, however, the people succeeded in taking hold of him, and they restored him to health by means of magic herbs. When he had recovered, he taught them the dances of the four groups of people whom he had seen in the mountain, and since that time the dances Mē'itla, Nō'otlam, Wihalait', and Cimhalai'det are performed every winter by the Tsimpcian.

It is difficult to decide whether the Tsimpcian or the Kwakiutl were the first to practice this custom. To answer this question it would be necessary to study the folk-lore of the Tsimpcian of the interior. The custom is not practiced by the Tlingit and Haida, but seems to obtain, to a certain extent, among the tribes of the west coast of Vancouver Island. Its origin and development are still obscure, but it is to be hoped that a further study of the folk-lore and language will clear up many doubtful points.

OF MEN WHO BECAME CANNIBALS
(Kwakiutl)

Once upon a time there was a woman who had married the spirit Baqbakuā'latlē, with whom she lived at the bottom of a lake. They had a son, whom they gave the name of his father. When he came to be grown up, he killed all people whom he met, tore out their eyes and fried them in the ashes of his fire. He enjoyed it to see them burst, and cried: "Ha! ha! Look, how my eyes burst!" Then he threw them into a basket. Besides, he cut the fingers, toes, and ears from the slain, and gathered them in separate baskets. Thus he killed all people except his uncle and the latter's son. But after a while he longed for their eyes and fingers. One night he seized a spear and flung it at his uncle, who happened to stand in a dark corner of the house. Therefore he missed him, and the uncle in defence pierced Baqbakuā'latlē's left side with a lance. The young man escaped, although severely hurt. The uncle said unto his wife: "Now stay here; I will pursue my nephew, and kill him." He followed the track of blood left by the young man, and found him on the shore of a lake. There he lay dying, and the diver (a bird) stood by him and tried to cure him. The uncle stepped up to Baqbakuā'latlē and said: "You wanted to kill me, but now you must die yourself." When he raised the lance to kill him, Baqbakuā'latlē asked him a few moments' grace. He said: "Do not kill me at once. First I will give you all my treasures." He told him where his baskets were concealed, and then the uncle killed him and burnt his corpse. When he blew upon the ashes, they were transformed into mosquitoes. From the finest ashes originated the sunflies. Then he went to search for his nephew's treasures, and when he found the baskets, filled with the ears, fingers, toes, and with the fried eyes, he became a cannibal himself.

Besides these spirits there is the crane, who can become the genius of a cannibal. Here is a tradition of the Wik'enoχ which treats of the initiation of a young cannibal by this being, the Hāoχhāoχ:—

Ꝁ'ōm′kīliky went into the woods to collect cedar bark. He had not been gone long when the spirit Hāoχhāoχ scented him. He smelled that the youth was clean and good, and rushed down upon him to carry him away. When Ꝁ'ōm′kīliky heard the flapping of the wings of the spirit, who had the shape of a crane, he almost fainted with fear. He hoped to recover his spirits by smoking a pipe of tobacco, but in vain. He fell down, and lay there like dead. The Hāoχhāoχ alighted upon him, and while the youth lay unconscious he infused him his spirit.

Ꝁ'ōm′kīliky's friends waited in vain for his return, and at last they went into the woods to look for him. They found him still unconscious. They sprinkled his face with cold water, but he did not awake. Then they carried him to the village, and took him into his father's hut. When he saw the men carrying his son into his house he thought that he was dead, and cried for grief. Soon, however, he perceived that Ꝁ'ōm′kīliky still breathed. He called the medicine-man, and entreated him to restore his son to health. The medicine-man ordered him to sweep the house, and to strew the floor with sand, so that the feet should not touch the former floor. He carried the youth into the woods, and stayed there for four days. Then he returned. After four days more had elapsed, Ꝁ'ōm′kīliky returned also. The medicine-man had given him the name Ꝕoāltχoā′oi.

And now he sang of the Hāoχhāoχ. All of a sudden he made a jump and attacked his father, who sat on the opposite side of the fire. He wanted to devour him. Ꝕoātlχoā′oi wore a ring of red cedar bark on his head, which fell down when he jumped up, and covered his mouth when he was just about to bite his father. Thus he bit a piece out of the ring. The people who were assembled in the house to hear his song did not know what to do in order to quiet him. His grandfather took a large black blanket which he wrapped around Ꝕoātlχoā′oi's head. In vain; he bit right through it. Then all the men escaped, for they feared to be attacked by the youth. When they stood on the street they heard him singing, and on peeping through the chinks of the walls they saw him climbing up the posts which carried the roof, and trying to crawl through the roof. Then they placed two watchmen by the side of the door, to prevent him from leaving the house, while the others climbed up on the roof and prevented him from removing the boards. When he quieted down, they picked up courage and entered the house. They threw a bearskin over him, under which he crawled about on the floor. When the men tried to hold him, they found that he was as slippery as a fish. Late in the evening he lay quiet, and the men did not know whether he was asleep or not. They made a jacket of cedar bark, and tried to put it on him, but he escaped. On the island *Nalkuit-qoi'as* (Mac Kjol Island) a number of women were curing salmon. He scented them, and rushed into the sea to devour them, but they escaped in a boat.

At last Ꝕoātlχoā′oi recovered. He spoke to his father: "If I should try again to attack you, do not resist me. Then I shall do you no harm." After a little while he fell into another trance. He lay flat on the floor, his face turned downward. The men threw a net made of cedar bark over him, and tried to catch him. Sometimes a man succeeded in putting his foot upon his neck, or to grasp his long black hair, but he succeeded in making his escape. He raced through the village, and bit whomsoever he saw.

When he recovered, he asked his father to give him boiled fish oil when he should fall into a new trance. In a trance he was able to scent men on long distances. One day he scented a boat which was still far distant, and smelled that they had a heavy load of clams on board.

THE BOY AND THE SHAMAN
(Aleut)

In a small barrabara, away from other barrabaras and other people, lived an old woman and her young grandson. While the boy was small, the grandmother supplied both with food and clothing by hunting and fishing. She also taught him how to hunt and fish; and when nearly full grown, she surprised him one morning by telling him that a one-hatch bidarka (which she had made unbeknown to him) was on the beach ready for him.

It was there, sure enough, equipped and ready for hunting. He was supremely happy; for he had obtained that which for years he had been looking forward to. Every morning he went out hunting and fishing, and in the evening returned loaded with fish and game. In a little while he became very skillful in the handling of the bidarka, and daily ventured farther and farther out to sea.

His grandmother called him one morning, and said to him: "Son, you may go anywhere, except into yonder bay, and you will be safe; if you ever go there, you will never return to me. Take this mink skin, put it into the nose of your bidarka; this bag containing four tiny bows and arrows keep about your person. Should you ever be in trouble, turn to them, and they will help you."

He promised never to venture inside the bay, accepted the gifts, and disposed of them as he was told.

In those days, when this boy lived, there were no winds at all; the waters were always smooth and calm. One could go long distances from shore, and not be in danger of the winds and the waves. Not many days after the promise to his grandmother, the boy, while pursuing a seal, went much farther from shore than one would dare go now, and when he finally stopped paddling, after killing the seal, he found himself at the mouth of the bay.

The interior of the bay looked so inviting and alluring that he laughed at his grandmother's fears, and steered for the beautiful island in the middle of the bay. He beached his bidarka, took the mink skin, and started for the summit of a hill where he noticed a barrabara. As he began to ascend, large rocks came rolling down, blocking his way and nearly crushing him. The farther up he went the more difficult and dangerous it became. In order to save himself he jumped into a hole. The rocks fell over the hole, covered and blocked it.

He tried vainly to get out; the rocks were too heavy to be pushed off, and the openings too small to crawl through. While thinking over the situation, the mink skin occurred to him. Seizing it, he commenced chewing and stretching it until he pulled it over his head. As he did that, he changed into a mink. By scratching and squeezing, leaping and dodging, he escaped from his prison, and reached the summit, where he was surprised to see that all the rocks came from the barrabara.

Taking off the mink skin and becoming a boy again, he went into the barrabara. On the floor sat a very large woman making mats. When she saw him, she screamed in a loud and angry voice:—

"Who told you to come here!"

Reaching behind her, she pulled out a long, sharp spear and threw it at him. Before the spear reached him, he changed himself into a mink; the spear went over his head, sticking into the wall. Quickly assuming his boyish shape, he grabbed the spear, and called to her: "Change and save yourself if you can!" and hurled it at her, cutting her in two.

A loud report and earthquake followed his action. The barrabara trembled, tumbled in, and he was again a prisoner. His mink skin came into good use; by scratching and dodging he managed to crawl out and run down to the shore, and, after pulling off the skin, pushed the bidarka out and started homeward.

He had not gone very far when he heard some one calling, and on looking around saw people on the shore motioning to him. An old man greeted him as he landed, and taking him by the hand, led him into a barrabara where sat several girls. Pointing to one of them, he said: "You can have her for a wife."

This made him very happy, and glad he did not obey his grandmother. A dish of seal meat was placed before him, and after eating, they all lay down to sleep. The following morning the old man asked him to go to the woods, and bring wood for sled runners. In his position of prospective son-in-law he could not refuse any request of his prospective father-in-law, so he went.

A gruesome sight met his gaze on entering the woods. Human bones and skeletons were scattered everywhere; and he began to fear lest another trap was laid for him. He went about his work, however, and the woods soon rang with the reports of his axe.

A very frightful and horrible noise coming from the interior of the woods made him stop. The nearer it came the more terrible it sounded. "It must be a wild beast coming to eat me up," he thought.

Soon a very ferocious beast appeared and came running towards him. The boy looked for his mink skin; it was not about him, for he had left it in the bidarka; but still he had his bows and arrows. Quickly pulling them out of the bag, he sent one tiny arrow into the side of the monster, knocking him over; and when another arrow pierced the other side, he ceased kicking. Approaching him to withdraw the arrows, the boy found him dead.

On his return to the barrabara, after finishing his work, the old man looked surprised and uneasy—the old man was a shaman, and had been in the habit of sending strangers into the woods to be killed by the monster, and then eating them —and asked the boy:—

"Did you see or hear anything strange in the woods?"

"No, I did not," the boy replied.

The morning of the second day, while the boy was eating breakfast, the old shaman from outside called to him:—

"The girls want you to come out and swim with them!"

To refuse would have been unmanly, so he went to the beach, undressed himself, taking, however, the mink skin; for he suspected trouble, and swam after the girls, who were some distance from him. As he advanced, they retreated; and when almost up to them, a big whale appeared between them, and before he knew what to do, he was in the whale's mouth. In there, the boy put on the mink skin, and when the whale appeared on the surface, the boy escaped through the blow-hole, and swam for the shore.

When the shaman saw him, he was vexed and troubled, saying to himself: "He is the first one that I could not overcome, but I will."

That evening he had again a supper of seal meat; his bride sat where he could see her, but he dared not talk to her.

Early next morning the old man called him to have another swim with the girls. On the beach was a large whale, and the girls were climbing on his tail. When they were all on, he switched his tail, sending them through the air some distance into the sea.

The girls dared the boy do likewise. Stripping himself, and unnoticed by them—they were quite a distance from him—he took a tiny arrow in each hand. Instead of at once climbing on the tail, he approached the head of the whale. Sticking the arrows into the head, he asked the girls:—

"Am I to get on here?"

"No, further down," they answered.

He stuck the arrows into the whale, as he moved down towards the tail, repeating the same question and receiving the same answer. When he finally stood on the tail, it did not move; for the whale was dead. The girls, after waiting some time, swam to the shore to report to the shaman, who returned with them only to find the whale lifeless. Furious was the shaman; and in his heart he swore he would yet eat the boy.

The following morning the old man asked the boy whether he had any relatives, mother or grandmother, whom he would like to go and see before he settled down with them.

"I have a grandmother," said the boy, and went off that day.

Paddling first on one side of the bidarka, and then on the other, he was making good progress, when all of a sudden the mink skin startled him by calling to him: "Look out, you are in danger!" He looked ahead; there was nothing dangerous there, so he paddled on. Again the mink skin called to him: "Look out, you are in danger!" Ahead everything was safe; but as he looked behind, he was almost overcome with fear; for a huge wave, high as a mountain, was coming his way, and would soon overtake and overwhelm him. As quickly as he could, he shot one of his arrows into the wave, breaking it, and he was once more safe.

Towards evening he steered for the shore, in order to eat and rest there, and when near the shore, a large sea monster appeared and swallowed bim, bidarka and all. He pulled out and put on the mink skin, and when an opportunity offered itself, he escaped through the monster's gills, and swam to the shore.

His grandmother, who was also a shaman, had been watching the grandson's doings, though far away, punished the monster by sending two large ravens to peck his eyes out.

Being on shore, and without a bidarka, the boy started to walk home. He did not take off the mink skin, and so was still a mink. On the way he came to a large lake, abounding in fish; there he stopped, fed on the fish he caught, and in a short time became acquainted with the minks of the neighborhood. This easy life pleased him so well that he decided to remain there; and there (in the neighborhood of Kodiak) he is at present. The shamans, only, can tell him apart from the other minks.

The Unnatural Uncle
(Aleut)

In a village lived a man, known to his neighbors as "Unnatural Uncle." When his nephews became a few years old, he would kill them. Two had already suffered death at his hands. After the second had disappeared, his wife went to the mother of the boys, and said: "Should another boy be born to you, let us conceal the fact from my husband, and make him believe the child a girl. In that case he will not harm him, and we may succeed in bringing him up."

Not long after the above conversation another nephew was born. Unnatural Uncle, hearing that a child was born, sent his wife to ascertain the sex of the child. She, as had been agreed upon, reported the child a girl. "Let her live," he said.

The two women tended and dressed the boy as if he were a girl. When he grew older, they told him to play with the girls, and impressed upon him that he should at all times imitate the ways, attitudes, and postures of the girls, especially when attending to the calls of nature. Unnatural Uncle watched the boy as he was growing up, and often wondered at his boyish looks. One day the boy, not knowing that his uncle was about and observing him, raised up his parka, and so exposed his body. "Ah," said Unnatural Uncle to his wife, on reaching home, "this is the way you have fooled me. But I know everything now. Go and tell my nephew I wish to see him." With tears in her eyes the poor woman delivered the message to the nephew, told him of the disappearance of his brothers, and of his probable fate. The father and mother of the boy wept bitterly, for they were certain he would never return. The boy himself, although frightened, assured his parents to the contrary, and begged them not to worry, for he would come back safe and sound.

"Did my brothers have any playthings?" he asked before going.

He was shown to a box where their things were kept. In it he found a piece of a knife, some eagle-down, and a sour cranberry. These he hid about his person, and went to meet his uncle. The latter greeted him, and said: "Nephew, let us go and fetch some wood."

When they came to a large forest, the boy remarked: "Here is good wood; let us take some of it, and go back."

"Oh, no! There is better wood farther on," said the uncle.

From the forest they stepped into a bare plain. "Let us go back. There is no wood here," called the boy. But the uncle motioned to him to come on, telling him that they would soon find better wood. A little later they came to a big log. "Here is what I want," exclaimed the uncle, and began splitting it. "Here, nephew, jump in, and get that wedge out," called the uncle to the boy, as one of the wedges fell in. When the boy did so, the man knocked out the other wedges; the log closed in on the boy, and held him fast. "Stay there!" said Unnatural Uncle, and walked off.

For some time the boy remained in this helpless condition, planning a means of escape. At last he thought of his sour cranberry, and, taking it in his hand, he rubbed with it the interior of the log from edge to edge. The sourness of the berry caused the log to open its mouth, thus freeing him.

On his way back to the village, he gathered a bundle of wood, which he left at his uncle's door, announcing the fact to him: "Here, uncle, I have brought you the wood." The latter was both surprised and vexed at his failure, and determined more than ever to kill the boy. His wife, however, warned him: "You had better not harm the boy; you have killed his brothers, and if you hurt him, you will come to grief."

"I will kill him, too," he savagely replied.

When the boy reached his father's home, he found them weeping and mourning. "Don't weep!" he pleaded. "He cannot hurt me; no matter where he takes me, I will always come back." In the morning he was again summoned to appear at his uncle's. Before going, he entreated his parents not to feel uneasy, assuring them that no harm would befall him, and that he would be back. The uncle called the boy to go with him after some ducks and eggs. They passed several places abounding in ducks and eggs, and each time that the boy suggested, "Let us take these and go back," the uncle replied: "Oh, no! There are better ducks and eggs farther on." At last they came to a steep bluff, and, looking down, saw a great many ducks and eggs. "Go down carefully, nephew, and gather those ducks and eggs. Be quick, and come back as soon as you can."

The boy saw the trap at a glance, and prepared for it by taking the eagle-down in each hand, between thumb and finger. As the boy took a step or two downward, the uncle gave him a push, causing him to lose his footing. "He will never come back alive from here," smiled the uncle to himself, as he walked back. If he had remained awhile longer and looked down before going, he would have seen the boy descending gently instead of falling. The eagle-down kept him up in the air, and he lighted at his own pleasure safe and sound. After gathering all the ducks and eggs he wanted, he ascended by holding up the down, as before, and blowing under it. Up, up he went, and in a short time stood on the summit. It was night before he sighted his uncle's home. At the door he deposited the birds and eggs, and shouted: "Here, uncle, are the ducks and eggs."

"What! back again!" exclaimed the man very much mortified. His wife again pleaded with him to leave the boy in peace. "You will come to grief, if you don't," she said. "No; he cannot hurt me," he replied angrily, and spent the remainder of the night thinking and planning.

Although he assured them that he would return, the boy's parents did not have much faith in it; for he found them on his return weeping for him. This grieved him. "Why do you weep?" he said. "Didn't I say I would come back? He can take me to no place from which I cannot come back."

In the evening of the third day the aunt appeared and said that her husband wished the boy. He told his parents not to be disturbed, and promised to come back soon. This time the uncle invited him to go with him after clams. The clams were very large, large enough to enclose a man. It was ebb tide, and they found plenty of clams not far from the beach. The boy suggested that they take these and go back, but the uncle put him off with, "There are better clams farther out." They waded into the water, and then the man noticed an extraordinarily large clam. "Take him," he said, but when the boy bent over, the clam took him in. So confident was Unnatural Uncle of his success this time that he uttered not a word, but with a triumphant grin on his face and a wave of his hand he walked away. The boy tried to force the valves apart, but not succeeding, he cut the ligament with his piece of a knife, compelling the clam to open up little by little until he was able to hop out. He gathered some clams, and left them at his uncle's door as if nothing had happened. The man, on hearing the boy's voice outside, was almost beside himself with rage. His wife did not attempt to pacify him. "I will say nothing more," she said. "I have warned you, and if you persist in your ways, you will suffer."

The next day Unnatural Uncle was busy making a box.

"What is it for?" asked his wife.

"A plaything for our nephew," he replied.

In the evening the boy was sent for. On leaving his parents, he said: "Do not feel uneasy about my absence. This time I may be away a long time, but I will come back nevertheless."

"Nephew, here is something to amuse you," said his uncle. "Get inside of it, so that I may see whether it fits you." It fitted him, so did the lid the box, and the rope the lid. He felt himself borne along, and from the noise of the waves he knew it was to the sea. The box was lowered, and with a shove it was set adrift. It was stormy, the waves beat over the box, and several times he gave himself up as lost. How long he drifted he had no idea; but at last he heard the waves dashing against the beach, and his heart rejoiced. Louder, and louder did the joyful peal sound. He gathered himself together for the sudden stop which soon came, only to feel himself afloat again the next moment. This experience he went through several times, before the box finally stopped and he realized he was on land once more.

As he lay there, many thoughts passed through his mind: where was he? was any one living there? would he be saved? or would the flood-tide set him adrift again? what were his people at home doing? These, and many other thoughts passed through his brain, when he was startled by hearing voices, which he recognized, a little later, as women's. This is what he heard:—

"I saw the box first," said one.

"No, I saw it first," said the other.

"I am sure I saw it before you," said the first speaker again, "and, therefore, it is mine."

"Well, you may have the box, but its contents shall belong to me," replied the other.

They picked up the box, and began to carry it, but finding it somewhat heavy and being anxious to know what it contained, they stopped to untie it.

"If there are many things in there, I shall have some of them," said the first speaker, who rued her bargain. The other one said nothing. Great was their surprise on beholding him. He was in turn surprised to see two such beautiful girls, the large village, the numerous people, and their peculiar appearance, for he was among the Eagle people in Eagle land. The full grown people, like the full grown eagles, had white faces and heads, while those of the young people, like those of young eagles, were dark. Eagle skins were hanging about all over the village; and it amused him to watch some of the people put on their eagle skins and change to eagles, and after flying around, take them off and become human beings again.

The girls, being the daughters of the village chief, led the boy to their father, each claiming him. When he had heard them both, the chief gave the boy to the older girl (the second speaker). With her he lived happily, but his thoughts would very often wander back to his former home, the people there, his parents; and the thought of his uncle's cruelty to them would make his heart ache. His wife noted these spells of depression, and questioned him about them until he told her of his parents and uncle. She, like a good wife, bade him cheer up, and then went to have a talk with her father. He sent for his son-in-law, and advised him to put on his (chief's) eagle skin, soar up high until he could see his village, fly over there, visit his parents, and bring them back with him. He did as he was told, and in a short time found himself in the village. Although he could see all other people, his parents were not in sight.

This was in the evening. During the night he went out to sea, brought back a large whale, and placed it on the beach, knowing that all the villagers would come out for the meat. The first person to come to the village beach in the morning was Unnatural Uncle; and when he saw the whale, he aroused the village, and a little later all, except the boy's father and mother, were there, cutting and storing up the whale. His parents were not permitted to come near the whale, and when some of the neighbors left some meat at their house, Unnatural Uncle scolded, and forbade it being done again. "I can forgive him the killing of my brothers, the attempts on my life, but I will revenge his treatment of my parents." With these thoughts in his mind, the eagle left his perch, and flew over to the crowd. He circled over its head a little while, and then made a swoop at his uncle. "Ah, he knows that I am chief, and the whale is mine, and he asks me for a piece of meat." Saying this, he threw a piece of meat at the eagle. The second time the eagle descended it was still nearer the man's head, but he tried to laugh it off, and turn it to his glory. The people, however, did not see it that way, and warned him to keep out of the eagle's clutches, for the eagle meant mischief. When the eagle dropped the third time, it was so near his head that he fell on his face. The fourth time the eagle swooped him, and flew off with him.

Not far from the shore was a high and steep rock, and on its summit the eagle put down the man, placing himself opposite. When he had taken off the skin, and disclosed himself, he said to his trembling uncle: "I could have forgiven you the death of my brothers, the four attempts on my life, but for the cruel treatment of my parents you shall pay. The whale I brought was for my parents and others, and not for you alone; but you took entire possession of it, and would not allow them even to approach it. I will not kill you without giving you a chance for your life. Swim back to the shore, and you shall be spared." As he could not swim, Unnatural Uncle supplicated his nephew to take him back, but the latter, putting on the eagle skin, and hardening his eagle heart, clutched him, and from a dizzy height in the air dropped him into the sea.

From the beach the crowd watched the fatal act, understood and appreciated it, and, till it was dark, continued observing, from the distance, the eagle. When all had retired, he pulled off the skin, and set out for his father's barrabara. He related to his parents his adventures, and invited them to accompany him to his adopted land, to which they gladly consented. Early in the morning he put on again his skin, and, taking a parent in each claw, flew with them to Eagle land, and there they are living now.

LOVERS
(Various)

TUTOKANULA AND TISAYAC
(Unidentified)

The vast ravine of *Yo Semite* (Grizzly Bear), formed by tearing apart the solid Sierras, is graced by many water-falls raining down the mile-high cliffs. The one called Bridal Veil has this tale attached to it. Centuries ago, in the shelter of this valley, lived Tutokanula and his tribe—a good hunter, he, a thoughtful saver of crops and game for winter, a wise chief, trusted and loved by his people. While hunting, one day, the tutelary spirit of the valley—the lovely Tisayac—revealed herself to him, and from that moment he knew no peace, nor did he care for the well-being of his people; for she was not as they were: her skin was white, her hair was golden, and her eyes like heaven; her speech was as a thrush-song and led him to her, but when he opened his arms she rose lighter than any bird and vanished in the sky.

Lacking his direction Yo Semite became a desert, and when Tisayac returned she wept to see the corn lands grown with bushes and bears rooting where the huts had been. On a mighty dome of rock she knelt and begged the Great Spirit to restore its virtue to the land. He did so, for, stooping from the sky, he spread new life of green on all the valley floor, and smiting the mountains he broke a channel for the pent-up meltings of the snows, and the water ran and leaped far down, pooling in a lake below and flowing off to gladden other land. The birds returned, the flowers sprang up, corn swayed in the breeze, and the people, coming back, gave the name of Tisayac to South Dome, where she had knelt.

Then came the chief home again, and, hearing that the spirit had appeared, was smitten with love more strong than ever. Climbing to the crest of a rock that spires three thousand feet above the valley, he carved his likeness there with his hunting-knife, so that his memory might live among his tribe. As he sat, tired with his work, at the foot of the Bridal Veil, he saw, with a rainbow arching around her, the form of

Tisayac shining from the water. She smiled on him and beckoned. His quest was at an end. With a cry of joy he sprang into the fall and disappeared with Tisayac. Two rainbows quivered on the falling water, and the sun went down.

MENTONEE AND THE YOUNG WARRIOR
(Siwash)

When the Siwash, as the Northwestern Indians called themselves, were few, Mount Hood was kept by the Spirit of Storms, who when he shook his robe caused rain or snow to fall over the land, while the Fire Spirit flashed his lightnings from Mount Adams. Across the vale between them stretched a mighty bridge of stone, joining peak to peak, and on this the Siwash laid his offering of salmon and dressed skins. Here, too, the tribal festivals were kept. The priestess of the arch—Mentonee, who fed the fire on the tribal altar "unimpassioned by a mortal throb"—had won the love of the wild tamanouses of the mountains, but she was careless alike of coaxing and threats, and her heart was as marble to them.

Jealous of each other, these two spirits fell to fighting, and, appalled by the whirl of fire and cloud, of splintering trees and crumbling rocks, the Indians fled in terror toward the lowlands, but she, unhurt and undaunted, kept in her place, and still offered praise to the one god. Yet she was not alone, for watchful in the shadow of a rock stood a warrior who had loved her so long, without the hope of lovers, that he, too, had outgrown fear. Though she had given him but passing words and never a smile, his own heart was the warmer and the heavier with its freight, and it was his way to be ever watching her in some place where she might not be troubled by the sight of him.

The war waxed fiercer, and at last the spirits met at the center of the arch, and in roar and quake and deluge the great bridge swayed and cracked. The young man sprang forward. He seized Mentonee in his arms. There was time for one embrace that cheated death of sorrow. Then, with a thunder like a bursting world, the miles of masonry crashed down and buried the two forever. The Columbia leaps the ruins of the bridge in the rapids that they call the Cascades, and the waters still brawl on, while the sulky tamanouses watch the whitened floods from their mountain-tops, knowing that never again will they see so fair a creature as Mentonee.

THE GROUSE-GIRL AND THE MEN
(Unidentified)

Two men, the older lame and unattractive, the younger sound and handsome, lived by themselves in a barrabara, far from other human beings. When they arose in the morning, they drank some oil—to keep hunger away the rest of the day—and then went out hunting; one to the hills, and the other to the beach. In the evening one returned with seal meat, while his partner brought bear meat. Many years they lived in this manner without seeing or even knowing that other people existed.

After the usual breakfast one morning, the older man went to the beach to hunt, and the younger man to the hills, and in the evening both returned loaded with seal and bear meat respectively. By rubbing together two sticks of wood, they soon had a fire over which they cooked some meat, and, after eating, put on their parkas and sat outside on the barrabara, with their faces toward the sea. While sitting there, a grouse appeared and lit on the barrabara, near the younger man, and commenced pecking. "Why does the grouse come here?" the man asked, and pushed her away. She flew up, but returned a moment later to the place occupied before. Seeing her there again, the handsome fellow said to the other one: "What is the matter with the bird? Her home is on the hills, and yet she is bothering here." He drove her off, but she, not discouraged, came back to him. "What does she want?" he exclaimed impatiently, and forced her away rather roughly. When she descended the fourth time, it was by the side of the lame man who took her in his hand, began stroking her, and finally decided to keep her as his pet. Before retiring, the lame man made a nest for the bird near him, and then all turned in for the night.

The next morning the men went hunting as usual. As they approached the barrabara in the evening, they were greatly surprised to see smoke coming out of it, and on entering to find it clean, a warm supper waiting for them, and a pair of new *torbarsar* (shoes made of sealskin) garters hanging over the lame man's bed. "Somebody has been here today," said the younger man; and although they looked outside and inside, they found no one. The grouse was on her nest, her head hidden under her drooping wings, and looked altogether tired. Perceiving her condition, the lame man remarked: "The bird has had nothing to eat or drink the whole day; she must be both hungry and thirsty."

This little excitement did not prevent them from enjoying their supper, nor did it disturb their sound sleep during the night; and the next morning they proceeded with their daily occupation. As the evening before, they found their home in order, the meat cooked, and a pair of new torbarsars hanging where the garters hung the day previous. The grouse was on her nest, her head under the drooping wings, but no one else was to be found, although they searched a long time. After eating their supper, the older man fed and played with the grouse, and then they all went to sleep.

On account of the stormy weather, the several days following the men remained at home. During that time the bird tried once more to gain the good grace of the handsome man, but he treated her roughly, and would not let her come near him, and she avoided him after this. The first favorable day the two men went in different directions to hunt. As soon as the younger man was out of sight, the lame man squatted down, saying: "I will watch today and see who cleans and cooks for us, and makes torbarsars for me." Slowly and cautiously he crawled back quite close to the barrabara, and waited. The morning passed without giving him a clue, but towards evening he saw smoke coming out of the smoke hole. He crept still closer, and heard footsteps within. While he lay there, guessing who it might be, a young and beautiful girl stepped out. Her face was white, hair and eyebrows black, the parka was of white grouse feathers, and the leggings of the fur seal torbarsars were white with various trimmings. He gazed at her, and when she went in, he followed her, watched her a moment at her work, and then seized her.

"*Ai-Ai-Y-a-h!*" she exclaimed. "You scared me. Let me go." Instead he drew her fondly to him, and when he did so, her face reddened with blushes.

"I will not let you go," he said; but when he noticed a grouse skin on the nest, he freed her, and although she begged to have the skin back, he took it outside, and hid it.

The handsome man was both scared and amazed, but he asked no questions. Since it was customary for a newly married man to stay at home with his wife for a certain time, it was a long time before the old man went out hunting again. When he did so, he always returned before his partner, and generally found a pair of torbarsars or some other present waiting for him; but the younger man found nothing.

Though the younger man asked no questions, and knew not who the girl was and where she came from, he did a great deal of thinking. It puzzled him to know why the girl preferred a lame, old man to him a young, handsome man. She did not like him, he knew, for she never made anything for him, while the lame man had presents forced on him. He finally decided to take matters in his own hands, and make the girl his wife. One night, when the married couple were asleep, he arose and killed the lame man. Going back to his bed, he called to the girl to leave her dead husband, and be his wife. This she refused to do. "You cannot go away from here," he said; "you will have to be my wife."

"I will never be your wife," she answered; and getting up, she searched for the grouse skin among her husband's things, and found it in his tool bag. This she hid under her parka. When he called her again, saying, "Come, you are my wife," she replied: "I came here to be your wife, but you did not take me. Three times I came to you, and three times you chased me away. The last time you hurt me. I will not be your wife now." While speaking, she pulled out the grouse skin, shook it three times, and, when she had finished, pulled it on herself, and flew out through the smoke hole, leaving the young, sound, and handsome man wifeless and partnerless.

Uchatngiak and the Goose Girl
(Aleut)

It was a very large settlement, and over it presided only one chief. This chief had a son whom, from babyhood, he kept secluded in a barrabara. Two men watched continuously over him, giving him no opportunity either to go or look out. The boy, Uchatngiak, as he grew up and heard the shouts of the men who were shooting ducks in the bay with their bows and arrows, the laughter of others, playing "*nabada*" (a stick is set up and stones thrown at it), the cheering of still others, testing their skill of marksmanship on a piece of kelp, tried in vain to guess the reason of his seclusion. One day in early spring, being very restless and hearing more noise than usual, he decided to see what was going on outside. While one man was after fresh water, he sent the other one to fetch him some roots, and in the mean time pulled out the seal-intestine window, and looked out. A rapturous sight greeted him: the green grass, the flowers just beginning to bloom, the clear sky overhead, the young men happy and sportive, hunting and playing games; he gazed till blinded by tears, then fell on his bed, and wept.

The guards on their return, finding him in this condition, were frightened, thinking he was ill, or what was worse, perhaps he had looked out; in that case they would be severely punished. He would not answer their many questions at first; but when he became composed, told them everything, and ordered them to go to his father, and say to him that he desired to go and stay outside. One of the men went to the chief, and reported to him what happened and how it happened, and delivered the son's message. The chief thought a while, and then said: "My son is now grown up, he may come and live outside."

The chief ordered some of his servants to dress his son in a sea-otter parka and torbarsars, to spread skins on the ground for him to walk on, to place a bearskin on the roof of the barrabara for him to sit on; others of his servants he sent through the village, inviting the people to come and see his son, concerning whom they knew nothing. Uchatngiak, seated on the barrabara, gazed with astonishment on all the people and wonders about him. Five white geese, who happened to fly by just then, had a special fascination for him, and he eyed them till they settled down some distance off. "People hunt them. I too will go and hunt them," thought he. Sending his guards away on different errands, he snatched a bow and arrow, and started after the geese.

When he came to the place where the geese seemed to alight, he saw a lake and in it five beautiful girls bathing and enjoying themselves. In order to get a better look at them, he began sneaking around the lake, and, while doing so, came across five white geese skins. Taking one, the smallest, he sat down at a distance to see what would happen. Pretty soon the girls, who were sisters, came out of the water, and walked to the place where they left their skins. The four older sisters were soon ready to fly, but waited impatiently for the youngest sister. "Do hurry, we must be going," they called.

"I have looked all around here for my skin, but I cannot find it," she weepingly said. The others joined with her in the fruitless search, until Uchatngiak was espied, when the four geese flew up and away, and the girl ran to him, and begged: "O give me back my skin." Looking at her beautiful form, he said: "No, I will not give it back to you." He dressed her in his parka and torbarsars, and asked her to come home with him. For ten days she lived with him in his barrabara before his mother learned the fact, but she said nothing. During the day Uchatngiak hunted, and his wife went to the lake to feed on the delicate grasses that geese like so well. In this manner the young couple lived happily together until the following spring. A son was born to them in the mean while.

Uchatngiak had a very meddlesome sister, who disliked her strange sister-in-law, and often, in speaking with other women, would remark that her sister-in-law had a peculiar mouth, resembling that of a goose, and that, whenever she laughed, she covered her mouth, so that no one could see her teeth. One day, while Uchatngiak was away from home, his sister called and shamefully abused his wife, and called her a goose. The wife endured the abuse a long time, and then, putting on her goose skin, flew out through the hole in the roof and away. An alarm was given, that a goose flew out of the chief's son's house; and some chased after her, but in vain. Uchatngiak, when he returned and found his wife gone, grieved for her, and complained bitterly.

Several years passed. The boy, who was now five years old, was in the habit of going everywhere with his father. One day they were on the beach, Uchatngiak was fixing his bidarka, and the boy was amusing himself with a bow and arrow; while there, five geese flew right over their heads, and lighted on the rocks near the point. The boy noticed them, and said: "Father, I will go and shoot them." Not returning soon, the father went to look for him, and could not find him, but in the distance saw the five white geese flying. "His mother joined her sisters, and they came and took my son from me!" he cried out, and felt very miserable and lonely.

This happened in the fall; and he decided to go immediately in search of his wife and son. He took with him a stone hatchet, five dried salmon, and one sour salmon. (Formerly, the Aleuts buried the salmon for the winter, and when they took them out, the salmon were "sour.") Eastward he went a half of the winter before anything unusual broke into the monotony of his journey. One day, while following a very narrow path, he came upon two fierce foxes fighting in the path. He asked them several times to let him pass, but they heeded him not; finally, one of the foxes said to him: "Give us your sour salmon, and we will let you pass." Dividing the salmon in two parts, he threw one part to one side and the other to the other side of the path; and while the foxes rushed for the fish, he passed on. From the top of the mountain which he ascended, he saw in the valley below smoke coming out of a small bar-rabara, and a path leading down to it. The path led him to the door of the barrabara, and when he pushed it in, he saw a very stout woman seated on the floor, making fine sinew threads. "May I come in?" he asked. Without raising her head, she replied: "If you are alive, you may, if a ghost, do not."

"I am alive," and walked in.

"What do you want?" she asked, still without raising her head.

"I wish to know where my wife and son are?"

"I will not tell you, but if you give me half of a dried salmon, I will tell you how you may find out."

He gave her what she asked, and when she had eaten it, she said: "Go to the top of yonder hill, there you will see two paths, one leading to the right and the other to the left. Follow the one to the right until you come to my brother who will tell you where they are." Giving her the other half of the salmon also, he walked up the hill, took the path to the right, and followed it many days without seeing a sign of habitation. At last, one evening, while in a very narrow path, he heard a noise and then some one singing very softly. The music led him to the beach where an old man sat, singing and chopping off chips from a large stick. On closer observation, he noted that the smallest chips on falling into the water turned to trout, the larger chips became humpback salmon, the still larger ones changed to dog-salmon, those next to the largest were transformed to king-salmon, and the largest chips swam away silver-salmon. He crept closely behind the old man, watched him, and thought: "If I could get the stone hatchet, he would be obliged to tell me where they are." The old man continued singing and chopping, and, once, as he raised up the hatchet to cut off a king-salmon, it slipped from his hand, falling at the feet of Uchatngiak. When the old man turned around, and saw the stranger, he said:—

"You have my hatchet."

"No, I have it not; but if you will tell me where my wife and son are, I will give you your old hatchet and a new one besides."

"Give them to me;" and when he had them, he said, "I am about to cut off a king-salmon. Just as soon as he appears in the water, clutch him and hold fast to him; he will take you to your wife and son."

He grabbed the salmon, the salmon seized his clothes, and away they went through weeds and kelp, current and stream, along the bottom of the sea, then gradually in shallow and shallower water and sandy bottom. Close to the shore he looked up and saw his son, with a bow and arrow in his hand, eying the salmon. With his feet he steered the salmon close to the boy who shot and killed the salmon, and, on pulling him out, was greatly surprised to see his father sticking on.

"Where is your mother?"

"In the barrabara," the boy replied.

"Go and tell her that I wish to see her."

"You had better wait outside until I go and see about it."

The boy started off, and, when he came near the barrabara, commenced to cry. Going to his aunt Akcheten, he said: "Uchatngiak fell down; go and bring him in." She pushed him aside, saying: "We left him afar off; and we cannot go now in winter and bring him in." From her he went to aunt Chavillo, Qulo, and Podonigyuk, who put him off in the same manner as aunt Akcheten. Leaving them, he approached his mother, saying, "Uchatngiak fell down; go and bring him in."

"Where is he?"

"Outside the barrabara."

She looked, and there, as the boy said, sat Uchatngiak. She seemed glad to see him, and began questioning him: "Why and how did you come here? You cannot live with us. This is "Bird Heaven." (The Aleuts believed that the birds, on leaving Alaska in the fall, went to a place somewhere above the earth, known as Bird Heaven or Bird Home.)

"I came to see my wife and son. Can you not manage to keep me with you a short time?" he pleaded.

They promised to keep him, if he would promise not to go out of the barrabara. The village in which he now found himself was very large, containing many inhabitants of various colors: some red, others black, still others a mixture of colors; in fact, people of all colors and shades conceivable. In the early spring evenings his wife, her sisters, and the boy, putting on their goose skins, would fly away and not return until dawn. Before going, they made him pledge not to leave the barrabara; but during the night, as he heard many people talking, and strange and mysterious noises outside, he wished that he could go out and solve the mystery. Later in the spring, instead of going in the evenings and returning in the mornings, his folks flew away in the morning, and remained away all day. He begged to be taken along, but they paid no attention to the request.

In one end of the village was an extraordinarily large barrabara, and thither, he noticed, the different people, his own among them, gathered and remained the whole day. Two days he observed them assemble without learning their doings; on the third day his curiosity overcame him. Sneaking out of the house, he crawled to the barrabara, and, pushing aside the grass and sticks, peeped in. The interior was filled with birds, dressing and painting themselves with the variously colored rocks lying about. Everybody was already dressed or dressing, except two who were still naked. Akcheten and Chavillo spied him, and, turning to Agoiyuan (his wife), said, "Uchatngiak is peeping." The alarm was given instantly, and the birds hurried to dress the two naked ones, sea-gull and raven. In the excitement the raven was painted black all over and the sea-gull all white, which colors they have retained to this day. Uchatngiak had seen enough, and hastened home; and when the family returned he was scolded severely, and told that the following day the whole village would depart. He pleaded not to be left behind until they finally consented to take him with them. The eagle was asked to take him on his back and carry him across safely; but when the raven heard of this arrangement, she came coaxing and begging to be allowed to carry him.

"You will soon tire, and you might hurt him," the sisters, refusing her, said.

"If I tire, and I will not, I will turn over, and you can all see."

She coaxed so long that they promised to let her try. The next day all the birds left Bird Heaven earthward. Uchatngiak was perched on the raven's back, with the other birds around them to render assistance should it be needed. When about half way across, the raven began to turn over, but soon steadied herself.

"Let the eagle carry him, let the eagle carry him; you are tired, you will drop him," they all began to clamor.

"I am not tired, and I can carry him myself," she haughtily replied.

They had gone only a little farther when, without warning, the raven went down with her burden into the deep sea. All the other birds hovered about the spot of the accident, ready to do what they could. The eagle had his claws in position to snatch Uchatngiak when he should come to the surface. But the same Uchatngiak never appeared; for he was changed to a white whale. The raven became a drifting, large-rooted tree-trunk. Seeing the sad ending, the geese left the mournful spot, and in time came to the earth where they laid eggs, and hatched them, and have continued doing so ever since.

OF JOURNEYS AND TRAVELERS
(Various)

THE TWO INQUISITIVE MEN
(Aleut)

There were two men; the name of one was Achayongch, the name of the other Achgoyan. They lived together, but spoke and looked at each other only when really compelled to do so. Anything happening at other places was known to them, and they generally went there to investigate. They went, looked, said not a word, did not a thing, and returned. One day, as they were sitting in their barrabara around the fire, their backs toward each other, and eating shell-fish, Achgoyan pulled out a feather from his hair, threw it from him, and said, "Achayongch, what shall we do? There is a man living over there on the other side. He hunts every day with his sling."

Achayongch was silent for a while, then he scratched his ear, and said, "I do not know what is the matter with me. There is much whistling in my ear."

Silence for a long time; finally Achgoyan, pulling out another feather from his hair, and throwing it from him, said, "Achayongch, what shall we do? There is a man living over there on the other side. He hunts every day with his sling."

After scratching his ear, Achayongch replied, "I do not know what is the matter. There is much whistling in my ear."

A third time Achgoyan threw away a feather, saying, "There is a man living on the other side whose name is Plochgoyuli. He hunts every day with his 'plochgo' (sling). We will go and see."

They set about preparing for the trip. On the canoe was piled the barrabara, the bugs and insects of the barrabara (they, being considered personal property, went with the house and person), the grave and remains of their wife. Achgoyan then thought that the canoe was sufficiently loaded; but on launching it was discovered too heavily loaded on one side; and in order to have it equally heavy on both sides, they dug up a little hillock, and put it on, and when they had filled hollow reeds with fresh water, started off.

Coming close to the other shore, they saw Plochgoyuli hunting ducks with his sling. He saw them too, knew the nature of their visit, and on that account threw rocks at them so as to destroy them. The first rock hit close to the canoe, and made Achgoyan exclaim, *"Ka! Ka! Ka! Ka!* It nearly hit." The second rock hit still closer, and he exclaimed again, *"Ka! Ka! Ka! Ka!"* and as the rocks continued coming, they steered their canoe around, but not before Plochgoyuli had damaged the canoe. On returning home, all the things were replaced.

A few days later they were sitting in the barrabara around the fire, their backs toward each other, eating shell-fish. Achgoyan pulled out a feather, and throwing it from him, said, "Achayongch, there is a man living on an island. He heats a bath, and catches codfish every day."

Achayongch scratched his ear, and replied, "I do not know what is the matter; but there is much whistling in my ear today."

A pause; then Achgoyan pulled out another feather, saying, "Achayongch, there is a man living on an island in the middle of the sea whose name is Petingyuwock. He heats a bath, and catches codfish every day."

"I do not know what is the matter; but there is much whistling in my ear to-day," answered Achayongch.

Silence for a long time; finally Achgoyan, pulling out a third feather, spoke up, "Achayongch, there is a man living on an island in the middle of the sea, whose name is Petingyuwock. He heats a bath, and catches codfish every day. Let us go and see."

They paddled off in the canoe, loaded with barrabara, bugs, grave, and hillock.

On reaching the island, they beached the canoe, and went into the barrabara. An old man who was sitting there exclaimed, *"Futi!* where is the man-smell coming from?"

"We came to see because we heard that there is a man living here who heats a bath, and catches codfish every day."

"The bath is ready," said Petingyuwock, and Achayongch and Achgoyan went in to take a bath. While they were bathing, the old man tied together a lot of thin, dried kelp, which he had kept to make clothes, into a long rope, and fastened one end of it to the canoe. That done, he roasted a codfish and gave it to the men when they came out of the bath. "There is a strong wind blowing. You had better hasten back," suggested the old man.

The men pushed off against a strong sea-breeze; and when quite a distance from the shore, the old man commenced pulling his end of the rope, gradually drawing them back, and when he had them close to the shore, asked them why they delayed, since the wind was freshening up every moment. A second time they started. This time they went about half way across before Petingyuwock, who was in the barrabara, began hauling in the rope until the canoe was on shore again. He then came out, and demanded to know why they did not go while there was yet time. The third time they paddled against such a strong breeze that with great difficulty headway was made at all. When half way across, the old man pulled again the rope, but the wind upset the canoe.

The grave of their wife became a porpoise. Achayongch and Achgoyan were cast on the shore, where they became two capes; and since then quiet and peace are unknown on capes; for the men were inquisitive.

THE ASCENT TO HEAVEN
(Tillamook)

Once upon a time there was a man who had two sons. One day he went out hunting and did not return. His elder son went in search of him, and soon discovered in the woods his headless body. In vain he searched for the missing head; he was unable to find it. Then he came to know that the people in heaven had killed his father, and he resolved to take revenge. He stayed in the forest for six days making arrows. Then he returned to his younger brother and told him that he had resolved to ascend to heaven in order to avenge the death of his father. His younger brother, whose name was *Qäxäaιcī'ya* (whose mother is a dog), resolved to accompany him. One half of his body was like that of a dog. They took their arrows and made themselves ready. They went into the woods to the place where the elder brother had found his father's body. The latter began to shoot his arrows towards the sky, but they fell down and did not reach the heavenly vault.

Then he asked his younger brother to shoot, and his arrows struck the sky. He continued shooting, each arrow hitting the notch of the preceding one. Thus he made a chain which soon began to approach the earth. When it reached half way from heaven to earth he asked his elder brother to help him, and both continued shooting until the chain of arrows touched the ground. Then they commenced to climb up. Before starting, the younger brother had warned the elder one not to look back, as else the arrows would break asunder and would fall to the ground. When he climbed up his tongue hung out like that of a dog. They sang while climbing up. Finally they reached heaven and found a trail, which they followed in order to search for their father's head. After a while they saw two women gathering fern-roots. In doing so they were performing a dance with their digging-sticks. Then the brothers hid behind a few bushes, and the younger one sent his soul [life] to the women. It ran about near them in the shape of a weasel. They tried to hit it with their sticks, but it dodged. When the young man's soul had seen what the women were doing, it returned to its owner. Then the young men stepped forth from their hiding-place and accosted the women. They asked, "Where is your canoe?" They replied, "We keep our canoe on the water. We never haul it ashore, and when we want to go aboard we jump into it." The young men next asked, "For whom are you digging roots here?" They replied, "A great shaman has been dancing for ten days. This is the last day of his performance, and the roots will be used in the concluding feast." They asked, "How do you distribute the roots?" They told them where they commenced, and that they gave everybody roots, except to the grubs who inhabited one house of the village. They also asked, "Do your eyes water on account of the smoke in your house?" The women replied that their eyes never watered. Upon their further questions, they told them that they were the chief's wives, and that they slept the one at his right side, the other at his left side, and they told their names. Then the young men killed the two women, took their roots, and put on their clothing. Then they went to the place where the canoe of the women was, and they jumped aboard. The elder brother touched the water with his feet, while the younger one jumped right into the canoe. They paddled towards the village and halted a short distance from the beach. Then they jumped ashore, the elder brother first. Again he touched the water with his feet. Then the chief, who was watching her, cried, "You have not been true to me!" He ran for his bow and arrow and was about to kill his supposed wife, but he was restrained by his people. He had arranged that so long as his wives remained true to him they should be able to jump from the canoe to the shore without touching the water, but that as soon as they were unfaithful they should be unable to do so. The younger brother cleared the distance without any difficulty. They entered the house and began preparing the roots. The younger brother was placing them in the smoke over the fire. While thus engaged he looked up and saw his father's head hanging from the roof of the house. Then tears streamed down his cheeks. When the people observed this they said, "What is the matter with our women today? Now her eyes water, although the smoke never affected her before this." The youth said, "The smoke made my eyes water," and the people were satisfied with this reply. When they were distributing the roots they gave some to the grubs, and the chief shouted, "Certainly my wives must have done something bad today. They are making mistake after mistake!" While they were moving about distributing the roots, they had great difficulty in hiding their knives. At first they tried to carry them under their arms, but, since they were visible there, they hid them in their clothing. When they were moving about a man named Qä'tcιa discovered the younger brother's knife, and their identity had nearly been disclosed. In the evening they lay down with the chief, one at his right side, the other at his left. When he was asleep they arose quietly and went down to the beach. They cut holes in the bottoms of all the canoes and then crept back stealthily to the chief's bed. Here the younger brother took his knife and severed the chief's head from his trunk. Then they climbed up to the roof, took their father's head, and made their escape. The people could not pursue them, because their canoes were all leaky.

They reached the place where the bodies of the two women whom they had killed were lying. They exchanged their clothes and washed the bodies in the river. Then the women resurrected. They married them and made their way back to the chain of arrows. They climbed down and then took the chain of arrows down. They went to the place where their father's body was lying. They put its head in place and washed it in the water of the river. Then their father came to life. They made him dance and sing, but when he moved, his head fell down again. They tried to tie it on with various kinds of plants. Finally they used bast of the cedar, which held it in place. Ever since that time their father has had a red head. He became the woodpecker.

The Journey Across the Ocean
(Unidentified)

O nce upon a time there were many people standing on the beach. They saw what they thought to be a whale drifting by, and many birds sitting on its back. Then five brothers launched their canoe and went out to tow the whale to the beach. When they had been gone a little while and approached nearer the floating object, one of the men said: "That is no whale," but the others did not believe him. They went on, and when they were near by they saw that it was no whale, but a canoe covered with whale skin on which birds were sitting. People from the other side of the ocean, the ᴌxuina'ē, were in it. When they saw this, they turned back as quickly as possible. The people from the other side of the ocean pursued them. The brothers had just time to reach the beach, when the other canoe overtook them. One of the five men jumped ashore, but the pursuers caused the water to draw back from the beach, and thus drew the canoe out into the sea. They took the four brothers who had remained in the canoe and began to return to their own country. They hunted whales while crossing the ocean, but whenever they were unsuccessful they cut pieces of flesh from the men whom they had captured and used it for bait. Finally nothing but their bones remained. Three of the brothers died, but the last, although nothing but his bones remained, was still alive.

The man who had escaped ran up to the house calling, "The men from the other side of the ocean have taken my brothers!" He went to the top of Bald Mountain, at the mouth of Salmon River, where he stayed twenty days fasting. Then he dreamed of his brothers. After this he returned to the village and asked all the people to accompany him across the ocean to see what had become of his brothers.

They fitted out their largest canoe and started out the next morning. At nightfall they stopped far out at sea. The mountains of their home had disappeared from their view. Early in the morning they traveled on and stopped again at night-time. Thus they traveled for many days, steering towards sunset. Finally they saw the land at the other side of the ocean. They found a kind of wood which they did not know. It looked like reed, but was as tall as a tree. They went ashore, and the man who had escaped from the canoe said: "I will go alone and look for my brothers." He went along the beach and finally found a house. He waited until the following morning, and then he saw smoke rising from the roof. He opened the door a little way and peeped into the room. He saw a few old blankets. There was no living person to be seen. Cautiously he entered, and saw that something was stirring under the blankets. He was frightened and was about to fly, but he took heart and looked more closely. He found the bones of his brothers under the blankets. They said, "Have you come, brother? You cannot help us now. We cannot move, and you cannot restore us to our former lives. But let us take revenge upon these people. Take some of them back with you across the ocean. Every day their women go out to gather skunk-cabbage. Two go in each canoe, and when they return they will all come ashore and carry the skunk-cabbage up to the house. One only will stay in her canoe. She is the chief's daughter. Her garments are covered with dentalia." The man left the house, returned to the canoe, and told his people what he had seen and heard. On the following day they hid in the woods. The women returned from gathering skunk-cabbage, and one girl only remained in the canoe. Then they launched their canoe, bailed it out, ran up to the girl, captured her and left the shore. They put her in the bottom of the canoe. She said, "Treat me well. I shall not attempt to run away." They returned across the ocean, traveling in the daytime and resting at night. They had been unable to take along the men whom the ʟxuin'ē had captured, as they were nothing but bones, which would have brought ill-luck to their canoe. On the third day at nightfall they began to see the mountains at the mouth of Salmon River, and on the fourth day, at the time of sunset, they reached their village. There the man married the daughter of the ʟxuin'ē chief.

After a short time she was with child. She used to go out to the beach, look towards sunset and say, "Where the sun sets is my father's house." Every day she did the same thing. One night the people went out to see what she was doing. They did not find her at the place where she was accustomed to sit, and on coming toward the spot they saw her walking down the river on the surface of the water. She reached the sea and went over breakers and over waves back to her father's house. They were unable to bring her back.

After she had arrived at her father's house she gave birth to a boy. When he began to grow up, he made a bow and arrow and shot birds. One day his mother told him that his father was a chief in a village on the other side of the ocean. She said, "I came back before you were born. I was pregnant with you for ten months. It may be that your father will come here some day to look for me. If you should ever see a man who does not belong to this side of the ocean, think that he is your father. Ask him where he comes from, and treat him kindly."

After a number of years the man asked his people to accompany him once more across the ocean. He wished to look for his wife. He filled his canoe with precious skins and blankets and started on his journey.

On arriving on the other side he concealed his canoe in the woods, left his people in charge of it, and went alone to look for his wife. He hid behind a hill under some bushes, where he was able to see all that was going on, while he himself was invisible. Finally he saw a boy coming, who was playing with his bow and arrows. The boy tried his strength, shooting as far as he could, and then gathering up his arrows. One arrow fell close to the man, who took it up. The boy ran after the arrow, and thus found his father. He asked, "To what tribe do you belong? You do not belong here." The man replied, "I belong to the other side of the ocean." Then the boy said, "Mother told me that she had carried me for ten months when she came here. She told me that if I should see a stranger I should treat him well, because he might be my father." Then the man was glad and said, "I am your father." He said to the boy, "Go home and tell your mother I am here. Is your grandfather at home?" "No; they have gone whaling," replied the boy. He returned to the house and found his mother sitting in company of many other women. He stepped up to her and whispered in her ear, "I found father; he wants to see you," and ran out of the house again. In order to avoid suspicion, the woman did not stir until midnight, when all the other women were sleeping, and then went out to see her husband. She said, "Have your people come with you?" He said, "Yes; they are waiting for me in the canoe."

She said, "Call them; I will give them to eat." At first they were afraid lest her father might kill them. But she reassured them, and called them in. Finally they concealed their bows and arrows and knives under their blankets and entered the house. After they had eaten, the woman's father returned, and when he saw the strangers he grew angry, but his daughter took him out of the house, and told him, "This is my husband. I love him. You shall not murder him. They are going to give you many fine presents." Then they became good friends. The strangers gave him many skins and blankets and dentalia. After a while they returned home, accompanied by the woman and her son. Her father gave her beautiful clothing and many dentalia to take with her.

THE TRAVELERS
(Unidentified)

Once upon a time there was a man and a woman. They had six children,—five boys and one girl. The children started to travel all over the world to play ball with the various tribes. As soon as they reached a village, they challenged the people and induced them to stake their daughters on the game. One of their number was the hummingbird. He was very swift, and therefore they won all the girls, whom they married. But they stayed nowhere more than one night. They always promised to return at an early day, but they did not intend to keep their word.

One day they met a man who asked them where they were going. They told him that they were playing ball in all the villages, and that they married the girls of the villages; they added that they deserted them after one night. The man went on to the next village in order to warn the people, who manned a boat and came across the river, intending to attack the brothers. But the latter caused the canoe to capsize in mid-river.

They traveled on and reached another village. Again they played at ball and won. But the people did not wish to surrender their girls to them. They invited them to a feast which was spread in a large house. They hired the bat, who, as soon as the brothers and their sister had entered, closed up all the chinks. Then the people transformed the house into a rock. The girl observed the transformation. She looked up and saw a little hole in the roof. She assumed the shape of the crane and flew away, leaving her brothers.

She returned towards her native village, and passed all the places where her brothers had played ball. There she found their children, and the nearer she approached her native country the older she found the children to be. She addressed them, singing, *"Anaxaguā'xogua anē'a!"* Finally she reached the house of her parents. Her mother was making a garment, which she was painting. The girl told her what had happened, but the old woman did not seem to pay any attention. At last, when she had finished the garment, she said to her daughter, "If I had accompanied you, that would not have happened. You did not know how to take care of your brothers." She put on the new garment, and they started in search of the lost brothers. The old woman was singing while they were walking along. When they reached the villages where the brothers had tarried on their outward journey, they found that their children were grown up. The girl was furious on account of the loss of her brothers, and upturned all the houses in these villages, but her mother asked her to desist. She said, "Wait until we reach the house in which your brothers are held captive." They traveled on, and the old woman saw all her grandchildren. Finally they reached the rock in which the brothers were imprisoned. Then the old woman upturned it by the power of her magic. Thus the young men were set free. The broken rock may still be seen at the mouth of the river.

THE SIX TRAVELERS
(Unidentified)

O nce upon a time there lived six men who wanted to travel in their canoe all over the world. They reached the lightning-door, which opened and closed with great rapidity and force. They went ashore, and one of them tried to pass through the door. He succeeded in jumping through it without being hurt. He found himself in a house, where he saw two blind women, who had a plentiful supply of whale meat. He took some of it and threw it out of the door. The first piece he threw passed through it, but the second was caught by the closing door. Then he watched his opportunity and jumped out of the house, when the door opened. It closed so rapidly that it cut off half of his back. He did not know what to do. But when he came to the canoe one of his companions said, "Let us put some mud on, which will heal it." They did so, and traveled on across the ocean.

In mid-ocean they saw a sea-otter swimming about. One of the men shot it, but it sank before they were able to reach it. After they had traveled for a long time they reached the opposite shore and saw a large village. When the people saw them coming, they rushed down to the shore, led by their chief, who threatened to attack the strangers. They asked, "Why do you wish to attack us? We did you no harm." He replied, "Yes, you did: you shot my dog." The men replied, "We shot no dog; where did you lose it?" The chief answered, "I sent it across the sea to hunt elk, and you shot it in mid-ocean." The men replied, "We shot no dog, only a sea-otter, which sank before we could reach it."

Then the chief said, "That was my dog." The men stated that they had not known it to be the chief's dog, and offered two slaves to make good the loss. Then they were received kindly by the chief, who showed them a cave in which they were to dwell. There was an opening to it on each side.

Early in the morning the chief sent his people into the house to kill the strangers before they awoke. The breath of his people was so hot that the house became very warm and almost stifled the men, who did not know how to escape. Finally one of the men called the bear to help them, but he was unable to assist them. Then he called the beaver, but to no better effect. He called the deer, which was also unable to help them. At last they called the raccoon, who began to sing, and suddenly a stream of water sprung forth from the wall of the cave, and all the people who had come into the house to kill the strangers were drowned. Then the chief thought of another way of getting rid of the men. He invited them to a game of hoops. He placed all his people in a row, he himself standing at the head. The strangers stood opposite, headed by the raccoon. Then the chief rolled the hoop, hoping that it would kill the strangers. It was made of lightning. The raccoon succeeded in stopping it with his pole.

Then the raccoon rolled back the lightning hoop, and it killed all the chief's people and the chief himself; only a little girl and a boy who had been left at home escaped. They grew up, and from them sprang all the water animals.

The six men launched their canoe, and continued their travels. After a while they saw a house. They landed, and went to see who lived in it. They found no one there, and were about to continue their travels, when one of the men remembered having seen a large supply of fish in the house. They returned and sat down near the fire. All of a sudden a basket filled with fish fell down from the loft. The chief said, "Put it back; maybe the people will return very soon, and they certainly would pursue us if they should find that we had stolen their fish." Then they put them back. After a while another basketful of fish fell down close to their feet. The chief said, "Let us eat of the fish, for we are hungry." After they had eaten, the men intended to carry baskets of fish down to their canoe. The chief took one basket and said, "I will take these fish; they are very good." At once he felt his hair pulled by invisible hands, and he was thrown down and his basket taken from him. He thought his people had done so, but on looking back he saw them still seated near the fire. Then he thought he had stumbled and fallen, the basket being very heavy. He took it up again, but as soon as he had turned towards the door he was thrown down once more and thoroughly beaten. His people had now finished eating. Each of them took a basket and turned towards the door. There they were thrown down at once and beaten by invisible hands. The baskets were taken away from them. Then they knew that the house was the abode of the shadows.

Then they left and traveled on for a long time. Their supply of provisions began to give out. They came to a country where the people had no mouths. They offered them a little of the fish they had left, but saw that the people merely smelled it and then threw it away. The chief of the travelers was surprised to see the mouthless people. He touched their faces in order to investigate if they had teeth, and when he found that they had teeth under the skin he resolved to cut open their faces. He took a stone, sharpened his knife, and opened the face of one of them. He told him to wash the wound he had made, and then to eat fish. After he had made a mouth for this one, all the others came to him, and asked him to do them the same favor. They paid him with fish and whale meat. He enjoyed this occupation, and made sport of the people, cutting some of the mouths so that they stretched from one ear to the other; others he slashed from nose to chin. Finally they left this place and traveled on.

After they had traveled for a long time they came to a house, which they entered. They met two old women, but did not see any provisions in the house. The chief wondered what they lived on, but the old women did not take any notice of the strangers. They made a large fire and put stones into it, talking among themselves, and the men did not understand what they said. The chief of the travelers looked about the house, and all of a sudden he saw that their canoe had been transferred to the top of the roof. He did not know how it came there. He told his companions to throw grass on the fire, so that the smoke should fill the house, and to take the canoe down as quietly as possible. He alone continued to stay in the house, and pretended to talk with his companions. Soon the men succeeded in launching their canoe, then the chief ran down to the beach, jumped aboard, and they paddled away as fast as they could. When the old women found that their victims had escaped they began to cry, and said, "Our good dinner has run away." They were cannibals.

The men traveled on, and one night after dark they heard singing and dancing on the beach. They went ashore, and asked whether they might stay in the village over night. They were invited to a house in which a shaman performed his dance. The latter disliked the arrival of the strangers, and forbade them to enter his house. Then the chief of the travelers grew angry. He went down to the beach with his men; they took their bows and arrows, returned to the house, and demanded to be admitted. He threatened to kill the whole tribe if they denied them admittance to the house. The shaman did not allow them to enter, and when the chief attacked the house he made him faint before he reached the door. His men poured water over his head, but were unable to restore him to life. Then the shaman said: "If you will give me two slaves, I will cure him." They promised to give him the slaves, and he cured the chief. They gave him the slaves, but then they killed him, entered the house, took away a large part of his property, and took three men and two women as slaves.

They traveled on, but the people whose shaman they had killed pursued them in ten canoes. Before they were able to overtake the travelers the latter reached a village where a powerful shaman lived, whom the chief of the travelers hired. He told them that the other shaman whom they had killed had returned to life and was pursuing them. Early the following morning the pursuers reached the village. The shaman whom the travelers had hired asked them to stay in the house while he stayed at the door waiting for their enemy. He kept his supernatural powers in a bag of sea-otter skin, which he opened as soon as the enemies came. When they saw the contents of the bag they fell down dead.

Then the men wished to return home; they turned their canoe, and began their homeward journey. After a while they arrived at a huge rock, on which they found a large amount of driftwood. They made a fire on the beach and fell asleep. When they were fast asleep the rock began to shake, and they discovered that they were camping on the house of the Killer Whale. After a short time the monster came forth from under the rock and began to devour the travelers. The chief jumped into a fissure of the rock, where the monster was unable to reach him, and stayed there until it had returned to its house. When it entered its abode, the rock was shaking violently. In the daytime a great many sea-lions came to the rock to bask on the beach and on the driftwood. As the chief was very skilful in hunting sea-lions, having learned that craft from his father, he killed two sea-lions and one seal with his arrows. He put them into his canoe, made a sail out of his blankets, and started home. He had hardly gone when the monster came out of its house. It saw the remains of its subjects, and intended to kill the man who had murdered them. It chased him, but he began to sing and to conjure the wind. When the monster had almost reached him, the wind began to blow stronger and stronger, and drove the canoe forward, so that the chief was able to escape the Killer Whale. When he reached land near his village, and was crossing the bar, his people saw him coming. He was obliged to lower his sail, as the wind was blowing a gale. His people perceived that he had some difficulty in crossing the bar, and one of their largest canoes went out to assist him. When they approached him the Killer Whale had almost reached the chief's canoe; therefore, in order to escape the monster, he hoisted his sail and succeeded in entering the river. The large canoe, which was managed by twenty people, was unable to escape, and they were devoured by the monster. The canoe was upset. The women were standing on the beach, and saw the canoe being upset and the monster returning to its home. The chief was very sad at having lost so many of his people and thought of revenge.

He went to Salmon River and hired a powerful shaman, whom he asked to break the rock under which the Killer Whale lived. All the people who lived on his river accompanied him when he went out to the rock.

They had four canoes lashed together and covered with a platform of planks, on which the shaman was dancing. When they approached the rock, the shaman ordered the people to hide their faces and to turn backward. They turned the canoes, and the shaman began his incantations, singing, "Throw up! throw up! throw up!" The rock began to shake, and finally jumped out of the water, and falling, killed the monster. The latter, however, had two young ones, which stayed at the bottom of the sea and were not hurt by the falling masses. After the rock had settled down, they returned to it and continued to live there.

A year had elapsed; the people did not know that the young ones were still alive. One day they went out hunting seals and sea-lions. When they came to the rock, the two Killer Whales came out and devoured all the people; only the chief's son escaped by hiding under the bailer of one of the canoes. Peeping out from it, he saw one of the monsters swallow his father. He cried for fear, and pushed his canoe out into the sea, hoping to make his escape. He had no paddles, and drifted about helplessly. After a while some people who had remained in the village saw the canoe drifting by, and went out to secure it. They found the chief's son, who was so badly frightened that he was hardly able to speak. When he had recovered he told them what had happened.